# Readings in
# **Introductory**
# **Sociology**

# Dennis H. Wrong

New York University

# Harry L. Gracey

Union College

# Readings in

# Introductory

# Sociology

The Macmillan Company, New York

Collier-Macmillan Limited, London

# Second Edition

# Preface

Most introductory sociology courses today include consideration of the nature of man as now conceived by sociologists; the basic concepts and perspective of sociology as the scientific study of man's social life; some reference to the most enduring ideas of the "founding fathers" of the field and their successors, the "second generation" of sociologists; and, usually central to the course, analyses of the important institutions, organizations, and processes of modern Western society. This book covers all these topics, with a large number of substantial readings on each. The teacher can, therefore, either use it to supplement his textbook, selecting from among the readings we offer in each of these areas, or adopt it as his text, using the introductions to help present a systematic overview of the field and the selections to provide basic facts, concepts, and theories that he will develop in his lectures.

In the Introduction, "What Is Sociology?" we present two readings that discuss the subject matter of sociology, the methods of study, and sociology's status as a humanistic discipline—part of man's age-old search for knowledge of himself. These readings are preceded by an introduction that brings in some aspects of the historical development of the field and changing concepts of its nature and purpose.

Part One, "Basic Concepts and Perspectives of Sociology," contains explanatory and analytic articles on the concepts that have become the common tools of sociological analysis: social action, the development of the self, norms, roles, values, groups, institutions, societies, and social change. In addition to introducing the particular readings in the section, the Introduction to Part One discusses the uniqueness of human nature and conduct in the perspective of biological evolution and summarizes the interrelations among the basic concepts of sociology. The concepts covered can be seen to range from the microsociological to the macrosociological, from those used to describe and analyze face-to-face interaction to those applied to organized social groups and the historical development of entire societies. These readings will be especially valuable to teachers using this book as a basic text, for here the student is given the distinctively sociological perspective on the life of the "human animal." It should be pointed out, however, that the selections in Part One do not simply give textbook expositions of the basic concepts; they also provide critical examinations of these concepts and examples of their use in sociological analysis. This part therefore should be a valuable addition to the standard textbook expositions of the basic concepts. As a whole it will give the student an appreciation of the wide range of sociological interest and the broad scope of sociological inquiry.

Part Two, "Industrial Society and the Origins of Sociology," provides substantial selections from the works of the classic sociologists, a feature not found in other anthologies. These readings depict the historical origins of scientific sociology in the "age of revolution," when Western society was in the process of transformation from a rural-agrarian life to today's urban-industrial world. The selections include discussions of concepts and theories which the classical sociologists developed to comprehend this transformation. Many of these are still very much at the heart of sociology, including alienation, anomie, social class, conflict, the Protestant ethic, the industrialization of the West under capitalism, and the meaning of science for modern life. These readings can be used as a unit, to provide a historical introduction to sociological analysis, or individually, in conjunction with those sections of Part Three that give contemporary applications of these and related concepts and theories. The Introduction to this part provides a brief summary of the central ideas of each selection, places the whole unit in historical perspective, and points out the contemporary relevance of the ideas discussed. This, plus the fact that many of the concepts and ideas discussed are not only part of sociology today but have found their way into popular discourse (witness the current revival of interest in the concept of alienation), puts an understanding and appreciation of classical sociology well within the capacities of today's students.

Part Three, "Sociology of Contemporary Society," constitutes 60 per cent of the book, reflecting the emphasis of most introductory courses. Here is the major "payoff" of the sociological enterprise: making sense out of life in today's society. Each section of this part consists of an interrelated group of essays analyzing a particular aspect of contemporary social life. Each section has a basic theme, or set of interrelated themes, which the selections develop with regard to that area of social life. These themes include the metropolitanization of community life; the bureaucratization of advanced societies and the problems this creates; the developing patterns of ethnic and race relations in modern societies; the characteristics of social classes in American society and the changing nature of its stratification system; the interrelations of government, business, and the military in the political economy of modern Western societies; the developing "totalization" and "massification" of these societies; and the role of sociology in the intellectual and political understanding of modern social life. Discussion of the nature and role of modern sociology is placed at the end because we feel the student will appreciate it after he has been introduced to sociological analysis itself. The Introduction to Part Three reviews the topics covered and the separate introductions for each of the sections forecast for the student the basic themes developed in the selections. The student thus enters each section prepared for the ideas he will meet there. The sections themselves have been arranged in a logical sequence, from the simpler to the more complex topics, and readings in each section have been ordered from the general to the specific.

Several sociological topics often given separate headings in anthologies and textbooks are included, although grouped differently. Population, for example, will be found discussed in Kingsley Davis' article in Part One. Social-psychological topics are considered throughout the book. These include treatment of the relationship between personality and role performance in Part Two, Weber's famous discussion of the relationship between the values of the Protestant and his behavior as a capitalist, and, in the entire second section in Part Two, discussions by the classical sociologists of the influence of society and culture on personality. Socialization is discussed in the first section of Part Three, especially in Harry Gracey's article on the kindergarten. Although considerations of the consequences of social arrangements for the individual are scattered throughout the readings in Part Three, the section "Man in Mass-Total Society" concentrates specifically on how trends in American society and culture affect the personality development of contemporary Americans. Social psychology, as the study of the interrelation of personality and social structure, is thus one of the themes pervading the entire book.

Sociologists have traditionally been concerned with the trends of change in industrial society, not merely with its origins and current features. A preoccupation with the shape of things to come was one of the defining characteristics of the work of the classical sociologists. Included are a number of readings that, in addition to analyzing present-day social realities, attempt to project the direction of change in contemporary society. Such attempts to anticipate the future draw on verified sociological knowledge of the past and present in order to establish the limits within which future changes are likely to take place. Sociology, as the study of social life, cannot ignore the shape of the future at a time when all men are conscious of unceasing social change as the central, disturbing fact of contemporary life.

Sociology is a subject vital to the intelligent understanding of life in society today. We have been guided in our selection of material by a desire to show the student the crucial relevance of sociology to his understanding of his world of experience. A special effort has been made to find intelligent and intelligible analyses of the basic areas of social experience of people living in today's advanced societies. We hope in this way to make sociology worthy of the respect of our students.

We wish to thank the authors and publishers of our selections for permission to reprint their material, thus making them more readily available to the beginning student. We also wish to thank our editor at Macmillan, Mr. Charles Smith, for his labors on behalf of this second edition.

D. H. W.<br>
H. L. G.

# Contents

# What Is Sociology?

## INTRODUCTION

Sociology is very much a product of modern history, seeking to provide new answers to old questions as well as answers to the new questions posed by the social changes and contacts between previously isolated peoples that have become the background of daily life in the twentieth century. Of course, long before 1837, when Auguste Comte coined the term *sociology,* the Greek philosophers, the Church Fathers, and the thinkers of the Enlightenment—to mention only the most outstanding figures of Western intellectual history—reflected on the origins and foundations of human society. Indeed the first amateur sociologist was the tribesman who first perceived in the social relations of his fellows an enduring pattern or structure that outlasted the particular individuals composing it at a given time.

In spite of their many penetrating insights into human customs and institutions, the early philosophers and theologians generally regarded human social relations as part of a divinely ordained cosmic order or as the expression of a fixed and timeless human nature. The political philosophers and classical economists, who were the immediate precursors of the founding fathers of sociology, had a narrow view of the social bonds uniting men, seeing them almost exclusively as political and economic relations. Thus Hobbes, Locke, Rousseau, and the other great seventeenth- and eighteenth-century political theorists thought of the relation between man and society largely in terms of the relation of the state to its subjects. Adam Smith and the classical economists, on the other hand, saw the contractual relations between traders in an exchange economy as the prototype of all social relations. Only after the social consequences of the great political and economic revolutions of the late eighteenth and early nineteenth centuries became fully evident was it possible for the structure of social relations to be perceived as an *autonomous* realm, a "variable" partially independent of political regimes and market relations. The disintegration of traditional European institutions as a result of the French Revolution and the industrial revolution made visible the existence of an order in men's social behavior that was independent of the statecraft of rulers and that could not be seen as the manifestation of an unchanging human nature.

The thinkers who were the first to conceive of the social order as a larger

1

whole encompassing the state, the economy, and all the other institutions of society are the men we honor today as the founding fathers of sociology: Henri Saint-Simon and Auguste Comte in France, Herbert Spencer in England, and Karl Marx in Germany. Comte and Spencer in particular saw the necessity for developing a new intellectual discipline—sociology—which would study the social order and seek to discover general principles and laws underlying it.

The historical changes which gave birth to sociology as a new perspective— and, eventually, a new discipline—have continued at an accelerating rate to transform Western industrial societies. Indeed, machine technology, the concentration of more and more people in large cities, representative government, the nation-state as the dominant form of political organization, and the substitution of secular values for religiously inspired ones are now spreading around the world. The conception of sociology as a continuing effort to understand these societal changes, from the time of the founding fathers to the present, has served as the main organizing principle of this book.

If sociology originated as a response to the birth pangs of the modern world in Western Europe, it is also true that the discovery of the "social" as an independent force shaping human experience had implications transcending the specific historical conditions under which it occurred. The sociological perspective has cast light on traditional as well as on modern societies, and it has also illuminated age-old questions about the nature of human nature and the origins of man and society. The sociological perspective has influenced the work of other social scientists and that of philosophers and historians as well. Indeed practitioners of these disciplines have made many important contributions to sociology itself.

C. Wright Mills points out in our first reading, that the enormous variety of social worlds that men have created has been the major stimulus to the social sciences as organized efforts to understand them. Their major, though by no means only, concern has been with societies caught up in the throes of *historical change*. Sociology, in particular, as the newest of the social sciences, emerged, as we have seen, in response to the social transformations of modern history. The idea of *social structure*, Mills argues, is central to sociology but is nowadays no longer confined to that discipline. Because human institutions have become more closely interrelated and bound together in modern nation-states, social structure—the pattern of their interrelatedness—has to be taken into account by economists and political scientists, and even by anthropologists studying the changes going on in the underdeveloped world. The nation-state, Mills insists, has become the "prime unit" for the study of the most significant problems in the social sciences. This common focus reduces, therefore, the separateness of each discipline and makes "sociological imagination" a requirement for all of them.

Systematic reflection on man and his works, however, long antedates the birth of social science. What, then, is the relationship of sociology, and of social science in general, to older traditions and ways of thinking about human affairs? How do the aims and methods of sociology and social science resemble or differ from the aims and methods of the humanities and the arts? How is social science related to man's age-old search for the good and the beautiful? How is sociology related to efforts to imagine the good society and to projects for making it a reality?

Robert Redfield stresses the role of creative imagination in social science.

He points out that some of the greatest works of social science increase our understanding of man and society in ways that do not depend on their logical rigor nor rely on formal research methods. Such works possess an originality and freshness of vision similar to that of great works of literature, although in presenting generalized descriptions of actual rather than fictional persons and groups they are, unmistakably, contributions to social science. Redfield suggests that the depth and originality of the social scientist's insight into his own humanity and his experience as a participant in his own society are prerequisites for significant new generalizations in social science that go beyond the patient accumulation of facts. No formal course of scientific training can equip the social scientist with the kind of insight that leads to intellectual creativity. Redfield ascribes a dual nature to social science, one displaying aspects of both the humanities and the physical sciences. Important as it is to train the social scientist in technical methods of collecting and recording data, social science, he contends, is also an art that cannot entirely be taught but depends upon the reflective use the scientist makes of his direct experience as a man participating in the life of his society.

# 1

# The Human Variety

### C. WRIGHT MILLS

## I

. . . What social science is properly about is the human variety, which consists of all the social worlds in which men have lived, are living, and might live. These worlds contain primitive communities that, so far as we know, have changed little in a thousand years; but also great power states that have, as it were, come suddenly into violent being. Byzantine and Europe, classical China and ancient Rome, the city of Los Angeles and the empire of ancient Peru—all the worlds men have known now lie before us, open to our scrutiny.

Within these worlds there are open-

country settlements and pressure groups and boys' gangs and Navajo oil men; air forces pointed to demolish metropolitan areas a hundred miles wide; policemen on a corner; intimate circles and publics seated in a room; criminal syndicates; masses thronged one night at the crossroads and squares of the cities of the world; Hopi children and slave dealers in Arabia and German parties and Polish classes and Mennonite schools and the mentally deranged in Tibet and radio networks reaching around the world. Racial stocks and ethnic groups are jumbled up in movie houses and also segregated; married happily and also hating systematically; a thousand detailed occupations are seated in businesses and industries, in governments and localities, in near-continent-wide nations. A million little bargains are transacted every day, and everywhere there are more 'small groups' than anyone could ever count.

The human variety also includes the variety of individual human beings; these too the sociological imagination must grasp and understand. In this imagination an Indian Brahmin of 1850 stands alongside a pioneer farmer of Illinois; an eighteenth-century English gentleman alongside an Australian aboriginal, together with a Chinese peasant of one hundred years ago, a politician in Bolivia today, a feudal knight of France, an English suffragette on hunger strike in 1914, a Hollywood starlet, a Roman patrician. To write of 'man' is to write of all these men and women—also of Goethe, and of the girl next door.

The social scientist seeks to understand the human variety in an orderly way, but considering the range and depth of this variety, he might well be asked: Is this really possible? Is not the confusion of the social sciences an inevitable reflection of what their practitioners are trying to study? My answer is that perhaps the variety is not as 'disorderly' as the mere listing of a small part of it makes it seem; perhaps not even as disorderly as it is often made to seem by the courses of study offered in colleges and universities. Order as well as disorder is relative to viewpoint: to come to an orderly understanding of men and societies requires a set of viewpoints that are simple enough to make understanding possible, yet comprehensive enough to permit us to include in our views the range and depth of the human variety. The struggle for such viewpoints is the first and continuing struggle of social science.

Any viewpoint, of course, rests upon a set of questions, and the over-all questions of the social sciences . . . come readily to the mind that has firm hold of the orienting conception of social science as the study of biography, of history, and of the problems of their intersection within social structure. To study these problems, to realize the human variety, requires that our work be continuously and closely related to the level of historical reality—and to the meanings of this reality for individual men and women. Our aim is to define this reality and to discern these meanings; it is in terms of them that the problems of classic social science are formulated, and thus the issues and troubles these problems incorporate are confronted. It requires that we seek a fully comparative understanding of the social structures that have appeared and do now exist in world history. It requires that smaller-scale milieux be selected and studied in terms of larger-scale historical structures. It requires that we avoid the arbitrary specialization of academic departments, that we specialize our work variously according to topic and above all according to problem, and that in doing so we draw upon the perspectives and ideas, the materials and the methods, of any and all suitable studies of man as an historical actor.

Historically, social scientists have paid most attention to political and economic institutions, but military and kinship, religious and educational institutions have also been much studied. Such classification according to the objective functions institutions generally serve is deceptively simple, but still it is handy. If we understand how these institutional orders are related to one another, we understand the social structure of a society. For 'social structure,' as the conception is most commonly used, refers to just that—to the combination of institutions classified according to the functions each performs. As such, it is the most inclusive working unit with which social scientists deal. Their broadest aim, accordingly, is to understand each of the varieties of social structure, in its components and in its totality. The term 'social structure' itself is quite variously defined, and other terms are used for the conception, but if the distinction between milieu and structure is kept in mind, along with the notion of institution, no one will fail to recognize the idea of social structure when he comes upon it.

## II

In our period, social structures are usually organized under a political state. In terms of power, and in many other interesting terms as well, the most inclusive unit of social structure is the nation-state. The nation-state is now the dominating form in world history and, as such, a major fact in the life of every man. The nation-state has split up and organized, in varying degree and manner, the 'civilizations' and continents of the world. The extent of its spread and the stages of its development are major clues to modern and now to world history. Within the nation-state, the political and military, cultural and economic means of decision and power are now organized; all the institutions and specific milieux in which most men live their public and private lives are now organized into one or the other of the nation-states.

Social scientists of course do not always study only national social structures. The point is that the nation-state is the frame within which they most often feel the need to formulate the problems of smaller and of larger units. Other 'units' are most readily understood as 'pre-national'—or as 'post-national.' For of course national units may 'belong' to one of the 'civilizations,' which usually means that their religious institutions are those of one or another of the 'world religions.' Such facts of 'civilization,' as well as many others, may suggest ways to compare the present-day variety of nation-states. But as used for example by writers like Arnold Toynbee, 'civilizations,' it seems to me, are much too sprawling and imprecise to be the prime units, the 'intelligible fields of study,' of the social sciences.

In choosing the national social structure as our generic working unit, we are adopting a suitable level of generality: one that enables us to avoid abandoning our problems and yet to include the structural forces obviously involved in many details and troubles of human conduct today. Moreover, the choice of national social structures enables us most readily to take up the major issues of public concern, for it is within and between the nation-states of the world that the effective means of power, and hence to a considerable extent of history-making, are now, for better or for worse, tightly organized.

It is of course true that not all nation-states are equal in their power to make history. Some are so small and dependent upon others that what happens within them can only be understood by studying The Great Power States. But that is merely another problem in the useful classification of our units—the nations—and in their necessarily comparative study. It is also true that all nation-states interact, and some clusters of them derive from similar contexts of tradition. But that is true of any sizable unit we might choose for social study. Moreover, especially since World War One, every nation-state capable of it has become increasingly self-sufficient.

Most economists and political scientists consider it obvious that their prime unit is the nation-state; even when they are concerned with 'the international economy' and 'international relations,' they must work closely in the terms of various and specific nation-states. The condition and the continuing practice of anthropologists are of course to study 'the whole' of a society or 'culture,' and in so far as they study modern societies they readily attempt, with varying success, to understand nations as wholes. But sociologists—or more exactly, research technicians—who do not have a very firm hold on the conception of social structure, often consider nations dubiously grand in scale. Apparently this is owing to a bias in favor of 'data collection' which can be less expensively indulged only in smaller-scale units. This means of course that their choice of units is not in accordance with what is needed for whatever problems they have chosen; instead both problem and unit are determined by their choice of method.

In a sense, this book as a whole is an argument against this bias. I think that when most social scientists come seriously to examine a significant problem, they find it most difficult to formulate in terms of any unit smaller than the nation-state. This is true for the study of stratification and of economic policy, of public opinion and the nature of political power, of work and leisure; even problems of municipal government cannot be adequately formulated without quite full reference to their national frame. The unit of the nation-state thus recommends itself by a good deal of empirical evidence available to anyone who is experienced in working on the problems of social science.

## III

The idea of social structure, along with the contention that it is the generic unit of social science, is historically most closely associated with sociology, and sociologists have been its classical exponents. The traditional subject matter of both sociology and anthropology has been the total society; or, as it is called by anthropologists, 'the culture.' What is specifically 'sociological' in the study of any particular feature of a total society is the continual effort to relate that feature to others, in order to gain a conception of the whole. The sociological imagination, I have noted, is in considerable part a result of training in this kind of effort. But nowadays such a view and such practice is by no means confined to sociologists and anthropologists. What was once a promise in these disciplines has become at least a faltering practice, as well as an intention, in the social sciences generally.

Cultural anthropology, in its classic tradition and in its current developments, does not seem to me in any fundamental way distinguishable from sociological study. Once upon a time, when there were few or no surveys of contemporary societies, anthropologists had to collect materials about preliterate peoples in out-of-the-way places. Other social sciences—notably history, demography and political science— have from their beginnings depended upon documentary materials accumulated in literate societies. And this fact tended to separate the disciplines. But now 'empirical surveys' of various sorts are used in all the social sciences, in fact the technique has been most fully developed by psychologists and sociologists in connection with historical societies. In recent years, too, anthropologists have of course studied advanced communities and even nation-states, often at a considerable distance; in turn, sociologists and economists have studied 'the undeveloped peoples.' There is neither a distinction in method nor a boundary of subject matter that truly distinguishes anthropology from economics and sociology today.

Most economics and political science has been concerned with special institutional areas of social structure. About the 'economy' and about 'the state,' political scientists to a lesser extent, and economists to a greater, have developed 'classic theories' that have persisted for generations of scholars. They have, in short, built models, although the political scientists (along with the sociologists) have traditionally been less aware of their model building than the economists have been. Classical theory, of course, consists of making up conceptions and assumptions, from which deductions and generalizations are drawn; these in turn are compared with a variety of empirical propositions. In these tasks, conceptions and procedures and even questions are at least implicitly codified.

This may be all very well. However, for economics certainly and for political science and sociology in due course, two developments tend to make less relevant formal models of state and economy having neat, which is to say formal—and largely mutually exclusive —boundaries: (1) the economic and political development of the so-called underdeveloped areas, and (2) trends of twentieth-century forms of 'the political economy'—both totalitarian and formally democratic. The aftermath of World War Two has been at once erosive and fructifying for alert economic

theorists, in fact, for all social scientists worthy of the title.

A 'theory of prices' that is merely economic may be logically neat, but it cannot be empirically adequate. Such a theory demands consideration of the administration of business institutions and the role of decision-makers within and between them; it requires attention to the psychology of expectations about costs, in particular about wages; to the fixing of prices by small business cartels whose leaders must be understood, etc. In a similar way, to understand 'the rate of interest' often requires knowledge of the official and personal traffic between bankers and government officials as well as impersonal economic mechanics.

There is nothing for it, I think, but for each social scientist to join social science, and with it to go fully comparative—and that, I believe, is now a quite strong drift of interest. Comparative work, both theoretical and empirical, is the most promising line of development for social science today; and such work can best be done within a unified social science.

# 2

# The Art of Social Science [1]

ROBERT REDFIELD

A dozen years ago I was a member of a committee of social scientists on social

Reprinted from *The American Journal of Sociology* 54 (November, 1948), pp. 181–190, by permission of the University of Chicago Press. Copyright 1948 by the University of Chicago Press. All rights reserved.
[1] A lecture delivered at the University of Chicago in May, 1948.

science method charged to appraise some outstanding published works of social science research. Our task was to find some good publications of social science research and then to discover in what their methodological virtue consisted. The first part of our task we passed on to the communities of social scientists themselves. We asked economists to name some outstanding work in their field, sociologists to pick a work in sociology, etc. We limited the choice to publications by living social scientists. Of the books or monographs that received the greatest number of nominations, three were then subjected to analysis and discussion. I participated in the study of the methodological virtues of *The Polish Peasant* by Thomas and Znaniecki and of Webb's *The Great Plains*. These were books nominated by sociologists and historians, respectively, as outstanding in merit.

A curious thing happened. Herbert Blumer, who analyzed *The Polish Peasant* for the committee, came to the conclusion that the method in that book was really unsuccessful because the general propositions set forth in the work could not be established by the particular facts adduced. The committee had to agree. Yet it remained with the impression that this was a very distinguished and important work. Webb's history of cultural transformation in the American West fared no better at the hands of the young historian who analyzed that work. He pointed out many undeniable failures of the author of *The Great Plains* to use and to interpret fully some of the evidence. And yet again a majority of the committee persisted in the impression that Webb's book was truly stimulating, original, and praiseworthy.

Of course one does not conclude from this experience that the failure of facts to support hypotheses, in whole or in part, is a virtue in social science or is to be recommended. No doubt these books would have been more highly praised had these defects been proved to be absent. But does not the experience suggest that there is something in social science which is good, perhaps essential, apart from success with formal method; that these works have virtues not wholly dependent on the

degree of success demonstrated in performing specified and formalized operations on restricted and precisely identified data?

I recall a comment I heard made by a distinguished social scientist whom I shall call A, about another distinguished social scientist whom I shall call B. A said of B: "He is very successful in spite of his method." Now, A was one who laid great stress on the obedience of the research worker to precise methods of operation with limited data, whereas B was much less so concerned. Yet A admired B, and the success he recognized in B was not worldly success but success in advancing our understanding and our control of man in society. Perhaps A felt that B's success was troubling to A's own views as to the importance of formal method. But A, a generous and able man, recognized something of virtue in B as a great student of man in society—a something other than methodological excellence.

What is that something? In attempting an answer here, I do not propose a separation between two ways of working in the scientific study of society. Nor do I deny that social science is dependent upon formal method. I seek rather to direct attention to an aspect of fruitful work in social science which is called for, in addition to formal method, if social science is to be most productive.

Let us here try to find out something about the nature of this nonformal aspect of social science through a consideration of three books about society that have long been recognized as important, influential, and meritorious: De Tocqueville's *Democracy in America*, Sumner's *Folkways*, and Veblen's *The Theory of the Leisure Class*. For from almost fifty to a hundred years these books have interested and have influenced many kinds of social scientists. Veblen and Sumner were economists, but the books they wrote are important for sociologists, anthropologists, historians, and other kinds of social scientists. De Tocqueville's book is a work interesting to political scientists as well as to historians of America, but it is quite as much a work in sociology, for De Tocqueville was concerned not so much in reporting what went on in the United States in 1830 as he was defining a sort of natural societal type: the democratic society, including in the type not merely its political institutions but also its moral, familial, and "cultural" institutions and attitudes, treated as a single whole.

None of these books tells very much about research method, in the sense of teaching special procedures of operation with certain kinds of data. There is nothing in any of them about kinship genealogies, or sampling, or guided interviews, or margins of error. There is nowhere in them any procedure, any kind of operation upon facts to reach conclusions which might not occur to any intelligent and generally educated person. Sumner made notes on the customs of exotic peoples as he read about them. Veblen's methods, as represented in *The Theory of the Leisure Class*, are no more formal than Sumner's. The factual substance of De Tocqueville's book is the record of his own observations as he traveled about America looking at what there was about him and talking to the people he met. If these books have merit, it is not by reason of any inventions or devices of method, for they exhibit none. Yet these are books which have for many years profoundly affected the course of social science and have contributed to our understanding of man in society. They might be even more important if they also made contributions to or through formal method, but, as they do not, something may be learned from them about that part of the study of society which is not formal method.

Perhaps these are not works of research. Perhaps for some "research" always means special procedures of operation which have to be learned or means analysis of some small set of facts or very limited problem. If this is your view of research, I shall not dispute it. Then the three books are not works of research. But what is there in them that is admired and that is valuable in the study of man in society that is not dependent upon formal method?

If these three classic books are not books in social science, what are they? They are surely not novels, or journalism, or yet belles-lettres. That they have qualities of literary style is true—and is not to be deplored—even Sumner's book impresses with the effective iteration of its terse, stark sentences. But the value of these books for the student of society lies not in any appeal they make to aesthetic sensibilities but for the illumination they throw upon man's nature or upon the nature of society. It is true that great novels do that too. But there are, of course, important differences between the books named, on the one hand, and, let us say, *War and Peace* and *The Remembrance of Things Past*, on the other. These last are works for social scientists to know about and to learn from, but they are not works of social science. They are not because neither Proust's book nor Tolstoi's is a generalized description of the nature of society stated at some remove from the personal experiences of the writer. De Tocqueville made his own observations, but he stated his results objectively in generalized and analytical terms making comparisons with other observations and conclusions easy. Tolstoi wrote about a real Russia during the real Napoleonic Wars, but his Pierres and Natashas are imagined, individual, personal, intimate, and ungeneralized. It is not difficult to distinguish the great analyses of society, as objectively studied and presented in generalized conclusions, from the works of personal record and of freely creative imagination.

Are the three books "objective" descriptions of society? In varying degree, but all three to some degree. Probably De Tocqueville, who of the three writers was least a professional social scientist, impresses one most with an air of severe detachment, of willingness to look at this social being, a democratic society, without blame or praise. De Tocqueville's work seems as objective as a social scientist might wish. Sumner, too, is describing, not evaluating, yet there is in the *Folkways* an undertone of patient scorn for the irrationality of man, for man's obedience to whatever folly his tradition may decree. Veblen seems the least objective. Below the forms of scientific analysis lies, urbanely and ironically disguised, the condemnation of a moralist. As a recent writer on Veblen has put it, he used "the realistic paraphernalia of scholarship" to attack the morality of capitalistic society.[2] Nevertheless, even Veblen's books presents a fresh description of a part of modern society, and the description is not that of a creative artist but of one who is responsible to facts studied and facts verifiable.

The three books are works which are not novels, which do not have much to say about formal procedures of research, and which, nevertheless, throw light upon man in society through the more or less objective presentation of generalized conclusions from the study of particular societies. In these respects they correspond with what is by at least some people called "scientific." What did the authors do that constitutes their contribution to the understanding of man in society?

It is surely not that these writers

[2] Daniel Aaron, "Thorstein Veblen—Moralist," *Antioch Review*, VII, No. 3 (Fall, 1947), 390.

have been proved to be invariably right. Indeed, in each case there are points in which in the later days they have been found wrong. Veblen's account overemphasizes competitiveness in terms of consumption and accepts a good deal of what was then current as to race and as to stages of social evolution which is now inacceptable today. Sumner's conception of the mores, immensely stimulating as it was, exaggerates the helplessness of men before tradition and is especially inadequate as a concept for understanding modern societies—as Myrdal has recently shown. And, although De Tocqueville's account of early American society is perceptive and revealing to a degree that is almost miraculous, there is certainly confusion in it between what is necessarily democratic and what is characteristic of the frontier and between what must be characteristic of any democracy and what happened to be in the Anglo-American tradition.

In three respects these books, which have nothing to teach about formal method, make great contributions to the understanding of man in society.

In the first place, each is an expression of some perception of human nature. In each case the writer has looked at people in a society, or in many societies, and has directly apprehended something about their ways of thinking and feeling which are characteristic of the human race under those particular circumstances. His central concern has not been some second- or third-hand index or sign of human nature, some check marks on a schedule or some numbered quantities of anything. He has looked at people with the vision of his own humanity.

Not all of what is called social science is concerned with human nature. The study of population is not concerned with it until matters of population policy are reached. Marginal analysis in economics is concerned with such a slender sliver of human nature, so artificially severed from the rest, that it, too, is unrepresentative of studies of human nature. And this is also of necessity true of much of the archeology of the North American Indian.

These last-mentioned kinds of investigation, worthy as they are, are the special or marginal cases that mark the outskirts of the study of man in society. The essential nature of man in society is his human nature and the expressions of that human nature in particular institutions. To find out the nature and significance of human nature there is no substitute for the human nature of the student himself. He must use his own humanity to understand humanity. To understand alien institutions, he must try to see in them the correspondences and the divergences they exhibit in relation to the institutions with which he is more closely familiar. To understand an alien culture, it is not, first of all, necessary to learn how to interview or how to make schedules for a house-to-house canvass, useful as these skills are. It is first needful to have experienced some culture—some culture which will serve as the touchstone in apprehending this new one.

One aspect of the great merit of the three works mentioned lies in the central attention directed by Sumner, Veblen, and De Tocqueville to the humanity of their subject matter and in the success each had in apprehending the particular facet of that humanity as it was shaped and conditioned by the surrounding circumstances. Sumner, looking especially at small, long-isolated societies or at the later little-changing societies derived from primitive conditions, saw the resulting creation, in each individual there born and reared, of motives and designs of life that were there, in the customs of that society, before him. He saw in human nature the extraordinary malleability of human nature and the precedence of cus-tom over habit. Veblen looked freshly at the behavior of consumers, saw them as people who actually do buy and consume, in their families and their communities, and recognized theretofore insufficiently recognized aspects of human nature in society. De Tocqueville touched Americans in their age of self-confidence and in a great number of true perceptions saw what their behavior meant to them and why. Just compare his success in using his own humanity with imagination, and yet with detachment, with Mrs. Trollope's failure to achieve understanding of these same people.

It is at this point that the methods of the social sciences—now using "method" in its broadest sense to include all the ways of thinking and even feeling about subject matter—approach the methods of the creative artist. Like the novelist, the scientific student of society must project the sympathetic understanding which he has of people with motives, desires, and moral judgments into the subject he is treating. Neither the one nor the other can get along without this gift, this means of understanding. But whereas the novelist may let his imagination run freely, once it is stimulated by personal experience and reading, the scientific student must constantly return to the particular men, the particular societies, he has chosen to investigate, test his insights by these, and report these particular facts with such specificity that his successor may repeat the testing. In spite of this all-important difference, the territories of the humanities and of the scientific study of man in society are in part the same. The subject matter of both is, centrally, man as a human being. Human beings are not the subject matter of physics and chemistry. So it would be error to build a social science upon the image of physics or chemistry. Social science is neither the same as the humanities nor the same as the physical sciences. It is a way of learning about man in society which uses the precise procedures and the objectivity characteristic of physics as far as these will helpfully go in studying human beings but no further; and which uses, indispensably, that personal direct apprehension of the human qualities of behavior and of institutions which is shared by the novelist.

A second observation may be made about the three books chosen. Each brings forward significant generalizations. In the case of Veblen's book, the general conceptions that are known by the phrases "pecuniary emulation," "vicarious consumption," etc., are, like the concepts in *Folkways*, names for new insights into persistent and widely inclusive aspects of man's nature in society. In reading these books, we catch a glimpse of the eternal in the light of the ephemeral. We see ourselves as exemplifications of patterns in nature. Social science is concerned with uniformities. The uniformities are exaggerated; they transcend the particularity of real experience and historic event; they claim more than each fact by itself would allow; they say: "If it were really like this, this would be the pattern." De Tocqueville, too, offers such patterns that go beyond the particular facts. Indeed, the case of De Tocqueville is particularly plain in this connection, for so interested is he in presenting a system of coherent generalizations as to the necessary nature of democratic society that in many passages he makes no reference at all to what he saw in the United States but derives one generalization as to the democratic society he conceives from some other generalization already brought forward. He is not, therefore, to be rejected as a contributor to the scientific understanding of society, for these deductions are tied to generalizations that in turn rest upon many particular observations of many particular men and events. The concept, like the novel, is a work of creative imagination but a work more closely and publicly bound to particular facts of observation and record.

Like the apprehension of the humanly significant, the making of the generalization is a work of imagination. Sumner did not find out that there is such a thing as the mores by learning and applying some method of research. He discovered it by watching the people around him and by using the observations recorded by other men and then by making a leap of thought across many diversities to apprehend the degree of uniformity that deserves the term "mores." In the reaching of a significant generalization as to man in society there is an exercise of a gift of apprehension so personal and so subtly creative that it cannot be expected to result merely from application of some formal method of research.

The three books show thinkers about man in society who have had some new and generalized apprehension of human nature or of human institutions. They have succeeded in communicating this apprehension in such a way as to show it to be both important and true. It is true in the sense that there are facts accessible that support it. It is not, of course, all the truth, and it may be that some other apprehension will come to appear "more true," that is, even more illuminating, as applied to some set of circumstances.

There is another quality in the thinking and the creating of the three writers that deserves recognition by itself: the freshness and independence of viewpoint with which each looked at his subject matter. One feels, in reading any one of the three books, how the writer saw what he saw with his own eyes, as if the previous views of it were suspect, just because they were previous. One feels in the case of each writer a discontent with the way some aspect of man in society was then being regarded, a clear-headed wilfulness to take another look for himself. There is a disposition to make the thing looked at a true part of the viewer's own being, to go beyond obedience to the existing writings on the subject. De Tocqueville was dissatisfied with the views of democracy current in his time: the passionate condemnations or the equally passionate espousals. He would go to the country where the angel or the monster was actually in course of development, and he would, he resolved coolly, look for neither monster nor angel; he would look at what he should find, and grasp it, in its whole and natural condition, as one would look at a newly arrived class of animal. He could weigh the good and the bad, then, after he had come to understand the natural circumstances that would produce the creature. Sumner's book is in one way a reaffirmation of a viewpoint then current and in another way a reaction against it. As the folkways come about by no man's planning but through the accidental interactions of men and the competition of alternative solutions, they are consistent with that conception of unrestrained individualistic competition which Sumner supported in the economic sphere. On the other hand, the *Folkways* reads as a reaction against the Age of Reason. It seems to say that men do not, after all, solve their problems by rational calculation of utilities. Looked at anew, the ways of men appear not reasonable but unreasonable and determined by pre-existing customs and moral judgments which make the calculation of utilities seem absurd. From this point of view the book is an act of rebellion. An economist looks for himself at the whole human scene and says, too emphatically, no doubt, what needs to be said to correct the preceding vision. Something not so different could be

said about the fresh look that Veblen took.

It may be objected that the qualities in these three works are qualities one may expect to find only in an occasional book written by some unusual mind. These books have passed beyond social science, or they fall short of it; and the humbler toiler in the vineyard cannot expect to learn from them anything that would help him in tending the vines of his more limited hypotheses or in pressing the wine of his more restricted conclusions.

Yet all three of the qualities found in these works may be emulated by the student of any human aspect of man in society. It is not only in good major works that there is found that human sympathy which is needful in apprehending a human reality. The exercise of this capacity is demanded in every study of a community; it is exacted in every consideration of an institution in which men with motives and desires like our own fulfil the roles and offices that make it up; it is required in every interview. One may be taught how to pursue a course of questioning, how to map a neighborhood, or how to tabulate and treat statistically the votes cast in an election; but to know how to do these things is not to be assured of meaningful conclusions. Besides these skills, one needs also the ability to enter imaginatively, boldly, and, at the same time, self-critically into that little fraction of the human comedy with which one has become scientifically concerned. One must become a part of the human relations one studies, while holding one's self also a little to one side, so as to suspend judgment as to the worth of one's first insight. Then one looks at the scene again; perhaps, guided by something one has known or read of human beings in some comparable situation, in some other place or age, one may get a second insight that better withstands reexamination and the test of particular observations. This procedure, call it method, non-method, or what you will, is an essential part of most of social science, great and small.

As for the exercise of the ability to see the general in the particular, is this not also demanded of anyone who takes a scientific attitude toward anything in human nature or society? We are not freed from the obligation to look for what may be widely true by the narrowness, in time and space, of the facts before us. Surely Sumner did not wait to conceive of the mores until he had piled up those five hundred pages of examples. Malinowski provided a clearer understanding of the nature of myth, in its resemblance to and its difference from folk tale, from the view he had of the stories told and the ways they were told in a small community in the South Seas. Webb, a historian rather than one of those students of society who more easily announce generalizations thought to be widely applicable, does not, in his *The Great Plains*, announce any; but the value of the work lies for many in the fact that it is easily read as an exemplification of the tendency of institutions adjusted to one environment to undergo change when imported into a new and of the effects of changes in technology upon human relations. The social scientist is always called upon to use his imagination as to the general that may lie within the immediate particulars. The formal method may lead him to these generalizations; after he has added up the cases, or completed the tests, he may for the first time see some correspondences that suggest a generalization. But it happens at least as often that he sees the generalization long before the formal methods have been carried out; the exercise of the formal method may then test the worth of his insight. And a significant generalization may appear without formal

method. The conceptions of marginal utility in economics and of the marginal man in sociology perhaps illustrate the development of a concept, on the one hand, with close dependence upon formal method and, on the other, without such dependence. In the latter case Park was struck by resemblances in the conduct of particular men and women whom he met, American Negroes, mission-educated Orientals, and second-generation immigrants: humane insight, guided by scientific imagination, then created the concept.

The third quality of good social science in its less formal aspects is freshness of vision. It is the looking at what one is studying as if the world's comprehension of it depended solely on one's own look. In taking such a look, one does not ignore the views that other men have taken of the subject matter or of similar subject matter. But these earlier views are challenged. Maybe, one says, it is not as my teachers told me I should find it. I will look for myself. One has perhaps heard something about folk society. But at this particular society with which I am concerned I will look for myself. Perhaps there is no folk society there. Perhaps there is something else, much nearer the truth.

It is difficult for teachers who have expounded their own views of some aspect of man in society to teach their successors to take some other view of it. Perhaps it cannot be taught. Yet somehow each generation of social scientists must rear a following generation of rebels. Now rebellion is not well inculated in the teaching of formal procedure. Indeed, an exclusive emphasis on formal procedure may cause atrophy of the scientific imagination. To train a man to perform a technique may result in making him satisfied with mastery of the technique. Having learned so much about field procedure, or statistics, or the situations in which interviews are held and recorded, or the criticism of documents, the new social scientist may come to feel that he has accomplished all the learning he needs. He may rest content in proficiency. Proficiency is excellent, but it must be combined with an imaginative dissatisfaction. In little investigations as in large ones, the situation studied demands a whole look and a free look.

It is equally doubtful whether one can give instruction in the exercise of humane insight or in recognizing the general in the particular when the generality is not thrust upon the student by a marked statistical predominance. These are qualities of the social science investigator that perhaps depend upon the accidents of natural endowment. Humane insight is a gift. The concept is a work of creative imagination; apprehension is a gift. In stressing the necessity, in good social science, for the investigator to think and to speculate independently and freely, in emphasizing the reliance of good social science upon the personal and human qualities of the investigator, one seems to be talking not about a science but about an art and to be saying that social science is also an art. It is an art in that the social scientist creates imaginatively out of his own human qualities brought into connection with the facts before him. It is an art in degree much greater than that in which physics and chemistry are arts, for the student of the atom or of the element is not required, when he confronts his subject matter, to become a person among persons, a creature of tradition and attitude in a community that exists in tradition and in attitude. With half his being the social scientist approaches his subject matter with a detachment he shares with the physicist. With the other half he approaches it with a human sympathy which he shares with the novelist. And it is an art to a greater degree than is physics or chemistry for the further reason that the relationships among the parts of a person or of a society are, as compared with physical relationships, much less susceptible of definitions, clear and machine precise. In spite of the great advances in formal method in social science, much of the understanding of persisting and general relationships depends upon a grasp that is intuitive and that is independent of or not fully dependent on some formal method. In advancing social science, we invent and practice techniques, and we also cultivate a humanistic art.

The nature of social science is double. In the circle of learning, its place adjoins the natural sciences, on the one hand, and the humanities, on the other. It is not a result of exceptional political ambition that political scientists and anthropologists are to be found included both in the Social Science Research Council and in the American Council of Learned Societies; it is a recognition of the double nature of social science. On the one hand, the student of society is called upon to apprehend the significant general characteristics of human beings with something of the same human insight which is practiced by a novelist or a dramatist. On the other hand, he is obliged to make his observations and his inferences as precise and as testable, and his generalizations as explicit and as compendent, as the examples of the natural sciences suggest and as his own different materials allow.

It is the example of the natural sciences which social scientists have on the whole striven to imitate. In the short history of social science its practitioners have turned their admiring gazes toward their neighbors on the scientific side. They have looked that way, perhaps, because the natural sciences were the current success. They have looked that way, surely, because when the students of human nature in society came to think of themselves as representing one or more disciplines, with professors and places in universities and in national councils, social science was not very scientific: it was speculative and imprecise. To achieve identity, it had to grow away from the making of personally conceived systems of abstract thought. It had to learn to build, a brick at a time, and to develop procedures that would make the building public and subject to testing.

But now the invention and the teaching of special procedures have received too exclusive an emphasis in the doing of social science and in the making of social scientists. In places the invention and the teaching of special procedures have gone ahead of the possibility of finding out anything very significant with their aid. It is certainly desirable to be precise, but it is quite as needful to be precise about something worth knowing. It is good to teach men and women who are to be social scientists how to use the instruments of observation and analysis that have been developed in their disciplines. But it is not good to neglect that other equally important side of social science.

To identify social science very closely with the physical sciences is to take one view of the education of social scientists: to think of that education chiefly in terms of formal method and formal knowledge of society already achieved and to be taught. Then programs for making social scientists will be made up of training in techniques and the opportunity to take part in some kind of research in which the procedures are already determined and the problems set by some established master. Then the holder of a fellowship will go to a school, where a way of working is well known and well fixed, and he will acquire the procedural competences taught at that school.

If this is all we do for young students of society, we are likely to have proficient technicians, but we are not likely to have great social scientists or to have many books written that are as illuminating and as influential as those by Sumner, Veblen, and De Tocqueville.

It would be well to give some attention to the humanistic aspect of social science. Part of the preparation of good social scientists is humanistic education. As what is called general education, or liberal education, is largely humanistic, it follows that the social scientist has two interests in liberal education. Like the physicist, like everybody else, the social scientist needs liberal education in his role as a citizen. But, in addition, he needs liberal humanistic education in his role as a social scientist.

The art of social science cannot be inculcated, but, like other arts, it can be encouraged to develop. The exercise of that art can be favored by humanistic education. If the social scientist is to apprehend, deeply and widely and correctly, persons and societies and cultures, then he needs experience, direct or vicarious, with persons, societies, and cultures. This experience is partly had through acquaintance with history, literature, biography, and ethnography. And if philosophy gives some experience in the art of formulating and in thinking about widely inclusive generalizations, then the social scientist needs acquaintance with philosophy. There is no longer any need to be fearful about philosophy. The time when young social science was struggling to make itself something different from philosophy is past. Now social science is something different. Now social scientists need to learn from philosophy, not to become philosophers, but to become better social scientists. The acquaintance with literature, biography, ethnography, and philosophy which is gained in that general education given in high schools and colleges is probably not rich enough or deep enough for some of those who are to become social scientists. The opportunities for advanced education given to some who appear to have exceptional gifts as students of man in society may well consist of the study of Chinese or East Indian culture, or of the novel in Western literature, or of the history of democracy.

The humanistic aspect of social science is the aspect of it that is today not well appreciated. Social science is essentially scientific in that its propositions describe, in general terms, natural phenomena; in that it returns again and again to special experience to verify and to modify these propositions. It tells what is, not what ought to be. It investigates nature. It strives for objectivity, accuracy, compendency. It employs hypotheses and formal evidence; it values negative cases; and, when it finds a hypothesis to be unsupported by the facts, it drops it for some other which is. But these are all aspects of social science so well known that it is tedious to list them again. What is less familiar, but equally true, is that to create the hypothesis, to reach the conclusion, to get, often, the very first real datum as to what are A's motives or what is the meaning of this odd custom or that too-familiar institution, requires on the part of one who studies persons and societies, and not rocks or proteins, a truly humanistic and freely imaginative insight into people, their conventions and interests and motives, and that this requirement in the social scientist calls for gifts and for a kind of education different from that required of any physicist and very similar to what is called for in a creative artist.

If this be seen, it may also be seen that the function of social science in our society is a double function. Social science is customarily explained and justified by reason of what social science contributes to the solution of particular problems that arise in the management of our society, as a help in getting particular things done. As social scientists we take satisfaction in the fact that today, as compared with thirty years ago, social scientists are employed because their employers think that their social science is applicable to some practical necessity. Some knowledge of techniques developed in social science may be used: to select taxicab drivers that are not likely to have accidents; to give vocational guidance; to discover why one business enterprise has labor troubles while a similar enterprise does not; to make more effective some governmental program carried into farming communities; to help the War Relocation Authority carry out its difficult task with Japanese-Americans.

All these contributions to efficiency and adjustment may be claimed with justice by social scientists. What is also to be claimed, and is less commonly stressed, is that social science contributes to that general understanding of the world around us which, as we say, "liberalizes," or "enriches." The relation of social science to humanistic learning is reciprocal. Social scientists need humanistic learning the better to be social scientists. And the understanding of society, personality, and human nature which is achieved by scientific methods returns to enrich that humanistic understanding without which none can become human and with which some few may become wise. Because its subject matter is humanity, the contribution of social science to general, liberal education is greater than is the contribution of those sciences with subject matter that is physical. In this respect also, creative artist and social scientist find themselves side by side. The artist may reveal something of universal human or social nature. So too may the social scientist. No one has ever applied, as a key to a lock, Sumner's *Folkways* or Tawney's *Religion and the Rise of Capitalism* or James's *The Varieties of Religious Experience*. These are not the works of social science that can be directly consulted and applied when a government office or a business concern has an immediate problem. But they are the books of lasting influence. Besides what influence they have upon those social scientists who come to work in the government office, or the business concern, in so far as they are read and understood and thought about by men and women who are not social scientists, or even as they are communicated indirectly by those who have read them to others, they are part of humanistic education, in the broad sense. Releasing us from our imprisonment in the particular, we are freed by seeing how we are exemplifications of the general. For how many young people has not Sumner's book, or Veblen's book, or some work by Freud, come as a swift widening of the doors of vision, truly a liberation, a seeing of one's self, perhaps for the first time, as sharing the experiences, the nature, of many other men and women? So I say that social science, as practiced, is something of an art and that, as its best works are communicated, it has something of the personal and social values of all the arts.

# Part One

# Basic Concepts and Perspectives of Sociology

## INTRODUCTION

Much of contemporary social science developed in reaction against conclusions about the nature of man and society advanced by the first post-Darwinian thinkers. Darwin showed that man's bodily structure was continuous with that of subhuman species and had evolved in accordance with the same laws. A host of philosophers, psychologists, sociologists, and natural scientists concluded that if man is an animal like other animals, albeit a specially gifted one, then biological laws governing all other living things must also apply to human nature, history, and society. Accordingly, they espoused a variety of theories of biological determinism in which processes occurring in human societies were interpreted as reflections of similar processes occurring in the animal world.

The social Darwinists argued that human society itself was an arena of ruthless competition between individuals, groups, and entire peoples that conformed to the same principles of natural selection, or "survival of the fittest," that Darwin had seen as the explanation for the evolution of different species. The unilinear evolutionists maintained that human societies, like the various species, develop through a series of stages, from simple to more complex organization. The eugenics movement insisted that man's heredity determined his behavior and that criminal behavior, creativity, and character were the result of differing heredities. Racial theorists extended this assumption to the achievements of whole peoples, arguing that varying *group* heredities accounted for the diverse customs and institutions of mankind, just as the varying behavior of animal species reflected their different heredities. The school of instinct psychologists claimed that all human conduct was the manifestation of instincts that man had acquired long ago when he first emerged as a distinct species adapted to a primeval environment.

The assaults on all these ideas by twentieth-century social science—often inspired, as in the case of the doctrines of racial difference, by moral outrage over their social and political consequences—have recreated a view of the uniqueness of man almost as pronounced as that held by Darwin's original theological opponents, who believed that man was the specially created possessor of a soul and had little in common with his fellow living creatures. Recognizing that man's brain and nervous system are as much the products of biological evolution as the crab's shell or the bird's wing, social scientists have insisted that the learning capacity of the human brain has enabled man to dispense with inherited instincts as the dominant mode of adapting to his environment. Man's unique achievements stem from learning rather than from heredity. Conceptual thought and speech, made possible by a superior brain, have created a gulf between man and the rest of the animal world. Men are able to communicate what they have learned to their fellows and to later generations. In this way they create a variety of cultures, or collective ways of life, shared by different groups of men. Man and society both depend for growth and survival on the resourcefulness of cultural tradition, rather than on the "blind" process of natural selection and biological evolution. The historical cultures men have created are so diverse in origin and content and in the patterns of change they have undergone that they cannot be subsumed under any law of evolution that implies a sequence of fixed stages paralleling the stages of development through which the various living species have passed. In short, an emphasis on the *discontinuities* rather than the *continuities* between human life and the animal world has become characteristic of social thought in recent decades.

Attempts to define the essence of man, that is, what is uniquely human (the *differentia specifica* of man, as Aristotle put it) are very old, long antedating the controversy over Darwinism. The Greek philosophers called man the "rational animal" singling out *reason* as his distinctive gift. This emphasis on reason is reflected in the name given the human species: *Homo sapiens,* or man, the wise one. Speech too has long been regarded as a peculiarly human capacity, although it has usually been mistakenly treated as a mere consequence of man's prior ability to think and reason. Possession of conscience, a "sense of right and wrong," has also often been selected as defining the line between man and other animals. Some nineteenth-century thinkers saw man's ability to reshape his material environment with the aid of tools as his outstanding peculiarity and christened him *Homo faber:* man, the maker of things, a definition central to the Marxist tradition. William James considered self-consciousness, as opposed to mere consciousness, as a distinctively human mental attribute. Alfred Korzybski, the founder of semantics, has called man the "time-binding animal," the only organism who lives in simultaneous awareness of the past and the future as well as the present. Norman O. Brown characterizes man as the "neurotic animal" or the "repressed animal," the only creature who is so torn by emotional conflict that he almost literally drives himself mad.[1] A great many sociologists and anthropologists have considered man's creation and perpetuation of *culture,* a body of socially transmitted habits, beliefs, and sentiments, as the most important distinction between the human and the animal.

All these efforts to define the uniquely human contain a good deal of truth, nor are they mutually exclusive. Yet they are clearly partial in arbitrarily selecting a single feature of human conduct and failing to show how it is related to other traits that differentiate men and animals. In the present century trends within a number of intellectual disciplines, from metaphysics to experimental psychology and physical anthropology, have converged in pointing to the crucial significance of the human ability to create symbols as the source of most human behavior that is not duplicated by lower species. George Herbert Mead, an American

---

[1] Norman O. Brown, *Life Against Death* (New York: Vintage Books, 1959), pp. 3–10.

philosopher and social psychologist,[2] argued that mind, self, and society are all necessary consequences of man's possession of language, which is essentially a set of vocal symbols that name and represent the multitudinous aspects of lived experience. We have included a selection on the social origins of the self from his most influential book in Section B. The rationality so stressed by the early philosophers; man's selfhood, which enables him to get outside of his own skin and to respond to himself as an object; and his social nature, through which he relates himself to others in subtle and complex ways that have no counterparts in the animal world, all these, Mead insists, are results of symbolic communication. Man is, as Ernst Cassirer christened him in another selection reprinted here, the *animal symbolicum*—the symbolic animal.

In recent years there have been some signs in the social sciences of a renewed interest in man's animal nature. In part, this is no doubt attributable to general tendencies in contemporary history—the savagery of recent wars and revolutions, the increased preoccupation with sexuality as Victorian taboos are relaxed, and the primitivism and eulogy of the irrational in much modern art—that have made us more receptive to the idea that our animal heritage has by no means been transcended. In social thought, Freud has long been a partial counterinfluence to the belief that man's essence lies in his successful conquest of the limits his biology imposes on his behavior. In the biological sciences themselves, recent discoveries have modified older views of human evolution. New fossil finds of early human and hominoid forms, for example, have made obsolete the assumption that man's body evolved to the point where he became capable of symbolizing and of creating culture but then stopped evolving because his new cultural or "superorganic" mode of existence freed him from the pressures of natural selection. It now appears far more probable that skills in communicating, making and using tools, planning for the future, and living cooperatively in social groups gave their possessors adaptive advantages, with the result that the bodily structures supporting these skills were increasingly selected for survival. Upright posture, bipedalism, the development of the hand as a grasping organ, the specialization of the jaws and vocal cords for speech, a more complex brain, nonseasonal sexuality, greater infantile helplessness—all these organic traits that define man as a separate species can no longer be regarded simply as preconditions for culture and human social life, but they are themselves products of a process of natural selection that favored increasing reliance on culture. Man's cultural and social history, in other words, has shaped his biological history. These newer views of the relation between man's biological evolution and culture are summarized by Robert Endleman in our first selection.

If man's very culture-creating capacity is rooted in his body, in the kind of peculiar mammalian animal that he is, then it is unlikely that human nature is as variable or human society as malleable as social scientists have sometimes contended. Extreme versions of cultural relativism that regarded man as capable of creating an almost infinite variety of possible ways of life are less plausible today than several decades ago. The reaction against biological determinism in the social sciences has occasionally overshot its mark. It indeed succeeded in thoroughly refuting the extreme hereditarianism and the superficially be-

[2] The work of Mead that has most influenced sociologists is *Mind, Self and Society* (Chicago: University of Chicago Press, 1934).

guiling Darwinian analogies that dominated social thought from the middle of the nineteenth century until roughly the 1920's. But the critics of biological determinism did not address themselves to the issue of what limits man's biology sets to his historical variability; they were, perhaps inevitably, more concerned with asserting the reality of human variability against those who denied or minimized it. Because they have indisputably won their battle, today it is possible for social scientists to return to consideration of what is constant in human nature and universal in human society and what bearing man's animal heritage has on these.

Endleman discusses here the origins of language in the course of man's evolution as a species, while Cassirer traces the "slow and continuous process" of the growth of the individual mind's capacity to symbolize through speech. In addition to relating man's symbolizing capacities to the "Human Revolution" —the adoption by man's protohuman ancestors of a new hunting way of life on the savannahs of East Africa—Endleman also describes the emergence under these conditions of the basic human character structure identified by Freud. The sexual division of labor between male hunters and female child-raisers, the role of vocalization in play and in the mother-child relationship, the bearing of the long period of infantile dependence required for the development of a symbol and tool-making brain on adult psychosexual relations, the origins of repression in infantile helplessness and the emotionally overburdened tie to the parent, are among the themes he develops. The interdependence between man's body and his psychic conflicts and their common origin in human evolution lead Endleman to question the utopian hopes of the Freudian Left, represented by Herbert Marcuse and Norman Brown, for the abolition of repression and the psychic liberation of mankind.[3]

Our readings in Section A deal with the biological and psychological origins of human nature and social life. While the authors are an anthropologisti-sociologist (Endleman) and a philosopher (Cassirer), they provide a general background to all of the social sciences. The readings in this section also introduce the student to the concept of culture, which is the generic term social scientists use to refer to everything men share as members of society as distinct from their biological heritage. Culture is man's social heritage and includes language, technology, the arts, and fundamental beliefs, as well as the patterns of social conduct with which sociologists are primarily concerned. The remaining sections in Part One deal with the basic concepts and approaches used by contemporary sociologists to describe and interpret the social world.

Sociology is a disciplined *perspective* on human social life. It is a way of examining the varied relations among people as we seek answers to questions that puzzle us about man and society. Some of these questions are of a *transhistorical* nature—that is, they are concerned with what all men and all societies have in common throughout time. Many of the questions to which we most urgently desire answers, however, are *historically specific*. They arise out of men's experiences living in particular historical epochs and types of

---

[3] See Brown, op. cit.; and Herbert Marcuse, *Eros and Civilization* (Boston: the Beacon Press, 1955). For a general discussion of the Freudian Left, see Paul A. Robinson, *The Freudian Left* (New York, Evanston, and London: Harper Colophon Books, 1969). One of the figures Robinson discusses is Géza Roheim, who is a major influence on Endleman and whose long out-of-print *The Origin and Function of Culture* has recently been reissued (Garden City, N.Y.: Doubleday Anchor Books, 1971).

society. We may want to know, for example, the origins of capitalism in modern Western history, the emerging pattern of race relations in twentieth-century America, the results of efforts to control population growth in countries where the death rate has rapidly declined, and the changing group interests that shape the programs of political parties.

The sociological perspective includes a set of *basic concepts* which sociologists employ in their inquiries. These concepts serve as lenses through which they examine the social world and try to understand it. The readings reprinted in Sections B, C, D, and E explain and illustrate the following basic concepts: *social action, social interaction, primary group, social norm, social role, social structure, institutions, and society.* All of these concepts are *universals;* they refer to features of social life found in all human societies.

In their universality they point to transhistorical aspects of social life. Several of them contain, in compressed form, an entire theory about some aspect of the nature of man and society. They represent, that is, an answer to some perennial question about human life. Thus, as we have previously seen, the concept of culture is a way of answering the ancient question "What is the *differentia specifica* of Man?" Similarly, the concept of social norm introduced in Section C is an assertion of the reality of man's moral nature, a denial that his behavior can be reduced to instinct, mechanical conditioning, rational calculation of self-interest, or the effects of coercion.

Although our basic concepts often imply answers to transhistorical questions about the general nature of man and society, they also are useful in answering specific historical questions about social life. We have called the basic concepts "lenses" through which the sociologist looks at social reality. To vary the metaphor, they are also the building blocks with which he constructs more elaborate conceptions of historically specific social phenomena, such as *bureaucracy, capitalism, mass society, class* and *caste,* or the *metropolitan community,* which are dealt with later in this book.

Concern with historically specific questions has always been a main focus of sociological inquiry because of the sociologist's inescapable involvement as man and citizen in the fate of his own country and era. We are all of us men embedded in history and our deepest curiosities and anxieties are often aroused by contemporary problems. Such a concern, however, in no sense condemns the sociologist to parochialism, to a narrow concentration on the here and now. For, as the work of Max Weber in particular shows, a full understanding of contemporary social life can only be achieved by comparing it and contrasting it with social life in other times and places. This is the meaning of the idea that the sociological perspective is *comparative.* As C. Wright Mills has said, the sociologist should "never think of describing an institution in twentieth-century America without trying to bear in mind similar institutions in other types of structures [societies] and periods." [4] Our sociological knowledge, therefore, is embodied both in transhistorical generalizations that are efforts to formulate timeless truths about man and society and in historically specific generalizations applicable only to life in particular changing societies. The sociologist, however, needs always to examine several societies even if his immediate aim is to define and isolate the unique features of one of them.

[4] C. Wright Mills, *The Sociological Imagination* (New York: Oxford University Press, 1959), p. 215.

The great French thinker Alexis de Tocqueville, who is not easily classifiable as a sociologist, a political scientist, or a historian, once wrote in reflecting on his classic *Democracy in America:*

In my work on America . . . though I seldom mentioned France, I did not write a page without thinking of her, and placing her as it were before me. And what I specifically tried to draw out, and to explain in the United States, was not the whole condition of that foreign society, but the points in which it differs from our own or resembled us. It is always by noting likenesses and contrasts that I succeeded in giving an interesting and accurate description of the New World. . . . I believe that this perpetual silent reference to France was a principal cause of the book's success.

This statement superbly summarizes the comparative approach to the study of human society that has become the hallmark of sociology. De Tocqueville regarded his comparative perspective as valuable because it illuminates both "likenesses *and* contrasts"—the similarities and the differences—between societies. The chief difference between de Tocqueville and the modern sociologist is that the latter substitutes for the former's "perpetual silent reference to France" a systematic, explicit comparative frame of reference. Our basic sociological concepts are an effort to build such a frame of reference. Let us review these concepts in detail.

*Social action* is behavior of individuals which is directed toward other people. *Social interaction* is two or more individuals responding to each other and mutually influencing one another's conduct.[5] Two pedestrians who collide accidentally while turning a street corner in opposite directions are not interacting socially, only physically. Two birds, however, who call to one another in the treetops are engaged in social interaction. Social interaction is the basic component of all the relationships, groups, and associations that constitute human society. Groups, associations, and societies are more or less complex patterns or networks of interactions among individuals. We have included as one of our readings a famous description of small, relatively undifferentiated, face-to-face groups—"primary groups" as he christened them—by the early twentieth century American sociologist, Charles Horton Cooley.

Sociologists are concerned with isolating and specifying the distinctive features of human social interaction. As we have seen, man's ability to create symbols, especially vocal symbols, of his experience is what chiefly distinguishes him from other animals. Symbolic communication, or symbolic interaction as some writers have called it, is the essence of human social behavior. Both W. J. H. Sprott and Peter Berger, in the readings presented here, describe the features of all human social interaction that depend on man's ability to communicate symbolically, and both acknowledge their indebtedness to the ideas of George Herbert Mead.[6]

Human social interaction both creates and is governed by *social norms*—rules or symbolized models of behavior present in the consciousness of men that guide and control their interactions. Social norms are an important part of the

[5] W. J. H. Sprott, in our first selection in Section B, does not distinguish between social action and social interaction, but uses the terms synonymously.
[6] An interesting attempt to arrive at a definition of the peculiar features of human social interaction which arrives at conclusions almost identical to those of the symbolic interactionists though starting from a quite different philosophical perspective is Jose Ortega y Gasset, *Man and People* (New York: W. W. Norton, 1957), pp. 72–89.

301.08  W944a2

c.1

culture men learn as members of a given society. Norms state the expectations people have of how others will behave toward them and toward one another. For example, we do not expect to be jostled in an unmannerly fashion when walking the streets, because we know that showing at least this minimal consideration for strangers is a widely accepted norm in American society. But our expectations are not merely predictions or anticipations of how others will act in the sense in which we expect the sun to rise in the East or material objects to behave in accordance with the laws of gravity. Our expectations of other people usually also amount to a *demand* that they be fulfilled. When the Admiral warns the sailors of the British fleet that "England expects every man to do his duty," or when a mother tells her children on their departure for school that she "expects" them to obey the teacher, it is clear that the Admiral and the mother are not merely voicing predictions about the behavior of the sailors and the children, but are trying to influence or control their behavior in advance.[7] Their admonitions clearly carry, at least implicitly, the suggestion that if the "expected" behavior is not forthcoming some penalty or *sanction* will be imposed upon the recalcitrant individual.

Norms are often classified according to the degree of severity, specificity, and certainty of the sanctions imposed if they are violated. *Laws* are norms that have been embodied in formal written statutes enforced by specially designated officials; the sanctions imposed on violators are decided upon by other specially designated officials or agencies such as judges, courts, and juries, or they may in some cases be themselves prescribed by statute. *Mores* are norms, the violation of which evokes a reaction of intense indignation and moral outrage from others, and the sanctions imposed are likely to be severe. *Custom* and *fashion* are norms which if not conformed to will be followed by milder and less certain sanctions such as ostracism and ridicule, which may nevertheless have psychologically devastating effects on the violator. The very complex relationship between norms—the detailed rules prescribed for behavior—and *values*, more general conceptions of what is good and desirable that may be invoked to justify particular norms, is explored by Judith Blake and Kingsley Davis in one of the readings in Section C.

Not all norms apply to every member of a group or society. Even in small informal groups and in primitive tribes, individuals differ in the parts they play in the total network of interactions among members. These different parts are what sociologists call *social roles*. Essentially, social roles are clusters of norms and expectations that apply to different classes of persons within a group or society. Thus in all societies somewhat different behavior is expected of men and women, the old and the young, and parents and children. Some differentiation of roles based on differences in sex, age, and kinship is a universal feature of human society. In the larger and more complex societies there is a much greater variety of roles—which is part of what we mean in describing them as complex societies. In the sphere of economic activities, the pattern of role differentiation is usually called the *division of labor*. Some examples of social roles in various known societies are *woman, father, adult, sorcerer, sage, beggar, nobleman, playboy, automobile salesman, physician, Catholic.* Obviously the

---

[7] This double sense in which we use the verb, *to expect,* is pointed out by Robert Cooley Angell, *Free Society and Moral Crisis* (Ann Arbor: University of Michigan Press, 1958), p. 34.

size of the categories of persons who fill these roles may vary from well over half the population in the case of *adult* to a single individual at any given time in the case of *head roles* in large organizations, such as the Pope of the Roman Catholic Church or the President of the United States. The norms and expectations that constitute a particular role may also govern one's interactions with only a few other people, as in the case of kinship roles, or with almost every person one encounters, as in the case of sex roles. Furthermore, the range of conduct prescribed by a role may be great, as for the roles of wife and priest, or a role may require little more than the occasional observance of a few simple rules, as in the case of customer or hotel guest.

The individual is likely to experience the demands and expectations of others most intensely in striving to fulfill the requirements of his social roles. Yet, as Peter Berger points out, he generally does not feel his role obligations as a coercive and tyrannical "power of society" limiting his freedom: often, "we *want* the parts that society has assigned to us." [8] Berger argues that our very sense of individual identity, our most intimate awareness of our self-hood, is shaped by the roles we play. That this shaping of self by role is rarely complete, however, is implied by Erving Goffman's concept of *role distance*, which he illustrates in the reading reprinted here with an account of the conduct of doctors and nurses during a surgical operation.

If the relation between the individual and society is illuminated by the concept of role, roles can also be examined in their mutual interrelationships. Roles are reciprocal in prescribing behavior toward persons in other roles whose behavior is similarly regulated. Thus one cannot describe the role of husband without at the same time describing the role of wife. The total pattern formed by a given arrangement of roles is a *social structure* or *social organization*. The study of such systems of linked roles differentiates sociology proper from social psychology, which is the study of the impact of social norms and roles on individual personality. Any recurring pattern of interaction among individuals playing different roles may be said to constitute a social structure. We may thus speak of the social structure of the American middle-class family, of a primitive tribe, of a ladies' bridge club, of Harvard University, and even of American society as a whole.

A *group* is a plurality of individuals in recurring interaction with one another, their interactions controlled by common norms and differentiated roles. The members of the group are at least to some degree aware of their membership and perceive the group as a coherent, relatively permanent entity. The group, in other words, possesses a common culture and a social structure and its members see it as a collectivity rather than merely as an aggregate of individuals. Cooley's "primary group" is the smallest and least structured but most universal type of group.

Those social structures specializing in such activities as economic production or the rearing of children that are found in nearly all societies are called *institutions*. Peter Blau describes *institutionalization* as a general process in one of our readings, and Hans Gerth and C. Wright Mills present a classification of the major institutional orders in another. The notion of specialized institutional orders does not imply, of course, that a particular order performs only a single activity or function. For example, churches may, as they did in the Middle Ages,

[8] Peter Berger, *Invitation to Sociology* (New York: Doubleday Anchor Books, 1963), p. 93.

engage in extensive economic activities. Armies perform educational activities when they conduct training schools. Nevertheless, the dominant function performed by churches is the organization of collective worship and by armies the organization and direction of violence; churches and armies were originally created to perform these dominant functions and still invoke them to justify their existence and whatever additional functions they have assumed. In simpler societies, that is, those with undifferentiated social structures, the kinship order encompasses economic production, religious worship, vocational training of children, and many other activities that are the province of specialized, non-familial institutions in the more complex societies. Institutions are central units of sociological analysis because they are organized to perpetuate themselves from one generation to the next. They thus give society its enduring structure even when, as Blau points out, after several generations, they have experienced a complete turnover in membership.

A society is simply the totality of the social relations and groups formed by a given population occupying a given territory. Where to draw the line between one society and another is largely a matter of convenience—for some purposes we may wish to speak of the United States as a single society, for others we may choose to speak of Western society, treating as a single entity the United States, Western (and even parts of Eastern) Europe, and overseas countries settled by Europeans. The nation-state is usually the largest social unit employed as a framework for analysis by sociologists studying contemporary societies.

In the final section of Part One we have included three essays discussing social change and its effects. Robert Redfield describes the kinds of human societies that existed before the "urban revolution," which marks the dividing line between civilized and primitive or folk societies. The transformation of previously isolated primitive societies into larger, more complex and dynamic civilized societies represents one of the major processes of social change in human history. It is rivaled in importance only by the industrial revolution of modern history, now spreading around the world as the newly independent "underdeveloped" countries of Asia and Africa seek to modernize their economic and social structures.

James C. Davies, in our last selection, advances a theory of those sudden, violent, politically instituted changes we call "revolutions," applying concepts derived largely from Marx and Tocqueville to three main empirical cases of violent political uprisings. The selection preceding it by Kingsley Davis, deals with a process of social change that, in contrast to political revolution, has been so slow and gradual throughout most of human history as to have been almost invisible in its effects until long afterward—the growth of population. In the last two-hundred years and especially in the last twenty, however, world population has grown at unprecedented rates as a result of a worldwide decline in death rates. Such rates of growth cannot continue without bringing about even more widespread poverty than at present and ultimately reversing the drop in death rates with famines and mass starvation, again becoming the major checks on population increase. Davis reviews the alternative possibility of ending the population explosion by adopting successful policies to reduce fertility or the birth rate. His conclusions are far from optimistic.

Sociologists study social reality at all the levels of scope and complexity suggested by the basic concepts here reviewed. Some concentrate on primary groups and face-to-face interpersonal relations *within* much larger social units. Such studies are sometimes called "microsociology" to distinguish them from "macro-sociology"—the study of large-scale social structures, major institutions, and their interrelations within whole societies. Sprott's account of his hypothetical pair of movie-going friends, many of Berger's illustrations of role theory, and Goffman's report on behavior in the operating room are examples of micro-sociological analysis. Parts Two and Three of this book emphasize readings that are macrosociological in character: the conception of industrial society as a whole, influencing the nature of all the individuals and groups within it, is the main organizing theme there. However, it should not be forgotten that such macrosociological units as nations, class systems, political economies, and large bureaucratic organizations are made up of microsociological interactions among concrete persons.

# A Human Nature and Social Origins

## 3

## Reflections on the Human Revolution

### ROBERT ENDLEMAN

In a brilliant paper in the June 1964 issue of *Current Anthropology* a linguist and an archaeologist, Charles Hockett and Robert Ascher, present a new interpretation of what they call "The Human Revolution." [1] They attempt to trace the origins of man by drawing on linguistics as well as the usual paleontological, archaeological and geological reconstructions. What they have come up with is of extraordinary significance

From *The Psychoanalytic Review* (Summer 1966), pp. 169–188. Reprinted by permission.
[1] Charles F. Hockett and Robert Ascher. The Human Revolution. *Current Anthropology*, Vol. 5, No. 3, June 1964. pp. 135–147; with commentaries by Weston LaBarre, Frank B. Livingstone, G. G. Simpson and others, and replies by Hockett and Ascher, pp. 147–168.

for psychoanalysis and points to the need for a further elaboration of their theory in the light of a psychoanalytically-oriented anthropology. Hockett and Ascher themselves do not employ a psychoanalytic approach or refer to psychodynamic mechanisms, but the addition of these latter would fill out some of the lacunae and puzzles posed by their interpretation and I think the time is ripe for just such a development in anthropology. First let me summarize Hockett and Ascher's hypotheses:

### 1.

Tree-living primate ancestors of both the modern apes and man, living in the East African forests, faced an ecological crisis in the Miocene age (the geological period estimated at about 28 to 12 million years ago). Due to climatic changes, the forests receded and gave way to open grassy savanna, and in the competitive struggle for the declining forest territories, weaker bands of these "apes" ("protohominoids") were forced to the edges of the forest groves, and thence to migrate across open savanna in quest of other grove territory in which to continue their traditional arboreal and vegetarian existence. As such grove-to-grove treks became progressively greater so did the premium on these apes' developing in more fully bipedal mode of locomotion (possibly but only intermittently used by their ancestors). Hence we have the development of the characteristically human foot (the only important human bodily specialization). This bipedality and the related fully erect posture were adaptive not only for locomotion, but for two other signifi-can reasons: the value of being able to see predators over the savanna grasses and of being able to free the already prehensile hands for carrying weapons, first of defense against the existing larger animal predators, later of offense against other (especially large) animals, now *objects* of predation. As the forests continued to recede, these "failures" who were forced out had in time to accept the savannas as their necessary habitat, and therefore to adapt to it and the predation conditions in it or else! Occasional tool and weapon-carrying by the tree-ancestors and relatives now became a constant necessity and weapons of defense became weapons of offense as these "waifs", to survive in the new environment, became hunters themselves and changed from the vegetarian diet of the trees to the carnivorous or omnivorous diet of the new life. *Carrying* thus produced the "hunting revolution" and the "failures" of the forest struggle were on their way to evolving into men. Carrying of weapons and carrying of food frees the mouth and the teeth, essential for the development of language. The hunting of larger animals, made possible by the carrying, first of *ad-hoc*, then of deliberately manufactured weapons, in turn requires social cooperation and co-ordination. Hand-signaling is not feasible if hands are carrying weapons or food or infants; visual attention meanwhile is focused on the prey and or other hunters; therefore the most feasible communication must be *auditory*. Hence selective survival chances go to those bands who further develop an already-existing primate system of vocal *calls* (something like that of the present-day gibbon).

Why should such a system of calls *need* to be further elaborated, in a direction that leads to language? Because social organization would necessarily have to become more complex under conditions of collective hunting of larger game animals, with its concomitant of a larger range of food-*sharing*, and hence a wider range of "socialization" among the band members. It is assumed that these would have needed to move about in bands of some size (10–30 members), for singly or in very small groups they would have had very poor chances of surviving against larger and more powerful predators better adapted to the savanna environment. It is also assumed that they would have transferred to the new environment habits of territoriality such primates tend to have in the trees: i.e., a safe "home-base" surrounded by a not-clearly bounded food-getting territory. Another factor: the adaptive development of fully erect posture (meaning that those who developed this feature had a better chance of surviving —and hence of passing erectness on to later generations—than those who did not) also brought about physical changes in the structure of the head, brain, face, jaws, and "organs of speech" that made distinctively human speech possible.

The development of true language

from an ape-type call system could have occurred like this: Calls are discrete vocal signals, each communicating the total Gestalt of a situation, e.g., "food here," "danger here," "I am here," etc. The first step toward language would be the *blending* of two different calls into a new composite, e.g. a new call indicating food *and* danger, using one constituent element of each of the old calls. While such blending must have occurred fortuitously thousands of times in the earlier tree life without being taken up and transmitted through the band, the new and socially more complex savanna life would put a premium upon the development of such innovations. Blending then institutes a process of *building* composite signals out of separate meaningful parts (linguists call this changing a *closed* system into an *open* one.) This opening up must have taken thousands of years, but once accomplished it is revolutionary, for new communication demands detailed conventions that cannot possibly be transmitted through the genes (presumably the main mechanism of earlier systems) and *must* be learned; therefore there is natural selection for greater learning capacity, hence of the bases in brain structure *for* such capacity. Opening up the system also involves *displacement:* that is, it makes possible something increasingly *necessary* in more complex social life: talking about *something* out of sight, in the past or future, or purely hypothetical or mythical. This is parallel to the elements of foresight and memory involved in carrying a weapon for which there is no *immediate* use, and each of these mental habits reinforces the other, and each is reciprocally related to the process of tool or weapon *manufacture*, as distinct from carrying sticks or stones only *used* as tools. During this process, probably taking hundreds of generations, the head-face-vocal-apparatus structure is changed to a form more like that of modern man, the use of such

blended-call pre-language increases the innervation of the vocal tract and enriches the cortical representation of that region. This sets the stage for the final development to language.

As "pre-language" (the system of multiple call-blend signals) develops, the number of different call-blends increases, until it reaches a point where it becomes difficult to distinguish some of them from others. Then by mutation, some individuals start to listen to, and to articulate, these call-Gestalten not as total units, but in terms of smaller constituent elements, discretely produced and heard, in varying arrangements, and the distinction between sound units ("phonological components" or "phonemes") and collections of sound units that have a minimum unit of meaning ("morphemes") is made. With this we have true language. If we take toolmaking and language as the criteria of humanity, then the ape-like ancestor has evolved into man.

As an aside, Hockett-Ascher mention another important by-product of man's erect posture: the change from a dorsal to a frontal position in coitus. Presumably the enlargement of the gluteus maximus produced by bipedal erectness made the old primate dorsal coital position awkward, and fostered the invention of the frontal position, almost unique to human beings. This position puts the adult male mate in a position to the adult female similar to that of the suckling infant, and can thereby enhance the diffusion and complexity of sexual feelings (a trend which probably had already begun with the non-seasonal year-round sexuality of advanced primates in tree life.) The importance of this phenomenon for the Oedipus complex is obvious.

Hockett and Ascher hypothesize that this whole evolutionary process—from the Miocene "waifs" to man—must have been *completed* by the beginning of the Pleistocene period (i.e., roughly a million years ago). That is, taking as "man" a generalized primate with one specialization (the human foot), with fully erect posture and bipedal gait, stereoscopic and color vision and very complex hand-eye-brain coordinations, a large complex brain, great learning capacity, the use and manufacture of tools, and language.

Weston LaBarre,[2] commenting on the Hockett-Ascher paper, notes that the shift to the frontal coital position must have a lot to do with the characteristically human development of *paternal feelings* toward offspring, the like of which we find in no other mammals, including our nearest primate relatives of today. He also sees another significance in the frontal position: a change in the role of the female in controlling the situation of sexual encounter. Whereas the primate female in dorsal position in effect controls the sexual situation, the human female in supine frontal position, if solitary, is vulnerable to any sexual encounter with the (usually) physically stronger male. This would help explain the development of institutions of male dominance, sexual possessiveness, familial protectiveness of the male toward the mate as well as the offspring, and also the necessity for sexual rules. Hunting males need social cooperation which unregulated sexuality would easily disrupt.

## 2.

Let us now consider some of the implications of this interpretation. First note that the last stage in the development from ape-like ancestor to man, as seen by Hockett and Ascher, is both a biological and a cultural process, and in a complex inter-causality involves all the elements that make us distinctively human: the use of hands to carry and use things like sticks and stones as tools

[2] *Current Anthropology*, Vol. 5, No. 3, June, 1964. pp. 147–150.

and weapons, then to *make* tools and weapons, with which man in turn *transforms* the environment rather than merely adapting to it; the freeing of the hands by the development of the specialized human foot; the transformation of man's ecological place dependent on both of these and the whole complex of hunting, its necessary social organization and the related social and sexual band relationships; the transformation and freeing of the face and mouth and head and brain; the development of more complex cortical processes; the increased duration and dependency of human infancy and the relation of this to the whole complex learning process; finally, the greater complexity of communication, culminating in the distinctively human phenomenon of language.

The implications of this postulated evolutionary process toward modern man ramify in all directions. Let us explore just a few.

First, the problems of human psychosexuality that are so central to psychoanalysis. The prolongation of infancy is made both *possible and necessary* by the evolutionary changes the authors are postulating: the great increase in the amount and variety of learning that can only be taught by other agents of the species (rather than transmitted through the genes), the greater complexity of band organization in the emerging hunting economy, the greater security-with-interdependency. This prolongation of infancy is one meaning of the phrase: "man is an infantilized ape." The other meaning is that man retains into adulthood traits that are infantile or embryonic in lower species, in particular the other higher primates (e.g., orthognathy, hairlessness, position of the foramen magnum, loss of pigmentation in skin, hair and eyes, the form of the pelvis, etc.). In the evolutionary progression from other mammals to primates to man, the duration of gestation increases, the typical number of offspring per birth declines, the period from birth to sexual maturity increases, and, even more dramatically, the period from birth to full adult growth increases. Further, the long prenatal period and the protracted and helpless infancy are prerequisites for the ultimately high development of the nervous system and mental capacities. But alongside this infantilism, man's sexuality is precocious. The sexual pattern is present in infants before the gonadal hormone is produced in adequate quantities. The female ovum is practically fully developed at the early age of five. That is, the Soma lags far behind the Germa in man, so that within the frame of his general infantilism, his sexuality is relatively precocious.[3] With man's great reproductive economy, heightened further by the advancements of culture, his precocious and lifelong sexuality must therefore be seen as a kind of "surplus" or "discretionary" sexuality (to borrow concepts from economics), and, as LaBarre points out, very significantly for the social life of man. Freud, of course, taught us to see this close linkage of the social and the sexual, the simplified formulation of which is to say that *all* social ties are basically libidinal ties.

In this context, consider one of Hockett and Ascher's main points: The relative verticality of tree-living primates (in contrast with infra-primate land mammals) was further developed by the Miocene "rejects" into a more completely frontal approach to the world, by the development of totally upright posture and bipedal gait. This frontal

[3] For the development of this theme, drawing on the work of the anatomist L. Bolk, see Géza Róheim, *Psychoanalysis and Anthropology*, New York: International Universities Press, 1950, especially pages 400–404; and its further implications: Weston LaBarre, *The Human Animal*, Chicago: University of Chicago Press, 1954, throughout, but especially pp. 150–156, 304–310.

approach is further extended to the change of position in coitus. Now an implication of these changes is that all relationships, mate-to-mate as well as parent-to-child, are now face-to-face relationships, and this I think is an important determinant of what I would call man's peculiarly polymorphous *sexual sociality*. Infantilization means a much greater continuity, in man, of infantile (indeed, embryonic) processes and attachments throughout life, than in any infra-human mammals. This means a greater diffusion of sexual-social feeling throughout the range of inter-individual relationships, which is another way of referring to the polymorphousness of infantile sexuality which persists (in the unconscious, if not overtly) throughout life. Add to this the convergence of mother-infant sexuality and mate-mate sexuality produced by the change to the frontal position in coitus, and we have the basis in evolution for the great extensiveness and displaceability of sexual-social ties that Freud taught us to recognize in man.

Róheim, in summarizing Bolk's evidence for the fetalization of man, argues that if a fetal quality becomes gradually permanent there must be an inhibitory factor that prevents the "normal" process of ontogenesis. Bolk assumes the cause must be endocrinological. In turn, such endocrine changes could come about through a change in *diet*. Now the transition from ape-like primate to man that the Hockett-Ascher reconstruction (in this respect in agreement with many other anthropological reconstructions) outlines, does in fact postulate a change of diet of major proportions: from the herbivorous one of the tree-dwellers, to the carnivorous one of land-living hunters. Here the pieces of the puzzle start to fit together. The diet change, of course, did not simply occur; it was a product of the whole complex of ecological, social and other body-structural changes, as Hockett and Ascher show.

The sexual-sociality of man, that is both infantile and precocious, is connected in turn with two other human phenomena: *language* and *play*. Hockett and Ascher's reconstruction of the possible line of development of language is ingenious, provocative, and internally consistent with the rest of their reconstruction of the "human revolution." But it is, I thing, incomplete. Language is an oral activity, most intensively developed in face-to-face contacts (in contrast with a call system, which operates primarily at a distance.) Perhaps then, the frontal coital position has as much to do with the development of language as the savanna hunting-organization. In turn, language is linked to the development of human sexuality through the phenomenon of *play*. Another way of talking about the persistence of man's infantile sexuality is to say that other animals grow up and *un*learn to play; *man never does*. Play is one of the more direct expressions of Eros. Since man's sexuality is both precocious and extravagantly out of line with reproductive necessities, the arena of play—as a channel for all this "surplus" sexuality —is greater and more complex in man than in other animals.

What are the connections between language and play? Hockett and Ascher make many references to play in their paper, but aside from noting that the introduction of pre-language into the new life of the apes-becoming-men, adds *verbal* to other types of play, they do not develop the connections. I do not think that a theory explaining the development from a call system to pre-language to language, *only* in terms of the *adaptive* value of the changes, is adequate. The assumption behind it (as of most anthropological "explanations" of cultural artifacts) is basically utilitarian. But what we know about Eros and play belies such assumptions.

Let us examine, instead, how play would be involved in the emergence of speech. First of all, innovations in vocalization (Hockett-Ascher refer to "generations of chattering") are as likely to come from play [4] as from such emergency situations as the need to communicate the simultaneous presence of food and danger. Play involves "playing around with" elements that are already given, trying them out in new combinations and sequences. Play may also involve body contact, as in fighting or sexual play (observable in nearly all mammals, and other animals as well), and one of the contexts for this is the mother-infant situation. In this situation the mother carries on a whole variety of vocalizations with the child. (Even in modern human mothers, there is still plenty of such phatic, prelinguistic vocalization with the child, as part of a general context of play, relaxation and erotic exchange.) Such vocalizations must surely have been at least the *materials* for innovation, out of which language developed, alongside of (not instead of) a call system. (There is no good reason to suppose that one excludes the other.)

Speech has been defined by Róheim as "orality coming to terms with reality." And what situation is more oral than infancy? The progressive lengthening of infancy and heightening of dependency must have increased the significance of Eros and play in the mother-child situation and encouraged a greater variety of vocalization. Sim-

[4] Once when I was explaining the intricacies of a particular Australian kinship system to an anthropology class, one student, in great annoyance, blurted out: "Why should they have developed such a complicated system? I don't see what *use* it is! Surely they're not just playing games!" Since the utilitarian value of having 16 marriage-classes is by no means self-evident (in fact it is demonstrably anti-utilitarian in some ways) and taking a Freudian view of the "not" in the student's question, maybe he was on the right track.

ilarly, in the same period, there would be extensions of this into the spheres of inter-peer juvenile play and adult play, including the sexual relationship, which, now involving the frontal position, brings the mating pair into face-to-face relationship. The latter has two significances: greater *oral* contact, and greater vocal communication.

It is interesting that all of these play situations, involving direct person-to-person contacts, would use vocalizations at low volume and probably relatively low pitch. LaBarre comments (on the Hockett-Ascher paper, *loc. cit.* p. 149–50) that there is a puzzling difference between calls (e.g. gibbon calls, or a human female's or juvenile's "piercing" scream) and ordinary speech language; i.e. that the pitch of calls is in frequencies around 3000 cycles per second, near the *top* of the range for the human ear, and the range to which the human ear is most sensitive (i.e. calls of this pitch can be heard over much longer distances than lower-pitched calls of the same amplitude). By contrast, ordinary human speech is mainly in the range below 1000 c.p.s. Then LaBarre asks:

Whence the massive flatting of speech-frequencies in man? Or did speech not arise out of "closed" primate call-systems after all, but rather from the lower frequencies of feckless play-chatter, where speech has remained ever since? [*loc. cit.* p. 150]

Although LaBarre introduces this query by referring to "one *minor* linguistic problem" (my emphasis), the question is a critical one in reference to the Hockett-Ascher theory. It is of course not a question which can be answered with any certitude, given present evidence. But I would raise the further question: why the *either-or* in LaBarre's question? Why must language have developed exclusively either from a call system, or from "feckless play-chattering"? Since existing infra-

human primates show both, and since the whole Hockett-Ascher thesis about steps in the change toward language rests on the assumption of something like a gibbon's call system in our "proto-hominoid" ancestors, we are certainly as justified in assuming "feckless play-chatter" in those same putative ancestors.

Hockett and Ascher refer to "generations of chattering . . . increasing the innervation of the vocal tract" . . . etc. Now "chattering" is clearly not "calling." But it is the sort of thing youngsters (or adults for that matter) do at play. (Listen at any cocktail party.) Some of the chattering may be imitative of calls used in "serious" (i.e. instrumental) situations, just as much else in play is imitative of serious activities on the physical action plane. So play is one context of which a repertoire of signal-calls could be elaborated by innovations consisting of playful new combinations. But I think alongside of the process of elaboration of call signals, *another* set of innovations must have occurred, within the context of erotic-play-chattering.

Someone may object at this point: "How can you talk about juvenile play being at *low* volume? Haven't you ever heard a gang of kids playing outdoors?" There indeed we find elements of the call system at work (at play, rather). And we can argue that modifications of a call system might well have come about in *that* kind of play situation too, as well as in such "serious" situations as the food-and-danger example.

There are all kinds of pre-linguistic vocalizations: imitations of sounds heard in the environment (the "bow-wow" theory of language origins traces it to such vocalizations); emotive ejaculations evoked by intense feelings of any kind (the "pooh-pooh"—or better, the "ai-yai-yai!" theory); expiratory sounds made to the accompaniment of physical exertions (the "yo-he-ho" theory); exclamations in sing-song spontaneously made in exultation over a successful feat (the "ta-ra-ra-boom-te-day" theory); sounds made by infants sucking or chewing at the mother's breast (the "chew" theory)—to which could be added the whole repertory of non-linguistic sounds and exclamations animals at all like human beings make in carrying out any of the body processes (eating, eliminating, copulating, to name the classic triad, but also including scratching, rubbing, grooming the body, etc.) Sounds made in fighting should also be added to the list. *Any and all of these could have, in fact must have, contributed to the repertory of sounds in early proto-language.* Many of these types of sounds must have been important parts of the content of vocalizations in sub-human play. Play activities of a cortically increasingly complex animal would then allow innovative elaborations of such "raw material", expansion of the repertoire, and then the chance for playful recombinations of the elements. Add to such recombination or blending the process of conventionalization, and the animal is on the way to human language. (Conventionalization means that a particular sound comes to be conventionally associated with a particular referent; at first by the close affinity between the sound and the activity or thing referred to; but later, when such phatic elements are blended and recombined in ever-more-complex ways, the relationship between the sound-combination and the thing referred to becomes "purely conventional"—i.e., there is no longer any obvious connection, and the association of sound and referent has to be *learned*.)

Let us retrace some of these connections, then: Ape-like primates become more infantilized as they evolve into man. This heightens the significance of infantile sexuality. The adoption of the frontal coital position fosters the as-similation of parent-infant sexuality with mate-mate sexuality. Constant non-seasonal mating abolishes the older mammal device of segregating mating from offspring-care activities. Heightened inter-individual dependency raises inter-individual empathy and communicability. Contexts of play are extended and elaborated, with the progressive juvenilization of the human animal. The range, number, and variety of vocalizations increases, and play (as well as certain "serious" emergency situations) increases the chances for innovations in the form of blendings and recombinations of elements. Playful innovations may come and go by the thousands, but the more complex conditions of social life start to put an evolutionary premium on (or select for) a more adequate communication system. Hence both a blending of call elements and a blending of phatic "chattering" elements take place, and through the imitativeness of play vocalization there is an interweaving of both processes.

The mother-infant situation—*not* typically a call situation— is important for language in yet another respect. Mammal teaching of the young is generally direct, behavioral, immediate in the situation involved (e.g. a cat teaching her kitten how to catch mice). As life for the proto-humans on the postulated Miocene savannas becomes more complex, socially and ecologically, there develops a need for more of the teaching to be *anticipatory* rather than contemporary with its uses, and more need to communicate *about* things, past, future, or potential. The various monistic theories of language origin are helpful in suggesting some ways in which early symbol-referent connections are made. However, we would still need something like the blending mechanism Hockett and Ascher postulate, before any purely ejaculatory, or exertion-respiratory, or onomatopoetic vocalizations, can reach the pre-linguistic level of call-blends, and thus provide the necessary displacement for anticipatory vocal-socialization. It seems reasonable then to postulate, alongside of Hockett-Ascher's call-blending, a similar blending of lower-frequency vocalizations of these latter types.

Psychodynamically, language means that symbol replaces object. We re-invest objects with libido by the meaning of words. But this implies the absence of *direct* cathexis with the objects. All this suggests a transformation of the animal's direct erotic relationship to the world, through a medium that holds out long-range potential for enormously greater mastery, but at this point stands *between* the animal (human being) and the object. Hence the magical quality of words. Language is bound up with repression, and can be regarded as one of those great compromise formations, at the cultural level, which permit much gratification of Eros while damming up other aspects.

A significant aspect of the linkage of language and repression is the phenomenon of negation. A call system may *imply* "Don't come near!" by a call signalling "Danger!" but by its nature, the call system communicates *positive* statements: "Here's food," "Here's danger" or "Here I am, over here!" etc., and not negative ones. However, the process of blending that Hockett and Ascher suggest starts a call system on the way to language, *introduces* the concept of negation. They suggest that if a call had elements ABCD and signified food; and another call with elements EFGH signified danger, a new situation including *both* food and danger might evoke a new call, that is a compromise between the two others, and consists of the elements ABGH. If this "caught on" and spread, there would now be *three* signals, *each* of them now having two units, AB with CD or GH and EF with GH. The implica-

tions of this are enormous, because *now* ABCD doesn't just mean "food", it means "food *and no danger*." Similarly, EFGH now means, not just "danger," but "danger *and no food*." Now it would become possible to have still a fourth signal: CDEF, meaning "*no* food and *no* danger." In other words, *the concept of negation has entered the signal system*. We can now raise the question: what are the preconditions for such conceptualization to occur, granted it *can* logically follow once a blend such as ABGH has occurred and then has been accepted and diffused throughout the community? Since the concept of negation does not appear in the unconscious, Freud argues [5] that it is tied up with the process of repression. Repression is the primal act of negation. At the same time, the *conscious* use of negation makes it possible to deal with the repressed material, so long as it is denied. Then the process that Hockett-Ascher describe, could be carried to its logical extension of "CD equals 'no danger'" *only* in an animal that has learned how to repress, that is, an animal that is human or close to human.

Norman Brown hypothesizes [6] that "formal logic and the law of contradiction are the rules whereby the mind submits to operate under general conditions of repression." Could not the hypothesis be extended to include all of language in general? In this view, language can arise only in an animal that has learned how to *repress*. What would have provoked the need to repress, in a proto-human animal? Very clearly, precisely the conditions we have been describing: a new challenging environment requiring more elaborate inter-individual dependency and co-

[5] Sigmund Freud: On Negation. *Collected Papers*, Vol. 5, London: Hogarth Press, pp. 181–185.
[6] Norman O. Brown: *Life Against Death*, p. 321.

operation, including the need to control intra-band aggression and sexuality, the developments in sexuality just described (which produce a conflict between parental and mate sexuality) combined with a heightening of libidinal attachments and their prolongation with the increasing infantilization of the human animal.

### 3.

Where does play fit in all this? I think the very difficulty we experience in seeing play elements or origins in "serious" customs or institutions, is a mark of that repression that is characteristic of the socialized man. One function of play is to evade such repression, with the excuse, "It's not serious, we don't mean it, we're just playing around, etc.," so that a portion of the repressed content can be expressed, usually disguised, but especially in some innocuous-looking form. Play is also the insurance that repression of unconscious forces is never quite complete (a totally repressed person cannot play at all, or enjoy others' play) so that some channels *are* open to reach those layers. Play is particularly the opportunity for creative forces of the unconscious. We can allow it, repressed human beings that we are, on the pretext that it is separate from things that "really" matter. All this suggests, then, that play is *antithetical* to the development of language, where language, built on repression, constitutes a formal system of constructs and categories that constrain and channelize the confrontation with "reality." Precisely so, and every language does constitute a certain arbitrary codification of reality that makes difficult, if not impossible, certain kinds of playful verbal elaborations or recombinations. Here poetry and myth attempt to come to the rescue—never entirely successfully—as preservers of pre-linguistic or non-linguistic play dealings with reality,

by verbal structures which defy the laws of logic, especially the law of contradiction, in ways analogous to the dream, that ever-renewed resource of the unconscious.

But I have argued earlier that play must have contributed, importantly, to the *origins of language*. Now we have a view of play which shows it as *antagonistic* to language. Both conditions, I would argue, are true, and they are connected: for play and language, just as myth and language, are in a dialectical relationship to each other, in a constant state of tension, language needing to formalize, i.e. constrain, repress and sublimate, the forces of play, yet still needing play for constant renewal and revitalization, and breaking through the rigidities of formalization, especially those involved in the process of negation and the linkage of language to the rules of formal logic. (As an aside, this is one reason that formally constructed artificial "universal" languages like Esperanto have been such dismal failures, for all their "reasonable" appeal; so too, the absurdities of language-translating machines.)

It seems entirely improbable that language, any more than other cultural creations, could have emerged *only* out of necessities (adaptiveness, etc.), and not also out of the arena of freedom whose epitome in activity is play. It is also improbable that anything so multifunctional as language could have come from only a single source. It may well have been "invented," as Hockett-Ascher argue, "only *once*" and then diffused (their arguments against the probability of parallel developments in different areas of the world, and later convergence, sound convincing), but this "invention" in a single population (a process which by their interpretation would require hundreds of generations) must very well have had a multiplicity of determinants (as all inventions, on close inspection, turn out to have). This would leave room for all of the factors that they indicate, and in addition *play* and its various ramifications, as I have attempted to show.

Let us return to the problems of psycho-sexuality, or sexual-sociality. Hockett-Ascher argue that in the emergence of a new ecological adaptation of the proto-hominoid ancestors to the savanna environment, vocal calls had to become elaborated because hands were occupied carrying weapons, tools, or food, while eyes were busy observing predators, objects of predation, and/or the other hunters. In my summary of their argument above, I had inadvertantly added ". . . hands carrying weapons, food, *or infants*" but on checking find that *"or infants"* does not appear in Hockett-Ascher's text. Thinking about this, we may say: with good reason. For what they describe are the circumstances of a group of *adult males* hunting large game, and adult males would not likely be carrying the infants. In other words, the elaboration of a closed to an open call system they relate to the *adult male activities of hunting*. This limitation makes it all the more imperative that we pay attention to the situation of adult females and offspring, in looking at the interrelated changes that our ancestors must have undergone during the period in question. Here we can refer again to my discussion of the mother-child situation, especially its elements of eroticism and play, as probable *additional* origins of the transformation toward language. Following Hockett-Ascher's type of reasoning: if the mother's hands are busy holding the infant, and her body busy giving it suck, her mouth and ears are free for other kinds of communication. However, the persistence to this day, of human mothers' babbling, cooing and gurgling and baby-talk to the child—in other words, pre-linguistic vocal communication—suggests that these phatic communications still have primacy for the adult female. By contrast, if *male*-interpersonal communications de-

veloped primarily out of the call system (i.e. *distance* rather than proximate communication) and with the development of the concept of negation through the blending process just described—with much less emphasis on direct body-contact phatic communication—perhaps we have here the roots of a very deep psychobiological sex difference, according to which the world of Logos has been universally, *predominantly* a male world, and the world of body-feeling predominantly a woman's world. (Granted, of course, that particular cultural configurations can accentuate or de-emphasize this difference.) The sheer physical dimorphism of human males and females, as LaBarre points out (*loc. cit.*), is surely attributable to selective adaptation to the sexual division of labor of the emergent hunting economy of the Miocene-Pliocene apes-becoming-men.

We must also consider, at this point, some further implications of the shift to the frontal position in intercourse, the universal (though not of course the exclusive) position used by human beings, and one which is almost a human monopoly. We have indicated that this shift promotes an assimilation, hence diffusion and confusion, of mother-child and male-female sexualities. Given human infantilization, and constant, precocious, ubiquitous and polymorphous human sexuality, this diffusion is bound to promote father-child, and *also mother-child* rivalries and animosities. For if to the female, the male in coitus is similar to a suckling child, *so*, in a sense, *is the female to the male*. For she, like a suckling infant, is receiving, through an erogenous body orifice, lifegiving substances from a protuberance of the face-to-face partner's body.[7] (In fact it could be argued that, in this specific respect, *she* is more like a suck-

---

[7] Roger W. Wescott suggests this analogy, in his comments on the Hockett-Ascher paper. *Current Anthropology*, Vol 5, No. 3, June, 1964. p. 164.

ling infant than he is!) And of course psychoanalysis has had a lot to tell us about the re-arousal of unconscious infantile fantasy in the sexual activities of human adults. The Hockett-Ascher observations now give us some *evolutionary* understanding of these phenomena, and of their pan-human universality. This is not just mammalian behavior, but the behavior of a very special primate. The universality of the primary incest taboos (mother-son, father-daughter, brother-sister, and we might as well add, their homosexual coordinates), and of Oedipal phenomena (ignoring their minor variations with social structure) are also now understandable in a new evolutionary light.[8]

[8] There have been repeated attempts, in recent anthropology, to "disprove" the universality of these phenomena. Malinowski's famous case (*Sex and Repression*, 1927) against the existence of Oedipus Complex in the Trobriand Islands, has, however been adequately refuted by Ernest Jones, and more conclusively, by Geza Roheim (*Psychoanalysis and Anthropology*, 1950); and the noted royal cases (Egypt, Peru, Polynesia) are just that—*royal* exceptions. Even the great modern instance of a society *deliberately* trying to do away with Oedipal involvements by doing away with the nuclear family altogether—the Israeli Kibbutz—has succeeded in doing neither, as is quite clear from Melford Spiro's reports, *Kibbutz: Venture in Utopia* and *Children of the Kibbutz*, which show that the family, though bereft of economic-productive functions and residential territoriality, is still an emotionally-significant structure in the lives of parents (including toward each other) and of children; and that Oedipal feelings, though lacking the intensity they show in other Western societies, through lack of hostility-guilt feelings toward the father, nevertheless do appear. As for incest taboo, the whole collective is so much like a family to the children, that they *spontaneously* institute taboos against sexual relations or marriage with others they have grown up with on the Kibbutz. (See Yonina Talmon: "Mate Selection in Collective Settlements," *American Sociological Review*, Vol. 29, July, 1964. pp. 491–508.) For a fuller discussion of incest taboos and Oedipus complex generally, see R. Endleman: *Personality and So-*

We have here, then, another angle of vision on the phenomenon of *repression*, that special human problem. Repression is the mechanism that an infantilized human ape with a burgeoning polymorphous sexuality imposes upon himself, with the aid of the terrifying and nurturant giant lover-haters, the parents, to regulate the potential chaos of indiscriminate Eros. Language flows from, and helps consolidate this process. Play helps in the development of language, but also works against it and against repression, in the service of the polymorphous unconscious forces. Repression institutes the incest taboos and resolves the Oedipus Complex, while play, and its derivatives in poetry and myth, repeatedly break through these constrictions. Repression makes possible the whole complex of mastery on which man embarked by changing from dinner to diner on the Miocene African savannas, and the peculiarly crazy "rationality" by which he has constructed a whole world around himself, substituting his man-made environment (culture) and the constrictions of Logos, for instinct and the predation conditions of nature.

## 4. Epilogue

These reflections have an obvious relevance to the great problems raised by Freud in *Civilization and its Discontents*, by Herbert Marcuse in *Eros and Civilization* and by Norman O. Brown in *Life Against Death*. How is a non-repressive civilization possible? If language, that *sine qua non* of humanity, emerges out of the dialectic of repression and play, then what are the implications? If culture is rooted in the repressive transformations of polymorphous sexuality, the heritage of the

*cial Life* (Random House, 1967), which also includes an extensive chapter on the Kibbutz.

peculiar primate evolution of man, then what?

Brown and Marcuse explore the radical implications of Freud's breakthrough, in opposition to the gloomy pessimism of *Civilization and its Discontents*. But alongside their fervent plea for the *potentiality* of a non-repressive civilization, marked by liberation of Eros made possible by following psychoanalytical insights to their farther conclusions, their recital of the repressive, indeed *diseased*, bases of past and existing civilizations, is itself gloomy in the extreme—perhaps even more gloomy than Freud's own vision.

Pushing back behind history to the evolutionary origins of man (as is now more possible by such synthetic reconstructions as Hockett and Ascher's) seems, on the basis of the reflections I have suggested, to offer small comfort for any optimistic view such as Brown's or Marcuse's, but only to make more explicable and consistent their kind of interpretation of history, by rooting it in biological and cultural evolution. If Hockett and Ascher's interpretation, with the addenda I have suggested above, are basically correct, then this is the way man has been, from his emergence anywhere from a million to seven million years ago. Anthropologists seem in essential agreement that there has been no further *biological* evolution of man since *homo sapiens* emerged and then survived as the only remaining hominid species on this planet; that the emergence of *culture*, as the peculiar characteristic of man, abolishes the necessity for further biological evolution of the species.

The implications of this idea can be read, however, in several ways. One is to emphasize elements of fixity: i.e., that the peculiar historical circumstances of man's evolution from a tree-living primate to a ground-living savanna hunter, had set, once and for all, the peculiar bio-cultural problems

of the species: i.e., infantilization, precocious and polymorphous sexuality, conflict-laden inter-individual intimacies and dependencies, communication necessities emerging in language, social control necessities favoring the process of repression, itself intimately tied to the development of language, and hence of the universal problems of culture. Freud, Marcuse, Brown—indeed, the whole corpus of critical reflections on our times—all document how we are still struggling with these same basic problems in the present desperate hour of civilization.

Another way to read the message of the end of biological evolution, however, is to emphasize its argument that *biological* evolution has stopped, has been rendered obsolete, because *cultural* evolution takes over. Man no longer (evolutionarily) adapts to the world, but instead proceeds to *transform* it. Earlier anthropological formulations of cultural evolution partook of the naive optimism of the Idea of Progress, later rejected as hopelessly out of touch with the desperate realities of the plight of man in "advanced" civilizations. Cultural evolutionism is today enjoying a revival in anthropology (partly in reaction against the anti-historical excesses of functionalist social anthropology), but in a greatly modified form, eschewing the grand simplicities of the 19th-century thinkers for more limited and more detailed regional reconstructions, and avoiding over-all progress formulations. However, cultural evolutionism of whatever stripe implies certain assumptions about the species nature of man, notably, for our concern, that man has the *potentiality* of transforming his own institutions. Hence no *particular civilization* has an ensured, inevitable holding power. Such a view is consistent with the faith of Brown and Marcuse that man *could* overcome the diseases of particular civilizations.

But then the question is: does the

potentiality to transform extend to the potentiality to conquer the disease of civilization *in general* (or to use the anthropologists' wider term, of *culture,* in general)? Brown and Marcuse are hopeful that it does, and draw upon their analyses of the *dialectical* interplay of repression and Eros to support such a faith. Their evidence, however, as already suggested, would appear to me to cast an enormous doubt on such possibilities, and to support instead the view that there is a great and tragic fixity to man's bio-cultural dilemmas, the evolutionary roots of which our present discussion has explored. What seems to me to be documented by their work, by Freud's, Roheim's, LaBarre's, and by the current anthropological evolutionary reconstructions, is the persistence in man's life of the same basic *conflicts* and *tensions,* never resolved, but re-expressed in changing transformations in different eras and cultures. *Plus ça change . . .*

That there *is* conflict and tension, rather than simple persistence of one set pattern or direction, can of course be read optimistically (*vide* Brown and Marcuse), that there *is* a chance for man really to liberate himself. Earlier cultural evolutionism (echoed in Freud's *Civilization and its Discontents*) assumed that man transformations of the world and civilization were necessarily the product of man's growing *intellectual* mastery—the forces that Brown brilliantly demonstrates as part of repressive culture, and more specifically, of anal-sadistic disease. May it not be possible, however, to have a new cultural evolutionism, in which the transforming mechanism in human potentiality is not intellectual mastery and its repression-based science and technology, but the forces of Eros and a science devoted to *its* cause, i.e., integrating the insights of the poets and mystics, along lines that Brown proposes? Hope springs eternal.

# 4

# A Clue to the Nature of Man: The Symbol

**ERNST CASSIRER**

. . . No longer in a merely physical universe, man lives in a symbolic universe. Language, myth, art, and religion are parts of this universe. They are the varied threads which weave the symbolic net, the tangled web of human experience. All human progress in thought and experience refines upon and strengthens this net. No longer can man confront reality immediately; he cannot see it, as it were, face to face.

Physical reality seems to recede in proportion as man's symbolic activity advances. Instead of dealing with the things themselves man is in a sense constantly conversing with himself. He has so enveloped himself in linguistic forms, in artistic images, in mythical symbols or religious rites that he cannot see or know anything except by the interposition of this artificial medium. His situation is the same in the theoretical as in the practical sphere. Even here man does not live in a world of hard facts, or according to his immediate needs and desires. He lives rather in the midst of imaginary emotions, in hopes and fears, in illusions and disillusions, in his fantasies and dreams. "What disturbs and alarms man," said Epictetus, "are not the things, but his opinions and fancies about the things."

From the point of view at which we have just arrived we may correct and enlarge the classical definition of man. In spite of all the efforts of modern irrationalism this definition of man as an *animal rationale* has not lost its force. Rationality is indeed an inherent feature of all human activities. Mythology itself is not simply a crude mass of superstitions or gross delusions. It is not merely chaotic, for it possesses a systematic or conceptual form. But, on the other hand, it would be impossible to characterize the structure of myth as rational. Language has often been identified with reason, or with the very source of reason. But it is easy to see that this definition fails to cover the whole field. It is a *pars pro toto*; it offers us a part for the whole. For side by side with conceptual language there is an emotional language; side by side with logical or scientific language there is a language of poetic imagination. Primarily language does not express thoughts or ideas, but feelings and affections. And even a religion "within the limits of pure reason" as conceived and worked out by Kant is no more than a mere abstraction. It conveys only the ideal shape, only the shadow, of what a genuine and concrete religious life is. The great thinkers who have defined man as an *animal rationale* were not empiricists, nor did they ever intend to give an empirical account of human nature. By this definition they were expressing rather a fundamental moral imperative. Reason is a very inadequate term with which to comprehend the forms of man's cultural life in all their richness and variety. But all these forms are symbolic forms. Hence, instead of defining man

as an *animal rationale*, we should define him as an *animal symbolicum*. By so doing we can designate his specific difference, and we can understand the new way open to man—the way to civilization.

## I

By our definition of man as an *animal symbolicum* we have arrived at our first point of departure for further investigations. But it now becomes imperative that we develop this definition somewhat in order to give it greater precision. That symbolic thought and symbolic behavior are among the most characteristic features of human life, and that the whole progress of human culture is based on these conditions, is undeniable. But are we entitled to consider them as the special endowment of man to the exclusion of all other organic beings? Is not symbolism a principle which we may trace back to a much deeper source, and which has a much broader range of applicability? If we answer this question in the negative we must, as it seems, confess our ignorance concerning many fundamental questions which have perennially occupied the center of attention in the philosophy of human culture. The question of the *origin* of language, of art, of religion becomes unanswerable, and we are left with human culture as a given fact which remains in a sense isolated and, therefore, unintelligible.

It is understandable that scientists have always refused to accept such a solution. They have made great efforts to connect the fact of symbolism with other well-known and more elementary facts. The problem has been felt to be of paramount importance, but unfortunately it has very rarely been approached with an entirely open mind. From the first it has been obscured and confused by other questions which belong to a quite different realm of discourse. Instead of giving us an unbiased description and analysis of the phenomena themselves the discussion of this problem has been converted into a metaphysical dispute. It has become the bone of contention between the different metaphysical systems: between idealism and materialism, spiritualism and naturalism. For all these systems the question of symbolism has become a crucial problem, on which the future shape of science and metaphysics has seemed to hinge.

With this aspect of the problem we are not concerned here, having set for ourselves a much more modest and concrete task. We shall attempt to describe the symbolic attitude of man in a more accurate manner in order to be able to contradistinguish it from other modes of symbolic behavior found throughout the animal kingdom. That animals do not always react to stimuli in a direct way, that they are capable of an indirect reaction, is evidently beyond question. The well-known experiments of Pavlov provide us with a rich body of empirical evidence concerning the so-called representative stimuli. In the case of the anthropoid apes a very interesting experimental study by Wolfe has shown the effectiveness of "token rewards." The animals learned to respond to tokens as substitute for food rewards in the same way in which they responded to food itself.[1] According to Wolfe the results of varied and protracted training experiments have demonstrated that symbolic processes occur in the behavior of anthropoid apes. Robert M. Yerkes, who describes these experiments in his latest book, draws from them an important general conclusion.

That they [symbolic processes] are relatively rare and difficult to observe is evi-

dent. One may fairly continue to question their existence, but I suspect that they presently will be identified as antecedents of human symbolic processes. Thus we leave this subject at a most exciting stage of development, when discoveries of moment seem imminent.[2]

It would be premature to make any predictions with regard to the future development of this problem. The field must be left open for future investigations. The interpretation of the experimental facts, on the other hand, always depends on certain fundamental concepts which have to be clarified before the empirical material can bear its fruit. Modern psychology and psychobiology take this fact into account. It seems to me highly significant that nowadays it is not the philosophers but the empirical observers and investigators who appear to be taking the leading roles in solving this problem. The latter tell us that after all the problem is not merely an empirical one but to a great degree a logical one. Georg Révész has recently published a series of articles in which he starts off with the proposition that the warmly debated question of so-called *animal language* cannot be solved on the basis of mere facts of animal psychology. Everyone who examines the different psychological theses and theories with an unbiased and critical mind must come at least to the conclusion that the problem cannot be cleared up by simply referring to forms of animal communication and to certain animal accomplishments which are gained by drill and training. All such accomplishments admit to the most contradictory interpretations. Hence it is necessary, first of all, to find a correct logical starting point, one which can lead us to a natural and sound interpretation

[1] J. B. Wolfe, "Effectiveness of Token-rewards for Chimpanzees," Comparative Psychology Monographs, 12, No. 5.

[2] Robert M. Yerkes, *Chimpanzees. A Laboratory Colony* (New Haven, Yale University Press, 1943), p. 189.

of the empirical facts. This starting point is the *definition of speech* (*die Begriffsbestimmung der Sprache*).[3] But instead of giving a ready-made definition of speech, it would be better perhaps to proceed along tentative lines. Speech is not a simple and uniform phenomenon. It consists of different elements which, both biologically and systematically, are not on the same level. We must try to find the order and interrelationships of the constituent elements; we must, as it were, distinguish the various geological strata of speech. The first and most fundamental stratum is evidently the language of the emotions. A great portion of all human utterance still belongs to this stratum. But there is a form of speech that shows us quite a different type. Here the word is by no means a mere interjection; it is not an involuntary expression of feeling, but a part of a sentence which has a definite syntactical and logical structure.[4] It is true that even in highly developed, in theoretical language the connection with the first element is not entirely broken off. Scarcely a sentence can be found—except perhaps the pure formal sentences of mathematics—without a certain affective or emotional tinge.[5] Analogies and parallels to emotional language may be found in abundance in the animal world. As regards chimpanzees Wolfgang Koehler states that they achieve a considerable degree of expression by means of gesture. Rage,

terror, despair, grief, pleading, desire, playfulness, and pleasure are readily expressed in this manner. Nevertheless one element, which is characteristic of and indispensable to all human language, is missing: we find no signs which have an objective reference or meaning. "It may be . taken as positively proved," say Koehler,

that their gamut of *phonetics* is entirely "subjective," and can only express emotions, never designate or describe objects. But they have so many phonetic elements which are also common to human languages, that their lack of articulate speech cannot be ascribed to *secondary* (gloss-labial) limitations. Their gestures too, of face and body like their expression in sound, never designate or "describe" objects (Bühler).[6]

## II

Here we touch upon the crucial point in our whole problem. The difference between *propositional language* and *emotional language* is the real landmark between the human and the animal world. All the theories and observations concerning animal language are wide of the mark if they fail to recognize this fundamental difference.[7]

[3] G. Révész, "Die menschlichen Kommunikationsformen und die sogenannte Tiersprache," *Proceedings of the Netherlands Akademie van Wetenschappen*, XLIII (1940), Nos. 9, 10; XLIV (1941), No. 1.

[4] For the distinction between mere emotive utterances and "the normal type of communication of ideas that is speech," see the introductory remarks of Edward Sapir, *Language* (New York, Harcourt, Brace, 1921).

[5] For further details see Charles Bally, *Le langage et la vie* (Paris, 1936).

[6] Wolfgang Koehler, "Zur Psychologie des Schimpansen," *Psychologische Forschung*, I (1921), 27. Cf. the English ed., *The Mentality of Apes* (New York, Harcourt, Brace, 1925), App., p. 317.

[7] An early attempt to make a sharp distinction between propositional and emotional language was made in the field of the psychopathology of language. The English neurologist Jackson introduced the term "propositional language" in order to account for some very interesting pathological phenomena. He found that many patients suffering from aphasia had by no means lost the use of speech but that they could not employ their words in an objective, propositional sense. Jackson's distinction proved to be very fruitful. It has played an important part in the further development of the psychopathology of language. For details see Cassirer, *Philosophie der symbolischen Formen*, III, Chap. vi, 237–323.

In all the literature of the subject there does not seem to be a single conclusive proof of the fact that any animal ever made the decisive step from subjective to objective, from affective to propositional language. Koehler insists emphatically that speech is definitely beyond the powers of anthropoid apes. He maintains that the lack of this invaluable technical aid and the great limitation of those very important components of thought, the so-called images, constitute the causes which prevent animals from ever achieving even the least beginnings of cultural development.[8] The same conclusion has been reached by Révész. Speech, he asserts, is an anthropological concept which accordingly should be entirely discarded from the study of animal psychology. If we proceed from a clear and precise definition of speech, all the other forms of utterances, which we also find in animals, are automatically eliminated.[9] Yerkes, who has studied the problem with special interest, speaks in a more positive tone. He is convinced that even with respect to language and symbolism there exists a close relationship between man and the anthropoid apes. "This suggests," he writes, "that we may have happened upon an early phylogenetic stage in the evolution of symbolic process. There is abundant evidence that various other types of sign process than the symbolic are of frequent occurrence and function effectively in the chimpanzee." [10] Yet all this remains definitely prelinguistic. Even in the judgment of Yerkes all these functional expressions are exceedingly rudimentary, simple, and of limited usefulness by comparison with human cognitive processes.[11] The genetic question is not to be confused here with the analytical and phenomenological question. The logical analysis of human speech always leads us to an element of prime importance which has no parallel in the animal world. The general theory of evolution in no sense stands in the way of the acknowledgment of this fact. Even in the field of the phenomena of organic nature we have learned that evolution does not exclude a sort of original creation. The fact of sudden mutation and of emergent evolution has to be admitted. Modern biology no longer speaks of evolution in terms of earlier Darwinism; nor does it explain the causes of evolution in the same way. We may readily admit that the anthropoid apes, in the development of certain symbolic processes, have made a significant forward step. But again we must insist that they did not reach the threshold of the human world. They entered, as it were, a blind alley.

For the sake of a clear statement of the problem we must carefully distinguish between *signs* and *symbols*. That we find rather complex systems of signs and signals in animal behavior seems to be an ascertained fact. We may even say that some animals, especially domesticated animals, are extremely susceptible to signs.[12] A dog will react to the slightest changes in the behavior of his master; he will even distinguish the expressions of a human

[8] Koehler, *The Mentality of Apes*, p. 277.
[9] Révész, *op. cit.*, XLIII, Pt. II (1940), 33.
[10] Yerkes and Nissen, "Prelinguistic Sign Behavior in Chimpanzee," *Science*, LXXXIX, 587.
[11] Yerkes, *Chimpanzees*, p. 189.

[12] This susceptibility has, for instance, been proved in the famous case of "clever Hans" which a few decades ago created something of a sensation among psychobiologists. Clever Hans was a horse which appeared to possess an astounding intelligence. He could even master rather complicated arithmetical problems, extract cube roots, and so on, stamping on the ground as many times as the solution of the problem required. A special committee of psychologists and other scientists was called on to investigate the case. It soon became clear that the animal reacted to certain involuntary movements of its owner. When the owner was absent or did not understand the question, the horse could not answer it.

face or the modulations of a human voice.[13] But it is a far cry from these phenomena to an understanding of symbolic and human speech. The famous experiments of Pavlov prove only that animals can easily be trained to react not merely to direct stimuli but to all sorts of mediate or representative stimuli. A bell, for example, may become a "sign for dinner," and an animal may be trained not to touch its food when this sign is absent. But from this we learn only that the experimenter, in this case, has succeeded in changing the food-situation of the animal. He has complicated this situation by voluntarily introducing into it a new element. All the phenomena which are commonly described as conditioned reflexes are not merely very far from but even opposed to the essential character of human symbolic thought. Symbols— in the proper sense of this term—cannot be reduced to mere signals. Signals and symbols belong to two different universes of discourse: a signal is a

part of the physical world of being; a symbol is a part of the human world of meaning. Signals are "operators"; symbols are "designators."[14] Signals, even when understood and used as such, have nevertheless a sort of physical or substantial being; symbols have only a functional value.

Bearing this distinction in mind, we can find an approach to one of the most controverted problems. The question of the *intelligence of animals* has always been one of the greatest puzzles of anthropological philsophy. Tremendous efforts, both of thought and observation, have been expended on answers to this question. But the ambiguity and vagueness of the very term "intelligence" has always stood in the way of a clear solution. How can we hope to answer a question whose import we do not understand? Metaphysicians and scientists, naturalists and theologians have used the word intelligence in varying and contradictory senses. Some psychologists and psychobiologists have flatly refused to speak of the intelligence of animals. In all animal behavior they saw only the play of a certain automatism. This thesis had behind it the authority of Descartes; yet it has been reasserted in modern psychology. "The animal," says E. L. Thorndike in his work on animal intelligence, "does not think one is like the other, nor does it, as is so often said, mistake one for the other. It does not think *about* it at all; it just thinks *it* . . . The idea that animals react to a particular and absolutely defined and realized sense-impression, and that a similar reaction to a sense-impression which varies from the first proves an association by similarity, is a myth." [15] Later and more exact ob-

[13] To illustrate this point I should like to mention another very revealing example. The psychologist, Dr. Pfungst, who had developed some new and interesting methods for the study of animal behavior, once told me that he had received a letter from a major about a curious problem. The major had a dog which accompanied him on his walks. Whenever the master got ready to go out the animal showed signs of great joy and excitement. But one day the major decided to try a little experiment. Pretending to go out, he put on his hat, took his cane, and made the customary preparations—without, however, any intention of going for a walk. To his great surprise the dog was not in the least deceived; he remained quietly in his corner. After a brief period of observation Dr. Pfungst was able to solve the mystery. In the major's room there was a desk with a drawer which contained some valuable and important documents. The major had formed the habit of rattling this drawer before leaving the house in order to make sure that it was locked. He did not do so the day he did not intend to go out. But for the dog this had become a signal, a necessary element of the walk-situation. Without this signal the dog did not react.

[14] For the distinction between operators and designators see Charles Morris, "The Foundation of the Theory of Signs," *Encyclopedia of the Unified Sciences* (1938).
[15] Edward L. Thorndike, *Animal Intelligence* (New York, Macmillan, 1911), pp. 119 ff.

servations led to a different conclusion. In the case of the higher animals it became clear that they were able to solve rather difficult problems and that these solutions were not brought about in a merely mechanical way, by trial and error. As Koehler points out, the most striking difference exists between a mere chance solution and a genuine solution, so that the one can easily be distinguished from the other. That at least some of the reactions of the higher animals are not merely a product of chance but guided by insight appears to be incontestable.[16] If by intelligence we understand either adjustment to the immediate environment or adaptive modification of environment, we must certainly ascribe to animals a comparatively highly developed intelligence. It must also be conceded that not all animal actions are governed by the presence of an immediate stimulus. The animal is capable of all sorts of detours in its reactions. It may learn not only to use implements but even to invent tools for its purposes. Hence some psychobiologists do not hesitate to speak of a creative or constructive imagination in animals.[17] But neither this intelligence nor this imagination is of the specifically human type. In short, we may say that the animal possesses a practical imagination and intelligence whereas man alone has developed a new form: *a symbolic imagination and intelligence.*

Moreover, in the mental development of the individual mind the transition from one form to the other—from a merely practical attitude to a symbolic attitude—is evident. But here this step is the final result of a slow and continuous process. By the usual methods of psychological observation it is not easy to distinguish the individual

stages of this complicated process. There is, however, another way to obtain full insight into the general character and paramount importance of this transition. Nature itself has here, so to speak, made an experiment capable of throwing unexpected light upon the point in question. We have the classical cases of Laura Bridgman and Helen Keller, two blind deaf-mute children, who by means of special methods learned to speak. Although both cases are well known and have often been treated in psychological literature,[18] I must nevertheless remind the reader of them once more because they contain perhaps the best illustration of the general problem with which we are here concerned. Mrs. Sullivan, the teacher of Helen Keller, has recorded the exact date on which the child really began to understand the meaning and function of human language. I quote her own words:

I must write you a line this morning because something very important has happened. Helen has taken the second great step in her education. She has learned that *everything has a name, and that the manual alphabet is the key to everything she wants to know.*

. . . This morning, while she was washing, she wanted to know the name for "water." When she wants to know the name of anything, she points to it and pats my hand. I spelled "w-a-t-e-r" and thought no more about it until after breakfast. . . . [Later on] we went out to the pump house, and I made Helen hold her mug under the spout while I pumped. As the cold water gushed forth, filling the mug, I spelled "w-a-t-e-r" in Helen's free hand. The word coming so close upon the sensation of cold water

[16] See Koehler, *op. cit.*, chap. vii, " 'Chance' and 'Imitation.' "
[17] See R. M. and A. W. Yerkes, *The Great Apes* (New Haven, Yale University Press, 1929), pp. 368 ff., 520 ff.

[18] For Laura Bridgman see Maud Howe and Florence Howe Hall, *Laura Bridgman* (Boston, 1903); Mary Swift Lamson, *Life and Education of Laura Dewey Bridgman* (Boston, 1881); Wilhelm Jerusalem, *Laura Bridgman, Erziehung einer Taubstumm-Blinden* (Berlin, 1905).

rushing over her hand seemed to startle her. She dropped the mug and stood as one transfixed. A new light came into her face. She spelled "water" several times. Then she dropped on the ground and asked for its name and pointed to the pump and the trellis and suddenly turning round she asked for my name. I spelled "teacher." All the way back to the house she was highly excited, and learned the name of every object she touched, so that in a few hours she had added thirty new words to her vocabulary. The next morning she got up like a radiant fairy. She has flitted from object to object, asking the name of everything and kissing me for very gladness. . . . Everything must have a name now. Wherever we go, she asks eagerly for the names of things she has not learned at home. She is anxious for her friends to spell, and eager to teach the letters to everyone she meets. She drops the signs and pantomime she used before, as soon as she has words to supply their place, and the acquirement of a new word affords her the liveliest pleasure. And we notice that her face grows more expressive each day.[19]

The decisive step leading from the use of signs and pantomime to the use of words, that is, of symbols, could scarcely be described in a more striking manner. What was the child's real discovery at this moment? Helen Keller had previously learned to combine a certain thing or event with a certain sign of the manual alphabet. A fixed association had been established between these things and certain tactile impressions. But a series of such associations, even if they are repeated and amplified, still does not imply an understanding of what human speech is and means. In order to arrive at such an understanding the child had to make a new and much more significant discovery. It had to understand that *every-thing has a name*—that the symbolic

function is not restricted to particular cases but is a principle of *universal* applicability which encompasses the whole field of human thought. In the case of Helen Keller this discovery came as a sudden shock. She was a girl seven years of age who, with the exception of defects in the use of certain sense organs, was in an excellent state of health and possessed of a highly developed mind. By the neglect of her education she had been very much retarded. Then, suddenly, the crucial development takes place. It works like an intellectual revolution. The child begins to see the world in a new light. It has learned the use of words not merely as mechanical signs or signals but as an entirely new instrument of thought. A new horizon is opened up, and henceforth the child will roam at will in this incomparably wider and freer area.

The same can be shown in the case of Laura Bridgman, though hers is a less spectacular story. Both in mental ability and in intellectual development Laura Bridgman was greatly inferior to Helen Keller. Her life and education do not contain the same dramatic elements we find in Helen Keller. Yet in both cases the same typical elements are present. After Laura Bridgman had learned the use of the finger-alphabet she, too, suddenly reached the point at which she began to understand the symbolism of human speech. In this respect we find a surprising parallelism between the two cases. "I shall never forget," write Miss Drew, one of the first teachers of Laura Bridgman, "the first meal taken after she appreciated the use of the finger-alphabet. Every article that she touched must have a name; and I was obliged to call some one to help me wait upon the other children, while she kept me busy in spelling the new words."[20]

[19] See Helen Keller, *The Story of My Life* (New York, Doubleday, Page & Co., 1902, 1903), Supplementary Account of Helen Keller's Life and Education, pp. 315 ff.

[20] See Mary Swift Lamson, *Life and Education of Laura Dewey Bridgman, the Deaf, Dumb, and Blind Girl* (Boston, Houghton, Mifflin Co., 1881), pp. 7 f.

## III

The principle of symbolism, with its universality, validity, and general applicability, is the magic word, the Open Sesame! giving access to the specifically human world, to the world of human culture. Once man is in possession of this magic key further progress is assured. Such progress is evidently not obstructed or made impossible by any lack in the sense material. The case of Helen Keller, who reached a very high degree of mental development and intellectual culture, shows us clearly and irrefutably that a human being in the construction of his human world is not dependent upon the quality of his sense material. If the theories of sensationalism were right, if every idea were nothing but a faint copy of an original sense impression, then the condition of a blind, deaf, and dumb child would indeed be desperate. For it would be deprived of the very sources of human knowledge; it would be, as it were, an exile from reality. But if we study Helen Keller's autobiography we are at once aware that this is untrue, and at the same time we understand why it is untrue. Human culture derives its specific character and its intellectual and moral values, not from the material of which it consists, but from its form, its architectural structure. And this form may be expressed in any sense material. Vocal language has a very great technical advantage over tactile language; but the technical defects of the latter do not destroy its essential use. The free development of symbolic thought and symbolic expression is not obstructed by the use of tactile signs in the place of vocal ones. If the child has succeeded in grasping the meaning of human language, it does not matter in which particular material this meaning is accessible to it. As the case of Helen Keller proves, man can construct his symbolic world out of the poorest and scantiest materials. The thing of vital importance is not the individual bricks and stones but their general *function* as architectural form. In the realm of speech it is their general symbolic function which vivifies the material signs and "makes them speak." Without this vivifying principle the human world would indeed remain deaf and mute. With this principle, even the world of a deaf, dumb, and blind child can become incomparably broader and richer than the world of the most highly developed animal.

Universal applicability, owing to the fact that everything has a name, is one of the greatest prerogatives of human symbolism. But it is not the only one. There is still another characteristic of symbols which accompanies and complements this one, and forms its necessary correlate. A symbol is not only universal but extremely variable. I can express the same meaning in various languages; and even within the limits of a single language a certain thought or idea may be expressed in quite different terms. A sign or signal is related to the thing to which it refers in a fixed and unique way. Any one concrete and individual sign refers to a certain individual thing. In Pavlov's experiments the dogs could easily be trained to reach for food only upon being given special signs; they would not eat until they heard a particular sound which could be chosen at the discretion of the experimenter. But this bears no analogy, as it has often been interpreted, to human symbolism; on the contrary, it is in opposition to symbolism. A genuine human symbol is characterized not by its uniformity but by its versatility. It is not rigid or inflexible but mobile. It is true that the full *awareness* of this mobility seems to be a rather late achievement in man's intellectual and cultural development. In primitive mentality this awareness is very seldom attained. Here the symbol is still regarded as a property of the thing like other physical properties. In mythical thought the name of a god is an integral part of the nature of the god. If I do not call the god by his right name, then the spell or prayer becomes ineffective. The same holds good for symbolic actions. A religious rite, a sacrifice, must always be performed in the same invariable way and in the same order if it is to have its effect. [21] Children are often greatly confused when they first learn that not every name of an object is a "proper name," that the same thing may have quite different names in different languages. They tend to think that a thing "is" what it is called. But this is only a first step. Every normal child will learn very soon that it can use various symbols to express the same wish or thought. For this variability and mobility there is apparently no parallel in the animal world. [22] Long before Laura Bridgman had learned to speak, she had developed a very curious mode of expression, a language of her own. This language did not consist of articulated sounds but only of various noises, which are described as "emotional noises." She was in the habit of uttering these sounds in the presence of certain persons. Thus they become entirely individualized; every person in her environment was greeted by a special noise. "Whenever she met unexpectedly an acquaintance," writes Dr. Lieber, "I found that she repeatedly uttered the word for that person before she began to speak. It was the utterance of pleasurable recognition." [23] But when by means of the finger alphabet the child had grasped the meaning of human language the case was altered. Now the sound really became a name: and this name was not bound to an in-

dividual person but could be changed if the circumstances seemed to require it. One day, for instance, Laura Bridgman had a letter from her former teacher, Miss Drew, who, in the meantime, by her marriage had become a Mrs. Morton. In this letter she was invited to visit her teacher. This gave her great pleasure, but she found fault with Miss Drew because she had signed the letter with her old name instead of using the name of her husband. She even said that now she must find another noise for her teacher, as the one for Drew must not be the same as that for Morton.[24] It is clear that the former "noises" have here undergone an important and very interesting change in meaning. They are no longer special utterances, inseparable from a particular concrete situation. They have become abstract names. For the new name invented by the child did not designate a new individual but the same individual in a new relationship.

## IV

Another important aspect of our general problem now emerges—the problem of the *dependence of relational thought upon symbolic thought*. Without a complex system of symbols relational thought cannot arise at all, much less reach its full development. It would not be correct to say that the mere *awareness* of relations presupposes an intellectual act, an act of logical or abstract thought. Such an awareness is necessary even in elementary acts of perception. The sensationalist theories used to describe perception as a mosaic or simple sense data. Thinkers of this persuasion constantly overlooked the fact that sensation itself is by no means a mere struggle or bundle of isolated impressions. Modern Gestalt psychology has corrected this view. It has shown that the very simplest perceptual processes imply fundamental structural

[21] For further details see Cassirer, *Sprache und Mythos* (Leipzig, 1925).
[22] For this problem see W. M. Urban, *Language and Reality*, Pt. I, iii, 95 ff.
[23] See Francis Lieber, "A Paper on the Vocal Sounds of Laura Bridgman," *Smithsonian Contributions to Knowledge*, II, Art. 2, p. 27.

[24] See Mary Swift Lamson, *op. cit.*, p. 84.

elements, certain patterns or configurations. This principle holds both for the human and the animal world. Even in comparatively low stages of animal life the presence of these structural elements—especially of spatial and optical structures—has been experimentally proved.[25] The mere awareness of relations cannot, therefore, be regarded as a specific feature of human consciousness. We do find, however, in man a special type of relational thought which has no parallel in the animal world. In man an ability to isolate relations—to consider them in their abstract meaning—has developed. In order to grasp this meaning man is no longer dependent upon concrete sense data, upon visual, auditory, tactile, kinesthetic data. He considers these relations "in themselves"—αὐτὸ καθ᾽ αυτό, as Plato said. Geometry is the classic example of this turning point in man's intellectual life. Even in elementary geometry we are not bound to the apprehension of concrete individual figures. We are not concerned with physical things or perceptual objects, for we are studying universal spatial relations for whose expression we have an adequate symbolism. Without the preliminary step of human language such an achievement would not be possible. In all the tests which have been made of the processes of abstraction or generalization in animals, this point has become evident. Koehler succeeded in showing the ability of chimpanzees to respond to the *relation* between two or more objects instead of to a particular object. Confronted by two food-containing boxes, the chimpanzee by reason of previous general training would constantly choose the larger—even though

the particular object might in a previous experiment have been rejected as the smaller of the pair. Similar capacity to respond to the nearer object, the brighter, the bluer, rather than to a particular box was demonstrated. Koehler's results were confirmed and extended by later experiments. It could be shown that the higher animals are capable of what has been called the "isolation of perceptual factors." They have the potentiality for singling out a particular perceptual quality of the experimental situation and reacting accordingly. In this sense animals are able to abstract color from size and shape or shape from size and color. In some experiments made by Mrs. Kohts a chimpanzee was able to select from a collection of objects varying extremely in visual qualities those which had some one quality in common; it could, for instance, pick out all objects of a given color and place them in a receiving box. These examples seem to prove that the higher animals are capable of that process which Hume in his theory of knowledge terms making a *"distinction of reason."* [26] But all the experimenters engaged in these investigations have also emphasized the rarity, the rudimentariness, and the imperfection of these processes. Even after they have learned to single out a particular quality and to reach toward this, animals are liable to all sorts of curious mistakes.[27] If there are certain traces of a *distinctio rationis* in the animal world, they are, as it were, nipped in the bud. They cannot develop because they do not possess that invaluable and indeed indispensable aid of human speech, of a system of symbols. . . .

---

[25] See Wolfgang Koehler, "Optische Untersuchungen am Schimpansen und am Haushuhn; Nachweis einfacher Strukturfunktionen beim Schimpansen und beim Haushuhn," *Abhandlungen der Berliner Akademie der Wissenschaften* (1915, 1918).

[26] Hume's theory of the "distinction of reason" is explained in his *Treatise of Human Nature*, Pt. I, sec. 7 (London, Green and Grosse, 1874), I, 332 ff.

[27] Examples are given by Yerkes in *Chimpanzees*, pp. 103 ff.

# B Social Action and the Development of the Self

## 5

### The Nature of Social Action

#### W. J. H. SPROTT

. . . If it is true that the natural sciences are, as it were, an elaboration of the day-to-day practical rules that everyone has to learn in order to cope with his physical environment, it is indeed the case that psychology and the social sciences are an elaboration of the day-to-day practical rules we have to apply in dealing with one another. It is true, of course, that while the non-specialists are applying such a general corpus of knowledge as has become common property the specialist in the natural sciences investigates new problems; and he makes discoveries which are surprising to his fellow men. And

From *Science and Social Action* by W. J. H. Sprott. Copyright © by C. A. Watts & Co. Ltd. Used by permission.

this is what makes it sound odd to say that his work is an "elaboration of day-to-day practical rules." I use the expression to link up the "pure" scientist with action. The surprises are due to the fact that the scientific discoverer in the field of the natural sciences is either handling old materials in a new way, or handling new materials altogether. He is enlarging the world in which we live and extending the scope of our action, much as the early explorers extended the world in which we live by discovering places previously unknown, and much as—in a microscopic region—the cook who discovers that the best way to cook brussels sprouts is to plunge them for five minutes into boiling water, is extending her culinary sphere and those of her friends to whom she reveals her secret.

Now with psychology and sociology all this seems to me to be different. If we say, very rightly, that psychology is the study of human behaviour, and sociology the study of social behaviour and its accompaniments, surely it is absurd to suggest that no one studied human beings and groups of human beings before Wundt and Comte. . . . Surely man was studying woman from the very beginning in the Garden of Eden. And as to social psychology, it was applied with some effect by the serpent. Social science was applied in action by the first administrator. Man has been studying man, and men have administered their fellows, ever since men emerged and lived in groups large enough to call for the concept of "society." And this has gone on down the ages. No wonder the self-conscious and explicit study of men and society brings with it so few surprises. Even psycho-analysis is really an elaboration of what was already known: namely that certain people give bona fide reasons for doing things—reasons which other people know to be false. Let me hasten to say that I am not minimizing the importance of this. All I am saying is that psychology and sociology are quite obviously elaborations of ideas which we inevitably get from our everyday social intercourse with other people like ourselves. Unlike the fields of natural science, we are not coming across new materials, new places, new techniques—or very rarely; we are ever defining our concepts about the same old thing. It is this that depresses many modern psychologists. They want something new, something startling. And where do they look? To physiology, of course. There they can find new physical materials, such as endocrine secretions, which influence human behaviour in unexpected ways. They study the physiology of conditioning and try

to reduce it to a system. They handle the body in new ways, giving it electric shocks, pumping in insulin, or severing brain-fibres by pre-frontal leucotomy; and the results are startling indeed. But psychology, in the sense that we usually understand it—the study of men's behaviour in terms of conscious and unconscious motives—does not spring from the study of their nervous systems; it springs from the inevitabilities of social action, and so, I shall suggest, does sociology. . . .

Let us now look more closely into the concept of social action. My first point is that all social action involves mutual adaptation. The conduct of A is determined by A's expectation of B's response, and B's response is determined by B's interpretation of A's conduct and the expectation he attributes to him, and also by his expectation of A's counter-response, and so on. This, as George Mead has pointed out, is true of the intercourse of animals below human level. The sexual, playful, and quarrelsome interaction of dogs and cats and birds all involve such mutual adaptation. So does the intercourse between humans and such domestic animals as interact with them. These range from such creatures as one can, as they say, "make pets of" to such creatures as one cannot because their interaction is limited to the mere approach to food and retreat from contact. With human beings the same "pet" level is found between mother and her infant child. With human beings, however, something else is present. At some point in the evolutionary series creatures emerged whose gestures became not merely significant in the sense of eliciting appropriate responses, but significant to themselves—the point at which a gesture is awarefully directed to the eliciting of a response. How this came about we do not know. To say that the fore-brain became bigger does not help us until we know what goes on inside it.

It may be that something like what George Mead suggested took place: that the turning point was the incipient adumbration in the actor of the response of the other, so that he, the actor, takes the role of the other in himself, thus paving the way for a contrast between his own "other" response, the *real* response of the other, and between both and his own spontaneous spring of activity. It may be that language, with its peculiar characteristics of being uttered and heard—both action and self-stimulus—by the actor, played a significant part in the development of man as such. We cannot go back and look. We can say that such feral men as have come to our notice—children brought up by animals or neglected by men—are scarcely human at all; but as for our own remote prehuman ancestry, we can but speculate. One thing seems to be plausible, and that is that only through social interaction at a level at which the awareful eliciting of counter-responses becomes possible do men become men, aware of themselves as separate beings having meaning intercourse with one another.

And what happens then? I think one can get some insight into this by examining one or two trivial and very familiar experiences—so trivial that I feel somewhat apologetic about bringing them to your attention.

Imagine two friends who have been so related for some time. The actions of each when they are together are mutually adapted. After a while each can, as we say, "count upon" the other. In fact it is not merely that A can guess what B will do, as a psychiatrist can guess at the likely response of his patient, and it is not merely that B can guess what A will do, as, indeed, the patient may guess at the likely conduct of the psychiatrist. There is more to it than that. A knows that B knows what A is likely to do, and B knows what A

expects B to expect. Something which one can call a mutually accepted system of expectations gets established. Each knows the other's little ways, and knows that the other knows his. There may, indeed, be unspoken secrets which each keeps from the other. Each has his own perspective in the duality; but for the relationship to persist there must be a mutual system controlling the conduct of both. The importance of this may indeed be realized when one reflects upon the common complaint you hear people make about some acquaintance: "Of course," they say, "you can't really make friends with him because he's so incalculable; you don't know what he's going to do next." Without a mutually accepted framework of behaviour no persistent social intercourse is possible. I would even extend this notion to hostility, though here there are complications. One enemy may destroy the other, and the relationship is at an end in default of one of the relata. The enemies may part and hate at a distance, and in some sense the relationship is at an end. They may, however, persist together or near at hand, and then, as we all know, for the mutual hate to be kept up, a mutually accepted system of not speaking or passing nasty remarks, or reciprocal head-tossing must be preserved. That, surely, is one of the reasons why a soft answer turneth away wrath. That is why it takes two to make a quarrel.

Corresponding to the overt mutual adjustments and registering their consistency over a period we can conveniently endow the interacting parties with "frames of reference." This intervening variable we can build into that other construct: "personality," in terms of which we explain the total behaviour of each. By saying that persistent social intercourse engenders frames of reference I mean that each participant views and thinks of the other in terms of those expectations which he has ac-

quired in the course of their friendship. Each will, as we say, "understand"
the other, interpreting his gestures
and his speech in terms of the mutual scheme which has become established.

And even this trivial example can be
carried a little further. The two parties
may, of course, interact to their mutual
satisfaction without either of them mentioning the matter either to the other
or to himself. On the other hand, they
may, when perhaps the expectations of
one are falsified: "I never expected you
to do such a thing" one might say; then
what I have called the scheme of accepted values may become symbolized
as "our friendship." Doubtless the symbol will be slightly different in one
from what it is in the other; but there
must be common constituents, otherwise neither will be intelligible to the
other. Again, it might be that one of
them wants to do something which will
cause pain to the other, something indeed which conflicts with their mutual
system. Then he may say to himself:
"I really ought not," or even, "I really
*cannot* do this or that. It would ruin
our friendship." Suppose, for instance,
it is their wont to go to the pictures
every Saturday night. Suppose A has
an enticing invitation for one Saturday
night. Will there not be a conflict in
A's mind? And, indeed, supposing both
A and B receive an invitation for a
Saturday night. Is it a gross exaggeration to suggest that they may say to
one another: "Well, of course it means
giving up *our* Saturday night's pictures"? Something has been ever so
slightly outraged. What, surely, has
happened is that this day-to-day mutual
scheme of inter-responses has become
externalized and now stands out against
them coercively. We are at once reminded of Durkheim's [1] definition of a

social fact: "Un fait social se reconnait au pouvoir de coercition externe
qu'il exerce ou est susceptible d'exercer
sur les individus; et la présence de ce
pouvoir se reconnait a son tour soit à
l'existance de quelque sanction deter-
minée, soit à la résistance que le fait
oppose à toute entreprise individuelle
qui tend à lui faire violence." [2]

This going to the pictures on a Saturday night is, when we come to think
of it, an institution of our society of
two. It would be "wrong" of A to act
in disaccord with its rules in despite of
B, and even slightly "wrong" of A and
B to alter it. And this, not only because
of a cultural standard of "friendship,"
—though of course any example I take
will in fact bring this wider context in
—but, I suggest, mainly because their
relationship cannot continue without
such mutually accepted norms. Certainly there are variations in the range
of permissible behaviour when you
compare two pairs of friends—as there
are when you compare two societies on
a larger scale—but some regulation
there must be for any social relationship to persist.

What I am trying to suggest to you
is that social institutions, law, and morality are the necessary products of all
persistent social intercourse. Embry-
onically they are there even at the prehuman level, but their symbolization in
language makes a vital difference.
Without language I do not see how
they could achieve the external validity
they do achieve.

This becomes even clearer if we take
a group larger than a pair. Imagine
four people setting up house together:

[1] *Règles de la Méthode Sociologique* (Presses
Universitaires, 1947 edition), p. 11.

[2] A social fact may be recognized by the coercive pressure which it brings to bear on the
individual from outside; and the presence of
this pressure can be detected either by the
existence of some determinate sanction, or
by the resistance which is set up against any
attempt by the individual to violate the
social fact.

it might be four students. Again mutual adaptation of each to each, and each, in a sense, to all, is essential. They cannot, we will suppose, all sit on the same chair; they cannot all get into the bath at the same time. Problems arise, and a mutually acceptable solution must be found. The seating arrangements, the bath rota, the rules for washing up, and the times for meals will become established institutions; and any new-comer will find himself confronted with an order—let us say, "a culture"—not of his devising, external and coercive, to which he has to submit. The order will be felt to be "right"; that accommodation of conflicting interests, which we call "justice," will be achieved. I mentioned the new-comer, who is confronted with a pattern of interaction. How is it conveyed to him? He might, of course, painstakingly watch and note the interlocking conduct, and form in his mind a patterned construct to represent it. More likely, of course, he will be told by the participants. "This," they might say, "is our way of life." It will have been symbolized.

And now increase this number. Let us suppose that the scheme is a success and that more students want to join. The group moves to larger quarters. They no longer, perhaps, consist of intimate friends, but acquaintances who have to be initiated. Mutual adjustment on a purely spontaneous basis becomes less reliable. The bath rota, the meal times, and so forth must be more strictly adhered to. Rules may even be written down on a sheet of paper and pinned up in the hall. Now let us suppose that in the early days each of our four friends took turns with the catering; there would not be much to do for four. But increased numbers, increased household expenses, increased responsibility for a larger establishment, present difficulties: One of their number might be specially

good at dealing with them, perhaps the one who suggested the scheme in the first place—the leader or the eldest. Here the staging of my example in student circles becomes a little unrealistic, but I will ask you to bear with me, because the unrealism is really unimportant for my purpose. Let us suppose that this skilful organizer takes on the organizing as a whole-time job. To keep him contributions must be made, perhaps larger numbers still might be needed. The group incorporates anyone who wishes to join. A room is set aside for the organizer, now called the Warden. Note what has happened. The spontaneously interacting group of people who have precipitated their own norms in the course of living together has grown into an "enterprise"—a going concern. Organization brings with it its stratification; a hierarchy is in the offing. Administration has begun. A post, a social position with its appropriate role, has been created. A *new form of social action has come into being.* And look into the future. Generations of members have passed through the group. Wardens have come and gone, each judged not by his charm but by his efficiency. The group is enlarged still further, and along come an accountant, a secretary, a matron, and a staff of waiters. There are so many in the community that the Warden, who now sits upon a dais, cannot know them all. They are just anonymous students, mere names upon alphabetical lists, allotted rooms in order of application. The group has a name, a badge, a tie and a yell. The picture of the founder hangs in a prominent place in the refectory. To go further would be frivolous. We might even imagine that when servants are in short supply, our establishment might capture the smaller hostel next door, incorporate it, and reduce its inhabitants to servitude.

Now I suggest that here we have, in

an example not so fictitious as to be quite absurd, something very like what I think Hegel and Engels had in mind when they spoke of increase in quantity often leading to a change in quality. The impersonal world of administration produces frames of reference different from those which are developed in purely personal intercourse. They are explicitly symbolized and are applied to a different kind of content. The administrator's frame of reference, when he is playing his role, is not of such a kind as is brought into action when he thinks of: "My friendship with dear old George, who is so charming even when he does get het up, though of course he only does it in order to tease me." It is not like that at all. Whether he thinks in pictures or words or both, he thinks of a larger scheme with a name attached to it—the hostel, the business, the county, the city, the country, the party. He thinks in terms of individuals occupying certain positions in the concern which, as position, are relatively permanent. He thinks of the occupants as functionaries rather than as personalities, though of course he recognizes their personalities as making them good or bad role-players. And beside the functionaries, whom he might possibly name, there are the anonymous many who are administered for his own benefit, for the benefit of someone else, or for their own benefit. Here language is essential to the working of the scheme. Communications must run backward and forward, couched in terms which are intelligible to the intercommunicants. This means that the frame of reference of all involved, the key men and the masses, must have common elements. They too must think in terms of the hostel, the business, the county, the city, the country, the party, or whatever type of concern they, as we say, belong to. In fact I would say that "belonging," in anything more than a purely classifica-

tory sense, positively *means* thinking in such terms.

But thinking in terms of the concern is by no means the whole story. In the first place, each member will see it from his own point of view; but their points of view must contain common elements for communication to be possible. The student thinks of himself as a student at Birmingham University, the lecturer as a lecturer at Birmingham University, the lab-steward as lab-steward at Birmingham University, and so on. They all mean something the same by "Birmingham University." Secondly, each will have an attitude towards the concern. He may identify himself with it and act with enthusiasm in terms of its regulations and in terms of his notion of the accepted ethos; he may dissociate himself from the concern, merely keeping the rules in order to avoid the consequences of breaking them; or he may be indifferent to the concern but keep the rules because life is simpler that way; or break them when he thinks he can get away with it. But whichever he does, he must have somewhat the same notion of the concern and its rules as his fellow members. The future history of the concern will of course in part depend on the proportions of those who identify themselves with it as compared with those who dissociate themselves from it, and the intensity of their feelings, which, in turn, will be largely dependent on their conscious or unconscious interests.

Now all the time we must remember that within the concern, whatever it may be, there is always personal intercourse going on, with its mutual adjustments, its private codes of behaviour, its crises, and their resolutions. The administrator has his wife, his daughter, his cronies, and his carpet slippers. Indeed, one of the administrated, meeting him *en pantouffles*, may say afterwards: "the old man was really quite human"—a significant phrase. And yet, again, these private affairs occur upon a public stage. Thus we must fuse or combine our frames of reference. Every man is both a "private person" and a "public personage"—using the latter phrase in no status-conferring sense. He is in love with, devoted to, or indifferent to, the woman with whom he shares his leisure hours; at the same time he is her husband, her fiancé, or her lover. One evening he is with his intimates, but has to leave them to take the chair at a meeting. He is having dinner with his friend Tom and is called away to a patient.

And so we might go on, but we must beware of imputing the analytical world view of the social scientist to the subjects of his study without qualification. A man's conduct is less awarefully governed than we are apt to imagine. It is ridiculous to suppose that a person says to himself: "Now I am a private person, now I am a civil servant, foreign secretary, dustman," or whatever position he may occupy. The analytic view is seen through the frame of reference of the sociologist. Nevertheless we can say that every man and woman is brought up to develop a kind of double world in which he or she lives: a world of immediacies set in a context of remoter relationships, institutions, beliefs, and concerns. . . . A man works beside Fred, a decent sort of chap even if he is a bit of a boozer; his face-to-face intercourse with Fred takes place in a context of the firm who employs them, and that is situated in a city, and the city in a country which has relations with other countries in the world. Sometimes the man thinks in terms of Fred's Freddishness, if I may be allowed the expression, sometimes in terms of "the country." He has learnt to handle Fred partly by past experience with other people, and partly by trial and error with Fred himself; he has learnt to think in terms of the firm and the country because these

concepts have been conveyed to him in language. In the latter case there is no direct contact because in some sense the firm and the country exist only in virtue of the agreed conventions of the people he meets and of multitudes of other people whom he does not meet. Of course there has to be a material substratum for it all; there have to be other human beings able to do things with their hands and with machines; there have to be materials to mould into the desired shapes; there have to be buildings in which this is done. Without all this the notion of "the firm" will not come into existence. All the same, the accumulation of these articles in one place is the result of social action. Our worker does not merely mean by "the firm" these physical things: he means the whole concern with its positions of manager and foreman, its profit-making, its clocking-in system, and so on, within which the men, machine and building have their meaning.

Now not all of the world-views I have been discussing are of equal importance to the sociologist. There are some which more closely approximate to the one he is trying to formulate. The world of the peasant may be limited by the boundaries of his village with a vague penumbra behind his religion and the fruits of his labour, a vague notion of distant co-believers and tax-collectors. He is more concerned with day-to-day personal contacts. The administrator, as we have seen, has a different and wider view. He thinks in terms of countries, of cities, of economic problems. He, indeed, has the sociological view. The sociologist, I suggest, is the specialist who tries to elaborate and make precise the administrative world-picture.

I have put the whole matter in this way because I want to make two points. In the first place, just as the first man who moulded metal was the first metal-

lurgist, so the first person who awarefully considered the character of the
person he was dealing with was the
first psychologist; and the first administrator, whether chief or warrior,
who thought in terms of the tribe, the
clan, or the army, was the first sociologist. Metallurgy, psychology, and sociology as scientific disciplines arise
when thought about these things becomes too complicated for the practical
man. In the second place, the emergence of psychology and sociology is a
natural development from the necessities of social action when performed by
creatures capable of reflection and symbolic registration.

We cannot penetrate the night of
time. We can, I think, plausibly assume that something like this happened. In the beginning was the word.
Our ancestors at some point or other
began to use words meaningfully and
not as mere emotive utterances. They
were then capable of symbolizing the
rules according to which their social
action was conducted, and handed on
these rules to their children. Then,
when technology enabled large numbers to keep together, a more complicated régime was necessary to ensure
their efficient co-operation, and this
means social action at the administrative level, with the appropriate conceptual superstructure. Once this is established and gets verbalized, then the ball
is set rolling from those distant ages
down to our own times. The whole apparatus of sociological analysis is there
from the start: law, morality, beliefs,
society, technology, economics, politics,
the in-group, the out-group, the face-to-
face group, the indirectly-related group,
the system of positions and accompanying roles, and moreover, even the
embryonic concept of status, whereby
some are accepted as higher than
others.

It will, I dare say, be objected that
I have concentrated too much on human beings interacting with one an-

other and that I have left their material
conditions out of account. This is only
because one cannot say everything at
once. Of course the development of
societies depends on material conditions, the appraisal of them as valuable
or indifferent, and the presence or absence of things to appraise. And each
generation is brought up to apprehend
the significance of the physical environment as understood by the technological standards of its parents. Their own
efforts will change the world both materially and evaluatively for their prog-
eny, often in ways which they did not
expect and the stage is set for another
act.

In stressing the vital importance of
men's *ideas* of the groups to which
they belong, I may be accused of treating the whole subject too mentalisti-
cally; I may be accused of idealism, in
some of the many senses of that term
of abuse. But surely mental talk is the
only talk we can use. Picture a little
boy in a forest; along the path comes
a man; the lad peeps out to see who is
coming so that he can prepare himself
for appropriate behaviour. It might be
his maternal uncle, it might be a relation with whom it is incumbent upon
him to joke or tell dirty stories, it
might be the chief. The boy will recognize the on-comer and act accordingly.
"He knows who it is, he has learnt
how to behave, he believes that certain
conduct is right and certain conduct is
wrong," we say. And will any physiological story about the intruder be
more helpful? X-ray him, subject him
to electroencephalography, dissect him,
tell us all you can about his physical
make-up, and now tell us whether he
really was the boy's maternal uncle or
not. And the boy himself? Look into
his fore-brain for traces and you will
have to interpret your findings in terms
of the boy's actual conduct. It may, of
course, well be that in the future we
shall be able to peer into the nervous
system of such a little boy and say,

*before* he acts: "See, that neural explosion is the maternal-uncle index; now he will be neurally caused to do so and so." But such predictive powers lie in the future. We can make our little curtsy to some useless but fashionable form of materialism and say what is doubtless true: "It all depends on our brains." Then we must pass on to talk in terms which are intelligible.

Again I may be accused of psychologism—of saying that we can understand and interpret social events by direct reference to human intentions. I am saying no such thing. Human intentions are certainly basic to social happenings, but the social happenings themselves are frequently—more often than not—unintended. Each of our two friends had intentions, but they did not intend to precipitate the coercive social fact of friendship. We intend to reap where we have sown, but we did not intend to make a dust-bowl. Men and women intend to have fewer children, they do not intend to alter the age-structure of the population. Once an agreed structure is established with its appropriate frames-of-reference, as a resultant of the interaction of individuals, whether the structure be tribalism, the slave state, feudalism, cap-

italism, or communism, individuals privately intend to do this or that within whatever context they may be operating. The result of the totality of their private intentions—desires for money, prestige, sexual intercourse, or the satisfaction of curiosity—will be the perpetuation, the alteration, the transformation, or the destruction of the social pattern. But the result cannot be attributed to the individual wishes of any one of them, save perhaps to a very few in key positions.

I have suggested, then, that social action takes place between persons who agree among themselves that they hold certain positions in a social structure. As participants in that structure they have been brought up to entertain certain beliefs. And they and their fellow participants are confronted by certain physical opportunities and hazards, including among them the number of participants there are.

Thus we have four aspects of social action to study: interaction itself; the social constructs within which it is performed; the beliefs which it produces and which in turn guide it; and the physical and demographic environment in which it takes place. . . .

# 6

# The Development of the Self in Social Interaction

GEORGE HERBERT MEAD

In our statement of the development of intelligence we have already suggested that the language process is essential for

Reprinted from *Mind, Self and Society* by George Herbert Mead by permission of The University of Chicago Press. Copyright © 1934 by The University of Chicago Press.

the development of the self. The self has a character which is different from that of the physiological organism proper. The self is something which has a development; it is not initially there, at birth, but arises in the process of social experience and activity, that is, develops in the given individual as a result of his relations to that process as a whole and to other individuals within that process.

. . . . . . . . . . . .

It is the characteristic of the self as an object to itself that I want to bring out. This characteristic is represented in the word "self," which is a reflexive, and indicates that which can be both subject and object. This type of object is essentially different from other objects, and in the past it has been distinguished as conscious, a term which indicates an experience with, an experience of, one's self. It was assumed that consciousness in some way carried this capacity of being an object to itself. In giving a behavioristic statement of consciousness we have to look for some sort of experience in which the physical organism can become an object to itself.[1]

When one is running to get away from someone who is chasing him, he is entirely occupied in this action, and his experience may be swallowed up in the objects about him, so that he has, at the time being, no consciousness of self at all. We must be, of course, very completely occupied to have that take place, but we can, I think, recognize that sort of a possible experience in which the self does not enter. We can, perhaps, get some light on that situation through those experiences in which in very intense action there appear in the experience of the individual, back of this intense action, memories and anticipations. Tolstoi as an officer in

[1] Man's behavior is such in his social group that he is able to become an object to himself, a fact which constitutes him a more advanced product of evolutionary development than are the lower animals. Fundamentally it is this social fact—and not his alleged possession of a soul or mind with which he, as an individual, has been mysteriously and supernaturally endowed, and with which the lower animals have not been endowed—that differentiates him from them.

the war gives an account of having pictures of his past experience in the midst of his most intense action. There are also pictures that flash into a person's mind when he is drowning. In such instances there is a contrast between an experience that is absolutely wound up in outside activity in which the self as an object does not enter, and an activity of memory and imagination in which the self is the principal object. The self is then entirely distinguishable from an organism that is surrounded by things and acts with reference to things, including parts of its own body. These latter may be objects like other objects, but they are just objects out there in the field, and they do not involve a self that is an object to the organism. This is, I think, frequently overlooked. It is that fact which makes our anthropomorphic reconstructions of animal life so fallacious. How can an individual get outside himself (experientially) in such a way as to become an object to himself? This is the essential psychological problem of selfhood or of self-consciousness; and its solution is to be found by referring to the process of social conduct or activity in which the given person or individual is implicated. The apparatus of reason would not be complete unless it swept itself into its own analysis of the field of experience; or unless the individual brought himself into the same experiential field as that of the other individual selves in relation to whom he acts in any given social situation. Reason cannot become impersonal unless it takes an objective, non-affective attitude toward itself; otherwise we have just consciousness, not *self*-consciousness. And it is necessary to rational conduct that the individual should thus take an objective, impersonal attitude toward himself, that he should become an object to himself. For the individual organism is obviously an essential and important fact or constituent element of the empirical situation in which it acts; and without taking objective account of itself as such, it cannot act intelligently, or rationally.

The individual experiences himself as such, not directly, but only indirectly, from the particular standpoints of other individual members of the same social group, or from the generalized standpoint of the social group as a whole to which he belongs. For he enters his own experience as a self or individual, not directly or immediately, not by becoming a subject to himself, but only in so far as he first becomes an object to himself just as other individuals are objects to him or in his experience; and he becomes an object to himself only by taking the attitudes of other individuals toward himself within a social environment or context of experience and behavior in which both he and they are involved.

The importance of what we term "communication" lies in the fact that it provides a form of behavior in which the organism or the individual may become an object to himself. It is that sort of communication which we have been discussing—not communication in the sense of the cluck of the hen to the chickens, or the bark of a wolf to the pack, or the lowing of a cow, but communication in the sense of significant symbols, communication which is directed not only to others but also to the individual himself. So far as that type of communication is a part of behavior it at least introduces a self. Of course, one may hear without listening; one may see things that he does not realize; do things that he is not really aware of. But it is where one does respond to that which he addresses to another and where that response of his own becomes a part of his conduct, where he not only hears himself but responds to himself, talks and replies to himself as truly as the other person

replies to him, that we have behavior in which the individuals become objects to themselves.

.    .    .    .    .    .    .    .    .    .

The self, as that which can be an object to itself, is essentially a social structure, and it arises in social experience. After a self has arisen, it in a certain sense provides for itself its social experiences, and so we can conceive of an absolutely solitary self. But it is impossible to conceive of a self arising outside of social experience. When it has arisen we can think of a person in solitary confinement for the rest of his life, but who still has himself as a companion, and is able to think and to converse with himself as he had communicated with others. That process to which I have just referred, of responding to one's self as another responds to it, taking part in one's own conversation with others, being aware of what one is saying and using that awareness of what one is saying to determine what one is going to say thereafter—that is a process with which we are all familiar. We are continually following up our own address to other persons by an understanding of what we are saying, and using that understanding in the direction of our continued speech. We are finding out what we are going to say, what we are going to do, by saying and doing, and in the process we are continually controlling the process itself. In the conversation of gestures what we say calls out a certain response in another and that in turn changes our own action, so that we shift from what we started to do because of the reply the other makes. The conversation of gestures is the beginning of communication. The individual comes to carry on a conversation of gestures with himself. He says something, and that calls out a certain reply in himself which makes him change what he was going to say. One starts to say something, we will presume an unpleasant something, but when he starts to say it he realizes it is cruel. The effect on himself of what he is saying checks him; there is here a conversation of gestures between the individual and himself. We mean by significant speech that the action is one that affects the individual himself, and that the effect upon the individual himself is part of the intelligent carrying-out of the conversation with others. Now we, so to speak, amputate that social phase and dispense with it for the time being, so that one is talking to one's self as one would talk to another person.

This process of abstraction cannot be carried on indefinitely. One inevitably seeks an audience, has to pour himself out to somebody. In reflective intelligence one thinks to act, and to act solely so that this action remains a part of a social process. Thinking becomes preparatory to social action. The very process of thinking is, of course, simply an inner conversation that goes on, but it is a conversation of gestures which in its completion implies the expression of that which one thinks to an audience. One separates the significance of what he is saying to others from the actual speech and gets it ready before saying it. He thinks it out, and perhaps writes it in the form of a book; but it is still a part of social intercourse in which one is addressing other persons and at the same time addressing one's self, and in which one controls the address to other persons by the response made to one's own gesture. That the person should be responding to himself is necessary to the self, and it is this sort of social conduct which provides behavior within which that self appears. I know of no other form of behavior than the linguistic in which the individual is an object to himself, and, so far as I can see, the individual is not a self in the reflexive sense unless he is an object to himself. It is this fact that gives a critical importance to communication, since this is a type of be-

havior in which the individual does so respond to himself.

We realize in everyday conduct and experience that an individual does not mean a great deal of what he is doing and saying. We frequently say that such an individual is not himself. We come away from an interview with a realization that we have left out important things, that there are parts of the self that did not get into what was said. What determines the amount of the self that gets into communication is the social experience itself. Of course, a good deal of the self does not need to get expression. We carry on a whole series of different relationships to different people. We are one thing to one man and another thing to another. There are parts of the self which exist only for the self in relationship to itself. We divide ourselves up in all sorts of different selves with reference to our acquaintances. We discuss politics with one and religion with another. There are all sorts of different selves answering to all sorts of different social reactions. It is the social process itself that is responsible for the appearance of the self; it is not there as a self apart from this type of experience.

A multiple personality is in a certain sense normal, as I have just pointed out. There is usually an organization of the whole self with reference to the community to which we belong, and the situation in which we find ourselves. What the society is, whether we are living with people of the present, people of our own imaginations, people of the past, varies, of course, with different individuals. Normally, within the sort of community as a whole to which we belong, there is a unified self, but that may be broken up.

.    .    .    .    .    .    .    .    .    .    .    .

The unity and structure of the complete self reflects the unity and structure of the social process as a whole; and each of the elementary selves of which it is composed reflects the unity and structure of one of the various aspects of that process in which the individual is implicated. In other words, the various elementary selves which constitute, or are organized into, a complete self are the various aspects of the structure of that complete self answering to the various aspects of the structure of the social process as a whole; the structure of the complete self is thus a reflection of the complete social process. The organization and unification of a social group is identical with the organization and unification of any one of the selves arising within the social process in which that group is engaged, or which it is carrying on.

The phenomenon of dissociation of personality is caused by a breaking up of the complete, unitary self into the component selves of which it is composed, and which respectively correspond to different aspects of the social process in which the person is involved, and within which his complete or unitary self has arisen; these aspects being the different social groups to which he belongs within that process.

. . . . . . . . . . . . .

We find in children . . . imaginary companions which a good many children produce in their own experience. They organize in this way the responses which they call out in other persons and call out also in themselves. Of course, this playing with an imaginary companion is only a peculiarly interesting phase of ordinary play. Play in this sense, especially the stage which precedes the organized games, is a play at something. A child plays at being a mother, at being a teacher, at being a policeman; that is, it is taking different rôles, as we say. We have something that suggests this in what we call the play of animals: a cat will play with her kittens, and dogs play with each other. Two dogs playing with each other will attack and defend, in a process which if carried through would amount to an actual fight. There is a combination of

responses which checks the depth of the bite. But we do not have in such a situation the dogs taking a definite rôle in the sense that a child deliberately takes the rôle of another. This tendency on the part of the children is what we are working with in the kindergarten where the rôles which the children assume are made the basis for training. When a child does assume a rôle he has in himself the stimuli which call out that particular response or group of responses. He may, of course, run away when he is chased, as the dog does, or he may turn around and strike back just as the dog does in his play. But that is not the same as playing at something. Children get together to "play Indian." This means that the child has a certain set of stimuli which call out in itself the responses that they would call out in others, and which answer to an Indian. In the play period the child utilizes his own responses to these stimuli which he makes use of in building a self. The response which he has a tendency to make to these stimuli organizes them. He plays that he is, for instance, offering himself something, and he buys it; he gives a letter to himself and takes it away; he addresses himself as a parent, as a teacher; he arrests himself as a policeman. He has a set of stimuli which call out in himself the sort of responses they call out in others. He takes this group of responses and organizes them into a certain whole. Such is the simplest form of being another to one's self. It involves a temporal situation. The child says something in one character and responds in another character, and then his responding in another character is a stimulus to himself in the first character, and so the conversation goes on. A certain organized structure arises in him and in his other which replies to it, and these carry on the conversation of gestures between themselves.

If we contrast play with the situation in an organized game, we note the essential difference that the child who plays in a game must be ready to take the attitude of everyone else involved in that game, and that these different rôles must have a definite relationship to each other. Taking a very simple game such as hide-and-seek, everyone with the exception of the one who is hiding is a person who is hunting. A child does not require more than the person who is hunted and the one who is hunting. If a child is playing in the first sense he just goes on playing, but there is no basic organization gained. In that early stage he passes from one rôle to another just as a whim takes him. But in a game where a number of individuals are involved, then the child taking one rôle must be ready to take the rôle of everyone else. If he gets in a baseball nine he must have the responses of each position involved in his own position. He must know what everyone else is going to do in order to carry out his own play. He has to take all of these rôles. They do not all have to be present in consciousness at the same time, but at some moments he has to have three or four individuals present in his own attitude, such as the one who is going to throw the ball, the one who is going to catch it, and so on. These responses must be, in some degree, present in his own make-up. In the game, then, there is a set of responses of such others so organized that the attitude of one calls out the appropriate attitudes of the other.

This organization is put in the form of the rules of the game. Children take a great interest in rules. They make rules on the spot in order to help themselves out of difficulties. Part of the enjoyment of the game is to get these rules. Now, the rules are the set of responses which a particular attitude calls out. You can demand a certain response in others if you take a certain attitude. These responses are all in yourself as well. There you get an organized set of such responses as that to

which I have referred, which is something more elaborate than the rôles found in play. Here there is just a set of responses that follow on each other indefinitely. At such a stage we speak of a child as not yet having a fully developed self. The child responds in a fairly intelligent fashion to the immediate stimuli that come to him, but they are not organized. He does not organize his life as we would like to have him do, namely, as a whole. There is just a set of responses of the type of play. The child reacts to a certain stimulus, and the reaction is in himself that is called out in others, but he is not a whole self. In his game he has to have an organization of these rôles; otherwise he cannot play the game. The game represents the passage in the life of the child from taking the rôle of others in play to the organized part that is essential to self-consciousness in the full sense of the term.

We were speaking of the social conditions under which the self arises as an object. In addition to language we found two illustrations, one in play and the other in the game, and I wish to summarize and expand my account on these points. I have spoken of these from the point of view of children. We can, of course, refer also to the attitudes of more primitive people out of which our civilization has arisen. A striking illustration of play as distinct from the game is found in the myths and various of the plays which primitive people carry out, especially in religious pageants. The pure play attitude which we find in the case of little children may not be found here, since the participants are adults, and undoubtedly the relationship of these play processes to that which they interpret is more or less in the minds of even the most primitive people. In the process of interpretation of such rituals, there is an organization of play which perhaps might be compared to that which is taking place in the kindergarten in dealing with the plays of little children, where these are made into a set that will have a definite structure or relationship. At least something of the same sort is found in the play of primitive people. This type of activity belongs, of course, not to the everyday life of the people in their dealing with the objects about them—there we have a more or less definitely developed self-consciousness—but in their attitudes toward the forces about them, the nature upon which they depend; in their attitude toward this nature which is vague and uncertain, there we have a much more primitive response; and that response finds its expression in taking the rôle of the other, playing at the expression of their gods and their heroes, going through certain rites which are the representation of what these individuals are supposed to be doing. The process is one which develops, to be sure, into a more or less definite technique and is controlled; and yet we can say that it has arisen out of situations similar to those in which little children play at being a parent, at being a teacher—vague personalities that are about them and which affect them and on which they depend. These are personalities which they take, rôles they play, and in so far control the development of their own personality. This outcome is just what the kindergarten works toward. It takes the characters of these various vague beings and gets them into such an organized social relationship to each other that they build up the character of the little child.[2] The very introduction of organization from outside supposes a lack of organization at this period in the child's experience. Over against such a situation of the little child and primitive people, we have the game as such.

The fundamental difference between the game and play is that in the latter the child must have the attitude of all the others involved in that game. The attitudes of the other players which the participant assumes organize into a sort of unit, and it is that organization which controls the response of the individual. The illustration used was of a person playing baseball. Each one of his own acts is determined by his assumption of the action of the others who are playing the game. What he does is controlled by his being everyone else on that team, at least in so far as those attitudes affect his own particular response. We get then an "other" which is an organization of the attitudes of those involved in the same process.

The organized community or social group which gives to the individual his unity of self may be called "the generalized other." The attitude of the generalized other is the attitude of the whole community.[3] Thus, for example, in the case of such a social group as a

[3] It is possible for inanimate objects, no less than for other human organisms, to form parts of the generalized and organized—the completely socialized—other for any given human individual, in so far as he responds to such objects socially or in a social fashion (by means of the mechanism of thought, the internalized conversation of gestures). Any thing—any object or set of objects, whether animate or inanimate, human or animal, or merely physical—toward which he acts, or to which he responds, socially, is an element in what for him is the generalized other; by taking the attitudes of which toward himself he becomes conscious of himself as an object or individual, and thus develops a self or personality. Thus, for example, the cult, in its primitive form, is merely the social embodiment of the relation between the given social group or community and its physical environment—an organized social means, adopted by the individual members of that group or community, of entering into social relations with that environment, or (in a sense) of carrying on conversations with it; and in this way that environment becomes part of the total generalized other for each of the individual members of the given social group or community.

[2] ["The Relation of Play to Education," *University of Chicago Record*, I (1896–97), 140 ff.]

ball team, the team is the generalized other in so far as it enters—as an organized process or social activity—into the experience of any one of the individual members of it.

If the given human individual is to develop a self in the fullest sense, it is not sufficient for him merely to take the attitudes of other human individuals toward himself and toward one another within the human social process, and to bring that social process as a whole into his individual experience merely in these terms: he must also, in the same way that he takes the attitudes of other individuals toward himself and toward one another, take their attitudes toward the various phases or aspects of the common social activity or set of social undertakings in which, as members of an organized society or social group, they are all engaged; and he must then, by generalizing these individual attitudes of that organized society or social group itself, as a whole, act toward different social projects which at any given time it is carrying out, or toward the various larger phases of the general social process which constitutes its life and of which these projects are specific manifestations. This getting of the broad activities of any given social whole or organized society as such within the experiential field of any one of the individuals involved or included in that whole is, in other words, the essential basis and prerequisite of the fullest development of that individual's self: only in so far as he takes the attitudes of the organized social group to which he belongs toward the organized, co-operative social activity or set of such activities in which that group as such is engaged, does he develop a complete self or possess the sort of complete self he has developed. And on the other hand, the complex co-operative processes and activities and institutional functionings of organized human society are also possible only in so far as every individual involved in them or belonging to that

society can take the general attitudes of all other such individuals with reference to these processes and activities and institutional functionings, and to the organized social whole of experiential relations and interactions thereby constituted—and can direct his own behavior accordingly.

It is in the form of the generalized other that the social process influences the behavior of the individuals involved in it and carrying it on, i.e., that the community exercises control over the conduct of its individual members; for it is in this form that the social process or community enters as a determining factor into the individual's thinking. In abstract thought the individual takes the attitude of the generalized other [4] toward himself, without reference to its expression in any particular other individuals; and in concrete thought he takes that attitude in so far as it is expressed in the attitudes toward his behavior of those other individuals with whom he is involved in the given social situation or act. But only by taking the attitude of the generalized other toward himself, in one or another of these ways, can he think at all; for only thus can thinking—or the internalized conversation of gestures which constitutes thinking—occur. And only through the taking by individuals of the attitude or attitudes of the generalized other toward themselves is the existence of a universe of discourse, as that system of common or social meanings which thinking presupposes at its context, rendered possible.

.    .    .    .    .    .    .    .    .    .

What goes to make up the organized self is the organization of the attitudes

[4] We have said that the internal conversation of the individual with himself in terms of words or significant gestures . . . is carried on by the individual from the standpoint of the "generalized other." And the more abstract that conversation is, the more abstract thinking happens to be, the further removed is the generalized other from any connection with particular individuals . . .

which are common to the group. A person is a personality because he belongs to a community, because he takes over the institutions of that community into his own conduct. He takes its language as a medium by which he gets his personality, and then through a process of taking the different rôles that all the others furnish he comes to get the attitude of the members of the community. Such, in a certain sense, is the structure of a man's personality. There are certain common responses which each individual has toward certain common things, and in so far as those common responses are awakened in the individual when he is affecting other persons he arouses his own self. The structure, then, on which the self is built is this response which is common to all, for one has to be a member of a community to be a self. Such responses are abstract attitudes, but they constitute just what we term a man's character. They give him what we term his principles, the acknowledged attitudes of all members of the community toward what are the values of that community. He is putting himself in the place of the generalized other, which represents the organized responses of all the members of the group. It is that which guides conduct controlled by principles, and a person who has such an organized group of responses is a man whom we say has character, in the moral sense.

. . . . . . . . . . .

I have so far emphasized what I have called the structures upon which the self is constructed, the framework of the self, as it were. Of course we are not only what is common to all: each one of the selves is different from everyone else; but there has to be such a common structure as I have sketched in order that we may be members of a community at all. We cannot be ourselves unless we are also members in whom there is a community of attitudes which control the attitudes of all. We can-

not have rights unless we have common attitudes. That which we have acquired as self-conscious persons makes us such members of society and gives us selves. Selves can only exist in definite relationships to other selves. No hard-and-fast line can be drawn between our own selves and the selves of others, since our own selves exist and enter as such into our experience only in so far as the selves of others exist and enter as such into our experience also. The individual possesses a self only in relation to the selves of the other members of his social group; and the structure of his self expresses or reflects the general behavior pattern of this social group to which he belongs, just as does the structure of the self of every other individual belonging to this social group.

. . . . . . . . . .

There is one other matter which I wish briefly to refer to now. The only way in which we can react against the disapproval of the entire community is by setting up a higher sort of community which in a certain sense outvotes the one we find. A person may reach a point of going against the whole world about him; he may stand out by himself over against it. But to do that he has to speak with the voice of reason to himself. He has to comprehend the voices of the past and of the future. That is the only way in which the self can get a voice which is more than the voice of the community. As a rule we assume that this general voice of the community is identical with the larger community of the past and the future; we assume that an organized custom represents what we call morality. The things one cannot do are those which everybody would condemn. If we take the attitude of the community over against our own responses, that is a true statement, but we must not forget this other capacity, that of replying to the community and insisting on the gesture of the community changing. We can reform the order of things;

we can insist on making the community standards better standards. We are not simply bound by the community. We are engaged in a conversation in which what we say is listened to by the community and its response is one which is affected by what we have to say. This is especially true in critical situations. A man rises up and defends himself for what he does; he has his "day in court"; he can present his views. He can perhaps change the attitude of the community toward himself. The process of conversation is one in which the individual has not only the right but the duty of talking to the community of which he is a part, and bringing about those changes which take place through the interaction of individuals. That is the way, of course, in which society gets ahead, by just such interactions as those in which some person thinks a thing out. We are continually changing our social system in some respects, and we are able to do that intelligently because we can think. . . .

# 7

# Primary Groups

## CHARLES HORTON COOLEY

By primary groups I mean those characterized by intimate face-to-face association and coöperation. They are primary in several senses, but chiefly in that they are fundamental in forming the social nature and ideals of the individual. The result of intimate association, psychologically, is a certain fusion of individualities in a common whole, so that one's very self, for many purposes at least, is the common life and purpose of the group. Perhaps the simplest way of describing this wholeness is by saying that it is a "we"; it involves the sort of sympathy and mutual identification for which "we" is the natural expression. One lives in the feeling of the whole and finds the chief aims of his will in that feeling.

It is not to be supposed that the unity

of the primary group is one of mere harmony and love. It is always a differentiated and usually a competitive unity, admitting of self-assertion and various appropriative passions; but these passions are socialized by sympathy, and come, or tend to come, under the discipline of a common spirit. The individual will be ambitious, but the chief object of his ambition will be some desired place in the thought of the others, and he will feel allegiance to common standards of service and fair play. So the boy will dispute with his fellows a place on the team, but above such disputes will place the common glory of his class and school.

The most important spheres of this intimate association and coöperation— though by no means the only ones— are the family, the play-group of children, and the neighborhood or community group of elders. These are practically universal, belonging to all times and all stages of development;

and are accordingly a chief basis of what is universal in human nature and human ideals. The best comparative studies of the family, such as those of Westermarck [1] or Howard,[2] show it to us as not only a universal institution, but as more alike the world over than the exaggeration of exceptional customs by an earlier school had led us to suppose. Nor can any one doubt the general prevalence of play-groups among children or of informal assemblies of various kinds among their elders. Such association is clearly the nursery of human nature in the world about us, and there is no apparent reason to suppose that the case has anywhere or at any time been essentially different.

As regards play, I might, were it not a matter of common observation, multiply illustrations of the universality and spontaneity of the group discussion and coöperation to which it gives rise. The general fact is that children, especially boys after about their twelfth year, live in fellowships in which their sympathy, ambition and honor are engaged even more, often, than they are in the family. Most of us can recall examples of the endurance by boys of injustice and even cruelty, rather than appeal from their fellows to parents or teachers—as, for instance, in the hazing so prevalent at schools, and so difficult, for this very reason, to suppress. And how elaborate the discussion, how cogent the public opinion, how hot the ambitions in these fellowships.

Nor is this facility of juvenile association, as is sometimes supposed, a trait peculiar to English and American boys; since experience among our immigrant population seems to show that the offspring of the more restrictive civilizations of the continent of Europe form self-governing play-groups with almost equal readiness. Thus Miss Jane Addams, after pointing out that the

"gang" is almost universal, speaks of the interminable discussion which every detail of the gang's activity receives, remarking that "in these social folk-motes, so to speak, the young citizen learns to act upon his own determination." [3]

Of the neighborhood group it may be said, in general, that from the time men formed permanent settlements upon the land, down, at least, to the rise of modern industrial cities, it has played a main part of the primary, heart-to-heart life of the people. Among our Teutonic forefathers the village community was apparently the chief sphere of sympathy and mutual aid for the commons all through the "dark" and middle ages, and for many purposes it remains so in rural districts at the present day. In some countries we still find it with all its ancient vitality, notably in Russia, where the mir, or self-governing village group, is the main theatre of life, along with the family, for perhaps fifty millions of peasants.

In our own life the intimacy of the neighborhood has been broken up by the growth of an intricate mesh of wider contacts which leaves us strangers to people who live in the same house. And even in the country the same principle is at work, though less obviously, diminishing our economic and spiritual community with our neighbors. How far this change is a healthy development, and how far a disease, is perhaps still uncertain.

Besides these almost universal kinds of primary association, there are many others whose form depends upon the particular state of civilization; the only essential thing, as I have said, being a certain intimacy and fusion of personalities. In our own society, being little bound by place, people easily form clubs, fraternal societies and the like, based on congeniality, which may give rise to real intimacy. Many such

[1] *The History of Human Marriage.*
[2] *A History of Matrimonial Institutions.*
[3] *Newer Ideals of Peace,* 177.

relations are formed at school and college, and among men and women brought together in the first instance by their occupations—as workmen in the same trade, or the like. Where there is a little common interest and activity, kindness grows like weeds by the roadside.

But the fact that the family and neighborhood groups are ascendant in the open and plastic time of childhood makes them even now incomparably more influential than all the rest.

Primary groups are primary in the sense that they give the individual his earliest and completest experience of social unity, and also in the sense that they do not change in the same degree as more elaborate relations, but form a comparatively permanent source out of which the latter are ever springing. Of course they are not independent of the larger society, but to some extent reflect its spirit; as the German family and the German school bear somewhat distinctly the print of German militarism. But this, after all, is like the tide setting back into creeks, and does not commonly go very far. Among the German, and still more among the Russian, peasantry are found habits of free co-operation and discussion almost uninfluenced by the character of the state; and it is a familiar and well-supported view that the village commune, self-governing as regards local affairs and habituated to discussion, is a very widespread institution in settled communities, and the continuator of a similar autonomy previously existing in the clan. "It is man who makes monarchies and establishes republics, but the commune seems to come directly from the hand of God." [4]

In our own cities the crowded tenements and the general economic and social confusion have sorely wounded the family and the neighborhood, but

[4] De Tocqueville, *Democracy in America*, vol. i, chap. 5.

it is remarkable, in view of these conditions, what vitality they show; and there is nothing upon which the conscience of the time is more determined than upon restoring them to health.

These groups, then, are springs of life, not only for the individual but for social institutions. They are only in part moulded by special traditions, and, in larger degree, express a universal nature. The religion or government of other civilizations may seem alien to us, but the children or the family group wear the common life, and with them we can always make ourselves at home.

By human nature, I suppose, we may understand those sentiments and impulses that are human in being superior to those of lower animals, and also in the sense that they belong to mankind at large, and not to any particular race or time. It means, particularly, sympathy and the innumerable sentiments into which sympathy enters, such as love, resentment, ambition, vanity, hero-worship, and the feeling of social right and wrong.

Human nature in this sense is justly regarded as a comparatively permanent element in society. Always and everywhere men seek honor and dread ridicule, defer to public opinion, cherish their goods and their children, and admire courage, generosity, and success. It is always safe to assume that people are and have been human. . . .

There is no better proof of this generic likeness of human nature than in the ease and joy with which the modern man makes himself at home in literature depicting the most remote and varied phases of life—in Homer, in the Nibelung tales, in the Hebrew Scriptures, in the legends of the American Indians, in stories of frontier life, of soldiers and sailors, of criminals and tramps, and so on. The more penetratingly any phase of human life is studied the more an essential likeness to ourselves is revealed.

To return to primary groups: the view here maintained is that human nature is not something existing separately in the individual, but a *group-nature or primary phase of society*, a relatively simple and general condition of the social mind. It is something more, on the one hand, than the mere instinct that is born in us—though that enters into it—and something less, on the other, than the more elaborate development of ideas and sentiments that makes up institutions. It is the nature which is developed and expressed in those simple, face-to-face groups that are somewhat alike in all societies; groups of the family, the playground, and the neighborhood. In the essential similarity of these is to be found the basis, in experience, for similar ideas and sentiments in the human mind. In these, everywhere, human nature comes into existence. Man does not have it at birth; he cannot acquire it except through fellowship, and it decays in isolation.

If this view does not recommend itself to common-sense I do not know that elaboration will be of much avail. It simply means the application at this point of the idea that society and individuals are inseparable phases of a common whole, so that wherever we find an individual fact we may look for a social fact to go with it. If there is a universal nature in persons there must be something universal in association to correspond to it.

What else can human nature be than a trait of primary groups? Surely not an attribute of the separate individual—supposing there were any such thing—since its typical characteristics, such as affection, ambition, vanity, and resentment, are inconceivable apart from society. If it belongs, then, to man in association, what kind or degree of association is required to develop it? Evidently nothing elaborate, because elaborate phases of society are transient and diverse, while human nature is comparatively stable and universal. In short the family and neighborhood life is essential to its genesis and nothing more is.

Here as everywhere in the study of society we must learn to see mankind in psychical wholes, rather than in artificial separation. We must see and feel the communal life of family and local groups as immediate facts, not as combinations of something else. And perhaps we shall do this best by recalling our own experience and extending it through sympathetic observation. What, in our life, is the family and the fellowship; what do we know of the we-feeling? Thought of this kind may help us to get a concrete perception of that primary group-nature of which everything social is the outgrowth.

# C Roles, Norms, and Values in Social Life

## 8

## Social Roles: Society in Man

PETER L. BERGER

. . . Role theory has been almost entirely an American intellectual development. Some of its germinal insights go back to William James, while its direct parents are two other American thinkers,' Charles Cooley and George Herbert Mead. It cannot be our purpose here to give a historical introduction to this quite fascinating portion of intellectual history. Rather than try this even in outline, we shall start more systematically by beginning our consideration of the import of role theory with another look at Thomas' concept of the definition of the situation.

From *Invitation to Sociology* by Peter L. Berger. Copyright © 1963 by Peter L. Berger. Reprinted by permission of Doubleday & Company, Inc. and Penguin Books, Ltd.

The reader will recall Thomas' understanding of the social situation as a sort of reality agreed upon *ad hoc* by those who participate in it, or, more exactly, those who do the defining of the situation. From the viewpoint of the individual participant this means that each situation he enters confronts him with specific expectations and demands of him specific responses to these expectations. As we have already seen, powerful pressures exist in just about any social situation to ensure that the proper responses are indeed forthcoming. Society can exist by virtue of the fact that most of the time most people's definitions of the most important situations at least coincide approximately. The motives of the publisher and writer of these lines may be rather different, but the ways the two define the situation in which this book is being produced are sufficiently similar for the joint venture to be possible. In similar fashion there may be quite divergent interests present in a classroom of students, some of them having little connection with the educational activity that is supposedly going on, but in most cases these interests (say, that one student came to study the subject being taught, while another simply registers for every course taken by a certain redhead he is pursuing) can coexist in the situation without destroying it. In other words, there is a certain amount of leeway in the extent to which response must meet expectation for a situation to remain sociologically viable. Of course, if the definitions of the situation are too widely discrepant, some form of social conflict or disorganization will inevitably result—say, if some students interpret the classroom meeting as a party, or if an author has no intention of producing a book but is using his contract with one publisher to put pressure on another.

While an average individual meets up with very different expectations in different areas of his life in society, the situations that produce these expectations fall into certain clusters. A student may take two courses from two different professors in two different departments, with considerable variations in the expectations met with in the two situations (say, as between formality or informality in the relations between professor and students). Nevertheless, the situations will be sufficiently similar to each other and to other classroom situations previously experienced to enable the student to carry into both situations essentially the same overall response. In other words, in both cases, with but a few modifications, he will be able to *play the role* of student. A role, then, may be defined as a typified response to a typified expectation. So-

ciety has predefined the fundamental typology. To use the language of the theater, from which the concept of role is derived, we can say that society provides the script for all the *dramatis personae*. The individual actors, therefore, need but slip into the roles already assigned to them before the curtain goes up. As long as they play their roles as provided for in this script, the social play can proceed as planned.

The role provides the pattern according to which the individual is to act in the particular situation. Roles, in society as in the theater, will vary in the exactness with which they lay down instructions for the actor. Taking occupational roles for an instance, a fairly minimal pattern goes into the role of garbage collector, while physicians or clergymen or officers have to acquire all kinds of distinctive mannerisms, speech and motor habits, such as military bearing, sanctimonious diction or bedside cheer. It would, however, be missing an essential aspect of the role if one regarded it merely as a regulatory pattern for externally visible actions. One feels more ardent by kissing, more humble by kneeling and more angry by shaking one's fist. That is, the kiss not only expresses ardor but manufactures it. Roles carry with them both certain actions and the emotions and attitudes that belong to these actions. The professor putting on an act that pretends to wisdom comes to feel wise. The preacher finds himself believing what he preaches. The soldier discovers martial stirrings in his breast as he puts on his uniform. In each case, while the emotion or attitude may have been present before the role was taken on, the latter inevitably strengthens what was there before. In many instances there is every reason to suppose that nothing at all anteceded the playing of the role in the actor's consciousness. In other words, one becomes wise by being appointed a professor, believing by engaging in activities that presuppose belief, and ready for battle by marching in formation.

Let us take an example. A man recently commissioned as an officer, especially if he came up through the ranks, will at first be at least slightly embarrassed by the salutes he now receives from the enlisted men he meets on his way. Probably he will respond to them in a friendly, almost apologetic manner. The new insignia on his uniform are at that point still something that he has merely put on, almost like a disguise. Indeed, the new officer may even tell himself and others that underneath he is still the same person, that he simply has new responsibilities (among which, *en passant*, is the duty to accept the salutes of enlisted men). This attitude is not likely to last very long. In order to carry out his new role of officer, our man must maintain a certain bearing. This bearing has quite definite implications. Despite all the double-talk in this area that is customary in so-called democratic armies, such as the American one, one of the fundamental implications is that an officer is a superior somebody, entitled to obedience and respect on the basis of this superiority. Every military salute given by an inferior in rank is an act of obeisance, received as a matter of course by the one who returns it. Thus, with every salute given and accepted (along, of course, with a hundred other ceremonial acts that enhance his new status) our man is fortified in his new bearing—and in its, as it were, ontological presuppositions. He not only acts like an officer, he feels like one. Gone are the embarrassment, the apologetic attitude, the I'm-just-another-guy-really grin. If on some occasion an enlisted man should fail to salute with the appropriate amount of enthusiasm or even commit the unthinkable act of failing to salute at all, our officer is not merely going to punish a violation of

military regulations. He will be driven with every fiber of his being to redress an offense against the appointed order of his cosmos.

It is important to stress in this illustration that only very rarely is such a process deliberate or based on reflection. Our man has not sat down and figured out all the things that ought to go into his new role, including the things that he ought to feel and believe. The strength of the process comes precisely from its unconscious, unreflecting character. He has become an officer almost as effortlessly as he grew into a person with blue eyes, brown hair and a height of six feet. Nor would it be correct to say that our man must be rather stupid and quite an exception among his comrades. On the contrary, the exception is the man who reflects on his roles and his role changes (a type, by the way, who would probably make a poor officer). Even very intelligent people, who faced with doubt about their roles in society, will involve themselves even more in the doubted activity rather than withdraw into reflection. The theologian who doubts his faith will pray more and increase his church attendance, the businessman beset by qualms about his rat-race activities starts going to the office on Sundays too, and the terrorist who suffers from nightmares volunteers for nocturnal executions. And, of course, they are perfectly correct in this course of action. Each role has its inner discipline, what Catholic monastics would call its "formation." The role forms, shapes, patterns both action and actor. It is very difficult to pretend in this world. Normally, one becomes what one plays at.

Every role in society has attached to it a certain identity. As we have seen, some of these identities are trivial and temporary ones, as in some occupations that demand little modification in the being of their practitioners. It is not difficult to change from garbage collector to night watchman. It is considerably more difficult to change from clergyman to officer. It is very, very difficult to change from Negro to white. And it is almost impossible to change from man to woman. These differences in the case of role changing ought not to blind us to the fact that even identities that we consider to be our essential selves have been socially assigned. Just as there are racial roles to be acquired and identified with, so there are sexual roles. To say "I am a man" is just as much a proclamation of role as to say "I am a colonel in the U.S. Army." We are well aware of the fact that one is born a male, while not even the most humorless martinet imagines himself to have been born with a golden eagle sitting on his umbilical cord. But to be biologically male is a far cry from the specific, socially defined (and, of course, socially relative) role that goes with the statement "I am a man." A male child does not have to learn to have an erection. But he must learn to be aggressive, to have ambitions, to compete with others, and to be suspicious of too much gentleness in himself. The male role in our society, however, requires all these things that one must learn, as does a male identity. To have an erection is not enough—if it were, regiments of psychotherapists would be out of work.

This significance of role theory could be summarized by saying that, in a sociological perspective, identity is socially bestowed, socially sustained and socially transformed. The example of the man in process of becoming an officer may suffice to illustrate the way in which identities are bestowed in adult life. However, even roles that are much more fundamentally part of what psychologists would call our personality than those associated with a particular adult activity are bestowed in very similar manner through a social process.

This has been demonstrated over and over again in studies of so-called socialization—the process by which a child learns to be a participant member of society.

Probably the most penetrating theoretical account of this process is the one given by Mead, in which the genesis of the self is interpreted as being one and the same event as the discovery of society. The child finds out who he is as he learns what society is. He learns to play roles properly belonging to him by learning, as Mead puts it, "to take the role of the other"—which, incidentally, is the crucial sociopsychological function of play, in which children masquerade with a variety of social roles and in doing so discover the significance of those being assigned to them. All this learning occurs, and can only occur, in interaction with other human beings, be it the parents or whoever else raises the child. The child first takes on roles *vis-à-vis* what Mead calls his "significant others," that is, those persons who deal with him intimately and whose attitudes are decisive for the formation of his conception of himself. Later, the child learns that the roles he plays are not only relevant to this intimate circle, but relate to the expectations directed toward him by society at large. This higher level of abstraction in the social response Mead calls the discovery of the "generalized other." That is, not only the child's mother expects him to be good, clean and truthful, society in general does so as well. Only when this general conception of society emerges is the child capable of forming a clear conception of himself. "Self" and "society," in the child's experience, are the two sides of the same coin.

In other words, identity is not something "given," but is bestowed in acts of social recognition. We become that as which we are addressed. The same idea is expressed in Cooley's well-known description of the self as a reflection in a looking glass. This does not mean, of course, that there are not certain characteristics an individual is born with, that are carried by his genetic heritage regardless of the social environment in which the latter will have to unfold itself. Our knowledge of man's biology does not as yet allow us a very clear picture of the extent to which this may be true. We do know, however, that the room for social formation within those genetic limits is very large indeed. Even with the biological questions left largely unsettled, we can say that to be human is to be recognized as human, just as to be a certain kind of man is to be recognized as such. The child deprived of human affection and attention becomes dehumanized. The child who is given respect comes to respect himself. A little boy considered to be a *schlemiel* becomes one, just as a grown-up treated as an awe-inspiring young god of war begins to think of himself and act as is appropriate to such a figure—and, indeed, merges his identity with one he is presented with in these expectations.

Identities are socially bestowed. They must also be socially sustained, and fairly steadily so. One cannot be human all by oneself and, apparently, one cannot hold on to any particular identity all by oneself. The self-image of the officer as an officer can be maintained only in a social context in which others are willing to recognize him in this identity. If this recognition is suddenly withdrawn, it usually does not take very long before the self-image collapses.

Cases of radical withdrawal of recognition by society can tell us much about the social character of identity. For example, a man turned overnight from a free citizen into a convict finds himself subjected at once to a massive assault on his previous conception of himself. He may try desperately to hold on to the latter, but in the absence of others in his immediate environment confirming his old identity he will find it almost impossible to maintain it within his own consciousness. With frightening speed he will discover that he is acting as a convict is supposed to, and feeling all the things that a convict is expected to feel. It would be a misleading perspective on this process to look upon it simply as one of the disintegration of personality. A more accurate way of seeing the phenomenon is as a reintegration of personality, no different in its sociopsychological dynamics from the process in which the old identity was integrated. It used to be that our man was treated by all the important people around him as responsible, dignified, considerate and aesthetically fastidious. Consequently he was able to be all these things. Now the walls of the prison separate him from those whose recognition sustained him in the exhibition of these traits. Instead he is now surrounded by people who treat him as irresponsible, swinish in behavior, only out for his own interests and careless of his appearance unless forced to take care by constant supervision. The new expectations are typified in the convict role that responds to them just as the old ones were integrated into a different pattern of conduct. In both cases, identity comes with conduct and conduct occurs in response to a specific social situation.

Extreme cases in which an individual is radically stripped of his old identity simply illustrate more sharply processes that occur in ordinary life. We live our everyday lives within a complex web of recognitions and nonrecognitions. We work better when we are given encouragement by our superiors. We find it hard to be anything but clumsy in a gathering where we know people have an image of us as awkward. We become wits when people expect us to be funny, and interesting characters when we know that such a reputation has preceded us. Intelligence, humor, manual skills, religious devotion and even sexual potency respond with equal alacrity to the expectations of others. This makes understandable the previously mentioned process by which individuals choose their associates in such a way that the latter sustain their self-interpretations. To put this succinctly, every act of social affiliation entails a choice of identity. Conversely every identity requires specific social affiliations for its survival. Birds of the same feather flock together not as a luxury but out of necessity. The intellectual becomes a slob after he is kidnapped by the army. The theological student progressively loses his sense of humor as he approaches ordination. The worker who breaks all norms finds that he breaks even more after he has been given a medal by management. The young man with anxieties about his virility becomes hell-on-wheels in bed when he finds a girl who sees him as an avatar of Don Giovanni. . . .

Such sociological perspective on the character of identity gives us a deeper understanding of the human meaning of prejudice. As a result, we obtain the chilling perception that the prejudging not only concerns the victim's external fate at the hands of his oppressors, but also his consciousness as it is shaped by their expectations. The most terrible thing that prejudice can do to a human being is to make him tend to become what the prejudiced image of him says that he is. The Jew in an anti-Semitic milieu must struggle hard not to become more and more like the anti-Semitic stereotype, as must the Negro in a racist situation. Significantly, this struggle will only have a chance of success when the individual is protected from succumbing to the prejudiced program for his personality by what we could call the counterrecognition of those within his immediate community.

The Gentile world might recognize him as but another despicable Jew of no consequence, and treat him accordingly, but this nonrecognition of his worth may be balanced by the counterrecognition of him within the Jewish community itself as, say, the greatest Talmudic scholar in Latvia.

In view of the sociopsychological dynamics of this deadly game of recognitions, it should not surprise us that the problem of "Jewish identity" arose only among modern Western Jews when assimilation into the surrounding Gentile society had begun to weaken the power of the Jewish community itself to bestow alternate identities on its members as against the identities assigned to them by anti-Semitism. As an individual is forced to gaze at himself in a mirror so constructed as to let him see a leering monster, he must frantically search for other men with other mirrors, unless he is to forget that he ever had another face. To put this a little differently, human dignity is a matter of social permission.

The same relationship between society and identity can be seen in cases where, for one reason or another, an individual's identity is drastically changed. The transformation of identity, just as its genesis and its maintenance, is a social process. We have already indicated the way in which any reinterpretation of the past, any "alternation" from one self-image to another, requires the presence of a group that conspires to bring about the metamorphosis. What anthropologists call a rite of passage involves the repudiation of an old identity (say, that of being a child) and the initiation into a new one (such as that of adult). Modern societies have milder rites of passage, as in the institution of the engagement, by which the individual is gently led by a general conspiracy of all concerned over the threshold between bachelor freedom and the captivity of marriage.

If it were not for this institution, many more would panic at the last moment before the enormity of what they are about to undertake.

We have also seen how "alternation" operates to change identities in such highly structured situations as religious training or psychoanalysis. Again taking the latter as a timely illustration, it involves an intensive social situation in which the individual is led to repudiate his past conception of himself and to take on a new identity, the one that has been programmed for him in the psychoanalytic ideology. What psychoanalysts call "transference," the intense social relationship between analyst and analysand, is essentially the creation of an artificial social milieu within which the alchemy of transformation can occur, that is, within which this alchemy can become plausible to the individual. The longer the relationship lasts and the more intensive it becomes, the more committed does the individual become to his new identity. Finally, when he is "cured," this new identity has indeed become what he is. It will not do, therefore, to dismiss with a Marxist guffaw the psychoanalyst's claim that his treatment is more effective if the patient sees him frequently, does so over a long time and pays a considerable fee. While it is obviously in the analyst's economic interest to hold to this position, it is quite plausible sociologically that the position is factually correct. What is actually "done" in psychoanalysis is that a new identity is constructed. The individual's commitment to this new identity will obviously increase the more intensively, the longer and the more painfully he invests in its manufacture. Certainly his capacity to reject the whole business as a fake has become rather minimal after an investment of several years of his life and thousands of dollars of hard-earned cash.

The same kind of "alchemistic" environment is established in situations of "group therapy." The recent popularity of the latter in American psychiatry can again not be interpreted simply as an economic rationalization. It has its sociological basis in the perfectly correct understanding that group pressures work effectively to make the individual accept the new mirror-image that is being presented to him. Erving Goffman, a contemporary sociologist, has given us a vivid description of how these pressures work in the context of a mental hospital, with the patients finally "selling out" to the psychiatric interpretation of their existence that is the common frame of reference of the "therapeutic" group.

The same process occurs whenever an entire group of individuals is to be "broken" and made to accept a new definition of themselves. It happens in basic training for draftees in the army; much more intensively in the training of personnel for a permanent career in the army, as at military academies. It happens in the indoctrination and "formation" program of cadres for totalitarian organizations, such as the Nazi SS or the Communist Party elite. It has happened for many centuries in monastic novitiates. It has recently been applied to the point of scientific precision in the "brainwashing" techniques employed against prisoners of totalitarian secret-police organizations. The violence of such procedures, as compared with the more routine initiations of society, is to be explained sociologically in terms of the radical degree of transformation of identity that is sought and the functional necessity in these cases that commitment to the transformed identity be foolproof against new "alternations."

Role theory, when pursued to its logical conclusions, does far more than provide us with a convenient shorthand for the description of various social activities. It gives us a sociological anthropology, that is, a view of man based on his existence in society. This view tells us that man plays dramatic parts in the grand play of society, and that, speaking sociologically, he *is* the masks that he must wear to do so. The human person also appears now in a dramatic context, true to its theatrical etymology (*persona*, the technical term given to the actors' masks in classical theater). The person is perceived as a repertoire of roles, each one properly equipped with a certain identity. The range of an individual person can be measured by the number of roles he is capable of playing. The person's biography now appears to us as an uninterrupted sequence of stage performances, played to different audiences, sometimes involving drastic changes of costume, always demanding that the actor *be* what he is playing.

Such a sociological view of personality is far more radical in its challenge to the way that we commonly think of ourselves than most psychological theories. It challenges radically one of the fondest presuppositions about the self —its continuity. Looked at sociologically, the self is no longer a solid, given entity that moves from one situation to another. It is rather a process, continuously created and re-created in each social situation that one enters, held together by the slender thread of memory. How slender this thread is, we have seen in our discussion of the reinterpretation of the past. Nor is it possible within this framework of understanding to take refuge in the unconscious as containing the "real" contents of the self, because the presumed unconscious self is just as subject to social production as is the so-called conscious one, as we have seen. In other words, man is not *also* a social being, but he is social in every aspect of his being that is open to empirical investigation. Still speaking sociologically, then, if one wants to ask who an individual "really" is in this kaleidoscope of roles and identities, one can answer only by enumerating the situations in which he is one thing and those in which he is another.

Now, it is clear that such transformations cannot occur *ad infinitum* and that some are easier than others. An individual becomes so habituated to certain identities that, even when his social situation changes, he has difficulty keeping up with the expectations newly directed toward him. The difficulties that healthy and previously highly active individuals have when they are forced to retire from their occupation show this very clearly. The transformability of the self depends not *only* on its social context, but also on the degree of its habituation to previous identities and perhaps also on certain genetically given traits. While these modifications in our model are necessary to avoid a radicalization of our position, they do not detract appreciably from the discontinuity of the self as revealed by sociological analysis.

If this not very edifying anthropological model is reminiscent of any other, it would be of that employed in early Buddhist psychology in India, in which the self was compared to a long row of candles, each of which lights the wick of its neighbor and is extinguished in that moment. The Buddhist psychologists used this picture to decry the Hindu notion of the transmigration of the soul, meaning to say thereby that there is no entity that passes from one candle to another. But the same picture fits our present anthropological model quite well.

One might obtain the impression from all of this that there is really no essential difference between most people and those afflicted with what psychiatry calls "multiple personality." If someone wanted to harp on the word "essential" here, the sociologist might agree with the statement. The actual difference, however, is that for "normal" people (that is, those so recognized by their society) there are strong pressures toward consistency in the various roles they play and the identities that go with these roles. These pressures are both external and internal. Externally the others with whom one must play one's social games, and on whose recognition one's own parts depend, demand that one present at least a relatively consistent picture to the world. A certain degree of role discrepancy may be permitted, but if certain tolerance limits are passed society will withdraw its recognition of the individual in question, defining him as a moral or psychological aberration. Thus society will allow an individual to be an emperor at work and a serf at home, but it will not permit him to impersonate a police officer or to wear the costume assigned to the other sex. In order to stay within the limits set to his masquerades, the individual may have to resort to complicated maneuvers to make sure that one role remains segregated from the other. The imperial role in the office is endangered by the appearance of one's wife at a director's meeting, or one's role in one circle as an accomplished *raconteur* is threatened by the intrusion of someone from that other circle in which one has been typed as the fellow who never opens his mouth without putting his foot into it. Such role segregation is increasingly possible in our contemporary urban civilization, with its anonymity and its means of rapid transportation, although even here there is a danger that people with contradictory images of oneself may suddenly bump into each other and endanger one's whole stage management. Wife and secretary might meet for coffee, and between them reduce both home-self and office-self to a pitiable shambles. At that point, for sure, one will re-

quire a psychotherapist to put a new Humpty Dumpty together again.

There are also internal pressures toward consistency, possibly based on very profound psychological needs to perceive oneself as a totality. Even the contemporary urban masquerader, who plays mutually irreconcilable roles in different areas of his life, may feel internal tensions though he can successfully control external ones by carefully segregating his several *mises en scène* from each other. To avoid such anxieties people commonly segregate their consciousness as well as their conduct. By this we do not mean that they "repress" their discrepant identities into some "unconscious," for within our model we have every reason to be suspicious of such concepts. We rather mean that they focus their attention only on that particular identity that, so to speak, they require at the moment. Other identities are forgotten for the duration of this particular act. The way in which socially disapproved sexual acts or morally questionable acts of any kind are segregated in consciousness may serve to illustrate this process. The man who engages in, say, homosexual masochism has a carefully constructed identity set aside for just these occasions. When any given occasion is over, he checks that identity again at the gate, so to speak, and returns home as affectionate father, responsible husband, perhaps even ardent lover of his wife. In the same way, the judge who sentences a man to death segregates the identity in which he does this from the rest of his consciousness, in which he is a kindly, tolerant and sensitive human being. The Nazi concentration-camp commander who writes sentimental letters to his children is but an extreme case of something that occurs all the time.

It would be a complete misunderstanding of what has just been said if the reader now thought that we are presenting a picture of society in which everybody schemes, plots and deliberately puts on disguises to fool his fellow men. On the contrary, role-playing and identity-building processes are generally unreflected and unplanned, almost automatic. The psychological needs for consistency of self-image just mentioned ensure this. Deliberate deception requires a degree of psychological self-control that few people are capable of. That is why insincerity is rather a rare phenomenon. Most people are sincere, because this is the easiest course to take psychologically. That is, they believe in their own act, conveniently forget the act that preceded it, and happily go through life in the conviction of being responsible in all its demands. Sincerity is the consciousness of the man who is taken in by his own act. Or as it has been put by David Riesman, the sincere man is the one who believes in his own propaganda. In view of the socio-psychological dynamics just discussed, it is much more likely that the Nazi murderers are sincere in their self-portrayals as having been bureaucrats faced with certain unpleasant exigencies that actually were distasteful to them than to assume that they say this only in order to gain sympathy from their judges. Their humane remorse is probably just as sincere as their erstwhile cruelty. As the Austrian novelist Robert Musil has put it, in every murderer's heart there is a spot in which he is eternally innocent. The seasons of life follow one another, and one must change one's face as one changes one's clothes. At the moment we are not concerned with the psychological difficulties or the ethical import of such "lack of character." We only want to stress that it is the customary procedure.

To tie up what has just been said about role theory with what was said in the preceding chapter about control systems we refer to what Hans Gerth and C. Wright Mills have called "person selection." Every social structure selects those persons that it needs for its functioning and eliminates in one way or another those that do not fit. If no persons are available to be selected, they will have to be invented—or rather, they will be produced in accordance with the required specifications. In this way, through its mechanisms of socialization and "formation," society manufactures the personnel it requies to keep going. The sociologist stands on its head the commonsense idea that certain institutions arise because there are certain persons around. On the contrary, fierce warriors appear because there are armies to be sent out, pious men because there are churches to be built, scholars because there are universities to be staffed, and murderers because there are killings to be performed. It is not correct to say that each society gets the men it deserves. Rather, each society produces the men it needs. We can derive some comfort from the fact that this production process sometimes runs into technical difficulties. We shall see later that it can also be sabotaged. For the moment, however, we can see that role theory and its concomitant perceptions add an important dimension to our sociological perspective on human existence.

# 9

# Norms, Values, and Sanctions

## JUDITH BLAKE AND KINGSLEY DAVIS

The meaning of "norm" in everyday usuage is ambiguous. It often refers to a statistical regularity, as when we say that one's temperature is "normal" or that a man who has been sick has resumed his "normal" activities. On the other hand, it may indicate an accepted standard or model, as in the phrase "set the norm" or "conform to ethical norms." In sociology the same ambiguity is found, although ostensibly, at least, when a formal definition is given, the second meaning is stipulated. Thus the term is presumably employed . . . to designate any standard or rule that states what human beings should or should not think, say, or do under given circumstances.

In this strict sociological usage, the most important element is the *should*, for it clearly implies two important propositions: first, that actual behavior *may* differ from the norm; second, that it *will* differ from the norm unless some effort or force is exerted to bring about conformity. The sociological use of the term generally assumes, without always saying so, that norms are shared to some extent. A purely private, or individual, view of what people should do or think is a norm, but unless it is shared by others, it has no social significance.

Anything in society which pertains to norms, including statements concerning their nature, rationalizations justifying them, and reactions to their violation, may be designated by the

adjective "normative." Employed in this way, the word is seen to refer to an entire aspect of human society. It also refers to an element in individual behavior, as when we say that someone's actions are influenced by "normative" factors.

Construed in this way, the normative aspect of human society and human behavior is broad in coverage but conceptually distinct. It embraces, for example, the notion of "values," which are the goals or principles in terms of which specific norms are claimed to be desirable. For example, the rule that political officials should be elected is justified, or "explained," by saying that popular election is necessary if "democracy" is to be realized. The rule itself is the norm, but the value, democracy, is part of the normative reasoning. Disembodied values—i.e., values without any norms through which they can be collectively achieved—are, like purely private norms, sociologically irrelevant.

The "normative" further embraces the inner and outer compulsions (generally called "sanctions") which tend to enforce conformity. A banker who embezzles funds must contend, even when he is successful, with the efforts of others to catch him and with his own ideas of the potential dangers if he is caught. His behavior is therefore "normatively oriented," not so much because of the sheer rule prohibiting embezzlement as because of the sanctions against violation of the rule.

## Why the Normative Plays a Crucial Role in Sociology

The reason that sociology has given a great deal of attention to norms is clear.

From "Norms, Values, and Sanctions" by Judith Blake and Kingsley Davis in *Handbook of Modern Sociology*, edited by Robert E. L. Faris. Copyright © 1964 by Rand McNally & Company. Reprinted by permission of Rand McNally & Company.

Human society, as distinct from insect and animal societies, is in part organized, and made possible by rules of behavior. By contrast, the intricate interactions of an ant colony or a beehive, like those of a prairie dog village, are governed mainly by instinctive reactions to natural and social stimuli. Such interactions may involve learning to some degree, but this learning, if it occurs, is mainly a matter of habituation to (hence remembrance of) particular environmental stimuli, to which a stereotyped response becomes affixed. In human groups, on the other hand, instinctive responses are channeled or even repressed by the enforcement of behavioral rules that are transmitted by symbolic communication. These rules differ in character from one group to another, and thus help to account for differences in behavior among human societies. For insects and animals, however, behavior tends to be nearly identical from one group to another within the same species, varying only with external conditions. Obviously, then, if the structure of human societies is to be understood, if human behavior is to be adequately explained, the normative aspect must be dealt with. A biologist, habituated to viewing behavior as a function of a physical organism reacting to physical stimuli presented by the environment and other organisms, is apt to bring the same outlook to his analysis of human conduct. If he does so in the concrete sense of offering a complete explanation of some social phenomenon, he is "biologizing" human society. This fallacy is no less bizarre than the opposite—namely, an explanation of some aspect of insect or animal society in terms of presumed norms governing behavior.

Not only does the role of norms account for the difference between human sociology and biology, but it helps account for the division of labor between sociology and economics. In general,

economics assumes a normative framework in terms of which the process of production and exchange takes place. Sociology, on the other hand, in trying to understand the way the entire society works (not merely its economic system) has to deal with the norms themselves. For instance, a popular economics textbook points out that in the United States the distribution of income is influenced by the fact that women and Negroes are kept out of certain good jobs and are sometimes paid less for the same job (Samuelson, 1961). If this fact were due to differences in capacity between the races or the sexes, it would come under the economic system of explanation, because the "human resources" available to enter into production would be different. But, finding that "there are numerous jobs which either sex or race can do equally well," the author attributes the discrimination to "prejudice" (pp. 126–127). As an economist he is not obliged to explain why this prejudice occurs (the word is not even in the index), although, as he says, it affects something he is concerned with, the distribution of income. He takes the prejudice for granted, whereas the sociologist must explain its existence by accounting for the norms governing differential hiring and pay. One way in which he does this is by examining nonoccupational roles. The norms governing women's participation in the labor force certainly have something to do with their particular role within the family.

If it be granted that social norms affect behavior, then the totality of norms, or at least the totality of major norms, within a society can be expected to have some consistency, or order. Otherwise, the social system would not approximate a "system," and the society would tend to fall to pieces and be absorbed by another one which was orderly. It follows that an important aspect of the study of social organization is the study of the "normative order."

## Values and Norms

So far we have tried to distinguish the normative factor in behavior and to assess the reasons for its importance to sociology. Let us now admit that this "factor" is quite diverse in character and try to distinguish some of its elements or parts.

Probably the greatest single distinction within the normative realm is that between something variously called values, sentiments, themes, or ethical principles, on the one hand, and the specific rules of conduct, thought, and speech on the other. The line between the two is always fuzzy (Is the doctrine of freedom of the press, for example, a norm or a value?), but the attempt to separate them has been made again and again in sociological and philosophical thought. Apparently the reasons for this effort have varied, but two seem to stand out. Investigators have felt it necessary to probe beyond external behavior to the motives that impel behavior. In addition, since subjective phenomena seem bewildering in the number and variety of their expressions, observers have felt it must be possible to reduce them to a few recurrent, underlying principles, or perhaps "real motives." In any case, the task of finding these subjective forces or entities has been complicated by the fact that human beings not only act but give reasons for their actions. An observer must therefore decide whether to accept the reason given or to judge that, through ignorance or deception, it is not the real one. Not only do persons give private reasons, but there are official versions of what are the proper reasons for given kinds of conduct.

An early attempt to separate the essential values from the kaleidoscope of external manifestations was made by Vilfredo Pareto. In his general treatise on sociology (1935) he not only distinguished basic subjective factors but sought to use them in the analysis of social structure and social change. Underlying the countless rules and rites, verbal arguments and rationalizations (or "derivations"), he thought he could distill a few recurrent motives, or themes, which he called "residues," and which he thought responded to corresponding sentiments. The social system was, for him, a "social equilibrium" consisting of these sentiments acting as forces, and "social dynamics" was, in large part, a matter of the "circulation of the elite" in which differential strength of the various sentiments among the social classes was the main explanatory principle (pp. 509–519, 885–1120, 1740–1929).

Pareto was a student of advanced societies and therefore had to deal with the limitless sophistries of thought which came from the mouths and pens of priests, philosophers, statesmen, scholars, journalists, scientists, and other literate specialists and pleaders. He had to deal with conflicts and differences of opinion. For this reason he had particularly to wrestle with the problem of how to cope with the verbal arguments and explanations in getting to the actual motives hidden behind them. For William Graham Sumner, on the other hand, the problem was somewhat different. This great student of the norms drew his materials mostly from reports about primitive tribes. He therefore was required to pay little or no attention to written expressions of human thought as objects of study and did not need to consider seriously the supernatural and magical explanations that primitive people gave for their norms. In contrast to Pareto, therefore, he barely recognized anything like general principles or abstract values, and when he did, he saw them as consequences rather than determinants of the norms themselves, which he called folk-ways and mores.

All are forced to conform, and the folk-ways dominate social life. They seem true and right, and arise into mores as the norm of welfare. Thence are produced faiths, ideas, doctrines, religions, and philosophies, according to the stage of civilization and the fashion of reflection and generalization (Sumner, 1906, p. 38).

Both Pareto and Sumner refused to take the explanations people give for their norms or their conduct at face value. But Pareto sought to find behind the explanations a few basic motives or sentiments, while Sumner emphasized the norms themselves, simply regarding the verbal expressions of people as part of the normative system.

It seems that in general the literature dealing with norms has followed both men in certain respects, regardless of whether or not it was actually influenced directly by them. There has been a tendency to draw materials and inspiration, as Sumner did, from studies of preliterate villagers. Hence conflict, deviation, and the complexity of verbal statement and argument have been minimized. This line of treatment has of course been prominent among the social anthropologists, but it has been present too in the work of Talcott Parsons and some of his students. Due to the emphasis on *different* societies in anthropological thought, the search for values tended to take a new turn. It became a search for the particular underlying values, cultural themes, or ethos of each particular society. This development raised in turn the question of whether the values of one society had any relation to the values of another. In other words, is cultural relativity absolute, or is there a single set of values of which those of different societies are simply variant expressions? Pareto had made it clear that he regarded the sentiments as having "social utility"; Sumner thought that the folk-ways and mores were adaptive, keeping the society in touch with reality and contributing to its survival. Presumably, in anthropological and sociological thought since Emile Durkheim and Bronislaw Malinowski, the values must have a *function* in society; but the question is obscure because, for many social scientists at least, what is taken as a value may be disfunctional, and what is functional may not be valued. . . .

There is, of course, a distinction to be made between the standards involved in judgments, on the one hand, and the application of those standards in specific judgments, on the other. Thus, in regard to social behavior, it is one thing to say that parents prefer sons to daughters, and quite another to say that parents feel they should treat their daughters in a certain way under given circumstances. Presumably, a preference for sons is a value, but it says nothing concrete concerning parental conduct and it has no sanctions. A norm, on the other hand, says that a given line of conduct must, or should, be followed. Thus a preference for sons in the United States does not mean that female infanticide is permitted or that boys are given more clothes. What, then, is the utility of the distinction between values and norms?

Whatever the utility may be, it surely is not that of designating cause and effect. Presumably a norm "exemplifies" a value, but this does not mean that the norm is *caused* by the value it exemplifies, or that the value is the motive and the norm simply the expression of this motive with respect to behavior. Such a mode of explanation is extremely tempting, not only because it is the way people think anyway—that is, the individual always has a reason for doing whatever he does—but also because it gives an unfailing mode of explaining norms and behavior. The flaw, however, lies in the question of logic and evidence. Can we accept as true people's verbal description of their values? These may be nothing more than a rationalization of the norms—as when, for instance, someone justifies the exclusion of married women from jobs on the ground that a woman's place is in the home. Can we adopt some indirect technique of getting verbal statements of values, thus deceiving the subject into revealing what he would not reveal if he knew our purpose? Such a technique still makes the assumption that the values are consciously held and are rationally connected with norms and conduct—an old-fashioned view controverted by voluminous evidence. Can we then take people's statements and *reinterpret* them to get at "underlying" values? Yes, provided we wish to make the questionable assumption that verbal statements inevitably reflect real values, and provided we admit that the process of symbolic reinterpretation in itself has no empirical controls and consequently may differ radically from one observer to another.

In practice, we tend to find the best evidence of values in the norms themselves. If people manifest a dislike of cheating in examinations, of dishonest advertising in business, and of unnecessary roughness in sports, we infer something like a value of "fair competition." Such a process of reasoning may help us to insert the motivational linkages and thus integrate a body of diverse information. At bottom, however, it is a classification. Its usefulness does not extend to causal explanation, because the inferred value comes only from the specific norms themselves and hence cannot be used as an explanation of those norms. In other words, unless we have evidence independent of the norms themselves, we cannot logically derive norms from values. Independent evidence, if obtainable, may show that the so-called values are nonexistent, that they are consequences of the

norms, or that they derive from a third factor which is also responsible for the norms.

It is the norms, not the values, that have the pressure of reality upon them. It is the norms that are enforced by sanctions, that are subject to the necessity of action and the agony of decision. It is therefore the norms that represent the cutting edge of social control. In this regard Sumner seems to have been more correct than some of his successors, for he emphasized the importance of the folkways and mores in understanding society rather than the vague, slippery ideologies, rationalizations, and generalizations people use in justifying their observance or nonobservance of norms.

A more satisfactory use of "values" in sociological analysis is to abandon them as causal agents and to recognize them frankly as sheer constructs by which we attempt to fill in the subjective linkages in the analysis of social causation. For example, the movement of peasants to cities during the process of industrialization is not "explained" by saying that they prefer the bright lights of the city to the drab monotony of the village. Only when the evolving economic and social situation in both the village and the city are taken into account can we begin to explain this recurrent major social phenomenon. It helps us understand the process, however, if we can get some inkling of how the peasant's feelings and thoughts take shape in view of these conditions; and so we try to put together a model of his mental reactions and test it out against various kinds of empirical evidence, including his verbal statements.

## The Fallacy of Normative Determinism

We raise the question of causation with respect to values and norms because we believe that conceptual distinctions unrelated to empirical investigation are empty exercises. For the same reason, we wish to push on to the wider question of normative causation in general, apart from the distinction between values and norms. In doing so, we come to one of the most confused and at the same time basic issues in sociology and social anthropology. No one can doubt that norms exercise *some* influence on behavior, but the question of *how much* influence they exercise is highly debatable. At times, sociologists and social anthropologists have seemed to adopt an extreme view by treating the normative system as the sole object of analysis or as the sole determinant of social phenomena. This has usually been done by implicit assumption and careless overstatement rather than by deliberate doctrine, and it has been camouflaged at times by a seemingly broader position of cultural determinism. At any rate, it is a position that affords a good point of departure in analyzing the interrelation between norms and other factors in behavior.

At its most naive level, normative determinism takes the fact that norms *are meant* to control behavior as the basis for assuming that they *do* control it. The only task of social science is then to discover the particular norms in any given society. By this reasoning, nearly all social scientists in Latin America are trained in the law rather than in statistics and social research. The law, being the crystallization of the normative order, is assumed to be what one needs to know. At a more sophisticated level, the assumption is made that the independent variable consists in "cultural configurations," "basic value-orientations," or "the institutional system," which determines everything else in a society. This has a doctrinal side—e.g., in statements about the nature of man—as well as a methodological side. An anthropologist states with approval that national character studies assume that

each member of a society is systematically representative of the cultural pattern of that society, so that the treatment accorded infant or immigrant, pupils or employees or rulers, is indicative of the culturally regular character-forming methods of that society (Mead, 1953, p. 643).

C. Kluckhohn expresses a common dictum when he says that the constants in human life from one society to another "arise out of the biological nature of the species" and its fixed environment, whereas the variations arise from culture. Each culture, he says, has a "grammar." "The function of linguistic grammar is to control the freedom of words so that there is no needless congestion of the communication traffic. The grammar of culture, in general, likewise makes for orderliness" (1959, pp. 273–274).

According to this view, the avenue to understanding actual societies is to understand their cultures. The term culture has a bewildering and altogether too convenient variety of definitions. Sometimes it is used so broadly as to cover all material products of man, all social behavior, all ideas and goals. Used in this way, it includes society itself, and therefore the cultural determinism of social phenomena becomes a tautology. Frequently, however, the term culture is used primarily in the sense of a normative system. In this case we get what may be called a "blueprint theory" of society, namely, that there is a set of "culture-patterns" which are, so to speak, laid down in advance and followed by the members of the society. The determinism implicit in this view is indicated by such phrases as "handed down," "shaped by his culture," "ultimate values," "culture-bound," "way of life," and others.

The way of life that is *handed down* as the social heritage of every people does more than *supply* a set of skills for making a living and a *set of blueprints* for human relations. Each different way of life *makes its own assumptions* about the ends and purposes of human existence . . . (Italics supplied) (C. Kluckhohn, 1959, p. 247).

Similarly, Parsons and his followers have placed heavy emphasis on value-orientations as the key to sociological analysis. In the hands of some, this emphasis gets translated into dogma; for example, "Values determine the choices men make, and the ends they live by" (Stein and Cloward, 1958, p. 263).

Under the assumption of the supremacy of the norms and "dominant" value-orientations, the chief research method of the social disciplines becomes that of questioning informants. The investigator asks a member of the society what people are *supposed* to do, and hence the normative pattern will emerge. The informant necessarily knows the "culture," because he lives it and is determined by it.

Any member of a group, provided that his position within that group is specified, is a perfect sample of the group-wide pattern on which he is acting as an informant (Mead, 1953, p. 648).

Furthermore, with this reliance on norms and values as determinants of social phenomena, peculiar importance is naturally given to "socialization," normally interpreted to mean the acquisition, or "internalization," of the norms. According to Parsons:

There is reason to believe that, among the learned elements of personality in certain respects the stablest and most enduring are the major value-orientation patterns and there is much evidence that these are "laid down" in childhood and are not on a large scale subject to drastic alteration during adult life. There is good reason to treat these patterns of value-orientation, as analyzed in terms of pattern variable combinations, as the core of what is sometimes called "basic personality structure" . . . (1951, p. 208).

Most of the sociologists and anthropologists who stress culture, culture patterns, norms, value-attitudes, and such concepts would deny that they are determinists. They would say they are abstracting—treating behavior *as if* it were determined by the normative system. In practice, however, the emphasis on values and norms leads, as critics have been quick to point out, to deficiencies in the scientific understanding of real societies. The gravest deficiency arises, ironically, in the failure to deal adequately with norms themselves. As long as the cultural configurations, basic value-attitudes, prevailing mores, or what not are taken as the starting point and principal determinant, they have the status of unanalyzed assumptions. The very questions that would enable us to understand the norms tend not to be asked, and certain facts about society become difficult, if not impossible, to comprehend. For instance, an assumption of normative primacy renders it difficult to explain deviancy and crime, although the real world plainly exhibits a great deal of normative violation. If one is to understand deviancy, one must ask why societies frequently reward violation more heavily than conformity to the norms; why legitimate authority is one of the most widespread bases of illegitimate power; why ego and alter so frequently disagree on norms applicable to their relationship; why any action, no matter how atrocious, can be justified in terms of the verbal formulas in which norms and values are couched. Furthermore, the origin and appearance of new norms and their constant change—again facts of social existence—become incomprehensible under an assumption of normative sovereignty. . . .

Presumably if one's interpretation is in terms of norms rather than values, one is on firmer ground. Yet the difficulty of proving the existence of the norm is great. As a consequence, there is a tendency to take regularities in behavior as the evidence of the norm. When this is done, to explain the behavior in terms of the norm is a redundancy. Seen in this light, statements such as the following are also redundant: "Knowledge of a culture makes it possible to predict a good many of the actions of any person who shares that culture" (C. Kluckhohn, 1949, p. 38). Why not simply say, "Knowledge of behavior in a society makes it possible to predict behavior in that society"? Of course, if norms are taken to be regularities of behavior, they have no analytical significance at all; they are then merely another name for behavior itself, and cannot contribute to an understanding of behavior.

## Types of Norms

The blueprint theory of society does not fit the facts of social existence. Societies as we know them are highly active and dynamic, filled with conflict, striving, deceit, cunning. Behavior in a given situation tends to be closely related to that situation, to be strongly affected by individual interests, to be unpredictable from a knowledge of the norms alone. Far from being fully determinant, the norms themselves tend to be a product of the constant interaction involving the interplay of interests, changing conditions, power, dominance, force, fraud, ignorance, and knowledge.

Furthermore it is surprising how simplified the view of culture and of the normative system tends to be in the hands of many who emphasize their role. To show this, let us attempt a brief listing of the variegated aspects of the norms—aspects seldom all dealt with in the social science literature. . . .

1. Content
   a. Societal requirement involved.

(Norms ordinarily concern some functional requirement such as reproduction, division of labor, allocation of power. Norms clustered around a given functional requirement are often collectively designated as "institutions.")
   b. Whether the norm relates to a goal or to the means.
   c. How the norm is stated—whether put negatively (should not) or positively (should).
2. Types of Sanctions
   a. Maximum or minimum.
   b. Reward or punishment. Repressive or restitutive (in the case of punishment).
   c. Specific or diffuse (may be both).
3. Acceptance of the Norm
   a. Extent of acceptance (accepted as obligatory by virtually everyone or accepted as obligatory by only certain groups, such as certain ethnic groups).
   b. Degree of acceptance (felt to be mildly obligatory or felt to be mandatory).
4. Mode of Transmission
   a. Primary socialization.
   b. Secondary socialization.
5. Source of Imputed Authority for the Norm
   a. Tradition.
   b. Law.
   c. A nonempirical or supernatural agency ("natural law," God, some member of a pantheon, ghosts, etc.).
   d. Public opinion.
6. Extent of Application of the Norm
   a. To which statuses does the norm apply? (The reader will note that the extent of application of a norm is different from the extent of its acceptance. A norm which applies only to the occupant of a particular status may nonetheless be accepted by everyone as the proper conduct for that status. Example: Everyone thinks a

judge should be fair and impartial.)
   b. To what groups does the norm apply?
7. Mode of Origination
   a. Formal enactment.
   b. Informal, traditional, accretion.
8. Formal Properties of the Statement of the Norm
   a. Explicit (a body of law, regulations, codes).
   b. Implicit ("gentlemen's agreements," rarely verbalized but understood ways of behaving and thinking).
   c. Vague, diffuse statement.
   d. Specific, detailed statement.
   e. Rigid (requires exact conformity).
   f. Flexible (latitude in the precision with which the normative demand must be met).

Clearly, these ways in which social norms can vary are interrelated. For example, a norm that is stated positively is, in effect, stated in terms of some *reward* for compliance, whereas a negative normative statement implies punishment. Moreover, maximum sanctions—either rewards or punishments—typically imply that the norm involved is widely accepted (in the society, or group, or organization under consideration) and that strong sentiments support it. A norm of this type will also very likely be one that individuals have learned early in life at a time (the period of "primary socialization") when they must accept social rules in a more unreflective fashion than later. Further, norms carrying maximum sanctions are usually felt by people to be inherently right (natural) rather than simply legitimated by reference to law, tradition, or public opinion. Also, for maximum sanctions actually to be applied, the norm must definitely specify the relevant status. For instance, even a so-called universal

in the United States such as the norm against killing another human being has so many legitimized exceptions that these must be clearly specified before sanctions can be brought to bear.

## Sanctions

People not only conform to rules themselves but, by means of their sanctioning of others' behavior, motivate others to conform also. In most cases sanctions are informal—an approving or contemptuous glance, an encouraging or derisive laugh, a sympathetic or embarrassed silence. Such seemingly trivial but pervasive sanctions enable human beings to control informally a share of their own actions and reactions and the actions and reactions of others. However, it is also true that behavior is frequently controlled by formal sanctions as well—by a medal or a jail, an honorary dinner or an electric chair, a parade or a court-martial. In the ordinary course of our lives, we tend to be more aware of the explicitly sanctioning nature of formal than of informal rewards and punishments. Indeed, the relatively unruffled fashion in which informal sanctions operate constitutes one of their most important societal functions—they control behavior in a relatively painless manner before more formal measures are necessary.

Yet every viable society must develop supports to help individuals *resist* this type of informal pressure as well as to help them conform to it, for such pressures never are so finely geared to changing situations that it is socially advantageous for individuals always to respond with gusto to sanctions of this type. To be sure, the system is partially self-corrective in that what is negatively sanctioned by one individual may be highly rewarded by another. But this capacity for self-correction is limited, because individuals deal with one another in terms of social roles which, by definition, tend to be highly standardized sets of expectations. Hence, one of the problems that every society faces constantly is that of assuring itself role flexibility in the face of changing conditions.

Since so many sanctions are informal and applied continuously in the course of daily living, we are all in effect constantly "administering" the normative order. There must accordingly be mechanisms to keep individuals *cognitively* primed or "briefed" about the norms (what the norms are, to whom they apply, in what situations, etc.) and, in addition, to keep people *emotionally* primed respecting the *legitimacy* of norms. By and large people must feel that behavior they are punishing or rewarding (either in themselves or others) is at least roughly the same as other people would punish or reward in similar situations. Yet, like any other set of rules, social norms are only approximations of how people should act. In specific situations, individuals must take many things into account, and, in particular, they are faced with the difficulty that adherence to the letter of a norm (or to the formal content of a number of different norms) may place them or others in situations having no apparent legitimacy at all. The result is that much of our lives is spent in seeking out the legitimacy of various courses of action and thereby inevitably redefining the legitimacy of specific norms—an example of how the effort at conformity with social rules provides a dynamic source of social change.

A significant share of orderly conduct is, however, a result of assessing the consequences for nonconformity rather than a result of the "internalization" of the norms as just discussed. In fact, individuals' internalization of norms is doubtless differentiated and segmental in most societies. Individuals are emotionally committed to some norms and others they merely conform to, if they conform at all, out of calculation and rational assessment. Such a criss-crossing of commitment and objectivity toward norms gives societies another source of change and of stability. There are some people who regard certain rules as "outdated" and "unjust" and make efforts to change the rules, and there are people who, feeling that the same rules are adequate and legitimate, resist this change. Because of this criss-crossing, many societies can undergo remarkable social transformations, all the while retaining an adequate degree of social control.

Much of modern sociological thinking has strongly emphasized the internalization of role expectations as the prime mover in social control, to the extent that the importance of calculation with respect to sanctions tends to be overlooked except as a last resort. Yet, we must never forget that social rules require doing what would ordinarily not be done if the rules did not exist. Since these rules therefore, by definition, have such a high nuisance value for human beings, it seems inconceivable that most people do not calculate extensively. . . .

# 10

## The Operating Room: A Study in Role Distance

ERVING GOFFMAN

### Surgery As an Activity System

I have suggested some cases where the scene of activity generates for the individual a self which he is apparently loath to accept openly for himself, since his conduct suggests that some disaffiliation exists between himself and his role. But a peek into some odd corner of social life provides no basis, perhaps, for generalizing about social life. As a test, then, of the notion of role distance (and role), let us take a scene in which activity generates a self for the individual that appears to be a most likely one for self-attachment. Let us take, for example, the activity system sustained during a surgical operation. The components consist of verbal and physical acts and the changing states of the organism undergoing the operation. Here, if anywhere in our society, we should find performers flushed with a feeling of the weight and dignity of their action. A Hollywood ideal is involved: the white-coated chief surgeon strides into the operating theater after the patient has been anesthetized and opened by assistants. A place is automatically made for him. He grunts a few abbreviated preliminaries, then deftly, almost silently, gets to work, serious, grim, competently living up to the image he and his team have of him, yet in a context where momentary failure to exhibit competence might permanently jeopardize the relation he is allowed to have to his role. Once the critical phase of the operation is quite over, he steps back and,

with a special compound of tiredness, strength, and disdain, rips off his gloves; he thus contaminates himself and abdicates his role, but at a time when his own labors put the others in a position to "close up." While he may be a father, a husband, or a baseball fan at home, he is here one and only one thing, a surgeon, and being a surgeon provides a fully rounded impression of the man. If the role perspective works, then, surely it works here, for in our society the surgeon, if anyone, is allowed and obliged to put himself into his work and gets a self out of it. . . .[1]

If we start with the situation of the lesser medical personnel,[2] the intern

[1] Much the same conceit has already been employed by Temple Burling in *Essays on Human Aspects of Administration*, Bulletin 25 (August 1953) of the New York State School of Industrial and Labor Relations, Cornell University, pp. 9–10. The fullest published accounts of conduct in the operating room that I know of are to be found in T. Burling, E. Lentz and R. Wilson, *The Give and Take in Hospitals* (New York: Putnam, 1956), Chap. 17, pp. 260–283, and R. Wilson, "Teamwork in the Operating Room," *Human Organization*, 12 (1954), pp. 9–14.

[2] My own material on interaction during surgery, from which all staff practices and verbal responses cited in this page are drawn, derives from brief observations to the medical building of a mental hospital and the operating rooms of a suburban community hospital. Not deriving from the most formal hospitals, these data load the facts a little in my favor.

I am grateful to Dr. Otis R. Farley, and his staff in the Medical and Surgical Branch of St. Elizabeth's Hospital, Washington, D.C., and to John F. Wight, Administrative Director, and Lenore Jones, Head Surgical Nurse, of Herrick Memorial Hospital, Berkeley, California, for full research freedom and great courtesy.

and the junior resident, the test will not be fair, for here, apparently, is a situation much like the ones previously mentioned. The tasks these juniors are given to do—such as passing hemostats, holding retractors, cutting small tied-off veins, swabbing the operating area before the operation, and perhaps suturing or closing at the end—are not large enough to support much of a surgical role. Furthermore, the junior person may find that he performs even these lowly tasks inadequately, and that the scrub nurse as well as the chief surgeon tells him so. And when the drama is over and the star performer has dropped his gloves and gown and walked out, the nurses may underline the intern's marginal position by lightly demanding his help in moving the body from the fixed table to the movable one, while automatically granting him a taste of the atmosphere they maintain when real doctors are absent. As for the intern himself, surgery is very likely *not* to be his chosen specialty; the three-month internship is a course requirement and he will shortly see the last of it. The intern may confirm all this ambivalence to his work on occasions away from the surgery floor, when he scathingly describes surgery as a plumber's craft exercised by mechanics who are told what to look for by internists.

The surgical junior, especially the intern, has, then, a humbling position during surgery. Whether as a protection against this condition or not, the medical juniors I observed, like overage merry-go-round riders, analysands, and carnival pitchmen, were not prepared to embrace their role fully; elaborate displays of role distance occurred.[3]

[3] Some of the interns I observed had plans to take a psychiatric residency and, apparently because of this, were doing their stint of surgical internship in the medical building of a mental hospital; they therefore had wider institutional support for their lack of interest in physical techniques.

A careful, bemused look on the face is sometimes found, implying, "This is not the real me." Sometimes the individual will allow himself to go "away," dropping off into a brown study that removes him from the continuity of events, increases the likelihood that his next contributory act will not quite fit into the flow of action, and effectively gives the appearance of occupational disaffection; brought back into play, he may be careful to evince little sign of chagrin. He may rest himself by leaning on the patient or by putting a foot on an inverted bucket but in a manner too contrived to allow the others to feel it is a matter of mere resting. Interestingly enough, he sometimes takes on the function of the jester, endangering his reputation with antics that temporarily place him in a doubtful and special position, yet through this providing the others present with a reminder of less exalted worlds:

CHIEF SURGEON JONES (*in this case a senior resident*): A small Richardson please.

SCRUB NURSE: Don't have one.

DR. JONES: O.K., then give me an Army and Navy.

SCRUB NURSE: It looks like we don't have one.

DR. JONES (*lightly joking*): No Army or Navy man here.

INTERN (*dryly*): No one in the armed forces, but Dr. Jones here is in the Boy Scouts.

SCRUB NURSE: Will there be more than three [sutures] more? We're running out of sutures.

CHIEF SURGEON: I don't know.

INTERN: We can finish up with Scotch tape.

INTERN (*looking for towel clamps around body*): Where in the world . . . . ?

SCRUB NURSE: Underneath the towel.

(*Intern turns to the nurse and in*

*slow measure makes a full cold bow to her.*)

SCRUB NURSE (*to intern*): Watch it, you're close to my table! [*A Mayo stand containing instruments whose asepsis she must guard and guarantee.*] (*Intern performs a mock gasp and clownishly draws back.*)

As I have suggested, just as we cannot use a child over four riding a merry-go-round as an exhibition of how to embrace an activity role, so also we cannot use the junior medical people on a surgical team. But surely the chief surgeon, at least, will demonstrate the embracing of a role. What we find, of course, is that even this central figure expresses considerable role distance.

Some examples may be cited. One can be found in medical etiquette. This body of custom requires that the surgeon, on leaving the operation, turn and thank his assistant, his anesthetist, and ordinarily his nurses as well. Where a team has worked together for a long time and where the members are of the same age-grade, the surgeon may guy this act, issuing the thanks in what he expects will be taken as an ironical and farcical tone of voice: "Miss Westly, you've done a simply wonderful job here." Similarly, there is a formal rule that in preparing a requested injection the nurse show the shelved vial to the surgeon before its sealed top is cracked off so that he can check its named contents and thereby take the responsibility on himself. If the surgeons are very busy at the time, this checking may be requested but not given. At other times, however, the checking may be guyed.

CIRCULATING NURSE: Dr. James, would you check this?

DR. JAMES (*in a loud ministerial voice, reading the label*): Three cubic centimeters of heparin at ten-milligram strength, put up by Invenex and held by Nurse Jackson at a forty-five-degree angle. That is right, Nurse Jackson.

Instead of employing technical terms at all times, he may tease the nurses by using homey appelations: "Give me the small knife, we'll get in just below the belly button"; and he may call the electric cauterizer by the apt name of "sizzler," ordering the assistant surgeon to "sizzle here, and here." Similarly, when a nurse allows her non-sterile undergown to be exposed a little, a surgeon may say in a pontifical and formal tone, "Nurse Bevan, can I call your attention to the anterior portion of your gown. It is exposing you. I trust you will correct this condition," thereby instituting social control, reference to the nurse's non-nursing attributes, and satire of the profession, all with one stroke. So, too, returning to the operating room with a question, "Dr. Williams?" may be answered by a phrase of self-satirization: "In person," or, "This is Dr. Williams." And a well-qualified surgeon, in taking the situated role of assistant surgeon for the duration of a particular operation, may tell the nurses, when they have been informed by the chief surgeon that two electric cauterizers will be employed, "I'm going to get one too, just like the big doctors, that's what I like to hear." A chief surgeon, then, may certainly express role distance. Why he does so, and with what effect, are clearly additional questions, and ought to be considered.

## The Functions of Role Distance for Surgery

I have suggested that in surgery, in a room that pridefully keeps out germs and gives equal medical treatment to bodies of different socio-economic status, there is no pretense at expressional asepsis. Role distance is routinely expressed.

But why should the individual be disinclined to embrace his role self? The situation of the junior medical man suggests that defensive activity is at work. We cannot say, however, that role distance protects the individual's ego, self-esteem, personality, or integrity from the implications of the situation without introducing constructs which have no place in a strictly sustained role perspective. We must find a way, then, of getting the ego back into society.

We can begin to do this by noting that when the individual withdraws from a situated self he does not draw into some psychological world that he creates himself but rather acts in the name of some other socially created identity. The liberty he takes in regard to a situated self is taken because of other, equally social, constraints. A first example of this is provided us when we try to obtain a systematic view of the functions performed by role distance in surgery, for immediately we see a paradoxical fact: one of the concerns that prevents the individual from fully accepting his situated self is his commitment to the situated activity system itself. We see this when we shift our point of view from the individual to the situated system and look at the functions that role distance serves for it. We find that certain maneuvers which act to integrate the system require for their execution individuals who do not fully embrace their situated selves. System-irrelevant roles can thus themselves be exploited for the system as a whole. In other words, one of the claims upon himself that the individual must balance against all others is the claim created by the over-all "needs"[4] of the situated activity system itself, apart from his particular role in it.

[4] In the sense used by Philip Selznick in "Foundations of the Theory of Organization," *American Sociological Review*, 13 (1948), pp. 29–30.

An illustration of these contingencies is provided by the chief surgeon. Like those in many other occupational positions, the chief surgeon finds that he has the obligation to direct and manage a particular activity system, in this case a surgical operation. He is obliged to see that the operation is effectively carried through, regardless of what this may sometimes express about himself.

Now for the surgical team to function usefully, each member, as already suggested, must sustain his capacity as a communicator, an individual capable of giving and receiving verbal communications and their substitutes. And, as in other activity systems, each member must be able to execute physical actions requiring some coolness and self-command. Anything that threatens either this verbal or physical poise threatens the participant's capacity to contribute, and hence the activity system itself. Each individual member of the surgical team must be in command of himself, and where he is not able to handle himself, others, especially the chief surgeon, must help him do it.

In order to ensure that the members of his team keep their heads during the operation, the chief surgeon finds himself under pressure to modulate his own demands and his own expectations of what is due him. If he exercises his situated rights openly to criticize incompetent conduct, the surgeon may only further weaken the defaulter's self-command and further endanger the particular operation. In short, the chief surgeon is likely to find himself with the situated role function of anxiety management[5] and may find that he must draw on his own dignity, on what

[5] This role function is one which the M.D. anesthetist often performs, or tries to perform, sometimes apparently quite intentionally, as a filler for a position that might otherwise not have enough weight for the person who fills it.

is owed his station, in order to fulfil this function. A kind of bargaining or bribery [6] occurs, whereby the surgeon receives a guarantee of equability from his team in return for being "a nice guy"—someone who does not press his rightful claims too far. Of course, the surgeon may save his dignity and lose the operation, but he is under pressure not to do so.

Given the conflict between correcting a subordinate and helping him maintain his poise, it is understandable that surgeons will employ joking means of negative sanction, so that it is difficult to determine whether the joke is a cover for the sanction, or the sanction a cover for the joke. In either case, some distance from usual surgical decorum is required:

(*Intern holds retractor at wrong end of incision and goes "away," being uninterested in the operation.*)
CHIEF SURGEON (*in mock English accent*): You don't have to hold that up there, old chap, perhaps down here. Going to sleep, old boy?

CHIEF SURGEON (*on being accidentally stabbed in the finger by the assistant surgeon, who is using the electric scalpel*): If I get syphalis [*sic*] I'll know where I got it from, and I'll have witnesses.

If some of these jokes seem weak and unnecessary, we must appreciate that to let a small error of conduct go by without comment has its own dangers, apart from what this laxness might mean for staff training. In the presence of a mistake, staff members can ready themselves for the occurrence of a corrective sanction, and unless something pertinent is said, this readiness may act as an anxiety-producing distraction. The

immediate expression of a joking sanction, however labored, grounds this sort of tension.

Just as a negative sanction may be toned down to prevent the offender from acting still more disruptively, so also direct commands may be softened into requests even though the surgeon's general occupational status and particular situated role empower him to command. Where he has a right to issue a peremptory order for an instrument, he may instead employ courtesies: "Let's have another Richardson," "Could I have a larger retractor." Instead of flaring up when no suitable ready-made instrument is available, he may choose to express a boyish mechanical ingenuity, constructing on the spot a make-do instrument.

I am suggesting that he who would effectively direct an operation at times may have to employ a touch so light as to embarrass the dark dignities of his position. In fact, we can expect that the more that is demanded from a subordinate in the way of delicacy, skill, and pure concentration, the more informal and friendly the superordinate is likely to become. If one person is to participate in a task as if he were an extension of another participant, opening himself up to the rapid and delicate feedback control that an individual ordinarily obtains only of and for himself, then, apparently, he must be favorably disposed to the person in command, for such cooperativeness is much easier to win than to exact.

I would like to note here that the chief surgeon may feel obliged to introduce distractions as well as to dispel them. When the spontaneous engagement of the participants in the task activity itself seems likely to tax them too much, the chief surgeon may distract them, for example, by joking. This is just the reverse of the process previously described. Thus, at a point of high tenseness, when a large renal tumor has been completely exposed

[6] The notion of "role bargain" is usefully developed in W. J. Goode, "A Theory of Role Strain," *American Sociological Review*, 25 (1960), pp. 483–496.

and was ready to be pierced by a drain-ing needle, a chief surgeon lightly warned before he pierced: "Now don't get too close." Another instance of this easing process is found in the fact that the others often seem to look to the chief surgeon to mark the end of a critical phase of action and the begin-ning of a less critical phase, one that can be used for a general letdown in the sustained concentration of attention and effort. In order to set the tone for these functionally useful relaxations, at the end of a phase of action, the sur-geon may stretch himself in a gawky, exaggerated, and clownish way and utter a supportive informality such as "okey-dokey" or "th-ar sh' be." Before the critical phase is begun, and after it has been terminated, he may engage others present in talk about last night's party, the recent ball game, or good places to fish.[7] And when the patient is being closed up and the critical work is quite over, the chief surgeon may initiate and tolerate joking with nurses, bantering with them about their lack of proficiency or about the operation not being nearly over. If no male nurse is present to lift the patient from the operating table to the trolley, the chief surgeon, if he is still in the operating room, may gallantly brush aside the efforts of one of the nurses and insist on lifting the heaviest part of the pa-tient, the middle, himself, acting now in the capacity of a protective male, not a medical person.

Just as the chief surgeon may mark the point where attentiveness may be usefully relaxed, so he, and sometimes others on the team, will put brackets around the central task activity with the result that the level of concern required for it will not be demanded of the team before matters actually get under way and after they have ended. This is nicely shown not merely in the ritual of tearing off one's gloves and im-mediately leaving the operating room, by which the chief surgeon tells the team that teacher is no longer checking up on them and they can relax, but also in the way in which the body is handled. During the operation, the body of the patient is the rightful focus of a great deal of respectful sustained considera-tion, technically based, especially in connection with the maintenance of asepsis, blood levels, and respiration. It is as if the body were a sacred object, regardless of the socioeconomic char-acter of its possessor, but in this case the consideration given is rational as well as ritual. As might be expected, then, before and after the operation proper there can be observed minor acts of desacralization, whereby the patient is reduced to more nearly pro-fane status. At the beginning of the task the surgeon may beat a tattoo on the leg of the anesthetized patient, and at the end he may irreverently pat the patient on the bottom, commenting that he is now better than new. The surgeon is not alone in this activity. While scrubbing the anesthetized patient, the nurse may lift up a foot by the toe and speak to it: "You're not sterile, are you?" In moving the now groggy pa-tient from the operating table to the trolley for the trip to the recovery room, the anesthetist, taking charge of

---

[7] Under strictest possible procedure, no talk-ing would be tolerated except when techni-cally necessary, since germs can apparently be spread through masks in this way. My own experience was in relatively informal hospitals where irrelevant talk and byplays did occur. Burling and Wilson report a simi-lar experience. Presumably the medical tra-ditions of different regions differ in this regard, as suggested by Eugene de Savitsch, *In Search of Complications* (New York: Simon and Schuster, 1940), pp. 374–375: "In a clinic or operating room almost any-where in the world all would be silence, soft lights, and sustained tension. In France every-body chatters away as merrily as in a cafe. While a brain tumor, for instance, is re-moved, the surgeon, his assistants, and the audience—if any—argue over the merits of the present cabinet, disclose the shortcom-ings of their wives, and exchange advice about stocks and bonds."

this relatively unskilled physical action, may obtain concerted effort from the other persons helping him by saying: "Ready, aim, fire." Similarly, in moving an anesthetized patient on his side for a thoracotomy, the anesthetist may say: "O.K., kids, are we ready to play flip flop? Ready? O.K."

In addition to maintaining the capacities and poise of other members of the team, the chief surgeon has, of course, an obligation to maintain his own. Moreover, he must be concerned not only with sustaining his own mobilization of personal resources, but also with the anxious attention that other members of the team might give to this. If they feel he is about to lose his temper, or that he has lost his skill, they themselves can become extremely uneasy and inefficient. Thus, when the surgeon runs into trouble that could cause his teammates a distracting and suppressed concern over how he might react to his trouble, we find him engaging in quite standard strategies of tension management, sometimes concealing his own real concerns to do so. He alludes openly to the incident in such a way as to rob it of its capacity to distract the team. When he drops an instrument, he may respond unseriously to his own action by a word such as "oopsadaisy." If he must give an order to one of his assistants which might leave the others not knowing if he were angry or not, he may deliver it in a false English accent, in adolescent slang, or in some other insulating way. Unable to find the right spot for a lumbar puncture, he may, after three tries, shake his head a little, as if to suggest that he, as a person sensitive to ideal standards, is still sensitive to them and yet in quiet control of himself, in short, that the implied discrediting of him has not made him lose poise.

Since the chief surgeon's own self-control is crucial in the operation, and since a question concerning it could

have such a disquieting effect upon the other members of the team, he may feel obliged to demonstrate that he is in possession of himself, not merely at times of crisis and trouble, but even at times when he would otherwise be silent and so be providing no information one way or the other about his state of mind. Thus, when puzzled about what to do, he may ruminate half out loud, ingenuously allowing others present a close glimpse of his thoughts. During quite delicate tasks, he may softly sing incongruous undignified tunes such as "He flies through the air with the greatest of ease." In clamping hemostats, he may let them go from his fingers, flipping them back upon the patient's body in a neat row with the verve and control that parking attendants manifest while parking cars, or merry-go-round managers display in collecting tickets while moving around on the turning platform.

What we have here is a kind of "externalization" of such feelings and thoughts as are likely to give security and confidence to the other members of the team. This externalization, as well as the constant cutting back of any distractive concern that might have arisen for the team in the course of action, also provides a constant stimulus to team members' attentiveness and task engagement, in both ways helping to hold them to the task as usable participants. Some surgeons, in fact, maintain something of a running line of patter during the operation, suggesting that whenever there is teamwork, someone is likely to have the role function of "talking it up."

We see that the chief surgeon is something of a host to persons at his party, as well as the director of his operating team. He is under pressure (however he responds to this pressure) to make sure that those at his table feel good about what is happening so that whatever their capacities they can better exploit them. And to do this morale-maintaining job, at least in America, the surgeon makes use of and draws upon activities not expected of one in his dignified position. When he himself does not perform the clown function, he may encourage someone else, such as the intern or circulating nurse, to take on the job.

In discussing the special responsibilities of the chief surgeon and his frequent need to draw on informality in order to meet these responsibilities, it was implied that the superordinate present may have some special reasons for exhibiting role distance. A further comment should be added concerning the relation between role distance and social ranking.

It seems characteristic of the formalities of a role that adherence to them must be allowed and confirmed by the others involved in the situation; this is one of the basic things we mean by the notion that something is formal and official. Adherence to formalities seems to guarantee the *status quo* of authority and social distance; under the guidance of this style, one can be assured that the others will not be able to move in on one. Reversing the role point of view, we can see that adherence to the formalities one owes to others can be a relatively protective matter, guaranteeing that one's conduct will have to be accepted by the others, and, often, that it will not be difficult to dissociate one's purely covert personal attachments from one's role projection. Finally, it should be added that in general we assume that it is to the advantage of the subordinate to decrease distance from the superordinate and to the advantage of the latter to sustain or increase it.

From these considerations it should be apparent that the exercise of role distance will take on quite different meanings, depending on the relative rank of the individual who exercises it.

Should a subordinate exercise role distance, this is likely to be seen as a sign of his refusal to keep his place (thereby moving toward greater intimacy with the superordinate, which the latter is likely to disapprove), or as rejection of authority,[8] or as evidence of low morale. On the other hand, the manifestations of role distance on the part of the superordinate is likely to express a willingness to relax the *status quo*, and this the subordinate is likely to approve because of its potential profitability for him. In the main, therefore, the expression of role distance is likely to be the prerogative of the superordinate in an interaction. In fact, since informality on the part of the inferior is so suspect, a tacit division of labor may arise, whereby the inferior contributes respect for the *status quo* on behalf of both parties, while the superior contributes a glaze of sociability that all can enjoy. Charm and colorful little informalities are thus usually the prerogatives of those in higher office, leading us mistakenly to assume that an individual's social graces helped him to his high position, instead of what is perhaps more likely, that the graces become possible for anyone who attains the office.[9] Hence, it is the surgeon, not the surgical nurse, who injects irony into medical etiquette. All

[8] For example, I know of a nurse who was transferred from an experimental surgery team, in part because she enacted simulated yawns, meant to be humorous, during the ticklish part of a delicate surgical technique, thereby showing role distance above her station.

[9] An empirical illustration of this is presented in an excellent paper by Rose Coser in which she demonstrates the special joking prerogatives of senior psychiatrists during ward meetings; see her "Laughter Among Colleagues," *Psychiatry*, 23 (1960), pp. 81–95. For further illustrations of role distance on the part of superordinates, see Ralph Turner, "The Navy Disbursing Officer as a Bureaucrat," *American Sociological Review*, 12 (1947), pp. 342–348.

of this, it may be added, fits other things we know about relations between unequals. It is the ship's captain who has a right to enter the territory of the ordinary seamen, the "fo'c'sle," not they to enter his. An officer has a right to penetrate the private life of a soldier serving under him, whereas the private does not have a similar right. In this connection, one student has been led to speak of the social distance between two individuals as being of different extent depending from whose place one starts.[10]

But, of course, subordinates can exercise much role distance, and not merely through grumbling. By sacrificing the seriousness of their claim to being treated as full-fledged persons, they can exercise liberties not given to social adults.

We can now see that with the chief surgeon on one side and the intern on the other there appears to be a standard distribution of role-distance rights and role-distance tendencies. The intern may sacrifice his character as a full and serious person, becoming, thereby, a half-child in the system, in return for which he is allowed to offend medical role requirements with impunity. The person with dominating status can also offend with impunity because his position gives others present a special reason for accepting the offense.

I would like to add that although the person who manifests much role distance may, in fact, be alienated from the role, still, the opposite can well be true: in some cases only those who feel secure in their attachment may be able to chance the expression of distance. And, in fact, in spite of interns, it appears that conformity to the prescriptive aspects of role often occurs most thoroughly at the neophyte level, when the individual must prove his compe-

[10] Donald MacRae, "Class Relationships and Ideology," *The Sociological Review*, n.s., 6 (1958), pp, 263–264.

tence, sincerity, and awareness of his place, leaving the showing of distance from a role to a time when he is firmly "validated" in that role.

Another peculiarity should be mentioned. To express role-irrelevant idiosyncracies of behavior is to expose oneself to the situation, making more of oneself available in it than is required by one's role. The executive's family picture on his desk, telling us that he is not to be considered entirely apart from his loved ones, also tells us, in a way, that they are in this occupation with him, and that they might understand his having to work late or open up his house to politically wise sociability.

The differing bases of role distance displayed by the chief surgeon and by the intern imply a division of labor or role differentiation. The nursing personnel exhibit a similar kind of differentiation among themselves: the division of labor and responsibility between the scrub nurse and the circulating nurse is associated with a difference in manifestation of role distance. The scrub nurse, in addition to her continued task obligation during the operation, may feel obliged to maintain the role function of standard-maintainer, policing the aseptic character of the order that is maintained, as well as keeping a Management's eye on the skills of the physicians. Any withdrawal of herself into the role of female might, therefore, jeopardize the situated system. The circulating nurse, on the other hand, has no such responsibilities, and, apparently, these sexual considerations can be displaced onto her. Further, not needing to be "in" the operation as must the scrub nurse, she can withdraw into herself, or into a conversation with the anesthetist or the nurses in the adjacent operating room, without jeopardizing matters. To place her in a female capacity does not reduce manpower. It is not surprising, therefore, that the circulating nurse, in addition to the intern, is allowed to be flighty—to act without character.

The division of role-function labor that I have described has a characteristic subtlety that should be mentioned again in conclusion. A person with a specialized task not only performs a service needed by the system but also provides a way of being, a selfhood, with which others in the system can identify, thus allowing them to sustain an image of themselves that would disrupt matters if sustained other than vicariously. The "good guy" informality of the chief surgeon can give his subordinates a feeling that they are not the sort to tolerate strict subordination, that in fact the surgeon must see this and has adjusted himself correspondingly, yet this is, of course, a vicarious rebelliousness carried out principally by the very agency against which one would ordinarily rebel. In the same way, the circulating nurse can establish the principle of female sexuality in which the surgical nurse can see her own reflection, even while the surgeon is calling her by a masculine last-name term of address and receiving a man-sized work contribution from her.

Some final points may now be mentioned concerning the function of role distance, now not merely in surgery but in situated systems in general.

First, by not demanding the full rights of his position, the individual finds that he is not completely committed to a particular standard of achievement; should an unanticipated discrediting of his capacity occur, he will not have committed himself and the others to a hopelessly compromised position. Second, it appears that social situations as such retain some weight and reality in their own right by drawing on role distance—on the margin of reservation the individual has placed between himself and his situated role.

An interesting confirmation of the functional significance of role distance in situated activity systems is to be had by examining situations where roles are played *at*.

There seems to be a little difficulty in getting stage actors to portray a character who is inflated with pomposity or bursting with emotion, and directors often have to restrain members of the cast from acting too broadly. The actor is apparently pleased to express before a large audience a lack of reservation which he would probably blush to express off the stage. However, this willingness to embrace a staged role is understandable. Since the actor's performed character is not his real one, he feels no need to safeguard himself by hedging his taken stand. Since the staged drama is not a real one, over-involvement will simply constitute the following of a script, not a threat to one's capacity to follow it. An acted lack of poise has none of the dysfunctions of real flustering.

More significant, there is the fact that in prisons and mental hospitals, where some inmates may constantly sustain a heroic edifice of withdrawal, uncooperativeness, insolence, and combativeness, the same inmates may be quite ready to engage in theatricals in which they enact excellent portraits of civil, sane, and compliant characters. But this very remarkable turnabout is understandable too. Since the staged circumstances of the portrayed character are not the inmate's real ones, he has no need (in the character's name) to exhibit distance from them, unless, of course, the script calls for it.

# D Social Structure and Institutions

## 11

## The Process of Institutionalization

### PETER H. BLAU

. . . Legitimate organizations are faced with the problem of their perpetuation through time. To be sure, all populations, animal as well as human, reproduce themselves, and no special arrangements are necessary to assure the survival of the species for many generations. The survival of a legitimate social order beyond the life span of individuals, however, does require special institutions. The basic cultural values and beliefs that are sacred or virtually sacred to people make them eager to preserve these ideas and ideals for future generations. The investments made in the organized patterns of social life that

From *Exchange and Power in Social Life* by Peter H. Blau. Copyright © 1964 by John Wiley & Sons, Inc., Publishers. Reprinted by permission of the publisher.

are legitimated by these values and embody them, and in the knowledge and technology that further the common welfare, make men interested in preserving those too. Formalized arrangements are instituted perpetuating the legitimate order and the social values that sustain it through time by making them independent of individual human beings. The organized community survives total turnover of its membership, often for many generations. . . . What persists are the principles governing social relations and patterns of conduct, and the reason for their persistence is that they have become institutionalized.

Institutionalization involves formalized procedures that perpetuate organizing principles of social life from generation to generation. Establishing a formal procedure requires an investment of resources, and it preserves and rigidifies patterns of social conduct and relations. Merely making explicit a course of action that has become customary entails effort and stabilizes it. Setting up rules to be consistently followed involves further costs and crystallizes the pattern of action further. The members of organizations sometimes operate under the guidance of superiors and on the basis of precedent without having written procedures to follow. Ascertaining the principles underlying their decisions and producing an official manual of procedures is a difficult task necessitating major investments, which are made in the hope of the future benefits resulting from having such formalized procedures. The explicitly formulated set of procedures, which are expected to govern the decisions of all members of the organization, and which can be readily taught to newcomers, are manifest in a pattern of actions and social interactions that are independent of the specific individuals who carry them out. Formalized rules make an organized pattern of social relations and conduct independent of particular human beings, which is the first requirement of a social institution. Other requirements of institutionalization are that the rules of conduct be legitimated by traditional values and enforced by powerful groups, thereby being made resistant against ready change.

There is a great diversity of social institutions. Examples are the dogma and ritual of a church, the form of government of a country, its laws and courts, the stock exchange that coordinates complex economic transactions, and monogamous marriage. What they all have in common is that legitimating values and formalized procedures perpetuate an organized pattern of social associations. The values that identify men in a society, and the dominant groups in particular, with their institutions and the advantages they derive from them make them interested in preserving these institutions for posterity. Sacred values are more important for the survival of some institutions, such as a church; material advantages are more important for the survival of others, such as a stock exchange; but all are legitimated by some common values. Two complementary social mechanisms preserve the institutions of men though they themselves die, external social arrangements that are historically transmitted and internalized social values that are transmitted in the process of socialization.

Social institutions constitute a historical reality that exists, at least in part, outside and independent of the human beings who make up societies. This historical reality is transmitted through oral traditions in nonliterate societies, but in literate societies it is primarily transmitted through written documents that embody the basic formalized values and norms of the communal life of men—their constitutions and their laws, their bibles and their commandments. To be sure, it is not the parchment or paper on which these documents are written that is of significance but the principles of human conduct they contain. The fact that these principles are written down, however, is of significance, since it assures their survival in fixed form and symbolizes the historical persistence of institutionalized principles of social life, independent of the specific human beings in whom these principles express themselves at any particular time.[1] Although these historical documents must

[1] The great importance rituals assume in nonliterate societies, compared to their lesser importance in modern societies, may be the result of a greater need for rituals to perpetuate institutionalized practices in the absence of written codes for doing so.

continue to be believed by people to govern social life, they do exert an influence of their own, as Durkheim has noted in his discussion of *written* dogmas and laws:

However well digested, they would of course remain dead letters if there were no one to conceive their significance and put them into practice. But though they are not self-sufficient, they are none the less in their own way factors of social activity. They have a manner of action of their own. Juridical relations are widely different depending on whether or not the law is written. Where there is a constituted code, jurisprudence is more regular but less flexible. . . . The material forms it assumes are thus not merely ineffective verbal combinations but active realities, since they produce effects which would not occur without their existence. They are not only external to individual consciousness, but this very externality establishes their specific qualities.[2]

Complementary to the historical transmission of the external forms of social institutions is the transmission of the basic cultural values and norms in the process of socialization that give these forms flesh and blood and continuing life, as it were. In the course of rearing their children, people inculcate in them their most profound values and beliefs, often without explicit intent. The dominant values and norms shared by the members of a society or its segments are, therefore, transmitted to succeeding generations. While the rebellion of children against their parents and, especially, the deprivations produced by political oppression or economic exploitation sometimes lead to the rejection of traditional values, only selected political or economic values are usually rejected. The major part of the cultural heritage tends to persist, even in periods of revolutionary transformations. In any case, the process of social-

ization results in many of the legitimating values of organized community life being passed on to future generations, and these are the institutionalized values that sustain and invigorate the external forms of institutions, which without them would be dead skeletons.

A third factor that supplements the other two in sustaining institutions is that they are rooted in the power structure. The cultural values and social arrangements that become institutionalized are those with which the dominant groups in the society are strongly identified, since these groups have the power to make their convictions prevail and to enforce the relevant social norms. Freedom of speech is institutionalized in a society, for example, if powerful groups value and defend it, even if the majority should care little about it or possibly deprecate it; when the powerful are no longer concerned with maintaining free speech its survival as an institution is imperiled. An institution exerts external constraints on succeeding generations in large part because, and as long as, powerful groups that can enforce institutional demands continue to be interested in its preservation. Powerful men and their wives are more likely than others to inculcate traditional values in their children in the process of socialization, inasmuch as the institutional structure embodying these values is the one on which their dominant position rests. Socialization, however, is not confined to childhood but occurs also later in life, notably when individuals join new groups, and members of lower strata who move up into dominant positions tend to be socialized by the established persons there to acquire a proper concern with traditional values and institutions. In brief, institutionalized patterns are typically those with which the dominant groups in a society are most identified, and these groups are the instruments of their historical perpetuation by enforc-

[2] Durkheim, *Suicide,* New York: Free Press, 1951, pp. 314–315.

ing the demands necessary for this purpose.[3]

Three conditions, therefore, must be met for aspects of social structures to become institutionalized, that is, to be perpetuated from one generation to the next. Patterns of organized community life must become formalized and part of the historical conditions that persist through time, the social values that legitimate these patterns must be transmitted in the process of socialization, and the society's dominant groups must be especially interested in the survival of these patterns. The historical forms without continued acceptance of the legitimating values become empty shells, and cultural values without institutional forms are ideals yet to be realized; both are required to maintain institutions, and so is their support by powerful groups. These factors can be illustrated with our political institutions. On the one hand, our Congressional form of government, the U.S. Constitution and laws, the various branches of government, and the election machinery, are formalized procedures embodied in documents and manifest in many organizations and agencies that persist as part of the historical reality, independent of the particular incumbents of the various offices. On the other hand, democratic and patriotic values, respect for the law and the mores that support it, as well as related values and norms, are transmitted to children in their homes and schools. Americans are born into a historical situation in which certain political forms exist, and they acquire, in their youth, values and norms that legitimate these institutional forms. The foundations of the authority of the law and of political authority are the historical traditions in which they are

grounded and the pertinent normative orientations that the members of our society have internalized in the course of socialization as part of their basic personality. The support of the nation's dominant groups, moveover, has sustained the American form of government and legal institutions even in periods when large-scale immigration filled the country with people from other traditions and with different orientations. Institutional constraints generally derive their distinctive force from the combination of being buttressed by the power structure and having twofold historical roots, in the traditions of society and in the childhood socialization experiences of its individual members.

Institutions reflect the historical dimension in social life, the impact of the past on the present. The relationship between institutions and social structure is in some ways parallel to that between social structure and human conduct. Institutions are those aspects of the social structure that persist for long periods of time, and the social structure consists of those patterns of conduct that prevail throughout a collectivity. Yet institutions exert traditional constraints on the social structure that exists at any one time, just as the social structure exerts external constraints on the behavior of individuals. Thus the values and norms shared by most members of a collectivity constitute external structural constraints for each one of them to which he must adapt. Similarly, the traditional values and their external institutional forms constitute a historical framework to which the social structure at any one time must adapt. Men collectively can change the social structure that restrains them, however, and communities in the course of time can change the institutions that confine their social life. In short, institutions impose historical limits on the social structure

[3] I am indebted to Arthur L. Stinchcombe for calling my attention to these points in a private communication.

which in turn exerts structural constraints on individual conduct.

The typology of social values as mediators of social transactions presented in the preceding section can be employed to classify social institutions. First, integrative institutions perpetuate particularistic values, maintain social solidarity, and preserve the distinctive character and identity of the social structure that differentiates it from others. The core of this institutional complex is the kinship system, which assures every member of the society an integrated position in a network of cohesive social relations and socioemotional support on the basis of ascribed qualities, and which preserves the distinctive social structure by transmitting cultural values and norms to succeeding generations as well as by reproducing the population biologically. Mate selection in accordance with the incest taboo recurrently establishes new particularistic ties of kinship allegiance between subgroups previously separated by these particularistic boundaries. Religious institutions constitute the second main component of this complex, since moral dogmas and hallowed symbols are fundamental elements of particularism and sacred ceremonies and rituals greatly strengthen commitment to the particularistic values they represent. Inasmuch as most religious bodies in the modern world cut across national boundaries, the common traditions and allegiances they create do too, and separate patriotic doctrines, symbols, and ceremonies—the Declaration of Independence, the Stars and Stripes, Fourth-of-July celebrations—develop to bolster national traditions, solidarity, and loyalty.

A second major type of institution functions to preserve the social arrangements that have been developed for the production and distribution of needed social facilities, contributions, and rewards of various kinds. This type includes, of course, the economic institutions in a society, but it also includes other institutions that are governed by universalistic standards of instrumental value. It encompasses educational institutions, through which technological skills and instrumental knowledge are transmitted to future generations, and which, in their higher branches, simultaneously serve the function of advancing knowledge through research. The stratification system too is part of this institutional complex, insofar as it entails an incentive system for recruiting and channeling men into occupations where they furnish diverse services. It is important in this connection to distinguish two aspects of social stratification.[4] On one hand, the stratification system consists of a hierarchy of social positions, not the persons who occupy them, that yield differential rewards. On the other hand, the class structure consists of actual collectivities of individuals, not abstract positions, who differ in wealth, power, and prestige. The stratification system is an institution, while class structure is not. Although not an institution, the class structure is instrumental in fortifying other institutions, as noted above, and important elements of it typically persist from generation to generation, just as institutions do, because wealth and consequently some aspects of class position can be inherited. The resulting rigidities in the class structure impede the function of the stratification system as a mechanism for distributing human resources, since hereditary status rewards are not effective incentives for achievement.

A third main set of institutions serves

[4] See Walter Buckley, "Social Stratification and the Functional Theory of Social Differentiation," *American Sociological Review*, 23 (1958), 369–375, and Kingsley Davis, "The Abominable Heresy," *American Sociological Review*, 24 (1959), 82-83.

to perpetuate the authority and organization necessary to mobilize resources and coordinate collective effort in the pursuit of social objectives. The prototype is the lasting political organization of a society, including not only its form of government and various specific political institutions, such as the legislature, but also such corollary institutions as the judiciary that maintains law and order, the military establishment that protects national security and strength, and the administrative agencies that implement the decisions of the government. To this set of institutions belong also the formal organizations that have become established outside the political arena in a society—like business concerns, unions, and professional associations—and notably the enduring principles of management and administration in terms of which they are governed. Private as well as public organizations are the instruments through which a community attains its social objectives, such as a higher standard of living, and their internal structure corresponds to the executive segment of a political system. Persisting organizations, therefore, are analytically part of the complex of political institutions.[5]

The cultural heritage of a society, finally, contains what may be called a "counterinstitutional component," consisting of those basic values and ideals that have not been realized and have not found expression in explicit institu-

tional forms, and which are the ultimate source of social change. The conflict between these as yet unrealized, but culturally legitimated, ideals and the actual conditions of social existence is at the base of social opposition to existing institutions. For this conflict to become activated typically requires that the diffuse discontent become focused in an opposition ideology. Although some opposition movements formulate revolutionary ideologies that reject many basic values and advocate the complete overthrow of many institutional arrangements, they do so within the framework of some of the ideals and ultimate objectives legitimated by the prevailing culture. Even the most radical revolutionary ideologies are not independent of and receive some legitimation from traditional social values. The very cultural values that legitimate existing institutions contain the seeds of their potential destruction, because the idealized expectations these values raise in the minds of men in order to justify the existing social order cannot be fully met by it and thus may serve as justification, if need be, for opposition to it.[6]

[6] The schema presented reveals some parallels to Parsons' schema of four functional imperatives—adaptation, goal gratification, integration, and latency—but there are also some fundamental differences; see Parsons and Neil J. Smelser, *Economy and Society*, New York: Free Press, 1956, pp. 16–28 and *passim*.

[5] See Parsons, *Structure and Process in Modern Societies*, New York: Free Press, 1960, pp. 41–44.

# 12

# Components of the Social Structure

## HANS GERTH AND C. WRIGHT MILLS

The sociologist . . . tries to "locate" the human being and his conduct in various institutions, never isolating the individual or the workings of his mind from his social and historical setting. He explains character and conduct in terms of these institutions, and of the total social structure which they form. He draws upon the experience of people as social persons rather than upon the physical and organic facts about people as animal organisms. . . .

We speak of roles as organized or instituted when they are guaranteed by authority. Thus, the cluster of roles enacted by the members of a household is guanteed by "parental authority": the "head" of the household may use sanctions against infractions of the role pattern. Thus, employees are subject to the control of owners and managers; soldiers are subject to the authority of the commanding officer; parishioners stand under the jurisdiction of church authorities. Whatever ends the organized and interacting partners may pursue and whatever means they may employ, "authority" exists: and whenever a role configuration is so guaranteed or stabilized by a "head" who wields authority over the "members" who enact the roles, the configuration may be called an institution.

The head of the institution, the king of a political order, or the father of a patriarchal kinship system is the most significant "other," of the persons following the institutional patterns. The

From *Character and Social Structure* by Hans Gerth and C. Wright Mills, copyright, © 1953 by Harcourt, Brace & World, Inc. and reprinted with their permission. Copyright © by Routledge and Kegan Paul, Ltd. Used by permission of the publisher.

kind of external sanction this head may take against those who do not meet their expected roles in expected manners may range from disapproval to expulsion or death. His expectations are treated as most important by persons so long as they are really involved in the institution as a going concern. In this way, then, as well as in others which in due course we shall take up, institutions are deeply relevant to our understanding of the person, and in turn to the entire character structure.

Just as role is the unit with which we build our conception of institutions, so institution is the unit with which we build the conception of social structure. There is more to a social structure than the interrelations of its institutions, but these institutions, in our view, do make up its basic framework. Our immediate aim, then, is to classify institutions in such a way as to enable us to construct types of social structure. . . .

An *institutional order*, as we shall use the phrase, consists of all those institutions within a social structure which have similar consequences and ends or which serve similar objective functions. However institutions may vary in size, recruitment, and composition of membership, in forms of control or proportions of permanent and transitory roles, as we examine the advanced societies of the modern Western world we can distinguish some five major institutional orders.

At least at first glance, we may classify most of the institutions as having to do with such ends as power, goods and services, violence, deities, and procreation. All those institutions which deal with the recurrent and collective worship of God or deities, for instance, we may call religious institutions; together they make up the religious order. Similarly, we may call those institutions that have to do with power, the political; with violence, the military; with procreation, the kinship; and with goods and services, the economic order. By delineating these institutional orders, which form the skeleton structure of the total society, we may conveniently analyze and compare different social structures. Any social *structure* [society], according to our conception, is made up of a certain combination or pattern of such institutional orders. . . .

1. The *political* order consists of those institutions within which men acquire, wield, or influence the distribution of power and authority within social structures.
2. The *economic* order is made up of those establishments by which men organize labor, resources, and technical implements in order to produce and distribute goods and services.
3. The *military* order is composed of institutions in which men organize legitimate violence and supervise its use.
4. The *kinship* order is made up of institutions which regulate and facilitate legitimate sexual intercourse, procreation, and the early rearing of children.
5. The *religious* order is composed of those institutions in which men organize and supervise the collective worship of God or deities, usually at regular occasions and at fixed places.

Some four qualifications or cautions about this way of classifying institutions must be kept in mind at all times, and although they will become clearer as we proceed with our work, we must state them at once:

I. The conception of social structures in terms of such functional institutional orders is, of course, suggested by modern society in which various institutional orders have reached a high degree of autonomy and in which the relative differentiation of ends has gone very far; so far in fact, that businessmen often engage in the pursuit of profits without consideration for the effects of business institutions upon other institutional orders; that is, they posture as purely economic man. Yet few, if any, modern claims for the *pure* autonomy of an institutional order have been realized. If they were, it would mean that one order was wholly segregated from all others; no social structure is so mechanically composed. Moreover, during the last half century, modern social structures have definitely tended to become more tightly integrated, and their various orders interlinked under more total control.

There are social structures in which the specialization of ends and institutions has not been pushed as far as in modern society. Business and private life, or the economic and kinship orders, are not segregated in peasant society. Farms provide members of peasant families with a household way of life in which economic production and family living are not only interrelated but in many respects identical. We may isolate one aspect of a society from another for the sake of analysis, but we have to realize that often, as in the peasant village and the garrison state, this analytical isolation is not experienced; life is an inseparable fusion. For example, the fact that ancient Israel had no distinct term for "religion" did not mean that there were no religious functions; on the contrary, there was little in this society that was not at least indirectly related to Yahweh and his commandments.

Therefore, our first caution is: In "less developed" societies than the mid-nineteenth-century West, as well as in more developed societies, any one of the functions we have isolated may *not* have autonomous institutions serving it. Just what institutional orders exist in a more or less autonomous way is a matter to be investigated in any given society. In some societies the institutions of the kinship order may perform functions which, in more segmented societies, are performed by specifically political institutions. Any classification of institutional orders in terms of function should be seen as an abstraction which sensitizes us to the possibilities and enables us to construct and to understand the concrete segments and specific functions of any given social structure.

II. The classification of institutional orders according to the *dominant* ends of the institutions composing them should not blind us to the fact that the activities and functions of an institution are not exhaustively characterized by its primary end. A religious institution, such as the Catholic Church, employs numerous specialized functionaries who devote themselves to the financial and property affairs of the institution; a monastery may specialize in the production and sale of "Chartreuse," and exquisite French liqueur; or it may engage in the brewing of beer, the printing of books, and so on. Yet, we shall not call such institutions "economic institutions"; for it is hardly satisfactory to account for the existence and shape of a "monk order" in terms of its economic pursuits, no matter how relevant economic activities may be for the religious organization. Monks who brew beer do not thereby constitute a brewery which just happens to recruit tonsured and celibate men as employees. The financial transactions of the Vatican do not make it a bank. That an army or a factory may employ religious leaders for morale-building purposes does not mean that the army

or the factory becomes a religious institution, but rather that the military order is able to use religious personnel for its own ends. That the dispute concerning the dogma of the Trinity was settled at Nicaea in A.D. 325 by monks armed with clubs does not make "military institutions" out of monasteries. Neither is the employment of practitioners of violence by business corporations or trade unions sufficient to turn such institutions into elements of the "military" order. An institution may enroll numerous agents and may comprise many specialized roles for the implementation of its dominant goal.

Many and varied activities are required to operate large institutions, and these activities often overlap with those of other orders; accordingly, the ends of one order often serve as the means of another. Nevertheless, we must first set up a scheme in which we attempt to define and classify institutions by their *dominant* functions before we can consider such problems of "overlap" and integration in a fruitful and systematic way.

III. Our classification of institutions into orders is in terms of their objective, social functions, not subjective, personal meanings of their members or leaders. Concretely, this means that whether or not the persons who enact roles making up the institutions within an order are aware of the order's ends, nevertheless, their conduct is so oriented. A Catholic cardinal, for example Richelieu, may have been personally motivated to win political power, and may even have spent most of his life in political rather than religious activities; but this does not make the churches under his authority part of the political order. Nor does it necessarily mean that the more political bishops are less effective in their religious roles than "more religious" bishops. The motives that are typical of persons playing roles in a given order are matters to be investigated in every case; they are not in any way settled by any objective definition of the dominant functions of institutional orders.

IV. Not all social experience and conduct are included in this scheme of institutional orders. The "dating" of young lovers and the behavior of "the man in the street" are not institutional conduct—although, of course, they are affected by several institutional orders. Yet, if we aim to grasp total societies, it is convenient to focus first on institutions and their settings rather than on the more amorphous and ephemeral modes of social interaction, however crucial these may at times be.

There are several aspects of social conduct which characterize all institutional orders, the most important being: technology, symbols, status, and education. All orders may be characterized by technological implements, by the modes of speech and symbols peculiar to them, by the distribution of prestige enjoyed by their members, and by the transmission of skills and values. We shall arbitrarily call these "spheres," in contradistinction to "orders," because they are, in our view, rarely or never autonomous as to the ends they serve and because any of them may be used within any one of our five orders.

1. "Symbols" may be visual or acoustic; they may be signs, signals, emblems, ceremonial, language, music, or other arts. Without such symbols we could not understand the conduct of human actors, and normally, their belief in and use of these symbols operate to uphold or justify the institutional order. The religious order has its sphere of theology, the elaboration, attenuation, and justification of God or deities; the military order has its startle commands; and the political order has its political formulae and rhetoric, in the name of which its agents exercise authority.

2. "Technology" refers to the implementation of conduct with tools, apparatus, machines, instruments, and physical devices of all sorts. In addition to such instrumentalities, the technological sphere refers to the skill, dexterity, or expertness with which persons meet their role demands. In this sense, "technique" is used by the violinist as well as by the skilled soldier; it is revealed by the surgeon's use of his tools, as well as by the priest handling such paraphernalia of worship as the chalice or the prayer wheel. Whenever we concentrate on the degree, or the absence, of skill with which roles are enacted, we may speak of the technological sphere, regardless of what the institutional context may be. Technology is never autonomous: it is always instituted in some specific order or orders. In modern industrial society, it is centered primarily in the economic and military orders, which not only stimulate it and "supervise" its production and distribution to other institutions, but are the orders in which it is most often used.

3. The "Status" sphere consists of agencies and means of distributing prestige, deference, or honor among the members of the social structure. Any role in any institutional order may be the basis for status claims, and the status sphere as a whole may be anchored primarily in any one order or in many specific combinations of institutional orders.

4. The "Educational" sphere consists of those institutions and activities concerned with the transmission of skills and values to those persons who have not yet acquired them.

A *social structure* [society] is composed of institutional orders and spheres. The precise weight which each institutional order and sphere has with reference to every other order and sphere, and the ways in which they are related with one another—these determine the unity and the composition of a social structure.

The analysis of social structure into orders, as we have said, does not decide what "orders" exist; only concrete investigation of different societies can do that. We shall not be surprised, of course, when we have to elaborate or simplify the classification of institutional orders sketched here. Social structures are not frozen, they may be static or dynamic, they have beginnings, duration, varying degrees of unity, and they may disintegrate.

These problems of the interrelations of institutional orders and of social change will be dealt with in due course. Here it is perhaps enough to remark that the warp of one institutional order may be the woof of another. Military men, for instance, becoming conscious of a scarcity of manpower, may be concerned about the declining health of the working classes because they anticipate an increasing percentage of men unfit for military service—a thought that may not enter the mind of the businessman, still thinking of the abundance of labor force. Similarly, businessmen, interested in educated labor for clerical jobs, many become much concerned with tax-supported high schools.

In their ramifications, then, institutional orders have definite bearings upon each other; tensions and conflicts arise, and practices lead to results which the practitioners neither intend nor foresee.

It is often convenient to examine these interrelations of institutional orders in terms of ends and means; often the activities which fulfill one institutional order's ends serve as means to the dominant ends of another order. When we focus upon such subsidiary aspects of institutions, we may economic order." The religious order What dominates in one order may, in a different order, merely implement. The political activities of businessmen and corporations may thus be understood as "political ramifications of the economic order." The religious order or the educational order may also have political ramifications: the political activities of religious and educational institutions and personnel. Similarly, we may speak of the educational and religious ramifications of the political order when focusing upon educational activities of politicians in party schools or the role of prayer and other religious activities in politics. Any given order may thus become the ramification of any other order. "Ramifications" may thus be defined as those activities which are ends in one order but which are used as the means of another institutional order. In total war, for example, all orders become ramifications of the military state, for the military impinges upon all other orders which thus become prerequisites for realizing or for limiting military ends.

# E Societies and Social Change

## 13

## Human Society Before the Urban Revolution

ROBERT REDFIELD

What can be said that is general and true about the condition of mankind before civilization? The question is directed to a time from five to six thousand years ago. At that time human populations were to be found on all the world's continents, with the possible exception of Australia. Greenland had not yet been invaded by man, and some of the islands of the Pacific were as yet without human occupants. But there were people in a great many widely scattered parts of the habitable earth, not very many of them in any one place, and not very many of them altogether. No city had yet been built anywhere.

The question is whether anything can

Reprinted from Robert Redfield: *The Primitive World and Its Transformation.* Copyright 1953 by Cornell University. Used by permission of Cornell University Press.

be said, with show of reason and evidence, about *all* the human beings that were there then, whether they lived in the arctic or in the tropics, whether they hunted, fished, or farmed, and whatever may have been the color of their skins, the languages they spoke, or the particular beliefs and customs that they had. The question demands a positive characterization of their manner of life. The description should be more than a mere statement of the things that those early men did not have that we today do have. It should say: this is what they did; this is how they felt; this is the way the world looked to them.

The question, so understood, appears to require more than can be provided from trustworthy evidence, but I do not think that it really does. It can be answered from two sources of information. The archaeologists dig up the material things that men of those times made and used, and from these things draw reasonable inferences about their manner of life. And, secondly, the ethnologists tell us a good deal about the ways of life of those people who until recent times have remained uncivilized: the primitive, the preliterate—or, to use the old-fashioned terms—the savage and the barbaric peoples. To learn what precivilized men were like, we may look to the accounts of the remains of ancient camps and settlements unaffected by cities, either because they were there before there were any cities anywhere, or because they stood remote and unreached by ancient cities already arisen. And also we may look to what has been written in great detail about many hundreds of present-day tribes and bands and villages, little communities of the never civilized. I do not assume that these latter people have experienced no changes in the several thousands of years since the first cities were built. The particular thoughts and beliefs of the present-day preliterates have probably changed a good deal during many hundreds of generations. The customs of these people are not "earlier" [1] than is our own civilization, for they have had as long a history as have we. But what I do assert is that the surviving primitive peoples have remained substantially unaffected by civilization. Insofar as the conditions of primitive life remain—in the smallness of the community, and in its isolation and nonliteracy—so, too, the kind of thoughts and beliefs, however changed in specific content, remain of a kind characteristic of primitive society. That there is such a kind is evidenced to us from the fact that we can generalize as to this manner of thought and belief from the surviving primitive peoples, in the face of

the very great variety of content of thought and belief which these exhibit. These surviving primitive peoples provide us with instances of that general and primordial kind of human living which it is my immediate purpose to describe.

Now it is fortunate for the present enterprise that these two sources of information, the archaeological and the ethnological, supplement each other. Where the former is weak, the latter is strong; and where the ethnologist may be insufficiently impressed by the influence of technology on the manner of life of a human community, the archaeologist can hardly fail to be impressed. This is what he sees: the material things. Moreover, of the many meanings which are locked in the artifacts that ancient peoples made, it is those meanings which relate to practical action, especially the getting of food, which communicate themselves most readily to the archaeologist who finds them. A Plains Indian medicine bundle or an Australian totemic design as an archaeological object by itself would convey only a little of the very great deal which the ethnologist who can talk to a living Indian or Australian can find out that it means. So the archaeologist's view of the manner of life of the precivilized peoples will emphasize the practical aspects of living and the material influences on change. An archaeologist should make a little effort to lean deliberately away from a materialist view of human life and a conception of history in simple terms of economic determinism. His work inclines him toward it. On the other hand, the ethnologist is often in a position where he can find out little or nothing of the history of the people he is studying, as they have written nothing down about it, having no means to do so; and so it may sometimes appear to him that they are to be explained chiefly in terms of the kinds of marriage choices he finds them making when he finds them,

[1] Melville Herskovits, Man and His Works (New York: A. A. Knopf, 1948), p. 71.

or the potlatches they give. In the absence of a history, the way the material conditions of living limited that people here or gave them a chance to develop something there may not be apparent.

Archaeologist and ethnologist, however, do often talk to each other, and indeed in some cases are the same person. So the separation of work, the difference in emphasis, is not so great as I have perhaps made it sound. In the attempt to characterize the precivilized manner of life, I will begin by following Childe, an archaeologist. Professor Childe is interested in the effects on human development of changes in the technology by which food is produced. He makes a separation of importance between that period in human history when men were hunters and fishers only (savagery), and that period when men had learned how to be agriculturalists or animal breeders (barbarism). The change from the one kind of life to the other he calls a revolution, "the food-producing revolution."

The discovery of how to produce food was, of course, of enormous importance in human history, and it is not too much to call it a revolution and to group it, as Childe does, with the "urban revolution," when civilization came into being, and with the industrial revolution of modern times. Yet certain qualifications or additions need to be made. It has been pointed out that the food-producing revolution was the more notable event in that from the condition of food collecting one could not predict that food producing would be achieved, but that when once food production had increased human population and made leisure possible, civilization was bound to come about.[2] And it is also necessary to recognize that

some of the changes charac̲t̲e̲.̲ each stage may have taken place, in one community or another, before the revolution in technology that Childe stresses had occurred there. Thus we know that a sedentary village life is possible to a people who know nothing of agriculture or animal husbandry. The fishing Indians of our Northwest coast lived a village life and developed certain aspects of their culture very highly. In prehistoric times there existed on the Scandinavian coast sessile communities, quite comparable with Neolithic farmers in the village character of life, with pottery and the polishing of flint, but without crops or herds.[3] Also, it is not unlikely that with the advent of agriculture there began some of those changes which we are able to see only when cities and writing have made them visible to us. The excavations in Iraq, already mentioned, suggest this possibility. As the changes in technology, so also the changes in the human mind which are the subject of these pages may have well begun before the urban revolution, even before the food-producing revolution.

Nevertheless, within the wide generalizations that I am here attempting, the food-producing revolution and the urban revolution may be considered as two parts of one great transformation. To one interested in changes in human habits and capacities of mind, the urban revolution is the more important part, for it is with the coming of city life that we are able to see novel and transforming attitudes taken toward life and the universe. That these novel attitudes began earlier is likely, and farther on in these pages indications will be drawn from present-day primitive societies that occasional beginnings of these civilized attitudes were to be found in the precivilized societies had we been there to look for them. The

[2] Sol Tax, "Revolution and the Process of Civilization," *Human Origins, An Introductory General Course in Anthropology, Selected Readings*, Series II (2nd ed.; Chicago: University of Chicago Press, 1946, mimeographed).

[3] Gutorm Gjessing, *Norges Steinalder* (Oslo: Taslum, 1945).

question as to the relative importance of Childe's two first revolutions may be set aside with this statement: the food-producing revolution was perhaps the turning point in the human career, but it was through the urban revolution that the consequences of the turn were realized.

Now let us attempt a characterization of mankind in precivilized times. Let us begin with the simple statement that in the primary condition of mankind the human community was small. As Childe says, writing of the food-collecting period, hunters and vegetable-food collectors usually live in small roving bands.[4] Even the more stable settlement of Pacific coast Indian fishing people, of recent times exceptionally well provided with food, includes hardly more than thirty occupied houses and several hundred people. Nor does the immediate transition to food producing increase substantially the size of the community, now a group of farmer's huts or a center of cattle raising.

On the whole the growth of population was not reflected so much in the enlargement of the settlement unit as in a multiplication of settlements. In ethnography neolithic villages can boast only a few hundred inhabitants. . . . In prehistoric Europe the largest neolithic village yet known, Barkaer in Jutland, comprised fifty-two small, one-roomed dwellings, but sixteen to thirty houses was a more normal figure; so the average local group in neolithic times would average two hundred to four hundred members.[5]

Certain food-producing town centers well on the way to civilization do give indication of larger populations, but hunters' bands or food producers' settlements are alike in general contrast

to the far larger community which has the ancient city with its seven thousand to twenty thousand inhabitants.[6] What is here worth emphasizing is that until the rise of civilization mankind lived in communities so small that every adult could, and no doubt did, know everybody else.

These communities were isolated from one another. Again Childe gives us to understand that the change in this regard with the coming of agriculture was a change in some degree, but at first not a radical change. Throughout both Paleolithic and Neolithic times each little group was largely self-contained and self-supported, as the surviving primitive societies, whether hunters or growers of vegetable or animal food, are largely self-contained and self-supported. The trade that occurred in Paleolithic times was chiefly trade in nonessentials; with Neolithic times the trade intensified and included some staple commodities, such as stone for querns and flint for hand axes.[7] But the trade did not greatly limit the essential separateness of the local community. The isolation of the Neolithic settlement continued into the medieval English village.[8] Villagers of primitives or peasants today are still relatively isolated, and, on the whole, when such people have more than casual association with outsiders, it is with people who are much like themselves, in neighboring bands or settlements that are like their own community.

So we may characterize mankind in its primary condition as living in small and isolated communities. These com-

[4] V. Gordon Childe, *Prehistoric Migrations in Europe* (Oslo: Aschehoug; Cambridge, Harvard University Press, 1950), p. 6.
[5] *Ibid.*, pp. 5–6.
[6] *Ibid.*, p. 11.
[7] Childe, *What Happened in History* (Harmondsworth, Middlesex: Penguin Books, 1942), p. 53; *Man Makes Himself* (2nd ed.; London: Watts and Co., 1941, first published in 1936), pp. 86–87.
[8] George C. Homans, *English Villagers of the Thirteenth Century* (Cambridge: Harvard University Press, 1941).

munities were of course without writing. I do not say more of this absence of literacy and literature; its importance as a criterion of primitive as contrasted with civilized living is familiar. To these qualities others may be added. The precivilized community was composed of one kind of people. If this fact is not to be deduced from the archaeologist's data, it follows from what we know of isolated primitive communities seen today. Small and isolated communities are intimate communities; people come to have the same ways of doing things; they marry with and live almost entirely with others like them in that community.

Next we may say that the members of the precivilized community had a strong sense of group solidarity. No doubt they thought of themselves as naturally belonging together, and so far as they were aware of people different from themselves, they thought their own ways to be better than those of the ways of others. These things also may be said, not only because they are necessary consequences of the isolation and the smallness of the community, but because we see them to be true of contemporary primitive communities. Civilized communities are more heterogeneous, and the sense of group solidarity is qualified by the number and variety of kinds of groups to which the individual makes attachment—or by the difficulty of making firm attachments to groups in some urban situations.

Let us follow Professor Childe further in his characterization of precivilized man. We see that now he must make increasing use of reasonable deduction and of the evidence from ethnology. He tells us that in the precivilized community there were no full-time specialists. He asserts this for the reason that in communities with simple hunting or even farming, "there simply will not be enough food to go round

unless every member of the group contributes to the supply." [9] In the primitive societies of the present day there are rarely full-time specialists. So the assumption is fairly well founded that in the early condition of mankind what men did was customarily different from what women did, but what one man did was much like what another did. There were men with special skills at activities carried on by all men, and there were probably shamans or other part-time practitioners in the spiritual and healing arts. Differences among individuals with respect to the depth of understanding of cosmogonic and religious ideas may have been very considerable. . . . But, on the whole, all men shared the same essential knowledge, practiced the same arts of life, had the same interests and similar experiences.

Yet another characteristic of precivilized living may be asserted. Within those early communities the relationships among people were primarily those of personal status. In a small and intimate community all people are known for their individual qualities of personality. Few or no strangers take part in the daily life. So men and women are seen as persons, not as parts of mechanical operations, as city people see so many of those around them. Indeed, this disposition to see what is around one as human and personal like oneself is not, in precivilized or primitive society, limited to people; a great deal of what we call "nature" is more or less so regarded. The cosmos is personal and humanlike.

Also in this connection it may be said that the groupings of people within the primitive community is one that depends on status and on role, not on mere practical usefulness. There are fathers, or older people, or shamans, or priests; each such kind of person is accorded prestige. In civilized soci-

[9] Childe, *Prehistoric Migrations*, p. 7.

eties the network of relationships of utility—the numbers and kinds of people who produce goods and services are so great and are at such remote distances—that many of the relationships that keep people provided with what they use are not involved in status at all, for those who use the goods. In primitive societies the status relationships are universal and dominant; the exceptions to be made would be those relatively few that arise out of trade with foreign communities.

Furthermore, in this personal universe where categories of relationships involve status, the forms and groupings of kinship provide the basic classifications. The original human society was one of kinsmen. Childe speaks of the "sentiment of kinship" [10] which in considerable part held the group together. Within the precivilized society, it is safe to assume that relationships were essentially familial. The primary arrangements of personal status and role are those connected with that universally persistent kind of family anthropologists now call "nuclear" and the extensions of this primary kinship into many, possibly even all, of the other relationships within the community. Moreover, the categories of kinship may include elements of nature, as some animals, and supernatural beings. Of course we cannot say just what were the kinship institutions in the thousands of bands and settlements that constituted precivilized society. In his latest book Childe [11] with ingenuity and prudence draws reasonable inferences as to elements of social organization in precivilized societies known only archaeologically. The result suggests the presence in one place of single-family households, in another of large households including several or many nuclear families, and a variety of forms

of marriage. Nevertheless the very smallness and isolation of the precivilized community everywhere allows us to say that in the early condition of humanity, the community, as well as the cosmos of which its members felt it to be a part, was essentially made up of personal relationships, and that the patterning of these relationships was primarily accomplished by developments derived from the differences of age, sex, and familial connection. Today, among western Australian peoples, "the whole society forms a body of relatives," [12] and the intimate connection between the body of relatives and nature, through the water hole or other center of animal multiplication, and the totemic rites, is familiar to readers of Australian ethnology.

What, essentially, held together this primordial human community? Was it the mutual usefulness to one another of those few hunters or fishers or farmers? To answer, Yes, is to recognize what is obviously true: "Cooperation is essential to secure food and shelter and for defense against foes, human and subhuman." [13] But to answer, Yes, is also to suggest a possible misconception. The "identity of economic interests" of which Childe writes in the paragraph in which he so interestingly characterizes the mode of life of man before civilization, is a fact which any of us would have observed had we been there to see the precivilized community, and which is an obvious inference from what we know more directly about it. But this does not mean that in those communities men worked primarily for material wealth. The incentives to work and to exchange labor and goods are, in primitive and precivilized society especially, various and chiefly noneco-

[10] *Ibid.*

[11] Childe, *Social Evolution* (London: Watts and Co., 1951).

[12] A. R. Radcliffe-Brown, "Three Tribes of Western Australia," *Journal of the Royal Anthropological Institute,* **XLIII** (1913), 150–151.

[13] Childe, *Prehistoric Migrations,* p. 7.

nomic (in the narrow sense). They arise from tradition, from a sense of obligation coming out of one's position in a system of status relationships, especially those of kinship, and from religious considerations and moral motivations of many kinds. The point has been put very convincingly by Karl Polanyi.[14] Let us then add to our characterization of the precivilized society that it was a society in which the economy was one determined by status (as contrasted with the society imagined and in part realized in nineteenth-century Europe and America, in which the economy was determined by the market). In the precivilized or the primitive society "man's economy is, as a rule, submerged in his social relations." [15] Essentially and primarily, man "does not aim at safeguarding his individual interest in the acquisition of material possessions, but rather at ensuring social good-will, social status, social assets. He values possessions primarily as a means to that end." We are talking now of a time before the acquisitive society.

To answer only that the precivilized community was held together by reason of mutual usefulness is to fail to say what it is that most importantly and characteristically holds such a community together. Indeed, Childe sees and states succinctly, in terms which Durkheim caused many of us to use, the difference in this regard between the precivilized settlement and the city. It is not the former, but the earliest cities that "illustrate a first approximation to an organic solidarity based upon functional complementarity and interdependence between all its members such as subsist between the

constituent cells of an organism." [16] It is the urban community that rests upon mutual usefulness. The primitive and precivilized communities are held together essentially by common understandings as to the ultimate nature and purpose of life. The precivilized society was like the present-day primitive society in those characteristics—isolation, smallness, homogeneity, persistence in the common effort to make a way of living under relatively stable circumstances—to which we have already attended, and therefore it was like the parallel societies which we can observe today in that its fundamental order was a matter of moral conviction. In both cases the society

exists not so much in the exchange of useful functions as in common understandings as to the ends given. The ends are not stated as matters of doctrine, but are implied by the many acts which make up the living that goes on in the society. Therefore, the morale of a folk society—its power to act consistently over periods of time and to meet crises effectively—is not dependent upon discipline exerted by force or upon devotion to some single principle of action, but to the concurrence and consistency of many or all of the actions and conceptions which make up the whole round of life.[17]

For the homogeneity of such a society is not that homogeneity in which everybody does the same thing at the same time.[18] The people are homogeneous in that they share the same tradition and have the same view of the good life. They do the same kinds of work and they worship and marry and feel shame or pride in the same way and under similar circumstances. But

[14] Karl Polanyi, *The Great Transformation* (New York and Toronto: Farrar & Rinehart, 1944).
[15] Polanyi, "Our Obsolete Market Mentality," *Commentary*, III (February, 1947, 112.
[16] Childe, *Prehistoric Migrations*, p. 16.
[17] Robert Redfield, "The Folk Society," *American Journal of Sociology*, LII (January, 1947), 299.
[18] Herbert Blumer, "Moulding of Mass Behavior through the Motion Picture," *Publications of the American Sociological Society*, XXIX (August, 1935), 115–127.

at any one time the members of a primitive community may be doing notably different things: the women looking for edible roots while the men hunt; some men out on a war party while others at home perform a rite for its success. And when there is a familial ceremonial, or a magico-religious ritual affecting the whole community, the differences in what is being done may be very great. In the activities to gain a material living, labor, as between man and man or woman and woman, may be divided. But the total specialization of function, as among people of different sexes and age-or-kinship positions, and as among participants in a rite, may be very considerable. The point to be stressed is that all these activities conduce to a purpose, express a view of man's duty, that all share, and to which each activity or element of institution contributes.

We can safely say these things of the precivilized societies as we can say them of the primitive societies because these things follow from the other characteristics which we have already conceded, and are attested in every very isolated, undisturbed primitive society we observe today. For the same reasons it is possible to add yet other attributes to the characterization. In the most primitive societies of living men into which we may enter and which we can come directly to understand, the controls of action are informal; they rest on the traditional obligations of largely inherited status, and are expressed in talk and gesture and in the patterns of reciprocal action. Political institutions are few and simple, or even entirely absent. The members of these societies "believe in the sacred things; their sense of right and wrong springs from the unconscious roots of social feeling, and is therefore unreasoned, compulsive and strong." [19] People do the kind

of things they do, not because somebody just thought up that kind of thing, or because anybody ordered them to do so, but because it seems to the people to flow from the very necessity of existence that they do that kind of thing. The reasons given after the thing is done, in the form of myth and the dress of ceremony, assert the rightness of the choice. Particular things are done as a result of decision as to that particular action, but as to the class of action, tradition is the source and the authority. "The Indians decide now to go on a hunt; but it is not a matter of debate whether one should, from time to time, hunt." [20] So the principles of rightness which underlie the activities are largely tacit. And they are not the subject of much explicit criticism, nor even of very much reflective thought. Institutions are not planned out, nor is their modification a matter of much deliberate choice and action. Legislation, though it may occur, is not the characteristic form of legal action in primitive societies. And, what Malinowski [21] refers to as "science" in connection with the primitive peoples is better distinguished as practical knowledge. And these things too may with confidence be attributed to the precivilized societies. Yet, because in them thought and action were largely traditional and uncritical, it does not follow that activities were automatic or empty of meaning. Rather we must suppose that activity with them as with us involved lively and variable subjective states. Ruth Bunzel, studying Pueblo potters, found that the Indian woman who was in fact copying the designs of other potters with only the smallest variation was unaware that she copied, condemned copying as wrong, and had a strong conviction that she was in fact

[19] A. L. Kroeber, *Anthropology* (New York: Harcourt, Brace and Co., 1948), p. 282.

[20] Redfield, *op. cit.*, p. 300.
[21] Bronislaw Malinowski, *Magic, Science and Religion* (Boston: Beacon Press, 1948).

inventive and creative. [22] And as for the meaning of life—that was, so to speak, guaranteed. One did what tradition said one did, making a multitude of interesting and particular choices. But all of it fell within and was motivated by the common understandings of the little community as to the nature and purpose of life.

The attempt to gather together some of the attributes of that form of human living which prevailed before the first civilizations arose may now be halted. . . . There results a picture, very generalized, of the organization of life, social control, and motivation among most of the societies of mankind during most of human history. The point upon which we are to insist . . . is that in this early condition of humanity the essential order of society, the nexus which held people together, was moral. Humanity attained its characteristic, long-enduring nature as a multitude of different but equivalent systems of relationships and institutions each expressive of a view of the good. Each precivilized society was held together by largely undeclared but continually realized ethical conceptions.

Professor Childe unfortunately happened upon a figure of comparison that leads in the direction just opposite to the truth when he wrote that the solidarity of the precivilized community was "really based on the same principles as that of a pack of wolves or a herd of sheep." [23] Even the little glimpses of religion and sense of obligation to do right which are accorded the archaeologist show us that twenty-five thousand years ago the order of society was moral order. That of wolves or sheep is not. Childe's facts prove that this was so and that his compari-

son of precivilized society with that of animals is misleading. Describing the wall paintings, the personal adornments, the trade in cowrie shells, and the hints these things give a life of the mind and the spirit among the Western Europeans of the Ice Age, Childe says, "Savagery produced a dazzling culture." [24] It is Childe who uses this adjective for the cultures at the end of the Ice Age that found expression in necklaces of animal teeth, in well-executed realistic paintings of the animals that were hunted, in stone-weighted skeletons of reindeer cast into a German lake, "presumably as an offering to the spirit of the herd or the genius of the land," according to Childe.

The antiquity of the moral order is not fully attested by archaeology. A people's conceptions as to the good are only meagerly represented in the material things that they make. A tribe of western Australia, the Pitjendadjara, today carry on a religious and moral life of great intensity, but they make and use material objects so few and so perishable that were these people exhibited to us only through archaeology, we would barely know that they had existed and we would know nothing of their moral life. As described by Charles P. Mountford in his charming book,[25] these aborigines perform their rites to increase animal and plant food, and they follow a morality of personal relations with dignity and conscience. Mountford says that they make but five tools: a spear, a spear thrower, a wooden carrying dish, a stone slab on which to grind food, and a digging stick. Perhaps this investigator overlooked some of the articles made by these aborigines, but it is certainly true that naked and wandering, with almost

[22] Ruth Bunzel, *The Pueblo Potter, A Study of Creative Imagination in Primitive Art* (Ph.D. dissertation, Columbia University, 1929), p. 52.
[23] Childe, *Prehistoric Migrations*, p. 7.

[24] Childe, *What Happened in History*, p. 35.
[25] Charles P. Mountford, *Brown Men and Red Sand* (Melbourne: Robertson and Mullens, 1948).

none of the material possessions and power which we associate with the development of humanity, they are nevertheless as human as are you and I.

We may suppose that fifty thousand years ago mankind had developed a variety of moral orders, each expressed in some local tradition, and comparable to what we find among aborigines today. Their development required both the organic evolution of human bodily and cerebral nature and also the accumulation of experience by tradition. As the tradition began to accumulate while the organic evolution was still going on, the moral order—and the technical order—began to be established among the apelike men of the early Pleistocene. On the other hand, until bodily and cerebral nature equivalent to that of men living today had been developed, we cannot fairly attribute to those earliest humanoid societies a moral order comparable, let us say, with that of the Australian blackfellow. Even in the case of so relatively late a being as Neanderthal man there was a factor of biological difference which would have limited the development of culture. But by a time seventy-five or fifty thousand years ago, the biological evolution of mankind had reached a point at which the genetic qualities necessary for the development of fully human life had been attained. This reaches the conclusion that for a period of time at least five times as long as the entire period of civilization man has had the capacity for a life governed by such moral orders as we see in primitive societies today. The men who left the paintings of Altamira were fully human and not very different from us. And I follow Eliseo Vivas when he writes:

That does not mean, of course, that they pursued the identical values and were capable of the same theoretical sophistication of which we are capable; it merely means that they probably had the same

degree of moral sensibility, though perhaps focused toward different objects than those toward which we, the men of contemporary technological society, focus ours.[26]

In recognizing that every precivilized society of the past fifty or seventy-five millenniums had a moral order to which the technical order was subordinate, I do not say that the religious and ethical systems of these societies were equally complex. Then, as now, there were "thin cultures" and "rich cultures." Childe sees certain of the mesolithic cultures as "thin" in comparison with the cultures that preceded them. It is not, of course, clear that the thinness lay in the moral life. Maybe they had a religious and personal life that is not represented in the archaeology. However this may be in that particular case, we are to recognize that the development of technology had, even in precivilized times, an important influence on the moral life. While the Australians show us how little material culture is needed for the development of a moral order, such a contrast as that between the Haida and the Paiute Indians reminds us that generally speaking a people desperately concerned with getting a living cannot develop a rich moral or esthetic life. The moral order of a hard-pressed people may be itself simple. But I insist that it is there in every case.

One other point is to be made about the moral orders that preceded civilization. Morality has had its developmental history. . . . When the moralities of primitive or precivilized peoples are judged by men of the present day, some are found to be better than others; and the judgment makes allowances for practical difficulties encountered by the primitive people. In primitive societies known today where the food quest

[26] Eliseo Vivas, The Moral Life and the Ethical Life (Chicago: University of Chicago Press, 1950), p. 105.

is all absorbing one does not condemn the people for failing to develop much creative art or for failing to show a particularly humane consideration for other people. The Siriono of Bolivia, as recently reported by Allen R. Holmberg,[27] live a harsh and precarious life in a tropical rain forest. They have their moral order—systems of intense inhibition as to sexual relations with certain relatives, ideas as to the rights and duties of relatives to share food, fearful attitudes toward invisible spirits, and so forth. But men's activities "remain on the same monotonous level day after day and year after year, and they are centered largely around the satisfaction of the basic needs of hunger, sex and avoidance of fatigue and pain." Holmberg saw a band of Indians walk out of a camp leaving a woman, sick to death, alone in her hammock. "Even the husband departed without saying goodbye." It is stern necessity that makes for this conduct; children, who can be cared for, are tenderly treated at much expenditure of effort. On the other hand, elsewhere we are reminded of the degree to which respect for personal integrity may develop among primitive food collectors. Among the Yagua, another people living under difficult conditions in the tropical forest of South America, although the entire clan lives in a single long house, Fejos tells us that the members of the large household "are able to obtain perfect privacy whenever they wish it by simply turning their faces to the wall of the house. Whenever a man, woman or child faces the wall, the others regard that individual as if he were no longer present." [28]

I turn now to the distinction between the technical order and the moral order, and from that proceed to contrast pre-civilized and primitive living with civilized living in terms of this distinction. Technical order and moral order name two contrasting aspects of all human societies. The phrases stand for two distinguishable ways in which the activities of men are co-ordinated. As used by C. H. Cooley [29] and R. E. Park,[30] "the moral order" refers to the organization of human sentiments into judgments as to what is right. Describing how the division of labor puts an organization of society based on occupation and vocational interests in place of an older kind of organization of society, Park contrasts these newer ties, based on common interests, with "forms of association like the neighborhood, which are based on contiguity, personal association, and the common ties of humanity." [31] The division of labor modifies this older moral order. Here we will extend the significance of the phrase, and make it cover all the binding together of men through implicit convictions as to what is right, through explicit ideals, or through similarities of conscience. The moral order is therefore always based on what is peculiarly human—sentiments, morality, conscience —and in the first place arises in the groups where people are intimately associated with one another. The word "values," [32] is a related conception, but the phrase "moral order" points to the nature of the bonds among men, rather than to a category of the content of culture. We may conceive of the moral

[27] Allen R. Holmberg, Nomads of the Long Bow, the Siriono of Eastern Bolivia, Smithsonian Institution, Institute of Social Anthropology, Pub. No. 10 (Washington, 1950).
[28] Paul Fejos, Ethnography of the Yagua (New York: Viking Fund, 1943).

[29] C. H. Cooley, Social Organization (New York: C. Scribner's Sons, 1909), p. 54.
[30] Robert Ezra Park, Human Communities (Glencoe, Ill.: Free Press, 1952), pp. 22–32, 35.
[31] Ibid., p. 24.
[32] Clyde Kluckhohn and others, "Values and Value-Orientation," The Theory of Social Action, ed. by Parsons and Shils (Cambridge: Harvard University Press, 1951).

order as equally present in those societies in which the rules for right conduct among men are supported by supernatural sanctions and in those in which the morality of human conduct is largely independent of the religion (in the sense of belief and cult about the supernatural). "Moral order" includes the binding sentiments of rightness that attend religion, the social solidarity that accompanies religious ritual, the sense of religious seriousness and obligation that strengthens men, and the effects of a belief in invisible beings that embody goodness. The moral order becomes vivid to us when we think of the Australian Arunta assembling, each man to do his part, denying himself food, making the sacred marks or performing the holy dances, that the witchetty-grub may become numerous and the whole band thus continue to find its food. Or of the old Chinese family performing the rituals for the ancestors. Or of the members of the boys' gang refusing, even in the face of threats from the police, to "tell on" a fellow member.

By a corresponding extension of another and more familiar term, all the other forms of co-ordination of activity which appear in human societies may be brought together and contrasted with the moral order under the phrase "the technical order." The bonds that co-ordinate the activities of men in the technical order do not rest on convictions as to the good life; they are not characterized by a foundation in human sentiments; they can exist even without the knowledge of those bound together that they are bound together. The technical order is that order which results from mutual usefulness, from deliberate coercion, or from the mere utilization of the same means. In the technical order men are bound by things, or are themselves things. They are organized by necessity or expediency. Think, if you will, of the orderly way in which

automobiles move in response to the traffic light or the policeman's whistle, or think of the flow of goods, services, and money among the people who together produce, distribute, and consume some commodity such as rubber.

Civilization may be thought of as the antithesis of the folk society. It may also, and consistently with the first antithesis, be thought of as the society in which the relations between technical order and moral order take forms radically different from the relationships between the two which prevail in precivilized society.

Civilization (conceived now as one single thing and not—as by Toynbee—as twenty-one different things) may be said to exist to the extent, to the degree, and in the respects in which a society has developed away from the kind of precivilized society which I have been describing. Civilization is, of course, things added to society: cities, writing, public works, the state, the market, and so forth. Another way of looking at it is from the base provided by the folk society. Then we may say that a society is civilized insofar as the community is no longer small, isolated, homogeneous and self-sufficient; as the division of labor is no longer simple; as impersonal relationships come to take the place of personal relationships; as familial connections come to be modified or supplanted by those of political affiliation or contract; and as thinking has become reflective and systematic. I do not mention all of the characteristics of folk societies which I named in foregoing paragraphs; these are enough to suggest the point of view we might adopt. If we do adopt this way of conceiving civilization, we shall think of Toynbee's twenty-one civilizations as different developments away from the folk society. We see then that civilizations do not depart from the nature of the folk society evenly or in the same way. In Chinese civilization the organization of social relationships according to the categories and attitudes of kinship retained its importance while philosophy and the fine arts passed through long histories of development. The Andean civilization developed political and administrative institutions of impressive complexity and far-reaching influence while yet the Indians who developed them were without writing. The Mayan peoples, in contrast, extended their political institutions little beyond that attained by the ordinary tribe while their intellectual specialists carried some parts of mathematics and astronomy to heights that astonish us. In short, the several civilizations start up from their folk bases into specialized developments in which some elements of the folk society are left behind while others are retained. Yet this fact does not destroy the impression that, as a manner of life taken as a whole, civilization is one kind of thing different from the life of the folk society.

The contrast between technical order and moral order helps us to understand the general kind of thing which is civilization. In the folk society the moral order is great and the technical order is small. In primitive and pre-civilized societies material tools are few and little natural power is used. Neither the formal regulations of the state or church nor the nonmoral ordering of behavior which occurs in the market plays an important part in these societies. It is civilization that develops them.

It is civilization, too, that develops those formal and apparent institutions which both express the moral order and are means toward its realization. The technical order appears not only in tools, power, and an interdependence of people chiefly or wholly impersonal and utilitarian, but also in greater and more varied apparatus for living—apparatus both physical and institutional. Under ten headings Childe [33] has sum-

marized the characteristics of civilized life whether lived at Uruk, Mohenjo-daro, or Uxmal among the Mayans. One, the reappearance of naturalistic art, has a significance not immediately plain, and may be a little doubtful. Of the other nine, six plainly announce the growth of the technical order: (1) the great increase in the size of the settlement (the material equipment for human association becomes far larger); (2) the institution of tribute or taxation with resulting central accumulation of capital; (3) monumental public works; (4) the art of writing; (5) the beginnings of such exact and predictive sciences as arithmetic, geometry, and astronomy; and (6) developed economic institutions making possible a greatly expanded foreign trade. Each of these six suggests the increasing complexity of social organization, and the remaining three criteria explicitly declare features of that social organization which are characteristic of civilization; (7) full-time technical specialists, as in metal working; (8) a privileged ruling class; and (9) the state, or the organization of society on a basis of residence in place of, or on top of, a basis of kinship.

In folk societies the moral order predominates over the technical order. It is not possible, however, simply to reverse this statement and declare that in civilizations the technical order predominates over the moral. In civiliza-

[33] Childe, "The Urban Revolution," *Town*

*Planning Review*, **XXI** (1950), 3–17. Childe says that these ten criteria are "all deducible from archaeological data." He must include in such data written records, for several of these criteria are made known to us only through written records. And this fact reminds us of the possibility that certain of these criteria of civilization—accumulation of capital, writing (insofar as begun on perishable materials), the beginnings of science, full-time specialists possibly, and a privileged ruling class—might have had their beginnings in the life of those Middle Eastern towns that preceded the building of the first true cities.

tion the technical order certainly becomes great. But we cannot truthfully say that in civilization the moral order becomes small. There are ways in civilization in which the moral order takes on new greatness. In civilization the relations between the two orders are varying and complex.

The great transformations of humanity are only in part reported in terms of the revolutions in technology with resulting increases in the number of people living together. There have also occurred changes in the thinking and valuing of men which may also be called "radical and indeed revolutionary innovations." Like changes in the technical order, these changes in the intellectual and moral habits of men become themselves generative of far-reaching changes in the nature of human living. They do not reveal themselves in events as visible and particular as do material inventions, or even always as increasing complexity in the systems of social relationships. Nor is it perhaps possible to associate the moral transformations with limited periods of time as we can associate technological revolutions with particular spans of years. Yet the attempt to identify some of the transformations in men's minds can be made.

One might begin such an attempt by examining the manner of life of the most primitive people we know today, and perhaps also something that is told us about ancient peoples, for evidence of the appearance of forms of thought, belief, or action which a little knowledge of the history of some civilization shows us became influential in changing human life. We see some far-reaching change in the moral or intellectual life of the Western world, perhaps, and so guided we return to the primitive societies to see if it had a beginning there. So we might come to some understanding of some of the relations in history between the two kinds of orders.

As to the trend of this relationship throughout history, I have one general impression. It is that the moral order begins as something pre-eminent but incapable of changing itself, and becomes perhaps less eminent but more independent. In folk society the moral rules bend, but men cannot make them afresh. In civilization the old moral orders suffer, but new states of mind are developed by which the moral order is, to some significant degree, taken in charge. The story of the moral order is attainment of some autonomy through much adversity.

# 14

# Population Policy: Stemming the Human Tide

KINGSLEY DAVIS

One of the most crucial issues in the world today is that of population control. Faced with the undesired consequences

From 1971 Britannica Yearbook of Science and the Future. Encyclopaedia Britannica, Inc. (Chicago), pp. 400–411.

of unprecedented and accelerating human multiplication, many countries are currently trying to curb their birthrates by supporting family-planning programs. For Homo sapiens, with his unique sociocultural apparatus, has suddenly achieved such a preeminent place in the organic world that he threatens to drive out all species except those he pets or eats.

In man's history, there have probably been two major jumps in the rate of population increase. One of these came with the invention of agriculture and animal husbandry some several thousand years ago; the other came with the Industrial Revolution beginning around 1750. Of the two jumps, the second is by far the greater. Over one-fifth of the earth's entire human increase has occurred in the last 220 years—less than one-tenth of 1% of man's history. In those 220 years the population has multiplied itself more than four and one-half times. Even within the modern era, the most recent periods have seen the most rapid growth. Nearly 40% of the increase after 1750 has occurred in 10% of the time, the two decades between 1950 and 1970. The number of people added in those 20 years is equal to the entire population of the world in 1825.

It takes little skill at arithmetic to see that this trend, if allowed to continue, will give the world an unworkable population within a short time. In only 150 years the total would be 57,000,000,000. Since the 3,600,000,000 on earth today are far too many—judging by the hundreds of millions who are impoverished, illiterate, unskilled, crowded, and plagued by deteriorating air, water, and soil—the question is not will the growth stop, but how. One hopes that this can be accomplished by drastically reducing fertility. If that should fail, the inevitable result will be a calamitous resurgence of the death rate.

## The Failure of Population Control

It is obvious that current efforts to curb population are not succeeding. Between 1960 and 1970, world population rose by approximately 600 million, a 20% increase in 10 years. This eclipsed the 488 million increase (19%) of the prior decade. Even in countries that have had a population-control policy, no appreciable decline in population growth can be demonstrated. In India, for example, the government began a population-control program in 1952, but the growth of the Indian population has been more rapid since that time than before. In Taiwan the long-time downward trend in population growth, which had occurred as a result of urban-industrial development, diminished after 1964, when a huge private program became fully operational.

According to some critics, current population policies are not succeeding because they are inadequate. If so, it is an old story; these are not the first population policies to be tried, nor are they the first to fail.

In the industrially advanced nations, the 19th century was a period of rapid population growth; economic success was accompanied by demographic expansion. The peoples of northwestern Europe and their offshoots overseas multiplied faster than the rest of the world. Whereas in 1750 they had represented approximately 21% of the world's population, by 1900 they accounted for about 32%. There was much debate over this growth, but on the whole it was academic; no real effort was made to stop the increase.

Around 1870, however, the birthrate in industrial countries began a long decline that lasted until about 1933. During the depression of the 1930s, fertility reached such a low point that, had it continued at that level, the populations of the urban-industrial nations would eventually have failed to replace themselves. This virtual cessation of population growth brought widespread alarm, and deliberate government policies to raise the birthrate were instituted in several developed countries, among them Germany, Italy, Japan, Sweden, and France. These policies failed; it

**Table 1**

Modern Growth of World's Population

| YEAR | POPULATION (IN 000,000) | DOUBLING TIME (IN YEARS) |
|------|------------------------|--------------------------|
| 1750 | 791 | |
| 1850 | 1,262 | 148 |
| 1900 | 1,650 | 129 |
| 1950 | 2,515 | 82 |
| 1970 | 3,628 | 38 |

Sources: Duran, *op. cit.*, except for 1970 estimate, which is by the author.

cannot be demonstrated that any of the measures had a significant positive effect. Beginning in the late 1930s birthrates began to rise, but they rose in countries that had no special pronatalist measures as well as in those with them.

In the meantime, the locus of population growth had shifted from the industrialized nations to the less developed countries. The reason was that advanced health techniques were being exported to the poorer nations. Mortality declined far more rapidly in the less developed two-thirds of the world than it had ever done in the industrial countries; it also declined at an earlier stage of economic development and independently of local economic advance or stagnation. This was especially marked after World War II, when large-scale international aid made it possible to bring machine-age medicine even to Stone Age aborigines.

In recent decades, the population in less developed areas has been growing almost twice as fast, on the average, as the population of the industrial nations. This does not mean that the industrial nations themselves have not been growing; they all had a baby boom after World War II that contributed to the recent acceleration of world population growth. However, by far the most spectacular increase has been in the less developed countries.

In these countries the skyrocketing population is a major obstacle to eco-nomic development. But the industrial countries are not exempt from the problems of population growth. Their lesser but still rapid increase robs their economic development of a large part of its value, since an increasing share of per capita income must be spent simply in coping with the nuisances and dangers created by a rising population multiplied by a rising use of material goods.

## Beginnings of Action

In the 1950s world leaders began to advocate population control, cautiously at first but with increasing vigor. Their aim was to get governments to act in three ways. First, for the sake of population control, old rules outlawing contraceptive information were to be eliminated. Second, governments in less developed countries were urged to undertake programs to spread knowledge and use of advanced contraceptive techniques. Third, the governments of industrial nations were asked to pour money into research on improved contraceptives, to install birth-control clinics for their own poor, to use part of their economic-aid funds to finance family-planning programs in less developed countries, and to influence such international agencies as the United Nations to further similar programs.

Although Puerto Rico passed enabling legislation in 1937 for the installation of contraceptive services in public health clinics, India was the first independent nation to start a national population-control program. In December 1952, Prime Minister Jawaharlal Nehru presented to Parliament India's first five-year plan, which called for $1 million to establish family-planning clinics throughout the country. Pakistan started a similar program in 1957, followed by South Korea in 1961, the United Arab Republic in 1966, and several other countries at more recent dates. The industrial nations proved anxious to help.

Sweden, for example, after a nation-wide fund-raising campaign in 1955–56, donated $77,360 to help start a family-planning scheme in Ceylon, with Swedish doctors investigating local birth-control attitudes and then teaching methods. An agreement was signed between the two governments in 1958.

Private U.S. foundations had long been active in assisting family-planning programs. As early as 1952, the Population Council was set up as an intermediary organization through which funds could be channeled for this purpose. Increasingly, however, the U.S. government was being put under pressure to help. In 1959, after a committee appointed by Pres. Dwight D. Eisenhower to review the activities of the Agency for International Development had recommended inclusion of family planning in AID's work, the president responded that birth control was not a proper concern for government. Although Eisenhower later changed his mind, this remark, together with a statement by the Catholic bishops of America opposing any use of public funds for birth control abroad, forced a showdown on the issue. The politicians of the day generally equivocated by misinterpreting the question as one of "compelling" other countries to adopt birth control, but the leaders of the movement were in no mood to be sidetracked. As a result of their persistent efforts, in February 1965 AID finally sent instructions to its missions abroad to provide assistance in family planning, although this assistance did not include contraceptive devices or equipment for their manufacture. Nevertheless, in only six years, U.S. officials had completely reversed themselves, going from political fear of mentioning birth control to an endeavor to join with those advocating such a policy.

During this period the subject of population growth also became an issue in the United Nations. After the administration of Pres. John F. Kennedy

had joined with Sweden in urging the UN to discuss the question, the General Assembly concluded its first debate devoted entirely to population on Dec. 18, 1962. It then adopted a resolution calling for intensified international cooperation "in the population field," but birth control and population limitation were not actually mentioned. A year later, however, the UN sponsored an Asian population conference—the first such conference of governments ever held—with a mandate to make recommendations for population policies. Then, in his June 1965 speech to the UN commemorating the 20th anniversary of that organization, Pres. Lyndon B. Johnson made the now-famous statement, "Let us act on the fact that less than five dollars invested in population control is worth a hundred dollars invested in economic growth." Subsequently, in December 1966, UN Secretary-General U Thant endorsed a Declaration on Population signed by 12 heads of state (later joined by 18 others) that called attention to the seriousness of the problem and approved family planning.

Meanwhile, in the same month as President Johnson's 20th anniversary speech to the UN, the U.S. Congress began public hearings on legislation that would give to federal agencies direct responsibilities in providing birth-control facilities. This was followed, on July 18, 1969, by Pres. Richard Nixon's historic population message to Congress, in which he pointed out that "many already impoverished nations are struggling under a handicap of intense population increase." He not only offered the cooperation of the United States in strengthening population and family programs abroad but also recommended that contraceptive services in the United States be expanded. Thus, by 1969 the advocates of a U.S. government population policy that had been rejected only 10 years before had achieved victory.

**Table 2**

Population Growth in Developed Regions Versus Less Developed Regions

| DECADE | PERCENTAGE OF WORLD'S POPULATION | | RATE OF INCREASE PER DECADE | |
|---|---|---|---|---|
|  | Developed | Less Developed | Developed | Less Developed |
| 1920–40 | 26.0 | 74.0 | 8.3 | 12.4 |
| 1940–60 | 29.7 | 70.3 | 8.9 | 18.5 |
| 1960–70 | 30.8 | 69.2 | 12.6 | 22.9 |

Note: Derived from data on populations of each country every 10 years, as given in the United Nations, *Demographic Yearbook*. The countries making up the "developed" and "less developed" categories are held constant for each decade but are allowed to change from one decade to another if their development justifies it. In 1920–30 the "developed" category included Canada, the United States, Australia, New Zealand, northwest Europe, and parts of central Europe. The U.S.S.R. was added in 1930; Czechoslovakia and Japan in 1940; Argentina, Israel, Italy, and Uruguay in 1950; and Chile, Poland, South Africa, Spain, Venezuela, and Yugoslavia in 1960. The "less developed" category includes the rest of the world in each decade.

Official programs to control fertility were amazingly popular.

Just at the moment of success, however, doubt was raised that this type of action would prove effective. An article, "Population Policy: Will Current Programs Succeed?" in the Nov. 10, 1967, issue of *Science*, pointed out that, if the goal is population control, family planning is not the means. This criticism rapidly gained wide assent.

**Family Planning: Is It Enough?**

Essentially, family planning is the use of contraceptives to ensure the desired number and spacing of births. The planned parenthood movement has concentrated on research to find a 100% effective contraceptive, clinics to supply contraceptive materials and instruction, and education to induce couples to use contraception so they will have only as many children as they want. Viewed from the standpoint of population control, however, family-planning programs have a fundamental flaw: they provide control for couples but not for societies. There has been considerable confusion over this distinction. Thus, the Declaration on Population, signed by 30 world leaders and endorsed by Secretary-General U Thant, says that a "great problem threatens the world. . . . the problem of unplanned population growth." One then expects the declaration to call for *population* planning, but actually it calls only for *family* planning, stating that "the opportunity [of parents] to decide the number and spacing of children is a basic human right."

According to the critics of the family-planning approach, undesired population growth is a collective rather than an individual problem. The number of children that a couple wants is not necessarily the number that, from society's point of view, it should have. To make individual decisions add up to a desirable population trend, a nation must find ways to influence those decisions in accordance with an overall plan. Otherwise, individual planning will merely result in collective nonplanning.

To demonstrate the ineffectiveness of family-planning programs for population control, the critics cite many surveys, taken all over the world, which show that the number of offspring couples want is enough to guarantee rapid population growth. In the United

States, for example, polls taken since the 1930s indicate that white women, on the average, want more than three children, and that there is a tendency for the number to rise. In 1961 the average white female under age 30 considered 3.6 children to be the ideal family size, while 52% of the women questioned said they wanted four or more. If these desires were achieved— if couples had as many children as they say they want—the U.S. population would be growing even more rapidly than it is. And this holds true for the industrialized countries generally.

In less developed societies, the desire for children is even greater. In Taiwan in 1967, for instance, 42% of the women under 40 who already had three children said they wanted more. A 1963 survey in Turkey found that over 42% of the women wanted four or more children. In an eastern Javan village, the average size for an "ideal" family was thought to be 4.3 children; in a Delhi, India, village, 4 children; and in a Mysore, India, village, 4.2. Furthermore, urbanization in the less developed countries brought only slight reductions in the desired number of children. In Bangalore, India, a city of over a million, the number of children desired by wives was 3.7; in seven capital cities of Latin America, it averaged 3.4.

This being the case, critics of family planning see no evidence that merely furnishing couples with efficient contraceptives will control population. If nothing is done beyond making contraceptives available, the birthrate will usually be well above the zero-population-growth level and, particularly in industrialized societies, will tend to rise when economic conditions are good. Couples can "plan" big families as well as small ones.

The defenders of the family-planning approach claim that it represents a first step in population control, that it has the advantage of being religiously and politically acceptable, and that, as societies modernize, couples will voluntarily bring down fertility to a reasonable level. To this, the critics reply that family planning is a way to avoid facing up to the revolutionary social changes required to bring fertility into balance with low mortality. Obviously, people must have some means to control their fertility, but the object of that control —the desired number of children— depends on other factors.

If people are sufficiently motivated, the argument continues, they will lower their fertility even without a government program to help them. The steady fall in birthrates in industrialized countries between 1870 and 1932 occurred while governments were trying to suppress birth control. In the teeth of official opposition, people reduced their fertility by postponing marriage, by not marrying at all, by getting abortions, or by using such simple contraceptive techniques as coitus interruptus, douches, and condoms, none of which requires the services of a clinic. They did this in order to take advantage of the opportunities of an industrializing society, where social position increasingly depended on education and achievement and where children were becoming economic liabilities rather than assets.

When the depression came in the 1930s, prospects seemed so poor that people postponed marriage and childbearing to a point where the population was in imminent danger of decreasing —but still without government-sponsored birth-control services. Thus, the post-World War II baby boom cannot be interpreted as the result of a decline in contraceptive technology or services. Rather, it was due to economic prosperity, which led people to plan larger families. In short, therefore, human fertility is directly related, not to the availability of contraceptive services or technology, but to social and economic conditions. And while couples may lower their fertility if conditions become bad enough, one of the goals of population policy is to prevent the uncontrolled population growth that will make conditions so bad that having a family seems pointless.

A further argument against the family-planning approach is that it is peculiarly unsuited to less developed countries. With its emphasis on a 100% sure, medically certified and supervised contraceptive, it requires a highly organized and expensive bureaucratic apparatus, deflects attention from institutional changes that would reduce the motivation to have large families, and makes contraception itself too cumbersome. In India, for example, the program of inserting intrauterine devices was a failure. In the absence of sufficient medical personnel, side effects went untreated and were magnified, in the popular mind, by rumors. Reliable follow-up and research were impossible. Even in the United States, this emphasis on the "perfect contraceptive" led to hasty introduction of the Pill, the medical wisdom of which is only now being questioned.

## New Solutions

The proponents of the family-planning approach stress that their policy has the advantage of being purely voluntary, but its critics say it is they, not the family planners, who wish to free people from the compulsions built into the old system. The old institutions were designed to ensure that people would have enough children to offset the high death rate. If population control is to be achieved, the institutions themselves must be altered.

The general principle underlying such changes should be to release people, especially women, from the social and economic coercion to marry and reproduce, and to offer them new opportunities outside the family. Suppose a Pakistani woman is given a perfect contraceptive and advised to have only two

children. What then? For thousands of years the Oriental woman's mission in life has been to bear and rear children. Unless she is given an attractive alternative, her life after bearing two children will be so empty that she will crave more.

There are many possibilities for change. Among the old compulsions is the ban on abortions, which forces women to bear children once they are conceived. Lifting the ban and subsidizing the costs of abortion would automatically provide a birth-control method that is 100% effective, regardless of the kind of contraceptive used, if any. The traditional discrimination against women in educational and occupational spheres has the effect of forcing them back into a family role for economic and emotional satisfaction. Removal of this discrimination would enable women to develop the same absorbing career interests and outside contacts that are now available to men. Again, instead of taxing single people more heavily than married individuals, and instead of taxing families in which the wife works more heavily than those in which she does not work, the taxing authorities could do the opposite. The military authorities could cease exempting men because they are fathers.

Positive incentives by advocates of effective population control include paying people to become sterilized (now practiced in some states of India); giving couples a bond or some other payment for each year they refrain from having children; offering career fellowships to men and women who remain single; providing tax incentives and child-care facilities for the working wife; providing recreational facilities and social life around the place of work; and giving special housing, recreational, and other advantages to childless people.

It is to be hoped that, if the traditional compulsions were removed and new and attractive alternatives to reproduction were provided, the birthrate could be reduced sufficiently to avoid the need for direct compulsory measures. If compulsory measures had to be adopted, they could be of two kinds: those relating to marriage and those relating specifically to reproduction. Couples might be required to furnish evidence of economic ability to support a family before being allowed to marry —a condition that would cause many marriages to be postponed or avoided. In addition, illegitimate pregnancy could be penalized, the girl being required to secure an abortion and the father being punished. Finally, women might be forbidden to have more than four children. In the United States during the four years 1965–68, nearly 15% of all births were of the fifth or higher order. If no woman with four children had been allowed to have another, the birthrate would have been 15.6 per 1,000 population instead of the actual 18.3, and the net reproduction rate—the generation replacement rate —would have been only 8% above unity instead of 27%.

Mention of such policies, whether of the positive or the punitive variety, seems immoral to many people. This is because traditional morality encourages reproduction. It is a system of inducing people to marry, rear children, and value family life. Any policy that will effectively discourage reproduction is therefore revolutionary. This is why no government, as yet, has seriously tried to achieve zero population growth.

The critics of the purely family-planning approach to population control are probably right, but the family planners, because they advocate only minimum changes in existing institutions and because they generally go along with religious beliefs and dogmas, are more readily accepted. It may be that, in the long run, the problems of population growth will force the adoption of effective control policies. As things stand, however, one can only conclude that any efforts likely to be made in the foreseeable future will be too feeble to avoid catastrophic rises in the death rate brought on by over-population.

## For Additional Reading:

1. BERELSON, BERNARD, et al. (ed.), *Family Planning and Population Programs* (University of Chicago Press, 1966).
2. BLAKE, JUDITH, "Population Policy for Americans: Is the Government Being Misled?," *Science* (May 2, 1969, pp. 522–529).
3. DAVIS, KINGSLEY, "Population Policy: Will Current Programs Succeed?," *Science* (Nov. 10, 1967, pp. 730–739).
4. DURAND, JOHN D., "The Modern Expansion of World Population," *Proceedings of the American Philosophical Society*, vol. iii, no. 3 (June 1967).
5. ERLICH, PAUL R., and ERLICH, ANNE H., *Population, Resources, Environment* (W. H. Freeman, 1970).
6. NAM, CHARLES B. (ed.), *Population and Society: A Textbook of Reading* (Houghton Mifflin, 1968).
7. PETERSON, WILLIAM, *Population*, 2nd ed. (Macmillan, 1969).

# 15

# Toward a Theory of Revolution

## JAMES C. DAVIES

In exhorting proletarians of all nations to unite in revolution, because they had nothing to lose but their chains, Marx and Engels most succinctly presented that theory of revolution which is recognized as their brain child. But this most famed thesis, that progressive degradation of the industrial working class would finally reach the point of despair and inevitable revolt, is not the only one that Marx fathered. In at least one essay he gave life to a quite antithetical idea. He described, as a precondition of widespread unrest, not progressive degradation of the proletariat but rather an improvement in workers' economic condition which did not keep pace with the growing welfare of capitalists and therefore produced social tension.

A noticeable increase in wages presupposes a rapid growth of productive capital. The rapid growth of productive capital brings about an equally rapid growth of wealth, luxury, social wants, social enjoyments. Thus, although the enjoyments of the workers have risen, the social satisfaction that they give has fallen in comparison with the increased enjoyments of the capitalist, which are inaccessible to the worker, in comparison with the state of development of society in general. Our desires and pleasures spring from society; we measure them, therefore, by society and not by the objects which serve for their satisfaction. Because they are of a social nature, they are of a relative nature.[1]

From the *American Sociological Review* (February 1962), pp. 5–19. Reprinted by permission.
[1] Karl Marx and Frederick Engels, "Wage Labour and Capital," *Selected Works in Two Volumes*, Moscow: Foreign Languages Publishing House, 1955, vol. 1, p. 94.

Marx's qualification here of his more frequent belief that degradation produces revolution is expressed as the main thesis by de Tocqueville in his study of the French Revolution. After a long review of economic and social decline in the seventeenth century and dynamic growth in the eighteenth, de Tocqueville concludes:

So it would appear that the French found their condition the more unsupportable in proportion to its improvement. . . . Revolutions are not always brought about by a gradual decline from bad to worse. Nations that have endured patiently and almost unconsciously the most overwhelming oppression often burst into rebellion against the yoke the moment it begins to grow lighter. The regime which is destroyed by a revolution is almost always as improvement on its immediate predecessor. . . . Evils which are patiently endured when they seem inevitable become intolerable when once the idea of escape from them is suggested.[2]

On the basis of de Tocqueville and Marx, we can choose one of these ideas or the other, which makes it hard to decide just when revolutions are more likely to occur—when there has been social and economic progress or when there has been regress. It appears that both ideas have explanatory and possibly predictive value, if there are juxtaposed and put in the proper time sequence.

Revolutions are most likely to occur

[2] A. de Tocqueville, *The Old Regime and the French Revolution* (trans. by John Bonner), N. Y.: Harper & Bros., 1856, p. 214.

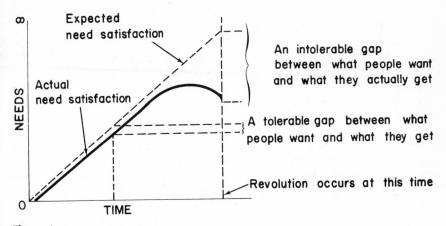

**Figure 1**
Need satisfaction and revolution.

when a prolonged period of objective economic and social development is followed by a short period of sharp reversal.[3] The all-important effect on the minds of people in a particular society is to produce, during the former period, an expectation of continued ability to satisfy needs—which continue to rise—and, during the latter, a mental state of anxiety and frustration when manifest reality breaks away from anticipated reality. The actual state of socioeconomic development is less significant than the expectation that past progress, now blocked, can and must continue in the future.

Political stability and instability are ultimately dependent on a state of mind, a mood, in a society. Satisfied or apathetic people who are poor in goods, status, and power can remain politically quiet and their opposites can revolt, just as, correlatively and more probably, dissatisfied poor can revolt and satisfied rich oppose revolution. It is the dissatisfied state of mind rather than the tangible provision of "ade-

quate" or "inadequate" supplies of food, equality, or liberty which produces the revolution. In actuality, there must be a joining of forces between dissatisfied, frustrated people who differ in their degree of objective, tangible welfare and status. Well-fed, well-educated, high-status individuals who rebel in the face of apathy among the objectively deprived can accomplish at most a coup d'état. The objectively deprived, when faced with solid opposition of people of wealth, status, and power, will be smashed in their rebellion as were peasants and Anabaptists by German noblemen in 1525 and East Germans by the Communist élite in 1953.

Before appraising this general notion in light of a series of revolutions, a word is in order as to why revolutions ordinarily do not occur when a society is generally impoverished—when, as de Tocqueville put it, evils that seem inevitable are patiently endured. They are endured in the extreme case because the physical and mental energies of people are totally employed in the process of merely staying alive.

. . . . . . . . . .

A revolutionary state of mind re-

[3] Revolutions are here defined as violent civil disturbances that cause the displacement of one ruling group by another that has a broader popular basis for support.

quires the continued, even habitual but dynamic expectation of greater opportunity to satisfy basic needs, which may range from merely physical (food, clothing, shelter, health, and safety from bodily harm) to social (the affectional ties of family and friends) to the need for equal dignity and justice. But the necessary additional ingredient is a persistent, unrelenting threat to the satisfaction of these needs: not a threat which actually returns people to a state of sheer survival but which puts them in the mental state where they believe they will not be able to satisfy one or more basic needs. Although physical deprivation in some degree may be threatened on the eve of all revolutions, it need not be the prime factor, as it surely was not in the American Revolution of 1775. The crucial factor is the vague or specific fear that ground gained over a long period of time will be quickly lost. This fear does not generate if there is continued opportunity to satisfy continually emerging needs; it generates when the existing government suppresses or is blamed for suppressing such opportunity.

. . . . . . . . . . .

## The Russian Revolution of 1917

In Russia's tangled history it is hard to decide when began the final upsurge of expectations that, when frustrated, produced the cataclysmic events of 1917. One can truly say that the real beginning was the slow modernization process begun by Peter the Great over two hundred years before the revolution. And surely the rationalist currents from France that slowly penetrated Russian intellectual life during the reign of Catherine the Great a hundred years before the revolution were necessary, lineal antecedents of the 1917 revolution.

Without denying that there was an accumulation of forces over at least a

200-year period,[4] we may nonetheless date the final upsurge as beginning with the 1861 emancipation of serfs and reaching a crest in the 1905 revolution.

The chronic and growing unrest of serfs before their emancipation in 1861 is an ironic commentary on the Marxian notion that human beings are what social institutions make them. Although serfdom had been shaping their personality since 1647, peasants became increasingly restive in the second quarter of the nineteenth century. The continued discontent of peasants after emancipation is an equally ironic commentary on the belief that relieving one profound frustration produces enduring contentment. Peasants rather quickly got over their joy at being untied from the soil after two hundred years. Instead of declining, rural violence increased. Having gained freedom but not much free land, peasants now had to rent or buy land to survive: virtual personal slavery was exchanged for financial servitude. Land pressure grew, reflected in a doubling of land prices between 1868 and 1897.

It is hard thus to tell whether the economic plight of peasants was much lessened after emancipation. A 1903 government study indicated that even with a normal harvest, average food intake per peasant was 30 per cent below the minimum for health. The only sure contrary item of evidence is that the peasant population grew, indicating at least increased ability of the land to support life . . .

The land-population pressure pushed people into towns and cities, where the rapid growth of industry truly afforded the chance for economic betterment.

[4] There is an excellent summary in B. Brutzkus, "The Historical Peculiarities of the Social and Economic Development of Russia," in R. Bendix and S. M. Lipset, *Class, Status, and Power*, Glencoe, Ill.: The Free Press, 1953, pp. 517–540.

One estimate of net annual income for a peasant family of five in the rich blackearth area in the late nineteenth century was 82 rubles. In contrast, a "good" wage for a male factory worker was about 168 rubles per year. It was this difference in the degree of poverty that produced almost a doubling of the urban population between 1878 and 1897. The number of industrial workers increased almost as rapidly. The city and the factory gave new hope. Strikes in the 1880s were met with brutal suppression but also with the beginning of factory legislation, including the requirement that wages be paid regularly and the abolition of child labor. The burgeoning proletariat remained comparatively contented until the eve of the 1905 revolution.

There is additional, non-economic evidence to support the view that 1861 to 1905 was the period of rising expectations that preceded the 1917 revolution. The administration of justice before the emancipation had largely been carried out by noblemen and landowners who embodied the law for their peasants. In 1864 justice was in principle no longer delegated to such private individuals. Trials became public, the jury system was introduced, and judges got tenure. Corporal punishment was alleviated by the elimination of running the gauntlet, lashing, and branding; caning persisted until 1904. Public joy at these reforms was widespread. For the intelligentsia, there was increased opportunity to think and write and to criticize established institutions, even sacrosanct absolutism itself.

But Tsarist autocracy had not quite abandoned the scene. Having inclined but not bowed, in granting the inevitable emancipation as an act not of justice but grace, it sought to maintain its absolutist principle by conceding reform without accepting anything like democratic authority. Radical political and economic criticism surged higher. Some strong efforts to raise the somewhat lowered floodgates began as early as 1866, after an unsuccessful attempt was made on the life of Alexander II, in whose name serfs had just gained emancipation. When the attempt succeeded fifteen years later, there was increasing state action under Alexander III to limit constantly rising expectations. By suppression and concession, the last Alexander succeeded in dying naturally in 1894.

When it became apparent that Nicholas II shared his father's ideas but not his forcefulness, opposition of the intelligentsia to absolutism joined with the demands of peasants and workers, who remained loyal to the Tsar but demanded economic reforms. Starting in 1904, there developed a "League of Deliverance" that coordinated efforts of at least seventeen other revolutionary, proletarian, or nationalist groups within the empire. Consensus on the need for drastic reform, both political and economic, established a many-ringed circus of groups sharing the same tent. These groups were geographically distributed from Finland to Armenia and ideologically from liberal constitutionalists to revolutionaries made prudent by the contrast between their own small forces and the power of Tsardom.

Events of 1904–5 mark the general downward turning point of expectations, which people increasingly saw as frustrated by the continuation of Tsardom. Two major and related occurrences made 1905 the point of no return. The first took place on the Bloody Sunday of January 22, 1905, when peaceful proletarian petitioners marched on the St. Petersburg palace and were killed by the hundreds. The myth that the Tsar was the gracious protector of his subjects, however surrounded he might be by malicious advisers, was quite shattered. The reac-

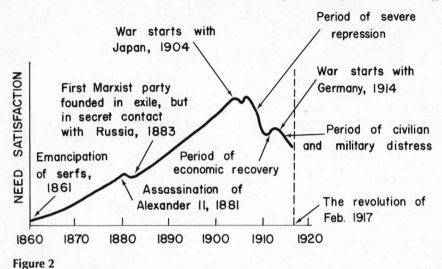

**Figure 2**

tion was immediate, bitter, and pro-longed and was not at all confined to the working class. Employers, mer-chants, and white-collar officials joined in the burgeoning of strikes which brought the economy to a virtual stand-still in October. Some employers even continued to pay wages to strikers. University students and faculties joined the revolution. After the great October strike, the peasants ominously sided with the workers and engaged in riots and assaults on landowners. Until peas-ants became involved, even some land-owners had sided with the revolution.

The other major occurrence was the disastrous defeat of the Russian army and navy in the 1904–5 war with Japan. Fundamentally an imperialist venture aspiring to hegemony over the people of Asia, the war was not regarded as a people's but as a Tsar's war, to save and spread absolutism. The military defeat itself probably had less portent than the return of shattered soldiers from a fight that was not for them. Hundreds of thousands, wounded or not, returned from the war as a visible, vocal, and ugly reminder to the entire populace of the weakness and selfish-ness of Tsarist absolutism.

The years from 1905 to 1917 formed an almost relentless procession of in-creasing misery and despair. Promising at last a constitutional government, the Tsar, in October, 1905, issued from on high a proclamation renouncing abso-lutism, granting law-making power to a duma, and guaranteeing freedom of speech, assembly, and association. The first two dumas, of 1906 and 1907, were dissolved for recalcitrance. The third was made pliant by reduced rep-resentation of workers and peasants and by the prosecution and conviction of protestants in the first two. The brief period of a free press was succeeded in 1907 by a reinstatement of censor-ship and confiscation of prohibited pub-lications. Trial of offenders against the Tsar was now conducted by courts martial. Whereas there had been only 26 executions of the death sentence, in the 13 years of Alexander II's firm rule (1881–94), there were 4,449 in the years 1905–10, in six years of Nicholas II's soft regimen.

But this "white terror," which caused despair among the workers and intelli-gentsia in the cities, was not the only face of misery. For the peasants, there was a bad harvest in 1906 followed by continued crop failures in several areas in 1907. To forestall action by the dumas, Stolypin decreed a series of agrarian reforms designed to break up the power of the rural communes by individualizing land ownership. Between these acts of God and government, peasants were so preoccupied with hunger or self-aggrandizement as to be dulled in their sensitivity to the revolutionary appeals of radical organizers.

After more than five years of degrading terror and misery, in 1910 the country appeared to have reached a condition of exhaustion. Political strikes had fallen off to a new low. As the economy recovered, the insouciance of hopelessness set in. Amongst the intelligentsia the mood was hedonism, or despair that often ended in suicide. Industrialists aligned themselves with the government. Workers worked. But an upturn of expectations, inadequately quashed by the police, was evidenced by a recrudescence of political strikes which, in the first half of 1914—on the eve of war—approached the peak of 1905. They sharply diminished during 1915 but grew again in 1916 and became a general strike in February 1917.

Figure 2 indicates the lesser waves in the tidal wave whose first trough is at the end of serfdom in 1861 and whose second is at the end of Tsardom in 1917. This fifty-six year period appears to constitute a single long phase in which popular gratification at the termination of one institution (serfdom) rather quickly was replaced with rising expectations which resulted from intensified industrialization and which were incompatible with the continuation of the inequitable and capricious power structure of Tsarist society. The small trough of frustration during the repression that followed the assassination of Alexander II seems to have only briefly interrupted the rise in popular demand

for more goods and more power. The trough in 1904 indicates the consequences of war with Japan. The 1905–6 trough reflects the repression of January 22, and after, and is followed by economic recovery. The final downturn, after the first year of war, was a consequence of the dislocations of the German attack on all kinds of concerted activities other than production for the prosecution of the war. Patriotism and governmental repression for a time smothered discontent. The inflation that developed in 1916 when goods, including food, became severely scarce began to make workers self-consciously discontented. The conduct of the war, including the growing brutality against reluctant, ill-provisioned troops, and the enormous loss of life, produced the same bitter frustration in the army. When civilian discontent reached the breaking point in February, 1917, it did not take long for it to spread rapidly into the armed forces. Thus began the second phase of the revolution that really started in 1905 and ended in death to the Tsar and Tsardom—but not to absolutism—when the Bolsheviks gained ascendancy over the moderates in October. A centuries-long history of absolutism appears to have made this post-Tsarist phase of it tragically inevitable.

## The Egyptian Revolution of 1952

The final slow upsurge of expectations in Egypt that culminated in the revolution began when that society became a nation in 1922, with the British grant of limited independence. British troops remained in Egypt to protect not only the Suez Canal but also, ostensibly, to prevent foreign aggression. The presence of foreign troops served only to heighten nationalist expectations, which were excited by the Wafd, the political organization that formed public opinion on national rather than religious grounds and helped establish a fairly unified community—in striking contrast to late-nineteenth century Russia.

But nationalist aspirations were not the only rising expectations in Egypt of the 1920s and 1930s. World War I had spurred industrialization, which opened opportunities for peasants to improve, somewhat, their way of life by working for wages in the cities and also opened great opportunities for entrepreneurs to get rich. The moderately wealthy got immoderately so in commodity market speculation, finance, and manufacture, and the uprooted peasants who were now employed, or at any rate living, in cities were relieved of at least the notion that poverty and boredom must be the will of Allah. But the incongruity of a money-based modern semi-feudality that was like a chariot with a gasoline engine evidently escaped the attention of ordinary people. The generation of the 1930s could see more rapid progress, even for themselves, than their parents had even envisioned. If conditions remained poor, they could always be blamed on the British, whose economic and military power remained visible and strong.

Economic progress continued, though unevenly, during World War II. Conventional exports, mostly cotton, actually declined, not even reaching depression levels until 1945, but direct employment by Allied military forces reached a peak of over 200,000 during the most intense part of the African war. Exports after the war rose steadily until 1948, dipped, and then rose sharply to a peak in 1951 as a consequence of the Korean war. But in 1945 over 250,000 wage earners—probably a third of the working force—became jobless. The cost of living by 1945 had risen to three times the index of 1937. Manual laborers were hit by unemployment; white collar workers and professionals probably more by inflation than unemployment. Meanwhile the number of millionaires in pounds sterling had increased eight times during the war.

Frustrations, exacerbated during the war by German and thereafter by Soviet propaganda, were at first deflected against the British but gradually shifted closer to home. Egyptian agitators began quoting the Koran in favor of a just, equalitarian society and against great differences in individual wealth. There was an ominous series of strikes, mostly in the textile mills, from 1945–8.

At least two factors stand out in the postponement of revolution. The first was the insatiable postwar world demand for cotton and textiles and the second was the surge of solidarity with king and country that followed the 1948 invasion of the new state of Israel. Israel now supplemented England as an object of deflected frustration. The disastrous defeat a year later, by a new nation with but a fifteenth of Egypt's population, was the beginning of the end. This little war had struck the peasant at his hearth, when a shortage of wheat and of oil for stoves provided a daily reminder of a weak and corrupt government. The defeat frustrated popular hopes for national glory and—with even more portent—humiliated the army and solidified it against the bureaucracy and the palace which had profiteered at the expense of national honor. In 1950 began for the first time a direct and open propaganda attack against the king himself. A series of peasant uprisings, even on the lands of the king, took place in 1951 along with some 49 strikes in the cities. The skyrocketing demand for cotton after the start of the Korean War in June, 1950 was followed by a collapse in March, 1952. The uncontrollable or uncontrolled riots in Cairo, on January 26, 1952, marked the fiery start of the revolution. The officers' coup in the early morning of July 23 only made it official.

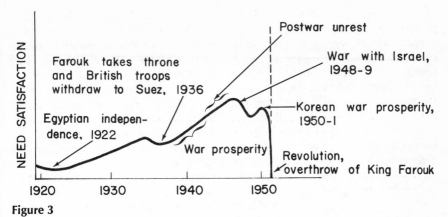

**Figure 3**

## Other Revolutions

The curve of rising expectations followed by their effective frustration is applicable to other revolutions and rebellions than just the three already considered. Leisler's Rebellion in the royal colony of New York in 1689 was a brief dress-rehearsal for the American Revolution eighty-six years later. In an effort to make the colony serve the crown better, duties had been raised and were being vigorously collected. The tanning of hides in the colony was forbidden, as was the distillation of liquor. An embargo was placed on unmilled grain, which hurt the farmers. After a long period of economic growth and substantial political autonomy, these new and burdensome regulations produced a popular rebellion that for a year displaced British sovereignty.

The American Revolution itself fits the J-curve and deserves more than the brief mention here given. Again prolonged economic growth and political autonomy produced continually rising expectations. They became acutely frustrated when, following the French and Indian War (which had cost England so much and the colonies so little), England began a series of largely economic regulations having the same purpose as those directed against New York

in the preceding century. From the 1763 Proclamation (closing to settlement land west of the Appalachians) to the Coercive Acts of April, 1774 (which among other things, in response to the December, 1773 Boston Tea Party, closed tight the port of Boston), Americans were beset with unaccustomed manifestations of British power and began to resist forcibly in 1775, on the Lexington-Concord road. A significant decline in trade with England in 1772 may have hastened the maturation of colonial rebelliousness.

The curve also fits the French Revolution, which again merits more mention than space here permits. Growing rural prosperity, marked by steadily rising land values in the eighteenth century, had progressed to the point where a third of French land was owned by peasant-proprietors. There were the beginnings of large-scale manufacture in the factory system. Constant pressure by the bourgeoisie against the state for reforms was met with considerable hospitality by a government already shifting from its old landed-aristocratic and clerical base to the growing middle class. Counter to these trends, which would *per se* avoid revolution, was the feudal reaction of the mid-eighteenth century, in which the dying nobility sought in numerous nagging ways to retain and reactivate its perquisites against a resentful peasantry and importunate bourgeoisie.

But expectations apparently continued rising until the growing opportunities and prosperity rather abruptly halted, about 1787. The fiscal crisis of the government is well known, much of it a consequence of a 1.5 billion livre deficit following intervention against Britain in the American war of independence. The threat to tax the nobility severely—after its virtual tax immunity—and the bourgeoisie more severely may indeed be said to have precipitated the revolution. But less well-known is the fact that 1787 was a bad harvest year and 1788 even worse; that by July, 1789 bread prices were higher than they had been in over 70 years; that an ill-timed trade treaty with England depressed the prices of French textiles; that a concurrent bumper grape crop depressed wine prices—all with the result of making desperate the plight of the large segment of the population now dependent on other producers for food. They had little money to buy even less bread. Nobles and bourgeosie were alienated from the government by the threat of taxation; workers and some peasants by the threat of starvation. A long period of halting but real progress for virtually all segments of the population was now abruptly ended in seqeunce of the government's efforts to meet its deficit and of economic crisis resulting from poor crops and poor tariff policy.

. . . . . . . . .

## Some Conclusions

The notion that revolutions need both a period of rising expectations and a succeeding period in which they are frustrated qualifies substantially the main Marxian notion that revolutions occur after progressive degradation and the de Tocqueville notion that they occur when conditions are improving.

By putting de Tocqueville before Marx but without abandoning either theory, we are better able to plot the antecedents of at least the disturbances here described.

Half of the general, if not common, sense of this revised notion lies in the uttter improbability of a revolution occurring in a society where there is the continued, unimpeded opportunity to satisfy new needs, new hopes, new expectations. Would Dorr's rebellion have become such if the established electorate and government had readily acceded to the suffrage demands of the unpropertied? Would the Russian Revolution have taken place if the Tsarist autocracy had, quite out of character, truly granted the popular demands for constitutional democracy in 1905? Would the Cairo riots of January, 1952 and the subsequent coup actually have occurred if Britain had departed from Egypt and if the Egyptian monarchy had established an equitable tax system and in other ways alleviated the poverty of urban masses and the shame of the military?

The other half of the sense of the notion has to do with the improbability of revolution taking place where there has been no hope, no period in which expectations have risen. Such a stability of expectations presupposes a static state of human aspirations that sometimes exists but is rare. Stability of expectations is not a stable social condition. Such was the case of American Indians (at least from our perspective) and perhaps Africans before white men with Bibles, guns, and other goods interrupted the stability of African society. Egypt was in such a condition, vis-à-vis modern aspirations, before Europe became interested in building a canal. Such stasis was the case in Nazi concentration camps, where conformism reached the point of inmates cooperating with guards even when the inmates were told to lie down so that they could be shot. But in the latter case there was a society with externally induced complete despair, and even in these camps there were occasional rebellions of sheer desperation. It is of course true that in a society less regimented than concentration camps, the rise of expectations can be frustrated successfully, thereby defeating rebellion just as the satisfaction of expectations does. This, however, requires the uninhibited exercise of brute force as it was used in suppressing the Hungarian rebellion of 1956. Failing the continued ability and persistent will of a ruling power to use such force, there appears to be no sure way to avoid revolution short of an effective, affirmative, and continuous response on the part of established governments to the almost continuously emerging needs of the governed.

# Part Two

# Industrial Society and the Origins of Sociology

## INTRODUCTION

Sociology was founded by a number of thinkers who lived through the last great transformation of Western European life, the change from agrarian society to modern industrial capitalism, which took place approximately between the years of 1780 and 1850. E. J. Hobsbawm has called this period the age of the "dual revolution." [1] During this time the industrial revolution took place in England and industrial capitalism gradually spread from there to the Continent, replacing preindustrial economies. The French Revolution of 1789 destroyed the old political regime of the monarchy and the nobility and replaced it with the first modern republican form of national government, and the idea of the modern democratic nation state was carried over much of the rest of Europe by the conquering Republican armies of Napoleon.

The first sociologists—Henri Comte de Saint-Simon and Auguste Comte in France, Herbert Spencer in England, and Karl Marx, the German who wrote his early works in Paris and his later studies in London—all lived through some part of this period of upheaval and revolution which brought about a total transformation of social life for Western man. The forms of this new society—commercial capitalism, the new machine technology, the large industrial city, and the modern nation state, with its elected representative government—gradually spread from France and England to Central and Southern Europe, Southern Scandinavia, and across the Atlantic to North America. The "second generation" of classical sociologists, including Emile Durkheim in France; Max Weber, Ferdinand Toennies, and Georg Simmel in Germany; and William Graham Sumner in the United States, experienced the later effects of these new social forces and analyzed their development and consequences for the lives of their contemporaries. These men were deeply and personally concerned with the problems the new social forms created for living what they considered a decent human life. Most of them viewed the scientific analysis of social life as a way of providing men with the knowledge necessary to improve their collective life.[2]

---

[1] E. J. Hobsbawm, *The Age of Revolution, 1789–1848* (New York and Cleveland: The World Publishing Company, 1962).
[2] Herbert Spencer and William Graham Sumner must be excepted from this concern. As strict social Darwinists, they felt men should not presume to interfere with the natural and necessary course of the development of society or social evolution.

Emile Durkheim's description of the life and work of Saint-Simon, whom he considers the first man to engage in systematic sociological analysis, shows all these aspects of classical sociology. Saint-Simon himself lived through the French Revolution and was transformed by it from a feudal nobleman to first a capitalist entrepreneur and then a student of the new society, known then as a "social philosopher." Saint-Simon's "philosophies," however, as Durkheim makes clear, were astute analyses of the social forces developing in European feudal society which eventually brought about the demise of that society and the rise of modern urban-industrial society. There were two main forces that Saint-Simon believed responsible for undermining and eventually destroying the old order in Europe. One of these was the free villages, communities which bought their political freedom from the feudal nobility and the medieval clergy and established themselves as centers of trade and handicraft manufacturing. Second, there were the physical and biological sciences, brought to Europe by the conquering Arabs at the apex of Islamic civilization and left in Europe after the waning of Saracen influence. The old society, he said, contained within it the seeds of the new, in the form of commerce and science, and therefore the seeds of its own destruction. Following the analytic history in which Saint-Simon explains how these forces helped bring about the transformation from feudal to modern society, Durkheim shows that he was concerned over the apparent instability of the new society and the problems this created for people living in this time of transition. Saint-Simon tried to discover the sources of this instability and thought he found some of them in the fact that lawyers, a group of functionaries developed in agrarian society to mediate the interests of the nobility and those of the rising commercial and industrial groups, dominated the postrevolutionary government of France. The new society, Saint-Simon said, was predominantly an industrial society, one in which the principal activity was production. As such, it could only be run effectively by those engaged in this activity—those he called the "industrials," meaning all those who carried on economically, and intellectually, productive activities. Saint-Simon's later works, Durkheim points out, contained the outlines of the industrially based organization of society which he felt had to replace the old political order before stability could be restored to European society.

Karl Marx spent his lifetime studying the new society of industrial capitalism, first in Germany, then in France, and finally in England, where he spent most of his working life and where he wrote his monumental three-volume study *Capital* There is only one small passage in all the volumes he produced, many of them with the help of his friend Friedrich Engels, in which Marx gives a formal statement of his theory of social structure and change. In this, a passage from *An Introduction to the Critique of Political Economy*, which is reprinted in this section, Marx presents the classic statement of the materialist theory of social structure and historical change. This is what might be called an "architectural" theory of the social structure in which all the institutions and activities of the society, such as the family, religion, politics, science, and philosophy, are seen to be built upon the foundation of the society's economy by the basic groups, social classes, which develop from the economy. The economy is seen as the "basic" institution in that it connects the society with its natural environment through the sustenance-producing activities of the group. The economy includes the technology available to the group and the division of labor, through which different people specialize in different aspects of the economic activities. Out of this division of labor develops the class system, which Marx sees as always containing two major classes—the owners of the means of economic production, such as land and tools, and the people who actually carry on the labor of economic production— the slaves in ancient society, the serfs in feudal society, and the wage laborers of capitalist society. It is out of this basic social structure, the class system, that all the other institutions of society develop, including the kinship system, the political system, and organized religion. All of society, then, reflects the basic class division, and Marx maintains that the important institutions, such as government and law, are controlled by the owning class, which becomes then the "ruling class," because the government represents their interests whenever they are opposed to those of the other classes. Social change occurs, in this theory, when changes in the economy and the technology lead to the development of a new division of labor, which gives birth to new social classes which become powerful and eventually challenge the ruling class for control of society, overthrow it, and establish themselves as the ruling class.

Marx and Engels, in the excerpt from *The Communist Manifesto* reprinted in this section, provide an example of this process in their analysis of how the bourgeoisie, or the commercial and manufacturing middle class, rose to power and created modern capitalist society. The bourgeoisie came into being with the development of trade and industry in the Middle Ages; eventually became strong enough, in numbers, money, and power, to challenge the political control of the nobility, clergy, and the monarchy; and eventually overthrew these ruling classes, establishing the new society of industrial capitalism. They became the ruling class and the economy which they represented, that of modern industry, became the dominant economic system of Western European countries. At the time Marx and Engels were writing, the middle of the nineteenth century, conditions of life for the urban factory workers in the industrial countries were probably at their worst. Open rebellions had been staged by hungry, overworked, and underpaid workers in the major industrial cities of England and France. Marx and Engels felt these uprisings were the beginning of the next revolutionary movement in history, one in which the proletariat, or working class, of the industrial countries would organize themselves, overthrow the bourgeois governments, and take control of these societies. They felt this would be a kind of "end of history," because the proletariat in capitalist society were the last exploited, underdog social class, and the society which they would create would be a classless society which would no longer breed exploitation and revolutionary change.

Max Weber, looking back on the origins of capitalism from the perspective of a century and a half, discerned another social force which had developed in the preindustrial society of Europe and which he felt had helped to create the society of modern industrial capitalism. This force was ascetic Protestantism, as preached and practiced by John Calvin, Martin Luther, and their followers. Weber was convinced that the modern European merchant and manufacturer was a unique kind of person in world history, and that ascetic Protestantism was responsible for some of the economically crucial character traits of this "new" man. Middle-class Protestants from the mid-fifteenth century on were relatively free men; they were generally engaged in individual business enterprises, they were not tied by bonds of slavery or serfdom to any master, and of course, they did not owe allegiance to the Pope and the hierarchy of the Roman Catholic Church, as did all other Europeans except the Jews. However, Weber points out, they created for themselves a bondage of another kind, that of the strict moral codes of early Protestant doctrines. This new moral code, or "Protestant ethic," as Weber calls it, had a great deal to do with the development of what he calls the spirit of modern capitalism. In the excerpt included here from Weber's book on this subject, he points out that the early Protestant (and he stresses these as characteristics of *early* Protestants, not necessarily Protestants of today, and not necessarily found *only* among Protestants today) believed that a lifetime of hard work in an occupation to which a person was "called" was the kind of behavior most pleasing to God. Protestants came to believe, Weber says, that success in worldly business endeavors was a sign that a man was looked upon with favor by God and would probably go to heaven after he died. At the same time, the Protestant was strictly forbidden to live in luxury or to make ostentatious display of material wealth. This meant, Weber says, that the Protestant capitalist, as distinct from capitalists who had appeared at previous times in world history, could not spend his profits on consumption for himself and his family. He was supposed to live austerely, or at least plainly, for too much comfort, it was believed, might make him slothful. The combined forces of the drive toward profit making as a sign of God's favor and the ban on spending for personal consumption beyond life's necessities led the Protestant capitalist to reinvest his profits. This reinvestment of profits in the business meant, of course, the expansion of the business and led to a cycle of economic growth which eventually made capitalism the dominant form of economic activity in Europe and created the large capital investments required in modern industrial economies. Protestantism even had a hand in providing labor for the business and industry of the capitalists, Weber feels, because Protestants who were not businessmen were enjoined by their ethic to work hard and diligently whatever their occupation. Protestant belief thus contributed to the creation of the disciplined industrial labor force needed for the modern economy.

The classical sociologists, as we have just seen, were interested in discovering how the modern world had come into being. They observed their societies to discover their dominant characteristics—industrial technology, capitalist market economies, large industrial cities, and republican nation states. Then they asked, "How did these arise?"—a question which led them into analytic history and comparative sociology. These same sociologists also asked another question, of equal importance in their own minds, which was, "What does it mean for the individual person to have to live in such a society?"

Erich Fromm explains very clearly the concept of "alienation" that Karl Marx developed in his early writings, while he was still living in Paris, to describe the consequences for the individual of life under industrial capitalism. In this society, Marx said, the workers in industry, who are a majority of the population, are "separated" from the product of their labor because they do not own it. Rather, the capitalist who owns the factory and buys their labor owns (or "expropriates," to use Marx's stronger term) what they produce, the product of their labor. Under capitalism, then, man is alienated from the product of his labor. But if this is true, man is also alienated from his work as an activity, because it does not bring him anything which is his, says Marx. One of Marx's basic philosophic assumptions, which he shares with many of the thinkers of his day and of our own day, is that work is man's basic self-defining activity: man *is Homo faber*, the animal that produces the means of his own livelihood. To remove intrinsic meaning from man's work, Marx believed, is to remove the keystone of meaning from his life. When work becomes meaningless, life becomes meaningless, and Marx felt that almost all work becomes meaningless in the economy of industrial capitalism

This concept of alienation has recently gained new popularity in industrial societies, both capitalist and socialist. It has, it would seem, a wider relevance than Marx himself gave it. It appears that the minute division of labor and the great size of industrial bureaucracies in all modern societies make it difficult for individuals to find meaning in their work. Psychologists, philosophers, and sociologists in such diverse modern nations as Poland, France, Yugoslavia, and the United States are studying this problem in its contemporary form: How modern industrial societies can be organized so that meaningful, self-defining, creative activities are available to individuals.

Modern societies have been referred to by sociologists as urban-industrial societies because they regard urbanism and industrialism as the defining characteristics of these societies. The early German sociologist Ferdinand Toennies observed the decline of peasant villages and the rise of cities and described this transition in his book *Gemeinschaft und Gesellschaft* (*Community and Society*), one of the classic sociological studies.[3] Georg Simmel, another German, outlined some of the consequences of urban life for the individual in his famous essay included here. The city dweller, Simmel says, is bombarded daily by a great multitude of stimuli, or sensory perceptions. The human psyche cannot, Simmel thinks, respond to all the sensory stimuli of the urban environment, so the urbanite must develop protective mechanisms. These involve a highly selective intellectual apparatus for deciding which stimuli call for a response and which do not, accompanied by a detached, blasé attitude toward the world. A major part of the "psychic stimulation" of the urban environment is, of course, provided by the great numbers of people with whom the city dweller comes briefly into contact. Under such conditions, Simmel contends, people soon become callous toward others, for it is just not possible to respond in a warm and friendly way to such large numbers of people or to be concerned about them in any genuine way. In fact, Simmel argues that this callousness actually masks a latent hostility toward other people which urban life produces in individuals. At the same time, Simmel points out, the city makes possible freedom which people cannot find in small communities where everyone knows everyone else, and everyone else's business. The privacy and freedom of action found in the city provide the person with greater chances to develop his individuality.

Emile Durkheim's study *Suicide*, from which an extract is reprinted here, is an acknowledged landmark of sociological research. In it Durkheim conceptualizes the act of killing oneself in sociological terms as the act of leaving society. Studying statistics from a great number of European countries over the last half of the nineteenth century, he finds that the rate of suicide increases with the advance of urban-industrial civilization. Durkheim came to feel that the new social order of modern industrial capitalism was creating a situation in which more and more people were choosing to kill themselves rather than live in their societies. Durkheim was much disturbed by a trend toward what he called *anomie*, a state in which group norms no longer provide effective limits to individual aspirations and actions, and which he thought responsible for the increased rates of self-destruction in the new society. He discovered in the course of his investigations that strong ties to social groups tended to "protect" people against self-destruction; the more groups a person was a member of, and the more com-

---

[3] Ferdinand Toennies, *Community and Society*, translated and edited by Charles P. Loomis (East Lansing, The Michigan State University Press, 1957).

pletely the group norms controlled his behavior, the less likely he was to leave the group by killing himself. Now the transition to the society of industrial capitalism, Durkheim pointed out, involved both the destruction of old social groups, such as the small peasant villages which people were leaving for the new industrial cities, and the loosening of the social ties of such surviving groups as the family and the church. By a loosening of social ties Durkheim usually means a decrease in the extent to which group norms control individual behavior. Under such anomic conditions, old norms, which had effectively limited human action and aspiration in the preindustrial world, no longer provided such limitations in the modern world, Durkheim thought, and the modern society had not as yet developed a new set of norms to guide indiviual behavior. Modern man, as a result, may have relatively limitless aspirations and when he cannot fulfill these may not feel effective group prohibitions of suicide as a response to his frustrations. Durkheim said anomie, or normlessness, was one of the dangerous characteristics of the modern world, and today statistics still show that the highest rates of suicide and other means of escape from social life, such as alcoholism, drug addiction, and psychosis, are found in the most advanced industrial countries.[4]

Science, one of the forces responsible for the creation of modern society, has often been looked to as a source of norms and values by which man can organize his world and live in the new society. Max Weber, in the last selection in this section, holds that this is a mistaken hope. Science, he maintains, cannot provide man with a new set of values by which to live in the new society. Science can supply knowledge of the world, and man can use this knowledge to predict the probable outcomes of actions he contemplates, but science cannot decide which actions are good and which are bad, or which should be taken and which should be avoided. Science, Weber avers, is the most effective method yet developed by man for understanding the world, both the physical and the social world, but it is not a source of morality. Science provides information with which man may implement his purposes, but these purposes arise from systems of values and beliefs outside the realm of science. Weber agrees with the Russian novelist Tolstoy that science cannot tell us how to live. He disagrees with Tolstoy, however, in the conclusion that science is therefore useless. With scientific knowledge of the world, Weber says, man can foresee some of the consequences of choosing one kind of action over another and can discover the most efficient means for carrying out the action he has decided upon. Weber sees very serious consequences in the fact that the modern way of knowing the world does not provide man with guidance for living in the world. The modern world is "disenchanted," Weber says, meaning that rational science has replaced metaphysical speculation, religious dogma, and magical thinking as the chief way of knowing the world. Organized religion, Weber thought, has lost its power to define ultimate goals and appropriate means for attaining them in the contemporary world of the twentieth century. Contemporary man, Weber believes, must find new ways of giving purpose and meaning to his life.

[4] An extremely interesting and very controversial study of modern society along these lines and a prescription for its reorganization to eliminate these problems is found in the book by Erich Fromm, *The Sane Society* (New York: Holt, Rinehart, & Winston, Inc. 1955).

# A Theories of the Origins of Industrial Capitalism

## 16

## Saint-Simon on the Origins of Industrial Society and Scientific Sociology

### EMILE DURKHEIM

### The Origins of Sociology in the Life and Work of Saint-Simon

[The system of Saint-Simon] had a success without equal in the history of the century. . . . Its author is so misunderstood and, besides, has so original a character that it warrants our pausing. Before studying the doctrine let us look at the man.

Claude Henri de Rouvroy, Count of Saint-Simon, was born on the 17th of October, 1750. He belonged to the fam-

From Emile Durkhein, *Socialism and Saint-Simon*. Edited and with an Introduction by Alvin W. Gouldner. Translated by Charlotte Sattler. Copyright © 1958 by The Antioch Press. Reprinted by permission of The Antioch Press.

ily of the author of the *Mémoires* [of the Court of Louis XIV], though of another branch. From infancy he evidenced rare energy and independence of character. At thirteen he refused to take his first communion. For this reason he was imprisoned in Saint-Lazare from which he escaped. Bitten by a mad dog, he himself cauterized the wound with a burning coal. One day when a coachman, in order to pass, was about to interrupt his play, he lay down on the ground in front of the moving carriage. Struck by the extraordinary nature of their child, his parents hurried his education—about which he later complained. "I was weighed down with teachers," said he, "without being left time to reflect on what they were teaching me." However, at an early age he made the acquaintance of d'Alembert who exerted considerable influence—and this undoubtedly is one of the causes which contributed to the development of his scientific mind. This is also, without doubt, the source of his plan—which his school inherited—to write the Encyclopedia of the eighteenth century in order to harmonize it with the new state of science.

He played successively, in the course of his life, the most diverse roles. To conform to the tradition of his family, he first tried an army career. A captain at the time when war [of national independence, 1776] broke out in America, he followed one of his relatives who was in command of the expeditionary force and took part in the war as a staff officer. In the battle of Saintes he was wounded and made prisoner. But on his return to France after peace was concluded, the *ennui* of garrison life became unbearable and he resolved to leave the army.

In the midst of all this the [French] Revolution broke out. He accepted it with enthusiasm but refused to play a role in it, believing that while the battle of parties lasted, former noblemen should keep their distance from public affairs. Still, he was not satisfied to stand by as an inactive witness or passive observer of the events that were unfolding and entered the revolutionary movement through another door. The former soldier made himself a business man and purchaser of national property. In this he was associated with a Prussian, the Count of Redern, who for this purpose placed at his disposal a sum of 500,000 francs. The undertaking which Saint-Simon was to direct alone succeeded beyond all expectations. However, in spite of the proof he thus gave of his confidence in the final triumph of the Revolution, he ended

by becoming suspect. Ordered arrested, he was imprisoned at Saint-Pélgie, then at Luxembourg, under the name of Jacques Bonhomme, which he had adopted for his business transactions. The 9th of Thermidor [general amnesty] happily came to deliver him. . . .

Then began the third phase in the life of Saint-Simon. The speculator was transformed into a grand lordly friend of luxury and learning. In his magnificent mansion on the Rue de Chabanais he held open house, but it was almost exclusively with artists and especially scholars that he surrounded himself. Monge and Lagrange were his principal companions. At the same time he helped very generously—and even more discretely—all young men of promise who were referred to him. Poisson and Dupuytren stayed with him a long time. He sought out these contacts in order to educate himself. He even went so far as to become a student again, and set up residence beside the École Polytechnique where he took courses. Then he moved—again for the same reason—near the École de Médecine. He even assumed the expenses of numerous experiments. I will not discuss his marriage which ended in amicable divorce at the end of a year, as it was an event without significance in his life.

But Saint-Simon's fortune was much too modest for this life of Maecenas to last. We can be sure that in 1797 he only possessed 144,000 livres. He lost his fortune knowingly, and by 1805 nothing was left. Then begins the last period of his life, when he produced all his works. But although productive, life did not cease being hard on this unfortunate thinker who more than once found himself with nothing to eat.

He sought a position, and through the intervention of the Comte de Ségur was named copyist to Mont-de-Pitié, with a stipend of a thousand francs a year. As duties occupied his whole day he was obliged to use his nights to pursue the personal works he had just begun. His health was in a deplorable state (he coughed blood) when chance placed in his path a man (Diard) who had formerly been in his service and who had become wealthy. This good man took him in and Saint-Simon was the guest of his former servant for four years, until 1810. It was at that time that he published his first great work: the *Introduction aux travaux scientifiques du XIXe siècle*. But Diard died, and living again presented difficulties for Saint-Simon. However, in 1814 he seems to have escaped them for a time, although it is not known just how. It is then that he successively had as secretaries Augustin Thierry and Auguste Comte. In 1817 his financial condition even permitted him to give the latter 300 francs a month. Some works he published at this time enjoyed great success and brought him important subscriptions for later works that he had in preparation. Among the subscribers are the names Vital Roux, Perior, de Broglie, La Fayette, La Rochefoucauld, etc. But the daring nature of the author's ideas ended by frightening them. For one thing, Saint-Simon led a very irregular life. He was always extravagant, and poverty began once more. At times during this period, he was tormented by hunger and could not always find—even among those he had previously helped—the assistance he might have expected. Dupuytren, who he had come across, offered him a hundred sous. Crushed, the philosopher surrendered to despair and on the 9th of March, 1823, shot himself. He lost an eye but his brain remained uninjured, and after 15 days the patient was better. This period of discouragement over, he returned to his work, and this time fortune was good to him. A small group of fervent disciples gathered around and maintained him until death, which occurred on the 19th of May, 1825. He died surrounded by friends, conversing with them about work undertaken in common, and about his next triumph.

It was, as one can see, a singularly unstable life. Nevertheless it was far from lacking in unity. What set its course from the first was the very character of Saint-Simon, which reappears —the same—in all the roles he successively played. What dominated him above all was a horror of everything common and vulgar and a passion for the great and new. From early infancy he had given indications of this. His faith in himself and the grandeur of his destiny were never belied. From the time he was fifteen his valet would awaken him every morning with the words: "Wake up, monsieur le comte, you have great things to do." Later, he related that he had a dream of Charlemagne, from whom his family claimed descent, and the great emperor said to him, "My son, your successes as a philosopher will equal mine as a soldier and statesman." Dedicating one of his books to a nephew, he wrote him, "My intention in dedicating my work to you is to urge you on to nobleness. It is an obligation for you to do great things." It is this passion that explains the lack of moderation he practiced in life, his wastefulness, and his debauchery, which did him the greatest harm in the eyes of his contemporaries. "I have made every effort," he wrote in another letter, "to excite you, that is to say, to make you mad—for madness, my dear Victor, is nothing but extreme ardor, and enhanced ardor, is indispensable for accomplishing great things. One does not enter the temple of glory except that he has escaped from the Petites-Maison." . . . Indeed, he exerted considerable influence on the most distinguished minds of his day: Poisson, Halévy, Olinde Rodrigues, Rouget de Lisle, and finally and above all, Auguste Comte, who owed him much more than he acknowledged.

But his career did not have a merely formal unity, due to the very personal mark his character placed on everything he did. Actually, in everything he undertook he pursued only one and the same end. . . . [he] was a man of a single idea. . . . To reorganize European societies by giving them science and industry as bases—that was the objective he never lost sight of. From the time of the American campaign it was on this that he reflected. At that time he was writing his father, "If I were in a calmer situation I would clarify my thoughts. They are still raw, but I have a clear expectation that after they have matured I should find myself in a condition to do a scientific work useful to humanity—which is the principal aim I am setting for my life." It is under the influence of this idea that he devoted himself both to scientific works and large economic enterprises. For his speculations on national possessions were not the only ones. In America he suggested to the viceroy of Mexico, a canal between the two oceans. He offered to build a canal from Madrid to the sea for the Spanish Government. Later he dreamed of a gigantic bank whose revenue would serve to execute useful works for humanity. . . . In any case, there is no doubt that the last part of his life . . . realizes an idea which is that of his life's work. . . .

To add a science to the list of sciences is always a very laborious operation, but more productive than the annexation of a new continent to old continents. And it is at once much more fruitful when the science has man for its object. It almost had to do violence to the human spirit and to triumph over the keenest resistance to make it understood that in order to act upon things it was first necessary to put them on trial [that is, to study them systematically and objectively]. The resistance

has been particularly stubborn when the material to be examined was ourselves, due to our tendency to place ourselves outside of things, to demand a place apart in the universe.

Saint-Simon was the first who resolutely freed himself from these prejudices. Although he may have had precursors, never had it been so clearly asserted that man and society could not be directed in their conduct unless one began by making them objects of science and further that this science could not rest on any other principles than do the sciences of nature. And this new science—he not only laid out its design but attempted to realize it in part. We can see here all that Auguste Comte, and consequently all that the thinkers of the nineteenth century, owe him. In him we encounter the seeds already developed of all the ideas which have fed the thinking of our time. We [find] in it positivist philosophy, positivist sociology. We will see that we will also find socialism in it. . . .

. . . Human sciences [according to Saint-Simon] have to be constructed in imitation of the other natural sciences, for man is only one part of nature. There are not two words in the world, one which depends on scientific observation, and the other which escapes it. The universe is one, and the same method must serve to explore it in all of its parts. Man and the universe, says Saint-Simon, are like a mechanism on two scales—the first is a reduction of the second but does not differ from it in nature. Man is related to the universe like "a watch enclosed within a great clock from which it receives movement." Since it is demonstrated that the positive method alone allows us to know the inorganic world, it follows that it alone is suited to the human world, also. The tendency of the human spirit since the fifteenth century "is to base all its reasoning on observed and examined facts. Already it has reorganized astronomy, physics and chemistry on this positive basis. . . . One concludes necessarily that physiology, of which the science of man is part, will be treated by the method adopted for the other physical sciences." . . . "The domain of physiology viewed as a whole is generally composed of all facts relating to organic beings." . . . Physiology consists of two parts: one which deals with individual organs, the other with social organs. "Physiology is not only the science which, addressing itself to our organs one by one, experiments on each of them . . . to better determine the spheres of activity. . . . It does not consist only in this comparative knowledge which draws from the study of plants and animals valuable ideas on the functions of the parts we possess in common with these different classes of organic beings." In addition to this special physiology there is another, a general physiology which, "rich in all the facts discovered through valuable pieces of work undertaken in these different directions, addresses itself to considerations of a higher order. It towers above individuals, looking upon them merely as organs of the social body, whose organic functions it must examine, just as specialized physiology studies those of individuals." . . . "Society is not at all a simple conglomeration of living beings whose actions have no other cause but the arbitrariness of individual wills, nor other result than ephemeral or unimportant accidents. On the contrary, society is above all a veritable organized machine, all of whose parts contribute in a different way to the movement of the whole. The gathering of men constitutes a veritable being whose existence is more or less certain or precarious according to whether its organs acquit themselves more or less regularly of the functions entrusted to them." This is the social organism.

This general and social physiology naturally embraces morality and politics which consequently must themselves become positive sciences. Once physiology is advanced, says Saint-Simon, "politics will become a science of observation, and political questions handled by those who would have studied the positive science of man by the same method and in the same way that today one treats those relating to other phenomena." And it is only when politics are dealt with in this manner, and when, as a result, it can be taught in schools like other sciences, that the European crisis can be resolved.

But this *sui generis* thing—the object of this new science—what is the proper perspective for it to be viewed in order to study it? Today it is generally acknowledged that to have as complete as possible knowledge of it, it must be considered successively from two different aspects. One can consider human societies at a determinate and fixed moment in their evolution and then examine how, in this phase, their different parts act and react on each other —in a word, how they contribute to the collective life. Or else, instead of fixing and immobilizing them artificially in one moment of time, one can follow them through the successive stages they have travelled in the course of history, and then propose to find how each stage has contributed to determine the one that followed. In the first case one attempts to determine the law of social organization at such and such a phase of historic development, while in the other, one inquires about the law according to which these different phases have succeeded each other, what is the order of succession and what accounts for this order—in other words, what is the law of progress. In the eyes of Saint-Simon the second point of view is the more important. . . .

In fact, according to him, the law of progress dominates us with an absolute necessity. We submit to it—we do not make it. We are its instruments—not its authors. "The supreme law of progress of the human spirit carries along and dominates everything; men are but its instruments. Although this force derives from us, it is no more in our power to withhold ourselves from its influence, or master its action, than to change at will the primary impulse which makes our planet revolve around the sun. All we can do is to obey this law by accounting for the course it directs, instead of being blindly pushed by it; and, incidentally, it is precisely in this that the great philosophic development reserved for the present era will consist." . . .

So we see both how the problem of social physiology is posed and by what method it must be resolved. Since the progress of human societies is subjected to a necessary law, the primary aim of science is to find this law. And once discovered, it will itself indicate the direction progress must follow. To discover the order in which humanity developed in the past, in order to determine what this development should become—that is the urgent question, *par excellence*, which imposes itself on a thinker. In this way politics can be treated scientifically. "The future consists of the last items of a series of which the first composed the past. When one has properly examined the first terms of a series, it is easy to postulate those following. Thus, from the past, deeply observed, one can with ease deduce the future." The fault of statesmen, usually, is to have their eyes fixed on the present. And thus they expose themselves to inevitable errors. For how, if one limits oneself to the consideration of so brief a period, distinguish "the remains of a past which was disappearing and the seeds of a future which is arising?" It is only by observing series of broadly extended facts, as a result of searching deeply

into the past, that one can disentangle among the various elements of the present those large with future from those which are no more than monuments of a past that has outlived itself. Since it will be easy to establish that the former belong to an ascending series and the latter to a regressive one, it will be relatively simple to make a selection and to orient progress. . . .

## Sociological Analysis of the Rise of Industrial Society

. . . We find the new science limited to a single and unique problem [the origins and development of industrial society] whose interest is more practical than speculative. But at least Saint-Simon undertakes to treat it according to the scientific and positive method whose fundamental rules we saw him formulate earlier. It is not a question of inventing a new system, created out of many pieces—as do utopians of the eighteenth century and other periods—but merely of discovering by observation what is in process of being worked out [in the new society-in-the-making]. "One does not create a system of social organization. One perceives the new chain of ideas and interests which has been formed, and points it out—that is all." . . . All one can do is to be aware of the direction the development is taking; next, to distinguish, among the elements of which the present is made up, those which are developing more and more—and developing more completely—and those which more and more are ceasing to be; finally, to recognize the future behind the survivals of the past which conceal it. To do these things, it is necessary to study the growth of our societies since they were definitively established. According to our author, it is in the Middle Ages—the eleventh and twelfth centuries—that they were formed with all their essential characteristics. That epoch is consequently "the most suitable point of departure" for "that philosophic observation of the past" which alone can enlighten the future. Let us see what societies were like at that time and how they evolved since.

What gave them an organized character when, toward the tenth century, they began to free themselves from the chaos produced by barbarian invasions, was that the social system revolved completely around two centers of gravity, distinct but closely associated. On the one hand, there were the chiefs of the army, who constituted what is since called feudalism, and to whom all of secular society was closely subjected. All property, real and personal, was in their hands, and workers —individually and collectively—were dependent upon them. On the other hand, there were the clergy, who controlled the spiritual direction of society, generally and specifically. Their doctrines and decisions served as guides to opinion; but what overwhelmingly established their authority was their absolute mastery over general and particular education. In other words, the entire economic life of society depended on the lords, and all intellectual life on the priests. The first ruled supremely over productive operations, the second over consciences. Thus all collective functions were strictly subjected either to military power or religious authority, and this double subjugation consituted the social organization [of feudalism]. . . . War was then chronic . . . consequently it was natural that only those capable of directing it were invested with the highest degree of authority and respect. Likewise, as the clergy was the only group which then possessed learning, it was out of real necessity that it exercised an absolute power over minds. Thus this two-pronged supremacy was based on the nature of things. It corresponded to a social superiority of these two classes which was real and which it merely expressed.

This is the origin. Let us now see what this organization became in the course of history.

It is a general rule that the apogee of a social system coincides with the beginning of its decadence. In the eleventh century, spiritual and temporal powers were definitively established; never was the authority of clergy and lords more undisputed. But coming into existence at that very moment were two new social forces. . . . These two forces were the free commune and exact science.

What had accounted for the strength of feudal organization was the subjugation of the industrial class by what then took its place, the military class. . . . All economic life was subordinated to the interests of war and warriors. But with the twelfth century began the great movement of the emancipation of the commune. Villages, by payment of silver, were freeing themselves from seigneurial tutelage. And they were totally composed of artisans and merchants. A whole segment of the economic structure thus found itself detached from the others who until then were forcing their control on it. . . . Liberated industry was going to be able freely to realize its own nature, to propose for itself purely industrial ends, which not only differed from but contradicted those the [feudal] system had forced upon it. A new force, *sui generis*, had entered the heart of the social body, and as by nature and origin it was foreign to the old organization— and could only disturb it—it was inevitable that its very presence would disconcert the latter's functioning and would develop only by destroying it.

At the same time the exact sciences were imported into Europe by the Arabs. The schools they founded in their conquered parts of Europe were quickly imitated elsewhere. Similar establishments arose in all occidental Europe, "observatories, dissection rooms, study rooms for natural history were set up in Italy, France, England, Germany. As early as the thirteenth century, Bacon was brilliantly cultivating the physical sciences." Gradually, in opposition to the clergy, a new body was forming, which like the preceding one aimed at directing the intellectual life of society. These were the scholars who, in their relation to the clerical class were in exactly the same situation as were the enfranchised communes—that is, the corporation of artisans and merchants —vis-à-vis feudalism. Thus two seeds of destruction were introduced into the theological-feudal system, and in fact from that moment the two forces which were the source of its strength began to grow weaker. . . .

Nevertheless, . . . it is only in the sixteenth century that the forces antagonistic to the old system found themselves strong enough to come into the open, in such a way that the results could be perceived by anyone. At first these forces were directed against theological rule; Luther and his co-reformers upset pontifical authority as a power in Europe. At the same time in a general way they undermined theological authority "by destroying the principle of blind faith, by replacing it with the right of examination which—restrained at first within quite narrow limits—was to inevitably increase . . . and finally to embrace an indefinite area." This two-fold change operated not only among the peoples converted to Protestantism, but even among those who remained Catholic. For once the principle was established, it extended well beyond the countries where it had first been proclaimed. As a result, the bond which tied individual consciences to ecclesiastical power—although not shattered—was loosened, and the moral unity of the social system definitely unsettled.

The entire sixteenth century was seized by this great intellectual revolu-

tion. But it was at its close that the struggle—began against spiritual power —proceeded against temporal power. It took place at almost the same time in France and in England. In both countries it was led by the common people, with one of the two branches of temporal power as leader. With the English, feudalism placed itself at their head to combat royal authority; in France royalty made itself their ally against feudal strength. Actually the coalition—in both peoples—had begun as early as the enfranchisement of the lower class, but it is only in the seventeenth century that the domestic rearrangements on both sides of the channel came into the open and battle was joined in broad daylight. Here Richelieu, then Louis XIV shattered seigneurial power; there [England], the Revolution of 1688 broke out, limiting royal authority as much as was possible without overturning the old organization. The final result of these events was a weakening of the military system in its entirety. It was weakened, first because it lost unity due to a schism between the two elements of which it was formed —and a system cannot be disunited without being enfeebled—and then because one of these elements departed from battle crushed. Therefore, although at this time feudalism—at least in France—seemed to burn with a strong flame, in reality these magnificent external appearances concealed a state of internal deterioration which events of the following century soon made clear. . . .

But at the same time that this regressive process was developing, another was occurring in reverse direction with no less significance. Industrial and scientific forces, once formed, did not manifest themselves exclusively by destructive effects, that is, by overthrowing the old social order. They gave rise to another. They did not limit themselves to detaching consciences and individual wills from the centers which until then, by providing a similar direction, had made a single body of them. But to the degree they acquired more energy, they themselves became foci of common action and centers of organization. Around them gradually formed the social elements which the old forces—more and more powerless to keep them subordinate—were allowing to escape. Under these new influences, a new social system was slowly arising in the bosom of the old, which was disintegrating.

As long as arts and crafts had been narrowly subordinated to theological and military authority, having to serve as instruments for ends which were not their own, they had been impeded in their progress. But as soon as they began to be free—thanks to the liberation of the common people [these free villagers engaged in commerce and industry]—they took flight and developed so quickly that they soon became a social force to be reckoned with. Little by little all society fell into dependence upon them, because nothing was any longer possible without them. Military force itself was subjected to them, once war became a complex and costly thing, once it demanded not merely native courage and a certain disposition of character, but money, machines, arms. More and more, improvements in industry, the inventions of science, and finally wealth, were proving more vital to success in arms than innate bravery. But when a class acquires greater importance and respect, when the functions it fulfills become more essential, it is inevitable for it to wield greater influence on the direction of society and increased political authority. This in fact is what occurred. Little by little one sees representatives of industry admitted to governmental councils, playing a greater and greater part, and as a result having a larger share in determining the general course of society. It

is especially in England that this phenomenon manifests itself. Gradually the common people—in other words, the classes which fulfill only economic functions—obtain first a consultative voice in the tax vote, then a deliberative voice, then the exclusive right to vote on budget. They substitute themselves for the old temporal power in one of its most important functions, and are able henceforth to act in conformity with their own interest in the direction of society; they modify its orientation, since they have altogether different ends than the military classes [feudal nobility]. In other words, the social system begins to revolve about a new center.

This is not all. One of the essential prerogatives of feudal power consisted in administering justice. Seigneurial justice was one of the essential characteristics of feudal organization. But once the villages were freed, one of the rights considered most important to achieve was the administration of justice. "From then on municipal [courts] were formed and entrusted with this care. Its members were designated by the citizens and for a limited term." . . . The appearance of these tribunals is an important event in the process of organization we are tracing. From this moment, in fact, the industrial class had a judiciary organ which was its own, in harmony with its special nature, and which contributed to complete the system which was in process of formation. . . .

Just as with industry, science, as it grew, developed an organization appropriate to its own character, and very different, consequently, from that permitted by theological authority. Scholars became esteemed personages whom royalty more and more made a habit of consulting. It is as a result of these repeated consultations that great scientific bodies were gradually established at the pinnacle of the system. These are the academies. Thereafter there arose all kinds "of special schools for science where the influence of theology and metaphysics were, so to speak, nil." "A larger and larger mass of scientific ideas entered ordinary education at the same time that religious doctrines gradually lost influence." Finally, just as with industry, this early organization did not remain confined to the higher levels of society, but extended to the mass of people. With respect to the body of scholars, they were in a state of subordination analogous to their former position vis-à-vis the body ecclesiastic. "The people, organized industrially, soon perceived that their usual works of art and craft were not at all in rapport with their theological ideas . . . and wherever they could be in contact with savants they lost the habit of consulting priests, and acquired the custom of placing themselves in touch with those who possessed positive [empirical, objective, scientific] knowledge." And since they found themselves benefitted by the counsel given them, they ended by according "the unanimous opinion of the scholars the same degree of confidence that in the Middle Ages they accorded the decisions of spiritual power. It is by a kind of faith of a new type that they successively accepted the movement of the earth, modern astronomical theory, the circulation of the blood, the identity of lightning and of electricity, etc., etc." "So it is proven," concludes Saint-Simon "that people have become spontaneously confident in and subordinate to their leaders in the fields of science, just as they are temporally with regard to their industrial leaders. I have, consequently, the right to conclude that confidence as well as social rankings are developed within the new system."

The results of this double evolution can be summarized as follows: In the measure that the ancient social system gave way, another was formed in the very bosom of the first. The old society

contained within itself a new society, in process of formation and every day acquiring more strength and consistency. But these two organizations are necessarily antagonistic to each other. They result from opposing forces and aim at contradictory ends. One is essentially aggressive, war-like, the other essentially peaceful. The one sees in other peoples enemies to destroy; the other tends to view them as collaborators in a common [economic] undertaking. One has conquest for its aim, the other, production. Similarly, in spiritual affairs the first calls on faith and imposes beliefs which it puts beyond discussion. The second calls on reason and even trust—it requires a type of intellectual subordination which is essential to rationality, a commitment to further exploration and testing. Thus these two societies could not coexist without contradicting each other. . . .

Such was the situation on the eve of the Revolution, and out of it the Revolution was born. "This tremendous crisis did not at all have its origin in this or that isolated fact. . . . It operated as an overturning of the political system for the single reason that the state of society to which the ancient order corresponded had totally changed in nature. A civil and moral revolution which had gradually developed for more than six centuries engendered and necessitated a political revolution. . . . If one insists on attributing the French Revolution to one source, it must be dated from the day the liberation of the communes and the cultivation of exact sciences in western Europe began." . . .

But on the land thus cleared, the Revolution built nothing new. It asserted that one was no longer obliged to accept the old beliefs but did not attempt to elaborate a new body of rational beliefs that all minds could accept. It destroyed the foundations on which political authority rested but failed to establish others of any stability. It proclaimed that political power was not to belong to those who had monopolized it until then, but did not assign it to any definite organ. . . . [and] the absence of organization from which industrial society suffered became far more perceptible once all that remained of the old had disappeared. The weak cohesion of this dawning society became a much graver social peril once the old social bonds were completely destroyed. . . . It is certainly from this that there stemmed a kind of uncertainty, an exasperated anguish, which is characteristic of the revolutionary epoch. . . .

But why had [the Revolution] stopped midway? What prevented it from ending in positive results? The explanation Saint-Simon gives deserves consideration.

It is in the nature of man, he says, to be unable to pass without intermediary from one doctrine to another, from one social system to a differing system. That is why the authority of science and industry would never have been able to replace that of clergy and feudalism unless—when the first began to arise and the second weaken—there had not constituted itself between the two "a temporal and spiritual power of an intermediary kind, illegitimate, transitory, whose unique role was to direct the transition from one social system to another." Thus between the feudal body and the industrial body appeared the class of lawyers. Lawyers, just as workers, had been at first merely agents of the lords. But gradually they formed a distinct class, whose autonomy kept growing, whose action, consequently, opposed feudal action and modified it "by the establishment of jurisprudence, which had merely been an organized system of barriers opposed to the exercise of force." An equity was then established which was not purely feudal, and military power found itself

subject to limitations and rules drawn in the interest of commercial men—for these latter necessarily profited from any restriction brought against the antagonistic power they fought. In the spiritual realm similarly, metaphysicians—rising from the very heart of theology—wedged themselves between positive science and clergy, inspired at once with the spirit of both. And without ceasing to base their reasoning on religious foundations, they nevertheless modified theological influence by establishing the right of examination in matters of law and morality.

These are the two intermediate and fused forces which occupied the political stage almost exclusively until the Revolution, because by their composite and ambiguous nature they corresponded better than all others to the equally ambiguous state of civilization. Without doubt they thus rendered the greatest services and contributed in large measure to the final liberation of science and industry. Thanks to one, the working world escaped feudal tribunals. Thanks to the other, the idea took hold more and more that society could maintain itself without individual consciences being subordinated to theological doctrines. Their authority was so great when the Revolution broke out that quite naturally people took direction from them. Manufacturers and scholars believed they could do no better than blindly entrust their cause to them. Thus the men of law and the metaphysically-trained almost exclusively composed the revolutionary assemblies and inspired their actions. . . . But if these lawyers and metaphysicians were admirably prepared and organized to lead this revolutionary work to its final goal, they possessed nothing of what was required to erect a new system. For, although they did not understand this, it was from the past, from the old order of things, that they inherited the whole groundwork of their doctrines.

How could jurists bring themselves to a conception of a social order different from the one they had just destroyed, since "their political opinions are inevitably deduced, for the most part, from Roman law, from the ordinances of our kings, from feudal customs—in a word, from all the legislation which preceded the "Revolution." How could metaphysicians—the entire philosophic school of the eighteenth century—establish a system of ideas and beliefs in harmony with a particular social condition when, under the influence of the theologic spirit which continued to animate them, they were aspiring in all practical questions to absolute solutions, independent of any consideration of time and place, any historic condition? The effective role of both was therefore reduced to merely destroying. "When they wished to go further, they were thrust into the absolute question of the best government imaginable, and—always controlled by the same habits—treated it as a question of jurisprudence and metaphysics. For the theory of the rights of man—which has always been the foundation of their work in general politics—is nothing other than an application of high metaphysics to high jurisprudence." . . .

Even as they stand, Saint-Simon's observations are noteworthy. But they represent still another significant point in the history of ideas. If, in fact, one relates them to what was previously said, one arrives at the conclusion that according to Saint-Simon, European societies have passed successively through three social systems; the theological or feudal, the metaphysical or juridical, and the positive. We recognize in this formula the famous law of three stages which Comte was to make the foundation of his doctrine. However, it is of Saint-Simonian origin. . . .

It would take too long to point out all the fertile ideas contained in this broad tableau of our historic develop-

ment. It is Saint-Simon who was the first, before Guizot, to understand the full social significance of the communal movement and the ties which bound it to the Revolution and to current problems. He was also the first to judge the work of the Revolution with the impartiality of history, without condemning it in general—as did the defenders of the old regime—and without systematically extolling it—as did the liberals of his time—and on this point again Comte was his heir. On the whole, one must admire his complete absence of all prejudice, and the feeling for historic continuity he discovered in the role of every period—even the most discredited, like the Middle Ages—in the uninterrupted course of transformations which bind the society of the tenth century to contemporary times.

## Saint-Simon's Proposed Organization of the Industrial System

Let us now return to the practical question noted in this historical analysis. Granted that our present societies contain in them two different, and even contradictory, social systems—one which is becoming weaker and weaker, the other emerging more and more—how can the crisis resulting from their antagonism be solved? . . .

It is neither possible nor useful to restore the old system in its entirety. But on the other hand we know that every eclectic combination is contradictory and incoherent, that a social organization cannot be regarded as stable except as it is entirely homogeneous. In other words, society must be based on only one of the two conflicting principles, and the other be excluded. It follows that modern societies will be definitely in equilibrium only when organized on a purely industrial basis. . . .

The most vital trait of this . . . organization is that its goal, and its exclusive goal, is to increase the control of man over things. "To concern itself only in acting on nature, in order to modify it as advantageously as possible for humankind," has been the unique task of the communes since their enfranchisement—that is, of the new society in process of formation. Instead of seeking to extend the national domain, instead of diverting the attention of men from worldly wealth, it addressed itself, on the contrary, to peacefully increasing their well-being through the development of arts, science and industry. It has had as its unique function the production of useful things for our worldly existence. Consequently, since all reform consists of extending to all of society what until now has been so only for a portion of it, the crisis will only be resolved when all social life converges toward this same goal, to the exclusion of every other. The only normal form that collective activity can take henceforth, is the industrial form. Society will be fully in harmony with itself only when it is totally industrialized. "The production of useful things is the only reasonable and positive end that political societies can set themselves." . . .

From this principle flows a significant conclusion. It is that "the producers of useful things—being the only useful people in society—are the only ones who should cooperate to regulate its course." It is therefore to them and them alone that law-making belongs. It is in their hands that all political power should be deposited. Since, hypothetically, the whole fabric of social life would be made up of industrial relationships, is it not obvious that only men of industry are in a position to direct it? The vital rationale consists of two stages: 1. Since in this system there is nothing more socially central than economic activity, the regulating organ of social functions should preside over the economic activity of society. There is no longer place for a central

organ with a differing objective since there is no longer other material in the common life; 2. This organ must necessarily be of the same nature as those which it is charged with regulating—that is to say, it must be composed exclusively of representatives of industrial life.

But what is understood by "industrial life?" . . . There are, says Saint-Simon, two major groups: one consists of the immense majority of the nation—that is to say, all workers—and which Saint-Simon calls national and industrial; and the other, which he labels antinational, because it is like a parasitic body whose presence only interrupts the play of social functions. In the latter are included noblemen . . . and "owners living like nobles, that is to say, doing nothing." . . . But it is important to note that it is not all capitalists who are placed beyond the pale of regular society, but only those who live on unearned income. As for those who themselves make their wealth productive, who enrich it with their toil—they are industrials. Consequently, industrial society comprises all those who actively participate in the economic life, whether they are owners or not. The fact of possessing does not provide access to it but does not preclude them from it. . . .

But if [some] owners are not to be considered producers, it is not the same with scholars, who are the indispensable auxiliaries of industry. "The social body," says Saint-Simon, "consists of two great families: that of intellectuals, or industrials of theory, and that of immediate producers, or scholars of application." Consequently they too have the right to be represented in the managing organs of society, and this representation is actually indispensable since industry cannot do without the knowledge of science. It is necessary therefore that the supreme council of industry be assisted by a supreme council of the learned. However, the two organs—though united—must be distinct, for the two functions—theory on one side and practice on the other—are too different to be fused. . . . Thinkers must be able to speculate with complete independence and without servilely capitulating to the needs of practice; but it is essential that the practical men decide finally on all that concerns execution. Moreover the two organs should not be placed on the same footing; there must exist between them a certain hierarchy. It is to the industrials that the principal role should belong, for it is on them that the existence of the thinkers depends. "Scholars render very important services to the industrial class, but receive services from it that are much more important. They receive existence. . . . The industrial class is the fundamental class, the providing class of society." The learned form but

"a secondary class." Between the two, finally, are the artists, whose position in the system is less clearly fixed. Occasionally Saint-Simon seems to treat them as a class apart, represented by a special organ in the managing centers of society; at other times they disappear into the industrial class.

In summary, granted that social functions can be only secular or spiritual—that is, turned towards thought or towards action—that in the present state of civilization the only rational form of the temporal is industry and of the spiritual, science, Saint-Simon concludes: 1. That normal society should consist only of producers and scholars; 2. That as a consequence it should be subordinated to directing organs composed of similar elements, with a certain preeminence of the first over the second. This is the fundamental principle of the new system. . . .

# 17

# Class Struggle and the Change from Feudalism to Capitalism

## KARL MARX AND FRIEDRICH ENGELS

### Theory of Social Structure and Change *

I was led by my studies to the conclusion that legal relations as well as forms of state could be neither understood by themselves nor explained by the so-called general progress of the human mind, but that they are rooted in the material conditions of life, which are summed up by Hegel after the fash-

* From Karl Marx, A Contribution to the Critique of Political Economy, Preface. First published in 1859.

ion of the English and French of the eighteenth century under the name "civil society"; the anatomy of that civil society is to be sought in political economy. The study of the latter, which I had taken up in Paris, I continued at Brussels, whither I immigrated on account of an order of expulsion issued by Mr. Guizot.

The general conclusion at which I arrived and which, once reached, continued to serve as the leading thread in my studies may be briefly summed up as follows: In the social production which men carry on they enter into definite relations that are indispensable and independent of their will; these relations of production correspond to a definite stage of development of their material powers of production. The sum total of these relations of production constitutes the economic structure of society—the real foundation, on which rise legal and political superstructures and to which correspond definite forms of social consciousness. The mode of production in material life determines the general character of the social, political, and spiritual processes of life. It is not the consciousness of men that determines their existence, but, on the contrary, their social existence determines their consciousness. At a certain stage of their development the material forces of production in society come into conflict with the existing relations of production, or—what is but a legal expression for the same thing—with the property relations within which they had been at work before. From forms of development of the forces of production these relations turn into their fetters. Then comes the period of social revolution. With the change of the economic foundation the entire immense superstructure is more or less rapidly transformed. In considering such transformations the distinction should always be made between the material transformation of the economic conditions of production, which can be determined with the precision of natural science, and the legal, political, religious, aesthetic, or philosophic—in short, ideological—forms in which men become conscious of this conflict and fight it out. Just as our opinion of an individual is not based on what he thinks of himself, so can we not judge such a period of transformation by its own consciousness; on the contrary, this consciousness must rather be explained from the contradictions of material life, from the existing conflict between the social forces of production and the relations of production. No social order ever disappears before all the productive forces for which there is room in it have been developed, and new, higher relations of production never appear before the material conditions of their existence have matured in the womb of the old society. Therefore mankind always takes up only such problems as it can solve, since, looking at the matter more closely, we will always find that the problem itself arises only when the material conditions necessary for its solution already exist or are at least in the process of formation. In broad outlines we can designate the Asiatic, the ancient, the feudal, and the modern bourgeois methods of production as so many epochs in the progress of the economic formation of society. The bourgeois relations of production are the last antagonistic form of the social process of production —antagonistic not in the sense of individual antagonism, but of one arising from conditions surrounding the life of individuals in society; at the same time the productive forces developing in the womb of bourgeois society create the material conditions for the solution of that antagonism. This social formation constitutes, therefore, the closing chapter of the prehistoric stage of human society.

## Class Conflict and Industrial Capitalism †

The history of all hitherto existing society is the history of class struggles.

Free man and slave, patrician and plebeian, lord and serf, guild master and journeyman, in a word, oppressor and oppressed, stood in constant opposition to one another, carried on an uninterrupted, now hidden, now open fight, a fight that each time ended either in a

† From Karl Marx and Friedrich Engels, *The Communist Manifesto*, Part I. First published in 1848.

revolutionary reconstitution of society at large or in the common ruin of the contending classes.

In the earlier epochs of history we find almost everywhere a complicated arrangement of society into various orders, a manifold gradation of social rank. In ancient Rome we have patricians, knights, plebeians, slaves; in the Middle Ages, feudal lords, vassals, guild masters, journeymen, apprentices, serfs; in almost all of these classes, again, subordinate gradations.

The modern bourgeois society that has sprouted from the ruins of feudal society has not done away with class antagonisms. It has but established new classes, new conditions of oppression, new forms of struggle in place of the old ones.

Our epoch, the epoch of the bourgeoisie, possesses, however, this distinctive feature: it has simplified the class antagonisms. Society as a whole is more and more splitting up into two great hostile camps, into two great classes directly facing each other: bourgeoisie and proletariat.[1]

From the serfs of the Middle Ages sprang the chartered burghers of the earliest towns. From these burgesses the first elements of the bourgeoisie were developed.

The discovery of America, the rounding of the Cape opened up fresh ground for the rising bourgeoisie. The East Indian and Chinese markets, the colonization of America, trade with the colonies, the increase in the means of exchange and in commodities generally, gave to commerce, to navigation, to industry an impulse never before known, and thereby, to the revolutionary ele-

ment in the tottering feudal society, a rapid development.

The feudal system of industry, under which industrial production was monopolized by closed guilds, now no longer sufficed for the growing wants of the new markets. The manufacturing system took its place. The guild masters were pushed on one side by the manufacturing middle class; division of labor between the different corporate guilds vanished in the face of division of labor in each single workshop.

Meantime the markets kept ever growing, the demand ever rising. Even manufacture no longer sufficed. Thereupon steam and machinery revolutionized industrial production. The place of manufacture was taken by the giant, modern industry, the place of the industrial middle class by industrial millionaires, the leaders of whole industrial armies, the modern bourgeois.

Modern industry has established the world market, for which the discovery of America paved the way. This market has given an immense development to commerce, to navigation, to communication by land. This development has, in its turn, reacted on the extension of industry; and in proportion as industry, commerce, navigation, railways extended, in the same proportion the bourgeoisie developed, increased its capital, and pushed into the background every class handed down from the Middle Ages.

We see, therefore, how the modern bourgeoisie is itself the product of a long course of development, of a series of revolutions in the modes of production and of exchange.

Each step in the development of the bourgeoisie was accompanied by a corresponding political advance of that class. An oppressed class under the sway of the feudal nobility, an armed and self-governing association in the medieval commune; here independent urban republic (as in Italy and Ger-

[1] By "bourgeoisie" is meant the class of modern capitalists, owners of the means of social production and employers of wage labor. By proletariat, the class of modern wage laborers who, having no means of production of their own, are reduced to selling their labor power in order to live.

many), there taxable "third estate" of the monarchy (as in France), afterwards, in the period of manufacture proper, serving either the semi-feudal or the absolute monarchy as a counterpoise against the nobility, and, in fact, cornerstone of the great monarchies in general, the bourgeoisie has at last, since the establishment of modern industry and of the world market, conquered for itself, in the modern representative state, exclusive political sway. The executive of the modern state is but a committee for managing the common affairs of the whole bourgeoisie.

The bourgeoisie, historically, has played a most revolutionary part.

The bourgeoisie, wherever it has got the upper hand, has put an end to all feudal, patriarchal, idyllic relations. It has pitilessly torn asunder the motley feudal ties that bound man to his "natural superiors," and has left remaining no other nexus between man and man than naked self-interest, than callous "cash payment." It has drowned the most heavenly ecstasies of religious fervor, of chivalrous enthusiasm, of Philistine sentimentalism in the icy water of egotistical calculation. It has resolved personal worth into exchange value and, in place of the numberless indefeasible chartered freedoms, has set up that single, unconscionable freedom—free trade. In one word, for exploitation, veiled by religious and political illusions, it has substituted naked, shameless, direct, brutal exploitation.

The bourgeoisie has stripped of its halo every occupation hitherto honored and looked up to with reverent awe. It has converted the physician, the lawyer, the priest, the poet, the man of science into its paid wage laborers.

The bourgeoisie has torn away from the family its sentimental veil, and has reduced the family relation to a mere money relation.

The bourgeoisie has disclosed how it came to pass that the brutal display of vigor in the Middle Ages, which reactionists so much admire, found its fitting complement in the most slothful indolence. It has been the first to show what man's activity can bring about. It has accomplished wonders far surpassing Egyptian pyramids, Roman aqueducts, and Gothic cathedrals; it has conducted expeditions that put in the shade all former exoduses of nations and crusades.

The bourgeoisie cannot exist without constantly revolutionizing the instruments of production, and thereby the relations of production, and with them the whole relations of society. Conservation of the old modes of production in unaltered form was, on the contrary, the first condition of existence for all earlier industrial classes. Constant revolutionizing of production, uninterrupted disturbance of all social conditions, everlasting uncertainty and agitation distinguish the bourgeois epoch from all earlier ones. All fixed, fast-frozen relations, with their train of ancient and venerable prejudices and opinions, are swept away, all new-formed ones become antiquated before they can ossify. All that is solid melts into air, all that is holy is profaned, and man is at last compelled to face with sober senses his real conditions of life and his relations with his kind.

The need of a constantly expanding market for its products chases the bourgeoisie over the whole surface of the globe. It must nestle everywhere, settle everywhere, establish connections everywhere.

The bourgeoisie has through its exploitation of the world market given a cosmopolitan character to production and consumption in every country. To the great chargrin of reactionists, it has drawn from under the feet of industry the national ground on which it stood. All old-established national industries have been destroyed or are daily being destroyed. They are dislodged by new industries, whose introduction becomes a life and death question for all civilized nations, by industries that no longer work up indigenous raw material, but raw material drawn from the remotest zones; industries whose products are consumed not only at home, but in every quarter of the globe. In place of the old wants, satisfied by the productions of the country, we find new wants, requiring for their satisfaction the products of distant lands and climes. In place of the old local and national seclusion and self-sufficiency we have intercourse in every direction, universal interdependence of nations. And as in material, so also in intellectual production. The intellectual creations of individual nations become common property. National one-sidedness and narrow-mindedness become more and more impossible, and from the numerous national and local literatures there arises a world literature.

The bourgeoisie, by the rapid improvement of all instruments of production, by the immensely facilitated means of communication, draws all, even the most barbarian, nations into civilization. The cheap prices of its commodities are the heavy artillery with which it batters down all Chinese walls, with which it forces the barbarians' intensely obstinate hatred of foreigners to capitulate. It compels all nations, on pain of extinction, to adopt the bourgeois mode of production; it compels them to introduce what it calls civilization into their midst, i.e., to become bourgeois themselves. In one word, it creates a world after its own image.

The bourgeoisie has subjected the country to the rule of the towns. It has created enormous cities, has greatly increased the urban population as compared with the rural, and has thus rescued a considerable part of the population from the idiocy of rural life. Just as it has made the country dependent on the towns, so it has made barbarian and semi-barbarian countries dependent on the civilized ones, nations of peasants on nations of bourgeois, the East on the West.

The bourgeoisie keeps more and more doing away with the scattered state of the population, of the means of production, and of property. It has agglomerated population, centralized means of production, and has concentrated property in a few hands. The necessary consequence of this was political centralization. Independent, or but loosely connected provinces, with separate interests, laws, governments and systems of taxation, became lumped together into one nation, with one government, one code of laws, one national class interest, one frontier, and one customs tariff.

The bourgeoisie, during its rule of scarce one hundred years, has created more massive and more colossal productive forces than have all preceding generations together. Subjection of nature's forces to man, machinery, application of chemistry to industry and agriculture, steam navigation, railways, electric telegraphs, clearing of whole continents for cultivation, canalization of rivers, whole populations conjured out of the ground—what earlier century had even a presentiment that such productive forces slumbered in the lap of social labor?

We see then: the means of production and of exchange, on whose foundation the bourgeoisie built itself up, were generated in feudal society. At a certain stage in the development of these means of production and of exchange, the conditions under which feudal society produced and exchanged, the feudal organization of agriculture and manufacturing industry, in one word, the feudal relations of property, became no longer compatible with the already developed productive forces; they became so many fetters. They had to be burst asunder; they were burst asunder.

Into their place stepped free competition, accompanied by a social and political constitution adapted to it, and by the economic and political sway of the bourgeois class.

A similar movement is going on before our own eyes. Modern bourgeois society with its relations of production, of exchange, and of property, a society that has conjured up such gigantic means of production and of exchange, is like the sorcerer who is no longer able to control the powers of the nether world whom he has called up by his spells. For many a decade past, the history of industry and commerce is but the history of the revolt of modern productive forces against modern conditions of production, against the property relations that are the conditions for the existence of the bourgeoisie and of its rule. It is enough to mention the commercial crises that by their periodic return put on its trial, each time more threateningly, the existence of the entire bourgeois society. In these crises a great part not only of the existing products but also of the previously created productive forces are periodically destroyed. In these crises there breaks out an epidemic that in all earlier epochs would have seemed an absurdity—the epidemic of overproduction. Society suddenly finds itself put back into a state of momentary barbarism; it appears as if a famine, a universal war of devastation had cut off the supply of every means of subsistence; industry and commerce seem to be destroyed; and why? Because there is too much civilization, too much means of subsistence, too much industry, too much commerce. The productive forces at the disposal of society no longer tend to further the development of the conditions of bourgeois property; on the contrary, they have become too powerful for these conditions, by which they are fettered, and as soon as they overcome these fetters they bring disorder into the whole of bourgeois society, endanger the existence of bour-

geois property. The conditions of bourgeois society are too narrow to comprise the wealth created by them. And how does the bourgeoisie get over these crises? On the one hand, by enforced destruction of a mass of productive forces; on the other, by the conquest of new markets, and by the more thorough exploitation of the old ones. That is to say, by paving the way for more extensive and more destructive crises, and by diminishing the means whereby crises are prevented.

The weapons with which the bourgeoisie felled feudalism to the ground are now turned against the bourgeoisie itself.

But not only has the bourgeoisie forged the weapons that bring death to itself; it has also called into existence the men who are to wield those weapons—the modern working class—the proletarians.

In proportion as the bourgeoisie, i.e., capital, is developed, in the same proportion is the proletariat, the modern working class, developed—a class of laborers, who live only so long as they find work, and who find work only so long as their labor increases capital. These laborers, who must sell themselves piecemeal, are a commodity, like every other article of commerce, and are consequently exposed to all the vicissitudes of competition, to all the fluctuations of the market.

Owing to the extensive use of machinery and to division of labor, the work of the proletarians has lost all individual character and, consequently, all charm for the workman. He becomes an appendage of the machine, and it is only the simplest, most monotonous, and most easily acquired knack that is required of him. Hence the cost of production of a workman is restricted, almost entirely, to the means of subsistence that he requires for his maintenance and for the propagation of his race. But the price of a commodity, and therefore also of labor, is equal to its cost of production. In proportion, therefore, as the repulsiveness of the work increases, the wage decreases. Nay, more, in proportion as the use of machinery and division of labor increases, in the same proportion the burden of toil also increases, whether by prolongation of the working hours, by increase of the work exacted in a given time, or by increased speed of the machinery, etc.

. Modern industry has converted the little workshop of the patriarchal master into the great factory of the industrial capitalist. Masses of laborers, crowded into the factory, are organized like soldiers. As privates of the industrial army they are placed under the command of a perfect hierarchy of officers and sergeants. Not only are they slaves of the bourgeois class, and of the bourgeois state; they are daily and hourly enslaved by the machine, by the overlooker, and, above all, by the individual bourgeois manufacturer himself. The more openly this despotism proclaims gain to be its end and aim, the more petty, the more hateful, and the more embittering it is.

The less the skill and exertion of strength implied in manual labor, in other words, the more modern industry becomes developed, the more is the labor of men superseded by that of women. Differences of age and sex have no longer any distinctive social validity for the working class. All are instruments of labor, more or less expensive to use, according to their age and sex.

No sooner is the exploitation of the laborer by the manufacturer over, to the extent that he receives his wages in cash, than he is set upon by the other portions of the bourgeoisie, the landlord, the shopkeeper, the pawnbroker, etc.

The lower strata of the middle class —the small trades-people, shopkeepers, and retired tradesmen generally, the

handicraftsmen and peasants—all these sink gradually into the proletariat, partly because their diminutive capital does not suffice for the scale on which modern industry is carried on, and is swamped in the competition with the large capitalists, partly because their specialized skill is rendered worthless by new methods of production. Thus the proletariat is recruited from all classes of the population.

The proletariat goes through various stages of development. With its birth begins its struggle with the bourgeoisie. At first the contest is carried on by individual laborers, then by the workpeople of a factory, then by the operatives of one trade, in one locality, against the individual bourgeois who directly exploits them. They direct their attacks not against the bourgeois conditions of production, but against the instruments of production themselves; they destroy imported wares that compete with their labor, they smash to pieces machinery, they set factories ablaze, they seek to restore by force the vanished status of the workman of the Middle Ages.

At this stage the laborers still form an incoherent mass scattered over the whole country and broken up by their mutual competition. If anywhere they unite to form more compact bodies, this is not yet the consequence of their own active union, but of the union of the bourgeoisie, which class, in order to attain its own political ends, is compelled to set the whole proletariat in motion, and is moreover yet, for a time, able to do so. At this stage, therefore, the proletarians do not fight their enemies, but the enemies of their enemies, the non-industrial bourgeois, the petty bourgeoisie. Thus the whole historical movement is concentrated in the hands of the bourgeoisie; every victory so obtained is a victory for the bourgeoisie.

But with the development of industry

the proletariat not only increases in number; it becomes concentrated in greater masses, its strength grows, and it feels that strength more. The various interests and conditions of life within the ranks of the proletariat are more and more equalized, in proportion as machinery obliterates all distinctions of labor and nearly everywhere reduces wages to the same low level. The growing competition among the bourgeois and the resulting commercial crises make the wages of the workers ever more fluctuating. The unceasing improvement of machinery, ever more rapidly developing, makes their livelihood more and more precarious; the collisions between individual workmen and individual bourgeois take more and more the character of collisions between two classes. Thereupon the workers begin to form combinations (trade unions) against the bourgeois; they club together in order to keep up the rate of wages; they found permanent associations in order to make provision beforehand for these occasional revolts. Here and there the contest breaks out into riots.

Now and then the workers are victorious, but only for a time. The real fruit of their battles lies not in the immediate result, but in the ever expanding union of the workers. This union is helped on by the improved means of communication that are created by modern industry and that place the workers of different localities in contact with one another. It was just this contact that was needed to centralize the numerous local struggles, all of the same character, into one national struggle between classes. But every class struggle is a political struggle. And that union, to attain which the burghers of the Middle Ages, with their miserable highways, required centuries, the modern proletarians, thanks to railways, achieve in a few years.

This organization of the proletarians into a class, and consequently into a political party, is continually being upset again by the competition between the workers themselves. But it ever rises up again, stronger, firmer, mightier. It compels legislative recognition of particular interests of the workers by taking advantage of the divisions among the bourgeoisie itself. Thus the ten-hour bill in England was carried.

Altogether collisions between the classes of the old society further, in many ways, the course of development of the proletariat. The bourgeoisie finds itself involved in a constant battle. At first with the aristocracy; later on, with those portions of the bourgeoisie itself whose interests have become antagonistic to the progress of industry; at all times, with the bourgeoisie of foreign countries. In all these battles it sees itself compelled to appeal to the proletariat, to ask for its help, and thus to drag it into the political arena. The bourgeoisie itself, therefore, supplies the proletariat with its own elements of political and general education: in other words, it furnishes the proletariat with weapons for fighting the bourgeoisie.

Further, as we have already seen, entire sections of the ruling classes are, by the advance of industry, precipitated into the proletariat, or are at least threatened in their conditions of existence. These also supply the proletariat with fresh elements of enlightenment and progress.

Finally, in times when the class struggle nears the decisive hour, the process of dissolution going on within the ruling class, in fact within the whole range of old society, assumes such a violent, glaring character that a small section of the ruling class cuts itself adrift and joins the revolutionary class, the class that holds the future in its hands. Just as, therefore, at an earlier period, a section of the nobility went over to the bourgeoisie, so now a portion of the bourgeoisie goes over to the proletariat, and in particular a portion of the bourgeois ideologists, who have raised themselves to the level of comprehending theoretically the historical movement as a whole.

Of all the classes that stand face to face with the bourgeoisie today, the proletariat alone is a really revolutionary class. The other classes decay and finally disappear in the face of modern industry; the proletariat is its special and essential product.

The lower-middle class, the small manufacturer, the shopkeeper, the artisan, the peasant, all these fight against the bourgeoisie, to save from extinction their existence as fractions of the middle class. They are therefore not revolutionary, but conservative. Nay, more, they are reactionary, for they try to roll back the wheel of history. If by chance they are revolutionary they are so only in view of their impending transfer into the proletariat; they thus defend not their present but their future interests, they desert their own standpoint to place themselves at that of the proletariat.

The "dangerous class," the social scum, that passively rotting mass thrown off by the lowest layers of old society, may, here and there, be swept into the movement by a proletarian revolution; its conditions of life, however, prepare it far more for the part of a bribed tool of reactionary intrigue.

In the conditions of the proletariat those of old society at large are already virtually swamped. The proletarian is without property; his relation to his wife and children has no longer anything in common with the bourgeois family relations; modern industrial labor, modern subjection to capital, the same in England as in France, in America as in Germany, has stripped him of every trace of national character. Law, morality, religion are to him so many bourgeois prejudices, be-

hind which lurk in ambush just as many bourgeois interests.

All the preceding classes that got the upper hand sought to fortify their already acquired status by subjecting society at large to their conditions of appropriation. The proletarians cannot become masters of their productive forces of society, except by abolishing their own previous mode of appropriation, and thereby also every other previous mode of appropriation. They have nothing of their own to secure and to fortify; their mission is to destroy all previous securities for, and insurances of, individual property.

All previous historical movements were movements of minorities, or in the interest of minorities. The proletarian movement is the self-conscious, independent movement of the immense majority, in the interests of the immense majority. The proletariat, the lowest stratum of our present society, cannot stir, cannot raise itself up, without the whole superincumbent strata of official society being sprung into the air.

Though not in substance, yet in form, the struggle of the proletariat with the bourgeoisie is at first a national struggle. The proletariat of each country must, of course, first of all settle matters with its own bourgeoisie.

In depicting the most general phases of the development of the proletariat, we traced the more or less veiled civil war, raging within existing society, up to the point where that war breaks out into open revolution, and where the violent overthrow of the bourgeoisie lays the foundation for the sway of the proletariat.

Hitherto every form of society has been based, as we have already seen, on the antagonism of oppressing and oppressed classes. But in order to oppress a class certain conditions must be assured to it under which it can, at least, continue its slavish existence. The serf, in the period of serfdom, raised himself to membership in the commune, just as the petty bourgeois, under the yoke of feudal absolutism, managed to develop into a bourgeois. The modern laborer, on the contrary, instead of rising with the progress of industry, sinks deeper and deeper below the conditions of existence of his own class. He becomes a pauper, and pauperism develops more rapidly than population and wealth. And here it becomes evident that the bourgeoisie is unfit any longer to be the ruling class in society, and to impose its conditions of existence upon society as an overriding law. It is unfit to rule because it is incompetent to assure an existence to its slave within his slavery, because it cannot help letting him sink into such a state that it has to feed him instead of being fed by him. Society can no longer live under this bourgeoisie: in other words, its existence is no longer compatible with society.

The essential condition for the existence, and for the sway of the bourgeois class, is the formation and augmentation of capital; the condition for capital is wage labor. Wage labor rests exclusively on competition between the laborers. The advance of industry, whose involuntary promoter is the bourgeoisie, replaces the isolation of the laborers, due to competition, by their revolutionary combination, due to association. The development of modern industry, therefore, cuts from under its feet the very foundation on which the bourgeoisie produces and appropriates products. What the bourgeoisie, therefore, produces, above all, is its own gravediggers. Its fall and the victory of the proletariat are equally inevitable.

# 18

# Protestantism and the Rise of Modern Capitalism

MAX WEBER

## The Uniqueness of Modern Capitalism

A product of modern European civilization, studying any problem of universal history, is bound to ask himself to what combination of circumstances the fact should be attributed that in Western civilization, and in Western civilization only, cultural phenomena have appeared which (as we like to

Reprinted with the permission of Charles Scribner's Sons from *The Protestant Ethic and the Spirit of Capitalism* by Max Weber. Translated by Talcott Parsons. Copyright © by George Allen & Unwin Ltd. Used by permission.

think) lie in a line of development having *universal* significance and value. . . .

. . . The Occident has developed capitalism both to a quantitative extent, and (carrying this quantitative development) in types, forms, and directions which have never existed elsewhere. All over the world there have been merchants, wholesale and retail, local and engaged in foreign trade. Loans of all kinds have been made, and there have been banks with the most various functions, at least comparable to ours of, say, the sixteenth century. . . . Whenever money finances of public bodies have existed, money-lenders have appeared, as in Babylon, Hellas, India, China, Rome. They have financed wars and piracy, contracts and building operations of all sorts. In overseas policy they have functioned as colonial entrepreneurs, as planters with slaves, or directly or indirectly forced labour, and have farmed domains, offices, and, above all, taxes. They have financed party leaders in elections and *condottieri* in civil wars. And, finally, they have been speculators in chances for pecuniary gain of all kinds. This kind of entrepreneur, the capitalistic adventurer, has existed everywhere. With the exception of trade and credit and banking transactions, their activities were predominantly of an irrational and speculative character, or directed to acquisition by force, above all the acqustion of booty, whether directly in war or in the form of continuous fiscal booty by exploitation of subjects.

The capitalism of promoters, large-scale speculators, concession hunters, and much modern financial capitalism even in peace time, but, above all, the capitalism especially concerned with exploiting wars, bears this stamp even in modern Western countries, and some, but only some, parts of large-scale international trade are closely related to it, to-day as always.

But in modern times the Occident has developed, in addition to this, a very different form of capitalism which has appeared nowhere else: the rational capitalistic organization of (formally) free labour. . . . Real domestic industries with free labour have definitely been proved to have existed in only a few isolated cases outside the Occident. . . .

Rational industrial organization, attuned to a regular market, and neither to political nor irrationally speculative opportunities for profit, is not, however, the only peculiarity of Western capitalism. The modern rational organ-

ization of the capitalistic enterprise would not have been possible without two other important factors in its development: the separation of business from the household, which completely dominates modern economic life, and closely connected with it, rational book-keeping. A spatial separation of places of work from those of residence exists elsewhere, as in the Oriental bazaar and in the *ergasteria* of other cultures. The development of capitalistic associations with their own accounts is also found in the Far East, the Near East, and in antiquity. But compared to the modern independence of business enterprises, those are only small beginnings. The reason for this was particularly that the indispensable requisites for this independence, our rational business book-keeping and our legal separation of corporate from personal property, were entirely lacking, or had only begun to develop. The tendency everywhere else was for acquisitive enterprises to arise as parts of a royal or manorial *household* (of the *oikos*), which is, as Rodbertus has perceived, with all its superficial similarity, a fundamentally different, even opposite, development.

However, all these peculiarities of Western capitalism have derived their significance in the last analysis only from their association with the capitalistic organization of labour. Even what is generally called commercialization, the development of negotiable securities and the rationalization of speculation, the exchanges, etc., is connected with it. For without the rational capitalistic organization of labour, all this, so far as it was possible at all, would have nothing like the same significance, above all for the social structure and all the specific problems of the modern Occident connected with it. Exact calculation—the basis of everything else —is only possible on a basis of free labour. . . .

Hence in a universal history of culture the central problem for us is . . . the origin of this sober bourgeois capitalism with its rational organization of free labour. Or in terms of cultural history, the problem is that of the origin of the Western bourgeois class and of its peculiarities. . . .

Now the peculiar modern Western form of capitalism has been, at first sight, strongly influenced by the development of technical possibilities. Its rationality is to-day essentially dependent on the calculability of the most important technical factors. But this means fundamentally that it is dependent on the peculiarities of modern science, especially the natural sciences based on mathematics and exact and rational experiment. On the other hand, the development of these sciences and of the technique resting upon them now receives important stimulation from these capitalistic interests in its practical economic application. It is true that the origin of Western science cannot be attributed to such interests. Calculation, even with decimals, and algebra have been carried on in India, where the decimal system was invented. But it was only made use of by developing capitalism in the West, while in India it led to no modern arithmetic or book-keeping. Neither was the origin of mathematics and mechanics determined by capitalistic interests. But the *technical* utilization of scientific knowledge, so important for the living conditions of the mass of people, was certainly encouraged by economic considerations, which were extremely favourable to it in the Occident. But this encouragement was derived from the peculiarities of the social structure of the Occident. We must hence ask, from *what* parts of that structure was it derived, since not all of them have been of equal importance?

Among those of undoubted importance are the rational structures of law and of administration. For modern rational capitalism has need, not only of the technical means of production, but of a calculable legal system and of administration in terms of formal rules. Without it adventurous and speculative trading capitalism and all sorts of politically determined capitalisms are possible, but no rational enterprise under individual initiative, with fixed capital and certainty of calculations. Such a legal system and such administration have been available for economic activity in a comparative state of legal and formalistic perfection only in the Occident. We must hence inquire where that law came from. Among other circumstances, capitalistic interests have in turn undoubtedly also helped, but by no means alone nor even principally, to prepare the way for the predominance in law and administration of a class of jurists specially trained in rational law. But these interests did not themselves create that law. Quite different forces were at work in this development. And why did not the capitalistic interests do the same in China or India? Why did not the scientific, the artistic, the political, or the economic development there enter upon that path or rationalization which is peculiar to the Occident?

For in all the above cases it is a question of the specific and peculiar rationalism of Western culture. Now by this term very different things may be understood, as the following discussion will repeatedly show. There is, for example, rationalization of mystical contemplation, that is of an attitude which, viewed from other departments of life, is especially irrational, just as much as there are rationalizations of economic life, of technique, of scientific research, of military training, of law and administration. Furthermore, each one of these fields may be rationalized in terms of very different ultimate values and ends, and what is rational from one point of view may well be irrational from another. Hence rationalizations of the most varied character have existed in various departments of life and in all areas of culture. To characterize their differences from the view-point of cultural history it is necessary to know what departments are rationalized, and in what direction. It is hence our first concern to work out and to explain genetically the special peculiarity of Occidental rationalism, and within this field that of the modern Occidental form. Every attempt at explanation must, recognizing the fundamental importance of the economic factor, above all take account of the economic conditions. But at the same time the opposite correlation must not be left out of consideration. For though the development of economic rationalism is partly dependent on rational technology and law, it is at the same time determined by the ability and disposition of men to adopt certain types of practical rational conduct. When these types have been obstructed by spiritual obstacles, the development of rational economic conduct has also met serious inner resistance. The magical and religious forces, and the ethical ideas of duty based upon them, have in the past always been among the most important formative influences on conduct. In the studies collected here we shall be concerned with . . . the influence of certain religious ideas on the development of an economic spirit, or the *ethos* of an economic system. In this case we are dealing with the connection of the spirit of modern economic life with the rational ethics of ascetic Protestantism. . . .

## Protestantism and Modern Capitalism

In order to understand the connection between the fundamental religious ideas of ascetic Protestantism and its maxims for everyday economic conduct, it is necessary to examine with

especial care such writings as have evidently been derived from ministerial practice. For a time in which the beyond meant everything, when the social position of the Christian depended upon his admission to the communion, the clergyman, through his ministry, Church discipline, and preaching, exercised an influence (as a glance at collections of *consilia, casus conscientiæ,* etc., shows) which we modern men are entirely unable to picture. In such a time the religious forces which express themselves through such channels are the decisive influences in the formation of national character. . . .

Since that side of English Puritanism which was derived from Calvinism gives the most consistent religious basis for the idea of the calling, we shall, . . . place one of its representatives at the centre of the discussion. Richard Baxter stands out above many other writers on Puritan ethics, both because of his eminently practical and realistic attitude, and, at the same time, because of the universal recognition accorded to his works, which have gone through many new editions and translations. He was a Presbyterian and an apologist of the Westminster Synod, but at the same time, like so many of the best spirits of his time, gradually grew away from the dogmas of pure Calvinism. At heart he opposed Cromwell's usurpation as he would any revolution. He was unfavourable to the sects and the fanatical enthusiasm of the saints, but was very broad-minded about external peculiarities and objective towards his opponents. He sought his field of labour most especially in the practical promotion of the moral life through the Church. In the pursuit of this end, as one of the most successful ministers known to history, he placed his services at the disposal of the Parliamentary Government, of Cromwell, and of the Restoration, until he retired from office under the last, before St. Bartholomew's day. His *Christian Directory* is the most complete compendium of Puritan ethics, and is continually adjusted to the practical experiences of his own ministerial activity. In comparison we shall make use of Spener's *Theologische Bedenken*, as representative of German Pietism, Barclay's *Apology* for the Quakers, and some other representatives of ascetic ethics, which, however, in the interest of space, will be limited as far as possible.

Now, in glancing at Baxter's *Saint's Everlasting Rest*, or his *Christian Directory*, or similar works of others, one is struck at first glance by the emphasis placed, in the discussion of wealth and its acquisition, on the ebionitic elements of the New Testament. Wealth as such is a great danger; its temptations never end, and its pursuit is not only senseless as compared with the dominating importance of the Kingdom of God, but it is morally suspect. Here asceticism seems to have turned much more sharply against the acquisition of earthly goods than it did in Calvin, who saw no hindrance to the effectiveness of the clergy in their wealth, but rather a thoroughly desirable enhancement of their prestige. Hence he permitted them to employ their means profitably. Examples of the condemnation of the pursuit of money and goods may be gathered without end from Puritan writings, and may be contrasted with the late mediæval ethical literature, which was much more openminded on this point.

Moreover, these doubts were meant with perfect seriousness; only it is necessary to examine them somewhat more closely in order to understand their true ethical significance and implications. The real moral objection is to relaxation in the security of possession, the enjoyment of wealth with the consequence of idleness and the temptations of the flesh, above all of distraction from the pursuit of a righteous life. In fact, it is only because possession involves this danger of relaxation that it is objectionable at all. For the saints' everlasting rest is in the next world; on earth man must, to be certain of his state of grace, "do the works of him who sent him, as long as it is yet day." Not leisure and enjoyment, but only activity serves to increase the glory of God, according to the definite manifestations of His will.

Waste of time is thus the first and in principle the deadliest of sins. The span of human life is infinitely short and precious to make sure of one's own election. Loss of time through sociability, idle talk, luxury, even more sleep than is necessary for health, six to at most eight hours, is worthy of absolute moral condemnation. It does not yet hold, with Franklin, that time is money, but the proposition is true in a certain spiritual sense. It is infinitely valuable because every hour lost is lost to labour for the glory of God. Thus inactive contemplation is also valueless, or even directly reprehensible if it is at the expense of one's daily work. For it is less pleasing to God than the active performance of His will in a calling. Besides, Sunday is provided for that, and, according to Baxter, it is always those who are not diligent in their callings who have no time for God when the occasion demands it.

Accordingly, Baxter's principal work is dominated by the continually repeated, often almost passionate preaching of hard, continuous bodily or mental labour. It is due to a combination of two different motives. Labour is, on the one hand, an approved ascetic technique, as it always has been in the Western Church, in sharp contrast not only to the Orient but to almost all monastic rules the world over. It is in particular the specific defence against all those temptations which Puritanism united under the name of the unclean life, whose rôle for it was by no means small. The sexual asceticism of Puritanism differs only in degree, not in fundamental principle, from that of monasticism; and on account of the Puritan conception of marriage, its practical influence is more far-reaching than that of the latter. For sexual intercourse is permitted, even within marriage, only as the means willed by God for the increase of His glory according to the commandment, "Be fruitful and multiply." Along with a moderate vegetable diet and cold baths, the same prescription is given for all sexual temptations as is used against religious doubts and a sense of moral unworthiness: "Work hard in your calling." But the most important thing was that even beyond that labour came to be considered in itself the end of life, ordained as such by God. St. Paul's "He who will not work shall not eat" holds unconditionally for everyone. Unwillingness to work is symptomatic of the lack of grace.

Here the difference from the mediæval view-point becomes quite evident. Thomas Aquinas also gave an interpretation of that statement of St. Paul. But for him labour is only necessary *naturali ratione* for the maintenance of individual and community. Where this end is achieved, the precept ceases to have any meaning. Moreover, it holds only for the race, not for every individual. It does not apply to anyone who can live without labour on his possessions, and of course contemplation, as a spiritual form of action in the Kingdom of God, takes precedence over the commandment in its literal sense. Moreover, for the popular theology of the time, the highest form of monastic productivity lay in the increase of the *Thesaurus ecclesiæ* through prayer and chant.

Now only do these exceptions to the duty to labour naturally no longer hold for Baxter, but he holds most emphatically that wealth does not exempt any-

one from the unconditional command. Even the wealthy shall not eat without working, for even though they do not need to labour to support their own needs, there is God's commandment which they, like the poor, must obey. For everyone without exception God's Providence has prepared a calling, which he should profess and in which he should labour. And this calling is not, as it was for the Lutheran, a fate to which he must submit and which he must make the best of, but God's commandment to the individual to work for the divine glory. This seemingly subtle difference had far-reaching psychological consequences, and became connected with a further development of the providential interpretation of the economic order which had begun in scholasticism.

The phenomenon of the division of labour and occupations in society had, among others, been interpreted by Thomas Aquinas, to whom we may most conveniently refer, as a direct consequence of the divine scheme of things. But the places assigned to each man in this cosmos follow *ex causis naturalibus* and are fortuitous (contingent in the Scholastic terminology). The differentiation of men into the classes and occupations established through historical development became for Luther, as we have seen, a direct result of the divine will. The perseverance of the individual in the place and within the limits which God had assigned to him was a religious duty. This was the more certainly the consequence since the relations of Lutheranism to the world were in general uncertain from the beginning and remained so. Ethical principles for the reform of the world could not be found in Luther's realm of ideas; in fact it never quite freed itself from Pauline indifference. Hence the world had to be accepted as it was, and this alone could be made a religious duty.

But in the Puritan view, the providential character of the play of private economic interests takes on a somewhat different emphasis. True to the Puritan tendency to pragmatic interpretations, the providential purpose of the division of labour is to be known by its fruits. On this point Baxter expresses himself in terms which more than once directly recall Adam Smith's well-known apotheosis of the division of labour. The specialization of occupations leads, since it makes the development of skill possible, to a quantitative and qualitative improvement in production, and thus serves the common good, which is identical with the good of the greatest possible number. So far, the motivation is purely utilitarian, and is closely related to the customary view-point of much of the secular literature of the time.

But the characteristic Puritan element appears when Baxter sets at the head of his discussion the statement that "outside of a well-marked calling the accomplishments of a man are only casual and irregular, and he spends more time in idleness than at work," and when he concludes it as follows: "and he [the specialized worker] will carry out his work in order while another remains in constant confusion, and his business knows neither time nor place . . . therefore is a certain calling the best for everyone." Irregular work, which the ordinary labourer is often forced to accept, is often unavoidable, but always an unwelcome state of transition. A man without a calling thus lacks the systematic, methodical character which is, as we have seen, demanded by worldly asceticism.

The Quaker ethic also holds that a man's life in his calling is an exercise in ascetic virtue, a proof of his state of grace through his conscientiousness, which is expressed in the care and method with which he pursues his calling. What God demands is not labour in itself, but rational labour in a call-

ing. In the Puritan concept of the calling the emphasis is always placed on this methodical character of worldly asceticism, not, as with Luther, on the acceptance of the lot which God has irretrievably assigned to man. . . .

Hence the question whether anyone may combine several callings is answered in the affirmative, if it is useful for the common good or one's own, and not injurious to anyone, and if it does not lead to unfaithfulness in one of the callings. Even a change of calling is by no means regarded as objectionable, if it is not thoughtless and is made for the purpose of pursuing a calling more pleasing to God, which means, on general principles, one more useful.

It is true that the usefulness of a calling, and thus its favour in the sight of God, is measured primarily in moral terms, and thus in terms of the importance of the goods produced in it for the community. But a further, and, above all, in practice the most important, criterion is found in private profitableness. For if that God, whose hand the Puritan sees in all the occurrences of life, shows one of His elect a chance of profit, he must do it with a purpose. Hence the faithful Christian must follow the call by taking advantage of the opportunity. "If God show you a way in which you may lawfully get more than in another way (without wrong to your soul or to any other), if you refuse this, and choose the less gainful way, you cross one of the ends of your calling, and you refuse to be God's steward, and to accept His gifts and use them for Him when He requireth it: you may labour to be rich for God, though not for the flesh and sin."

Wealth is thus bad ethically only in so far as it is a temptation to idleness and sinful enjoyment of life, and its acquisition is bad only when it is with the purpose of later living merrily and without care. But as a performance of duty in a calling it is not only morally permissible, but actually enjoined. The parable of the servant who was rejected because he did not increase the talent which was entrusted to him seemed to say so directly. To wish to be poor was, it was often argued, the same as wishing to be unhealthy; it is objectionable as a glorification of works and derogatory to the glory of God. Especially begging, on the part of one able to work, is not only the sin of slothfulness, but a violation of the duty of brotherly love according to the Apostle's own word.

The emphasis on the ascetic importance of a fixed calling provided an ethical justification of the modern specialized division of labour. In a similar way the providential interpretation of profit-making justified the activities of the business man. The superior indulgence of the *seigneur* and the parvenu ostentation of the *nouveau riche* are equally detestable to asceticism. But, on the other hand, it has the highest ethical appreciation of the sober, middle-class, self-made man. "God blesseth His trade" is a stock remark about those good men who had successfully followed the divine hints. The whole power of the God of the Old Testament, who rewards His people for their obedience in this life, necessarily exercised a similar influence on the Puritan who, following Baxter's advice, compared his own state of grace with that of the heroes of the Bible, and in the process interpreted the statements of the Scriptures as the articles of a book of statutes. . . .

In addition to the relationships already pointed out, it is important for the general inner attitude of the Puritans, above all, that the belief that they were God's chosen people saw in them a great renaissance. Even the kindly Baxter thanked God that he was born in England, and thus in the true Church, and nowhere else. This thankfulness for one's own perfection by the grace of God penetrated the attitude toward life of the Puritan middle class, and played its part in developing that formalistic, hard, correct character which was peculiar to the men of that heroic age of capitalism.

Let us now try to clarify the points in which the Puritan idea of the calling and the premium it placed upon ascetic conduct was bound directly to influence the development of a capitalistic way of life. As we have seen, this asceticism turned with all its force against one thing: the spontaneous enjoyment of life and all it had to offer. This is perhaps most characteristically brought out in the struggle over the *Book of Sports* which James I and Charles I made into law expressly as a means of counteracting Puritanism, and which the latter ordered to be read from all the pulpits. The fanatical opposition of the Puritans to the ordinances of the King, permitting certain popular amusements on Sunday outside of Church hours by law, was not only explained by the disturbance of the Sabbath rest, but also by resentment against the intentional diversion from the ordered life of the saint, which it caused. And, on his side, the King's threats of severe punishment for every attack on the legality of those sports were motivated by his purpose of breaking the anti-authoritarian ascetic tendency of Puritanism, which was so dangerous to the State. The feudal and monarchical forces protected the pleasure seekers against the rising middle-class morality and the anti-authoritarian ascetic conventicles, just as to-day capitalistic society tends to protect those willing to work against the class morality of the proletariat and the anti-authoritarian trade union.

As against this the Puritans upheld their decisive characteristic, the principle of ascetic conduct. For otherwise the Puritan aversion to sport, even for the Quakers, was by no means simply one of principle. Sport was accepted if it served a rational purpose, that of recreation necessary for physical efficiency. But as a means for the spontaneous expression of undisciplined impulses, it was under suspicion; and in so far as it became purely a means of enjoyment, or awakened pride, raw instincts or the irrational gambling instinct, it was of course strictly condemned. Impulsive enjoyment of life, which leads away both from work in a calling and from religion, was as such the enemy of rational asceticism, whether in the form of seigneurial sports, or the enjoyment of the dance-hall or the public-house of the common man. . . .

Its attitude was thus suspicious and often hostile to the aspects of culture without any immediate religious value. It is not, however, true that the ideals of Puritanism implied a solemn, narrow-minded contempt of culture. Quite the contrary is the case at least for science, with the exception of the hatred of Scholasticism. Moreover, the great men of the Puritan movement were thoroughly steeped in the culture of the Renaissance. The sermons of the Presbyterian divines abound with classical allusions, and even the Radicals, although they objected to it, were not ashamed to display that kind of learning in theological polemics. Perhaps no country was ever so full of graduates as New England in the first generation of its existence. The satire of their opponents, such as, for instance, Butler's *Hudibras*, also attacks primarily the pendantry and highly trained dialectics of the Puritans. This is partially due to the religious valuation of knowledge which followed from their attitude to the Catholic *fides implicita*.

But the situation is quite different when one looks at non-scientific literature, and especially the fine arts. Here asceticism descended like a frost on

the life of "Merrie old England." And not only worldly merriment felt its effect. The Puritan's ferocious hatred of everything which smacked of superstition, of all survivals of magical or sacramental salvation, applied to the Christmas festivities and the May Pole and all spontaneous religious art. . . .

The theatre was obnoxious to the Puritans, and with the strict exclusion of the erotic and of nudity from the realm of toleration, a radical view of either literature or art could not exist. The conceptions of idle talk, of superfluities, and of vain ostentation, all designations of an irrational attitude without objective purpose, thus not ascetic, and especially not serving the glory of God, but of man, were always at hand to serve in deciding in favour of sober utility as against any artistic tendencies. This was especially true in the case of decoration of the person, for instance clothing. That powerful tendency toward uniformity of life, which to-day so immensely aids the capitalistic interest in the standardization of production, had its ideal foundations in the repudiation of all idolatry of the flesh. . . .

Although we cannot here enter upon a discussion of the influence of Puritanism in all these directions, we should call attention to the fact that the toleration of pleasure in cultural goods, which contributed to purely æsthetic or athletic enjoyment, certainly always ran up against one characteristic limitation: they must not cost anything. Man is only a trustee of the goods which have come to him through God's grace. He must, like the servant in the parable, give an account of every penny entrusted to him, and it is at least hazardous to spend any of it for a purpose which does not serve the glory of God but only one's own enjoyment. What person, who keeps his eyes open, has not met representatives of this view-point even in the present?

The idea of a man's duty to his possessions, to which he subordinates himself as an obedient steward, or even as an acquisitive machine, bears with chilling weight on his life. The greater the possessions the heavier, if the ascetic attitude toward life stands the test, the feeling of responsibility for them, for holding them undiminished for the glory of God and increasing them by restless effort. . . .

This worldly Protestant asceticism, as we may recapitulate up to this point, acted powerfully against the spontaneous enjoyment of possessions; it restricted consumption, especially of luxuries. On the other hand, it had the psychological effect of freeing the acquisition of goods from the inhibitions of traditionalistic ethics. It broke the bonds of the impulse of acquisition in that it not only legalized it, but (in the sense discussed) looked upon it as directly willed by God. The campaign against the temptations of the flesh, and the dependence on external things, was, as besides the Puritans the great Quaker apologist Barclay expressly says, not a struggle against the rational acquistion, but against the irrational use of wealth.

But this irrational use was exemplified in the outward forms of luxury which their code condemned as idolatry of the flesh, however natural they had appeared to the feudal mind. On the other hand, they approved the rational and utilitarian uses of wealth which were willed by God for the needs of the individual and the community. They did not wish to impose mortification on the man of wealth, but the use of his means for necessary and practical things. The idea of comfort characteristically limits the extent of ethically permissible expenditures. It is naturally no accident that the development of a manner of living consistent with that idea may be observed earliest and most clearly among the most consistent representatives of this whole attitude toward life. Over against the glitter and ostentation of feudal magnificence, which, resting on an unsound economic basis, prefers a sordid elegance to a sober simplicity, they set the clean and solid comfort of the middle-class home as an ideal.

On the side of the production of private wealth, asceticism condemned both dishonesty and impulsive avarice. What was condemned as covetousness, Mammonism, etc., was the pursuit of riches for their own sake. For wealth in itself was a temptation. But here asceticism was the power "which ever seeks the good but ever creates evil"; what was evil in its sense was possession and its temptations. For, in conformity with the Old Testament and in analogy to the ethical valuation of good works, asceticism looked upon the pursuit of wealth as an end in itself as highly reprehensible; but the attainment of it as a fruit of labour in a calling was a sign of God's blessing. And even more important: the religious valuation of restless, continuous, systematic work in a worldly calling, as the highest means to asceticism, and at the same time the surest and most evident proof of rebirth and genuine faith, must have been the most powerful conceivable lever for the expansion of that attitude toward life which we have here called the spirit of capitalism.

When the limitation of consumption is combined with this release of acquisitive activity, the inevitable practical result is obvious: accumulation of capital through ascetic compulsion to save. The restraints which were imposed upon the consumption of wealth naturally served to increase it by making possible the productive investment of capital. How strong this influence was is not, unfortunately, susceptible of exact statistical demonstration. In New England the connection is so evident that it did not escape the eye of so discerning a historian as Doyle. But also in Holland, which was really only dominated by strict Calvinism for seven years, the greater simplicity of life in the more seriously religious circles, in combination with great wealth, led to an excessive propensity to accumulation. . . .

As far as the influence of the Puritan outlook extended, under all circumstances—and this is, of course, much more important than the mere encouragement of capital accumulation—it favoured the development of a rational bourgeois economic life; it was the most important, and above all the only consistent influence in the development of that life. It stood at the cradle of the modern economic man.

To be sure, these Puritanical ideals tended to give way under excessive pressure from the temptations of wealth, as the Puritans themselves knew very well. With great regularity we find the most genuine adherents of Puritanism among the classes which were rising from the lowly status, the small bourgeois and farmers, while the *beati possidentes,* even among Quakers, are often found tending to repudiate the old ideals. It was the same fate which again and again befell the predecessor of this worldly asceticism, the monastic asceticism of the Middle Ages. In the latter case, when rational economic activity had worked out its full effects by strict regulation of conduct and limitation of consumption, the wealth accumulated either succumbed directly to the nobility, as in the time before the Reformation, or monastic discipline threatened to break down, and one of the numerous reformations became necessary.

In fact the whole history of monasticism is in a certain sense the history of a continual struggle with the problem of the secularizing influence of wealth. The same is true on a grand scale of the worldly asceticism of Puritanism.

The great revival of Methodism, which preceded the expansion of English industry toward the end of the eighteenth century, may well be compared with such a monastic reform. We may hence quote here a passage from John Wesley himself which might well serve as a motto for everything which has been said above. For it shows that the leaders of these ascetic movements understood the seemingly paradoxical relationships which we have here analysed perfectly well, and in the same sense that we have given them. He wrote:

I fear, wherever riches have increased, the essence of religion has decreased in the same proportion. Therefore I do not see how it is possible, in the nature of things, for any revival of true religion to continue long. For religion must necessarily produce both industry and frugality, and these cannot but produce riches. But as riches increase, so will pride, anger, and love of the world in all its branches. How then is it possible that Methodism, that is, a religion of the heart, though it flourishes now as a green bay tree, should continue in this state? For the Methodists in every place grow diligent and frugal; consequently they increase in goods. Hence they proportionately increase in pride, in anger, in the desire of the flesh, the desire of the eyes, and the pride of life. So, although the form of religion remains, the spirit is swiftly vanishing away. Is there no way to prevent this—this continual decay of pure religion? We ought not to prevent people from being diligent and frugal; *we must exhort all Christians to gain all they can, and to save all they can; that is, in effect, to grow rich.* . . .

What the great religious epoch of the seventeenth century bequeathed to its utilitarian successor was, . . . above all an amazingly good, we may even say a pharisaically good, conscience in the acquisition of money, so long as it took place legally. . . .

A specifically bourgeois economic ethic had grown up. With the consciousness of standing in the fullness of God's grace and being visibly blessed by Him, the bourgeois business man, as long as he remained within the bounds of formal correctness, as long as his moral conduct was spotless and the use to which he put his wealth was not objectionable, could follow his pecuniary interests as he would and feel that he was fulfilling a duty in doing so. The power of religious asceticism provided him in addition with sober, conscientious, and unusually industrious workmen, who clung to their work as to a life purpose willed by God.

Finally, it gave him the comforting assurance that the unequal distribution of the goods of this world was a special dispensation of Divine Providence, which in these differences, as in particular grace, pursued secret ends unknown to men. Calvin himself had made the much-quoted statement that only when the people, i.e. the mass of labourers and craftsmen, were poor did they remain obedient to God. In the Netherlands (Pieter de la Court and others), that had been secularized to the effect that the mass of men only labour when necessity forces them to do so. This formulation of a leading idea of capitalistic economy later entered into the current theories of the productivity of low wages. Here also, with the dying out of the religious root, the utilitarian interpretation crept in unnoticed, in the line of development which we have again and again observed. . . .

Now naturally the whole ascetic literature of almost all denominations is saturated with the idea that faithful labour, even at low wages, on the part of those whom life offers no other opportunities, is highly pleasing to God. In this respect Protestant Asceticism added in itself nothing new. But it not only deepened this idea most powerfully, it also created the force which was alone decisive for its effectiveness: the psychological sanction of it through the conception of this labour as a calling, as the best, often in the last analy-

sis the only means of attaining certainty of grace. And on the other hand it legalized the exploitation of this specific willingness to work, in that it also interpreted the employer's business activity as a calling. It is obvious how powerfully the exclusive search for the Kingdom of God only through the fulfilment of duty in the calling, and the strict asceticism which Church discipline naturally imposed, especially on the propertyless classes, was bound to affect the productivity of labour in the capitalistic sense of the word. The treatment of labour as a calling became as characteristic of the modern worker as the corresponding attitude toward acquisition of the business man. It was a perception of this situation, new at his time, which caused so able an observer as Sir William Petty to attribute the economic power of Holland in the seventeenth century to the fact that the very numerous dissenters in that country (Calvinists and Baptists) "are for the most part thinking, sober men, and such as believe that Labour and Industry is their duty towards God." . . .

One of the fundamental elements of the spirit of modern capitalism, and not only of that but of all modern culture: rational conduct on the basis of the idea of the calling, was born—that is what this discussion has sought to demonstrate—from the spirit of Christian asceticism. . . .

The Puritan wanted to work in a calling; we are forced to do so. For when asceticism was carried out of monastic cells into everyday life, and began to dominate worldly morality, it did its part in building the tremendous cosmos of the modern economic order. This order is now bound to the technical and economic conditions of machine production which to-day determine the lives of all the individuals who are born into this mechanism, not only those directly concerned with economic acquisition, with irresistible force. Perhaps it will so determine them until the last ton of fossilized coal is burnt. In Baxter's view the care for external goods should only lie on the shoulders of the "saint like a light cloak, which can be thrown aside at any moment." But fate decreed that the cloak should become an iron cage.

Since asceticism undertook to remodel the world and to work out its ideals in the world, material goods have gained an increasing and finally an inexorable power over the lives of men as at no previous period in history. Today the spirit of religious asceticism—whether finally, who knows?—has escaped from the cage. But victorious capitalism, since it rests on mechanical foundations, needs its support no longer. The rosy blush of its laughing heir, the Enlightenment, seems also to be irretrievably fading, and the idea of duty in one's calling prowls about in our lives like the ghost of dead religious beliefs. Where the fulfilment of the calling cannot directly be related to the highest spiritual and cultural values, or when, on the other hand, it need not be felt simply as economic compulsion, the individual generally abandons the attempt to justify it at all. In the field of its highest development, in the United States, the pursuit of wealth, stripped of its religious and ethical meaning, tends to become associated with purely mundane passions, which often actually give it the character of sport.

No one knows who will live in this cage in the future, or whether at the end of this tremendous development entirely new prophets will arise, or there will be a great rebirth of old ideas and ideals, or, if neither, mechanized petrification, embellished with a sort of convulsive self-importance. For of the last stage of this cultural development, it might well be truly said: "Specialists without spirit, sensualists without heart; this nullity imagines that it has attained a level of civilization never before achieved."

But this bring us to the world of judgments of value and of faith, with which this purely historical discussion need not be burdened. The next task would be rather to show the significance of ascetic rationalism, which has only been touched in the foregoing sketch, for the content of practical social ethics, thus for the types or organization and the functions of social groups from the conventicle to the State. Then its relations to humanistic rationalism, its ideals of life and cultural influence; further to the development of philosophical and scientific empiricism, to technical development and to spiritual ideals would have to be analysed. Then its historical development from the mediæval beginnings of worldly asceticism to its dissolution into pure utilitarianism would have to be traced out through all the areas of ascetic religion. Only then could the quantitative cultural significance of ascetic Protestantism in its relation to the other plastic elements of modern culture be estimated.

Here we have only attempted to trace the fact and the direction of its influence to their motives in one, though a very important point. But it would also further be necessary to investigate how Protestant Asceticism was in turn influenced in its development and its character by the totality of social conditions, especially economic. The modern man is in general, even with the best will, unable to give religious ideas a significance for culture and national character which they deserve. But it is, of course, not my aim to substitute for a one-sided materialistic an equally one-sided spiritualistic causal interpretation of culture and of history. Each is equally possible, but each, if it does not serve as the preparation, but as the conclusion of an investigation, accomplishes equally little in the interest of historical truth.

# B Theories of the Human Consequences of the Industrial Transformation

## 19

### Karl Marx's Theory of Alienation

ERICH FROMM

Marx's central criticism of capitalism is not the injustice in the distribution of wealth; it is the perversion of labor into forced, alienated, meaningless labor, hence the transformation of man into a "crippled monstrosity." Marx's concept of labor as an expression of man's individuality is succinctly expressed in his vision of the complete abolition of the lifelong submersion of a man in one occupation. Since the aim of human development is that of the development of the total, universal man, man must be emancipated from the crippling influence of specialization. In all previous societies, Marx writes, man has been

a hunter, a fisherman, a shepherd, or a critical critic, and must remain so if he does not want to lose his means of liveli-

From *Marx's Concept of Man* by Erich Fromm. Copyright © 1961 by Erich Fromm. Used by permission.

hood; while in communist society, where nobody has one exclusive sphere of activity but each can become accomplished in any branch he wishes, society regulates the general production and thus makes it possible for me to do one thing today and another tomorrow, to hunt in the morning, fish in the afternoon, rear cattle in the evening, criticize after dinner, just as I have a mind, without ever becoming hunter, fisherman, shepherd or critic.[1]

There is no greater misunderstanding or misrepresentation of Marx than that which is to be found, implicitly or explicitly, in the thought of the Soviet Communists, the reformist socialists, and the capitalist opponents of socialism alike, all of whom assume that Marx wanted only the economic improvement of the working class, and

[1] *German Ideology*, p. 22.

that he wanted to abolish private property so that the worker would own what the capitalist now has. The truth is that for Marx the situation of a worker in a Russian "socialist" factory, a British state-owned factory, or an American factory such as General Motors, would appear essentially the same. This, Marx expresses very clearly in the following:

> An enforced *increase in wages* (disregarding the other difficulties, and especially that such an anomaly could only be maintained by force) would be nothing more than a *better remuneration of slaves,* and would not restore, either to the worker or to the work, their human significance and worth.
> Even the *equality of incomes* which Proudhon demands would only change the relation of the present-day worker to his work into a relation of all men to work. Society would then be conceived as an abstract capitalist.[2]

The central theme of Marx is the transformation of alienated, meaningless labor into productive, free labor, not the better payment of alienated labor by a private or "abstract" state capitalism.

The concept of the active, productive man who grasps and embraces the objective world with his own powers cannot be fully understood without the concept of the *negation of productivity: alienation.* For Marx the history of mankind is a history of the increasing development of man, and at the same time of increasing alienation. His concept of socialism is the emancipation from alienation, the return of man to himself, his self-realization.

Alienation (or "estrangement") means, for Marx, that man does *not* experience himself as the acting agent in his grasp of the world, but that the world (nature, others, and he himself) remain alien to him. They stand above

and against him as objects, even though they may be objects of his own creation. Alienation is essentially experiencing the world and oneself passively, receptively, as the subject separated from the object.

The whole concept of alienation found its first expression in Western thought in the Old Testament concept of idolatry.[3] The essence of what the prophets call "idolatry" is not that man worships many gods instead of only one. It is that the idols are the work of man's own hands—they are things, and man bows down and worships things; worships that which he has created himself. In doing so he transforms himself into a thing. He transfers to the things of his creation the attributes of his own life, and instead of experiencing himself as the creating person, he is in touch with himself only by the worship of the idol. He has become estranged from his own life forces, from the wealth of his own potentialities, and is in touch with himself only in the indirect way of submission to life frozen in the idols.[4]

The deadness and emptiness of the

[2] *Economic and Philosophic Manuscripts of 1845* (E.P. MSS.), p. 107.

[3] The connection between alienation and idolatry has also been emphasized by Paul Tillich in *Der Mensch im Christentum und im Marxismus,* Düsseldorf, 1953, p. 14. Tillich also points out in another lecture, "Protestantische Vision," that the concept of alienation in substance is to be found also in Augustine's thinking. Löwith also has pointed out that what Marx fights against are not the gods, but the idols [cf. *Von Hegel zu Nietzsche,* l.c., p. 378].

[4] This is, incidentally, also the psychology of the fanatic. He is empty, dead, depressed, but in order to compensate for the state of depression and inner deadness, he chooses an idol, be it the state, a party, an idea, the church, or God. He makes this idol into the absolute, and submits to it in an absolute way. In doing so his life attains meaning, and he finds excitement in the submission to the chosen idol. His excitement, however, does not stem from joy in productive relatedness; it is intense, yet cold excitement built upon inner deadness or, if one would want to put it symbolically, it is "burning ice."

idol is expressed in the Old Testament: "Eyes they have and they do not see, ears they have and they do not hear," etc. The more man transfers his own powers to the idols, the poorer he himself becomes, and the more dependent on the idols, so that they permit him to redeem a small part of what was originally his. The idols can be a god-like figure, the state, the church, a person, possession. Idolatry changes its objects; it is by no means to be found only in those forms in which the idol has a so-called religious meaning. Idolatry is always the worship of something into which man has put his own creative powers, and to which he now submits, instead of experiencing himself in his creating act. Among the many forms of alienation, the most frequent one is alienation in language. If I express a feeling with a word, let us say, if I say "I love you," the word is meant to be an indication of the reality which exists within myself, the power of my loving. The *word* "love" is meant to be a symbol of the *fact* love, but as soon as it is spoken it tends to assume a life of its own, it becomes a reality. I am under the illusion that the saying of the word is the equivalent of the experience, and soon I say the word and feel nothing, except the *thought* of love which the word expresses. The alienation of language shows the whole complexity of alienation. Language is one of the most precious human achievements; to avoid alienation by not speaking would be foolish—yet one must be always aware of the danger of the spoken word, that it threatens to substitute itself for the living experience. The same holds true for all other achievements of man; ideas, art, any kind of man-made objects. They are man's creations; they are valuable aids for life, yet each one of them is also a trap, a temptation to confuse life with things, experience with artifacts, feeling with surrender and submission.

The thinkers of the eighteenth and nineteenth centuries criticized their age for its increasing rigidity, emptiness, and deadness. In Goethe's thinking the very same concept of productivity that is central in Spinoza as well as in Hegel and Marx, was a cornerstone. "The divine," he says, "is effective in that which is alive, but not in that which is dead. It is in that which is becoming and evolving, but not in that which is completed and rigid. That is why *reason*, in its tendency toward the divine, deals only with that which is becoming, and which is alive, while the *intellect* deals with that which is completed and rigid, in order to use it." [5]

We find similar criticisms in Schiller and Fichte, and then in Hegel and in Marx, who makes a general criticism that in his time "truth is without passion, and passion is without truth." [6]

Essentially the whole existentialist philosophy, from Kierkegaard on, is, as Paul Tillich puts it, "an over one-hundred-years-old movement of rebellion against the dehumanization of man in industrial society." Actually, the concept of alienation is, in nontheistic language, the equivalent of what in theistic language would be called "sin": man's relinquishment of himself, of God within himself.

The thinker who coined the concept of alienation was Hegel. To him the history of man was at the same time the history of man's alienation (Entfremdung). "What the mind really strives for," he wrote in *The Philosophy of History*, "is the realization of its notion; but in doing so it hides that goal from its own vision and is proud and well satisfied in this alienation from its own essence." [7] For Marx, as

[5] Eckermann's conversation with Goethe, February 18, 1829, published in Leipzig, 1894, page 47. [My translation—E.F.]
[6] *18th Brumaire of Louis Bonaparte.*
[7] *The Philosophy of History*, translated by J. Sibree, The Colonial Press, New York, 1899.

for Hegel, the concept of alienation is based on the distinction between existence and essence, on the fact that man's existence is alienated from his essence, that in reality he is not what he potentially is, or, to put it differently, that *he is not what he ought to be, and that he ought to be that which he could be.*

For Marx the process of alienation is expressed in work and in the division of labor. Work is for him the active relatedness of man to nature, the creation of a new world, including the creation of man himself. (Intellectual activity is of course, for Marx, always work, like manual or artistic activity.) But as private property and the division of labor develop, labor loses its character of being an expression of man's powers; labor and its products assume an existence separate from man, his will and his planning. "The object produced by labor, its product, now stands opposed to it as an *alien being*, as a *power independent* of the producer. The product of labor is labor which has been embodied in an object and turned into a physical thing; this product is an *objectification* of labor." [8] Labor is alienated because the work has ceased to be a part of the worker's nature and "consequently, he does not fulfill himself in his work but denies himself, has a feeling of misery rather than well-being, does not develop freely his mental and physical energies but is physically exhausted and mentally debased. The worker therefore feels himself at home only during his leisure time, whereas at work he feels homeless." [9] Thus, in the act of production the relationship of the worker to his own activity is experienced "as something alien and not belonging to him, activity as suffering (passivity), strength as powerlessness, creation as emas-

culation." [10] While man thus becomes alienated from himself, the product of labor becomes "an alien object which dominates him. This relationship is at the same time the relationship to the sensuous external world, to natural objects, as an alien and hostile world." [11] Marx stresses two points: (1) in the process of work, and especially of work under the conditions of capitalism, man is estranged from his own creative powers, and (2) the *objects* of his own work become alien beings, and eventually rule over him, become powers independent of the producer. "The laborer exists for the process of production, and not the process of production for the laborer." [12]

A misunderstanding of Marx on this point is widespread, even among socialists. It is believed that Marx spoke primarily of the *economic* exploitation of the worker, and the fact that his share of the product was not as large as it should be, or that the product should belong to him, instead of to the capitalist. But as I have shown before, the state as a capitalist, as in the Soviet Union, would not have been any more welcome to Marx than the private capitalist. He is not concerned primarily with the equalization of income. He is concerned with the liberation of man from a kind of work which destroys his individuality, which transforms him into a thing, and which makes him into the slave of things. Just as Kierkegaard was concerned with the salvation of the individual, so Marx was, and his criticism of capitalist society is directed not at its method of distribution of income, but its mode of production, its destruction of individuality and its enslavement of man, not by the capitalist, but the enslavement of man—worker *and* capitalist—by things and circumstances of their own making.

[8] *E.P. MSS.*, p. 95.
[9] *E.P. MSS.*, p. 98.

[10] *E.P. MSS.*, p. 99.
[11] *E.P. MSS.*, p. 99.
[12] *Capital I*, l.c. p. 536.

Marx goes still further. In unalienated work man not only realizes himself as an individual, but also as a species-being. For Marx, as for Hegel and many other thinkers of the enlightenment, each individual represented the species, that is to say, humanity as a whole, the universality of man: the development of man leads to the unfolding of his whole humanity. In the process of work he

no longer reproduces himself merely intellectually, as in consciousness, but actively and in a real sense, and he sees his own reflection in a world which he has constructed. While, therefore, alienated labor takes away the object of production from man, it also takes away his *species life*, his real objectivity as a species-being, and changes his advantage over animals into a disadvantage in so far as his inorganic body, nature, is taken from him. Just as alienated labor transforms free and self-directed activity into a means, so it transforms the species life of man into a means of physical existence. Consciousness, which man has from his species, is transformed through alienation so that species life becomes only a means for him.[13]

As I indicated before, Marx assumed that the alienation of work, while existing throughout history, reaches its peak in capitalist society, and that the working class is the most alienated one. This assumption was based on the idea that the worker, having no part in the direction of the work, being "employed" as part of the machines he serves, is transformed into a thing in its dependence on capital. Hence, for Marx, "the emancipation of society from private property, from servitude, takes the political form of the *emancipation of the workers*; not in the sense that only the latter's emancipation is involved, but because this emancipation includes the *emancipation of humanity as a whole*. For all

human servitude is involved in the relation of the worker to production, and all types of servitude are only modifications or consequences of this relation." [14]

Again it must be emphasized that Marx's aim is not limited to the emancipation of the working class, but the emancipation of the human being through the restitution of the unalienated and hence free activity of all men, and a society in which man, and not the production of things, is the aim, in which man ceases to be "a crippled monstrosity, and becomes a fully developed human being." [15] Marx's concept of the alienated product of labor is expressed in one of the most fundamental points developed in *Capital*, in what he calls "the fetishism of commodities." Capitalist production transforms the relations of individuals into qualities of things themselves, and this transformation constitutes the nature of the commodity in capitalist production. "It cannot be otherwise in a mode of production in which the laborer exists to satisfy the need of self-expansion of existing values, instead of on the contrary, material wealth existing to satisfy the needs of development on the part of the laborer. As in religion man is governed by the products of his own brain, so in capitalist production he is governed by the products of his own hands." [16] "Machinery is adapted to the weakness of the human being, in order to turn the weak human being into a machine." [17]

The alienation of work in man's production is much greater than it was when production was by handicraft and manufacture [literally, making-by-hand]. "In handicrafts and manufacture, the workman makes use of a tool; in the factory the machine makes use of him. There the movements of the

[13] *E.P. MSS.*, pp. 102–3.

[14] *E.P. MSS.*, p. 107.
[15] *Capital I*, l.c. p. 396.
[16] *Capital I*, l.c. p. 680–1.
[17] *E.P. MSS.*, p. 143.

instrument of labor proceed from him; here it is the movement of the machines that he must follow. In manufacture, the workmen are parts of a living mechanism; in the factory we have a lifeless mechanism, independent of the workman, who becomes its mere living appendage." [18] It is of the utmost importance for the understanding of Marx to see how the concept of alienation was and remained the focal point in the thinking of the young Marx who wrote the *Economic and Philosophical Manuscripts*, and of the "old" Marx who wrote *Capital*. Aside from the examples already given, the following passages, one from the *Manuscripts*, the other from *Capital*, ought to make this continuity quite clear:

This fact simply implies that the object produced by labor, its product, now stands opposed to it as an *alien being*, as a *power independent* of the producer. The product of labor is labor which has been embodied in an object and turned into a physical thing; this product is an *objectification* of labor. The performance of work is at the same time its objectification. The performance of work appears in the sphere of political economy as a *vitiation* of the worker, objectification as a *loss* and as *servitude to the object*, and appropriation as *alienation*.[19]

This is what Marx wrote in *Capital*:

Within the capitalist system all methods for raising the social productiveness of labor are brought about at the cost of the individual laborer; all means for the development of production transform themselves into means of domination over, and exploitation of, the producers; they mutilate the laborer into a fragment of a man, degrade him to the level of an appendage of a machine, destroy every remnant of charm in his work and turn it into a hated toil; they estrange from him the intellectual potentialities of the labor process in the same proportion as

science is incorporated in it as an independent power.[20]

Again the role of private property (of course not as property of objects of use, but as capital which hires labor) was already clearly seen in its alienating functioning by the young Marx: "*Private property*," he wrote, "is therefore the product, the necessary result, of *alienated labor*, of the external relation of the worker to nature and to himself. *Private property* is thus derived from the analysis of the concept of *alienated labor*; that is, alienated man, alienated labor, alienated life, and estranged man." [21]

It is not only that the world of things becomes the ruler of man, but also that the *social and political circumstances* which he creates become his masters. "This consolidation of what we ourselves produce, which turns into an objective power above us, growing out of our control, thwarting our expectations, bringing to naught our calculations, is one of the chief factors in historical development up to now." [22] The alienated man, who believes that he has become the master of nature, has become the slave of things and of circumstances, the powerless appendage of a world which is at the same time the frozen expression of his own powers.

For Marx, alienation in the process of work, from the product of work and from circumstances, is inseparably connected with alienation from oneself, from one's fellow man and from nature.

A direct consequence of the alienation of man from the product of his labor, from his life activity and from his species life is that *man is alienated* from other men. When man confronts himself, he also confronts *other* men. What is true of man's relationship to his work, to the product of his work and to himself, is also

[18] *Capital I*, l.c. p. 461–2.
[19] *E.P. MSS.*, p. 95.
[20] *Capital I*, l.c. p. 708.
[21] *E.P. MSS.*, pp. 105–6.
[22] *German Ideology*, l.c. p. 23.

true of his relationship to other men, to their labor and to the objects of their labor. In general, the statement that man is alienated from his species life means that each man is alienated from others, and that each of the others is likewise alienated from human life.[23]

The alienated man is not only alienated from other men; he is alienated from the essence of humanity, from his "species-being," both in his natural and spiritual qualities. This alienation from the human essence leads to an existential egotism, described by Marx as man's human essence becoming "a *means* for his *individual existence*. It [alienated labor] alienates from man his own body, external nature, his mental life and his *human* life." [24]

Marx's concept touches here the Kantian principle that man must always be an end in himself, and never a means to an end. But he amplifies this principle by stating that man's human essence must never become a means for individual existence. The contrast between Marx's view and Communist totalitarianism could hardly be expressed more radically; humanity in man, says Marx, must not even become a *means* to his individual existence; how much less could it be considered a means for the state, the class, or the nation.

Alienation leads to the perversion of all values. By making economy and its values—"gain, work, thrift, and sobriety" [25]—the supreme aim of life, man fails to develop the truly moral values, "the riches of a good conscience, of virtue, etc., but how can I be virtuous if I am not alive, and how can I have a good conscience if I am not aware of anything?" [26] In a state of alienation each sphere of life, the economic and the moral, is independent from the other, "each is concentrated on a spe-

cific area of alienated activity and is itself alienated from the other." [27]

Marx recognized what becomes of human needs in an alienated world, and he actually foresaw with amazing clarity the completion of this process as it is visible only today. While in a socialist perspective the main importance should be attributed "to the *wealth* of human needs, and consequently also to a *new mode of production* and to a new *object* of production," to "a new manifestation of *human* powers and a new enrichment of the human being," [28] in the alienated world of capitalism needs are not expressions of man's latent powers, that is, they are not *human* needs; in capitalism

every man speculates upon creating a *new* need in another in order to force him to a new sacrifice, to place him in a new dependence, and to entice him into a new kind of pleasure and thereby into economic ruin. Everyone tries to establish over others an *alien* power in order to find there the satisfaction of his own egotistic need. With the mass of objects, therefore, there also increases the realm of alien entities to which man is subjected. Every new product is a new *potentiality* of mutual deceit and robbery. Man becomes increasingly poor as a man; he has increasing need of *money* in order to take possession of the hostile being. The power of his *money* diminishes directly with the growth of the quantity of production, i.e., his need increases with the increasing *power* of money. The need for money is therefore the real need created by the modern economy, and the only need which it creates. The *quantity* of money becomes increasingly its only important quality. Just as it reduces every entity to its abstraction, so it reduces itself in its own development to a *quantitative* entity. Excess and immoderation become its true standard. This is shown subjectively, partly in the fact that the expansion of production and of needs becomes an *ingenious* and always *calculat-*

[23] *E.P. MSS.*, p. 103.
[24] *E.P. MSS.*, p. 103.
[25] *E.P. MSS.*, p. 146.
[26] *E.P. MSS.*, p. 146.

[27] *E.P. MSS.*, p. 146.
[28] *E.P. MSS.*, p. 140.

*ing* subservience to inhuman, depraved, unnatural, and *imaginary* appetites. Private property does not know how to change crude need into *human* need; its *idealism* is *fantasy, caprice* and *fancy*. No eunuch flatters his tyrant more shamefully or seeks by more infamous means to stimulate his jaded appetite, in order to gain some favor, than does the eunuch of industry, the entrepreneur, in order to acquire a few silver coins or to charm the gold from the purse of his dearly beloved neighbor. (Every product is a bait by means of which the individual tries to entice the essence of the other person, his money. Every real or potential need is a weakness which will draw the bird into the lime. Universal exploitation of human communal life. As every imperfection of man is a bond with heaven, a point at which his heart is accessible to the priest, so every want is an opportunity for approaching one's neighbor with an air of friendship, and saying, "Dear friend, I will give you what you need, but you know the *conditio sine qua non*. You know what ink you must use in signing yourself over to me. I shall swindle you while providing your enjoyment.") The entrepreneur accedes to the most depraved fancies of his needs, awakens unhealthy appetites in him, and watches for every weakness in order, later, to claim the remuneration for this labor of love.[29]

The man who has thus become subject to his alienated needs is *"a mentally* and *physically dehumanized* being . . . the *self-conscious* and *self-acting commodity*."[30] This commodity-man knows only one way of relating himself to the world outside, by having it and by consuming (using) it. The more alienated he is, the more sense of having and using constitutes his relationship to the world. "The less you *are*, the less you express your life, the more you *have*, the greater is your *alienated* life and the greater is the saving of your alienated being."[31]

There is only one correction which

history has made in Marx's concept of alienation; Marx believed that the working class was the most alienated class, hence that the emancipation from alienation would necessarily start with the liberation of the working class. Marx did not foresee the extent to which alienation was to become the fate of the vast majority of people, especially of the ever-increasing segment of the population which manipulate symbols and men, rather than machines. If anything, the clerk, the salesman, the executive, are even more alienated today than the skilled manual worker. The latter's functioning still depends on the expression of certain personal qualities like skill, reliability, etc., and he is not forced to sell his "personality," his smile, his opinions in the bargain; the symbol manipulators are hired not only for their skill, but for all those personality qualities which make them "attractive personality packages," easy to handle and to manipulate. They are the true "organization men"—more so than the skilled laborer—their idol being the corporation. But as far as consumption is concerned, there is no difference between manual workers and the members of the bureaucracy. They all crave for things, new things, to have and to use. They are the passive recipients, the consumers, chained and weakened by the very things which satisfy their synthetic needs. They are not related to the world productively, grasping it in its full reality and in this process becoming one with it; they worship things, the machines which produce the things —and in this alienated world they feel as strangers and quite alone. In spite of Marx's underestimating the role of the bureaucracy, his general description could nevertheless have been written today: "Production does not simply produce man as a *commodity*, the *commodity-man*, man in the role of commodity; it produces him in keeping with this role as a *spiritually* and physically *dehumanized* being—[the] im-

29 *E.P. MSS.*, pp. 140–2.
30 *E.P. MSS.*, p. 111.
31 *E.P. MSS.*, p. 144.

morality, deformity, the hebetation of the workers and the capitalists. Its product is the *self-conscious* and *self-acting commodity* . . . the human commodity." [32]

To what extent things and circumstances of our own making have become our masters, Marx could hardly have foreseen; yet nothing could prove his prophecy more drastically than the fact that the whole human race is today the prisoner of the nuclear weapons it has created, and of the political institutions which are equally of its own making. A frightened mankind waits anxiously to see whether it will be saved from the power of the things it has created, from the blind action of the bureaucracies it has appointed.

# 20

# The Metropolis and Mental Life

### GEORG SIMMEL

The deepest problems of modern life derive from the claim of the individual to preserve the autonomy and individuality of his existence in the face of overwhelming social forces, of historical heritage, of external culture, and of the technique of life. The fight with nature which primitive man has to wage for his *bodily* existence attains in this modern form its latest transformation. The eighteenth century called upon man to free himself of all the historical bonds in the state and in religion, in morals and in economics. Man's nature, originally good and common to all, should develop unhampered. In addition to more liberty, the nineteenth century demanded the functional specialization of man and his work; this specialization makes one individual incomparable to another, and each of them indispensable to the highest possible extent. However, this specialization makes each man the more directly

Reprinted by permission of the publisher from *The Sociology of Georg Simmel* edited by Kurt Wolff. Copyright 1950 by The Free Press, A Corporation.

[32] *E.P. MSS.*, p. 111.

dependent upon the supplementary activities of all others. Nietzsche sees the full development of the individual conditioned by the most ruthless struggle of individuals; socialism believes in the suppression of all competition for the same reason. Be that as it may, in all these positions the same basic motive is at work: the person resists to being leveled down and worn out by a social-technological mechanism. An inquiry into the inner meaning of specifically modern life and its products, into the soul of the cultural body, so to speak, must seek to solve the equation which structures like the metropolis set up between the individual and the super-individual contents of life. Such an inquiry must answer the question of how the personality accommodates itself in the adjustments to external forces. This will be my task today.

The psychological basis of the metropolitan type of individuality consists in the *intensification of nervous stimulation* which results from the swift and uninterrupted change of outer and inner stimuli. Man is a differentiating creature. His mind is stimulated by the difference between a momentary impression and the one which preceded it. Lasting impressions, impressions which differ only slightly from one another, impressions which take a regular and habitual course and show regular and habitual contrasts—all these use up, so to speak, less consciousness than does the rapid crowding of changing images, the sharp discontinuity in the grasp of a single glance, and the unexpectedness of onrushing impressions. These are the psychological conditions which the metropolis creates. With each crossing of the street, with the tempo and multiplicity of economic, occupational and social life, the city sets up a deep contrast with small town and rural life with reference to the sensory foundations of psychic life. The metropolis exacts from man as a discriminating creature a different amount of consciousness than does rural life. Here the rhythm of life and sensory mental imagery flows more slowly, more habitually, and more evenly. Precisely in this connection the sophisticated character of metropolitan psychic life becomes understandable—as over against small town life which rests more upon deeply felt and emotional relationships. These latter are rooted in the more unconscious layers of the psyche and grow most readily in the steady rhythm of uninterrupted habituations. The intellect, however, has its locus in the transparent, conscious, higher layers of the psyche; it is the most adaptable of our inner forces. In order to accommodate to change and to the contrast of phenomena, the intellect does not require any shocks and inner upheavals; it is only through such upheavals that the more conservative mind could accommodate to the metropolitan rhythm of events. Thus the metropolitan type of man—which, of course, exists in a thousand individual variants—develops an organ protecting him against the threatening currents and discrepancies

of his external environment which would uproot him. He reacts with his head instead of his heart. In this an increased awareness assumes the psychic prerogative. Metropolitan life, thus, underlies a heightened awareness and a predominance of intelligence in metropolitan man. The reaction to metropolitan phenomena is shifted to that organ which is least sensitive and quite remote from the depth of the personality. Intellectuality is thus seen to preserve subjective life against the overwhelming power of metropolitan life, and intellectuality branches out in many directions and is integrated with numerous discrete phenomena.

The metropolis has always been the seat of the money economy. Here the multiplicity and concentration of economic exchange gives an importance to the means of exchange which the scantiness of rural commerce would not have allowed. Money economy and the dominance of the intellect are intrinsically connected. They share a matter-of-fact attitude in dealing with men and with things; and, in this attitude, a formal justice is often coupled with an inconsiderate hardness. The intellectually sophisticated person is indifferent to all genuine individuality, because relationships and reactions result from it which cannot be exhausted with logical operations. In the same manner, the individuality of phenomena is not commensurate with the pecuniary principle. Money is concerned only with what is common to all: it asks for the exchange value, it reduces all quality and individuality to the question: How much? All intimate emotional relations between persons are founded in their individuality, whereas in rational relations man is reckoned with like a number, like an element which is in itself indifferent. Only the objective measurable achievement is of interest. Thus metropolitan man reckons with his merchants and customers, his domestic servants and often even with persons with whom he is obliged to have social intercourse. These features of intellectuality contrast with the nature of the small circle in which the inevitable knowledge of individuality as inevitably produces a warmer tone of behavior, a behavior which is beyond a mere objective balancing of service and return. In the sphere of the economic psychology of the small group it is of importance that under primitive conditions production serves the customer who orders the good, so that the producer and the consumer are acquainted. The modern metropolis, however, is supplied almost entirely by production for the market, that is, for entirely unknown purchasers who never personally enter the producer's actual field of vision. Through this anonymity the interests of each party acquire an unmerciful matter-of-factness; and the intellectually calculating economic egoisms of both parties need not fear any deflection because of the imponderables of personal relationships. The money economy dominates the metropolis; it has displaced the last survivals of domestic production and the direct barter of goods; it minimizes, from day to day, the amount of work ordered by customers. The matter-of-fact attitude is obviously so intimately interrelated with the money economy, which is dominant in the metropolis, that nobody can say whether the intellectualistic mentality first promoted the money economy or whether the latter determined the former. The metropolitan way of life is certainly the most fertile soil for this reciprocity, a point which I shall document merely by citing the dictum of the most eminent English constitutional historian: throughout the whole course of English history, London has never acted as England's heart but often as England's intellect and always as her money-bag!

In certain seemingly insignificant traits, which lie upon the surface of life, the same psychic currents characteristically unite. Modern mind has become more and more calculating. The calculative exactness of practical life which the money economy has brought about corresponds to the ideal of natural science: to transform the world into an arithmetic problem, to fix every part of the world by mathematical formulas. Only money economy has filled the days of so many people with weighing, calculating, with numerical determinations, with a reduction of qualitative values to quantitative ones. Through the calculative nature of money a new precision, a certainty in the definition of identities and differences, an unambiguousness in agreements and arrangements has been brought about in the relations of life-elements—just as externally this precision has been effected by the universal diffusion of pocket watches. However, the conditions of metropolitan life are at once cause and effect of this trait. The relationships and affairs of the typical metropolitan usually are so varied and complex that without the strictest punctuality in promises and services the whole structure would break down into an inextricable chaos. Above all, this necessity is brought about by the aggregation of so many people with such differentiated interests, who must integrate their relations and activities into a highly complex organism. If all clocks and watches in Berlin would suddenly go wrong in different ways, even if only by one hour, all economic life and communication of the city would be disrupted for a long time. In addition an apparently mere external factor: long distances, would make all waiting and broken appointments result in an ill-afforded waste of time. Thus, the technique of metropolitan life is unimaginable without the most punctual integration of all activities and mutual relations into a stable and impersonal time schedule. Here again the general conclusions of this entire task of reflection become obvious, namely, that from each point on the surface of existence—however closely attached to the surface alone—one may drop a sounding into the depth of the psyche so that all the most banal externalities of life finally are connected with the ultimate decisions concerning the meaning and style of life. Punctuality, calculability, exactness are forced upon life by the complexity and extension of metropolitan existence and are not only the most intimately connected with its money economy and intellectualistic character. These traits must also color the contents of life and favor the exclusion of those irrational, instinctive, sovereign traits and impulses which aim at determining the mode of life from within, instead of receiving the general and precisely schematized form of life from without. Even though sovereign types of personality, characterized by irrational impulses, are by no means impossible in the city, they are, nevertheless, opposed to typical city life. The passionate hatred of men like Ruskin and Nietzsche for the metropolis is understandable in these terms. Their natures discovered the value of life alone in the unschematized existence which cannot be defined with precision for all alike. From the same source of this hatred of the metropolis surged their hatred of money economy and of the intellectualism of modern existence.

The same factors which have thus coalesced into the exactness and minute precision of the form of life have coalesced into a structure of the highest impersonality; on the other hand, they have promoted a highly personal subjectivity. There is perhaps no psychic phenomenon which has been so unconditionally reserved to the metropolis as has the blasé attitude. The blasé attitude results first from the rapidly changing and closely compressed contrasting stimulations of the nerves. From this, the enhancement of metropolitan intellectuality, also, seems originally to stem. Therefore, stupid people who are not intellectually alive in the first place usually are not exactly blasé.

A life in boundless pursuit of pleasure makes one blasé because it agitates the nerves to their strongest reactivity for such a long time that they finally cease to react at all. In the same way, through the rapidity and contradictoriness of their changes, more harmless impressions force such violent responses, tearing the nerves so brutally hither and thither that their last reserves of strength are spent; and if one remains in the same milieu they have no time to gather new strength. An incapacity thus emerges to react to new sensations with the appropriate energy. This constitutes that blasé attitude which, in fact, every metropolitan child shows when compared with children of quieter and less changeable milieus.

This physiological source of the metropolitan blasé attitude is joined by another source which flows from the money economy. The essence of the blasé attitude consists in the blunting of discrimination. This does not mean that the objects are not perceived, as is the case with the half-wit, but rather that the meaning and differing values of things, and thereby the things themselves, are experienced as insubstantial. They appear to the blasé person in an evenly flat and gray tone; no one object deserves preference over any other. This mood is the faithful subjective reflection of the completely internalized money economy. By being the equivalent to all the manifold things in one and the same way, money becomes the most frightful leveler. For money expresses all qualitative differences of things in terms of "how much?" Money, with all its colorlessness and indifference, becomes the common denominator of all values; irreparably it hollows out the core of things, their individuality, their specific value, and their incomparability. All things float with equal specific gravity in the constantly moving stream of money. All things lie on the same level and differ from one another only in the size of the area which they cover. In the individual case this coloration, or rather discoloration, of things through their money equivalence may be unnoticeably minute. However, through the relations of the rich to the objects to be had for money, perhaps even through the total character which the mentality of the contemporary public everywhere imparts to these objects, the exclusively pecuniary evaluation of objects has become quite considerable. The large cities, the main seats of the money exchange, bring the purchasibility of things to the fore much more impressively than do smaller localities. That is why cities are also the genuine locale of the blasé attitude. In the blasé attitude the concentration of men and things stimulates the nervous system of the individual to its highest achievement so that it attains its peak. Through the mere quantitative intensification of the same conditioning factors this achievement is transformed into its opposite and appears in the peculiar adjustment of the blasé attitude. In this phenomenon the nerves find in the refusal to react to their stimulation the last possibility of accommodating to the contents and forms of metropolitan life. The self-preservation of certain personalities is bought at the price of devaluating the whole objective world, a devaluation which in the end unavoidably drags one's own personality down into a feeling of the same worthlessness.

Whereas the subject of this form of existence has to come to terms with it entirely for himself, his self-preservation in the face of the large city demands from him a no less negative behavior of a social nature. This mental attitude of metropolitans toward one another we may designate, from a formal point of view, as reserve. If so many inner reactions were responses to the continuous external contacts with innumerable people as are those in the small town, where one knows almost everybody one meets and where one has a positive relation to almost everyone, one would be completely atomized internally and come to an unimaginable psychic state. Partly this psychological fact, partly the right to distrust which men have in the face of the touch-and-go elements of metropolitan life, necessitates our reserve. As a result of this reserve we frequently do not even know by sight those who have been our neighbors for years. And it is this reserve which in the eyes of the small-town people makes us appear to be cold and heartless. Indeed, if I do not deceive myself, the inner aspect of this outer reserve is not only indifference but, more often than we are aware, it is a slight aversion, a mutual strangeness and repulsion, which will break into hatred and fight at the moment of a closer contact, however caused. The whole inner organization of such an extensive communicative life rests upon an extremely varied hierarchy of sympathies, indifferences, and aversions of the briefest as well as of the most permanent nature. The sphere of indifference in this hierarchy is not as large as might appear on the surface. Our psychic activity still responds to almost every impression of somebody else with a somewhat distinct feeling. The unconscious, fluid and changing character of this impression seems to result in a state of indifference. Actually this indifference would be just as unnatural as the diffusion of indiscriminate mutual suggestion would be unbearable. From both these typical dangers of the metropolis, indifference and indiscriminate suggestibility, antipathy protects us. A latent antipathy and the preparatory stage of practical antagonism effect the distances and aversions without which this mode of life could not at all be led. The extent and the mixture of this style of life, the rhythm of its emergence and disappearance, the forms in which it is satisfied—all these, with the unifying motives in the narrower sense, form the inseparable whole of the metropolitan style of life. What appears in the metropolitan style of life directly as dissociation is in reality only one of its elemental forms of socialization.

This reserve with its overtone of hidden aversion appears in turn as the form or the cloak of a more general mental phenomenon of the metropolis: it grants to the individual a kind and an amount of personal freedom which has no analogy whatsoever under other conditions. The metropolis goes back to one of the large developmental tendencies of social life as such, to one of the few tendencies for which an approximately universal formula can be discovered. The earliest phase of social formations found in historical as well as in contemporary social structures is this: a relatively small circle firmly closed against neighboring, strange, or in some way antagonistic circles. However, this circle is closely coherent and allows its individual members only a narrow field for the development of unique qualities and free, self-responsible movements. Political and kinship groups, parties and religious associations begin in this way. The self-preservation of very young associations requires the establishment of strict boundaries and a centripetal unity. Therefore they cannot allow the individual freedom and unique inner and outer development. From this stage social development proceeds at once in two different, yet corresponding, directions. To the extent to which the group grows—numerically, spatially, in significance and in content of life—to the same degree the group's direct, inner unity loosens, and the rigidity of the original demarcation against others is softened through mutual relations and connections. At the same time, the individual gains freedom of movement, far beyond the first jealous delimitation. The individual also gains a specific individuality to which the division of labor in the enlarged group gives both occasion and necessity. The state and Christianity, guilds and political parties, and innumerable other groups have developed according to this formula, however much, of course, the special conditions and forces of the respective groups have modified the general scheme. This scheme seems to me distinctly recognizable also in the evolution of individuality within urban life. The small-town life in Antiquity and in the Middle Ages set barriers against movement and relations of the individual toward the outside, and it set up barriers against individual independence and differentiation within the individual self. These barriers were such that under them modern man could not have breathed. Even today a metropolitan man who is placed in a small town feels a restriction similar, at least, in kind. The smaller the circle which forms our milieu is, and the more restricted those relations to others are which dissolve the boundaries of the individual, the more anxiously the circle guards the achievements, the conduct of life, and the outlook of the individual, and the more readily a quantitative specialization would break up the framework of the whole little circle.

The ancient *polis* in this respect seems to have had the very character of a small town. The constant threat to its existence at the hands of enemies from near and afar effected strict coherence in political and military respects, a supervision of the citizen by the citizen, a jealousy of the whole against the individual whose particular life was suppressed to such a degree that he could compensate only by acting as a despot in his own household. The tremendous agitation and excitement, the unique colorfulness of Athenian life, can perhaps be understood in terms of the fact that a people of incomparably individualized personalities struggled against the constant inner and outer pressure of a de-individualizing small town. This produced a tense atmosphere in which the weaker individuals were suppressed and those of stronger natures were incited to prove themselves in the most passionate manner. This is precisely why it was that there blossomed in Athens what must be called, without defining it exactly, "the general human character" in the intellectual development of our species. For we maintain factual as well as historical validity for the following connection: the most extensive and the most general contents and forms of life are most intimately connected with the most individual ones. They have a preparatory stage in common, that is, they find their enemy in narrow formations and groupings the maintenance of which places both of them into a state of defense against expanse and generality lying without and the freely moving individuality within. Just as in the feudal age, the "free" man was the one who stood under the law of the land, that is, under the law of the largest social orbit, and the unfree man was the one who derived his right merely from the narrow circle of a feudal association and was excluded from the larger social orbit—so today metropolitan man is "free" in a spiritualized and refined sense, in contrast to the pettiness and prejudices which hem in the small-town man. For the reciprocal reserve and indifference and the intellectual life conditions of large circles

are never felt more strongly by the individual in their impact upon independence than in the thickest crowd of the big city. This is because the bodily proximity and narrowness of space makes the mental distance only the more visible. It is obviously only the obverse of this freedom if, under certain circumstances, one nowhere feels as lonely and lost as in the metropolitan crowd. For here as elsewhere it is by no means necessary that the freedom of man be reflected in his emotional life as comfort.

It is not only the immediate size of the area and the number of persons which, because of the universal historical correlation between the enlargement of the circle and the personal inner and outer freedom, has made the metropolis the locale of freedom. It is rather in transcending this visible expanse that any given city becomes the seat of cosmopolitanism. The horizon of the city expands in a manner comparable to the way in which wealth develops; a certain amount of property increases in a quasi-automatical way in ever more rapid progression. As soon as a certain limit has been passed, the economic, personal, and intellectual relations of the citizenry, the sphere of intellectual predominance of the city over its hinterland, grow as in geometrical progression. Every gain in dynamic extension becomes a step, not for an equal, but for a new and larger extension. From every thread spinning out of the city, ever new threads grow as if by themselves, just as within the city the unearned increment of ground rent, through the mere increase in communication, brings the owner automatically increasing profits. At this point, the quantitative aspect of life is transformed directly into qualitative traits of character. The sphere of life of the small town is, in the main, self-contained and autarchic. For it is the decisive nature of the metropolis that its inner life overflows by waves into a far-flung national or international area. Weimar is not an example to the contrary, since its significance was hinged upon individual personalities and died with them; whereas the metropolis is indeed characterized by its essential independence even from the most eminent individual personalities. This is the counterpart to the independence, and it is the price the individual pays for the independence, which he enjoys in the metropolis. The most significant characteristic of the metropolis is this functional extension beyond its physical boundaries. And this efficacy reacts in turn and gives weight, importance, and responsibility to metropolitan life. Man does not end with the limits of his body or the area comprising his immediate activity. Rather is the range of the person constituted by the sum of effects emanating from him temporally and spatially. In the same way, a city consists of its total effects which extend beyond its immediate confines. Only this range is the city's actual extent in which its existence is expressed. This fact makes it obvious that individual freedom, the logical and historical complement of such extension, is not to be understood only in the negative sense of mere freedom of mobility and elimination of prejudices and petty philistinism. The essential point is that the particularity and incomparability, which ultimately every human being possesses, be somehow expressed in the working-out of a way of life. That we follow the laws of our own nature—and this after all is freedom—becomes obvious and convincing to ourselves and to others only if the expressions of this nature differ from the expressions of others. Only our unmistakability proves that our way of life has not been superimposed by others.

Cities are, first, of all, seats of the highest economic division of labor.

They produce thereby such extreme phenomena as in Paris the remunerative occupation of the *quatorzième*. They are persons who identify themselves by signs on their residences and who are ready at the dinner hour in correct attire, so that they can be quickly called upon if a dinner party should consist of thirteen persons. In the measure of its expansion, the city offers more and more the decisive conditions of the division of labor. It offers a circle which through its size can absorb a highly diverse variety of services. At the same time, the concentration of individuals and their struggle for customers compel the individual to specialize in a function from which he cannot be readily displaced by another. It is decisive that city life has transformed the struggle with nature for livelihood into an inter-human struggle for gain, which here is not granted by nature but by other men. For specialization does not flow only from the competition for gain but also from the underlying fact that the seller must always seek to call forth new and differentiated needs of the lured customer. In order to find a source of income which is not yet exhausted, and to find a function which cannot readily be displaced, it is necessary to specialize in one's services. This process promotes differentiation, refinement, and the enrichment of the public's needs, which obviously must lead to growing personal differences within this public.

All this forms the transition to the individualization of mental and psychic traits which the city occasions in proportion to its size. There is a whole series of obvious causes underlying this process. First, one must meet the difficulty of asserting his own personality within the dimensions of metropolitan life. Where the quantitative increase in importance and the expense of energy reach their limits, one seizes upon qualitative differentiation in order somehow to attract the attention of the social circle by playing upon its sensitivity for differences. Finally, man is tempted to adopt the most tendentious peculiarities, that is, the specifically metropolitan extravagances of mannerism, caprice, and preciousness. Now, the meaning of these extravagances does not at all lie in the contents of such behavior, but rather in its form of "being different," of standing out in a striking manner and thereby attracting attention. For many character types, ultimately the only means of saving for themselves some modicum of self-esteem and the sense of filling a position is indirect, through the awareness of others. In the same sense a seemingly insignificant factor is operating, the cumulative effects of which are, however, still noticeable. I refer to the brevity and scarcity of the inter-human contacts granted to the metropolitan man, as compared with social intercourse in the small town. The temptation to appear "to the point," to appear concentrated and strikingly characteristic, lies much closer to the individual in brief metropolitan contacts than in an atmosphere in which frequent and prolonged association assures the personality of an unambiguous image of himself in the eyes of the other.

The most profound reason, however, why the metropolis conduces to the urge for the most individual personal existence—no matter whether justified and successful—appears to me to be the following: the development of modern culture is characterized by the preponderance of what one may call the "objective spirit" over the "subjective spirit." This is to say, in language as well as in law, in the technique of production as well as in art, in science as well as in the objects of domestic environment, there is embodied a sum of spirit. The individual in his intellectual development follows the growth of this spirit very imperfectly and at an ever

increasing distance. If, for instance, we view the immense culture which for the last hundred years has been embodied in things and in knowledge, in institutions and in comforts, and if we compare all this with the cultural progress of the individual during the same period—at least in high status groups —a frightful disproportion in growth between the two becomes evident. Indeed, at some points we notice a retrogression in the culture of the individual with reference to spirituality, delicacy, and idealism. This discrepancy results essentially from the growing division of labor. For the division of labor demands from the individual an ever more one-sided accomplishment, and the greatest advance in a one-sided pursuit only too frequently means dearth to the personality of the individual. In any case, he can cope less and less with the overgrowth of objective culture. The individual is reduced to a negligible quantity, perhaps less in his consciousness than in his practice and in the totality of his obscure emotional states that are derived from this practice. The individual has become a mere cog in an enormous organization of things and powers which tear from his hands all progress, spirituality, and value in order to transform them from their subjective form into the form of a purely objective life. It needs merely to be pointed out that the metropolis is the genuine arena of this culture which outgrows all personal life. Here in buildings and educational institutions, in the wonders and comforts of space-conquering technology, in the formations of community life, and in the visible institutions of the state, is offered such an overwhelming fullness of crystallized and impersonalized spirit that the personality, so to speak, cannot maintain itself under its impact. On the one hand, life is made infinitely easy for the personality in that stimulations, interests, uses of time and consciousness are offered to it from all sides. They carry the person as if in a stream, and one needs hardly to swim for oneself. On the other hand, however, life is composed more and more of these impersonal contents and offerings which tend to displace the genuine personal colorations and incomparabilities. This results in the individual's summoning the utmost in uniqueness and particularization, in order to preserve his most personal core. He has to exaggerate this personal element in order to remain audible even to himself. The atrophy of individual culture through the hypertrophy of objective culture is one reason for the bitter hatred which the preachers of the most extreme individualism, above all Nietzsche, harbor against the metropolis. But it is, indeed, also a reason why these preachers are so passionately loved in the metropolis and why they appear to the metropolitan man as the prophets and saviors of his most unsatisfied yearnings.

If one asks for the historical position of these two forms of individualism which are nourished by the quantitative relation of the metropolis, namely, individual independence and the elaboration of individuality itself, then the metropolis assumes an entirely new rank order in the world history of the spirit. The eighteenth century found the individual in oppressive bonds which had become meaningless—bonds of a political, agrarian, guild, and religious character. They were restraints which, so to speak, forced upon man an unnatural form and outmoded, unjust inequalities. In this situation the cry for liberty and equality arose, the belief in the individual's full freedom of movement in all social and intellectual relationships. Freedom would at once permit the noble substance common to all to come to the fore, a substance which nature had deposited in every man and which society and history had only deformed. Besides this eighteenth-century ideal of liberalism, in the nineteenth century, through Goethe and Romanticism, on the one hand, and through the economic division of labor, on the other hand, another ideal arose: individuals liberated from historical bonds now wished to distinguish themselves from one another. The carrier of man's values is no longer the "general human being" in every individual, but rather man's qualitative uniqueness and irreplaceability. The external and internal history of our time takes its course within the struggle and in the changing entanglements of these two ways of defining the individual's role in the whole of society. It is the function of the metropolis to provide the arena for this struggle and its reconciliation. For the metropolis presents the peculiar conditions which are revealed to us as the opportunities and the stimuli for the development of both these ways af allocating ro¹es to men. Therewith these conditions gain a unique place, pregnant with inestimable meanings for the development of psychic existence. The metropolis reveals itself as one of those great historical formations in which opposing streams which enclose life unfold, as well as join one another with equal right. However, in this process the currents of life, whether their individual phenomena touch us sympathetically or antipathetically, entirely transcend the sphere for which the judge's attitude is appropriate. Since such forces of life have grown into the roots and into the crown of the whole of the historical life in which we, in our fleeting existence, as a cell, belong only as a part, it is not our task either to accuse or to pardon, but only to understand.

# 21

## The Anomie of Modern Life

### EMILE DURKHEIM

No living being can be happy or even exist unless his needs are sufficiently proportioned to his means. In other words, if his needs require more than can be granted, or even merely something of a different sort, they will be under continual friction and can only function painfully. Movements incapable of production without pain tend not to be reproduced. Unsatisfied tendencies atrophy, and as the impulse to live is merely the result of all the rest, it is bound to weaken as the others relax.

In the animal, at least in a normal condition, this equilibrium is established with automatic spontaneity because the animal depends on purely material conditions. All the organism needs is that the supplies of substance and energy constantly employed in the vital process should be periodically renewed by equivalent quantities; that replacement be equivalent to use. When the void created by existence in its own resources is filled, the animal, satisfied, asks nothing further. Its power of reflection is not sufficiently developed to imagine other ends than those implicit in its physical nature. On the other hand, as the work demanded of each organ itself depends on the general state of vital energy and the needs of organic equilibrium, use is regulated in turn by replacement and the balance is automatic. The limits of one are those of the other; both are fundamental to the constitution of the existence in question, which cannot exceed them.

Reprinted by permission of the publisher from *Suicide* by Emile Durkheim. Translated by John A. Spaulding and George Simpson. Copyright 1951 by The Free Press, A Corporation.

This is not the case with man, because most of his needs are not dependent on his body or not to the same degree. Strictly speaking, we may consider that the quantity of material supplies necessary to the physical maintenance of a human life is subject to computation, though this be less exact than in the preceding case and a wider margin left for the free combinations of the will; for beyond the indispensable minimum which satisfies nature when instinctive, a more awakened reflection suggests better conditions, seemingly desirable ends craving fulfillment. Such appetites, however, admittedly sooner or later reach a limit which they cannot pass. But how determine the quantity of well-being, comfort or luxury legitimately to be craved by a human being? Nothing appears in man's organic nor in his psychological constitution which sets a limit to such tendencies. The functioning of individual life does not require them to cease at one point rather than at another; the proof being that they have constantly increased since the beginnings of history, receiving more complete satisfaction, yet with no weakening of average health. Above all, how establish their proper variation with different conditions of life, occupations, relative importance of services, etc.? In no society are they equally satisfied in the different stages of the social hierarchy. Yet human nature is substantially the same among all men, in its essential qualities. It is not human nature which can assign the variable limits necessary to our needs. They are thus unlimited so far as they depend on the individual alone. Irrespective of any external regulatory force, our capacity for feeling is in it-self an insatiable and bottomless abyss.

But if nothing external can restrain this capacity, it can only be a source of torment to itself. Unlimited desires are insatiable by definition and insatia-bility is rightly considered a sign of morbidity. Being unlimited, they con-stantly and infinitely surpass the means at their command; they cannot be quenched. Inextinguishable thirst is constantly renewed torture. It has been claimed, indeed, that human activity naturally aspires beyond assignable limits and sets itself unattainable goals. But how can such an undetermined state be any more reconciled with the conditions of mental life than with the demands of physical life? All man's pleasure in acting, moving and exert-ing himself implies the sense that his efforts are not in vain and that by walk-ing he has advanced. However, one does not advance when one walks to-ward no goal, or—which is the same thing—when his goal is infinity. Since the distance between us and it is always the same, whatever road we take, we might as well have made the motions without progress from the spot. Even our glances behind and our feeling of pride at the distance covered can cause only deceptive satisfaction, since the remaining distance is not proportion-ately reduced. To pursue a goal which is by definition unattainable is to con-demn oneself to a state of perpetual unhappiness. Of course, man may hope contrary to all reason, and hope has its pleasures even when unreasonable. It may sustain him for a time; but it can-not survive the repeated disappoint-ments of experience indefinitely. What more can the future offer him than the past, since he can never reach a tena-ble condition nor even approach the glimpsed ideal? Thus, the more one has, the more one wants, since satisfac-tions received only stimulate instead of filling needs. Shall action as such be

considered agreeable? First, only on condition of blindness to its useless-ness. Secondly, for this pleasure to be felt and to temper and half veil the ac-companying painful unrest, such un-ending motion must at least always be easy and unhampered. If it is inter-fered with only restlesness is left, with the lack of ease which it, itself, entails. But it would be a miracle if no insur-mountable obstacle were ever encoun-tered. Our thread of life on these con-ditions is pretty thin, breakable at any instant.

To achieve any other result, the pas-sions first must be limited. Only then can they be harmonized with the facul-ties and satisfied. But since the individ-ual has no way of limiting them, this must be done by some force exterior to him. A regulative force must play the same role for moral needs which the organism plays for physical needs. This means that the force can only be moral. The awakening of conscience inter-rupted the state of equilibrium of the animal's dormant existence; only con-science, therefore, can furnish the means to re-establish it. Physical re-straint would be ineffective; hearts can-not be touched by physio-chemical forces. So far as the appetites are not automatically restrained by physiolog-ical mechanisms, they can be halted only by a limit that they recognize as just. Men would never consent to re-strict their desires if they felt justified in passing the assigned limit. But, for reasons given above, they cannot as-sign themselves this law of justice. So they must receive it from an authority which they respect, to which they yield spontaneously. Either directly and as a whole, or through the agency of one of its organs, society alone can play this moderating role; for it is the only moral power superior to the individual, the authority of which he accepts. It alone has the power necessary to stipu-late law and to set the point beyond which the passions must not go. Finally, it alone can estimate the reward to be prospectively offered to every class of human functionary, in the name of the common interest.

As a matter of fact, at every moment of history there is a dim perception, in the moral consciousness of societies, of the respective value of different social services, the relative reward due to each, and the consequent degree of comfort appropriate on the average to workers in each occupation. The different functions are graded in public opinion and a certain coefficient of well-being assigned to each, according to its place in the hierarchy. According to accepted ideas, for example, a certain way of living is considered the upper limit to which a workman may aspire in his efforts to improve his existence, and there is another limit below which he is not willingly permitted to fall unless he has seriously demeaned himself. Both differ for city and country workers, for the domestic servant and the day-laborer, for the business clerk and the official, etc. Likewise the man of wealth is reproved if he lives the life of a poor man, but also if he seeks the refinements of luxury overmuch. Economists may protest in vain; public feeling will always be scandalized if an individual spends too much wealth for wholly superfluous use, and it even seems that this severity relaxes only in times of moral disturbance.[1] A genuine regimen exists, therefore, although not always legally formulated, which fixes with relative precision the maximum degree of ease of living to which each social class may legitimately aspire. However, there is nothing immutable about such a scale. It changes with the increase or decrease of collective revenue and the changes occurring in the

moral ideas of society. Thus what appears luxury to one period no longer does so to another; and the well-being which for long periods was granted to a class only by exception and supererogation, finally appears strictly necessary and equitable.

Under this pressure, each in his sphere vaguely realizes the extreme limit set to his ambitions and aspires to nothing beyond. At least if he respects regulations and is docile to collective authority, that is, has a wholesome moral constitution, he feels that it is not well to ask more. Thus, an end and goal are set to the passions. Truly, there is nothing rigid nor absolute about such determination. The economic ideal assigned each class of citizens is itself confined to certain limits, within which the desires have free range. But it is not infinite. This relative limitation and the moderation it involves, make men contented with their lot while stimulating them moderately to improve it; and this average contentment causes the feeling of calm, active happiness, the pleasure in existing and living which characterizes health for societies as well as for individuals. Each person is then at least, generally speaking, in harmony with his condition, and desires only what he may legitimately hope for as the normal reward of his activity. Besides, this does not condemn man to a sort of immobility. He may seek to give beauty to his life; but his attempts in this direction may fail without causing him to despair. For, loving what he has and not fixing his desire solely on what he lacks, his wishes and hopes may fail of what he has happened to aspire to, without his being wholly destitute. He has the essentials. The equilibrium of his happiness is secure because it is defined, and a few mishaps cannot disconcert him.

But it would be of little use for everyone to recognize the justice of the

---

[1] Actually, this is a purely moral reprobation and can hardly be judicially implemented. We do not consider any reestablishment of sumptuary laws desirable or even possible.

hierarchy of functions established by public opinion, if he did not also consider the distribution of these functions just. The workman is not in harmony with his social position if he is not convinced that he has his desserts. If he feels justified in occupying another, what he has would not satisfy him. So it is not enough for the average level of needs for each social condition to be regulated by public opinion, but another, more precise rule, must fix the way in which these conditions are open to individuals. There is no society in which such regulation does not exist. It varies with times and places. Once it regarded birth as the almost exclusive principle of social classification; today it recognizes no other inherent inequality than hereditary fortune and merit. But in all these various forms its object is unchanged. It is also only possible, everywhere, as a restriction upon individuals imposed by superior authority, that is, by collective authority. For it can be established only by requiring of one or another group of men, usually of all, sacrifices and concessions in the name of the public interest.

Some, to be sure, have thought that this moral pressure would become unnecessary if men's economic circumstances were only no longer determined by heredity. If inheritance were abolished, the argument runs, if everyone began life with equal resources and if the competitive struggle were fought out on a basis of perfect equality, no one could think its results unjust. Each would instinctively feel that things are as they should be.

Truly, the nearer this ideal equality were approached, the less social restraint will be necessary. But it is only a matter of degree. One sort of heredity will always exist, that of natural talent. Intelligence, taste, scientific, artistic, literary or industrial ability, courage and manual dexterity are gifts received by each of us at birth, as the

heir to wealth receives his capital or as the nobleman formerly received his title and function. A moral discipline will therefore still be required to make those less favored by nature accept the lesser advantages which they owe to the chance of birth. Shall it be demanded that all have an equal share and that no advantage be given those more useful and deserving? But then there would have to be a discipline far stronger to make these accept a treatment merely equal to that of the mediocre and incapable.

But like the one first mentioned, this discipline can be useful only if considered just by the peoples subject to it. When it is maintained only by custom and force, peace and harmony are illusory; the spirit of unrest and discontent are latent; appetites superficially restrained are ready to revolt. This happened in Rome and Greece when the faiths underlying the old organization of the patricians and plebeians were shaken, and in our modern societies when aristocratic prejudices began to lose their old ascendancy. But this state of upheaval is exceptional; it occurs only when society is passing through some abnormal crisis. In normal conditions the collective order is regarded as just by the great majority of persons. Therefore, when we say that an authority is necessary to impose this order on individuals, we certainly do not mean that violence is the only means of establishing it. Since this regulation is meant to restrain individual passions, it must come from a power which dominates individuals; but this power must also be obeyed through respect, not fear.

It is not true, then, that human activity can be released from all restraint. Nothing in the world can enjoy such a privilege. All existence being a part of the universe is relative to the remainder; its nature and method of manifestation accordingly depend not only on itself but on other beings, who consequently restrain and regulate it. Here there are only differences of degree and form between the mineral realm and the thinking person. Man's characteristic privilege is that the bond he accepts is not physical but moral; that is, social. He is governed not by a material environment brutally imposed on him, but by a conscience superior to his own, the superiority of which he feels. Because the greater, better part of his existence transcends the body, he escapes the body's yoke, but is subject to that of society.

But when society is disturbed by some painful crisis or by beneficent but abrupt transitions, it is momentarily incapable of exercising this influence; thence come the sudden rises in the curve of suicides which we have pointed out above.

In the case of economic disasters, indeed, something like a declassification occurs which suddenly casts certain individuals into a lower state than their previous one. Then they must reduce their requirements, restrain their needs, learn greater self-control. All the advantages of social influence are lost so far as they are concerned; their moral education has to be recommenced. But society cannot adjust them instantaneously to this new life and teach them to practice the increased self-repression to which they are unaccustomed. So they are not adjusted to the condition forced on them, and its very prospect is intolerable; hence the suffering which detaches them from a reduced existence even before they have made trial of it.

It is the same if the source of the crisis is an abrupt growth of power and wealth. Then, truly, as the conditions of life are changed, the standard according to which needs were regulated can no longer remain the same; for it varies with social resources, since it largely determines the share of each

class of producers. The scale is upset; but a new scale cannot be immediately improvised. Time is required for the public conscience to reclassify men and things. So long as the social forces thus freed have not regained equilibrium, their respective values are unknown and so all regulation is lacking for a time. The limits are unknown between the possible and the impossible, what is just and what is unjust, legitimate claims and hopes and those which are immoderate. Consequently, there is no restraint upon aspirations. If the disturbance is profound, it affects even the principles controlling the distribution of men among various occupations. since the relations between various parts of society are necessarily modified, the ideas expressing these relations must change. Some particular class especially favored by the crisis is no longer resigned to its former lot, and, on the other hand, the example of its greater good fortune arouses all sorts of jealousy below and about it. Appetites, not being controlled by a public opinion become disoriented, no longer recognize the limits proper to them. Besides, they are at the same time seized by a sort of natural erethism simply by the greater intensity of public life. With increased prosperity desires increase. At the very moment when traditional rules have lost their authority, the richer prize offered these appetites stimulates them and makes them more exigent and impatient of control. The state of de-regulation or anomy is thus further heightened by passions being less disciplined, precisely when they need more disciplining.

But then their very demands make fulfillment impossible. Overweening ambition always exceeds the results obtained, great as they may be, since there is no warning to pause here. Nothing gives satisfaction and all this agitation is uninterruptedly maintained without appeasement. Above all, since this race for an unattainable goal can give no other pleasure but that of the race itself, if it is one, once it is interrupted the participants are left empty-handed. At the same time the struggle grows more violent and painful, both from being less controlled and because competition is greater. All classes contend among themselves because no established classification any longer exists. Effort grows, just when it becomes less productive. How could the desire to live not be weakened under such conditions?

This explanation is confirmed by the remarkable immunity of poor countries. Poverty protects against suicide because it is a restraint in itself. No matter how one acts, desires have to depend upon resources to some extent; actual possessions are partly the criterion of those aspired to. So the less one has the less he is tempted to extend the range of his needs indefinitely. Lack of power, compelling moderation, accustoms men to it, while nothing excites envy if no one has superfluity. Wealth, on the other hand, by the power it bestows, deceives us into believing that we depend on ourselves only. Reducing the resistance we encounter from objects, it suggests the possibility of unlimited success against them. The less limited one feels, the more intolerable all limitation appears. Not without reason, therefore, have so many religions dwelt on the advantages and moral value of poverty. It is actually the best school for teaching self-restraint. Forcing us to constant self-discipline, it prepares us to accept collective discipline with equanimity, while wealth, exalting the individual, may always arouse the spirit of rebellion which is the very source of immorality. This, of course, is no reason why humanity should not improve its material condition. But though the moral danger involved in every growth of prosperity is not irremediable, it should not be forgotten.

If anomy [normlessness: lack of rules governing behavior] never appeared except, as in the above instances, in intermittent spurts and acute crisis, it might cause the social suicide-rate to vary from time to time, but it would not be a regular, constant factor. In one sphere of social life, however—the sphere of trade and industry—it is actually in a chronic state.

For a whole century, economic progress has mainly consisted in freeing industrial relations from all regulation. Until very recently, it was the function of a whole system of moral forces to exert this discipline. First, the influence of religion was felt alike by workers and masters, the poor and the rich. It consoled the former and taught them contentment with their lot by informing them of the providential nature of the social order, that the share of each class was assigned by God himself, and by holding out the hope for just compensation in a world to come in return for the inequalities of this world. It governed the latter, recalling that worldly interests are not man's entire lot, that they must be subordinate to other and higher interests, and that they should therefore not be pursued without rule or measure. Temporal power, in turn, restrained the scope of economic functions by its supremacy over them and by the relatively subordinate role it assigned them. Finally, within the business world proper, the occupational groups by regulating salaries, the price of products and production itself, indirectly fixed the average level of income on which needs are partially based by the very force of circumstances. However, we do not mean to propose this organization as a model. Clearly it would be inadequate to existing societies without great changes. What we stress is its existence, the fact of its useful influence, and that nothing today has come to take its place.

Actually, religion has lost most of

its power. And government, instead of regulating economic life, has become its tool and servant. The most opposite schools, orthodox economists and extreme socialists, unite to reduce government to the role of a more or less passive intermediary among the various social functions. The former wish to make it simply the guardian of individual contracts; the latter leave it the task of doing the collective bookkeeping, that is, of recording the demands of consumers, transmitting them to producers, inventorying the total revenue and distributing it according to a fixed formula. But both refuse it any power to subordinate other social organs to itself and to make them converge toward one dominant aim. On both sides nations are declared to have the single or chief purpose of achieving industrial prosperity; such is the implication of the dogma of economic materialism, the basis of both apparently opposed systems. And as these theories merely express the state of opinion, industry, instead of being still regarded as a means to an end transcending itself, has become the supreme end of individuals and societies alike. Thereupon the appetites thus excited have become freed of any limiting authority. By sanctifying them, so to speak, this apotheosis of well-being has placed them above all human law. Their restraint seems like a sort of sacrilege. For this reason, even the purely utilitarian regulation of them exercised by the industrial world itself through the medium of occupational groups has been unable to persist. Ultimately, this liberation of desires has been made worse by the very development of industry and the almost infinite extension of the market. So long as the producer could gain his profits only in his immediate neighborhood, the restricted amount of possible gain could not much overexcite ambition. Now that he may assume to have almost the entire world as his customer,

how could passions accept their former confinement in the face of such limitless prospects?

Such is the source of the excitment predominating in this part of society, and which has thence extended to the other parts. There, the state of crisis and anomy is constant and, so to speak, normal. From top to bottom of the ladder, greed is aroused without knowing where to find ultimate foothold. Nothing can calm it, since its goal is far beyond all it can attain. Reality seems valueless by comparison with the dreams of fevered imaginations; reality is therefore abandoned, but so too is possibility abandoned when it in turn becomes reality. A thirst arises for novelties, unfamiliar pleasures, nameless sensations, all of which lose their savor once known. Henceforth one has no strength to endure the least reverse. The whole fever subsides and the sterility of all the tumult is apparent, and it is seen that all these new sensations in their infinite quantity cannot form a solid foundation of happiness to support one during days of trial. The wise man, knowing how to enjoy achieved results without having constantly to replace them with others, finds in them an attachment to life in the hour of difficulty. But the man who has always pinned all his hopes on the future and lived with his eyes fixed upon it, has nothing in the past as a comfort against the present's afflictions, for the past was nothing to him but a series of hastily experienced stages. What blinded him to himself was his expectation always to find further on the happiness he had so far missed. Now he is stopped in his tracks; from now on nothing remains behind or ahead of him to fix his gaze upon. Weariness alone, moreover, is enough to bring disillusionment, for he cannot in the end escape the futility of an endless pursuit.

We may even wonder if this moral state is not principally what makes economic catastrophes of our day so fertile in suicides. In societies where a man is subjected to a healthy discipline, he submits more readily to the blows of chance. The necessary effort for sustaining a little more discomfort costs him relatively little, since he is used to discomfort and constraint. But when every constraint is hateful in itself, how can closer constraint not seem intolerable? There is no tendency to resignation in the feverish impatience of men's lives. When there is no other aim but to outstrip constantly the point arrived at, how painful to be thrown back! Now this very lack of organization characterizing our economic condition throws the door wide to every sort of adventure. Since imagination is hungry for novelty, and ungoverned, it gropes at random. Setbacks necessarily increase with risks and thus crises multiply, just when they are becoming more destructive.

Yet these dispositions are so inbred that society has grown to accept them and is accustomed to think them normal. It is everlastingly repeated that it is man's nature to be eternally dissatisfied, constantly to advance, without relief or rest, toward an indefinite goal. The longing for infinity is daily represented as a mark of moral distinction, whereas it can only appear within unregulated consciences which elevate to a rule the lack of rule from which they suffer. The doctrine of the most ruthless and swift progress has become an article of faith. But other theories appear parallel with those praising the advantages of instability, which, generalizing the situation that gives them birth, declare life evil, claim that it is richer in grief than in pleasure and that it attracts men only by false claims. Since this disorder is greatest in the economic world, it has most victims there.

Industrial and commercial functions are really among the occupations which furnish the greatest number of suicides. . . . Almost on a level with the liberal professions, they sometimes surpass them; they are especially more afflicted than agriculture, where the old regulative forces still make their appearance felt most and where the fever of business has least penetrated. Here is best recalled what was once the general constitution of the economic order. And the divergence would be yet greater if, among the suicides of industry, employees were distinguished from workmen, for the former are probably most stricken by the state of anomy. The enormous rate of those with independent means (720 per million) sufficiently shows that the possessors of most comfort suffer most. Everything that enforces subordination attenuates the effects of this state. At least the horizon of the lower classes is limited by those above them, and for this same reason their desires are more modest. Those who have only empty space above them are almost inevitably lost in it, if no force restrains them.

# 22

# Science and the Disenchantment of the World

## MAX WEBER

Scientific progress is a fraction, the most important fraction, of the process of intellectualization which we have been undergoing for thousands of years and which nowadays is usually judged in such an extremely negative way. Let us first clarify what this intellectualist rationalization, created by science and by scientifically oriented technology, means practically.

Does it mean that we, today, for instance, everyone sitting in this hall, have a greater knowledge of the conditions of life under which we exist than has an American Indian or a Hottentot? Hardly. Unless he is a physicist, one who rides on the streetcar has no idea how the car happened to get into motion. And he does not need to know. He is satisfied that he may 'count' on the behavior of the streetcar, and he orients his conduct according to this expectation; but he knows nothing about what it takes to produce such a car so that it can move. The savage knows incomparably more about his tools. When we spend money today I bet that even if there are colleagues of political economy here in the hall, almost every one of them will hold a different answer in readiness to the question: How does it happen that one can buy something for money—sometimes more and sometimes less? The savage knows what he does in order to get his daily food and which institutions serve him in this pursuit. The increasing intellectualization and rationalization do *not*, therefore, indicate an increased and general knowledge of the conditions under which one lives.

It means something else, namely, the knowledge or belief that if one but wished one *could* learn it at any time. Hence, it means that principally there are no mysterious incalculable forces that come into play, but rather that one can, in principle, master all things by calculation. This means that the world is disenchanted. One need no longer have recourse to magical means in order to master or implore the spirits, as did the savage, for whom such mysterious powers existed. Technical means and calculations perform the service. This above all is what intellectualization means.

Now, this process of disenchantment, which has continued to exist in Occidental culture for millennia, and, in general, this 'progress,' to which science belongs as a link and motive force, do they have any meanings that go beyond the purely practical and technical? . . . What is the value of science?

Here the contrast between the past and the present is tremendous. You will recall the wonderful image at the beginning of the seventh book of Plato's *Republic*: those enchained cavemen whose faces are turned toward the stone wall before them. Behind them lies the source of the light which they cannot see. They are concerned only with the shadowy images that this light throws upon the wall, and they seek to fathom their interrelations. Finally one of them succeeds in shattering his fetters, turns around, and sees the sun. Blinded, he gropes about and stammers of what he saw. The others say he is raving. But gradually he learns to behold the light, and then his task is to

From *From Max Weber, Essays in Sociology,* edited and translated by H. H. Gerth and C. Wright Mills. Copyright © 1946 by Oxford University Press, Inc. Reprinted by permission.

descend to the cavemen and to lead them to the light. He is the philosopher; the sun, however, is the truth of science, which alone seizes not upon illusions and shadows but upon the true being.

Well, who today views science in such a manner? Today youth feels rather the reverse: the intellectual constructions of science constitute an unreal realm of artificial abstractions, which with their bony hands seek to grasp the blood-and-the-sap of true life without ever catching up with it. But here in life, in what for Plato was the play of shadows on the walls of the cave, genuine reality is pulsating; and the rest are derivatives of life, lifeless ghosts, and nothing else. How did this change come about?

Plato's passionate enthusiasm in *The Republic* must, in the last analysis, be explained by the fact that for the first time the *concept*, one of the great tools of all scientific knowledge, had been consciously discovered. Socrates had discovered it in its bearing. He was not the only man in the world to discover it. In India one finds the beginnings of a logic that is quite similar to that of Aristotle's. But nowhere else do we find this realization of the significance of the concept. In Greece, for the first time, appeared a handy means by which one could put the logical screws upon somebody so that he could not come out without admitting either that he knew nothing or that this and nothing else was truth, the *eternal* truth that never would vanish as the doings of the blind men vanish. That was the tremendous experience which dawned upon the disciples of Socrates. And from this it seemed to follow that if one only found the right concept of the beautiful, the good, or, for instance, of bravery, of the soul—or whatever—that then one could also grasp its true being. And this, in turn, seemed to open the way for knowing and for teaching how to act rightly in life and, above

all, how to act as a citizen of the state; for this question was everything to the Hellenic man, whose thinking was political throughout. And for these reasons one engaged in science.

The second great tool of scientific work, the rational experiment, made its appearance at the side of this discovery of the Hellenic spirit during the Renaissance period. The experiment is a means of reliably controlling experience. Without it, present-day empirical science would be impossible. There were experiments earlier; for instance, in India physiological experiments were made in the service of ascetic yoga technique; in Hellenic antiquity, mathematical experiments were made for purposes of war technology; and in the Middle Ages, for purposes of mining. But to raise the experiment to a principle of research was the achievement of the Renaissance. They were the great innovators in *art*, who were the pioneers of experiment. Leonardo and his like and, above all, the sixteenth-century experimenters in music with their experimental pianos were characteristic. From these circles the experiment entered science, especially through Galileo, and it entered theory through Bacon; and then it was taken over by the various exact disciplines of the continental universities, first of all those of Italy and then those of the Netherlands.

What did science mean to these men who stood at the threshold of modern times? To artistic experimenters of the type of Leonardo and the musical innovators, science meant the path to *true* art, and that meant for them the path to true *nature*. Art was to be raised to the rank of a science, and this meant at the same time and above all to raise the artist to the rank of the doctor, socially and with reference to the meaning of his life. This is the ambition on which, for instance, Leonardo's sketch book was based. And today? 'Science as the way to nature' would sound like blasphemy to youth. Today, youth proclaims the opposite: redemption from the intellectualism of science in order to return to one's own nature and therewith to nature in general. Science as a way to art? Here no criticism is even needed.

But during the period of the rise of the exact sciences one expected a great deal more. If you recall Swammerdam's statement, 'Here I bring you the proof of God's providence in the anatomy of a louse,' you will see what the scientific worker, influenced (indirectly) by Protestantism and Puritanism, conceived to be his task: to show the path to God. People no longer found this path among the philosophers, with their concepts and deductions. All pietist theology of the time, above all Spener, knew that God was not to be found along the road by which the Middle Ages had sought him. God is hidden, His ways are not our ways, His thoughts are not our thoughts. In the exact sciences, however, where one could physically grasp His works, one hoped to come upon the traces of what He planned for the world. And today? Who—aside from certain big children who are indeed found in the natural sciences—still believes that the findings of astronomy, biology, physics, or chemistry could teach us anything about the *meaning* of the world? If there is any such 'meaning,' along what road could one come upon its tracks? If these natural sciences lead to anything in this way, they are apt to make the belief that there is such a thing as the 'meaning' of the universe die out at its very roots.

And finally, science as a way 'to God'? Science, this specifically irreligious power? That science today is irreligious no one will doubt in his innermost being, even if he will not admit it to himself. Redemption from the rationalism and intellectualism of

science is [considered] the fundamental presupposition of living in union with the divine. . . . The only thing that is strange is the method that is now followed: the spheres of the irrational, the only spheres that intellectualism has not yet touched, are now raised into consciousness and put under its lens. For in practice this is where the modern intellectualist form of romantic irrationalism leads. This method of emancipation from intellectualism may well bring about the very opposite of what those who take to it conceive as its goal.

After Nietzsche's devastating criticism of those 'last men' who "invented happiness," I may leave aside altogether the naive optimism in which science—that is, the technique of mastering life which rests upon science—has been celebrated as the way to happiness. Who believes in this?—aside from a few big children in university chairs or editorial offices. Let us resume our argument.

Under these internal presuppositions, what is the meaning of science as a vocation, now after all these former illusions, the 'way to true being,' the 'way to true art,' the 'way to true nature,' the 'way to true God,' the 'way to true happiness,' have been dispelled? Tolstoi has given the simplest answer, with the words: 'Science is meaningless because it gives no answer to our question, the only question important for us: "What shall we do and how shall we live?"' That science does not give an answer to this is indisputable. The only question that remains is the sense in which science gives 'no' answer, and whether or not science might yet be of some use to the one who puts the question correctly.

Today one usually speaks of science as 'free from presuppositions.' Is there such a thing? It depends upon what one understands thereby. All scientific work presupposes that the rules of logic and method are valid; these are the general foundations of our orientation in the world; and, at least for our special question, these presuppositions are the least problematic aspect of science. Science further presupposes that what is yielded by scientific work is important in the sense that it is 'worth being known.' In this, obviously, are contained all our problems. For this presupposition cannot be proved by scientific means. It can only be *interpreted* with reference to its ultimate meaning, which we must reject or accept according to our ultimate position towards life.

Furthermore, the nature of the relationship of scientific work and its presuppositions varies widely according to their structure. The natural sciences, for instance, physics, chemistry, and astronomy, presuppose as self-evident that it is worth while to know the ultimate laws of cosmic events as far as science can construe them. This is the case not only because with such knowledge one can attain technical results but for its own sake, if the quest for such knowledge is to be a 'vocation.' Yet this presupposition can by no means be proved. And still less can it be proved that the existence of the world which these sciences describe is worth while, that it has any 'meaning,' or that it makes sense to live in such a world. Science does not ask for the answers to such questions. . . . Natural science gives us an answer to the question of what we must do if we wish to master life technically. It leaves quite aside, or assumes for its purposes, whether we should and do wish to master life technically and whether it ultimately makes sense to do so. . . .

First, of course, science contributes to the technology of controlling life by calculating external objects as well as man's activities. . . .

Second, science can contribute . . . methods of thinking, the tools and the training for thought. . . .

Fortunately, however, the contribution of science does not reach its limit with this. We are in a position to help you to a third objective: to gain *clarity*. Of course, it is presupposed that we ourselves possess clarity. As far as this is the case, we can make clear to you the following:

In practice, you can take this or that position when concerned with a problem of value—for simplicity's sake, please think of social phenomena as examples. *If* you take such and such a stand, then, according to scientific experience, you have to use such and such a *means* in order to carry out your conviction practically. Now, these means are perhaps such that you believe you must reject them. Then you simply must choose between the end and the inevitable means. Does the end 'justify' the means? Or does it not? The teacher can confront you with the necessity of this choice. He cannot do more, so long as he wishes to remain a teacher and not to become a demagogue. He can, of course, also tell you that if you want such and such an end, then you must take into the bargain the subsidiary consequences which according to all experience will occur. Again we find ourselves in the same situation as before. These are still problems that can also emerge for the technician, who in numerous instances has to make decisions according to the principle of the lesser evil or of the relatively best. Only to him one thing, the main thing, is usually given, namely, the end. But as soon as truly 'ultimate' problems are at stake for us this is not the case. With this, at long last, we come to the final service that science as such can render to the aim of clarity, and at the same time we come to the limits of science.

Besides we can and we should state: In terms of its meaning, such and such a practical stand can be derived with inner consistency, and hence integrity, from this or that ultimate *weltanschau-*

*liche* position. Perhaps it can only be derived from one such fundamental position, or maybe from several, but it cannot be derived from these or those other positions. Figuratively speaking, you serve this god and you offend the other god when you decide to adhere to this position. And if you remain faithful to yourself, you will necessarily come to certain final conclusions that subjectively make sense. This much, in principle at least, can be accomplished. Philosophy, as a special discipline, and the essentially philosophical discussions of principles in the other sciences attempt to achieve this. Thus, if we are competent in our pursuit (which must be presupposed here) we can force the individual, or at least we can help him, to give himself an *account of the ultimate meaning of his own conduct.* This appears to me as not so trifling a thing to do, even for one's own personal life. Again, I am tempted to say of a teacher who succeeds in this: he stands in the service of 'moral' forces: he fulfils the duty of bringing about the self-clarification and a sense of responsibility. And I believe he will be the more able to accomplish this, the more conscientiously he avoids the desire personally to impose upon or suggest to his audience his own stand.

This proposition, which I present here, always takes its point of departure from the one fundamental fact, that so long as life remains immanent and is interpreted in its own terms, it knows only of an unceasing struggle of these gods with one another. Or speaking directly, the ultimately possible attitudes toward life are irreconcilable and hence their struggle can never be brought to a final conclusion. Thus it is necessary to make a decisive choice. Whether, under such conditions, science is a worthwhile 'vocation' for somebody, and whether science itself has an objectively valuable 'vocation' are again value judgments about which

nothing can be said in the lecture-room. To affirm the value of science is a presupposition for teaching there. I personally by my very work answer in the affirmative, and I also do so from precisely the standpoint that hates intellectualism as the worst devil, as youth does today, or usually only fancies it does. In that case the word holds for these youths: 'Mind you, the devil is old; grow old to understand him.' This does not mean age in the sense of the birth certificate. It means that if one wishes to settle with this devil, one must not take to flight before him as so many like to do nowadays. First of all, one has to see the devil's ways to the end in order to realize his power and his limitations.

Science today is a vocation organized in special disciplines in the service of self-clarification and knowledge of interrelated facts. It is not the gift of grace of seers and prophets dispensing sacred values and revelations, nor does it partake of the contemplation of sages and philosophers about the meaning of the universe. This, to be sure, is the inescapable condition of our historical situation. We cannot evade it so long as we remain true to ourselves. And if Tolstoi's question recurs to you: as science does not, who is to answer the question: 'What shall we do, and, how shall we arrange our lives?' or, in the words used here tonight: 'Which of the warring gods should we serve? Or should we serve perhaps an entirely different god, and who is he?' then one can say that only a prophet or a savior can give the answers. If there is no such man, or if his message is no longer believed in, then you will certainly not compel him to appear on this earth by having thousands of professors, as privileged hirelings of the state, attempt as petty prophets in their lecture-rooms to take over his role. All they will accomplish is to show that they are unaware of the decisive state of affairs: the prophet for whom so many of our younger generation yearn simply does not exist. But this knowledge in its forceful significance has never become vital for them. The inward interest of a truly religiously 'musical' man can never be served by veiling to him and to others the fundamental fact that he is destined to live in a godless and prophetless time by giving him the *ersatz* of armchair prophecy. The integrity of his religious organ, it seems to me, must rebel against this. . . .

The fate of our times is characterized by rationalization and intellectualization and, above all, by the "disenchantment of the world.' Precisely the ultimate and most sublime values have retreated from public life either into the transcendental realm of mystic life or into the brotherliness of direct and personal human relations. It is not accidental that our greatest art is intimate and not monumental, nor is it accidental that today only within the smallest and intimate circles, in personal human situations, in *pianissimo*, that something is pulsating that corresponds to the prophetic *pneuma*, which in former times swept through the great communities like a firebrand, welding them together. If we attempt to force and to 'invent' a monumental style in art, such miserable monstrosities are produced as the many monuments of the last twenty years. If one tries intellectually to construe new religions without a new and genuine prophecy, then, in an inner sense, something similar will result, but with still worse effects. And academic prophecy, finally, will create only fanatical sects but never a genuine community.

To the person who cannot bear the fate of the times like a man, one must say: may he rather return silently, without the usual publicity build-up of renegades, but simply and plainly. The arms of the old churches are opened widely and compassionately for him. After all, they do not make it hard for him. One way or another he has to bring his 'intellectual sacrifice'—that is inevitable. If he can really do it, we shall not rebuke him. For such an intellectual sacrifice in favor of an unconditional religious devotion is ethically quite a different matter than the evasion of the plain duty of intellectual integrity, which sets in if one lacks the courage to clarify one's own ultimate standpoint and rather facilitates this duty by feeble relative judgments. In my eyes, such religious return stands higher than the academic prophecy, which does not clearly realize that in the lecture-rooms of the university no other virtue holds but plain intellectual integrity. Integrity, however, compels us to state that for the many who today tarry for new prophets and saviors, the situation is the same as resounds in the beautiful Edomite watchman's song of the period of exile that has been included among Isaiah's oracles: "He calleth to me out of Seir, Watchman, what of the night? The watchman said, The morning cometh, and also the night: if ye will enquire, enquire ye: return, come."

The people to whom this was said has enquired and tarried for more than two millennia, and we are shaken when we realize its fate. From this we want to draw the lesson that nothing is gained by yearning and tarrying alone, and we shall act differently. We shall set to work and meet the 'demands of the day,' in human relations as well as in our vocation. This, however, is plain and simple, if each finds and obeys the demon who holds the fibers of his very life.

# Part Three

# Sociology of
# Contemporary Society

## INTRODUCTION

Life in contemporary society is, of course, the subject of most sociological analysis. Sociologists describe and explain the structure and change of contemporary social life, including the kinds of groups, social processes, and institutions that are predominant in today's world. Sociologists in North America and Western Europe generally concentrate on the study of their own urban-industrial societies, describing and explaining these as they move toward the metropolitan, bureaucratic, automated world which some have called the "postmodern" society.[1] The groups of essays in this, the largest section of the book, describe and explain some important aspects of life in this society.

Scientific analysis of any kind is a cooperative, progressive endeavor in which descriptions are made more accurate and explanations more complete as scientists check and expand one another's observations. The social sciences, however, have the special problem that their subject matter is today in the process of transformation as they observe it. The social scientist is very much in the position described by the ancient Greek philosopher Heraclitus, who likened life to a river and pointed out that a man, here an observer of life, could never step into the "same" river twice, for each time he walked into it it would actually be a different river, the part which he had originally observed having already moved on toward the sea. The sociologist studying social classes or suburban communities in America, for example, should know that what he is looking at has probably changed since the last group of sociologists studied it, and will be still different if he comes back to restudy it in a few years.[2]

Sociologists and other social scientists must have the courage to face this rapid obsolescence of their data. At the same time, they need to concentrate on the discovery of basic processes at work in contemporary social life so they can identify the overall trends of change in the postmodern society. In this way their studies become less time-bound and more relevant to the developing

[1] See, for example, David Cooperman and E. V. Walter, *Power and Civilization*, Part II, "The Postmodern World" (New York: Thomas Y. Crowell, 1962).

[2] Perhaps even more intriguing is the possibility that social life may be changed as a result of being observed and reported upon by sociologists. For a good discussion of this question, see John R. Seeley, "Social Science? Some Probative Problems" in Maurice R. Stein and Arthur J. Vidich, editors, *Sociology on Trial* (Englewood Cliffs, N.J.: Prentice-Hall, 1963).

future, as it can be discerned in the living present. For Part Three, the largest portion of the book, we have sought analyses which not only describe aspects of society today, but which also attempt to project its future trends. In other words the selections here are both fundamental, in that they deal with basic processes, groups, and institutions of modern society, and future-oriented, in that they attempt to describe what our social life is becoming.

It is revealing, in light of these goals, to compare Robert Heilbroner's essay "The Future of Capitalism" with the work of the classical sociologists Saint-Simon, Marx, and Weber. Heilbroner attempts to identify the forces at work in society today which may be bringing about its transformation into a new form of human society. The classical sociologists, it will be remembered, looked back into feudal society to discover the forces which had been at work there bringing about the transformation to industrial capitalism. Not all social science can be so grandly speculative as this, but social scientists must be aware that the object of their study, present-day society, is in the process of changing into something different even as they are examining it.

This part of the book concentrates on those groups, processes, and institutions that are most important to the postmodern societies coming into existence in North America and Western Europe. The dominant forms of social organization in this kind of society include the metropolis, bureaucracy, social classes, and ethnic groups; basic institutions of contemporary social life include the family, education, the economy, the state, and the military; and fundamental social processes include socialization, stratification, conflict, and change. Although important sociological studies exist of industrial socialist societies and nonindustrial societies of the underdeveloped "third world," they are not represented here owing to lack of space. We believe, however, that postmodern societies of the West show some important trends which will develop in advanced societies generally. These include metropolitanization, bureaucratization, and totalization, all of which are described in readings we have selected. Let us now briefly review the topics which are discussed in the readings of this section.

Families and schools are groups within which the young are *socialized,* that is, prepared for adult life in society as it is presently organized. The kinship and educational systems of our societies are therefore secondary institutions that prepare people for life in society but do not significantly shape the overall structure of society or determine the direction of its change. Religion is also regarded, at least in the United States, as an important socializing institution: Americans report they go to church because it is good for the children to have some religious training. The groups forming these institutions—churches, schools, particular families—prepare individuals to take roles and enact them successfully in a society whose basic structure and direction of change are mainly determined by people's activities in the primary institutions: the economy, government, and the military. Youth is the period of life in which people are making the transition from these socialization institutions to participation in the major institutions of society and the creation of their own families. Thus the problems of youth, the problems of "growing up American," for example, help show us some of the strains contemporary social life imposes on individuals. The study of adolescence, therefore, promises to tell us as much about the kind of society in which we live as about a particular period of life in this society.

The community is the habitat of the members of a society, the physical and social environment in which they carry out the important activities of their lives—earning a living, raising their families, governing themselves, and educating their children. For primitive man the community—that is, the roving band or the settled village—often constituted the largest social unit and so was synonymous with "society" as a whole. In feudal Europe the communities were the manors of the nobility and clergy or the towns of the tradesmen and merchants. Industrialization created the factory city as the place of residence of most members of early modern society. Postmodern society is in the process of metropolitanization as most communities are developing into metropolitan areas which fan out around large central cities and come to include satellite cities, suburbs, and even country towns within the web of their social and economic, though not political, organization. Sociological studies of communities are consequently recognizing that particular cities, towns, and villages have to be understood in their metropolitan contexts as specialized parts of the social and economic life of the entire metropolitan area into which they are being integrated. The habitat of postmodern man is becoming the highly integrated metropolitan complex rather than the distinctive and separate individual communities of the past.

Bureacracy is the typical form of group structure in most institutional areas of advanced industrial societies. The economy, the government, the military, education, and even religion become bureaucratically organized in both socialist and capitalist countries as they develop toward the advanced industrial form of society. In fact, the only institutional area which has not become bureaucratically organized in advanced societies is the kinship system. Families survive as one of the few nonbureaucratic groups in postmodern society. The trend toward bureaucratization has numerous causes, among the most important of which are the increasing size of the population and the increasing complexity of modern technology. Bureaucracy is the only form of social organization that has so far been invented to handle the large-scale administrative tasks which increasing size and complexity create for modern man in most areas of his social life. Bureaucracy's ability to organize the activities of many different people toward the accomplishment of some common end—such as producing and selling automobiles, governing a city, or fighting a war—results from its formal, rational organization in which the activities of the participants are governed by sets of rigid rules. Interaction among bureaucratic role players is standardized and impersonal, based on strictly limited areas of competence in which the bureaucrat is expected to be an expert. The effectiveness of bureaucracy comes from the specialization of each participant in some small area of activity in which he becomes an expert, and the coordination of the efforts of many such experts toward the achievement of a common goal. Bureaucracy is becoming the organizational environment of postmodern man, and understanding its functioning and its effects on people is necessary for any grasp of the structure of contemporary society and the psychology of contemporary man.

Social class, religion, race, and national origin have long provided bases of group organization in the large nations of Western Europe and North America. Relations among the different classes, races, and ethnic groups (those sharing a common national origin, language, and religion) have provided some of the basic dynamics of conflict, accommodation, and change in the lives of these nations. The United States of America and Canada, for example, were first settled by people from many European countries; in America some people imported African Negroes to work the plantations of the Southern states. Orientals were later brought to the United States to provide labor for the economic enterprises of the Western states. Negroes and Orientals today constitute segregated groups forced to live apart from the "white," or Caucasian, populations in residential and general social segregation. The Caucasian populations of these countries are themselves divided into different ethnic groups, each with its distinctive subculture. The French-Canadians; the Jews of large cities in the United States and Canada; and people of Italian, Irish, German, Scandinavian, Polish, and Hungarian backgrounds have formed social groups in cities and towns of different parts of these countries. To a greater or lesser degree, these ethnic groups have created organizations in which they carry on separate social lives and through which they promote their interests. Negroes, the most numerous racial minority in the United States, have recently begun creating and using organizations of their own to promote the interests of the group as a whole. Racial and ethnic groups will probably continue for some time to provide important forms of association for their members and the dynamics of group conflict in the United States and Canada.

Social class divisions have developed along similar lines in the various industrial capitalist nations of the West. These include an upper class of industrialists, financiers, and merchants, the owners of the means of economic production and exchange; a broad middle class of managers, government officials, small merchants, professional people, salesmen, clerks, and other lower white-collar workers; a working class of factory operatives, laborers, and service workers; and a lower class of people employed in marginal and seasonal work or unable to obtain employment at all. Western European nations have small classes of aristocrats, generally landowners whose estates and titles are survivals from preindustrial society. The extent to which the different classes have formed themselves into social groups actively promoting their common economic interests has differed from class to class and from one time to another. The upper classes have generally formed informal, loose associations of overlapping groups whose unity is based on common social backgrounds of the members and their common interests. The working class in these countries has occasionally formed revolutionary groups seeking to take power by force, but in the recent past has more commonly formed political parties to seek power through the electoral processes. In all countries of the West the working class has formed labor unions through which it seeks to promote the economic and sometimes political interests of its members. Some parts of the middle class, notably such high-status professional people as doctors and lawyers, have formed strong associations to protect and promote the interests of their professions as they see them. Managers, small merchants, government officials, and white-collar workers have not, for the most part, formed groups to promote their common class interests. Today, class-based social groups appear to be diminishing in number and importance even though major economic inequalities continue to exist in most societies of the West.

The political, economic, and military institutions of the industrial capitalist countries are the primary institutional areas of these societies. Men's actions in the groups which make up these institutions generally shape the organization and functioning of the societies as a whole and the personal experience of the people living in them. These societies, in fact, are in a permanent state of change arising from men's activities in these institutional areas. Other institutions, including the family, education, and religion, must change to accommodate themselves to changes in social life caused by the operation of the primary institutions, although their adaptive changes, as in the case of changes in the birth rate, eventually react on the primary institutions. Economic institutions include all the groups engaged in the production and distribution of material goods and related services in the society. Political institutions include all groups involved in the processes of distribution and exercise of legitimate power in the society. Military institutions include the groups which control the most powerful of the legitimate means of violence in the society.

We have included a discussion of the basic institutions under the single heading of "The Political Economy" because they all must be considered in their interrelations in order to understand their organization and operation today. Western European and North American countries are all welfare states today in which the national governments have formally assumed responsibility for assuring by one means or another the economic well-being of the population and the efficient functioning of the national economy as a whole. The military services, since World War II and during the long cold war, have become the largest branch of the federal government in the United States, and a major influence in the national economy. They spend over sixty billion dollars a year, about twenty-five billion of which is spent for procurements from private business and industry. The business corporations themselves exercise significant social, as well as economic, influence through their pricing, investment, and production decisions, which are privately made within the corporations but have great public consequences. The economies of the advanced industrial capitalist countries are becoming more and more organized into a small number of very large corporations. The largest 150 corporations in the United States control over 60 per cent of the productive assets of that country and about 25 per cent of those of the entire noncommunist world.[3] These corporations are becoming truly international organizations with significant economic interests in so many countries that they cannot be said to "belong" to any one country. Sociologists are just beginning to study this new form of social organization in the world.

The character of social life in a particular era is determined by the structure and processes of interaction in the major social groups and institutions of that period. In assessing the nature of social experience for the individual in our society, it is necessary to summarize its basic trends and point out their consequences for the individual participant in social life. Social scientists and social commentators have in recent years pointed out trends toward what have been called the "organized," or "total," society and the "mass" society.[4] By organized society, or total society, they refer to the tendency for social life to become organized into large-scale, impersonal bureaucracies. In bureaucracies power is vested in the top positions; the people in these positions make the basic

[3] See, for example, the essays in Andrew Hacker, editor, *The Corporation Take-Over* (New York: Harper & Row, 1964).
[4] See, for example, C. Wright Mills, *The Power Elite* (New York: Oxford University Press, 1956); Paul Goodman, "Youth in the Organized Society," *Commentary*, February 1960, pp. 95–107; and Harold L. Wilensky, "Mass Society and Mass Culture," *American Sociological Review*, 29 (April 1964), pp. 173–196. Many essays on these topics are collected in Phillip Olsen, editor, *America As a Mass Society* (New York: The Free Press, 1963).

decisions for the organization and these are passed down as orders to people in subordinate positions. The activities of most participants in bureaucracies are determined by these orders and the formal rules which define the rights and duties of their positions. A kind of bureaucratic totalism develops when most people's lives become organized by large bureaucracies and they as individuals are relatively powerless. If at the same time other groups in society, such as associations, informal groups, and interest groups are disappearing or else becoming large-scale bureaucracies themselves, some sociologists feel we have the conditions for the development of the mass society. This is a society in which, outside of the formal organization of the bureaucracies and the personal privacy of the home, social life becomes atomized into a mass of unorganized, only casually related individuals. Mass communication, including television, radio, newspapers, and large-circulation magazines, are seen as the means by which a leveling to a common "mass culture" occurs for these highly differentiated, unrelated individuals. A mass-total society, then, is one in which the individuals are relatively powerless, relate to others primarily in limited bureaucratic roles, and are reduced to a common cultural level by the agencies of the mass media.

Sociology is one of man's instruments for understanding his collective life. Its purposes include discovering the basic character and changes in societies and assessing the consequences of these for man's life. With his perspective on the whole of social life, we feel the sociologist has a special responsibility of trying to discern the basic direction of social change and to show contemporary man the kind of society he is creating by his current activities. This is certainly one of the important roles of sociology in modern society.

# A The Family, Education, and Youth

## INTRODUCTION

Kinship and education are the basic socialization institutions of contemporary society; and youth is the time in life when people are completing this socialization and moving toward adulthood. The family provides new members for society, as well as the very earliest training of new members in the society's culture. It is the one institution that is not becoming bureaucratically organized, and thus is one of the few sources of intimate, personal, emotionally involving and expressive social interaction in postmodern society. Education, on the other hand, is becoming one of the major "industries" of contemporary Western societies in the sense that, as more people are going to school for longer periods of time, educational organizations are becoming major employers and spenders of private and public money. Youth is a transitional period between childhood and adulthood which, in our society, has developed a number of *subcultures* or special worlds within the larger society, such as those of "teenagers," "juvenile delinquents," and "hippies." Some aspects of these subcultures have been adopted in the larger society, thereby making it possible for older people to participate in them.

Dennis Wrong, in his review of Philippe Ariès' history of the family, *Centuries of Childhood*, reminds us that the family as we know it is actually a recent social invention. The premodern "household" of late medieval times was a very loosely defined unit including parents and their children, perhaps some other blood relatives, business associates such as apprentices and journeymen in the household of a master artisan, and servants of the house, among whom social and sexual relations were often what to us would appear unstructured and promiscuous. According to Ariès, childhood in premodern Europe was not perceived as a special period of life; children were actually thought of and treated as "little adults."

Leo Zakuta describes the trend toward social equality between husbands and wives, and the decreasing social distance between parents and children in the nuclear family that is becoming typical of urban North America. This family contrasts strikingly with the large households of premodern Europe and with the extended families of primitive peoples which might include as many as sixty people, and corresponds, it is interesting to note, to the biologically based "family unit" which has been identified as characteristic of higher primates and some other mammals. The free choice of partners in forming this union, the small size of the family unit, and the increasing physical mobility of the family in modern America, Zakuta claims, all contribute to increasing the intimacy and emotional interdependence of family members. This, he believes, has led to the extension of the ideal of romantic love from courtship into the married life of the couple and to closer, less authoritarian relations between parents and their children.

Harry Gracey provides a case study of socialization processes in American elementary schools today. The first thing children are asked to learn in school, he claims, is how to play the *role of student*. With an account of a day in a kindergarten, he shows that this role includes conformity to an adult-imposed routine, unquestioning obedience to authority, participation in rituals which have no intrinsic meaning for the children, and their creation of private, meaningful social interaction in the interstices of a social and physical environment imposed by adults. Gracey contends that these requirements of the student role are commensurate with the requirements of role playing in bureaucracies generally, and that school today involves preparation for a social life which will be spent mostly in large bureaucratic organizations.

Ulf Hannerz lived in the Washington, D.C. black ghetto for two years studying the subculture there and paying particular attention of the socialization of boys in that community. It has been argued, most notably in the American government's Moynihan Reports on the Negro family, that because a permanent father was so often lacking boys growing up in the black inner-city neighborhoods were deprived of male models necessary for their socialization. It was contended that such deprivation would put these boys at a distinct disadvantage in making their way in the adult world, especially outside the ghetto. Hannerz, by contrast, found through his participant observation in the ghetto community itself, that while the actual fathers were often absent from homes with children, there were many males in the local community with whom the boys did interact and from whom they apparently learned the norms of masculine behavior in the subculture. Hannerz also observed that the boys' mothers and other female relatives with whom they had close relationships treated them as boys, or men-children, expecting their behavior to be different from the girls. In this way, the women showed the growing boys what was expected from men in the community.

Jesse Pitts discusses the goals of the hippie part of the contemporary youth subculture, the "counterculture" as it is sometimes called. The hippies have "dropped out" of the larger society in the sense of withdrawing from participation in most of its institutions and organizations. They have rejected many of the dominant values of the larger society, especially its materialism, emphasis on worldly success, and its active, achieving orientation toward the world. These youth, living together in communities and "communes" in the slums of large cities, near the campuses of university towns, and in the countryside of the West, are developing new cultures with different values, beliefs and practices. Pitts summarizes some of these new hippie cultural values in the concept of the "contrameritocracy" referring to the hippie preference for passivity rather than activity, inward contemplation and conversation rather than outward manipulation of the world, and cooperation rather than competition in their relations among themselves, as well as relationships based on what people are rather than what they do in particular instrumental roles. All of these "hippie values," Pitts points out, are the opposite of the dominant values of modern Western cultures, especially as exemplified in American society.

Bennett Berger's view of contemporary youth from the perspective of today's university campus shows him a variety of old and new patterns of adolescent behavior coexisting in this social setting. Some youth, he observes, are still coming to college to acquire an education in the accepted way of sitting in classes, listening to professors, reading books, writing papers, and taking examinations. For these, the college performs its traditional task of preparing them for adult life and principally for their careers in the larger society. Other young people, Berger observes, are looking at the college as a social context for identity acquisition, as a setting in which they can discover themselves and perhaps educate each other through contemplation and intense, intimate group experiences like those of the encounter groups. Other students and young faculty have also founded the "free universities" which exist near many of the campuses as a means of providing classes in subjects they want, taught in a style in which they feel comfortable. Berger contends that a good portion of the youth on the university campus today have no intention of leaving the "youth culture" at all, but plan to establish it as a permanent way of life, a kind of "almost endless adolescence" as he calls it, which people never leave to take up roles in the institutions of the larger society.

# 23

# A Brief Social History of the Family

### DENNIS H. WRONG

The average social scientist is thoroughly ignorant of Western social history. He is likely to know more about the kinship system of the Trobriand Islanders and the sexual mores of the Eskimos than he knows of the attitudes toward children or the kind of school system that existed in western Europe before the 19th century. Philippe Ariès'

*Centuries of Childhood*, which intensively explores the last subjects, among others, is bound therefore to come as something of a revelation, casting a new light on the contemporary sociologist's favorite generalizations about recent trends in parent-child relations, the connection between the family and the larger society, and the "socialization" of the young in general.

That marriage and the family are universal institutions and that all societies must make provision for the maintenance and socialization of children (which, indeed, is what primarily accounts for the universality of marriage and the family) are today sociological commonplaces. It is also well known that our contemporary laws governing marriage, divorce and the rights and obligations of parenthood, our kinship nomenclature and the balance we strike between the family group created by marriage and the extended family of affinal relatives ("in-laws") are deeply rooted in the Western past, stemming from Hebrew, Christian and classical influences. Demographic historians have, however, only recently become fully aware of the distinctiveness of the Western family as an enduring "structural type" when contrasted with the joint family systems of the great Asian civilizations. The Western family, they have concluded, stresses to a unique degree the priority of the marriage relation over ties of unilateral descent and thus grants greater economic and residential independence to the married pair and their offspring than is common in the Orient, where the nuclear group is absorbed into a larger household of paternal kin.

The interest of demographic historians has centered on the different effects of the Western and Asian family systems on the level of the birth rate and attitudes toward procreation, a difference that may have considerable bearing on the future of the underdeveloped countries now experiencing a population explosion that began in the West nearly two centuries ago. The Western family type was, of course, firmly established long before Europe's demographic revolution, and it may well have provided a favorable setting for the eventual mass adoption of birth control that has curtailed rapid Western growth in the present century. In fact, the recent work of several demographic and economic historians contains the germs of a "familistic" theory,

not only of the Western population transition but also of the genesis of capitalism and the Industrial Revolution themselves, which have so often been treated as independent causes of demographic change.

Ariès is a demographic historian, the author of an important study of French population since the 18th century. It was "the study of modern demographic phenomena," he tells us, that led him to conclude that "the family occupied a tremendous place in our industrial societies and that it had perhaps never before exercised so much influence over the human condition." Such a conclusion flatly contradicts the widely held view that the family has suffered a decline in industrial society, that—in the language of an influential school of family sociologists—it has been "losing its functions" and becoming in consequence a less significant focus of our lives. Accordingly, although Ariès' point of departure was demographic history, he has gone beyond it in an attempt "to look back into our past to find out whether the idea of the family had not been born comparatively recently. . . ." The result is a book that, although of limited interest to the population specialist, is endlessly fascinating to students of the family, of life in the premodern West in general and of the changing sensibilities of Western man as expressed in his manners, morals, art and religion.

The hard facts of demography and the only slightly less firm data on the formal structure of the family are quickly passed over as the author attempts to trace a moral revolution in the evaluation of childhood, the treatment of children and the significance attached to family life. Personal memoirs and correspondence, family portraits, the echoes of the past buried in colloquial speech, the subjects and genres of classical painting, religious and "profane" iconography, manuals of etiquette, the published sermons of moralists, old school registers, official histories of educational institutions— these are his sources, as they must necessarily be those of social historians studying beliefs and customs that were so taken for granted as the backdrop of daily life they left few enduring records of their existence in an age antedating universal literacy, the ubiquity of the printing press and the omnivorous fact-collecting of modern social science.

How did our European cultural and biological ancestors evaluate childhood as a period of life in the 16th, 17th and 18th centuries, the era that is the seedbed of so much of the "modern" and the graveyard of so much of the "medieval"? When did they first begin to see childhood as an irrecoverably precious age, worthy of celebration and fixation in art, requiring enrichment by parental solicitude and protection from too early exposure to the corruptions and workaday cynicism of adult life? Was the late medieval and early modern world addicted to the extreme age-grading we take so much for granted today? ("How old are you?" is usually the first question we put to a child we have just met.) How did the grouping of children into school classes differentiated by both age level and progressively more "advanced" subjects of study evolve— a feature of modern schooling that has not been questioned even by the most radical educational reformers? Is the notion of the family as the arena of an intense "private life," a fortress protecting the individuality of the person, truly an ancient heritage of Western culture, as is so often assumed by writers bewailing the forces of "mass society" that are today allegedly breaching its walls?

These are the main questions to which Ariès addresses himself. His answers reveal a fundamental change of outlook, a transformation of sensibility, that took place in the period he covers.

This change occurred within the structural type of the Western family institution, which remained constant throughout. Ariès' data therefore suggest that crucial historical shifts in feeling and imagination may escape the notice of contemporary sociologists whose "structural bias" disposes them to stress enduring institutional forms subject at most to gradual modifications of type. "Not that the family did not exist as a reality," he observes of the period preceding the changes he has described, "but it did not exist as a concept."

Nor does Ariès find that the demographic changes of the early modern period account for the revolution in sensibility he records; it would be highly plausible to interpret an increased concern with childhood and a new solicitude for children as results of the decline in infant mortality that made it easier for parents to cherish each child as an irreplaceable individual by reducing the risk of early death and the resulting shock of bereavement. But Ariès finds that the new interest in the child preceded by more than a century the medical and public health discoveries that decisively reduced infant mortality. He suggests, in fact, that the causal link may have run in the other direction, with increased concern for children producing a state of mind favorable to all hygienic precautions and to the rapid spread of such particular innovations as smallpox vaccination.

*Centuries of Childhood* is divided into three sections. The first deals with "the idea of childhood." Evidence ranging from iconography depicting the "ages of life" to the history of games and children's dress is surveyed to show the evolution from the complete lack of attribution of any special character to childhood in medieval society to the intense preoccupation with the physical, moral and—more recently—psychological welfare of children that had developed by the 18th century and still obsesses us today. The second section, occupying roughly half the book, is a history of schooling from the Middle Ages to the end of the *ancien régime*, comprehensively tracing the growth of different types of school and their curriculums, the origins of the school class, the progress of discipline and the development of age-grading in education. The book's final section discusses the family, particularly the "concept of the family." We are shown the metamorphosis of the great, sprawling aristocratic and midd-class households of the late Middle Ages, scarcely distinguishing between members of the family, servants and regular visitors, into the sharply defined unit of the married couple and their children, ensconced in the absolute privacy of their "home," that constitutes the modern family.

Ariès draws his material primarily from French sources, particularly in the section on the school, although he makes a sustained effort to cover developments in England as well. Germany, Switzerland, the Low Countries and Italy are referred to occasionally, usually when the evidence is iconographic. The Latin texts of the Church fathers and the later Renaissance humanists were influential, of course, throughout western Europe, so that much of Ariès' account of early postmedieval society refers to general conditions and needs no specific geographic reference.

Artists in the Middle Ages were not even capable of correctly drawing children. They pictured them as little men, fully equipped with the muscular development and bodily proportions of adults. And children were pictured only in religious art; although adult portraiture was popular, no effort was made to preserve the transitory likeness of the child until funeral effigies of dead children became common in the 16th century. Before this time and for a con-

siderable period afterward in the lower classes and rural areas, the child was regarded at most as a charming little plaything, a domestic pet, and his death was not much more of an occasion for grief and mourning than is that of a pet dog or cat today.

In the Middle Ages children were weaned rather later—at about the age of seven—than is the custom today, but as soon as weaning was completed they were removed from the care of their mothers or nurses and plunged straight into adult life. There were no special games or pastimes considered to be exclusively appropriate for children. Games like blindman's buff or hide-and-seek, which later were regarded solely as childish diversions, and which are still part of the strangely traditional and autonomous culture of childhood, were originally played by adults too. Conversely, children of five and six played chess, danced complicated ballet steps and learned to perform on the lute and violin.

No effort was made to conceal the facts of sexuality from small children. Their sex organs were fondled and joked about by adults. The lack of privacy in the medieval household, where any room might serve temporarily as a bedroom and where adults and children commonly shared the same bed, made it difficult for adults to conceal their sexual activities from children; indeed, they had little inclination to do so. Freud's once shocking discovery of infantile and childish curiosity about sex was no more than a rediscovery of what medieval parents and nurses matter-of-factly assumed. In this sense the now vanished Victorian belief in childish innocence did not exist in medieval society, although open references to sexuality before children were permitted because it was thought that children lacked all true sexual motivation before the age of puberty. There was no awareness of the connection between infantile and adult sexuality on which psycho-analysis so strongly insists.

The change from the casual medieval attitude toward childhood to our current tense concern with it passed through several stages. By the 16th century adult expressions of pleasure at the playfulness and prattling of small children, a pleasure that had previously "formed part of the huge domain of unexpressed feelings," amounted virtually to a "cult of the child" in upper-class families. No less a personage than Montaigne protested irritably: "I cannot abide that passion for caressing newborn children, which have neither mental activities nor recognizable bodily shape by which to make themselves lovable, and I have never willingly suffered them to be fed in my presence." Yet, as Ariès points out, Montaigne's very annoyance at the "coddling" of children "was as novel as 'coddling,' and even more foreign . . . to the indifferent attitude of people in the Middle Ages." His wish to segregate children from adults was shared by the 17th-century moralists and pedagogues whose "fondness for children and its special nature no longer found expression in amusement and 'coddling' but in psychological interest and moral solicitude."

These moralists and pedagogues—of whom the Jesuits and the Jansenists of Port Royal were the most important in France—eventually won the day. Their victory resulted in the creation of a system of schooling conceived of as being a careful, methodical preparation of the child for adult life. The contrast with the old free mingling of children and adults in the Middle Ages could scarcely have been greater. Moreover, the goals of education were no longer merely intellectual or vocational but included the shaping of the child's moral character as well. Thus the school became a thoroughly authoritarian institution in which a corps of disciplinarian masters ruled

over a "proletariat" of powerless children. The old freebootery of student life in the Middle Ages—next to which the much deplored hedonism and irresponsibility of our contemporary adolescent and college-age youth seem tame —became a thing of the past. The shutting off of the child in a separate, hierarchical world outside the family reached its zenith in the boarding schools of the 19th century, of which the great English public schools are the best-known examples. The reaction to this incarceration of the child in educational prisons came at the end of the 19th century, when "the family was substituted for the school as the predominant moral setting."

Most of the developments I have summarized applied to boys alone. Girls remained comparatively undifferentiated from women for a longer time: in dress; in the more tenacious belief that, except for religious instruction, they needed no special education outside the family, which effectively delayed the extension of schooling to girls until the late 18th and early 19th centuries; and in the survival through the 17th century of an exceedingly early age at marriage for females—13- and 14-year-old brides were by no means uncommon.

The interest in childhood, first manifest in the 16th century, was part of a developing interest in the family—that is, the "nuclear family" of parents and children—that originated in the 15th century, coinciding with a decline in the value attached to the hereditary line. The hereditary line had been glorified in medieval society, although it had never been the basis for the household group and so lacked the "functional" economic and child-rearing significance of the Oriental unilineal descent group. The Church disapproved of the emphasis on the "pagan" blood ties of the hereditary line, but it did not assume full control of marriage, transforming it into a sacrament, until the 13th century. And it was not until the 16th century that the family became a theme of religious iconography. At the same time, the practice of private family prayers and worship became common, indicating the new value attached to a group that had previously "existed in silence," failing to "awaken feelings strong enough to inspire poet or artist."

But before the family could come to be regarded as the virtual extension of the self that it is today, or even the lair from which one sallied forth to engage the outside world of the Victorian period, more mundane changes in the conditions of life had to take place. The houses of the rich until the end of the 17th century "sheltered, apart from the family proper, a whole population of servants, employees, clerics, clerks, shopkeepers, apprentices and so on." No clear distinctions were made between social, professional and private life, which brought together much the same people in any case. All activities were carried on in the family's living quarters, where the same rooms served successively—and often simultaneously —as salons, offices and bedrooms. It was the social (and often enough sexual) promiscuity of life in the big houses that spurred the clerical pedagogues to their task of building a school system that would effectively remove the child from the family during what were regarded as his formative years. In spite of the earlier development of new emotional relation between parents and children, it was not until the 18th century that "the family began to hold society at a distance, to push it back beyond a steadily extending zone of private life." The change was reflected in the new structure of the house: the old all-purpose rooms disappeared to be replaced by specialized bedrooms and dining rooms, and the rooms now opened off a central corridor, so that it was no longer necessary to pass through each room in traversing the house. Privacy and domesticity, those two prized and interlinked modern values, were born together.

It is not feasible to summarize all the information assembled by Ariès that challenges the stereotyped view of the past held even by most scholars and social scientists. One major conclusion suggests itself, although my own ignorance may have given me an exaggerated view of its novelty. We are accustomed to regarding the Middle Ages as an "age of faith" and to seeing our subsequent history as a steady movement away from a spiritually unified medieval Christendom toward the pluralistic, secularized, science-centered world of the present. The Renaissance, the Reformation, the Enlightenment and the Industrial Revolution are seen as successive stages in this movement. But Ariès' data suggest that Christian ideas and sensibility had little vital influence on social relations and daily life until the 16th century. Although the Church was a crucial unifying and centralizing institution in the polycentric world of medieval feudalism, its relation to daily life, to the web of custom, resembled more closely the relation of the Catholic Church today to the syncretic culture of the part-Indian, part-Negro populations of Central America than it resembled the later clerical reshaping of domestic habits achieved by the reformers of the Reformation and the Counter Reformation. Thus our modern sensibility, while it may properly be described as post-Christian, is in no sense postmedieval. In our attitudes toward the family and childhood we stand in vital respects closer to Christian thought and feeling, even in its more moralistic and puritanical forms that we see ourselves as reacting against, than to the gay, casual, frequently coarse outlook of the Middle Ages, which cannot even be characterized as the reverse of "child-centered" since it lacked any distinct conception of childhood.

Social history of the kind Ariès gives us reveals more fully than other kinds of history the value of what is called historical perspective. It does so because in exploring the world of childhood and the family, a world in which we are all intimately involved, it succeeds in communicating more profoundly a sense of the strangeness of time and change in the life of man and society. Our familiarity with the subject is enhanced because it is the life of our own historical ancestors that is described in *Centuries of Childhood*. Echoes of that life persist today in the form of beliefs, archaisms of speech and minor customs, twisted and distorted in the crucible of historical transformation, surviving in "form"

but not in "function," as the anthropologist would put it. Yet the very fact that this is so, that we are tied to the men and women of the Middle Ages by a thread of cultural continuity, enables us to experience more deeply what the anthropologist calls "culture shock" in confronting these lives so different from ours and yet marked with faint but decisive traces of similarity. No reading of anthropological materials on the kinship systems and domestic lives of primitive peoples can have such an impact. Nor, with all his opportunities for field observation, is it as easy for the anthropologist to succeed in discovering in his data "the tremor of life that he can feel in his own existence," to quote Ariès' brilliant summation of the ultimate aim of the social historian.

# 24

# Equality in North American Marriages

## LEO ZAKUTA

During the past several generations there have been important changes in North American family relationships. While this essay emphasizes the husband-wife relation, its main perspectives also apply to the relations between parents and children. The "data" presented here come from the casual observations of family life that are made by everyone, rather than from a formal empirical study of the family. Accordingly, I am assuming that these observations of the North American, urban, middle-class family—the only one that

Reprinted from *Social Research*, 30 (Summer, 1963), pp. 157–170, with permission of the author and the publisher.

I know at first hand—are sufficiently well known that they can be discussed here without that careful documentation of actual behavior that eventually will be necessary.

My central point is that certain changes in the behavior of family members toward each other stem from alterations in their mutual sentiments—or feelings toward one another; these feelings, in turn, are closely linked to shifts in their standards and forms of family organization. For the sake of economy, these standards and forms will be taken as given, as will be the general conditions out of which they arise: namely, the growth of democratic ideology, cities, and industry; the mobility and mixture of people; and the development of an essentially new society. I will not try to explain why the values and forms have changed, but will simply describe the new ones briefly and concentrate on how they have affected family sentiments and thereby behavior.

## Ideological Changes and Romantic Marriage

I have been trying in vain to recall from whom I first heard the suggestion that our fiction—popular as well as "serious"—provides an intriguing symptom of how significantly the married relation has changed in our society. The argument, which is perhaps familiar, goes as follows: In the past, love stories were ordinarily about courtship, and they usually concluded with marriage. The emotional relations of the married were of much less consuming interest, presumably on the assumption that they contained little of comparable fascination. In contrast, today's fiction, drama, and movies frequently center on the emotional relation between husband and wife; typically, they are already married when the story begins. The inference obviously is that those intense feelings which we think of as romance now occur much more often within marriage than they once did. If this inference is valid, why does contemporary marriage produce feelings of romantic involvement or such distress at their departure that the couple may dissolve or seriously consider dissolving their marriage? To pursue this question one must find the structural and ideological conditions which seem most closely associated with romance in general first, then those with its growing importance in contemporary marriage.

In general, romance seems to occur where the partners feel that they choose each other freely rather than where others, usually the parents, do the choosing. (Whether the choice is really "free" is not only beyond proof but, from the perspective of the social scientist, as totally irrelevant as whether man's will is really "free." It is the actor's sense or feeling of being free to choose that matters, just as a man's view of whether another's will is free or not governs his feelings and behavior towards him.)

The suggestion that romantic feelings are linked to a sense of free choice raises a parenthetical quarrel and question. The quarrel is with those exhortatory treatises on marriage and the family, unfortunately so numerous in the social sciences, that almost invariably warn the reader about the "romantic fallacy" and the dangers of "building" a marriage on so feeble a foundation as romance instead of on presumably more solid stuff, such as similar views about money, in-laws, child-rearing, and religion. One wonders how many of these writers have been sufficiently inspired by their own preaching to put it into practice.

The quarrel aside, the question is: If the "romantic fallacy" refers to expectations that are quite unlikely to be realized, why select these as if they were somehow unique? Are people not constantly launching new enterprises, activities, and organizations with the highest (one could almost say the "wildest") of hopes, some of which we label "utopian"? And don't many of these bodies, like most marriages, survive despite the subsequent abatement of their members' initial hopes? But who in our fraternity is ready to counsel against this general human tendency? Perhaps romance or falling in love may occur whenever people commit themselves, with a sense of free choice, to any undertaking about which they have great expectations. If so, the numerous parallels which have been drawn between "conversion" and "falling in love" should not be surprising.

Returning to the main question, how does the sense of free choice affect romance in marriage? Many obvious circumstances make divorce or separation seem much more feasible to a contemporary couple than to their grandparents and thus give them a greater feeling of choice than was once the case. The argument, however, that ideological and structural changes are responsible for the development of, or concern about, romance in marriage must rest on some distinctive grounds. These are more easily seen if we compare those two familiar models—the "patriarchal" and "contemporary" family types.

Three structural changes from the first type to the second seem to be closely linked to the growing importance of romantic feelings within marriage. They are, in ascending order of importance: the family's smaller size, the greater mobility of the family, and the equality of the married couple. These features have been termed structural solely as a matter of economy; properly, they should be called "ideological-structural," since each one of the changes in family form has occurred because the people concerned felt that they should.

The family's contraction results from fewer children and fewer relatives in the household. As a result, the child may become more deeply involved with the fewer remaining adults so that in his subsequent marriage he seeks the intensity of emotional involvement which he has already experienced. Framed in this way—the more adults in the family, the greater the dispersal of emotional involvement—this argument does not seem very convincing. The reduction in family size may not be important in itself. But it has been accompanied by another, though somewhat unrelated, change, which has made it important—the growing equality between parents and children which tends to intensify their mutual involvement by lowering the barriers that authority usually creates. Once the generations can become closer, numbers become important because the typical family contains fewer adults to serve as the focus for the children's involvement.

The family's greater mobility also tends to intensify the mutual involvement of its members by throwing them together more than would a more stable existence. If the unit which moves is usually the nuclear family, then it cuts itself off from its closest relatives as well as from its whole network of friends and acquaintances. Weakened ties with outsiders increase the members' mutual dependence and reduce their avenues of escape from one another. Although many families may not move, the growth of so many large organizations, including government, with their numerous branches probably means that increasing numbers regard relocation as a distinct possibility. If so, it need not be actually moving, but merely the prospect that heightens the married couple's feeling of how much their happiness hinges on the "success" of this one tie which not only endures when all others are severed but which, by the very breaking of other ties, becomes all the more important. Under these circumstances, would they not count somewhat more heavily on the congeniality of this relation?

It is the third condition of equality that merits the most serious consideration. Its general effect is similar to that of the other two—it brings people together more often and more intimately. Status differences everywhere seem to inhibit free and easy association, and the more pronounced they are, the more separate are the parties, except where their association is formally specified. This principle is built into the official military structure in the form of separate messes that limit extracurricular association and therefore presumably personal involvement across hierarchical levels. We see it arise somewhat more spontaneously in the cafeterias of work organizations and in relations between racial and ethnic groups—in the latter cases, it is called segregation.

*Consequences of inequality.* In an apparent paradox, the barriers to ease and intimacy are often less where the status differences are very great, so that a man may have a much freer and easier relation with his slave or servant than he does with his employee or even with his children, or, in some family systems, with his mistress than with his wife. These considerations, incidentally, should warn us against dismissing too lightly the statements of those white Southerners who claim that they love their Negroes. Before condemning the unspoken qualification, "in their place," as hypocrisy, we should ask if this is really very different from the parent who loves his children but who would be furious if they began to do certain things conventionally reserved for adults. P. G. Wodehouse has persistently rung one change on this theme in the delicately balanced relations between Jeeves, the manservant who is equal to every occasion, and his master, Bertie Wooster, who is equal to none of them. Jeeves' invariable way of demonstrating his displeasure with his master—of punishing him, as we say in our flat sociological speech—is by a cool but courteous refusal to exceed his station by offering the advice and suggestions that Bertie requires to cope with his current crisis. Thus, as in many accounts of the Negro in the old South and of others in servitude, Jeeves owes not only his intimacy with his master but also his considerable influence over him to the fact that he not only knows his place, but likes it.

What permits ease and intimacy in these various instances is, of course, that status differences are so large and clear that a more relaxed relation brings no suggestion of fundamental equality between the parties. Furthermore, the relaxation of formalities in relations of this type is ostensibly subject to the pleasure of the superior, and the parties do not associate as equals in any of the situations in which friends ordinarily meet. These considerations indicate that the links between friendship, sociability, and equality deserve a comprehensive examination.

The main point, however, is that if separate activities and restrained relations arise out of status differences, then separation and restraint should be much more prominent in the "patriarchal" than in the "contemporary" family. A casual glance at Toronto's large, post-war, Italian immigrant district shows how obviously they are more prominent. True to the traditions of their Italian patriarchal rural society, males congregate sociably in exclusively masculine groups in the streets and restaurants and the women presumably stay home. If the customers in the restaurants are couples, it is fairly certain that they are not first generation Italians. That the present Toronto pattern is not unusual is clear from William F. Whyte's portrait of comparable Italian groups in Boston in the 1930s.[1] His account, by the way, suggests another parallel between the gang and family. In both cases, the lower status members stay close to home, while the others feel free to roam. The Italian segregation of the sexes has innumerable counterparts the world over, including the British working man's pub and the exclusively male clubs of his "betters." (It is tempting to observe how neatly the proverbial closeness between the British wife and

[1] *Street Corner Society* (Chicago: University of Chicago, 1943).

her "mum" and the alleged fondness of Englishmen for their dogs both fit into the general pattern. But this may be merely circulating the stereotype.)

If status differences lead to segregation because people usually seek the companionship of their "equals," then the marital relation in the patriarchal family should display the same kind of separation in matters of sex and companionship as it does in most other activities. And, by all accounts, it does. Allowing for whatever exaggeration is introduced to achieve humor or drama, the stories, movies, and literature of continental Europe in the Victorian age or of contemporary rural society in France, Italy, and elsewhere indicate both the prevalence and the relative openness—the two are obviously interdependent—of extra-marital affairs for men. The relatively open acceptance of prostitution and of having a mistress on the grounds that "boys will be boys" or, less indulgently perhaps, "men are like that," coupled with the clear understanding that girls should be "ladylike," suggests once more the link with status differences. Again, it is the higher status category that is permitted freedom; who can roam, perhaps symbolically; and who at least feel that they have a choice that is less readily available to the lower status group.

One test of this general argument would involve looking at family systems with varying degrees of status difference between the spouses in order to examine the accompanying patterns of sexual fidelity. Thus, in the traditional Chinese family, in which the husband's standing was especially lofty, concubinage was apparently much more acceptable than was its counterpart in Europe, and the concubine's position was correspondingly higher. In the Chinese family, though below the level of a wife, the concubine was often brought into the household and, significantly, her children were considered legitimate. Wifely infidelity, as one would expect, was regarded as more outrageous and disastrous than it was in the European family. The elevated status of the Japanese *geisha* is another case in point. (It would be interesting to know how the occupation of the *geisha* has been affected by the reported rapid "Westernization" of the Japanese family.) Whether polygamy is a further point along this same continuum should be relatively easy to determine by determining whether it is always associated with even greater male dominance.

The contemporary "American" pattern, in which husband and wife are much closer in standing, fits neatly into this scheme on the other side of this argument. Whether extra-marital affairs are less frequent in this system is impossible to say because of their more clandestine nature, but the secrecy itself is the best evidence of its greater unacceptability to all concerned. Were it possible to know, one would expect that infidelity is also more evenly distributed between the sexes in this system than in the patriarchal.

I have pursued this theme in order to show both the extent of separation between wives and husbands in the patriarchal system as well as the link between separateness and relative rank. Relations between the sexes, married or unmarried, between the old and young, and between countless other groups all display essentially the same pattern. Our assumptions about what it is natural for people to do together obviously involve assumptions about their relative status. In most parts of the world, as introductory sociology students soon learn, men and women do not ordinarily dance, walk, or spend their leisure time together. Frequently, they do not even eat together—that seemingly universal expression of equality—and, in the more patriarchal homes in the North American society, parents and children eat separately much more regularly. Finally, our conventional assumption that sex relations, at least in marriage, are highly personal hardly corresponds to that of many males in the more patriarchal societies who make the distinction between duty and pleasure or between work and play that so often differentiates the formal from the informal.

*Consequences of equality.* The extended remarks about the consequences of inequality are a background against which we can see more clearly the consequences, in sentiment and behavior, of greater equality. For various reasons, the status of women and wives in Western and Westernized societies has increased considerably while that of men and husbands has dropped somewhat so that a woman's relationship to them in marriage has become much closer to equal. By reducing the distance which inequality imposes, both the range of association and of reciprocal emotional involvement increase. By emotional involvement, I refer not only to feelings of affection but also to their opposite. Both are likely to grow within the same relation. The central argument is that since mutual involvement increases and becomes more complex, feelings of antagonism and hatred are also likely to become intensified. (The reciprocity of involvement requires emphasis to distinguish these instances from those enduring relations characterized by intense involvement on one side and a much more casual attitude on the other. These asymmetrical feelings are common in authority relations, in which the superior ordinarily looms much larger in the mind of his subordinate than vice versa. Employees and boss, child and parent, and wife and husband in the older family system of the Orient are all instances of this type of unequal emotional involvement.)

As their positions become more equal, the prospect of informal or sociable association seems more natural and appealing to husbands and wives. In effect, they now view their prospective relation in terms of something like friendship, the main requisite of which is, of course, status equality. As a result, wives and husbands tend to leave their sexually compartmentalized worlds and to do many things together which their grandparents did not. Ideologically, this change is expressed in such phrases as "partnership, companionship," and even "togetherness." Their companionship, we have seen, is fostered not only by their greater equality but also by being more cut off from relatives and friends, including the adult kin who have disappeared from the household. The possibilities of friendship—perhaps it had better be called companionship—are further augmented by some blurring of their former distinctive roles and activities. Not only is the wife freer to venture from the home to work for pay, or on behalf of "worthy causes," or simply to play—all, incidentally, formerly reserved for higher status groups, either men or women of the wealthy leisure class—but her husband is also more likely to participate in the formerly exclusively wifely tasks—in the kitchen, nursery, or even in public by sharing the shopping. Thus, like friends and equals, they do numerous similar things, many of them together.

The combination of these conditions —a smaller, more mobile, and more equalitarian family—leads not only to a more informal, intimate, and complex marital relation; it also leads to a new conception of what that relation ought to be, that is, to new standards of what constitutes a successful marriage. Both partners are likely to expect and to want the more intense mutual involvement that the altered structure of the marriage relation facilitates and to judge the success of their marriage in terms of the extent and the character of that involvement. Under these circumstances, the sense of personal congeniality or, in the more usual phrase, "compatibility," becomes a, or perhaps the, central criterion on which the partners assess the success of their marriage and decide on its future.

Those who regard these developments with dismay or distaste usually conclude that marriage has come to mean less to the contemporary couple since so many do decide to terminate it. The advocates of the new often argue, on the other hand, that these decisions indicate the very opposite; namely, that people now expect more from their marriage and are unwilling to settle for the unhappy relations that previous generations endured. But this argument, like any evaluative one, is insoluble and beside the point. It is not a matter of greater or lesser expectations but of different ones. And the heavy emphasis placed on personal congeniality means that many of the relations that do not measure up to the expectations of at least one of the partners will be terminated.

Furthermore, the new marital structure and expectations create additional hazards to the permanence of the relation. By facilitating very strong involvement, they are likely to lead, at least on occasion, to more intense antagonism and bitter clashes. Feelings of equality contribute to this possibility by removing or threatening to remove ultimate authority from the husband and thereby open the way to struggle for power, since the right to decide is no longer vested in a position but in each individual's conviction of what should be done. Finally, if their relation "goes sour" chronically, both partners are likely to feel the consequences as more devastating than did their grandparents. Unlike the latter, they

have fewer avenues of escape from each other, they face the agonies of decision about the formal status of their marriage, and their deeper mutual involvement tends to produce stronger friction and animosity. It is therefore hardly surprising that, under these conditions, so many contemporary couples find their marriages too intolerable to endure. (In addition, if equality tends to reduce or conceal the incidence of husbands' infidelity, it simultaneously increases its seriousness as an offence and thus its threat to the continuation of the marriage.)

Thus instead of regarding a "high" rate of divorce and separation as a somewhat alien virus which has managed to infect the North American marriage system, we may, perhaps more profitably, view it as an inevitable outcome of the distinctive ideology, structure, and sentiments of that system.

I have suggested previously that the sense of free choice seems a necessary condition for romance—whether before or within marriage. Several obvious conditions provide this sense to the contemporary married couple. Among them are, of course, the greater prevalence and acceptability of divorce, one further instance of how an effect is also a cause, as well as the greater earning power of women, that facilitates the step for both partners. If I seem to have underemphasized this last condition, it was mainly out of reluctance to overemphasize it. While it seems extremely important, its exact significance is very difficult to determine since divorce and women's earning power have both risen considerably over the long run. Unless one can somehow separate these variables, precise statements about their relation seem impossible. These considerations naturally lead to speculation about Hollywood, where both divorce and the earning power of women seem to have reached unprecedented heights. Here is the community in which the status and income of women is least dependent on their husbands and where equality between the married partners and the sense of free choice about continuing the marriage are at a peak. It is under these circumstances, I would guess, that the concern about romance in marriage is most intense since the feeling of great freedom makes the continuity of the marriage contingent on little else. And despite all of the tongue-clucking about Hollywood, it seems clear that marriage still rates very highly there. How else can we account for Hollywood's apparently endless optimism about marriage in the face of such seemingly overwhelming odds?

The shifts in the standards and structure within the family, and more generally between the sexes, and between adults and children have several other effects on sentiments and behavior that seem worthy of note. As a result of the diminishing status distance between the sexes, in general, and between the various age levels, males and females seem increasingly at ease with each other and so do the young with their elders, though the reverse is not necessarily as true.

More specifically, greater equality seems to reduce the fear, deference, and perhaps even awe that children once had toward their parents and possibly wives toward their husbands. The contemporary father who lectures his son, "I would never have dared speak to *my* father as you do to me," may be doing something more than repeating a universal and timeless lament of fathers; he may, for a change in this endless litany, be uttering a simple truth. Correspondingly, husbands are more likely to be attentive and sensitive to the wishes, tastes, and viewpoints of their wives and children than they have been in the past, one example of which is the new ideology of sex

relations in the twentieth century.[2] Status equality seems to be the central condition for reciprocal sensitivity to the wishes and feelings of others. And this is a point that warrants fuller examination than is possible in this short essay.

How these shifts in structure and sentiment affect the cohesion of the family merits some special consideration. In this matter I take as my whipping boy George Homans, as a perverse repayment for the considerable debt that this paper obviously owes him. In *The Human Group* he refers to the contemporary family as one of "low integration" and to its more patriarchal predecessor as one of "high intergration." [3] But is "integration," or whatever we call the binding ties, all of a piece and thus simply a matter of more or less? In the older family type, cohesion or integration depended more heavily on specialized and physically interdependent roles with a fairly clear, if elaborate, chain of command, as well as, of course, considerable emotional involvement and interdependence. In the contemporary family, specialized roles, physical interdependence, and authority are all still of central importance, but the balance has been shifting away from these aspects towards the emotional involvement on which the cohesion of more informal groups depends. In brief, the family has been

[2] Significantly, that ideology emphasizes "sensitivity" for the male, "freedom" for the woman, and reduction of the traditional or stereotyped differences in their sexual roles and responses. And, as might be expected, the evidence of Alfred Kinsey and his associates strongly suggests that these modes of behavior are much more prevalent in the middle class, especially among the more highly educated.

[3] *The Human Group* (New York: Harcourt, Brace, 1950), p. 280. The essay's general indebtedness to the writings of Ernest Burgess and Talcott Parsons on the family and marriage will be sufficiently obvious to most readers so that specific references have seemed unnecessary.

moving away from the elaborate, formal, and involuntary structure characteristic of large and stable organizations toward the smaller, more intense,
and more volatile association composed
of freely consenting equals which is
characteristic of more informal groups.

## Conclusion

I will conclude with a venture into
the more fanciful, where the sociologist can treat more easily than he can
test. If changes in the relations between
the sexes can affect their conscious sentiments toward each other, then why
can they not similarly affect those feelings that are more buried and which
are manifested only indirectly in overt
behavior? If males have experienced
a loss of status relative to females,
then one should expect that at least
some—like any group which has suffered a loss of status—would exhibit
various forms of compensation for the
loss and resentment toward the
usurpers, and that these forms would
be perhaps partly in the realm of
fantasy.

Possibly the popularity of magazines
of the *Playboy* type represents such a
reaction. After all, the central themes
of these magazines can be interpreted
easily enough in terms of both compensation and resentment. There is
self-enhancement through the vicarious
association with the habits and objects
of the rich and lofty. But the outstanding "plaything" of the "playboy" is
women. His sure and easy "way with
women" is perhaps his chief qualification for solid standing as a "playboy."
The growing discrepancy between the
fantasy—the smooth, self-assured, sophisticated, and uninvolved male mastery of uniformly devoted and eager
women—and the increasingly free and
equal relations between the sexes may
be the source of the apparent popularity of these periodicals. Another branch
of this type of periodical—a "lower"
one by popular repute—expresses the
male's resentment much more directly,
sexual "sadism" permitting him to participate vicariously in a more vigorous
revenge on those who have robbed him
of his glorious partimony.

# 25

# Learning the Student Role: Kindergarten As Academic Boot Camp *

**HARRY  L.  GRACEY**

## Introduction

Education must be considered one of
the major institutions of social life

* This article is based on research conducted with the Bank Street College of
Education under NIMH Grant No. 9135.
The study is more fully reported in Harry
L. Gracey, *The Civil Structure and Ideology
of an Elementary School*, Chicago, University of Chicago Press, 1972.

today. Along with the family and organized religion, however, it is a "secondary institution," one in which
people are prepared for life in society
as it is presently organized. The main
dimensions of modern life, that is, the
nature of society as a whole, is determined principally by the "primary
institutions," which today are the economy, the political system, and the

military establishment. Education has been defined by sociologists, classical and contemporary, as an institution which serves society by socializing people into it through a formalized, standardized procedure. At the beginning of this century Emile Durkheim told student teachers at the University of Paris that education "consists of a methodical socialization of the younger generation." He went on to add:

It is the influence exercised by adult generations on those that are not ready for social life. Its object is to arouse and to develop in the child a certain number of physical, intellectual, and moral states that are demanded of him by the political society as a whole and by the special milieu for which he is specifically destined. . . . To the egotistic and asocial being that has just been born, (society) must, as rapidly as possible, add another, capable of leading a moral and social life. Such is the work of education.[1]

The educational process, Durkheim said, "is above all the means by which society perpetually recreates the conditions of its very existence." [2] The contemporary educational sociologist, Wilbur Brookover, offers a similar formulation in his recent textbook definition of education:

Actually, therefore, in the broadest sense education is synonymous with socialization. It includes any social behavior that assists in the induction of the child into membership in the society or any behavior by which the society perpetuates itself through the next generation.[3]

The educational institution is, then, one of the ways in which society is perpetuated through the systematic socializa-

tion of the young, while the nature of the society which is being perpetuated —its organization and operation, its values, beliefs and ways of living—are determined by the primary institutions. The educational system, like other secondary institutions, *serves* the society which is *created* by the operation of the economy, the political system, and the military establishment.

Schools, the social organizations of the educational institution, are today for the most part large bureaucracies run by specially trained and certified people. There are few places left in modern societies where formal teaching and learning is carried on in small, isolated groups, like the rural, one-room schoolhouses of the last century. Schools are large, formal organizations which tend to be parts of larger organizations, local community School Districts. These School Districts are bureaucratically organized and their operations are supervised by state and local governments. In this context, as Brookover says:

the term education is used . . . to refer to a system of schools, in which specifically designated persons are expected to teach children and youth certain types of acceptable behavior. The school system becomes a . . . unit in the total social structure and is recognized by the members of the society as a separate social institution. Within this structure a portion of the total socialization process occurs.[4]

Education is the part of the socialization process which takes place in the schools; and these are, more and more today, bureacracies within bureaucracies.

Kindergarten is generally conceived by educators as a year of preparation for school. It is thought of as a year in which small children, five or six years old, are prepared socially and emotionally for the academic learning

[1] Emile Durkheim, *Sociology and Education* (New York: The Free Press, 1956), pp. 71–72.
[2] *Ibid.*, p. 123.
[3] Wilbur Brookover, *The Sociology of Education* (New York: American Book Company, 1957), p. 4.
[4] *Ibid.*, p. 6.

which will take place over the next twelve years. It is expected that a foundation of behavior and attitudes will be laid in kindergarten on which the children can acquire the skills and knowledge they will be taught in the grades. A booklet prepared for parents by the staff of a suburban New York school system says that the kindergarten experience will stimulate the child's desire to learn and cultivate the skills he will need for learning in the rest of his school career. It claims that the child will find opportunities for physical growth, for satisfying his "need for self-expression," acquire some knowledge, and provide opportunities for creative activity. It concludes, "The most important benefit that your five-year-old will receive from kindergarten is the opportunity to live and grow happily and purposefully with others in a small society." The kindergarten teachers in one of the elementary schools in this community, one we shall call the Wilbur Wright School, said their goals were to see that the children "grew" in all ways: physically, of course, emotionally, socially, and academically. They said they wanted children to like school as a result of their kindergarten experiences and that they wanted them to learn to get along with others.

None of these goals, however, is unique to kndergarten; each of them is held to some extent by teachers in the other six grades at the Wright School. And growth would occur, but differently, even if the child did not attend school. The children already know how to get along with others, in their families and their play groups. The unique job of the kindergarten in the educational division of labor seems rather to be teaching children the student role. The student role is the repertoire of behavior and attitudes regarded by educators as appropriate to children in school. Observation in the kindergartens of the Wilbur Wright School revealed a great variety of activities

through which children are shown and then drilled in the behavior and attitudes defined as appropriate for school and thereby induced to learn the role of student. Observations of the kindergartens and interviews with the teachers both pointed to the teaching and learning of classroom routines as the main element of the student role. The teachers expended most of their efforts, for the first half of the year at least, in training the children to follow the routines which teachers created. The children were, in a very real sense, *drilled* in tasks and activities created by the teachers for their own purposes and beginning and ending quite arbitrarily (from the child's point of view) at the command of the teacher. One teacher remarked that she hated September, because during the first month "everything has to be done rigidly, and repeatedly, until they know exactly what they're supposed to do." However, "by January," she said, "they know exactly what to do [during the day] and I don't have to be after them all the time." Classroom routines were introduced gradually from the beginning of the year in all the kindergartens, and the children were drilled in them as long as was necessary to achieve regular compliance. By the end of the school year, the successful kindergarten teacher has a well-organized group of children. They follow classroom routines automatically, having learned all the command signals and the expected responses to them. They have, in our terms, learned the student role. The following observation shows one such classroom operating at optimum organization on an afternoon late in May. It is the class of an experienced and respected kindergarten teacher.

### An Afternoon in Kindergarten

At about 12:20 in the afternoon on a day in the last week of May, Edith Kerr leaves the teachers' room where she has been having lunch and walks to her classroom at the far end of the primary wing of Wright School. A group of five- and six-year-olds peers at her through the glass doors leading from the hall cloakroom to the play area outside. Entering her room, she straightens some material in the "book corner" of the room, arranges music on the piano, takes colored paper from her closet and places it on one of the shelves under the window. Her room is divided into a number of activity areas through the arrangement of furniture and play equipment. Two easels and a paint table near the door create a kind of passageway inside the room. A wedge-shaped area just inside the front door is made into a teacher's area by the placing of "her" things there: her desk, file, and piano. To the left is the book corner, marked off from the rest of the room by a puppet stage and a movable chalkboard. In it are a display rack of picture books, a record player, and a stack of children's records. To the right of the entrance are the sink and clean-up area. Four large round tables with six chairs at each for the children are placed near the walls about halfway down the length of the room, two on each side, leaving a large open area in the center for group games, block building, and toy truck driving. Windows stretch down the length of both walls, starting about three feet from the floor and extending almost to the high ceilings. Under the windows are long shelves on which are kept all the toys, games, blocks, paper, paints and other equipment of the kindergarten. The left rear corner of the room is a play store with shelves, merchandise, and cash register; the right rear corner is a play kitchen with stove, sink, ironing board, and bassinette with baby dolls in it. This area is partly shielded from the rest of the room by a large standing display rack for posters and children's art work. A sandbox is found against

the back wall between these two areas. The room is light, brightly colored and filled with things adults feel five- and six-year-olds will find interesting and pleasing.

At 12:25 Edith opens the outside door and admits the waiting children. They hang their sweaters on hooks outside the door and then go to the center of the room and arrange themselves in a semi-circle on the floor, facing the teacher's chair which she has placed in the center of the floor. Edith follows them in and sits in her chair checking attendance while waiting for the bell to ring. When she has finished attendance, which she takes by sight, she asks the children what the date is, what day and month it is, how many children are enrolled in the class, how many are present, and how many are absent.

The bell rings at 12:30 and the teacher puts away her attendance book. She introduces a visitor, who is sitting against the right wall taking notes, as someone who wants to learn about schools and children. She then goes to the back of the room and takes down a large chart labeled "Helping Hands." Bringing it to the center of the room, she tells the children it is time to change jobs. Each child is assigned some task on the chart by placing his name, lettered on a paper "hand," next to a picture signifying the task—e.g., a broom, a blackboard, a milk bottle, a flag, and a Bible. She asks the children who wants each of the jobs and rearranges their "hands" accordingly. Returning to her chair, Edith announces, "One person should tell us what happened to Mark." A girl raises her hand, and when called on says, "Mark fell and hit his head and had to go to the hospital." The teacher adds that Mark's mother had written saying he was in the hospital.

During this time the children have been interacting among themselves, in their semi-circle. Children have whispered to their neighbors, poked one another, made general comments to the group, waved to friends on the other side of the circle. None of this has been disruptive, and the teacher has ignored it for the most part. The children seem to know just how much of each kind of interaction is permitted—they may greet in a soft voice someone who sits next to them, for example, but may not shout greetings to a friend who sits across the circle, so they confine themselves to waving and remain well within understood limits.

At 12:35 two children arrive. Edith asks them why they are late and then sends them to join the circle on the floor. The other children vie with each other to tell the newcomers what happened to Mark. When this leads to a general disorder Edith asks, "Who has serious time?" The children become quiet and a girl raises her hand. Edith nods and the child gets a Bible and hands it to Edith. She reads the Twenty-third Psalm while the children sit quietly. Edith helps the child in charge begin reciting the Lord's Prayer, the other children follow along for the first unit of sounds, and then trail off as Edith finishes for them. Everyone stands and faces the American flag hung to the right of the door. Edith leads the pledge to the flag, with the children again following the familiar sounds as far as they remember them. Edith then asks the girl in charge what song she wants and the child replies, "My Country." Edith goes to the piano and plays "America," singing as the children follow her words.

Edith returns to her chair in the center of the room and the children sit again in the semi-circle on the floor. It is 12:40 when she tells the children, "Let's have boys' sharing time first." She calls the name of the first boy sitting on the end of the circle, and he comes up to her with a toy helicopter. He turns and holds it up for the other

children to see. He says, "It's a helicopter." Edith asks, "What is it used for?" and he replies, "For the army. Carry men. For the war." Other children join in, "For shooting submarines." "To bring back men from space when they are in the ocean." Edith sends the boy back to the circle and asks the next boy if he has something. He replies "No" and she passes on to the next. He says "Yes" and brings a bird's nest to her. He holds it for the class to see, and the teacher asks, "What kind of bird made the nest?" The boy replies, "My friend says a rain bird made it." Edith asks what the nest is made of and different children reply, "mud," "leaves" and "sticks." There is also a bit of moss woven into the nest and Edith tries to describe it to the children. They, however, are more interested in seeing if anything is inside it, and Edith lets the boy carry it around the semi-circle showing the children its insides. Edith tells the children of some baby robins in a nest in her yard, and some of the children tell about baby birds they have seen. Some children are asking about a small object in the nest which they say looks like an egg, but all have seen the nest now and Edith calls on the next boy. A number of children say, "I know what Michael has, but I'm not telling." Michael brings a book to the teacher and then goes back to his place in the circle of children. Edith reads the last page of the book to the class. Some children tell of books which they have at home. Edith calls the next boy, and three children call out, "I know what David has." "He always has the same thing." "It's a bang-bang." David goes to his table and gets a box which he brings to Edith. He opens it and shows the teacher a scale-model of an old-fashioned dueling pistol. When David does not turn around to the class, Edith tells him, "Show it to the children," and he does. One child says, "Mr. Johnson [the principal] said no guns." Edith replies, "Yes, how many of you know that?" Most of the children in the circle raise their hands. She continues, "That you aren't supposed to bring guns to school?" She calls the next boy on the circle and he brings two large toy soldiers to her which the children enthusiastically identify as being from "Babes in Toyland." The next boy brings an American flag to Edith and shows it to the class. She asks him what the stars and stripes stand for and admonishes him to treat it carefully. "Why should you treat it carefully?" she asks the boy. "Because it's our flag," he replies. She congratulates him, saying, "That's right."

"Show and Tell" lasted twenty minutes and during the last ten one girl in particular announced that she knew what each child called upon had to show. Edith asked her to be quiet each time she spoke out, but she was not content, continuing to offer her comment at each "show." Four children from other classes had come into the room to bring something from another teacher or to ask for something from Edith. Those with requests were asked to return later if the item wasn't readily available.

Edith now asks if any of the children told their mothers about their trip to the local zoo the previous day. Many children raise their hands. As Edith calls on them, they tell what they liked in the zoo. Some children cannot wait to be called on, and they call out things to the teacher, who asks them to be quiet. After a few of the animals are mentioned, one child says, "I liked the spooky house," and the others chime in to agree with him, some pantomiming fear and horror. Edith is puzzled, and asks what this was. When half the children try to tell her at once, she raises her hand for quiet, then calls on individual children. One says, "The house with nobody in it"; another,

"The dark little house." Edith asks where it was in the zoo, but the children cannot describe its location in any way which she can understand. Edith makes some jokes but they involve adult abstractions which the children cannot grasp. The children have become quite noisy now, speaking out to make both relevant and irrelevant comments, and three little girls have become particularly assertive.

Edith gets up from her seat at 1:10 and goes to the book corner, where she puts a record on the player. As it begins a story about the trip to the zoo, she returns to the circle and asks the children to go sit at the tables. She divides them among the tables in such a way as to indicate that they don't have regular seats. When the children are all seated at the four tables, five or six to a table, the teacher asks, "Who wants to be the first one?" One of the noisy girls comes to the center of the room. The voice on the record is giving directions for imitating an ostrich and the girl follows them, walking around the center of the room holding her ankles with her hands. Edith replays the record, and all the children, table by table, imitate ostriches down the center of the room and back. Edith removes her shoes and shows that she can be an ostrich too. This is apparently a familiar game, for a number of children are calling out, "Can we have the crab?" Edith asks one of the children to do a crab "so we can all remember how," and then plays the part of the record with music for imitating crabs by. The children from the first table line up across the room, hands and feet on the floor and faces pointing toward the ceiling. After they have "walked" down the room and back in this posture they sit at their table and the children of the next table play "crab." The children love this; they run from their tables, dance about on the floor waiting for their turns and are generally exuberant. Children ask for the "inch worm" and the game is played again with the children squirming down the floor. As a conclusion Edith shows them a new animal imitation, the "lame dog." The children all hobble down the floor on three "legs," table by table, to the accompaniment of the record.

At 1:30 Edith has the children line up in the center of the room; she says, "Table one, line up in front of me," and children ask, "What are we going to do?" Then she moves a few steps to the side and says, "Table two over here, line up next to table one," and more children ask, "What for?" She does this for table three and table four and each time the children ask, "Why, what are we going to do?" When the children are lined up in four lines of five each, spaced so that they are not touching one another, Edith puts on a new record and leads the class in calisthenics, to the accompaniment of the record. The children just jump around every which way in their places instead of doing the exercises, and by the time the record is finished, Edith, the only one following it, seems exhausted. She is apparently adopting the President's new "Physical Fitness" program in her classroom.

At 1:35 Edith pulls her chair to the easels and calls the children to sit on the floor in front of her, table by table. When they are all seated she asks, "What are you going to do for worktime today?" Different children raise their hands and tell Edith what they are going to draw. Most are going to make pictures of animals they saw in the zoo. Edith asks if they want to make pictures to send to Mark in the hospital, and the children agree to this. Edith gives drawing paper to the children, calling them to her one by one. After getting a piece of paper, the children go to the crayon box on the right-hand shelves, select a number of colors, and go to the tables, where they begin

drawing. Edith is again trying to quiet the perpetually talking girls. She keeps two of them standing by her so they won't disrupt the others. She asks them, "Why do you feel you have to talk all the time," and then scolds them for not listening to her. Then she sends them to their tables to draw,

Most of the children are drawing at their tables, sitting or kneeling in their chairs. They are all working very industriously and, engrossed in their work, very quietly. Three girls have chosen to paint at the easels, and having donned their smocks, they are busily mixing colors and intently applying them to their pictures. If the children at the tables are primitives and neo-realists in their animal depictions, these girls at the easels are the class abstract-expressionists, with their broad-stroked, colorful paintings.

Edith asks of the children generally, "What color should I make the cover of Mark's book?" Brown and green are suggested by some children "because Mark likes them." The other children are puzzled as to just what is going on and ask, "What book?" or "What does she mean?" Edith explains what she thought was clear to them already, that they are all going to put their pictures together in a "book" to be sent to Mark. She goes to a small table in the play-kitchen corner and tells the children to bring her their pictures when they are finished and she will write their message for Mark on them.

By 1:50 most children have finished their pictures and given them to Edith. She talks with some of them as she ties the bundle of pictures together—answering questions, listening, carrying on conversations. The children are playing in various parts of the room with toys, games and blocks which they have taken off the shelves. They also move from table to table examining each other's pictures, offering compliments and suggestions. Three girls at a table are cutting up colored paper for a collage. Another girl is walking about the room in a pair of high heels with a woman's purse over her arm. Three boys are playing in the center of the room with the large block set, with which they are building walk-ways and walking on them. Edith is very much concerned about their safety and comes over a number of times to fuss over them. Two or three other boys are pushing trucks around the center of the room, and mild altercations occur when they drive through the block constructions. Some boys and girl are playing at the toy store, two girls are serving "tea" in the play kitchen and one is washing a doll baby. Two boys have elected to clean the room, and with large sponges they wash the movable blackboard, the puppet stage, and then begin on the tables. They run into resistance from the children who are working with construction toys on the tables and do not want to dismantle their structures. The class is like a room full of bees, each intent on pursuing some activity, occasionally bumping into one another, but just veering off in another direction without serious altercation. At 2:05 the custodian arrives pushing a cart loaded with half-pint milk containers. He places a tray of cartons on the counter next to the sink, then leaves. His coming and going is unnoticed in the room (as, incidentally, is the presence of the observer, who is completely ignored by the children for the entire afternoon).

At 2:15 Edith walks to the entrance of the room, switches off the lights, and sits at the piano and plays. The children begin spontaneously singing the song, which is "Clean up, clean up. Everybody clean up." Edith walks around the room supervising the clean-up. Some children put their toys, the blocks, puzzles, games, and so on back on their shelves under the windows.

The children making a collage keep right on working. A child from another class comes in to borrow the 45-rpm adaptor for the record player. At more urging from Edith the rest of the children shelve their toys and work. The children are sitting around their tables now and Edith asks, "What record would you like to hear while you have your milk?" There is some confusion and no general consensus, so Edith drops the subject and begins to call the children, table by table, to come get their milk. "Table one," she says, and the five children come to the sink, wash their hands and dry them, pick up a carton of milk and a straw, and take it back to their table. Two talking girls wander about the room interfering with the children getting their milk and Edith calls out to them to "settle down." As the children sit many of them call out to Edith the name of the record they want to hear. When all the children are seated at tables with milk, Edith plays one of these records called "Bozo and the Birds" and shows the children pictures in a book which go with the record. The record recites, and the book shows the adventures of a clown, Bozo, as he walks through a woods meeting many different kinds of birds who, of course, display the characteristics of many kinds of people or, more accurately, different stereotypes. As children finish their milk they take blankets or pads from the shelves under the windows and lie on them in the center of the room, where Edith sits on her chair showing the pictures. By 2:30 half the class is lying on the floor on their blankets, the record is still playing and the teacher is turning the pages of the book. The child who came in previously returns the 45-rpm adaptor, and one of the kindergarteners tells Edith what the boy's name is and where he lives.

The record ends at 2:40. Edith says, "Children, down on your blankets."

All the class is lying on blankets now, Edith refuses to answer the various questions individual children put to her because, she tells them, "it's rest time now." Instead she talks very softly about what they will do tomorrow. They are going to work with clay, she says. The children lie quietly and listen. One of the boys raises his hand and when called on tells Edith, "The animals in the zoo looked so hungry yesterday." Edith asks the children what they think about this and a number try to volunteer opinions, but Edith accepts only those offered in a "rest-time tone," that is, softly and quietly. After a brief discussion of animal feeding, Edith calls the names of the two children on milk detail and has them collect empty milk cartons from the tables and return them to the tray. She asks the two children on clean-up detail to clean up the room. Then she gets up from her chair and goes to the door to turn on the lights. At this signal the children all get up from the floor and return their blankets and pads to the shelf. It is raining (the reason for no outside play this afternoon) and cars driven by mothers clog the school drive and line up along the street. One of the talkative little girls comes over to Edith and pointing out the window says, "Mrs. Kerr, see my mother in the new Cadillac?"

At 2:50 Edith sits at the piano and plays. The children sit on the floor in the center of the room and sing. They have a repertoire of songs about animals, including one in which each child sings a refrain alone. They know these by heart and sing along through the ringing of the 2:55 bell. When the song is finished, Edith gets up and coming to the group says, "Okay, rhyming words to get your coats today." The children raise their hands and as Edith calls on them, they tell her two rhyming words, after which they are allowed to go into the hall to get their

coats and sweaters. They return to the room with these and sit at their tables. At 2:59 Edith says, "When you have your coats on, you may line up at the door." Half of the children go to the door and stand in a long line. When the three o'clock bell rings, Edith returns to the piano and plays. The children sing a song called "Goodbye," after which Edith sends them out.

## Training for Learning and for Life

The day in kindergarten at Wright School illustrates both the content of the student role as it has been learned by these children and the processes by which the teacher has brought about this learning, or, "taught" them the student role. The children have learned to go through routines and to follow orders with unquestioning obedience, even when these make no sense to them. They have been disciplined to do as they are told by an authoritative person without significant protest. Edith has developed this discipline in the children by creating and enforcing a rigid social structure in the classroom through which she effectively controls the behavior of most of the children for most of the school day. The "living with others in a small society" which the school pamphlet tells parents is the most important thing the children will learn in kindergarten can be seen now in its operational meaning, which is learning to live by the routines imposed by the school. This learning appears to be the principal content of the student role.

Children who submit to school-imposed discipline and come to identify with it, so that being a "good student" comes to be an important part of their developing identities, *become* the good students by the school's definitions. Those who submit to the routines of the school but do not come to identify with them will be adequate students who find the more important part of their identities elsewhere, such as in the play group outside school. Children who refuse to submit to the school routines are rebels, who become known as "bad students" and often "problem children" in the school, for they do not learn the academic curriculum and their behavior is often disruptive in the classroom. Today schools engage clinical psychologists in part to help teachers deal with such children.

In looking at Edith's kindergarten at Wright School, it is interesting to ask how the children learn this role of student—come to accept school-imposed routines—and what, exactly, it involves in terms of behavior and attitudes. The most prominent features of the classroom are its physical and social structures. The room is carefully furnished and arranged in ways adults feel will interest children. The play store and play kitchen in the back of the room, for example, imply that children are interested in mimicking these activities of the adult world. The only space left for the children to create something of their own is the empty center of the room, and the materials at their disposal are the blocks, whose use causes anxiety on the part of the teacher. The room, being carefully organized physically by the adults, leaves little room for the creation of physical organization on the part of the children.

The social structure created by Edith is a far more powerful and subtle force for fitting the children to the student role. This structure is established by the very rigid and tightly controlled set of rituals and routines through which the children are put during the day. There is first the rigid "locating procedure" in which the children are asked to find themselves in terms of the month, date, day of the week, and the number of the class who are present and absent. This puts them solidly in the real world as defined by adults. The

day is then divided into six periods whose activities are for the most part determined by the teacher. In Edith's kindergarten the children went through Serious Time, which opens the school day, Sharing Time, Play Time (which in clear weather would be spent outside), Work Time, Clean-up Time, after which they have their milk, and Rest Time, after which they go home. The teacher has programmed activities for each of these Times.

Occasionally the class is allowed limited discretion to choose between proffered activities, such as stories or records, but original ideas for activities are never solicited from them. Opportunity for free individual action is open only once in the day, during the part of Work Time left after the general class assignment has been completed (on the day reported the class assignment was drawing animal pictures for the absent Mark). Spontaneous interests or observations from the children are never developed by the teacher. It seems that her schedule just does not allow room for developing such unplanned events. During Sharing Time, for example, the child who brought a bird's nest told Edith, in reply to her question of what kind of bird made it, "My friend says it's a rain bird." Edith does not think to ask about this bird, probably because the answer is "childish," that is, not given in accepted adult categories of birds. The children then express great interest in an object in the nest, but the teacher ignores this interest, probably because the object is uninteresting to her. The soldiers from "Babes in Toyland" strike a responsive note in the children, but this is not used for a discussion of any kind. The soldiers are treated in the same way as objects which bring little interest from the children. Finally, at the end of Sharing Time the child-world of perception literally erupts in the class with the recollection of "the spooky house" at the zoo. Apparently this made more of an impression on the children than did any of the animals, but Edith is unable to make any sense of it for herself. The tightly imposed order of the class begins to break down as the children discover a universe of discourse of their own and begin talking excitedly with one another. The teacher is effectively excluded from this child's world of perception and for a moment she fails to dominate the classroom situation. She reasserts control, however, by taking the children to the next activity she has planned for the day. It seems never to have occurred to Edith that there might be a meaningful learning experience for the children in re-creating the "spooky house" in the classroom. It seems fair to say that this would have offered an exercise in spontaneous self-expression and an opportunity for real creativity on the part of the children. Instead, they are taken through a canned animal imitation procedure, an activity which they apparently enjoy, but which is also imposed upon them rather than created by them.

While children's perceptions of the world and opportunities for genuine spontaneity and creativity are being systematically eliminated from the kindergarten, unquestioned obedience to authority and rote learning of meaningless material are being encouraged. When the children are called to line up in the center of the room they ask "Why?" and "What for?" as they are in the very process of complying. They have learned to go smoothly through a programmed day, regardless of whether parts of the program make any sense to them or not. Here the student role involves what might be called "doing what you're told and never mind why." Activities which might "make sense" to the children are effectively ruled out and they are forced or induced to participate in activities which may be "senseless," such as the calisthenics.

At the same time the children are being taught by rote meaningless sounds in the ritual oaths and songs, such as the Lord's Prayer, the Pledge to the Flag, and "America." As they go through the grades children learn more and more of the sounds of these ritual oaths, but the fact that they have often learned meaningless sounds rather than meaningful statements is shown when they are asked to write these out in the sixth grade; they write them as groups of sounds rather than as a series of words, according to the sixth grade teachers at Wright School. Probably much learning in the elementary grades is of this character, that is, having no intrinsic meaning to the children, but rather being tasks inexplicably required of them by authoritative adults. Listening to sixth grade children read social studies reports, for example, in which they have copied material from encyclopedias about a particular country, an observer often gets the feeling that he is watching an activity which has no intrinsic meaning for the child. The child who reads, "Switzerland grows wheat and cows and grass and makes a lot of cheese" knows the dictionary meaning of each of these words but may very well have no conception at all of this "thing" called Switzerland. He is simply carrying out a task assigned by the teacher *because* it is assigned, and this may be its only "meaning" for him.

Another type of learning which takes place in kindergarten is seen in children who take advantage of the "holes" in the adult social structure to create activities of their own, during Work Time or out-of-doors during Play Time. Here the children are learning to carve out a small world of their own within the world created by adults. They very quickly learn that if they keep within permissible limits of noise and action they can play much as they please. Small groups of children formed during the year in Edith's kindergarten who played together at these times, developing semi-independent little groups in which they created their own worlds in the interstices of the adult-imposed physical and social world. These groups remind the sociological observer very much of the so-called "informal groups" which adults develop in factories and offices of large bureaucracies.[5] Here too, within authoritatively imposed social organizations people find "holes" to create little subworlds which support informal, friendly, nonofficial behavior. Forming and participating in such groups seems to be as much part of the student role as it is of the role of bureaucrat.

The kindergarten has been conceived of here as the year in which children are prepared for their schooling by learning the role of student. In the classrooms of the rest of the school grades, the children will be asked to submit to systems and routines imposed by the teachers and the curriculum. The days will be much like those of kindergarten, except that academic subjects will be substituted for the activities of the kindergarten. Once out of the school system, young adults will more than likely find themselves working in large-scale bureaucratic organizations, perhaps on the assembly line in the factory, perhaps in the paper routines of the white collar occupations, where they will be required to submit to rigid routines imposed by "the company" which may make little sense to them. Those who can operate well in this situation will be successful bureaucratic functionaries. Kindergarten, therefore, can be seen as preparing children not only for participation in the bureaucratic organization of large modern school systems, but also for the large-scale occupational bureaucracies of modern society.

# 26

# Roots of Black Manhood

### ULF HANNERZ

Some 5.7 million people were simply not counted in the 1960 census, and most of them, it now appears, were Negro men living in northern cities. This statistical oversight, if that is what it was, is not unique to the government's census takers. Ever since the beginnings of the scholarly study of black people in the Americas, there

[5] See, for example, Peter M. Blau, *Bureaucracy in Modern Society* (New York: Random House, 1956), Chapter 3.

has been an interesting fascination with the differences between the family life of Negroes and that of their white counterparts, the chief difference being seen as the dominant, not to say dominating, role of women in black families.

From E. Franklin Frazier's pioneering 1932 study of *The Negro Family in Chicago* through Melville Herskovits' *The Myth of the Negro Past* in 1941 to the so-called Moynihan Report of 1965, social scientists have been repeatedly rediscovering, analyzing and worrying over the crucial role of the mother (or grandmother) in the family structure of blacks in the New World. Herskovits saw the centrality of the mother as an African vestige, typical of the polygynous marriage in which every woman, with her offspring, formed a separate unit. Frazier is generally regarded as the first to ascribe to the institution of slavery itself the strongest influence in undermining the stability of marriage, an influence that was later reinforced when blacks encountered what Frazier perceived as the peculiarly urban evils of anonymity, disorganization and the lack of social support and controls. Moynihan, like Frazier, sees the matriarchal family as being practically without strengths, at least in the context of the larger American society, but his Report emphasizes the ways in which employer discrimination and, more recently, welfare policies have contributed to the breaking up (or foreclosure) of the male-dominated family unit among blacks.

In all of these studies, however, the black *man*—as son, lover, husband, father, grandfather—is a distant and shadowy figure "out there somewhere" . . . if only because his major characteristic as far as the household is concerned is his marginality or absence.

I do not mean to suggest that the black man is undiscovered territory. Obviously he is not. His popular image was fixed for one (long) era in *Uncle Tom's Cabin* and prophetically fashioned for our own time in Norman Mailer's essay "The White Negro." Here is Mailer's Hipster, modeled on the Negro: "Sharing a collective disbelief in the words of men who had too much money and controlled too many things, they knew almost as powerful a disbelief in the socially monolithic ideas of the single mate, the solid family and the respectable love life." And here is Mailer's black man:

Knowing in the cells of his existence that life was war, nothing but war, the Negro (all exceptions admitted) could rarely afford the sophisticated inhibitions of civilization, and so he kept for his survival the art of the primitive, he lived in the enormous present, he subsisted for his Saturday night kicks, relinquishing the pleasures of the mind for the more obligatory pleasures of the body, and in his music he gave voice to the character and quality of his existence, to his rage and the infinite variations of joy, lust, languor, growl, cramp, pinch, scream and despair of his orgasm.

Certainly there is poetic exaggeration in Mailer's description, and perhaps a conscious effort to mythicize his subject; and certainly too there is a great deal of stereotyping in the general public's imagery of the people of the black ghetto. But hardly anyone acquainted with life in the ghetto can fail to see that Mailer's portrait captures much of the reality as well. Lee Rainwater's sketch of the "expressive life-style" of the black male shows a trained social scientist's analysis that is remarkably similar to Mailer's. And undoubtedly there *is* a sizable segment of the black male population that is strongly concerned with sex, drinking, sharp clothes and "trouble"; and among these men one finds many of those who are only marginally involved with married life. Of course, ghetto life styles are heterogeneous, and there are many men who live according to "mainstream" values; but it is to the ones who do not that we should turn our attention if we want to understand what kinds of masculinity go with the female-dominated family.

This essay is an attempt to outline the social processes within the ghetto communities of the northern United States whereby the identity of street-corner males is established and maintained. To set the stage and state the issues involved in this essay, I'd like to look at the views of two other observers of the ghetto male. One is Charles Keil, whose *Urban Blues* (1966) is a study of the bluesman as a "culture hero." According to Keil, the urban blues singer, with his emphasis on sexuality, "trouble" and flashy clothes, manifests a cultural model of maleness that is highly valued by ghetto dwellers and relatively independent of the mainstream cultural tradition. Keil criticizes a number of authors who, without cavilling at this description of the male role, tend to see it as rooted in the individual's anxiety about his masculinity. This, Keil finds, is unacceptably ethnocentric:

Any sound analysis of Negro masculinity should first deal with the statements and responses of Negro women, the conscious motives of the men themselves and the Negro cultural tradition. Applied in this setting, psychological theory may then be able to provide important new insights in place of basic and unfortunate distortions.

Keil, then, comes out clearly for a cultural interpretation of the male role we are interested in here. But Elliot Liebow in *Tally's Corner* (1967), a study resulting from the author's participation in a research project that definitely considered ghetto life more in terms of social problems than as a culture, reaches conclusions which, in some of their most succinct formulations, quite clearly contradict Keil's:

Similarities between the lower-class Negro father and son . . . do not result from "cultural transmission" but from the fact that the son goes out and independently experiences the same failures, in the same areas, and for much the same reasons as his father.

Thus father and son are "independently produced look-alikes." With this goes the view that the emphasis on sexual ability, drinking and so forth is a set of compensatory self-deceptions which can only unsuccessfully veil the streetcorner male's awareness of his failure.

Keil and Liebow, as reviewed here,

may be taken as representatives of two significantly different opinions on why black people in the ghettos, and in particular the males, behave differently than other Americans. One emphasizes a cultural determinism internal to the ghetto, the other an economic determinism in the relationship between the ghetto and the wider society. It is easy to see how the two views relate to one's perspective on the determinants of the domestic structure of ghetto dwellers. And it is also easy to see how these perspectives have considerable bearing on public policy, especially if it is believed that the ghetto family structure somehow prevents full participation by its members in the larger American society and economy. If it is held, for example, that broad social and economic factors, and particularly poverty, make ghetto families the way they are—and this seems to be the majority opinion among social scientists concerned with this area—then public policy should concentrate on mitigating or removing those elements that distort the lives of black people. But if the style of life in the ghetto is culturally determined and more or less independent of other "outside" factors, then public policy will have to take a different course, or drop the problem altogether *qua* problem.

Admittedly, the present opportunity structure places serious obstacles in the way of many ghetto dwellers, making a mainstream life-style difficult to accomplish. And if research is to influence public policy, it is particularly important to point to the wider structural influences that *can* be changed in order to give equal opportunity to ghetto dwellers. Yet some of the studies emphasizing such macrostructural determinants have resulted in somewhat crude conceptualizations that are hardly warranted by the facts and which in the light of anthropological theory appear very oversimplified.

First of all, let us dispose of some of the apparent opposition between the two points of view represented by Keil and Liebow. There is not necessarily any direct conflict between ecological-economic and cultural explanations; the tendency to create such a conflict in much of the current literature on poverty involves a false dichotomy. In anthropology, it is a commonplace that culture is usually both inherited and influenced by the community's relationship to its environment. Economic determinism and cultural determinism can go hand in hand in a stable environment. Since the ecological niche of ghetto dwellers has long remained relatively unchanged, there seems to be no reason why their adaptation should not have become in some ways cultural. It is possible, of course, that the first stage in the evolution of the specifically ghetto life-style consisted of a multiplicity of identical but largely independent adaptations from the existing cultural background—mainstream or otherwise—to the given opportunity structure, as Liebow suggests. But the second stage of adaptation—by the following generations—involves a perception of the first-stage adaptation as a normal condition, a state of affairs which from then on can be expected. What was at first independent adaptation becomes transformed into a ghetto heritage of assumptions about the nature of man and society.

Yet Liebow implies that father and son are independently produced as streetcorner men, and that transmission of a ghetto-specific culture has a negligible influence. To those adhering to this belief, strong evidence in its favor is seen in the fact that ghetto dwellers —both men and women—often express conventional sentiments about sex and other matters. Most ghetto dwellers would certainly agree, at times at least, that education is a good thing, that gambling and drinking are bad, if not

sinful, and that a man and a woman should be true to each other. Finding such opinions, and heeding Keil's admonition to listen to the statements and responses of the black people themselves, one may be led to doubt that there is much of a specific ghetto culture. But then, after having observed behavior among these same people that often and clearly contradicts their stated values, one has to ask two questions: Is there any reason to believe that ghetto-specific behavior is cultural? And, if it *is* cultural, what is the nature of the coexistence of mainstream culture and ghetto-specific culture in the black ghetto?

To answer the first question, one might look at the kinds of communications that are passed around in the ghetto relating to notions of maleness. One set of relationships in which such communications occur frequently is the family; another is the male peer group.

## Deficient Masculinity?

Much has been made of the notion that young boys in the ghetto, growing up in matrifocal households, are somehow deficient in or uncertain about their masculinity, because their fathers are absent or peripheral in household affairs. It is said that they lack the role models necessary for learning male behavior; there is a lack of the kind of information about the nature of masculinity which a father would transmit unintentionally merely by going about his life at home. The boys therefore supposedly experience a great deal of sex-role anxiety as a result of this cultural vacuum. It is possible that such a view contains more than a grain of truth in the case of some quite isolated female-headed households. Generally speaking, however, there may be less to it than meets the eye. First of all, a female-headed household without an adult male in residence but where young children are growing up—and where, therefore, it is likely that the mother is still rather young—is seldom one where adult males are totally absent. More or less steady boyfriends (sometimes including the separated father) go in and out. Even if these men do not assume a central household role, the boys can obviously use them as source material for the identification of male behavior. To be sure, the model is not a conventional middle-class one, but it still shows what males are like.

Furthermore, men are not the only ones who teach boys about masculinity. Although role-modeling is probably essential, other social processes can contribute to identity formation. Mothers, grandmothers, aunts and sisters who have observed men at close range have formed expectations about the typical behavior of men which they express and which influence the boys in the household. The boys will come to share in the women's imagery of men, and often they will find that men who are not regarded as good household partners (that is, "good" in the conventional sense) are still held to be attractive company. Thus the view is easily imparted that the hard men, good talkers, clothes-horses and all, are not altogether unsuccessful as men. The women also act more directly toward the boys in these terms—they have expectations of what men will do, and whether they wish the boys to live up (or down) to the expectations, they instruct them in the model. Boys are advised not to "mess with" girls, but at the same time it is emphasized that messing around is the natural thing they will otherwise go out and do—and when the boys start their early adventures with the other sex, the older women may scold them but at the same time point out, not without satisfaction, that "boys will be boys." This kind of maternal (or at least adult female) instruction of young males is obviously a kind of altercast-

ing, or more exactly, socialization to an alter role—that is, women cast boys in the role complementary to their own according to their experience of man-woman relationships. One single mother of three boys and two girls put it this way:

You know, you just got to act a little bit tougher with boys than with girls, 'cause they just ain't the same. Girls do what you tell them to do and don't get into no trouble, but you just can't be sure about the boys. I mean, you think they're OK and next thing you find out they're playing hookey and drinking wine and maybe stealing things from cars and what not. There's just something bad about boys here, you know. But what can you say when many of them are just like their daddies? That's the man in them coming out. You can't really fight it, you know that's the way it is. They know, too, But you just got to be tougher.

This is in some ways an antagonistic socialization, but it is built upon an expectation that it would be unnatural for men not to turn out to be in some ways bad—that is fighters, drinkers, lady killers and so forth. There is one thing worse than a no-good man—the sissy, who is his opposite. A boy who seems weak is often reprimanded and ridiculed not only by his peers but also by adults, including his mother and older sisters. The combination of role-modeling by peripheral fathers or temporary boyfriends with altercasting by adult women certainly provides for a measure of male role socialization within the family.

And yet, when I said that the view of the lack of models in the family was too narrow, I was not referring to the observers' lack of insight into many matrifocal ghetto families as much as I was to the emphasis they placed on the family as *the* information storage unit of a community's culture. I believe it is an ethnocentrism on the part of middle-class commentators to take it for granted that if information about sex roles is not transmitted from father to son within the family, it is not transmitted from generation to generation at all. In American sociology, no less than in the popular mind, there is what Ray Birdwhistell has termed a "sentimental model" of family life, according to which the family is an inward-turning isolated unit, meeting most of the needs of its members, and certainly their needs for sociability and affection. The "sentimental model" is hardly ever realistic even as far as middle-class American families are concerned, and it has even less relevance for black ghetto life. Ghetto children live and learn out on the streets just about as much as within the confines of the home. Even if mothers, aunts and sisters do not have streetcorner men as partners, there is an ample supply of them on the front stoop or down at the corner. Many of these men have such a regular attendance record as to become quite familiar to children and are frequently very friendly with them. Again, therefore, there is no lack of adult men to show a young boy what men are like. It seems rather unlikely that one can deny all role-modeling effect of these men on their young neighbors. They may be missing in the United States census records, but they are not missing in the ghetto community.

Much of the information gained about sex roles outside the family comes not from adult to child, however, but from persons in the same age-grade or only slightly higher. The idea of culture being stored in lower age-grades must be taken seriously. Many ghetto children start participating in the peer groups of the neighborhood at an early age, often under the watchful eye of an elder brother or sister. In this way they are initiated into the culture of the peer group by interacting with children —predominantly of the same sex—

who are only a little older than they are. And in the peer-group culture of the boys, the male sex role is a fairly constant topic of concern. Some observers have felt that this is another consequence of the alleged sex role anxiety of ghetto boys. This may be true, of course, at least in that it may have had an important part in the development of male peer-group life as a dominant element of ghetto social structure. Today, however, such a simple psychosocial explanation will not do. Most ghetto boys can hardly avoid associating with other boys, and once they are in the group, they are efficiently socialized into a high degree of concern with their sex role. Much of the joking, the verbal contests and the more or less obscene songs among small ghetto boys, serve to alienate them from dependence on mother figures and train them to the exploitative, somewhat antagonistic attitude toward women which is typical of streetcorner men.

## "Mother!"

This is not to say that the cultural messages are always very neat and clearcut. In the case of the kind of insult contest called "playing the dozens," "sounding" or (in Washington, D.C.) "joning," a form of ritualized interaction which is particularly common among boys in the early teens, the communication is highly ambiguous. When one boy says something unfavorable about another's mother, the other boy is expected either to answer in kind or to fight in defense of his honor (on which apparently that of his mother reflects). But the lasting impression is that there is something wrong about mothers—they are not as good as they ought to be ("Anybody can get pussy from your mother"), they take over male items of behavior and by implication too much of the male role ("Your mother smokes a pipe"). If standing up for one's family is the manifest expected consequence of "the dozens," then a latent function is a strengthening of the belief that ghetto women are not what they ought to be. The other point of significance is that the criteria of judgment about what a good woman should be like are apparently like those of the larger society. She should not be promiscuous, and she should stick to the mainstream female role and not be too dominant.

The boys, then, are learning and strengthening a cultural ambivalence involving contradictions between ideal and reality in female behavior. I will return to a discussion of such cultural ambivalence later. But the point remains that even this game involves continuous learning and strengthening of a cultural definition of what women are like that is in some ways complementary to the definition of what men are like. And much of the songs, the talk and the action—fighting, sneaking away with girls into a park or an alley or drinking out of half-empty wine bottles stolen from or given away by adult men—are quite clearly preparations for the streetcorner male role. If boys and men show anxiety about their masculinity, one may suspect that this is induced as much by existing cultural standards as by the alleged nonexistence of models.

This socialization within the male peer group is a continuing process; the talk that goes on, continuously or intermittently, at the street corner or on the front steps may deal occasionally with a football game or a human-interest story from the afternoon newspaper, but more often there are tales from personal experience about adventures of drinking (often involving the police), about women won and lost, about feminine fickleness and the masculine guile (which sometimes triumphs over it), about clothing, or there may simply be comments on the women passing down

the street. "Hi ugly . . . don't try to swing what you ain't got."

This sociability among the men seems to be a culture-building process. Shared definitions of reality are created out of the selected experiences of the participants. Women are nagging and hypocritical; you can't expect a union with one of them to last forever. Men are dogs; they have to run after many women. There is something about being a man and drinking liquor; booze makes hair grow on your chest. The regularity with which the same topics appear in conversation indicates that they have been established as the expected and appropriate subjects in this situation, to the exclusion of other topics.

• Mack asked me did I screw his daughter, so I asked: "I don't know, what's her name?" And then when I heard that gal was his daughter all right, I says, "Well, Mack, I didn't really have to take it. 'cause it was given to me." I thought Mack sounded like his daughter was some goddam white gal. But Mack says, "Well, I just wanted to hear it from you." Of course, I didn't know that was Mack's gal, 'cause she was married and had a kid, and so she had a different name. But then you know the day after when I was out there a car drove by, and somebody called my name from it, you know, "hi darling," and that was her right there. So the fellow I was with says, "Watch out, Buddy will shoot your ass off." Buddy, that's her husband. So I says, "Yeah, but he got to find me first!"

• Let me tell you fellows, I've been arrested for drunkenness more than two hundred times over the last few years, and I've used every name in the book. I remember once I told them I was Jasper Gonzales, and then I forgot what I had told them, you know. So I was sitting there waiting, and they came in and called "Jasper Gonzales," and nobody answered. I had forgotten that's what I said, and to tell you the truth, I didn't know how to spell it. So anyway, nobody answered, and there they were calling "Jasper Gonzales. Jasper Gonzales!" So I thought that must be me, so I answered. But they had been calling a lot of times before that. So the judge said, "Mr. Gonzales, are you of Spanish descent?" And I said, "Yes, your honor, I came to this country thirty-four years ago." And of course I was only thirty-five, but you see I had this beard then, and I looked pretty bad, dirty and everything, you know, so I looked like sixty. And so he said, "We don't have a record on you. This is the first time you have been arrested?" So I said, "Yes, your honor, nothing like this happened to me before. But my wife was sick, and then I lost my job you know, and I felt kind of bad. But it's the first time I ever got drunk." So he said, "Well, Mr. Gonzales, I'll let you go, 'cause you are not like the rest of them here. But let this be a warning to you." So I said, "Yes, your honor." And then I went out, and so I said to myself, "I'll have to celebrate this." So I went across the street from the court, and you know there are four liquor stores there, and I got a pint of wine and next thing I was drunk as a pig.

• Were you here that time a couple of weeks ago when these three chicks from North Carolina were up here visiting Miss Gladys? They were really gorgeous, about 30–35. So Charlie says why don't we step by the house and he and Jimmy and Deekay can go out and buy them a drink. So they say they have to go and see this cousin first, but then they'll be back. But then Brenda (Charlie's wife) comes back before they do, and so these girls walk back and forth in front of the house, and Charlie can't do a thing about it, except hope they won't knock on his door. And then Jimmy and Deekay come and pick them up, and Fats is also there, and the three of them go off with these chicks, and

there is Charlie looking through his window, and there is Brenda looking at them too, and asking Charlie does he know who the chicks are.

Groups of one's friends give some stability and social sanction to the meanings that streetcorner men attach to their experiences—meanings that may themselves have been learned in the same or preceding peer groups. They, probably more than families, are information storage units for the ghetto-specific male role. At the same time, they are self-perpetuating because they provide the most satisfactory contexts for legitimizing the realities involved. In other words, they suggest a program for maleness, but they also offer a haven of understanding for those who follow that program and are criticized for it or feel doubts about it. For of course all streetcorner males are more or less constantly exposed to the definitions and values of the mainstream cultural apparatus, and so some cultural ambivalence can hardly be avoided. Thus, if a man is a dog for running after women—as he is often said to be among ghetto dwellers—he wants to talk about it with other dogs who appreciate that this is a fact of life. If it is natural for men to drink, let it happen among other people who understand the nature of masculinity. In this way the group maintains constructions of reality, and life according to this reality maintains the group.

It is hard to avoid the conclusion, then, that there is a cultural element involved in the sex roles of streetcorner males, because expectations about sex are manifestly shared and transmitted rather than individually evolved. (If the latter had been the case, of course, it would have been less accurate to speak of these as roles, since roles are by definition cultural.) This takes us to the second question stated above, about the coexistence of conventional and ghetto-specific cultures. Streetcorner men certainly are aware of the male ideal of mainstream America—providing well for one's family, remaining faithful to one's spouse, staying out of trouble, etc. —and now and then every one of them states it as his own ideal. What we find here, then, may be seen as a bicultural situation. Mainstream culture and ghetto-specific culture provide different models for living, models familiar to everyone in the ghetto. Actual behavior may lean more toward one model or more toward the other, or it may be some kind of mixture, at one point or over time. The ghetto-specific culture, including the streetcorner male role, is adapted to the situation and the experience of the ghetto dweller; it tends to involve relatively little idealization but offers shared expectations concerning self, others and the environment. The mainstream culture, from the ghetto dweller's point of view, often involves idealization, but there is less real expectation that life will actually follow the paths suggested by those ideals. This is not to say that the ghetto-specific culture offers no values of its own at all, or that nothing of mainstream culture ever appears realistic in the ghetto; but in those areas of life where the two cultures exist side by side as alternative guides to action (for naturally, the ghetto-specific culture, as distinct from mainstream culture, is not a "complete" culture covering all areas of life), the ghetto-specific culture is often taken to forecast what one can actually expect from life, while the mainstream norms are held up as perhaps ultimately more valid but less attainable under the given situational constraints. "Sure it would be good to have a good job and a good home and your kids in college and all that, but you got to be yourself and do what you know." Of course, this often makes the ghetto-specific cultural expectations into self-fulfilling prophecies, as ghetto dwellers try to attain what they believe they can attain; but, to be sure, self-

fulfilling prophecies and realistic assessments may well coincide.

## "Be Yourself"

On the whole, one may say that both mainstream culture and ghetto-specific culture are transmitted within many ghetto families. I have noted how socialization into the ghetto male role within the household is largely an informal process, in which young boys may pick up bits and pieces of information about masculinity from the women in the house as well as from males who may make their entrances and exits. On the other hand, when adult women—usually mothers or grandmothers—really "tell the boys how to behave," they often try to instill in them mainstream, not to say puritanical norms—drinking is bad, sex is dirty and so forth. The male peer groups, as we have seen, are the strongholds of streetcorner maleness, although there are times when men cuss each other out for being "no good." Finally, of course, mainstream culture is transmitted in contacts with the outside world, such as in school or through the mass media. It should be added, though, that the latter may be used selectively to strengthen some elements of the streetcorner male role; ghetto men are drawn to Westerns, war movies and crime stories both in the movie house and on their TV sets.

Yet, even if the nature of men's allegiance to the two cultures makes it reasonably possible to adhere, after a fashion, to both at the same time, the bicultural situation of streetcorner males involves some ambivalence. The rejection of mainstream culture as a guide to action rather than only a lofty ideal is usually less than complete. Of course, acting according to one or the other of the two cultures to a great extent involves bowing to the demands of the social context, and so a man whose concerns in the peer-group milieu are drinking and philandering will try to be "good" in the company of his mother or his wife and children, even if a complete switch is hard to bring about. There are also peer groups, of course, that are more mainstream-oriented than others, although even the members of these groups are affected by streetcorner definitions of maleness. To some extent, then, the varying allegiance of different peer groups to the two cultures is largely a difference of degree, as the following statement by a young man implies.

Those fellows down at the corner there just keep drinking and drinking. You know, I think it's pretty natural for a man to drink, but they don't try to do nothing about it, they just drink every hour of the day, every day of the week. My crowd, we drink during the weekend, but we can be on our jobs again when Monday comes.

However, although where one is or who one is with does bring some order into this picture of bicultural ambivalence, it is still one of less than perfect stability. The drift between contexts is itself not something to which men are committed by demands somehow inherent in the social structure. Ghetto men may spend more time with the family, or more time with the peer group, and the extent to which they choose one or the other, and make a concomitant cultural selection, still appears to depend much on personal attachment to roles, and to changes in them. The social alignments of a few men may illustrate this. One man, Norman Hawkins, a construction laborer, spends practically all his leisure time at home with his family, only occasionally joining in the streetcorner conversations and behavior of the peer group to which his neighbor, Harry Jones, belongs. Harry Jones, also a construction worker, is also married and has a family but stays on the periphery of household life, although he lives with his wife and children. Some of the other

men in the group are unmarried or separated and so seldom play the "family man" role which Harry Jones takes on now and then. Harry's younger brother, Carl, also with a family, used to participate intensively in peer group life until his drinking led to a serious ailment, and after he recuperated from this he started spending much less time with his male friends and more with his family. Bee Jay, a middle-aged bachelor who was raised by his grandmother, had a job at the post office and had little to do with street life until she died. Since then, he has become deeply involved with a tough, hard-drinking group and now suffers from chronic health problems connected with his alcoholism. Thus we can see how the life careers of some ghetto men take them through many and partly unpredictable shifts and drifts between mainstream and ghetto-specific cultures, while others remain quite stable in one allegiance or another.

## Two Cultures

The sociocultural situation in the black ghetto is clearly complicated. The community shows a great heterogeneity of life-styles; individuals become committed in some degree to different ways of being by the impersonally-enforced structural arrangements to which they are subjected, but unpredictable contingencies have an influence, and their personal attachments to life-styles also vary. The socioeconomic conditions impose limits on the kinds of life ghetto dwellers may have, but these kinds of life are culturally transmitted and shared as many individuals in the present, and many in the past, live or have lived under the same premises. When the latter is the case, it is hardly possible to invent new adaptations again and again, as men are always observing each other and interacting with each other. The implication of some of Frazier's writings, that ghetto dwellers create their way of life in a cultural limbo—an idea which has had more modern expressions—appears as unacceptable in this case as in any other situation where people live together, and in particular where generations live together. The behavior of the streetcorner male is a natural pattern of masculinity with which ghetto dwellers grow up and which to some extent they grow into. To see it only as a complex of unsuccessful attempts at hiding failures by self-deception seems, for many of the men involved, to be too much psychologizing and too little sociology. But this does not mean that the attachment to the ghetto-specific culture is very strong among its bearers.

The question whether streetcorner males have mainstream culture or a specific ghetto culture, then, is best answered by saying that they have both, in different ways. There can be little doubt that this is the understanding most in line with that contemporary trend in anthropological thought which emphasizes the sharing of cultural imagery, of expectations and definitions of reality, as the medium whereby individuals in a community interact. It is noteworthy that many of the commentators who have been most skeptical of the idea of a ghetto-specific culture, or more generally a "culture of poverty," have been those who have taken a more narrow view of culture as a set of values about which an older generation consciously instructs the younger ones in the community.

Obviously, the answer to whether there is a ghetto-specific culture or not will depend to some extent on what we shall mean by culture. Perhaps this is too important a question to be affected by a mere terminological quibble, and perhaps social policy, in some areas, may well proceed unaffected by the questions raised by a ghetto-specific culture. On the other hand, in an anthropological study of community life, the wider view of cultural sharing and transmission which has been used here will have to play a part in our picture of the ghetto, including that of what ghetto males are like.

## 27

# The Hippies as Contrameritocracy

### JESSE R. PITTS

Hippies seem to fascinate the mass media somewhat less than they did a year or two ago. But they have not disappeared. Older Hippies, who refused to reconvert to straight society, have moved from Haight Ashbury to Big Sur or other places more removed from the tourist trade. "Communes" have sprung

From *Dissent* (1969), pp. 326–337. Reprinted by permission.

up in rural or urban settings, and Hippies are less noticeable now that some of their fashions have become part of youth culture. Some say that Hippies have become Yippies: they have renounced nonviolence and political indifference in favor of active provocation and resistance. Others say the Yippies are an invention of the mass media. The "mother-fucker" wing of SDS seems to consist of "Hipster"-type Hippies attracted by the pornography of violence.

But regardless of the vagaries of fashion that permit successive cohorts of youth to differentiate themselves from one another, the Hippie phenomenon seems here to stay, not merely as a variety of the perennial bohemian fringe well described some years ago by Ned Polsky in this magazine,[1] but as a social movement of some significance.

It is likely that Hippies, ostentatiously doing their thing even in Traverse City, Michigan, are an intrinsic part of the postindustrial world. My hypothesis is that there is developing in the United States (and probably in other industrialized countries of the West) a *contrameritocracy* which offers the failures or dropouts of the achievement society a haven that neutralizes the pains of failure. Until now this antiachievement society was located either at the very top or bottom. At the upperclass level we had "café society," at the bottom disorganized working-class elements and hoboes. (The underworld, by contrast, has an achievement orientation.) By its nature, the upper class cannot endorse the achievement criteria of the middle class. It must shift the grounds of status from occupational achievement to family-rooted superiorities: ancientness of dynasty, graceful living, and a commitment to *noblesse oblige*. Style is more important than the consequences of action. The upper class also supports the more high-brow forms of art; for this appreciation seems to require special gifts not available to conventional middle-class patrons. In its struggle against the middle class it is often led to disparage the values of hard work, thrift, and personal restraint in favor of an ethic of prowess flowing from inherent traits of personality ("breeding"). The "Jet Set" is the

militant expression of the antiachievement aspect of the upper-class ethos.

In the past few years, however, the Jet Set has become more and more a transmission belt into some sections, of the middle class for fashions, mannerisms, and ideology originating mainly in the Hippie movement. This is because the Hippie movement has become the effective center of the contrameritocracy in the United States and probably also in England, though in Japan, Germany, Italy, and France, New Left patterns have been more important. The New Left copes with the threat of failure by asserting that opportunity for achievement does not really exist, since it is monopolized by a nation's power elite. The Hippie movement claims that the opportunities offered by the meritocracy must not be pursued if man is to save his soul. It has become the effective center of the contrameritocracy, because its values and behavior patterns permit a thorough and enthusiastic alienation, and because its critique, whatever its "scientific" value, offers a disturbing challenge to society.

It is my contention that the Hippie movement is made up of youths who are overcommitted to the basic middle-class values but are unwilling to realize those values in the occupational world. Since their attachment to middle-class values makes them unwilling to enter the world of juvenile delinquency, there remain for them the patterns of heroic value commitment and expressive behavior, through which they align their stand with that of the upper class— but without the latter's devotion to graceful living and essential conservatism. The Hippie movement is a religious sect through which the members reach what they feel to be the highest levels of value achievement, and thus they attempt to bring salvation to the corrupt society that rejects them. The use of the adjective "religious" is justified by the constant reference in the

[1] "The Village Beat Scene; Summer 1960," by Ned Polsky. DISSENT Summer 1961.

Hippie movement to nonrational, non-empirical forces, its concern with the ultimate ends and meanings of life, and its relative immunity to organizational failure. To describe the Hippie movement as "religious" is also warranted by the fact that members of the movement are willing to give its basic values primacy in guiding their personal development, regardless of loss or disapproval.

Hippies give absolute allegiance to two values: universal love and the unique value of the individual. Of the Christian religions, Eastern-Orthodox Catholicism is the most collectively oriented and Puritanism the most individualistic.

The Hippie movement, I would suggest, represents a further emphasis on this individualism. For the Puritan ethos the value of the individual in his uniqueness lies in his imitation of Christ, his struggle to act continuously in such a way as to be consistent with the search for the City of Light; but this struggle is hampered, of course, by inner temptations representing the weight of the flesh. In the Puritan ethos there is one strain implying that actions of the elect have an inherent goodness; and then, in its liberal version this becomes the belief that all men are intrinsically good and that with effort, learning, and self-control anyone can succeed in "realizing himself." But whether fundamentalist or liberal, the Puritan ethos is suspicious of pleasure and holds that the direction of the good lies away from gratification of the flesh. The uniqueness of the individual resides in the unpredictable diversity of his struggles with the world and the flesh. An act, to be good, must be a personal effort rather than represent compliance with Church and State. While "nobody can tell you what to do" in any particular situation, the direction is nevertheless clear and common to all men: they must build the City of God on earth.

Though it has roots in the Puritan ethos, the Hippie conception of uniqueness is different. For the Hippie all men are good if only they give way to their nature, as against the pressures of the social structure. Hence, uniqueness will be found in the cultivation of sincerity and spontaneity. Since all individuals are equally valuable and worthy of love, the desires of each merit realization. Nor is there suspicion of pleasure as a guide to action, and of sensual pleasure in particular. But sensual pleasure is seen not so much in its hedonistic light (there is some of this, no doubt) but as a sign of what the individual needs, and a guarantee against domination by others. One must always do what one wants to do; anything else is subordination and loss of independence, *ergo* loss of individuality. Self-expression should know only one limit dictated by the love of others: the other's need for his own self expression.

The high valuation of love is in line with all the major religions. In the Hippie movement this is not to remain an abstract dedication to others but must become a warm openness toward all human beings such as precludes competitiveness at any level. In the Western world, at least, men are supposed to love their families and be receptive to outsiders, but they are also supposed to be able to enter into limited relations that are dominated by objectively measured exchanges. Outside the family and friendship, direct expression of the value of love is limited to a willingness to cooperate on the neighborhood or job level, or to a general respect for the rules of the game even if cheating would bring immediate returns. But the Hippie commitment to love goes beyond all this: it implies a permanent willingness to share all of one's possessions with anyone who might require them. It also implies a refusal to judge anyone or to give a person a label like thief, convict, addict, because the code of love requires that the individual always be given another chance—and without expecting anything in return. In fact, love is seen by the Hippies as the normal expression of man unless he is hampered and perverted by social structure: the meritocratic rat race destroys love. The Hippie community, which assembles those who dedicate themselves to the value of love, takes on a special sanctity, for it demonstrates the possibility of creating groups where men can be together without conformity, discrimination, or jealousy. Within the group all resources are shared and a good deal of time is spent in the sheer enjoyment of each other's company.

The value of the individual and the value of love find their first combined specifications in the cult of sincerity, the cult of independence, and the imperative of "keeping your cool." The valuation of sincerity is definitely in line with the Puritan ethos, not just in the "I cannot tell a lie" sense but, more important, as part of the search for inner consistency—since every action must reflect the election of the soul. Embracing this value with a vengeance, Hippies turn it against the adult world; they describe the relations between adults— with their mental reservations, their limited commitments, their unwillingness to raise issues irrelevant to an immediate problem—as "playing games."

Love is to be shared with all mankind, by contrast with the narrow capacities of the adults who are usually limited to family, friends, ethnic, and national similars. The Hippies want all relationships to be total or at least potentially total. No role differemtiation for them: merely human beings, face-to-face, intent on love rather than on manipulating each other for selfish ends.

Another specification in line with the American ethos is the Hippies' high valuation of independence. A man and a woman should be financially and emotionally independent from any other man or woman. This does not preclude developing attachments to particular individuals, but those attachments must involve complete reciprocity and never act as binding obligations upon the other. In order to be valid, a relationship must be totally spontaneous and sincere (there is a tendency to see these two kinds of behavior as synonymous). In the optic of universal love, whether one has a special attachment to someone else is not crucial. What replaces love between man and woman is not hatred or indifference, but simply universal love. If anything, romantic love is under some suspicion, for it tends to withdraw people from the magic circle of universal love. One should not be "hung up" on anything or anybody, one should "keep his cool."

The imperative of "keeping your cool" is strangely in line with the Puritan norm of self-control, although it is certainly not the English version of self-control with its inhibition of aggression and sexual expression. More than a restraint upon self-expression, it is a warning that one should be able to disconnect any relationship that turns out to be upsetting. One should never be so "hung up" on anything, or on any single relationship, that one is led to lose one's temper or feel inordinate grief; one should not allow anyone to possess another human being. Thus, the world can never threaten the Hippie effectively. Is not this antagonism to the "ties of the flesh" very similar to the attitude of the Puritan divines in the 17th century?

Another meaning of "cool" is awareness. The Hippie must never be "taken in" by society, but he must at all times keep his distance from the role relationships he may be compelled to enter. "To be cool" is to dominate through intelligence and analysis any potentially distasteful involvement in the world. In Puritanism potential conflicts between high valuation of the individual and high valuation of universal love are limited by the doctrine of original sin, which states that in and of himself the individual cannot reach perfection: he needs the aid of grace which permits him access to a perfection the model of which is outside the individual. Through denial of the self-directed impulse the individual demonstrates his state of grace, and the universal principles of morality (the Kantian categorical imperative) provide the rationale of self-restraint. Service combines inner direction and integration into the community, without foregoing the disruptive potentials of both the economic entrepreneur and the moral entrepreneur à la Thoreau.

Having abandoned the concept of original sin, the Hippies deny the relevance of any universal standard of morality. A person must do his own thing: only thus can he realize the good within him. Caught between what the sociologist must see as the conflicts inherent in a doctrine that stresses values impossible of simultaneous maximization (the cult of personal experience or independence and the cult of community, the cult of spontaneity and the high valuation on keeping cool), there is a tendency among Hippies toward a split in values: some choose an individualistic and hedonistic pattern, which Norman Mailer described as the "hipster" life, and others a mystic pattern that strives to deny ego needs or fuses them into the needs of the group. The latter part of the Hippie movement has been attracted by Eastern philosophies, mainly Hindu or Taoist, for they structure a system of thought in which intuition, vision, telepathy, and modulated emotion are preferred ways to the truth. These philosophies hold out the promise that man may rinse the soul of Ego in the narrower and greedy sense of the term.

The resolution of these contradictions, and the cohabitation of both the hipster and the mystic in the same communities, will be easier if spontaneous and sincere action stays away from places where facilities are scarce and where the pleasure of one may lessen the opportunities of the other. It will also be easier if one avoids complex forms of cooperative action where the pay-off is long in coming and where those who possess the highest technical skills must make sure they have the cooperation of the less skillful. Luckily, the most valued activity for the Hippie is the expression, and hopefully the creative expression, of inner moods through various art forms, or simply and more frequently, through the spontaneity of the "scene." And here the Hippies part from the Puritan ethos with its emphasis on active mastery of the environment. We have instead a primacy of expressive activities, which is reflected in the Hippies' devotion to culture, especially to culture of an avant-garde type. In painting their tastes go from the most advanced abstractionists to op and pop art. In writing there are a series of seers such as Kerouac (less liked now that he has become too establishment-oriented), Alan Ginsberg, Ferlinghetti, Herman Hesse, Corso, Burroughs, Ken Kesey, Selby, Tolkien, Kahlil Gibran. All poetry either far-out in style or sexual in content will be appreciated or given the benefit of the doubt. Poetry is preferred to novels because it is less rational in construction, more spontaneous, and apparently does not take as long to write. Many Hippies, when asked what they do, will answer "I write"; they usually mean poetry.

A function of this cult of culture is to upgrade the self-imputed status of the Hippie. Not only is he superior to all members of society who do not share his interest, but he is also superior to those who do not give to this interest the same dedication.

Yet the cult of culture requires less effort than might be thought. In many ways Hippies have a relation to high-brow culture similar to that of upper-class people. They know the writers and the artists, or know someone who claims to know them. There is a set vocabulary to assimilate and use at proper moments. There are taste leaders who give the proper cues as to what should be admired. Above all, Hippies see themselves as creators in their own right, even if the only object of their creation is their own mood when under the influence of drugs.

Any group whose ideas deviate significantly from the surrounding community has the problem of maintaining solidarity among members whose reason for belonging lies precisely in their social maladjustment. The cohesion and continuity of the group will be furthered if it develops a high ethnocentrism and reduces its relationships to the outside world as much as possible to martyrdom and proselytism.

The high ethnocentrism in the Hippie community leads to two consequences. The first is its justification of an exploitative relation to the outside world. Sponging on welfare and petty thievery in record shops, bookstores, university libraries, and supermarkets is accepted because, supposedly, there is a state of war between the square (or "straight") world and the Hippies, a war that is the sole responsibility of the former. Friendly patrons can be used without any commitment on the Hippie's part, since fundamentally they are still the enemy and, after all, they are repaid by the pleasure derived from giving. It encourages a feeling of mutual dependence, the fraternity of the trenches. Merely by belonging to the group, the Hippie gets a feeling of being one of the chosen few. Tolerance is justified because the failings of the chosen are minor in comparison with the importance of being among the chosen.

Two ideological tenets reinforce this ethnocentrism. One is "catastrophism,"

the belief that the world is soon to be obliterated because squares in their ignorance, folly, and meanness are bound to unleash atomic war, thereby making nonsense of middle-class planning and postponement of gratification. The second belief is "miserabilism" or "pastoralism," which states that the more outside the system an individual is, the less likely is his native goodness to be corrupted. And since the Hippie identifies with the Noble Savage, he can worship his own group without having to bear the burden of the sin of pride. Examples of the Noble Savage are the Negro, the itinerant worker, and, more recently, the Indian.

The tense relationship between the outside world and the Hippie community is maintained by "blowing people's minds," the use of drugs, and work avoidance. "Blowing people's minds" is the obverse of "keeping your cool": its purpose is to shock, disconcert, and thus help disintegrate the "unhealthy" psychological structures of outsiders.

Always permissible against squares, this is supposed to force people to face the futility of their present course of action and make them accept the new wisdom incarnated in the act that "blew their mind." The capacity to blow people's minds has been the only approved way to express aggression,[2] because in its essence it is supposed to be an act of love. Retelling of occasions where "blowing someone's mind" was

[2] The past tense seems indicated here because there seems to have been a shift away from nonviolence, e.g. the recent Chicago (August 1968) slogan "Kill the Pigs" (the police). It is difficult to determine, however, whether this was a slogan pushed mainly by the SDS, Maoists, and Trotskyites, and to what extent it was taken up by the new Yippies, the old-style Hippies, and the "straight" McCarthy youth. Furthermore, the slogan seems often part of the pornography of violence rather than an effective commitment. The police, unfortunately, do not always seem aware of the difference.

done successfully against squares is one of the ways prestige is built. And "blowing people's minds" has the advantage of shying clear of police reprisal: it may shock, it may be an act of exquisite cruelty, but it is unlikely to be a legal misdemeanor.

Squares have their minds blown when Hippies offer the spectacle of their decorative spontaneity, in their clothing, hair styles, profanity, public love-making or undressing, gifts of flowers to policemen, sleeping in the streets, in the frenzy and bawdiness of their music, integrated love-making, and self-righteous begging. The "love-in" becomes a sort of Hippie revival meeting. Blowing people's minds is the way to proselytize the world; but it is not an attempt to influence through dialectic, for the choice of the true way must remain one's own. To influence someone is to restrict his freedom.

Releasing the primacy of expressive activities need not result in the kind of achievement valued by squares: the drug cult is proof that one can gain pleasure without having to pay the price of work and self-denial, and that the road to happiness is not through competition. When one has some marijuana one shares it with others, and when they have some they reciprocate.

It is the secret weed around which rituals of solidarity and mutual love are organized, for Hippies believe that taking drugs together can lead people to mystical kinds of experiences that may link them forever, even if they should never again see each other. Drugs prove that the inner state (pleasure, revelation) is the important goal, rather than trying to modify the outside world.

A frequent belief among Hippies is that we do not normally use more than 10 percent of our brain power, and that drugs, especially of the LSD variety, permit the expansion of one's consciousness by going beyond the structures of thought derived from role playing and "status games." Thus drug takers are privy to a wisdom that is beyond the grasp of any square, however learned he may be.[3]

Drugs play a major role in cementing the solidarity of the Hippie community. For new members the use of drugs becomes a rite of passage, a way of teaching proper techniques of appreciation. It also serves as a sign of mutual recognition among Hippies and a way to maintain the hostility of the square community.

Avoidance of work is equally crucial to the integration of the Hippie community. As the opposite of spontaneity, work is a constraint upon one's fulfillment because it subverts the individual in his uniqueness. Hippies reject the alienation of work because it always requires some and often much self-denial.

Hippies also reject the commitment to exchange that is implicit in work. While the classical Puritan ethos sees in work the idea of service, for the Hippie the impersonality of the market to which work is oriented either directly or implicitly condemns work as a force separating individuals from one another.

The worst form of work is, of course, that which is most common in the modern world, work in the bureaucratic context, which is said to heighten impersonality and subordination and to remove people from nature. The Hippie might try his hand at some craft which puts him into intimate relation with wood, stone, plants—but not with IBM cards and paper clips. To paint, carve, write, or play music is not to work but, on the contrary, to do what one wants, regardless of whether others like the product or not.

Beatniks of the type described by Polsky in 1961 went to great extremes

[3] It is conceivable that drugs may not be necessary anymore, say some of the older Hippies. They were a shortcut, a way of discovering where "it was at," but the true sage should be able to gain peace and wisdom without them.

to avoid work, but Hippies will occasionally work at some semiskilled jobs. Men may do house painting and decorating, janitoring, cab driving, bartending, and mail delivery. Girls will do waitressing,[4] Kelly girling, thesis typing, modeling, or clerking.

The Hippie movement serves to mitigate the impact of deviance from the total society. Although the group is economically parasitic upon the society, it discourages among its members gross stealing and swindling. It is uncool to steal from persons, though all right to steal from supermarkets that overcharge the poor.

While there are many deviant behavior patterns Hippies will tolerate, they definitely do not encourage "hard drug" addiction. Even "pot heads" (people who smoke marijuana so as to be "high" through most of the day) and "speed freaks" (amphetamine addicts) will find a subtle pressure to limit their drug intake to group occasions. Although Hippies have no Kantian principles of sexual morality, they consider rather "uncool" seduction, satyriasis, pedophilia, rape. There is even some muted social pressure against homosexuality as a dominant sexual adjustment. Indeed, all the evidence points to a relatively low rate of sexual activity, considering the lack of moral censure and the ready opportunities; the levels are certainly well below those entertained by "square" fantasies. There are known cases of beautiful girls having lived many months in Hippie communities and remaining virgins. And Hippie girls will not prostitute themselves (turn themselves into an object), even though this is often an easy source of funds and need not assume the sordid trappings of "hustling."

At least until 1967 it was considered quite uncool to provoke the wrath of the police. The taboo against aggression insures that whatever provocation takes place will be verbal, indirect, and not likely to start the night sticks swinging. Except for the possession of drugs, the Hippie will seldom engage in obvious violations of the law. He is more likely to specialize in nondelictual delinquency which thrills the doer, shocks the onlooker if he's around, but rarely triggers the apparatus of justice. Dealing in marijuana and LSD is usually the worst felony committed, and the result is a very low arrest and conviction rate. Hence the delinquencies the Hippie community allows and/or fosters are unlikely to make a return to middle-class society difficult.

The educative impact of the Hippie community has two aspects: first, just by being a member, the Hippie experiences a relief from the self-deprecation that often has characterized these individuals before they joined the movement.

The refusal of career commitments becomes a conformity to the antiwork ideology. Failure becomes a mark of purity: paranoia, the assumed reality of police harassment, passivity kindness. Depersonalization and twilight states can be explained by the use of drugs. Impotence and nymphomania can be seen as expressions of sexual freedom. Homosexual trends can be talked out and even occasionally acted out in festive group occasions without shame and panic.[5]

The tolerance and lack of aggressiveness of the Hippies serve as tranquilizers on many personalities suspicious or anxiety-ridden in their interpersonal relations. The "saints" of the movement often do have a self-confident and benign quality that facilitates their rapport with an "uptight" neophyte. The importance of the group as a shelter, a source of nurturance, and a solvent of

---

[4] In bohemian bars and coffee shops, this may even have some prestige because it transforms the waitress into a priestess of the Rhythm and Blues cult.

[5] This is often the latent function or at least the unexpected consequence of the "orgy."

guilt facilitates a strong transference for a personality that has gained new self-esteem.

The Hippie collective offers the neophyte the possibility of increasing his rate of interaction with others—and at his own speed. "Keeping your cool" promotes a degree of self-control in personalities where this capacity has often been lacking. A legitimated self learns dissent without fearing exclusion. And then, like the child who discovers his parents are not perfect, the Hippie discovers the discrepancy between the values of the group and the limits of its organization.[6] For eventually he comes to realize that there are freaks and scoundrels as well as saints among the chosen, and that the difference from the square world is perhaps not so great as he first thought. A lasting heterosexual commitment; the subsequent realization that if one wants a good job, it is necessary to complete one's education and/or accept certain bureaucratic disciplines; a growing realization that one is not so young anymore and that the millennium is not for tomorrow—all these can lead the Hippie to "sell out" and rejoin the meritocracy.

Thus in the social reconversion of the Hippie his group experience will have been useful, and its cultivation of highbrow culture will have helped him maintain a familiarity with the academic atmosphere that is handy when he re-enlists in college. Sponsors on the fringe of the movement can often help him obtain a job in the mass communication industries, from managing record shops to writing advertising copy.

Evidence on the postgraduate lives of

Hippies is not easy to assemble. In 1967 a list was made of 67 Hippies who used to come to the Ibiza-Formentera islands every summer or live there all year around but had not shown up that summer. They had been described by informants as hard-core Hippies, whose period of activity in the movement ranged from one to four years. These Hippies were mostly American and British. Out of 25 women, one was dead, nine had married within the group, and another was living with a French sculptor. All but one of the husbands now hold relatively steady middle-class jobs. Of the 15 girls not known to be married, only six were involved in the type of employment that might permit the continuation of Hippie Life: three were photographers' models, two were night-club dancers, and one was a translator in Ibiza. Of the 42 men, one was dead, and only six could be said to be still pursuing the Hippie life. This does not mean that the teachers, the manager-owners of the macrobiotic restaurant, the published novelist, the American who had become an interior decorator in Germany, the nightclub manager in New York, have become entirely "straight." Some of these "reconverted" 35 have joined "swinging bohemia" and others "proper bohemia." What is crucial here is the assumption of a full-time job, i.e., coming to terms with the dominant society in ways other than sponging or part-time low-skill employment. Nor will the return to the community necessarily mean a simple conformity. There is more likely to be a marginal adjustment, and a potential relapse.

Over the last few years there has been a considerable increase in college enrollment in the Western world and especially in the U.S., drawn mainly from the lower-middle or working class. Once enrolled in college, these students benefit from a status that is already higher than that of their parents. Yet a good

[6] One of the major problems of the Hippie movement, as of all religious sects, is that success means wider membership, division of labor, hierarchy, all of which make much more difficult the indifferentiated and immediately-felt fraternity of the "tribe." There is a tendency for communities to explode and fragment when they reach a certain size.

number will not be able to maintain themselves in college and will have to settle for occupations involving a return to the status of their parents. Even a student from a middle-middle-class home who has entered a prestige Ivy League university will be exposed to this possibility. And since lower-middle- and even middle-middle-class families do not have the means to cushion the downward mobility of their children, achievement anxiety is likely to be most common among students from these two groups.

Only rarely will a student who has been able to enter college or graduate school fail because of lack of I.Q. He is much more likely to fail because of an incapacity to efficiently mobilize for the completion of tasks. College and graduate education require a capacity to work without direct supervision and to bear professional authority without fawning or rebellion, and perhaps most of all an ego strong enough to withstand the judgment of competent specialists. Given the crucial nature of the university degrees as passports to middle-middle- and upper-middle-class positions, and the broad equality of opportunity that exists in the university, the adolescent faces the possibility of a failure that could seem the failure of his whole personality. The better the university, the more talented and understanding the teaching staff and the psychological services, the more difficult it is to find excuses for one's failures. There is no place to hide.

Most students who drop out manage to reduce their level of aspiration without excessive bitterness. But those students who come from families with a strong desire for upward mobility, and whose status is threatened by discrepancies in income, occupation, style of life, and ethnic origin, are likely to experience a more difficult problem of identity. They are not as likely to find in their parents the models they need to balance their aspirations and their effective potential. The pressures of the meritocracy find a weaker ego structure, a greater fear of judgment, a greater anxiety as to what the future may contain. If the students come from non-religious, unitarian, "liberal," or radical homes, the response is likely to take the form of a New Left or Hippie commitment. And indeed, it is among the latter that we should find the bulk of the militants of the contrameritocracy.

Since those who choose the Hippie mode of adjustment as a *dominant* behavior pattern will represent no more than 1 percent of the student body, it is necessary to inquire why so small a movement has had such an impact upon the youth society and why it has become the *dominant* mode of bohemia.

Some of the impact upon youth can be explained by factors common to other movements: the chance to be taken seriously, to live dangerously (it takes "heart" to live the Hippie way), and the denial of competitive achievement.

The themes of love and total acceptance of the whole personality give legitimacy to the prolongation of a teen-age kind of gang that is immune to the centrifugal forces of heterosexual commitments and differential school and occupational achievements. Thus, while the Hippies attempt a "primarization of life" as their response to the increasing pressures of the meritocracy, they shift the grounds of achievement from areas where it is scarce and competitive to areas of the inner self where everybody can win.

Security and nurturance are offered without the member having to pay the price of conformity. Here is an opportunity for American youth to experience a peer group with which he is likely to have had little or no contact: a peer group where solidarity is untrammeled by any achievement criteria like sports, sexual prowess, fad leader-ship, etc.

Other "exclusives" of the Hippie movement are the heavy public expo-sure through the popularity of the Rock band and of young bards like the Beetles, Bob Dylan, Donovan, Joan Baez, Jimi Hendrix. Their music and songs are a self-righteous exaltation of love and animal spirits against the dull requirements of social structure. The Hippie cult of spontaneity and inde-pendence strikes a responsive chord among adolescents struggling to estab-lish their identity amid the pressures of school and family.

While Rock bands and bards sing the joy of having one's "mojo" working, the attitude of the Hippies toward sex suc-ceeds in removing some, if not much, of the confusion and anxiety attending sexuality among adolescents. And just as Puritanism began the movement to-ward a single sex standard (men abstain-ing as well as women), so the Hippies continue it (women enjoying sex as freely as men). The result is the same: a step toward effective equality between men and women. But the content of premarital sex—for this is the type of sex they are really concerned about—has been transformed. Sex has been demythified or desacralized. Hippies distinguish between "fucking" which is sheer sensual enjoyment,[7] without any commitment, and "making love," where there is some commitment even if it does not result in a lasting relationship. Hippie girls seem usually to prefer "making love," yet they can also indulge in the more detached type of sexual intercourse without feeling shame. Sex must be free, i.e., a woman must fully want it rather than merely bear it, con-sent to it, be seduced, or forced into it. To that extent even "fucking" is spirit-ualized, an act of the total self. Con-

trary to public fantasies, the end result of Hippie social pressure (not alto-gether intended) is not some loose promiscuity but more or less stable relationships, which are entered into on the basis of psychological compatibility without any fog of sexual deprivation and obsession.

For many boys the end of the "seduc-tion imperative" must indeed be a relief, but the main beneficiaries of the Hippie sexual patterns are the women. The Hippies at once upgrade the classical "female" values of love, nurturance, ex-pressiveness, while also offering girls more opportunities for rejecting the traditional female role.

Hippie life seems to resolve some of the strains that women experience in a period of changing sex roles: at once encouraged to be active and self-reliant in studies, job hunting, and choice of lover(s)—yet expected to be passive, attractive, and loyal to men even at the cost of some personal satisfaction. The Hippie woman *seems* to secure sexual satisfaction without shame, and to be free without loneliness. She can express "masculine trends" without fear of male rejection. Since it is easier for girls to find jobs in the square world—em-ployers being easier on the females of pariah groups—many a Hippie girl winds up as the breadwinner of the couple. Having set out to be an amazon she discovers she has become another Jewish mother.

Hence the Hippie movement is a preferred mode of deviance for girls, and their ratio in the Hippie com-munity (two or three boys for every girl) is much higher than in other pat-terns of deviance such as alcoholism, hard-drug addiction, suicide, profes-sional crime, or juvenile delinquency.

The most telling appeal of the Hippie movement is that it can relieve the pain of failure in the occupational world. Through drug experiences, for example, it has created a new respect among its

---

[7] The evidence collected so far does not seem to point to special success in attaining high levels of sexual enjoyment.

members for the nonrational and non-empirical aspects of human experience that challenge the value of occupational achievement and emphasize how much man deludes himself in thinking he can control his "social" destiny. Astrology, numerology, the whole folklore of good and bad "vibrations" are further instances of nonrational and nonempirical phenomena to which Hippies give credence. An air-tight system of beliefs thereby transforms the losers, the dispossessed, the subordinates, and the judged into a blessed group. Although in bureaucratic, capitalistic, war mongering Babylon they seem to be chained, they are superior to their captors and no prison can hold their souls. The first are really the last and the last the first, because they will not sell their birthright for the pottage of success. The Hippie belief system does not, like the radical political movements, have to suffer the consequences of the failures of ideology in Soviet Russia, China, or Cuba. It does not even have to achieve any concrete political goal, because on its own terms organizational success or failure means nothing.

One of the weaknesses of the American New Left is its youth orientation: every year brings its devotees closer to the fatal age of thirty. But the Hippies are on firmer ground for they deny the relevance of age, just as they deny the relevance of sex and status categories. And by declaring age irrelevant, they not only declare irrelevant the disabilities the square world attaches to age; they also offer their members eternal youth. Youth is transformed into a motivational category: the elect have it forever.

With all their potential appeal the Hippies have influenced so far only a small fraction of the Youth Society. Most lower-middle- and middle-middle-class youths have satisfactory family relations and have made sex-role identifications which permit integration to

occupational, marital, and community roles, and have ambitions that are within reach of their intellect and will power. Nevertheless, meritocratic pressures keep bearing down harder on the Youth Society and may make it vulnerable to the Hippie appeal if alternate structures do not appear.

Hippie Styles have radiated upward to older bohemia as it receives the mature failures and the temporary failures. The latter come to visit more than to stay. Their anger against the world that has passed them by, or friends who went on to better things, dissipates progressively as they learn the meaninglessness of what the squares call success. A whole world of freedom and new pleasures seems within easy reach. Although older bohemians tend to be sarcastic about Hippies (as the latter tend to be toward teenie-boppers, i.e. Hippies of high school age), they still feel obliged to defend them against the squares. Defending the Hippies is like the Hippies defending the Negroes, a way of validating one's group without seeming to.

The crucial appeal of the Hippies for older bohemia is that they offer the chance of renewed youth, a still open future. Hippies will relate to people whose age varies from 14 to 80, and bohemia will relate to the older Hippies (20 to 25).

Bohemia is, of course, an institution that antedates the Hippie movement by more than a century. Some of the Hippie themes, as Bennett Berger has pointed out, are as old as bohemia. What the Hippies have brought to bohemia is a mass base for the development of the underground press, a new militancy, an increase in self-righteousness, a relief from the ghetto feeling. The stress on high culture and the occasional interchange with the Jet Set permit condescension toward the middle-class meritocracy. Even if average in the occupational world, the bohemian is always culturally superior to the readers of the Time-Life art section.

Through mass media channels and the numerous shops that have sprung up in suburbia and around campuses, the Hippie movement has been providing a series of statements and attitudes, a style the young striver, at least in the professional, mass media, and intellectual trades (i.e. frequently high-ambition and high-uncertainty trades) can use as an *insurance policy against failure*. The heightening of meritocratic pressures leads to an increased need for a center that can reduce the tensions induced by frustrations while nevertheless keeping the individual from quitting. The Judeo-Christian churches used to provide this center for strivers and failures of all classes. Essentially, they were able to proclaim the salvation of those who had the proper motivation regardless of their success or lack of it in this vale of tears and thereby to reduce human failure to insignificance in the eyes of God.

It is largely in this sense that the Hippie movement—with mystique that places its basic dogmas outside the realm of rational discourse—can be termed a religious movement. It offers a way to *supreme success*, i.e. sincere, spontaneous, loving self-expression, doing what you want to do, if only you give up the games of bureaucratic existence.

Like all churches, the Hippie movement has a small core of devotees and theologians, its phonies and its saints, and a large mass of vacation, weekend, and Sunday members who return on Monday to the uncharitable competitive world of the job or graduate school. The Hippie commitment expresses itself through a nonactivist support for pacifism, the underdog, the rebellious youth; a style of life that dismisses as many of the conspicuous aspects of status as is possible; a pattern of speech that allows for the maximum amount of self-revelation and the maximum amount of support for others (we are

all sinners and love children together); a preference for direct confrontation rather than manipulation; a permissive attitude toward sex of which their somewhat over-weight wives do not seem to take notice or advantage; an attitude toward work that at once runs it down yet tries to make of it as much as possible a personal experience; a willingness to change career lines once one feels that there is little to be learned or created; a liking for the novel, the disconcerting, the far-out; a preference for marijuana and LSD as tranquilizers or as recreation, and for interactive adventure rather than getting things done; a tendency to transform the friendship network into a sort of Jewish family; in short an aesthetic and sentimental attitude toward life.

It is at least conceivable that the Hippie movement represents a groping toward a necessary adjustment of our social structure to the growing rationalization and "disenchantment" of life on the one hand and, on the other, to the decline in the *quality* of community experience that one can secure outside one's immediate family. So far, all the evidence points to the fact that the meritocracy, far from making life easier for the highly educated, increases the burdens upon those who have to assume high-uncertainty decisions.

Hippieism (or another movement less burdened by the contradictions between its ethics and the structural cost of living) may do for professional life and the increasing range of professionalized occupations what increased capital wealth, scientific technology, and the prestige of entrepreneurship did for bankruptcy: diminish its sting, make it a normal cost of business innovation to be assumed not just by the entrepreneur and his family, but also by the total society. The result was an increased rate of economic change and great increases in productivity. Thus Hippieism may decrease the cost of social change and create a sort of permanent revolution of manners and mores, more effective than political revolution.

Hippieism continues the Puritan tradition by putting the "burden of proof" upon the collectivity for the social forms that constrain the individual. It attempts to increase the capacity of people to relate more quickly at a level where they can give each other a support that is commensurate to the strains placed upon them by the meritocracy. Hence it may turn out to be necessary to the continued existence of the meritocracy. Just as Christianity, a religion proclaming the supremacy of the meek and the downtrodden, became the religion of some of the best officers and civil servants of the Empire, so Hippieism, instead of drawing only on the failures and semifailures of the system, may become a creed of its more effective servants. It serves as a response in the incessant search of mankind for forms of order which require less violence, less pain, and less contempt.

# 28

## Almost Endless Adolescence

### BENNETT M. BERGER

The problem of student unrest is rooted in the prolongation of adolescence in industrialized countries. But it should be understood that "adolescence" is only minimally a biological category; there are only a very few years between the onset of puberty and the achievement of the growth and strength it takes to do a man's or woman's work. As we know, however, culture has a habit of violating nature. Proto-adolescent behavior now begins even before puberty (which itself is occurring earlier) with the action—and the orientation—we call "pre-adolescent," while at the other end, technological, economic and social developments conspire to prolong the dependence of the young, to exclude them from many of the privileges and responsibilities of adult life, and therefore to *juvenilize* * them.

The casual evidence in support of this deep institutionalization of adolescence is diffuse and quite remarkable. It includes such spectacles as 6-foot, 200-pound "boys" who in another time and place might be founders of dynasties and world-conquerors (like Alexander of Macedon) cavorting on the fraternity house lawn hurling orange peels and bags of water at each other, while tolerant local police, who chucklingly *approve*, direct traffic around the battlefield. It includes the preservation of childlike cadence and intonation in voices otherwise physically mature. It includes the common—and growing—practice (even in official university documents) of opposing the word "student" to the word "adult"—as if students were by definition not adults, even as the median age of university students rises

* "Juvenilize": a verb I have devised to describe a process through which "childish"

behavior is induced or prolonged in persons who, in terms of their organic development, are capable of participating in adult affairs. If the process exists, there ought to a verb to describe it.

with the increase of the graduate student population.

Adolescence, then, is not the relatively fleeting "transitional stage" of textbook and popular lore but a substantial segment of life which may last 15 or 20 years, and if the meaning of adolescence is extended only slightly, it can last longer than that. I have in mind the age-graded norms and restrictions in those professions which require long years of advanced training, and in which the system of sponsorship makes the advancement of one's career dependent upon being somebody's "boy" perhaps well on toward one's middle-age—a fact not uncharacteristic of university faculties.

Much of the discussion of "youth culture" in recent years reflects the prolongation of adolescence, since it is not surprising that a period of life which may last from age 12 to age 35 might develop its own cultural style, its own traditions and its own sources of motivation, satisfaction—and dissatisfaction. There is thus an enormous stratum of persons caught in the tension between their experience of peak physical strength and sexual energy on the one hand, and their public definition as culturally "immature" on the other.

This tension is exacerbated by a contradictory tendency: while modern industrial conditions promote juvenilization and the prolongation of dependence, they also create an "older," more experienced youthful cohort. They have more and earlier experience with sex and drugs; they are far better educated than their parents were; urban life sophisticates them more quickly; television brings into their homes worlds of experience that would otherwise remain alien to them. Young people, then, are faced not only with the ambiguity of the adolescent role itself and its prolongation but with forces and conditions that, at least in some ways, make for *earlier* maturity. The youthful popula-

tion is a potentially explosive stratum because this society is ill-equipped to accommodate it within the status system.

Erik Erikson's well-known theory of the "psycho-social moratorium" of adolescence takes the facts of adolescent prolongation and transforms them into a triumph of civilization. By emphasizing the increased time provided for young persons to postpone commitments, to try on social roles and to play the game called "the search for identity," Erikson suggests that the moratorium on lasting adult responsibilities contributes to the development and elaboration of personal individuality. I have no wish to quarrel with Erikson's general thesis here; I have done so elsewhere. Instead, I want to emphasize a fact that is seemingly contradictory to Erikson's observations about the moratorium on adult commitments. Namely, there have actually been increasing and clearly documented pressures on young people for earlier and earlier occupational planning and choice. "Benjamin," ask that famous Graduate's parents repeatedly, "what are you going to *do?*" And the question is echoed by millions of prosperous American parents who, despite their affluence, cannot assure the future economic position of their heirs.

Logically, of course, prolonged identity play and early occupational choice cannot be encouraged at the same time; the fact is, they are. And like other ambiguous values (and most moral values are ambiguous, or can be made so), this pair permit different groups of youngsters to rationalize or justify the kinds of adaptations that differing circumstances in fact constrain them to make. The public attention generated by protesting youth in recent years (hippies, the New Left, black militants) obscures the fact that the majority of young people are still apparently able to tolerate the tensions of prolonged adolescence, to adjust to the adolescent role (primarily, student), to take some satisfaction from the gains it provides in irresponsibility (i.e., "freedom") and to sail smoothly through high school into college where they choose the majors, get the grades and eventually the certifications for the occupations which they want, which want them and which higher education is equipped to provide them—degrees in education, business, engineering, dentistry and so on.

For others, however, the search for identity (quote, unquote) functions as a substitute for an occupational orientation; it gives them something "serious" to do while coping with their problems of sex, education, family and career. In college most of these people tend to major in the humanities or social sciences (particularly sociology) where they may take 10 years or more between the time they enter as freshmen, drop out, return, graduate and go on to pursue graduate degrees or give up on them entirely. I will return to this matter, but for the moment I want to make two general points: (1) that the contradictions create understandable tensions in the young and feed their appetite to discover "hypocrisy" in their elders; (2) that this condition is largely beyond the control of the universities; it is generated by the exigencies of a "post-industrial" society which uses institutions of higher education as warehouses for the temporary storage of a population it knows not what else to do with.

The situation has become critical over the past 10 years because the enormous numbers of the young (even small percentages of which yield formidable numbers of troops for worthy causes) and their concentration (in schools and cities) have promoted easy communication and a sense of group solidarity among them. Numbers, concentration and communication regarding common grievances have made increasingly viable, in almost precisely the

way in which Karl Marx described the development of class consciousness among workers, the creation and maintenance of "deviant subcultures" of youth.

This youthful population is "available" for recruitment to moral causes because their marginal, ambiguous position in the social structure renders them sensitive to moral inconsistencies (note their talent for perceiving "hypocrisy"), because the major framework of their experience ("education") emphasizes "ideal" aspects of the culture and because their exclusion from adult responsibilities means that they are generally unrestrained by the institutional ties and commitments which normally function as a brake upon purely moral feeling; they also have the time for it.

The two great public issues of the decade (the Vietnam war and the rights of despised minorities) have been especially suited to enlist the militant predispositions of the young precisely because these issues are clearly moral issues. To take a strong "position" on these issues requires no great *expertise* or familiarity with arcane facts. And the moral fervor involved in taking such a position nicely reflects our traditional age-graded culture to the extent that it identifies virtue with "idealism," unspoiledness and innocence, precisely the qualities adults like to associate with the young.

It is almost as if the young, in the unconscious division of labor which occurs in all societies, were delegated the role of "moral organ" of society—what with all the grown-ups being too busy running the bureaucracies of the world (with their inevitable compromises, deals, gives and takes) to concern themselves with "ideals." This even makes a sort of good structural sense because the unanchored character of the young (that is, their relative unfetteredness to family, community and career) fits them to perform their "ideal" functions—in the same sense and for the same reason that Plato denied normal family life to his philosopher-kings and the Roman Catholic Church denies it to their priests.

It is the combination of moral sensitivity and alienation that accounts both for the extreme juvenophile postures of moral critics like Edgar Friedenberg, Paul Goodman and John Seeley (which sometimes reach the belief that the young are simply better people than the old or middle-aged, and hence even a belief in juvenocracy) and the fear of and hostility toward militant youth by writers epitomized by Lewis Feuer in his new book on student movements. In the latter view, the idealism of the young becomes corrupt, violent, terroristic and destructive precisely because, alienated, detached from institutions, youth are not "responsible"—that is, not accountable for the consequences of their moral zealotry upon the groups and organizations affected by it.

So one is tempted to say that society may just have to accept youth's irresponsibility if it values their moral contributions. But evidence suggests that adult society is in general sympathetic neither to their moral proddings nor toward granting the young any greater responsibility in public affairs. Research by English sociologist Frank Musgrove clearly documents that adults are unwilling to grant real responsibilities any earlier to the young, and there is good reason to believe the same is true in the United States, as is suggested by the repeated failures, until last year, of the movement to lower the voting age to 18. And as for the "idealism" of youth, when it goes beyond the innocent virtues of praising honesty, being loyal, true and brave and helping old ladies across the street, to serious moral involvements promoting their own group interests ("student power") or those of the domestic or "third world" dispos-

sessed, the shine of their "idealism" is likely to tarnish rather quickly.

Moreover, the moral activism of youth *is* sometimes vulnerable to attack on several counts. The "morality" of a political action, for example, is weakened when it has a self-congratulatory character (and the tendency to produce a holier-than-thou vanity in the actor). It also loses something when it does not involve substantial risk of personal interests or freedom (as it unambiguously *does* with the young only in the case of draft resisters). In the end, along with the society's prolongation of adolescence and encouragement of "the search for identity," continuing praise of the young for their "idealism" (except when it becomes serious) and continuing appeals to them to behave "responsibly"—in the face of repeated refusal to grant them real responsibilities (except in war)—are understandable as parts of the cultural armory supporting the process of juvenilization.

Colleges, universities and their environs are the places apparently designated by society as the primary locations where this armory is to be expended. It is clear that the schools, particularly institutions of higher learning, are increasingly being asked by society to perform a kind of holding operation for it. The major propaganda campaign to encourage students not to drop out of high school is significant less for the jobs which staying that last year or two in high school will qualify one for than it is for the reduced pressure it creates on labor markets unable to absorb unskilled 16- and 17-year-olds. The military institutions, through the draft, help store (and train) much of the working-class young, and the colleges and universities prepare many of the heirs of the middle classes for careers in business, the professions and the semiprofessions. But higher education also gets the lion's share of the identity seekers: those sensitive children of the affluent, less interested in preparing themselves for occupations which the universities are competent to prepare them for than in transcending or trading in the stigmata of their bourgeois backgrounds (work ethic, money-grubbing, status-seeking) for a more "meaningful" life.

It is these students who are heavily represented among the student activists and among whom the cry for "relevance" is heard most insistently. Does it seem odd that this cry should be coming from those students who are *least* interested in the curricula whose relevance is palpable, at least with respect to occupations? Not if one observes that many of these students are, in a sense, classically "intellectuals"—that is, oriented toward statuses or positions for which the universities (as well as other major institutions) have seldom been able or competent to provide certification.

The statuses such students want are those to which one appoints oneself or which one drifts into: artist, critic, writer, intellectual, journalist, revolutionist, philosopher. And these statuses have been undermined for two generations or more by technical and bureaucratic élites whose training has become increasingly specialized and "scientific." In this context the cry for relevance is a protest against technical, value-neutral education whose product (salable skills or the posture of uncommitment) contributes nothing to the search by these students for "identity" and "meaningful experience."

Adding final insult to the injury of the threatened replacement of traditional humanistic intellectuals by technical élites is the ironic transformation of some of their traditional curricula (social sciences particularly) into instruments useful to the "power structure" or "the establishment" in pursuing its own ends. It makes no sense to call a curriculum "irrelevant" and then to turn right around and accuse its chief practitioners of "selling out"; the powerful do not squander their money so easily. The ironic point, then, is not that these curricula are "irrelevant" but that they are far *too* relevant to the support of interests to which the left is opposed.

The villains here are the methodological orthodoxies of the social sciences: their commitment to objectivity, detachment and the "separation" between facts and values. In the view of radical students, these orthodoxies rationalize the official diffidence of social scientists regarding the social consequences of their research, a diffidence which (conveniently—and profitably—for social scientists, goes the argument) promotes the interests of the established and the powerful. This is far from the whole truth, of course. There is plenty of research, supported by establishments, whose results offer the establishment little comfort. But like other "nonpartisan" or value-neutral practices and procedures, the methodological orthodoxies of the social sciences do tend in general to support established interests, simply because the powerful, in command of greater resources and facilities, are better able to make use of "facts" than the weak, and because avoidance of ideological controversy tends to perpetuate the inequities of the status quo.

But the demands for a more activist and "committed" social science and for social scientists to function as advocates for oppressed and subordinated groups may not be the best way of correcting the inequities. A thorough *doctrinal* politicization of social science in the university is likely to mean the total loss of whatever little insulation remains against the ideological controversies rending the larger society; and the probable result would be that the university, instead of being more liberal than the society as a whole, would more accurately reflect the still-burgeoning reactionary mood of the country.

For students who tend to be "around" a university for a long time—the 10-year period mentioned earlier is not uncommon—the university tends to become a kind of "home territory," the place where they really live. They experience the university less as an élite training institution than as a political community in which "members" have a kind of quasi-"citizenship" which, if one believes in democratic process, means a right to a legitimate political voice in its government.

This conception of the university is quite discrepant with the conception held by most faculty members and administrators. To most faculty members the university is the élite training institution to which students who are both willing and able come to absorb intellectual disciplines—"ologies"—taught by skilled and certified professionals whose competences are defined by and limited to those certifications. But which way one sees the university—as a political community or as an élite training institution—is not purely a matter of ideological preference.

The fact seems to be that where training and certification and performance in politically neutral skills are clearest, the more conservative view is virtually unchallenged. This is true not only for dentistry and mathematics but for athletics, too. Presumably many militant blacks are not for any kind of a quota system with respect to varsity teams, and presumably football players in the huddle do not demand a voice in the decisions that shape their lives. But where what one's education confers upon one is a smattering of "high culture" or "civilized manners" or the detached sensibility and ethics of a science whose benefits, like other wealth, are not equitably distributed—in short, where the main result of liberal education is *Weltanschauung*—it indeed has "political" consequences.

These consequences were not con-

troversial so long as the culture of the university was fairly homogeneous and so long as the "aliens" it admitted were eager to absorb that culture. They have become controversial in recent years because the democratization of higher education has revealed the "class" character of academic culture and because of the appearance on the campus of students who do not share and/or do not aspire to that culture. These newcomers have arrived in sufficiently large numbers to mount a serious challenge to the hegemony of traditional academic culture.

Despite their many differences, the new militant "ethnic" students and their supporters among "white radicals," "street people," hippies and other young people on the left have in common their anti-academicism, which is the campus version of the anti-establishment outlook. This is true notwithstanding the fact that the academy has been the most liberal sector of establishment thought and the most sympathetic to at least some of the aspirations of dissident students. Partly, of course, their hostility to the academy is rooted in the fact that the university is where they're at, the institutional location in which they have to work through their prolonged adolescence and the problems associated with it. But beyond this, there is real conflict between the traditional criteria of academic performance and what dissident students ·demand from academic life.

Research suggests that most of the white radical students have grown up in a milieu where "intellectual" matters were discussed, where books were probably present in their homes, where middle-class manners and style were their birthright, and where, therefore, they learned how to "talk"—that is, where they developed the sort of verbal facility enabling them to do well enough in high school and to seem like promising "college material" if only because they look and sound much like college students have always looked and sounded. With the ascendence of the view that everybody has a right to a higher education (along with the fact that there's no place else to send well-born adolescents), most of them wind up in colleges and universities.

Some of them, despite their verbal facility, are not really bright; many others, despite their ability to get good college grades, strongly resist "conforming" to many of the requirements for professional certification which they demean as mere "socialization." Confronted by academic demands for rigor in their thinking, for sufficient discipline to master a systematic body of knowledge, for evidence that they can maintain a line of logical thinking beyond one or two propositions, and bring evidence systematically to bear upon a problem, many of them are found seriously wanting—some because they are not bright enough, others because they think it a point of honor to resist the intellectual demands made on them.

When their numbers are large enough to enable them to turn to each other for mutual support, it is not surprising that they should collectively turn against the system of criteria which derogates them and, in a manner not unanalogous to the "reaction formation" of slum delinquents who develop a subculture in opposition to middle-class school norms which judge them inadequate, develop an anti-academic viewpoint which defines abstraction, logical order, detachment, objectivity and systematic thinking as the cognitive armory of a repressive society, productive of alienation, personal rigidity and truncated capacity for feeling.

Preoccupied as most of these students are with "identity problems" and moral protest, it is again not surprising that many of them should be less interested in the mastery of academic disciplines, even if they have the ability, than in pursuing what they are likely to call "gut-issues" or nitty-gritty. The kinds of problems they apparently are interested in studying can be inferred from the examination of almost any "Free University" brochure, and what these add up to is a sort of extension division for the underground: practical, topical "rap sessions" on Vietnam, civil rights, encounter groups, pottery, psychedelics, macrobiotics, Eastern religion, rock music and so on.

In the conflict with the established interests of science and scholarship in the university, radical students do win significant victories. New courses do get approved; experimental curricula do get tried out; students do get appointed to important committees; greater weight is attached to teaching in the appointment and promotion of faculty members. But large numbers of these radical students, exhausted by conflict and depressed by negative criticism, drop out of school. In dropping out, however, they do not immediately disappear into the labor market. They tend to remain in the university community, employed occasionally or part time in dead-end jobs, living in furnished rooms or communal houses near the university, and most important for my purposes here, still participating in the marginal student culture which they know so well.

Their participation in this culture is made possible to some extent by the fact that their youth protects them from the degrading consequences of being poor and having no regular or "approved" status in the community. Part of the age-grading system which postpones adulthood is the temporary protection of the young against the stigmata which, for older people, are normally attached to poverty. But over time, this group of "nonstudents" can be regarded as downward mobile, and thereby hangs an interesting prospect.

The United States has no major tradition of large-scale downward mobility.

The only major image of intergenerational decline is associated with decadent aristocratic families in ruined Southern mansions. Given the general tendency for downwardly mobile groups to resent the system which derogates them, and given the fact that the channels of upward mobility today are largely through higher education, the hostility to the university of these radical, middle-class "nonstudents" is probably maintained even after they leave it. The irony is that in dropping out, the hippie and New Left children of the middle classes provide opportunity for the upward mobility of the new black and other ambitious "disadvantaged" students.

The blacks and other ethnic militants are presently using higher education in a manner different from that in which their predecessors from the lower class used it. For earlier ethnics, the university served as a channel of mobility for *individuals* from the talented poor; today, it is sought as a means of collective mobility. There are two aspects to this movement. There is the emphasis on ethnic studies programs designed to provide the members of the respective ethnic groups with a sense of pride in their history and culture, and there are the demands that the university play a more active role in ameliorating suffering in the ghettos, not merely through programs of research which exploit the cooperation of ghetto residents without helping them measurably, but by taking the university off the campus, bringing it to them, in their terms, on their turf, for their own purposes.

In the struggle to achieve the ends of the militants, black and white, the traditional university is very vulnerable because the militants have great leverage. Just as the blacks can conceivably turn the urban core into a guerrilla battleground, militant students can bring the universities to the proverbial grinding halt. Continual rallies, classroom disruptions, picket lines, building

seizures, student intimidation and general paranoia (to say nothing of the almost continual meetings by faculty and administration committees to cope with the crises and the continual corridor and coffee room gossip by knots of faculty members) can bring the teaching and other academic functions of the university to a virtual standstill.

This prospect raises seriously for the first time the question of whether the traditional university, as we know it, is an expendable institution. And another question, as well: Is it possible that a decision has been made somewhere that it is better to risk the destruction of the university by confining the unrest to the campus than to allow it to spill over into more critical institutions? Pickets, sit-ins, building seizures and non-negotiable demands are one thing on the campuses. Imagine them at C.B.S. on Madison Avenue: no TV until S.D.S. gets equal time; at the Stock Exchange: the ticker tape does not roll until corporation X gets rid of its South African holdings; at the headquarters of the Bank of America: no depositors get through the doors until interest-free loans are made to renovate the ghettos. There would be machine guns in the streets in no time at all!

In 1969, despite the tear gas and the National Guard, it is still hard to imagine tanks and machine guns used against student radicals so long as their militance is confined to the campus. Because if they do close the universities down, exactly who would miss them? The most practical functions the university performs and its activities which are most directly relevant to the national economy (engineering, science, law, medicine, etc.) could be transferred to the private sector. The beginnings of such a transfer are apparent already in the educational functions carried on by private foundations, institutes and industrial corporations.

And if the departments of English and history and political science and sociology and art and so on closed tight shut tomorrow, who would miss them? Aside from the implication of some social science departments in the military-industrial complex, the studies in humanities and social science departments are civilized luxuries with very few sources of government or business support. The student radicals have little sympathy for them and there is probably even less sympathy for them among the students' severest critics. These days, even conservative legislators, in the same breath that they denounce student militance, will quickly add, "Of course, this doesn't mean that there isn't plenty wrong with the university; there is." And if the student revolution can be bought off by substituting Bob Dylan for Dylan Thomas, McLuhan for Freud, Marcuse for Plato, rock for Bach, black culture for Greek culture, rap sessions for formal examinations, how many will care? Who needs high culture anyway? For the radicals it's an instrument of class oppression, and their oppressors, at least in America, have never been too keen on it anyway, except as a tax dodge.

Short of machine guns in the streets and outright revolution, what one can expect to see over the next decade in academic life is greater adaptation by the university to the new kinds of students it must serve and to the new publics whose anticipated support or hostility it must take into account in its planning. By the new students I mean ghetto youth, middle-class white radicals and the identity seekers. By the new publics I mean those millions of citizens whose taxes support the great state universities but who never thought of the university as "theirs" until its politicization encouraged ambitious politicians to call this fact to their attention. Having once been reminded (by Governor Reagan and others), the voters are not likely to forget it soon.

If it comes about, this adaptation is likely to occur in a manner not dissimilar to that in which the major political parties have adapted to third-party movements in the larger political community: by isolating the *most* radical through the adoption of some of their programs and demands, while at the same time adopting severe and punitive policies toward the more intransigent and violence-prone who are still unsatisfied.

For ghetto youth then, there will be more ethnic studies programs and compensatory admissions and grading policies and practices and more energetic recruiting of ethnic students and faculty. But there will be less indecision or tolerance in the handling of sit-ins, seizures and other disruptions. For the radicals (ethnic as well as middle-class white), there will be greater emphasis on programs granting academic credit for extension-type activities such as tutoring of ghetto children, neighborhood seminars on consumer savvy and community organization. For the identity seekers there will be more encounter groups, more classes emphasizing "openness and honesty" in dialogue, more experiments with less structured curricula and residential communities, more "retreats," more student-initiated courses on subjects which engage their sense of "relevance" to their interests, from sex to drugs to rock. For all, there will be further loosening of the *in loco parentis* restrictions which hardly anybody in the university believes in anymore, and a little more student power (at least influence) on faculty and administrative committees. All this, combined with a more effective public-relations campaign explaining the mission of the university and its problems in coping with the consequences of prolonged adolescence, may just bring about a semblance of peace on the campus. But without peace in Vietnam, it will be an uneasy peace at best.

There will be opposition. Academic conservatives will see in these new programs the prospect of the dilution or outright abandonment of traditional standards of scholarship. The legitimation of ethnicity, the amelioration of suffering by the poor and the search for identity by the young may all be noble endeavors, they will say, but the major functions of the university are the creation and transmission of systematic bodies of abstract knowledge. Political conservatives will see in these programs harbingers of social changes which they oppose. Militant students imply more leaders and troops for restive ghettos; "the search for identity" and the self-exploratory activities the phrase suggests are redolent of the "liberalism," "permissiveness" and self-indulgence offensive to the traditional Protestant ethic which "made this country great."

Yet academic conservatives might well be reminded that the university is facing radically transformed constituencies, that academic disciplines which are well institutionalized and "traditional" today were themselves academically born in the blood of earlier periods of such transformations and that they were initially opposed by still more "traditional" fields. Political conservatives might well be reminded that student unrest was not invented by outside agitators, that its source is in social conditions conservatives affirm and that it is not repressible short of military measures. The alternatives to the adaptable university involve blood on the quad and an expendable university.

# B The Community

## INTRODUCTION

Communities are populations that occupy a common territory and gain a living from the environment through their cooperative efforts. For primitive man the community was often simply a temporary settlement of a few families, who stopped in one place until they used up the available food supply, hunting birds and animals and gathering whatever fruits, nuts, and roots grew there, and then moved to a new location for a new supply of food. Permanent settlements of large populations became possible with the invention of agriculture. In general the more fertile and extensive the farmland and the more efficient the means of transportation, the larger the human settlements that became possible. In larger settlements a more complex division of labor developed and men became more dependent upon one another. The large cities of modern society require a high degree of coordination of individual activities in order to achieve the intricate integration of the whole required for their effective functioning.

The community, or the neighborhood if the settlement is very large, is the next social group beyond the family that the individual encounters as he grows up. The sociologist Charles Horton Cooley pointed out the importance of the small community or neighborhood in the formation of individual personality and in socializing children and young people to the culture of the group. The quality of community life, therefore, affects the development of individual personality as well as the group's efficiency in gaining a living from nature.

Sidney Aronson takes a fresh look at the city, the dominant form of community life in today's industrialized societies, reminding us that the city has always been the center of man's civilization, the place where all the arts and artifacts of civilized cultures have been created. He points out that they serve as the creative centers of societies because of the great variety of stimuli they provide man, the wide range of choices they present to urban dwellers, and the possibility of finding audiences or associates for almost any kind of activity. Variety, stimulation, creativity, and privacy, Aronson reminds us, are positive values of urban life which tend to be ignored by critics of cities today.

While the world is becoming urbanized today, the advanced industrial countries are becoming metropolitanized. William Dobriner shows how the communities of the United States, for example, are becoming organized into metropolitan areas around a small number of major cities. In such metropolitan areas a division of labor develops between communities. Central cities about which the metropolitan areas are integrated specialize in finance, in wholesale and retail trade, and, to a certain extent, in manufacturing. Smaller cities become specialized manufacturing satellites of the central cities, or sometimes residential suburbs, while new suburbs spring up rapidly in a "residential ring" of the metropolitan area. Communities on the "rur-urban fringe" of the metropolitan area may become residences of executives and professionals who can afford to travel long distances to work in the central cities, homes of people working in the satellite cities, or specialized suppliers of agricultural products or recreational facilities to the populations of the metropolitan areas. Small towns beyond the metropolitan areas, many of which are losing population even as the national population grows, sometimes disappear altogether, as when dams are built across valleys to provide water and electric power for the city and areas of the countryside are reforested to furnish recreation facilities for city people.

Dennis Wrong reviews the sociological literature on the residential suburbs of American cities and points out that many characteristics sociologists have attributed specifically to "suburban living" have been simply life-ways of the middle class, which was moving to the suburbs from the central cities in great numbers immediately after World War II. The high degree of physical and social mobility characteristic of their lives, Wrong says, accounts for much of the insecurity, status seeking, compulsive conformity, and "togetherness" which sociologists found in the lives of these people. Today, Wrong points out, even the middle-class character of the suburbs is changing as working-class families move into them in larger and larger numbers.

Arthur Vidich and Joseph Bensman describe the integration of the small country town into the metropolitan economy. The town they studied specialized in one agricultural product, milk, which was sold on a metropolitan market, while most of the products consumed by the community were imported from the metropolitan centers. The country town was also a residence for families of men working in the industries of nearby cities. The small town, Vidich and Bensman point out, even imports its image of itself from the urban centers. Articles, stories in magazines, and programs on radio and television which describe and evaluate small-town life are assembled in the editorial rooms and studios located in the metropolitan centers and transmitted to the countryside.

# 29

# The City: Illusion and Reality

### SIDNEY M. ARONSON

How different would our view of the city be, had the Jewish scribes who wrote the Book of Genesis been urban dwellers rather than members of a no-

From *Dissent*, 1971. Reprinted by permission.

madic, desert tribe; had they located paradise amid the marketplace or the theatre of a thriving town rather than in a pastoral Garden of Eden; had they not held up to an impressionable posterity the "cities of the valley"—Sodom and Gemorah—as archetypal images of appalling evil? We can only speculate on the answers to such questions while knowing full well that we are both the spiritual and lineal descendants of people who deeply distrusted the life of cities and who imaged the Golden Age of freedom and happiness as a sylvan oasis. The City of God was a self-evident self-contradiction.

Historical attempts to deal with the city's origins have always been in the nature of guesswork and ingenious speculation based on the most fragmentary of evidence. For the first few thousand years of its existence the archaelogical record of city life is a record more of gaps than of facts. Nor has the analysis of the modern city always been on firmer ground informed as so much of it has been, especially in America, by the anti-urban bias that pervades so much of our history and our social attitudes, a bias that has effectively obscured the nature of the city and led to an obsession with its worst features to the almost complete neglect of its best. The standard, contemporary sociological view of the city sees it rather as a human theatre of horrors than as the matrix of inexhaustible choices and opportunities, the provider of endless stimulation, and the seedbed of all that goes by the name "civilization."

Yet the city's origin and its early history may be worth brief attention if only because such an examination may uncover aspects of the city which have too long been obscured or casually assumed. Then too, an historical perspective should make it easier to avoid that reverse evolutionary thinking which, beginning with Hesiod and the Book of Genesis, has placed man's Golden Age in the past and has gone on to yearn for what Roger Starr has called the "City of the Imagination." This is not to deny the real things that are wrong with the cities of today but to suggest that that is only one facet of the story and not perhaps the most important one.

For most of his time on earth man was a roving hunter and predator, forced to wander and to forage for food because the latter was so limited and the competition for it so fierce that even the most bountifully supplied areas could support no more than a handful of people. The first permanent settlements (not cities, to be sure) probably began as resting places in a nomadic existence and as burial sites. At some point in the development of man's mind, he had attributed to the spirits of the dead such powers over the living that the former had to be ceremonially buried, commemorated, and propitiated. What converted these temporary settlements into permanent ones was that series of events, occurring during the Neolithic Period, which we are justified in calling the "Agricultural Revolution": the domestication of plants and animals and, ultimately, man himself.

The resulting increased food production made possible the support of a larger population than ever before and made it both necessary and possible to excuse some of the adult population from the food-growing process and to divert their energies to the process and storage of food and to the maintenance of the settlement itself. While the greater food supply made such specialization possible, the specialization, in its turn, led to more efficient food production and utilization thus setting in motion those cycles, vicious or beneficial depending on one's point of view, that have remained with us to this day. Lewis Mumford's definition of the city as a container of containers reflects implicitly the greater complexity and differentiation of village life.

The invention of the plow and, perhaps, of the political institution of kingship made it possible for the village to develop into the town, and ultimately the city, by producing, on the one hand, a food surplus large enough to free whole groups from direct involvement with food production and, on the other, by creating an instrumentality that could effectively organize and utilize surplus resources. In consequence the village artisan, once a part-time peasant, became a full-time craftsman producing for a more or less dependable "market." It was not long thereafter that fairs and regular markets supplanted the system of barter between individuals.

Whether between the village and the true city there is an homology or only an analogy remains a matter of dispute among historians and urbanists but we know that in the city the natural features of the landscape to which the villages resorted for protection gave way to well-planned fortresses or citadels, temporary markets, to permanent, regulated ones (the sine qua non of a city for Max Weber), and wooden altars to imposing stone temples. At this point in history political institutions were not differentiated from religious ones—the king was at the same time the chief priest of the cult and was often himself considered divine—and under the threat of religious sanction the people of the city and the surrounding hinterland that depended on it (the suburbs of an earlier era) could be made to build those imposing monuments that ever since have denoted the beginnings of civilization. Civilization is coeval with the city; the etymological connection between the two words is far from gratuitous.

For Emile Durkheim, on the other hand, the key to urbanism was not in monuments or material artifacts but in the social processes that underlay them and, specifically, in the division of labor that made possible such complex living arrangements. For Durkheim the city was, above all, a place where different people did different things and by so doing developed relationships of mutual interdependence. But this is tantamount to saying that the city by its very nature creates diversity. For the division of labor, by producing dif-

ferent kinds of work, created different personalities since every work situation shapes human character congruent with its own demands. Thus, the greater the variety of social processes in a society, the more distinctive and varied are the psychological types that it exhibits. What could truly be said of the peasant, that he "looks into his neighbor's face and sees his own image" was no longer true for the city dweller. The city thus became an inexhaustible spectacle.

Concomitent with this increase in size and diversity that in part defines the city went an equal increase in "impersonality" or "anonymity." Where a large population inhabits a confined area (and most premodern cities were quite small in area primarily because of the needs of defense), it becomes impossible for the individual, in Weber's terms, to have "personal reciprocal acquaintance" of all or any substantial part of his fellow inhabitants. In other words, the individual often finds himself a stranger in his own city, an insight forcefully developed by Weber's contemporary Georg Simmel.

In considering those features of the city that seemed to make urban living so eminently desirable to many of our ancestors, we must be careful to distinguish between the advantages of life in permanent settlements as such from the advantages to be derived from living in true cities. Many of the benefits of settled life were available to the inhabitants of hamlets and villages in almost equal measure to city dwellers. These included a respite from wandering, relative safety, and the comforts of a permanent dwelling. What the city added to these and what the village and hamlet could never supply were diversity, a superabundance of choices, an incomparable range of opportunities: economic, political, artistic, and religious; and a setting in which one could exploit and exchange the fruits of one's creativity, whatever its form. Further-more, there was the stimulation that inevitably arose from living among diverse types of people, of being at the center of power, commerce, and the arts, of meeting visitors from the other great cities of the world. To live in a city was thus to be present at the creation and the endless recreation of all that the word civilization connotes.

But the advantages of life in permanent settlements were not all on the side of the city nor did the advantages of the city necessarily increase in lineal fashion as the latter grew larger. Village life meant more comfortable and secure living for its inhabitants at the same time that its small size permitted villages the luxury of certain dangerous habits. The sloppy housekeeping customs villagers carried over from their nomadic past were tolerable in the relatively uncrowded conditions of village life. Nor did villages and small towns present the kind of tempting targets to marauders as did wealthy and populous cities. If the city nurtured civilization it also and simultaneously encouraged warfare, often for the same reasons.

Cities were thus beset by hazards within and enemies without. The more people were crowded into urban centers the more hazardous did the traditional habits of housekeeping become. The disposal of refuse was not perceived as a problem by the early urbanite, in fact, in the ancient city, human excreta and other wastes were customarily thrown into the street in front of one's dwelling and were removed only through biological degrading and the medium of rain, or, occasionally, of flooding. The hazards to health posed by this method of waste disposal are obvious and plagues were correspondingly common. The appearance of New York City's streets during the sanitation strike of early 1969 may give one a faint idea of what the streets of ancient metropoli

were like year after year, although, in fairness, most of the waste produced in the premodern city was of an organic character and did ultimately decay.

Even the introduction of indoor plumbing—which occurred as early as the Minoan Period (circa 3000 B.C.), did little to improve the problem of waste disposal since it was available only to the rich while the poor continued to use the streets as a convenient refuse dump. This was true even in Athens of Pericles and the Rome of the Empire. Meanwhile, the invention of the high-rise apartment building—the Roman "Insula"—so discouraged what little care had been exercised in the process of garbage disposal that new laws had to be passed, forbidding the emptying of chamber pots from the upper story windows of such buildings onto whatever unfortunates happened to be passing in the streets below. And, as has been a persistent irony of technological innovation, what improved one condition simultaneously worsened another: the water which flushed privies in Roman Insulae was later used for washing and cooking drawn as it was from the same conduits and streams. And so the city became the seedbed of disease and pestilence as well as of civilzation, able to maintain its population only as a result of high birth rates and of a constant influx of rural inhabitans drawn by the city's myriad attractions and opportunities.

The greatest threat to early cities was, however, other cities. "In reality," wrote Plato, "every city is in a natural state of war with every other." For urbanization and the political development that accompanied it also produced the capacity to organize larger and more effective armies than ever before. In consequence, cities, the storehouses of wealth and political power, became irresistible targets for those who sought one or another or both. The history of civilization is replete with the sacking and plundering of great cities, the slaughter and enslavement of their inhabitants. In premodern time Babylon, Nineveh, Carthage, Rome, Jerusalem, Ch'angan, Baghdad, and Constantinople all suffered such a fate at least once.

One of the more paradoxical aspects of the city's history, considering its seminal role in the rise of civilization, is what a relatively small percentage of the world's total population has actually resided in cities. Most of the people who have ever inhabited this planet have not been urbanites. Until the 19th century all but a relatively few of the world's cities, by the standards of today, were no larger than fair-sized towns. The earliest cities, those that arose some 5,000 to 8,000 years ago in the Mesopotamian culture area, probably did not contain populations much in excess of 5,000. Even in the first millennium B.C., when city life was at least 2,000 years old it was only the exceptional urban center that could boast a population larger than some 30,000, although Periclean Athens at the height of its power and influence may have had a population of as much as 300,000 including slaves and metics. The only two premodern cities that seem at all comparable to those of the industrial age are Rome of the second century A.D. (especially the period of Trajan) and Ch'angan of the first half of the T'ang Dynasty, each of which appears to have had a million or more inhabitants. But even in the heyday of the Roman Empire and the urban development it fostered most cities were modest in size and most Romans did not live in them. With the invasions from the North, the disintegration of the Roman Empire, and the consequent disruption of commerce, urban life in Western Europe entered on a half-millennium period of decline as many city-dwellers returned to the towns and the countryside and took up once again an agricultural life. Many cities, including

Rome itself, were reduced to a fraction of the population they had once supported. It was not until the 10th century, with the reopening of the Mediterranean to western traders and the general revival of economic life consequent upon that event, that cities entered upon a renaissance. Most of the later Medieval and Renaissance cities of Europe contained fewer than 50,000 inhabitants. As had always been the case up to that time the vast majority of the world's population lived physically if not politically, economically, and spiritually apart from the cities.

The Industrial Revolution radically and rapidly changed that state of affairs. Just as the expansion of commerce and trade had spurred urbanization in the preindustrial age so did industrialization lead, everywhere in the world, to the rise and growth of the modern city. Beginning in England in the late 18th century the Industrial Revolution spread first to Western Europe and then to America despite Thomas Jefferson's admonition to "let our workshops remain in Europe." It brought in its wake a profound and thoroughgoing restructuring of virtually every human activity and social institution—in agriculture, manufacturing, business organization, transportation, communication, government, religion, and family life. The city-building which the Industrial Revolution set in motion differed from that of the preindustrial age in that industrialization and its accompanying changes made possible the concentration of millions of people within the metropolis itself and of further millions, economically and socially dependent on the city, in adjacent suburbs. We have at last reached the point at which every region of the world has its megalopolis and it has become customary to speak of the "urbanization of the world," to refer to the spread and growth of cities as "irreversible and inexorable" and to predict that eventually three fourths of the world's population will live in cities of more than 500,000 inhabitants.

The industrial metropolis that was often superimposed on an existing pre-industrial city overwhelmed existing urban institutions that had, at best, been no more than adequate to their tasks. This would have been true even if the source of the rapidly increasing urban population had been primarily or entirely from the natural increase of the existing urban population (that is, from an accelerating increase of the birth rate over the death rate). But, in fact, most of the tens of millions who flooded into the cities in the aftermath of industrialization were drawn from the ranks of peasants, farmers, and landless agricultural laborers for whom the countryside had no further use or who had no further use for the countryside. Throughout the Western world, and especially in the United States, the rustic, the yokel, the country bumpkin —scarcely characterized by "urbanity" —became the typical new city dweller. In the American case the inevitable problems posed by the differing values and life styles of urban-born and rural-born groups were aggravated by the fact of the huge foreign immigration that began in earnest after the mid-1840's. Yet, the peasant is always a foreigner in the city and European cities were not appreciably better off simply because of their greater ethnic homogeneity. In every major city the problem of acculturation of rural immigrants has been a real and pressing one. In American society the movement from rural areas to the cities has gone on virtually to the present day although, since the 1920's, the chief source of this migration has shifted from foreign-born peasants to native-born rural blacks.

The great transformation of the city in the drive toward mature industrialization was experienced so acutely by both Eurpean and American sociologists that it became a dominant concern—almost

an obsession—of modern sociology (an intellectual activity which is itself a product of the conflict of ideologies that ushered in the industrial age). Many sociologists, writing from the essentially Romantic ideological position, deplored the loss of warm, intimate, primary group relations and that sense of belonging to an organic, solidary community which they believed—or affected to believe—to have characterized earlier small town and rural life. In its place they depicted a fragmented and impersonal urban society in which isolated, anonymous individuals had only the most temporary and superficial contact with one another.

Following the first World War, Robert Park and his colleagues at the University of Chicago, strongly influenced by the German tradition of Tonnies and Simmel, tried to provide the empirical evidence that would support the more philosophical and impressionistic analyses of the European sociological Romantics. In the America of Harding and Coolidge—the redoubt of "normalcy"—they found cities (more particularly, Chicago) characterized by slums and racial ghettos, by bohemias and skid rows, by crime and delinquency, by jack-rollers and hoboes, by prostitutes, taxi-dancers, and schizophrenics. Although the members of the Chicago School felt bound by the canons of dispassionate scientific inquiry to maintain a semblance of objectivity in their writings they could scarcely conceal their dismay. Surely this was not what Durkheim meant when he said that the moral order of modern society was based on the division of social labor. Urban dwellers seemed able to sustain only impersonal, fleeting, and exploitative relations with one another. City dwellers, wrote Park, were like so many guests in a hotel "meeting but not knowing one another."

Thus, the Chicago School brought the prestige of science (in an age enamored of science and "scientism") to the support of an anti-urban tradition in America that long antedated the development of sociology and that had numbered among its adherents some of America's most creative and influential thinkers. Surely the city has changed (if not always for the better) since Jefferson in the early 19th century warned of its poverty, depravity, and corruption but that characterization of American urban life has enjoyed remarkable continuity both in our philosophical and literary traditions. This may suggest that the preindustrial city despite several millennia of history had still not become the truly congenial home for man or there may even be biological reasons, as some evolutionary biologists have suggested, why even confirmed and satisfied city dwellers yearn for the quiet and beauty of the countryside even though their only real concession to such a desire may be a tree planted in the back yard of a Manhattan brownstone. The rapid and momentous changes wrought by the Industrial Revolution were, in most instances, forced upon a set of living and working arrangements that had never been able to make its residents feel "urbane."

And so instead of celebrants the American city has had little but critics —often vitriolic ones—from Thomas Jefferson to Frank Lloyd Wright and Lewis Mumford. The case for the city as a kind of a 20th century version of Dante's Inferno is too well known and too depressing to bear detailed review here. Any hardened urbanite would readily recognize the chief counts of the indictment: poverty, ugliness, filth, violence, substandard housing, foul air, nerve shattering noise, political corruption (the shame of the cities for Lincoln Steffens and the Muckrakers of the Progressive Era), crime, drug addiction, mutual fear, crowds, loneliness, exasperating traffic jams, inadequate health and welfare services, inade-

quate transportation facilities, mediocre public schools, a criminal justice system so overburdened and ineffectual that all but a handful of crimes go unpunished, and everywhere a pervasive incivility of man to man. As has always been so, these failings and inadequacies are not evenly distributed among all the residents and residential areas of the city but fall most heavily on the poor and, especially, on the blacks and other ethnic minorities who form an ever increasing proportion of the United States' central city's population.

Even those problems once thought definitely solved threaten to recur. The provision of enclosed sewer systems, first introduced in mid-19th century London (such a system had existed in Kanossos of the Minoans but that was in another country and besides, the civilization was dead), and the later chemical purification of water effectively put an end to the ages-old threat of cholera and typhus epidemics. But now detergent residues flood the sewers and even seep into the drinking water of cities and the ground water of the countryside itself. Natural epidemics may thus be replaced by man-made epidemics. Solid wastes, most of which used to be organic in character, now are composed largely of glass, metal, and plastic containers that will not decay for hundreds of years, if ever, leading to the creation of unsightly and undisposable mountains of refuse. And the excreta deposited every day by scores of thousands of pet dogs on the streets of every major American city serves to give each resident and visitor a faint idea of what the streets of most ancient cities probably were like.

As though this indictment were not devastating enough there are those who believe that the city's greatest offense is the absence of "community" or, in other terms, the presence of widespread "anomie," social disorganization or social and psychological isolation. In the eyes of its authors, the City of the Imagination was always characterized by geographically compact, close-knit groups of kinsmen and neighbors who satisfied the ubiquitous and imperious human need for emotional warmth, friendship, and protection. In such an ideal city all the needs of its inhabitants were satisfied by those who knew and cared for the individual personally without any intervention by formal, impersonal service organizations. Paradoxically unlike most of the other urban maladies, it is the economically better-off residents who are said to suffer most acutely from the decline of the old neighborhood community. Although those who hold this view do not specify by what processes it comes to pass, they appear to believe that poverty, crowding, and the deprivation of human dignity encourage the development of communal sentiments and institutions. Would Katherine Genovese, the most striking symbol of the breakdown of community in the American city, have been saved from death had she resided in a black or Puerto Rican ghetto rather than in a middle-class white neighborhood?

It was the German philosopher-sociologist Georg Simmel who, in his 1918 essay "The Metropolis and Mental Life," provided the first coherent characterization of the city as an arena of impersonality, secondary relationships, and anomie. (In fact Simmel did not use the word "anomie" but his characterization is close enough to the accepted meaning of that word so that we may use the latter as a convenient shorthand.) Twenty years later his student, Louis Wirth, repeated and embellished Simmel's analysis in his well-known article, "Urbanism as a Way of Life." It was through Wirth and his writings that this ideological position (for that is what it is) passed into the main stream of American sociology under the guise of factual descriptions.

Precisely because this ideology has been so prominent and persistent both in American sociology and popular social criticism it deserves some close scrutiny.

There is little doubt that the quantitative increase in the population of a city ultimately causes qualitative changes in the life of the city's inhabitants, a point that Marx made in a more general sense in the mid-19th century. At some critical point in the growth of a city (it is not necessary for the argument to be able to identify that point precisely), it becomes impossible for every inhabitant to know everyone else even by reputation. Attention to sheer numbers does not, of course, deny the importance of other sociological variables in understanding the life of a city or the attitudes of its inhabitants. Once passed the critical point cities become composed essentially of strangers, that is, individuals who tend to be suspicious of and even hostile to those they do not know personally. When, in addition, the strangers are of different races, ethnic groups, or social classes competing for scarce and limited resources the possibilities of misunderstanding and conflict increase exponentially.

The effect of increasing numbers on the character of urban life is to increase the probability that certain events or types of events will occur and that certain conditions will prevail while decreasing the probability of certain other kinds of events. For example, increasing the numbers and thus the density of a population of any given area will increase the probability of a high noise level, of large accumulations of refuse, of traffic jams, of overcrowded public transportation facilities at peak travel hours, of crowding in stores on weekends, and of long ticket lines for popular plays, movies, and sporting events. The very same conditions will, on the other hand, decrease the probability that any two randomly selected inhabitants will meet on the street and will similarly decrease the likelihood that one will be intimately acquainted with all of one's coworkers or physically close neighbors. Furthermore, an increase in the number of inhabitants will tend to increase the absolute numerical representation of many types of people whose proportion of the total population may be very small. Thus, every city of substantial size has its set population of psychopaths, drug addicts, hoodlums, lovers, lawyers, prostitutes, homosexuals, hippies, and so on *ad infinitum*. Finally, as with all voluntary migrations, that to the city was selective and thus increased some probabilities while decreasing others. Historically, it has always been the younger, the more energetic, the more ambitious, the more restless (accounting perhaps for the competitive atmosphere associated with cities), and the more unscrupulous who have been attracted to the city; but also those whose deviance or idiosyncracies could only be tolerated in the atmosphere of privacy (for which anonymity is but a pejorative name) that the numbers, the diversity, and the psychological distance of the city makes possible.

But these very same factors account for the existence of an entirely different city: the city of the museum and the cathedral, of the playhouse and concert hall, of the bookstore and the research laboratory, in summary, that seedbed and storehouse of the products of man's most creative impulses. Cities provide not only the time but the physical and psychological conditions necessary for the creation of art: large numbers of people from whom the gifted can be selected; teachers and critics; physical facilities and money; literacy; the stimulation of exhibits and performances and of people meeting people. While some of the opportunities offered by the city attract the anti-social, others attract another kind of deviant: the talented provincial. And, in fact, the two are often the same. Essential for the crea-

tion of art or of any high culture is the availability of audiences—those willing and able to buy or support the work of artists. Much has been made of the fact that relative to the total population of a city the proportion who support the "art trade" is small; that may well be but the absolute number is large, large enough to provide an adequate market for most creative artists. The village, the town, even small cities produce only the dilettante and the amateur, not the artist; orchestras and theatrical performances, but not music or drama. First rate artists may be found in towns and small cities but only after they have been formed in the crucible of the metropolis.

Once the city is viewed as composed of an almost infinite number of publics making almost an infinite number of choices, many of the amenities and delights of urbanity become clear. The diversity of publics is assured by that very migration to the industrial city that has made it into a living ethnographic museum. For example, the glossary in Kate Simon's *New York Places and Pleasures* directs the reader to places that sell attayef, barracuda loafs, bialys, boccie balls, bouillabaisse, brioche, cherimoyas, cholent, chladdegh ring, couscous, decoupage, fhidara, ipon, kimchee, kompe, kouraber, and scores of other things that demonstrate that the city remains what it has always been: the great bazaar of infinite choices. Indeed, the audiences for such urban amenities gradually grow larger not only because the cosmopolitanism of the city exposes people to the exotic but also because the increasing prosperity makes it possible for many who previously could not afford to be part of a particular audience to join in. As Roger Starr has observed, the increase in the number of customers for the products of the city further alienates its critics either because the latter, usually arguing from an aristocratic position, object to the leveling of taste or because they are inconvenienced by the heavy demand. They are totally unaware that the essential diversity of city life depends on the existence of many substantial publics. For example, even with an attendance of 250,000 the New York flower show of 1970 lost money. The greatest threat to urbanity would seem to lie not in the excessive size of publics but in the danger that those publics will not be large and diverse enough to sustain the multiplicity of markets and choices.

This image of the city as a crosscutting system of publics, markets, and choices clearly runs counter to the prevailing dreary view that social *dis*-organization is the defining characteristic of city life, if indeed, disorganization can be a defining characteristic of any viable institution. Present evidence suggests that the city still *is* viable, though ailing. From this point of view the *organization* of urban life seems a far more prominent characteristic than its *dis*-organization.

Unfortunately, not all urbanites share equally in the remarkable range of choices offered by the city. True, the decades since 1940 have produced a growing middle class which is both able and eager to enjoy the diversity of city life and to make use of the choices it offers. But for the poor, the excluded, and the disadvantaged the city remains a giant tease, offering much enticement but little fulfillment. The future of the city depends heavily on the capacity of its leadership to make those groups into publics able to participate in the city's diversity and able to make meaningful choices from among alternatives which it offers.

At the same time as the city increases the chances the individual will be able to satisfy his tastes and interests whatever they may be, it is also able, for the same reasons, to satisfy the human need for other people. Since its very invention the city has been a gathering place for different kinds of people, and the industrial metropolis especially, as we have seen, attracts and concentrates every conceivable personality type. This means that any individual urbanite, whatever his attitudes and behavior idiosyncracies, has a reasonable chance to find congenial others to share those attitudes and idiosyncracies. The other side of that cohesion and face-to-face intimacy so extolled by the champions of the village and the small town was that it forcibly imposed a set of attitudes and values on all its members and inhibited the expression of any views and feelings that were not consonant with the dominant ethos. It is not accidental that the one aspect of the small town that is not idealized by its nostalgic defenders is the difficulty of escaping the watchful eye of the community. Sherwood Anderson's *Winesburg, Ohio* serves as a model of the small town's hostility not only to deviance but to difference.

Despite this, critics of the city continue to "view with alarm" what they call the impersonal, fragmented quality of urban life and compare it unfavorably with the warm, face-to-face relationships they believe to have characterized villages, towns, and even the urban neighborhoods of half a century or more ago. They contend that the extended family, the single most important primary group, has disintegrated and dispersed under the impact of large scale industrialization as its constituent units, responding to opportunities presented by economic development, have scattered across the landscape. Although more recent studies have demonstrated that the American conjugal family is less isolated than once believed and although new types of primary groups have been discovered by sociologists, the latter have tended to see these as "temporary systems," shifting task and friendship groupings, grounded either in work situations or informal activities rather than in perduring groups such as the nuclear family. Sociologists, bemused by the confusion between physical and psychological closeness, have almost completely overlooked how large scale urban life makes it possible for the urbanite to take advantage of the multitude of human choices the city offers him.

The urbanite can become an integral part of a network of satisfying human relationships precisely because there exists in the city publics of every conceivable taste and interest and because forms of transportation and communication—especially the telephone—makes it possible for the individual to extend his range of personal associations far beyond the limits of his physical area of residence ("his neighborhood" in its original meaning). Unlike the town dweller, the urbanite can form primary groups based on personal attraction and shared interests rather than solely on the accident of physical propinquity. The very density of urban population makes it impossible to know all one's physical neighbors even if one wished to do so and makes of every street and virtually every building a physical point at which dozens or even hundreds of social networks intersect.

Some sociologists now speak of "dispersed" social networks to denote that many urbanites form primary groups with others who are scattered throughout the metropolitan area, groups which interact as much over the telephone as in face-to-face gatherings. From the point of view of the individual such groups constitute his "psychological neighborhood" as opposed to his physical neighborhood of residence. Modern transportation, of course, makes it possible for such groups to foregather in person but it seems doubtful that such dispersed groups could long remain cohesive without the communication made possible by the telephone. The city has not lost community, it has rather developed a different kind of community more appropriate to its physical setting.

Sociologists have only recently discovered these "telephone communities" (as Suzanne Keller calls them) and their precise character still remains obscure. I myself have discovered one such "neighborhood" that consists of a group of elderly widows living alone who maintain scheduled daily telephone contact as a means of insuring the safety, health, and emotional security of the group's members. The telephone also plays a key role in maintaining the cohesion of physically dispersed families: private telephone calls seem to be made most frequently among close relatives with mother-daughter calls probably the most frequent of all.

Of course, psychological closeness not dependent on the telephone is also possible in the modern city and probably exists in a few neighborhoods such as the Chinatowns of New York and San Francisco and the Italian North End of Boston. In addition, the communes that have recently sprung up in various parts of the country represent a new form of primary group, one that differs both from the preindustrial extended family and the conjugal family of industrial society. What the future of this new form will be and how successful it will be in meeting psychological as well as the physical needs of its members remains to be seen.

If we are to believe the ideology which has come to surround it, rural life provided emotional security at the expense of privacy and individuality; the modern city, on the other hand, can provide both physical privacy, even amidst high density living, and intimacy within one's psychological neighborhood or neighborhoods. Needless to say, this arrangement does not always work satisfactorily: there are times, as the Genovese case showed us, when a neighbor in the old fashioned sense of the word is sorely needed. But it is just as easy to blame such incidents on the lack of adequate police protection, a protection needed the more as the meaning of "community" shifts from physical to psychological and as many of the activities that used to be the province of informal neighborhood groupings are assumd by large-scale, bureaucratic governmental organizations. Moreover, in the modern industrial city it is virtually impossible to determine who speaks for "the community" since each psychological neighborhood draws its residents from diverse parts of the metropolitan area.

Those critics engaged in writing the city's obituary speak as though the chief hope of the future lies in alternative living arrangements. Much has been made of the recent census findings (both 1960 and 1970) that show decline in the population of many American central cities and a more than corresponding rise in the suburban population. Yet many of those who flock to the suburbs are the middle and upper middle class supporters of the "art trade" and the "great bazaar." To ask how quickly such people would live in small towns not situated near a major metropolis is at the same time to answer the question. Those who have chosen suburban life have not created new institutions but have tended to make second-hand imitations of existing urban forms. The suburban shopping center offers convenience and adequate parking space but at the price of a narrower range of choices than those offered by central city department stores and specialty shops. Suburbs are widely believed to offer superior public education and that belief has itself been a major motive for the exodus from the central city. But except for towns such as Newton, Massachusetts and Scarsdale, New York, there is precious little evidence for the superiority of suburban over central city schools. We now know that middle-class suburban schools at-

tract eager, highly motivated, well socialized white students; but the quality of education in blue collar suburbs is no better than that of urban schools which cater to similar populations.

It is, of course, possible that increasing dissatisfaction with the quality of urban life may produce a new migration out toward the suburbs and exurbs which, in its magnitude, may be comparable to that which created the industrial city as we know it. Some demographers and sociologists have claimed to see evidence of such a migration in the results of the 1970 census, results which disclosed that America's suburban population (exceeding 71 million) is now its largest single sector. In comparison, the central cities now contain some 59 million people while another 71 million live in the nation's smaller cities, towns, and genuinely rural areas. Should such a suburban or exurban migration prove, in fact, to be the trend of the future, the ultimate result will be the gradual filling of the relatively sparsely settled countryside, the still further diffusion of standardized housing developments and shopping centers, a still greater dependence on the automobile, and the total uglification of the American landscape. It may be little enough to say in its favor, but at least the concentration of the American population in large metropolitan areas has preserved a real distinction between the urban and the rural. That in itself may be a positive value.

But perhaps the most remarkable tribute to the city is the ability of its inhabitants to endure and to surmount virtually every catastrophe, every abomination, every one of the many affronts to their senses, to adapt to each successive trial, to survive and, by surviving, to triumph. As always, wars remain the greatest threat to the city, yet war has come to be accepted, much as fire used to be, as the "ultimate municipal germicide." The typical New Yorker, that intrepid veteran of municipal crises, has become a master of survival. At the Museum of Modern Art recently, I observed an elderly woman demonstrating to a companion the best way to keep a robber from making off with a handbag. Millions of subway riders know that any day they may be trapped in their trains and forced to exit through the labyrinth of tracks, tunnels, and underground passageways—as many thousands already have. And all city dwellers know that from time to time, as the result of strikes, job actions, and political disputes they will have to make do for shorter or longer periods without essential services. The dream of permanently leaving New York is but the New Yorker's latest wish-fulfilling fantasy and has replaced the older dream of leaving the employ of another and starting one's own business.

Recently, in the *New York Times*, John Canaday wrote something that may sum up both the glory and the horror of the contemporary American city. He wrote of the increase in his rent, the mugging of his mother-in-law, of subway delays, and of a pickpocket in the elevator, but then he added: "in how

many towns outside New York would 15th century prayer books and Japanese screens attract the large audiences they do here?" Where else but in New York or, more generally, in a true city? Such experiences incarnate the uniqueness of the urban experience: the coexistence at the same time in the same place of the wonders and the terrors of human life—the visionary and his audience side by side with the criminal and his victims.

Speculation over the supposed obsolescence of the city and its ultimate decline seems both premature and unfruitful. Around the world a new wave of the great urban migration is gathering force and the clamor for those products of civilization that only the city can provide rises apace. Robert Park, despite his concern over the city's anomie, was one of the first to realize that as a result of living in the city man produced civilization. The end of the city might well signify the end of that civilization. The task of this generation is not to bury or to replace the city but to humanize it, to make of it a decent home for all its residents, to make it urbane as well as urban.

# 30

# The Growth and Structure of Metropolitan Areas

### WILLIAM M. DOBRINER

In 1900, metropolitan areas claimed 31 percent of the total population. Today, 2 out of 3 Americans live in urban places, but over 60 percent of the total population lives in metropoli-

William M. Dobriner, *Class in Suburbia*, © 1963. By permission of Prentice-Hall, Inc., Englewood Cliffs, N.J.

tan areas. Census forecasts suggest that by 1975 the population of the United States will exceed 220 million, an increase of roughly 40 million over 1960, 63 percent of whom will live in metropolitan areas.

The growth of metropolitan centers, however, is merely one facet of the urban revolution of the last sixty years. Although metropolitan areas have demonstrated amazing growth, the component parts are by no means growing at the same rate. In 1900, for example, the population of the *central cities* of metropolitan areas constituted 61.9 percent of the total metropolitan unit while the suburban and fringe areas outside of the cities were only 38.1 percent of the total area. By 1960, however, the picture had changed. Central cities claimed barely half of the total population of metropolitan areas.

The 1960 Census for the New York Standard Metropolitan Statistical Area dramatically illustrates the national trend. While New York City lost a total of 109,973 persons between 1950 and 1960, its suburban counties were registering spectacular gains. Nassau County increased 93 percent over the decade. Rockland 53 percent, Suffolk 141 percent, and Westchester 29 percent. In this manner, while New York City lost about one and a half percent of its population during the decade, its suburbs increased by 75 percent.

From 1900 until 1920 central cities were growing faster than their tributary rings. However, in each decade since 1920 the rings have been growing faster than the central cities. Thus, the comparative growth rates between central cities and their rings have now become considerable. In the decade between 1940 and 1950, rings grew almost two and a half times as fast as central cities. The result has been that the suburban population alone is estimated at more than 50 million. The trends in the New York metropolitan area are clearly reflected on the national level. According to the 1960 Census, about 84 percent of the 28 million population increase during the decade 1950–60 occurred in the nation's metropolitan areas. However, the increase in these areas from 89,316,903 in 1950 to 112,885,178 in 1960 (26.4 percent)

saw the suburban rings growing at a much faster rate than central cities. The increase of central cities in the decade (5.6 million) to a total of 58 million by 1960 constituted a 10.7 percent increase; in contrast, outlying suburban areas grew from 36.9 million population in 1950 to 54.9 million in 1960 for an increase of 48.6 percent.

The growth rates for central cities are clearly continuing to decline. Indeed, the trend is for the central cities of the largest metropolitan areas to have even slower rates of growth than the central cities of smaller metropolitan areas. We have already noted that New York City lost population during the 1950–1960 decade. In the five metropolitan areas of 3,000,000 or more the growth in central cities was only 1 percent. In contrast, however, the growth of the suburban rings of these great metropolitan centers was 71 percent. As size declines, the growth rate of central cities increased in relation to the suburban areas. In the case of the smaller metropolitan areas of less than 100,000, the growth rate (29 percent exceeded the suburban rate (11 percent).

It is clear that population is moving toward the suburbs and the claim of central cities is decreasing. For the country as a whole, the outlying rings of metropolitan centers accounted for about two thirds of the total U.S. population increase since 1950 and for more than three-fourths of the total increase within metropolitan areas. Furthermore, the trend of central city loss and suburban gain is expected to continue. By 1975, the Committee for Economic Development estimates the central city population will have dropped to 42 percent of the metropolitan total, while the suburban and fringe areas outside will have grown to 57 percent of the entire metropolitan complex. This almost reverses the central city-suburban population proportions established for metropolitan areas at the turn of the century.

Although cities, as a distinguishable community form, have existed for over five thousand years, the city in its metropolitan guise is scarcely one hundred years old. . . . the metropolitan area may be regarded as a vast spatial structure consisting of functionally interdependent economic, political, and social subsystems. The result may be a super-organized concentration that takes in portions of two or three states in a highly specialized and differentiated functional integration of areas that go well beyond the political limits of the core city.

Indeed, the process of metropolitan growth has proceeded so far that the unit "metropolitan area" in the aforementioned sense may no longer apply to the larger, integrated metropolitan aggregates that are flowing into each other across the nation. The "boundaries" of metropolitan areas are fusing to form super-metropolitan entities that have been called "strip cities" or, as Jean Gottmann has termed the integration of metropolitan areas from southern New Hampshire all the way to the Appalachian foothills in Virginia, "Megalopolis."

According to a study made by *U.S. News and World Report* (Sept. 18, 1961; see Figure 1) the thirteen major "strip cities" in the United States—Boston to Washington, Albany to Erie, Cleveland to Pittsburgh, Toledo to Cincinnati, Detroit to Muskegon, Chicago–Gary to Milwaukee, St. Louis to Peoria, Seattle to Eugene, San Francisco to San Diego, Kansas City to Sioux Falls, Fort Worth–Dallas–San Antonio–Houston, Miami–Tampa–Jacksonville, and Atlanta to Raleigh—contain half the population of the country (89,395,496) and have increased more than 25 percent from 1950. Of the total 212 metropolitan areas in the nation, 119 fall within 13 giant strip city pat-

terns. Not only did half of the population live within these super-metropolitan constellations, but 109 billion dollars in retail trade at 54.7 percent of the total consumer market was expended there. . . .

Although their language varies, ecologists, demographers, economists, sociologists, and political scientists *think* of the metropolitan area in terms of three differentiated zones. We can, therefore, assume that this view of metropolitan centers is generally useful. Since there is general agreement that the zones *are there*, but not complete accord on the terms used to describe these areas, we shall identify them as (1) the Central Core, (2) the Suburban Zone, and (3) the Rural-Urban Fringe. Having identified these zones, however, the logical task is to inquire into those factors which have led to the three-ring view of metropolitan centers. In the interest of brevity we shall take the central city—the core area—as a given quantity and shall concentrate our discussion on the communities and zones which lie beyond the core city. . . .

All of these views of the suburbs, which are representative of the literature, rest heavily on two basic characteristics—characteristics which critically, or as Martin says "definitively," differentiate the suburb from all other forms of community organization. These are: the physical and political separation of the suburb from the central city, and the economic dependence of the suburb on the core city as particularly seen in the suburban commuting pattern. Suburbs may indeed be much more than this, but if a community is to be regarded as suburban in its simplest and most elementary form, it must be physically removed from the central city and it must rely heavily on the urban economy. . . .

Satellites [smaller manufacturing cities of a metropolitan area] tend to

**Figure 1**
The thirteen major strip cities in the United States. (*Courtesy of the Department of Commerce, Bureau of the Census.*)

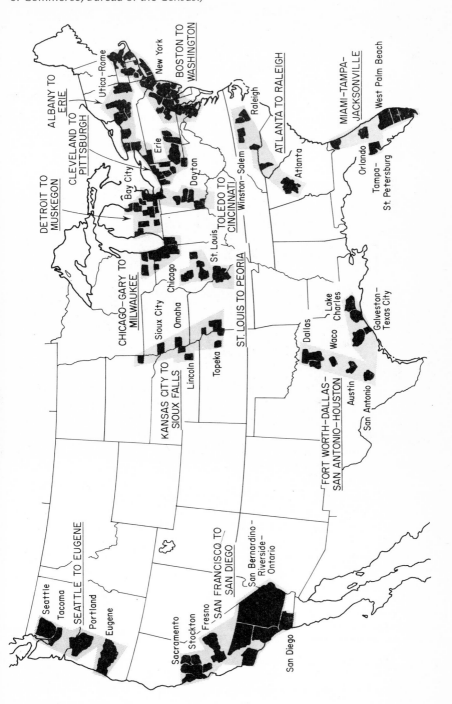

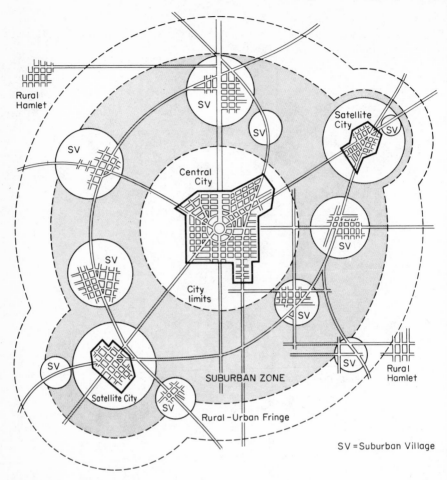

**Figure 2**
A model metropolitan area showing the relationship between the central city,
the suburban zone, and the rural-urban fringe.

be older than residential suburbs and
are found most often in industrialized
sections of the northeast and north-
central areas of the nation. In addition,
suburbs and satellite cities tend to have
contrasting types of populations. In
general, satellites contain younger
populations than do residential suburbs with a trend toward the lower
socioeconomic class and status groups.
Along similar lines, the population of
satellite cities, contrasted with a model
residential suburb, have a lower average education, lower average rent

levels, high proportions of foreign-born
whites, higher fertility rates, higher
percentages of tenant-occupied buildings, and a work force in which two out
of three workers are in the blue collar
occupations.

In contrasting the comparative
growth rates of residential suburbs and
the employing satellites, Schnore demonstrated that the suburbs were growing almost twice as fast as the satellites.
Furthermore, the suburbs were becoming even more residential in character,
while the satellite areas, in addition to

the central cities, were becoming more industrialized.

In the zonal view of the patterning of metropolitan areas [see Figure 2] Zone I consists of the densely populated and highly commercialized and industrialized core, while Zone II consists of a belt of rapidly growing suburban communities and industrialized satellite cities. Of the two, suburbs and satellites, the suburbs seem to predominate slightly on the national average. Beyond the suburban belt lies the third zone of the metropolitan area which goes by a variety of names. Some call it "the rural ring," "urban fringe," "the outer ring," "the rural-urban fringe," and the like. We have called it the "rural-urban fringe" and by that we identify it as the last belt or area in which metropolitan or urban patterns are still evident. Essentially this belt consists of a geographic area in which the prevailing use of land is neither clearly urban nor suburban (residential, industrial, commercial) or rural (agricultural). It is that area where the expanding metropolis is currently waging its imperialistic war. This is the belt where the new suburban colonies and satellite cities will emerge in a few years. Thus, from an ecological view, the rural-urban fringe represents that spatial dimension of the entire area in which new urban functions, largely in the form of suburban residential areas and employing satellites, eat into the rural countryside. As such, it is a heterogeneous area of instability and change. On one side of the illusive and fragmentary boundary of the urban fringe lies the ring of suburban villages and satellite cities and on the other, beyond suburbia and the interurban railways, past the commuter railroad, the expressway and parkway systems, the mass-produced subdivisions, the land opens up and the signs of the city fade. Beyond the rural-urban fringe all volatile and unstable, lie the small villages, the pokey economies, and the sleepy roadways of rural America. . . .

# 31

## Suburbs and Myths of Suburbia

### DENNIS H. WRONG

Suburbia is no longer a very fashionable topic. In the 1950's, social critics and sociologists subjected the growing numbers of suburban dwellers to endless scrutiny, seeing them as especially representative of an affluent postwar America whose complacency and flaccidity were mirrored in Eisenhower's Presidency. The suburb was the new habitat of the American middle class, whose taste, intellect, spiritual vigor and mental health were savagely attacked in best-selling assaults, both journalistic and fictional, on "split-level traps," "cracks in the picture window," and "gray flannel-suited" commuters. Social scientists, meanwhile, discovered new "styles of life" developing in the suburbs and linked suburban expansion to the revival of the Republican party, higher birth rates and the upward mobility of the erstwhile urban masses.

An image of the suburbanite as a new kind of American possessing a distinctive outlook shaped by his residential environment emerged from these accounts. He was pictured as a former plebeian city-dweller who, benefiting from postwar prosperity, fled to the suburbs to escape his origins. He changed his political affiliation from Democratic to Republican to express his sense of social elevation and refurbished his religious and ethnic loyalties by rejoining the church and choosing to live among those of like background, seeking in particular communities that excluded Negroes and other minorities. His insecurity about his newly won higher status revealed itself, however, in the frantic pursuit of material status symbols purchased to impress his neighbors, who were similarly striving to impress him. The inevitable result was a pervasive standardization of life externally manifested in the monotonous similarity of houses, furnishings, clothing, gardens, and cars. The cultural and leisure pursuits of suburbanites were also uniform: watching TV, reading mass magazines and the latest bestsellers, gardening, and outdoor barbecuing.

But common interests and possessions failed to create true "togetherness" in suburbia, for they existed in the context of the wary status-seeking that had motivated the move to the suburbs in the first place. And in spite of the proclaimed virtues of roots and local community spirit, each suburb remained a temporary resting place for many of its residents, who on climbing still higher up the social ladder were apt to move to a more prestigious, higher-income suburb and start the whole process all over again. This transience gave the busy suburban social life, both informal and in such organized groups as the church, the PTA, the women's clubs, a synthetic and compulsive quality, belying the vaunted neighborliness so often extolled in contrast to the cold impersonality of city life.

This portrait of the suburban lifestyle possessed an initial plausibility, because it managed to link all the new developments in American life during the late 1940's and the 1950's to suburbanization. The postwar economic boom was bringing relative affluence to many who had not previously known it, the moderation of class conflicts in our politics enabled the Republicans to win office under Eisenhower, obsession with the Cold War created a spirit of political timidity, marriage rates and birth rates were soaring to the highest levels in two generations, there was evidence of a religious revival in the land, and the mass media, particularly the new medium of television, were reaching more and more Americans. All of these trends seemed to attain their maximum intensity in suburbia and the mass migration to the suburbs after 1945 represented one of the largest and most visible population movements in American history. Whether described in the neutral language of the sociologists or in the satirical and rejecting epithets of social critics deprived temporarily of their usual targets of political attack, the suburbs seemed to exhibit all that was most contemporary and most typical in American life. Thus was born a composite portrait of suburbanism as a way of life that has been dubbed by those who have recently challenged its accuracy the "myth of suburbia."

All this seems very passé nowadays. With the return to power of the Democratic party in 1960, the growth of the civil rights movement, and the rediscovery of poverty, our attention today is directed to social problems arising out of inequality and economic deprivation rather than to the psychological burdens of newly won affluence. The Negroes and the poor are overwhelmingly concentrated in the center of the city or in such rural slums as those in Appalachia rather than in the outlying metropolitan districts. Moreover, the cities, responding to the flight of so many of their former inhabitants to the suburbs, have launched programs of urban renewal that have created a host of new and hotly debated political issues. Sociologists have turned to the investigation of blue-collar rather than white-collar ways of life. And social critics now assail middle-class America less for its allegedly trivial leisure pursuits and compulsive conformism than on moral grounds, charging it with racial bigotry and insensitivity to the sufferings of the urban poor and the Negroes trapped in black ghettoes.

Yet a social reality does not simply disappear when the spotlight of publicity is no longer focused upon it. The suburbs are still very much with us. Nor has the process of suburbanization slowed up: there is every indication that the movement of population to the suburbs has continued and will continue during the sixties at a rate equal to or surpassing that of the forties and fifties. By 1960, just over one fifth of the American people (roughly forty million of them) lived in the suburbs; by 1970 the proportion is likely to be closer to one third. Politically, the suburbs stand to gain the most from the reapportionment of congressional and state legislative districts required by recent Supreme Court and lower court decisions, even though few of the cases heard by the courts were suits brought by suburban voters. It is therefore worth taking another look at received views of the suburban way of life, examining not only their validity when first put forward but also how continuing suburban growth and change affect their accuracy as descriptions of social reality.

A suburb is an area adjacent to the political boundaries of a city that is more densely settled than the open countryside, but less so than the central city. It depends on the city economically and culturally; politically, however, it is a self-governing municipality. A suburb, then, is a *place* defined by its location in relation to a city, both geographically and along transportation lines. This elementary fact needs to be stressed in view of the prevalent tendency to treat suburbia as if it were a state of mind or a moral and spiritual condition. Thus defined, virtually all cities and towns in the United States—large, middle-sized, and small—have in the present century produced suburbs forming a population belt encircling their original political boundaries. But the distinctive social and political outlook that commentators have attributed to suburbia is clearly intended to characterize chiefly the suburban populations surrounding the metropolitan giants among American cities. At the 1960 census, twenty-one million people (about 12 percent of the total American population) lived in the suburban belt surrounding the central cities of our ten largest metropolitan areas. This figure, however, includes residents of industrial suburbs with working-class populations engaged in varied economic activities, whereas the popular generalizations about suburbia apply only to middle-class residential or "dormitory" suburbs whose inhabitants commute some distance to work, usually to the central city.

Most of the earlier accounts of the suburbs failed to distinguish between the traits of their residents that were acquired as a result of living in suburban communities with their special relation to cities, and traits that suburban migrants possessed before moving to the suburbs and continued to share after moving with fellow-citizens who remained in the city. Just as "urban" attitudes may exist in rural areas—say, among Great Plains farmers, a fair number of whom are today sufficiently prosperous and literate to own private planes, vacation in Hawaii, and subscribe to the Book-of-the-Month Club —so may the so-called suburban way of life flourish outside of the suburbs. Urban tastes and attitudes, nevertheless, could scarcely have *originated* outside of those dense concentrations of people of different occupations that we call cities. It is far less certain, on the other hand, that the outlook imputed to suburbia could have developed only in the special physical and demographic setting of the suburbs.

Sociologists who have continued to study the suburbs have recently concentrated their efforts on debunking the so-called "myth of suburbia" created by the popular writers of the 1950's and earlier sociological studies. Bennett Berger, for example, investigated a new working-class "mass-produced" suburb in California and found little evidence among its residents of the changes in attitudes and behavior alleged to result from the move to the suburbs. Their class identification remained working-class, their occupational and income aspirations were no higher than formerly, they did not participate more actively in the church or in other local community affairs, they regarded the suburb as their permanent home, and they continued to vote regularly for the Democratic party. William Dobriner, studying Levittown, Long Island, found that since 1950 Levittown has been "steadily drifting from monolithic homogeneity into heterogeneity" as far as the income, occupational, and even ethnic and religious composition of its population is concerned. S. D. Clark, a Canadian sociologist, has, in effect, insisted that the move to the suburbs is largely a search for cheap family housing and that status-seeking and mobility striving do not have to be invoked to account for it. Finally, Herbert Gans has criticized the general proposition that location, population density, and housing have the influence on attitudes and ways of life assumed by many writers on urban communities, whether slums, residential neighborhoods in the city or suburbs. Gans argues that the styles of life associated with the upper-middle, lower-middle, and working classes are determined by social and economic conditions having little to do with place of residence within the metropolitan community.

The enormous pluralities won by Eisenhower in the two Presidential elections of the 1950's gave rise to the claim that migrants to the suburbs were prone to change their party preferences from Democratic to Republican. But detailed analyses of the vote in 1952 and 1956 suggest that most of the suburban Republicans would have voted for Eisenhower even if they had remained in the city. Indeed, voters resembling the migrants in their social and economic characteristics who did remain voted just as overwhelmingly for Eisenhower, cutting deeply into the "normal" Democratic big-city majorities. Moreover, it is now plain that 1952 and 1956 were what Angus Campbell and his associates at the University of Michigan Survey Research Center call "deviating elections," elections in which the result was determined largely by the personal popularity of one candidate rather than by regular party preferences. In the more normal 1960 Presidential election, Nixon was unable to hold the huge suburban margins run up by Eisenhower, and in 1964, central cities and suburbs alike, outside of the South, were carried by the Democrats in the Johnson landslide.

Both Angus Campbell and political scientist Robert C. Wood have shown that migrants to the suburbs in the 1950's were indeed more likely to vote Republican, but not because of the impact of suburbia on their political preferences. Rather, Republicans were more likely to move to the suburbs than Democrats with the same social and economic characteristics, perhaps because big-city Republicans more often came from families who had grown up in traditionally Republican small towns and rural areas a generation or more ago. Such family histories would explain both their Republicanism and their greater disposition to move to the suburbs in an attempt to recapture something of the uncongested, small-town atmosphere of their forebears. Angus Campbell has also shown that movers to the suburbs, though preponderantly Republican, had not achieved greater upward social mobility than those they left behind them in the city. So much for the view that suburban Republicanism is the result of party-switching reflecting the new conservatism of the upward mobile.

The high birth rates of the 1950's, linked by many commentators to the family and child-centered way of life of suburbanites, have declined in the 1960's and many demographers expect them to decline still further. TV sets are now as ubiquitous in city neighborhoods and even in the slums as in the suburbs. Studies of local government have shown suburbanites to be just as apathetic as residents of city wards and small towns when it comes to voting in local elections and participating in civic affairs. The trend toward increased church attendance by Americans has leveled off in recent years. Sociological studies have shown that *all* Americans, whether they live in the suburbs, the city, or the country, attach greater significance to their religious affiliations than was the case before World War II. More new churches and synagogues have certainly been built in the suburbs, but this is to be expected, because the suburbs have been growing more rapidly than other areas and does not result from any stimulus to greater religious activity peculiar to the suburban environment.

Social scientists, of course, greatly enjoy debunking popular myths. Some of them, indeed, appear to believe that the refutation of common beliefs about contemporary society provides the main justification for the existence of social science. (Sometimes it almost seems as if social scientists initially help create new stereotypes in order to make work for other social scientists in testing and correcting them.) Debunking is clearly not enough, for one also wants to know why a particular myth won such wide currency. The myth of suburbia may be no more than a mid-twentieth-century version of the old intellectual's game of deriding the middle class (*épater le bourgeois*), but even so it possessed and still possesses in many circles a surface plausibility that needs to be accounted for.

The myth partly owes its origin to emphasis on extreme and vivid cases in the earlier accounts of the suburbs. The various Levittowns, Park Forest, Illinois, as described by William H. Whyte in *The Organization Man,* the mass-produced housing developments quickly thrown up by private realtors described by John Keats in *The Crack in the Picture Window*—these are the initial sources of the myth. It is relatively easy to show that mass-produced or "packaged" suburbs, springing up overnight like earlier boomtowns, are not the only, or even the most typical, kind of suburb. Their standardized house-types all similarly priced and the absence of the contrasts between old and new residents found in most communities obviously promote the social homogeneity and the busy creation of new formal and informal groups that have been seen as characteristic of suburbia in general. Yet there are many other kinds of suburbs: traditional, upper-class suburbs, often dating back to the turn of the century; old rural towns that have gradually been engulfed by migrants from the city; stable, middle-income residential suburbs with individually styled houses, in addition to industrial satellites with noncommuting working-class populations. All have been increasing in population in the past two decades, though not necessarily at the same rate.

If the suburbs have long been more heterogeneous than the myths of suburbia suggest, it is also the case that they have been becoming even more heterogeneous. Suburbanization is, after all, a *process*, and one that is by no means completed. William Dobriner's study of Levittown, Long Island, built in the late 1940's, finds that commuting to the central city—that presumably universal characteristic of suburbanites—is less common than formerly as a growing number of Levittown residents take shorter journeys to work, often to new industrial cities within the suburban ring. Dobriner concludes that the suburbs are losing their sociological distinctiveness and becoming merely the most recent extensions of the city. "In our efforts to capture the sociological soul of the suburbs," he writes, "perhaps we turned away from the basic and most fascinating question . . . the way in which cities create suburbs only to turn them into cities in their own image."

Yet suburban life possesses one unique feature that helps explain the resonance of the myth: what Dobriner calls the "visibility principle." Middle-class ways of life that are concealed from public view in city apartments or residential backstreets become highly visible in the suburbs, with their open lawns and gardens, on-the-street parking, backyard barbecue pits and swimming pools and, more important, the more informal visiting and friendship patterns that are possible in a smaller, less-densely settled and more like-minded community than a city neighborhood. The suburb is middle-class America fully exposed to public observation. Take the status-seeking, for example, that is alleged to be a peculiar trait of the suburban style of life. In the city there is not only less op-

portunity publicly to display one's possessions as "status symbols," but there is far less incentive to do so when they will be observed by the vulgar throng in all its variety, as well as by one's own circle of class and ethnic equals, one's own "reference group," to use the sociological term. In the suburb, surrounded by neighbors of similar class and ethnic background, this inhibition disappears. It is not that suburban life breeds a frenetic concern with status lacking in city-dwellers; it is merely that the status-seeking propensities of the latter must necessarily be expressed in more limited, less public ways.

Although there is little difference between suburban communities and many home-owning middle-class residential neighborhoods inside the city line (except for the local government independence of the former), the suburbs are more visible to strangers. They are located in proximity to major highways and transportation lines into the city and, in the case of new subdivisions, have been suddenly and dramatically created by bulldozing out of existence areas of the nearby countryside long visited by city-dwellers for picnics and walks through the woods on Sunday outings. On the other hand, middle-class residential neighborhoods in the city are often isolated from the rest of the city and protected from close contact with it by ecological barriers: hills in San Francisco or Montreal, ravines in Washington or Toronto, lake-shore enclaves in Chicago or Detroit.

From a broader perspective, it is clear that the myth of suburbia very well suited the prevailing style of cultural criticism during the politically quiescent 1950's. In the 1920's, also a decade of political complacency, intellectuals assailed the philistinism, sexual puritanism, and moral hypocrisy of the American middle class, seeing the small town or city as the place of residence of most Americans and the breeding ground of these attitudes. Suburbia played a similar role in the 1950's with Whyte's organization man replacing Sinclair Lewis' Babbitt, and the oppressive togetherness of the suburb supplanting the xenophobic provinciality of Main Street, as targets of satire. Conversely, celebrators of the American way of life saw the small town in the 1920's and the suburb in the 1950's as the locus of its virtues: in the earlier period *Saturday Evening Post* covers of frame houses and tree-lined streets played the same symbolic role as glossy advertising layouts depicting ranch-house living thirty years later. With civil rights, poverty, and international peace becoming major political issues in the 1960's, delineation of the suburban life-style have lost the immediacy and sense of relevance they possessed a decade ago, just as the Depression and the New Deal ended the *Zeitgeist* of the 1920's and the cultural revolt against the small town that played so large a part in it.

Yet the small town was indeed becoming a backwater of American life by the 1930's as more and more Americans moved to metropolitan areas, whereas the suburbs are still expanding and even now contain more Americans than central cities, small urban communities, or rural areas. We cannot therefore dismiss them as objects of interest, regarding the obsession with them in the 1950's as no more than a fad of yesterday. The image of a homogenized suburban sameness was always a caricature and is becoming an even more distorted one with the passage of time. The increasing heterogeneity of suburbia, however, means merely that the distinction between *suburbanization* and *urbanization* as social processes is becoming a less meaningful one. The continuing growth and differentiation of cities remains one of the most significant social trends of our time.

# 32

# The Country Town and the Mass Society

## ARTHUR J. VIDICH AND JOSEPH BENSMAN

### The Ambivalent Attitude to Mass Society

Springdalers have a decided respect for the great institutions that characterize American society. The efficiency, organizational ability and farflung activities of giant government and busi-

Selections from Arthur J. Vidich and Joseph Bensman, *Small Town in Mass Society: Class, Power, and Religion in a Rural Community* (rev. edn. copyright © 1968 by Princeton University Press; Princeton Paperback, 1968), pp. 79–93, 95–102, 104–105. Reprinted by permission of Princeton University Press.

ness enterprise inspire them with awe. The military might of the nation and the productive capacity of industry lend a Springdaler a sense of pride and security, and the continuous development and successful application of science assure him that he is a participant in the most forward-looking and progressive country in the world. Anyone who would attack the great institutions of America would have no audience in Springdale: "Everybody knows this country wouldn't be what it is if it weren't for free enterprise and the democratic form of government." When the Springdaler is on the defensive he will tell the critic, "If you don't like it here you can go back to where you came from."

The Springdaler also sees that the urban and metropolitan society is technically and culturally superior to his own community. He sees this in his everyday life when he confronts the fact that his community [a small country town of 3000 people] cannot provide him with everything he needs: almost everyone goes to the city for shopping or entertainment; large numbers of people are dependent on the radio and television; and everyone realizes that rural life would be drastically altered without cars and refrigerators. Springdalers clearly realize how much of local life is based on the modern techniques, equipment and products which originate in distant places.

The community is constantly dependent on cultural and material imports and welcomes these as a way of "keeping up with the times." However, they believe that the very technical and cultural factors that make for the superiority of the "outside" also account for the problems of living that cities exhibit. The "city masses," while they have easier access to progress, are also the ready-made victims of the negative aspects of progress. In contrast, rural life, because it is geographically distant, can enjoy progress and avoid the worst features of the industrial mass society; Springdalers can believe that they are in a position to choose and utilize only the best of two worlds, that the importations, if properly chosen, need not affect the inner life of the community.

Because it is possible to choose only the best, the Springdaler can believe, that in spite of some disadvantages, his is the better of two worlds. This belief in the autonomy or, at worst, the self-selective dependency of rural life makes it possible for the community member publicly to voice the following conceptions concerning the relationships between his town and mass society:

1. That the basic traditions of American society—"grassroots democracy," free and open expression, individualism—are most firmly located in rural society. The American heritage is better preserved in the small town because it can resist bad city influences and thereby preserve the best of the past.
2. That the future hope of American society lies in rural life because it has resisted all "isms" and constitutes the only major bulwark against them.
3. That much of the progress of society is the result of rural talent which has migrated to the cities. In this way rural society has a positive influence on urban life; rural migrants account for the virtues of city life. "Everyone knows that most of the outstanding men in the country were raised in small towns" and Springdalers proudly point to several local names that have made good on the outside.
4. That "when you live in a small town you can take or leave the big cities —go there when you want to and always come back without having to live as they do." There is the belief that "if more people lived in small towns, you wouldn't have all those problems."

These summarize the types of beliefs that are frequently stated in public situations. The observer who is willing to go beyond the public statements discovers that Springdale has a great variety of direct and intimate connections with a wide range of institutions of the mass society. Moreover, these institutions affect many phases of the community, have consequences for its internal local functioning and in some ways control the direction of social change within it.

Springdale is connected with the mass society in a variety of different forms. The cumulative effect of these various connections makes possible the continuous transmission of outside policies, programs and trends into the community, even though the effects of the transmission and the transmitting agents themselves are not always seen. Outside influences can be transmitted directly by a socially visible agent such as the extension specialist who lives in the community for the purpose of acting upon it. Outside interests and influences can also be expressed indirectly through members of the community: policies and programs of relatively invisible outside interests are transmitted by *heads* of local branches of state and national organizations, by *heads* of local businesses dependent on outside resources and by *heads* of churches attached to larger organizations. In some instances the community is affected by the consequences of decisions made by business and government which are made with specific reference to the community, i.e., the decision to build a state road through the community or the decision to close down a factory. Plans and decisions that refer directly to the community are made from a distance by invisible agents and institutions. Perhaps most important are the mass decisions of business and government which are transmitted to the rural scene by the consequences of changes in prices, costs and communications. These affect the town even though they are not explicitly directed at it, and they comprise the invisible social chain reactions of decisions that are made in centers of power in government, business and industry. The invisible social chain reactions emanating from the outside no doubt alter the life of the community more seriously than the action of visible agents such as the extension specialist.

These types of transmission do not represent mutually exclusive channels, but rather exist in complex interrelationship with each other. They merely suggest the major ways in which the community is influenced by dynamics which occur in the institutions of mass society. How these combined dynamics in their various combinations affect the fabric of life in Springdale can be seen by examining the way in which cultural importations and economic and political connections shape the character of community life. In their net effect they influence the psychological dimensions of the community.

## Cultural Importations from Mass Society

The external agents of cultural diffusion range from specific observable individuals placed in the local community by outside institutions to the impact of mass media of communications and successive waves of migration. The consequence of these modes of diffusion lies in the effect which they have on local styles of living.

*Formal Organizations.* The adult extension program of the land grant college is mediated at the local level by the county agent and the home demonstration agent who respectively are concerned with farming methods and production, and patterns of home-making and family life. These agents carry out their program through the Farm and Home Bureau organizations. In Springdale township these agencies have a membership of 300–400 adults. The county agent is primarily concerned with introducing modern methods of farm production and operation and with fostering political consciousness among the farmers. As a type of executive secretary to the local Farm Bureau, whose officers are local farmers, the agent acts as an advisor in planning the organization's program, which includes such items as production and marketing problems, parity price problems and taxation problems.

The organizational structure of the Home Bureau parallels the Farm Bureau. From skills and techniques and personnel available at the extension center, local programs consist, for example, of furniture refinishing or aluminum working as well as discussions on such topics as child-rearing, nutrition, penal institutions and interior design. The Home Bureau extension specialist trains a local woman in information and techniques which are reported back to the local club. This program, geared as it is to modern home-making, child-rearing and the feminine role, has the effect of introducing new styles and standards of taste and consumption for the membership.

Other institutional connectors similar to the above in organizational structure account for the introduction of still other social values and social definitions. The 4-H Club, the Future Farmers of America and the Boy and Girl Scouts, as well as the Masons, Odd Fellows, American Legion, Grange and other local branches of national organizations and their auxiliaries, relate the Springdaler to the larger society through the social meanings and styles of activity defined in the programs, procedures and rituals of the national headquarters. State and national conventions, but not office holding, of these as well as church organizations directly link individuals to the outside. In effect these arrangements regularize and institutionalize the communication and organizational nexus between the small town and the point of origin of new ideas and values.

New cultural standards are also imported by agents who are not permanent residents of the town or who have only a transient relationship with it. These include the teachers at the central school, many of whom view their jobs as a temporary interlude in a progression of experience which will lead to a position in a city system. The other agents of contact are a wide variety of salesmen and "experts" who have a regular or irregular contact with business, government and private organizations. From the surrounding urban centers and the regional sales offices of farm implement and automobile manufacturers and nationally branded products, modern methods of merchandizing and business practice are introduced. Experts in civil defense, evangelism, fire-fighting, gardening, charity drives, traffic control and youth recreation introduce new techniques and programs to the local community. This great variety and diversity of semi-permanent and changing contacts in their cumulative effect act as a perpetual blood transfusion to local society. The net effect that these agents have as transmitters of life styles depends in a measure on their position and prestige in the community. The differential effect of these cultural contacts is treated below.

*The Mass Media.* Social diffusion through the symbols and pictorial images of the mass media of communications has permeated the community, reducing the local paper to reporting of social items and local news already known by everyone. Few individuals read only the local weekly paper; the majority subscribe to dailies published in surrounding cities and in the large metropolitan areas. This press, itself part of larger newspaper combines, presents an image of the passing scene in its news and nationally syndicated features to which the population of an entire region is exposed.

The mass culture and mass advertising of television and radio reach Springdale in all their variety. Television, particularly, is significant in its impact because for the first time the higher art forms such as ballet, opera and plays are visible to a broad rural audience. National events such as party conventions, inaugurations and investigative hearings are visible now to an audience which was previously far removed from the national centers of action and drama. Because of the relative geographic isolation of Springdale, television has made available entirely new areas of entertainment, information and education. It has created new leisure-time interests, has introduced new modes of leisure-time consumption and has led to the acceptance of standardized entertainment models. Wrestling, Arthur Godfrey and Howdy-Doody are common symbols of entertainment. Equally available and pervasive among the classes and individuals to whom they appeal are pocket books, comic books, and horror and sex stories. Micky Spillane, Willie Mays, Davy Crockett and other nationally prominent personages as well as nationally branded products are as well known and available to the small town as they are to the big city. The intrusion of the mass media is so overwhelming that little scope is left for the expression of local cultural and artistic forms.

However, the diffusion of the printed word is not limited to the mass media; it is present also in the realm of education, both religious and secular. The state department of education syllabus defines minimum standards and content for subject matter instruction. Courses of Sunday School instruction are available for all age levels, and each faith secures its material from its own national religious press. In each of these major institutional areas the standards and *content* of instruction are defined in sources available only in standardized form. . . .

*The Immigrant As Cultural Carrier.* Specific individuals are carriers of cultural diffusion, and the volume and extent of migration in and out of the community suggests the degree and intimacy of its contact with the mass society. In a community which is regarded as stable and relatively unchanging by its own inhabitants, only 25 percent of its population was born locally. Another 25 percent has moved into the community since 1946 and 55 percent are new to the community since 1920. Moreover, of the 45 percent who have moved to the community since 1932, more than 30 percent have lived for a year or longer in cities with populations in excess of 25,000; 7 percent in cities with populations in excess of one-half million.

Each decade and each generation introduces a new layer of immigrants to the community. The agricultural and business prosperity of the 1940's and early 1950's has brought city dwellers to farms and to businesses on main street, and the housing shortage has led workers to reclaim long-abandoned farm dwellings. The 12 percent of new people who moved into Springdale in the Thirties came in response to the effects of the depression. From 1918 to 1928 the Poles moved onto farms abandoned by descendants of original settlers. Indeed, the ebb and flow of migration extends back to such eras of political and economic upheaval as the depression of the 1890's, the civil war, the depression of the 1830's and the mass movement of people during the Indian Wars and the opening of the territory in the early 1800's. Each new wave of migrants, bringing with it the fashions and thought styles of other places, influences the cultural development of the community.

The cumulative consequences of these channels of diffusion and the quantity and quality of the "material" diffused denies the existence of a culture indigenous to the small town. In almost all aspects of culture, even to speech forms, and including technology, literature, fashions and fads, as well as patterns of consumption, to mention a few, the small town tends to reflect the contemporary mass society.

Basically, an historically indigenous local culture does not seem to exist. The cultural imports of each decade and generation and the successive waves of migration associated with each combine to produce a local culture consisting of layers or segments of the mass culture of successive historical eras. In the small town the remaining elements of the gay-ninety culture are juxtaposed against the modern central school. The newer cultural importations frequently come in conflict with the older importations of other eras. The conflict between "spurious" and "genuine" culture appears to be a conflict between two different ages of "spurious" culture.

## The Economic Nexus: Occupational Gatekeepers to the Mass Society

Simply because individuals pursue given occupations, their interconnections with mass society follow given patterns. They may be direct employees of specific organizations of the mass society; they may be the objects and targets of the programs of mass organizations; they may be trained by and in great institutions or their skills may be utilized only in urban areas. Because of these occupational characteristics they are specially qualified, accessible and available as transmitters of specific organizational and cultural contacts and contents.

Because these individuals in their occupational roles as gatekeepers are treated as specialists by both the community and mass society, occupation even more than life style becomes a crucial dimension of community life. The content, quality and amount of cultural importation accounted for by an individual is a function of the specific occupational nexus which he has to both the community and mass society.

*The Professionals.* A number of institutional representatives who are residents of the town receive their position in the community by virtue of their connections with outside agencies. Their position in the community is secured in part by the institution to which they are connected and by the evaluation of the role they are imputed to have in the agency which they locally represent.

The group of individuals who possess a borrowed prestige based on their external affiliations fall largely in the professional category. They are individuals who uniformly possess a college education. Among their ranks are included lawyers, ministers, doctors, teachers, engineers, and a variety of field representatives of state and federal agencies who settle in the community for occupational purposes. All of these individuals, except one or two, have migrated to the community as adults. In addition to the prestige which they are accorded by virtue of being "educated," their overwhelming characteristic as a group lies in the influence which they have in mediating between the town and the larger society. They possess the knowledge and techniques necessary for connecting the small town to the intricate organization of the mass bureaucratic society. They possess "contacts" with outside agencies and their role requires an ability to understand "official" documents and forms, and to write appropriate letters to appropriate bureaus. Thus, for example, the lawyer is counsel to political bodies as well as to free associations and other local organizations, in which capacities he gains an extensive and intimate knowledge of affairs of the town and thereby acquires a position of influence. In like manner the technical knowledge of state educational regulations and policies possessed by the high-school principal is indispensable to the locally constituted school board.

In addition to the prestige and influence which segments of this group possess by virture of their education and institutional role, they are accorded a respect and, in some cases, awe because of the power which they are imputed to have in manipulating the outside world; they can accomplish things for the community which no one else can.

Moreover, this professional group as a whole, including the relatively transient teaching staff, are felt to have access to styles of taste and consumption which are considered different from those available to the rest of the community. As a result these institutional connectors are considered outside the ordinary realm of prestige assignments and social stratification. That is, their social position in the community is not guaranteed by conforming to standards which are indigenous to the community but, rather, by imputed conformance to "alien" or "exotic" standards of urban life.

As a result of this dual position, individuals in this group, especially those who have come from or have resided for some time outside the community, are able to influence styles of consumption and thought in the community. They do this in three main areas of activity: in organizational activities, community projects and social fashions. They have been prime movers in setting up a formal program of youth recreation and in vigorously participating in and supporting local cultural activities such as plays, recitals and educational talks. In the P.T.A. they constitute the block favoring those modern methods and programs which bring the outside world to the small town—talks by foreign university students, race relations discussions and socio-dramas in dating and parent-child relationships. Ideas for the development of a community center and adult education programs emanate from and are supported by them. In terms of dress styles and personal adornment as well as home furnishings and styles of party giving, this group is in the forefront of innovation.

This innovating group of middle-class newcomers is supported by a group of college-educated locals who act as a bridge between the new standards and local society. In supporting these new standards, the local group absorbs some of the resentment which is directed at the innovating group by both the farmers and merchants. . . .

It must be noted that the professionals' psychological orientation to accentuate the "elite" cultural values of mass society is more than merely a product of their residence, education or background in the mass society. The limitations on economic success and the limited professional opportunities in the community means that the drive toward success through work and investment is not fully available to them. The possession of alien cultural standards makes it possible for the professionals to reject the success drive by accepting meaningful standards alternative to those available to the rest of the community; they distinguish themselves in the community by their identification with external values.

*Businessmen.* For storekeepers, filling station operators, appliance dealers, automobile and farm equipment dealers and feed mill operators, the external world is a source of supply for the goods and commodities which they sell on the local market. Their position in relation to their source of supply and the overall condition of the national economy determines the level of their business activity, ceilings on their potential income, and hence indirectly their style of life. To analyze this group we must consider separately the position of the independent shopkeeper, the businessman who operates on a franchise and the feed mill and farm implement dealer.

The shopkeepers who make up the bulk of the business community have experienced a slow and gradual decline in their class position relative to other groups in the community. This is mainly due to the breakdown of their monopolistic position with respect to the local market, but it is also related to the rise of other groups. The development of the automobile, the appearance of the chain stores in surrounding areas and the expansion of mail order sales have placed them in a competitively disadvantageous position. Moreover, the nationally branded and advertised product, with its fixed profit margin determined by the producer, has tended in a general way to determine his volume/profit ratio in a way increasingly disadvantageous to him. His decrease in profits in relation to volume has driven him to greater competition with other local shopkeepers—a competition which takes place in the form of despecialization, greater reliance on credit trade and keeping his shop open for long hours. The first two of these responses to his dilemma have further depressed his profit/volume ratio: in the one case by reducing his return on his investment and in the other case by increased losses due to bad debts. He keeps his business open in an effort to improve his investment/profit ratio and this he can do only by staying in the store himself. . . .

The position of the businessman who operates on a *franchise* is more obviously linked to the mass society. Usually he not only has a single source of supply, but also his source of supply (a petroleum company, for example) specifies the business practices and standards which must be maintained in order to retain the franchise. If the retail outlet is owned by the supplier (as with some filling stations) rents may be charged on a sliding scale according to volume of business—less volume, less rent—with the consequence that the profit margin of the local operator is not fixed. . . . As individuals they are relatively unimportant to the community since there is a high rate of turnover of franchises.

There are three individuals in the business class who are exceptions. These are the feed mill operators and the farm implement dealers who in Springdale

consist of one feed mill operator located on the periphery of the township, one implement dealer located in the village, and one large-scale combined feed mill, housing supply and farm implement partnership. Because they service an agricultural industry which since the early Forties has been prosperous, they are favorably situated in the local economy.

In terms of their customer relationships they are most intimately tied to the farmers, especially to the prosperous farmers, who do most of the buying. Because of their market position their economic fate is intimately related to that of the farmers. In the period of farm ascendancy at the time of the study, they too were prosperous and exhibited all of the same aspects of expansion, investment and opportunity-consciousness already described for the farmer. In addition, however, because they are businessmen and the most successful businessmen, they have achieved the respect, admiration and enmity of the business community as well as of the town at large.

They are the most heavily capitalized group of individuals in the community and play an important credit function in the local agricultural economy. Because of the farmer's economic dependence on them and the interlocking character of their mutual fate, the feed mill and the implement dealers identify themselves with the farmer's interests. In local politics they are in a position to provide the leadership in organizing the farmer's interests and frequently act as spokesman for the farm community. . . .

*Industrial Workers.* Industrial workers represent a curious gap in the relationship of the rural community to mass society. Individuals who live in Springdale but work outside on products which are geared to a national market are not understandable to other members of the community because the rural community lacks the perceptual apparatus necessary to understand industry and the industrial process. The industrial worker lives in the community, but the occupational basis of his existence is not subject to the social pigeon-holing by others necessary to making judgments and assessments of him.

Industrial workers consist mainly of individuals and their families who have migrated to the community in an effort to escape city life and to seek cheaper housing as well as land for home gardens. Due to the ecological conditions of the rural community (a large number of abandoned farm dwellings and the breakup of large houses into apartments), in-migrating as well as native industrial workers live in a scattered pattern throughout the township. As a consequence of their work routine, which involves, in addition to their work in a factory, one or two hours of commuting plus, in many cases, the operation of an extensive garden, home improvements and the care of livestock or a secondary occupation, this group tends to be relatively socially isolated in its day-to-day contact with the rest of the community. Their work carries them to the city where they can do their shopping and engage in city activities. As individuals some of the industrial workers strive to become involved in community activities and many of them maintain an affiliation with one of the local churches. . . .

*Farmers.* As noted earlier, there are two classes of farmers, the rational and the traditional. A major difference between them is the way they organize their production in relation to the mass market and government regulations.

Those who gear themselves to the mass market address themselves to favorably pegged prices, subsidies and quotas. As a consequence when prices and regulations are favorable they accept the favorable environment as a condition for their operations. They invest and expand, work hard and are successful. Their success stimulates confidence and buoyancy and produces an expansionist psychology. . . .

To show how the internal status position of the farmer is related to the institutional structure of the larger society, account must be taken of the fluctuations in the agricultural economy over the past thirty years. The agricultural depression beginning after World War I and extending to the beginning of World War II placed the farmer in a depressed (indebted) economic position. The decline of the farmer in Springdale was more extreme than in the nation at large during this period because Springdale is a marginal agricultural area with relatively poor land and a high rate of feed purchases. Farmers were either dispossessed, displaced or they retrenched to a heavily indebted minimum standard of consumption and operation. In this period the farmer verged on being declassed or actually was declassed.

Today the farmer is an important and ascendant segment of the rural middle class. From a position of near bankruptcy in 1933 he had risen (at the time of the field work for this study) to a position of heavy capitalization and social prominence. His rise coincided with the rationalization of marketing procedures (The Federal Milk Price Order in the New York Milk Shed), federal agricultural policies, and the rise in the market value of his products since the early 1940's. Specific agricultural policies which have contributed to his rise include the price support program, farm credit programs, and fertilizer and other land improvement give-aways. A little recognized source of preferential treatment given him by an outside agency lies in the structure of United States income tax laws, which allow for rapid depreciation of plant and equipment, little accountability on cash sales and a broad base of allowable operating expenses.

Although the status of all farmers is equally linked to decisions and policies of these larger institutional structures (the price structure and federal agricultural legislation), all farmers do not equally orient their operations to legislation and regulations oriented to them. At this point the rate of status ascendancy of the individual farmer is probably directly related to the extent to which he accepts the preferential treatment accorded him in these larger policy decisions. Those who have been most swift and efficient in adjusting to the changing conditions of the agricultural economy over the past twenty years constitute the most rapidly ascending segment of farmers.

As a consequence of the character of the institutional connectors which link the farmer to the great society, the status of the farmer relative to other local groups is relatively independent of local community forces. By the same token, his status is directly related to price structures and mass decisions and policies. Alterations in these external forces, such as a tumbling in farm prices, can cause an upheaval in the status of the local community.

## The Political Surrender to Mass Society

Local political institutions consist of a village board, a town board and local committees of the Republican and Democratic parties. The jurisdiction of the village board includes powers of control and regulation over a variety of community facilities and services—street lighting, water supply, fire protection, village roads, street signs and parks. To carry out the functions empowered to it, it possesses the power of taxation. The town board is concerned chiefly with fire protection, the construction and maintenance of roads;

through its participation on the county board of supervisors, it participates in programs connected with welfare, penal and other county services.

However, at almost every point in this seemingly broad base of political domain the village and town boards adjust their action to either the regulations and laws defined by state and federal agencies which claim parallel functions on a statewide or nationwide basis or to the fact that outside agencies have the power to withhold subsidies to local political institutions.

Local assessment scales and tax rates are oriented to state equalization formulas which partially provide the standardized basis on which subsidies are dispersed by the state. State highway construction and development programs largely present local political agencies with the alternative of either accepting or rejecting proposed road plans and programs formulated by the state highway department.

The village board, more than the town board, is dependent on its own taxable resources (taxes account for almost half its revenues) and best illustrates the major dimensions of local political action. The village board in Springdale accepts few of the powers given to it. Instead, it orients its action to the facilities and subsidies controlled and dispensed by other agencies and, by virtue of this, forfeits its own political power. Solutions to the problem of fire protection are found in agreements with regionally organized fire districts. In matters pertaining to road signs and street signs action typically takes the form of petitioning state agencies to fulfill desired goals "without cost to the taxpaper." On roads built and maintained by the state there is no recourse but to accept the state traffic bureau's standards of safety. A problem such as snow removal is solved by dealing directly with the foreman of the state highway maintenance crew through personal contacts: "If you treat him right, you can get him to come in and clear the village roads." In other areas of power where there are no parallel state agencies, such as for garbage collections or parks, the village board abdicates its responsibility.

As a consequence of this pattern of dependence, many important decisions are made for Springdale by outside agencies. Decisions which are made locally tend to consist of approving the requirements of administrative or state laws. In short the program and policies of local political bodies are determined largely by acceptance · of grants-in-aid offered them—i.e., in order to get the subsidy specific types of decisions must be made—and by facilities and services made available to them by outside sources.

Psychologically this dependence leads to an habituation to outside control to the point where the town and village governments find it hard to act even where they have the power. Legal jurisdictions have been supplanted by psychological jurisdictions to such an extent that local political action is almost exclusively oriented to and predicated on seeking favors, subsidies and special treatment from outside agencies. The narrowing of legal jurisdictions by psychologically imposed limits leads to an inability to cope with local problems if outside resources are not available.

Power in local political affairs, then, tends to be based on accessibility to sources of decision in larger institutions. Frequently this accessibility consists merely of the knowledge of the source, or it may mean a personal contact, or an ability to correspond to get necessary information. Under these circumstances, power in the political arena is delegated to those with contacts in and knowledge of the outer world and to those who are experts in formal communication with impersonal bureaucratic offices. These are, on the individual level, the lawyer and, on an institutional level, the political party. The lawyer gains his paramountcy through technical knowledge and personalized non-party contacts up the political hierarchy with other lawyers. He is the mediator between the local party and the party hierarchy, and transforms his personalized contacts into political indispensability in the local community. His access to outside sources of power determines his power and predominance in the local community.

## The Social Psychological Consequences of the Rural Surrender

A central fact of rural life, then, is its dependence on the institutions and dynamics of urban and mass society. The recognition of this dependence and the powerlessness associated with it give to the agents and institutions of the great society a degree of respect and admiration which, however, does not always connote approval. Rather, there is a high degree of ambivalence with respect to these agents and institutions. They have respect because of their power and wealth, and because their norms have the legitimacy of acceptance in wide areas of the society at large. On the other hand, the very dominance of the mass institutions causes resentments, since, in the light of this dominance, rural life in its immediacy is devalued. Hence, for example, although the standards of the land grant college are accepted, the institution and its agents may be resented for the role they play in innovation.

The phenomenon of psychological ambivalence to the mass society is particularly reinforced by the fact that slight changes in the policies and dynamics of the mass institutions can have profound effects on the rural way of life and on its major social and economic classes—i.e., parity policies, industrial relocations, new state roads and state subsidization formulas. In response to these conditions, the members of the rural community and their political spokesmen resent their dependency and powerlessness and channelize it into anti-urban politics and policies. In relation to the outer world, there exist two types of political victory; when rural rather than urban areas get a disproportionately large share of the benefits of the state budget and when the city can be made the object of investigation on grounds of corruption or vice by politicians surrounded by a halo of rural images. At the same time a personal identification with important urban political officials lends an individual prestige in the rural community.

But this continuous transvaluation of the attitudes toward urban life and its representatives are never so simple as the dependence-resentment mechanism would suggest. For such political and psychological currents are supported by intricately articulated images of the mass society and rural self images . . . which for the purposes of this discussion can be termed counterimages.

These images, themselves, are a product of complex institutional developments and reflect the process of urban penetration. For it is uniquely ironical that the self-image of the rural community and its image of urban life are in part the products of the penetration of urban mass media. Through these media the people of Springdale see urban life dominated by crime, dirt, filth, immorality, vice, corruption and anti-Americanism. The urban center is seen as a jungle of man's inhumanity to man; the large political center as a "dog-eat-dog" world of investigations and counterinvestigations with few clearly defined heroes. It sees the urban middle classes confronted by appar-

ently hopeless personal problems and moving from crisis to crisis without end. It is because of the mechanism of resentment that the Springdaler can see wide class differences in urban society and be unaware of class in his own environment.

Contrariwise, the mass media frequently present rural life in idyllic terms. The *Saturday Evening Post* cover brings forth the image of the cracker barrel, the virtues of life close to soil and stream and of healthy, simple, family living. The weekly press carries syndicated columnists who extol the virtues of ruralism. Political as well as feature speakers who come to town invariably reinforce the town's image of itself: "The false life of cities," "If America were made up of small towns like Springdale, this would be a better country." "The goodness of America lies in the small town where life and nature meet to make for genuine living." The urban man of knowledge and the university scientist verbalize their own image of rural life and in doing so shape the self-image of the rural audience. . . .

The farmer [for example] is strong, self-reliant and capable. He is warm, affectionate and devoted but these characteristics are frequently hidden under a crusty, gruff exterior. He is a good businessman and a sharp trader capable in the final analysis of outwitting others, especially the city slicker. Outside of a few old gossips, community life is richly warm and filled with a wide variety of social interchange, gatherings and genuinely spontaneous self-expression. The rural dweller is religious, moral and upright, though capable of "cutting-up" in a way which is both amusing and tolerable. . . .

From the standpoint of the producer of mass media, to complete the picture, the image presented of rural life and life in general reflects not only his estimate of his audience (since not all of the mass media are specifically aimed at the rural market) but also the psychological climate of the urban centers where images of rural life are produced. The romanticization of rural life in press and radio reflects the need of the urban dweller to conceive of rural life as simpler and freer from the complexities, tensions and anxieties which he faces in his own world. Rural life is thus conceived as a counter-image which highlights his own situation. However, when presented to the rural resident, it serves as an image which enables the rural dweller to form symbolic and ideological resistance to urban society. It is thus through the mass media that the negative reactions to mass society of both the rural and urban dweller are linked; and it is as sets of similar responses to the negative aspects of urbanism that both urban and rural dwellers find a common symbolic meeting ground. . . .

Hence, those factors which appear to be decisive in determining the action of the rural community are factors which originate in areas outside the rural community. Thus, even when the rural community attacks the urban mass society, the nature of the attack, its intensity and the situations which bring it forth are, in large part, the products of urban mass society. Rural life, then, can be seen as one area in which the dynamics of modern urban mass society are worked out. . . .

# C Bureaucracy

## INTRODUCTION

Bureaucracy is a form of social organization which men have invented for carrying out administrative tasks in large, complex societies. Bureaucracy was used by the ancient Egyptians for organizing the complex economy of the Nile Valley and the empire; the emperors and empresses of ancient China used a bureaucratic form of organization to govern their vast empires; and the Romans used bureaucracy to administer their far-flung territories, as well as to organize the provision of large cities and the command of the Legions. Today, as human societies become large and complex the world over, most of the important areas of social life within them are becoming bureaucratically organized.

The governments of modern cities and nations are composed of large numbers of administrative bureaucracies through which all the varied tasks of government are carried out. Business enterprises in the capitalist nations are becoming organized into large-scale corporate bureaucracies, the largest of which employ more people and have larger budgets than states of the United States and half the nations of the world. In socialist countries, economic activity is organized in the bureaucracies of the national government. Modern military establishments are the epitome of authoritarian bureaucracies, where total control is vested in the top positions and relations between superior and subordinate are almost purely ones of command and obedience. Education systems, even when administered on the local community level as in the United States, develop into bureaucracies simply because the communities are large and the task of educating people for life in our technologically advanced society is very complex, requiring the services of many specialists whose activities must be integrated. The modern university is a vast bureaucratic structure administering the education of as many as forty thousand students at a time. Religious denominations in modern Western societies find they must organize central bureaucracies to administer standard policies throughout the denomination. The Roman Catholic Church provides one of the oldest models of bureaucratically organized religious groups.

Max Weber was the first sociologist to make a systematic study of bureaucratic organization, both in ancient societies and in the modern West. It is his contention that bureaucracy provides the most efficient means for carrying out large-scale administrative tasks. He attributes the efficiency of bureaucracy to the basic characteristics of its structure, which he identifies as the distribution of the work in a fixed division of labor among offices, a hierarchical ordering of offices so that the work of each employee is supervised by another, a set of formal, rational rules which govern the work of all employees, objectivity and impersonality in the conduct of the affairs of each office, the filling of positions in the bureaucracy by people possessing the certified technical qualifications to carry out the work, and the definition of bureaucratic office holding as a secure full-time career for the individual in order to motivate him to work efficiently. Weber shows how each of these basic characteristics of bureaucratic organizations contributes to the overall efficiency and effectiveness of administration.

Seymour Martin Lipset discusses the common predicament of a new group of top officers coming into a bureaucratic organization and finding that career bureaucrats have effective control. The new top officers find they must somehow gain the cooperation of these bureaucrats before they can use the organization to carry out new programs they wish to institute. Lipset provides a case study of this process in a Canadian provincial government bureaucracy which had developed under many years of conservative government rule and was suddenly asked, as the result of a socialist party election victory, to administer a series of radical government programs. The resistance which the newly elected politicians met from the bureaucrats in this case is not different in kind from that which might be met by a new group of officers taking charge of a business corporation with the goal of changing its ways of operating, or by a new president of a large university wishing to reform its educational program.

Chris Argyris offers a theory of the psychological consequences of participation in bureaucratic organizations, asking what effects these organizations have on the personalities of their office holders. Using criteria of personal maturity derived from the psychiatric theories of Harry Stack Sullivan, Argyris shows that these criteria are incompatible, theoretically, with the behavior required of individuals in the lower positions of bureaucracies. If this kind of bureaucratic work is inimical to mature personality development, then Argyris has identified a basic problem for individuals in advanced industrial societies.

Alfred Weber, the younger brother of Max Weber, discusses the implications of bureaucracy for the continuation of freedom in modern societies. The hierarchical organization of bureaucracy, he points out, requires the making of decisions and the exercise of control over the organization by those in top positions, leaving those in lower positions generally powerless. This centralization has the further consequence of discouraging individual initiative in the development of new ideas and practices in the organization. The standardization of bureaucratic procedures and practices has the consequence, Weber claims, of developing uniformity in thought and behavior throughout the society. Weber sees these consequences of bureaucracy in advanced capitalist and socialist countries today and argues that only a structural reorganization of these societies can preserve freedom in the modern world.

# 33

# Formal Characteristics of Bureaucracy

## MAX WEBER

Modern officialdom functions in the following specific manner:

I. There is the principle of fixed and official jurisdictional areas, which are generally ordered by rules, that is, by laws or administrative regulations. (1.) The regular activities required for the purposes of the bureaucratically governed structure are distributed in a fixed way as official duties. (2.) The authority to give the commands required for the discharge of these duties is distributed in a stable way and is strictly delimited by rules concerning the coercive means, physical, sacerdotal, or otherwise, which may be placed at the disposal of officials. (3.) Methodical provision is made for the regular and continuous fulfilment of these duties and for the execution of the corresponding rights; only persons who have the generally regulated qualifications to serve are employed.

In public and lawful government these three elements constitute 'bureaucratic authority.' In private economic domination, they constitute bureaucratic 'management.' Bureaucracy, thus understood, is fully developed in political and ecclesiastical communities only in the modern state, and, in the private economy, only in the most advanced institutions of capitalism. Permanent and public office authority, with fixed jurisdiction, is not the historical rule but rather the exception. This is so even in large political structures such as those of the ancient Orient, the Germanic and Mongolian empires of con-

From *From Max Weber: Essays in Sociology*, edited and translated by H. H. Gerth and C. Wright Mills. Copyright © 1946 by Oxford University Press, Inc. Reprinted by permission.

quest, or of many feudal structures of state. In all these cases, the ruler executes the most important measures through personal trustees, table-companions, or court-servants. Their commissions and authority are not precisely delimited and are temporarily called into being for each case.

II. The principles of office hierarchy and of levels of graded authority mean a firmly ordered system of super- and subordination in which there is a supervision of the lower offices by the higher ones. Such a system offers the governed the possibility of appealing the decision of a lower office to its higher authority, in a definitely regulated manner. With the full development of the bureaucratic type, the office hierarchy is monocratically organized. The principle of hierarchical office authority is found in all bureaucratic structures: in state and ecclesiastical structures as well as in large party organizations and private enterprises. It does not matter for the character of bureaucracy whether its authority is called 'private' or 'public.'

When the principle of jurisdictional 'competency' is fully carried through, hierarchical subordination—at least in public office—does not mean that the 'higher' authority is simply authorized to take over the business of the 'lower.' Indeed, the opposite is the rule. Once established and having fulfilled its task, an office tends to continue in existence and be held by another incumbent.

III. The management of the modern office is based upon written documents ('the files'), which are preserved in their original or draught form. There is, therefore, a staff of subaltern officials and scribes of all sorts. The body of officials actively engaged in a 'public' office, along with the respective apparatus of material implements and the files, make up a 'bureau.' In private enterprise, 'the bureau' is often called 'the office.'

In principle, the modern organization of the civil service separates the bureau from the private domicile of the official, and, in general, bureaucracy segregates official activity as something distinct from the sphere of private life. Public monies and equipment are divorced from the private property of the official. This condition is everywhere the product of a long development. Nowadays, it is found in public as well as in private enterprises; in the latter, the principle extends even to the leading entrepreneur. In principle, the executive office is separated from the household, business from private correspondence, and business assets from private fortunes. The more consistently the modern type of business management has been carried through the more are these separations the case. The beginnings of this process are to be found as early as the Middle Ages.

It is the peculiarity of the modern entrepreneur that he conducts himself as the 'first official' of his enterprise, in the very same way in which the ruler of a specifically modern bureaucratic state spoke of himself as 'the first servant' of the state. The idea that the bureau activities of the state are intrinsically different in character from the management of private economic offices is a continental European notion and, by the way of contrast, is totally foreign to the American way.

IV. Office management, at least all specialized office management—and such management is distinctly modern —usually presupposes a thorough and expert training. This increasingly holds for the modern executive and employee of private enterprises, in the same manner as it holds for the state official.

V. When the office is fully developed, official activity demands the full working capacity of the official, irrespective of the fact that his obligatory time in the bureau may be firmly delimited. In the normal case, this is only the product of a long development, in the public as well as in the private office. Formerly, in all cases, the normal state of affairs was reversed: official business was discharged as a secondary activity.

VI. The management of the office follows general rules, which are more or less stable, more or less exhaustive, and which can be learned. Knowledge of these rules represents a special technical learning which the officials possess. It involves jurisprudence, or administrative or business management.

The reduction of modern office management to rules is deeply embedded in its very nature. The theory of modern public administration, for instance, assumes that the authority to order certain matters by decree—which has been legally granted to public authorities— does not entitle the bureau to regulate the matter by commands given for each case, but only to regulate the matter abstractly. This stands in extreme contrast to the regulation of all relationships through individual privileges and bestowals of favor, which is absolutely dominant in patrimonialism, at least in so far as such relationships are not fixed by sacred tradition.

All this results in the following for the internal and external position of the official.

I. Office holding is a 'vocation.' This is shown, first, in the requirement of a firmly prescribed course of training, which demands the entire capacity for work for a long period of time, and in the generally prescribed and special examinations which are prerequisites of employment. Furthermore, the position of the official is in the nature of a duty. This determines the internal structure of his relations, in the following manner: Legally and actually, office holding is not considered a source to be exploited for rents or emoluments, as was normally the case during the Middle Ages and frequently up to the threshold of recent times. Nor is office holding considered a usual exchange of services for equivalents, as is the case with free labor contracts. Entrance into an office, including one in the private economy, is considered an acceptance of a specific obligation of faithful management in return for a secure existence. It is decisive for the specific nature of modern loyalty to an office that, in the pure type, it does not establish a relationship to a *person*, like the vassal's or disciple's faith in feudal or in patrimonial relations of authority. Modern loyalty is devoted to impersonal and functional purposes. Behind the functional purposes, of course, 'ideas of culture-values' usually stand. These are *ersatz* for the earthly or supra-mundane personal master: ideas such as 'state,' 'church,' 'community,' 'party,' or 'enterprise' are thought of as being realized in a community; they provide an ideological halo for the master.

The political official—at least in the fully developed modern state—is not considered the personal servant of a ruler. Today, the bishop, the priest, and the preacher are in fact no longer, as in early Christian times, holders of purely personal charisma. The supra-mundane and sacred values which they offer are given to everybody who seems to be worthy of them and who asks for them. In former times, such leaders acted upon the personal command of their master; in principle, they were responsible only to him. Nowadays, in spite of the partial survival of the old theory, such religious leaders are officials in the service of a functional purpose, which in the present-day 'church' has become routinized and, in turn, ideologically hallowed.

II. The personal position of the official is patterned in the following way:

(1.) Whether he is in a private office or a public bureau, the modern official always strives and usually enjoys a distinct *social esteem* as compared with the governed. His social position is guaranteed by the prescriptive rules of rank order and, for the political official, by special definitions of the criminal code against 'insults of officials' and 'contempt' of state and church authorities.

The actual social position of the official is normally highest where, as in old civilized countries, the following conditions prevail: a strong demand for administration by trained experts; a strong and stable social differentiation, where the official predominantly derives from socially and economically privileged strata because of the social distribution of power; or where the costliness of the required training and status conventions are binding upon him. The possession of educational certificates—to be discussed elsewhere —are usually linked with qualification for office. Naturally, such certificates or patents enhance the 'status element' in the social position of the official. For the rest this status factor in individual cases is explicitly and impassively acknowledged; for example, in the prescription that the acceptance or rejection of an aspirant to an official career depends upon the consent ('election') of the members of the official body. This is the case in the German army with the officer corps. Similar phenomena, which promote this guild-like closure of officialdom, are typically found in patrimonial and, particularly, in prebendal officialdoms of the past. The desire to resurrect such phenomena in changed forms is by no means infrequent among modern bureaucrats. For instance, they have played a role among the demands of the quite proletarian and expert officials (the *tretyj* element) during the Russian revolution.

Usually the social esteem of the officials as such is especially low where the demand for expert administration and the dominance of status conventions are weak. This is especially the case in the United States; it is often the case in new settlements by virtue of their wide fields for profit-making and the great instability of their social stratification.

(2.) The pure type of bureaucratic official is *appointed* by a superior authority. An official elected by the governed is not a purely bureaucratic figure. Of course, the formal existence of an election does not by itself mean that no appointment hides behind the election—in the state, especially, appointment by party chiefs. Whether or not this is the case does not depend upon legal statutes but upon the way in which the party mechanism functions. Once firmly organized, the parties can turn a formally free election into the mere acclamation of a candidate designated by the party chief. As a rule, however, a formally free election is turned into a fight, conducted according to definite rules, for votes in favor of one of two designated candidates.

In all circumstances, the designation of officials by means of an election among the governed modifies the strictness of hierarchical subordination. In principle, an official who is so elected has an autonomous position opposite the superordinate official. The elected official does not derive his position 'from above' but 'from below,' or at least not from a superior authority of the official hierarchy but from powerful party men ('bosses'), who also determine his further career. The career of the elected official is not, or at least not primarily, dependent upon his chief in the administration. The official who is not elected but appointed by a chief normally functions more exactly, from a technical point of view, because, all other circumstances being equal, it is more likely that purely functional points of consideration and qualities will determine his selection and career.

As laymen, the governed can become acquainted with the extent to which a candidate is expertly qualified for office only in terms of experience, and hence only after his service. Moreover, in every sort of selection of officials by election, parties quite naturally give decisive weight not to expert considerations but to the services a follower renders to the party boss. This holds for all kinds of procurement of officials by elections, for the designation of formally free, elected officials by party bosses when they determine the slate of candidates, or the free appointment by a chief who has himself been elected. The contrast, however, is relative: substantially similar conditions hold where legitimate monarchs and their subordinates appoint officials, except that the influence of the followings are then less controllable.

Where the demand for administration by trained experts is considerable, and the party followings have to recognize an intellectually developed, educated, and freely moving 'public opinion,' the use of unqualified officials falls back upon the party in power at the next election. Naturally, this is more likely to happen when the officials are appointed by the chief. The demand for a trained administration now exists in the United States, but in the large cities, where immigrant votes are 'corraled,' there is, of course, no educated public opinion. Therefore, popular elections of the administrative chief and also of his subordinate officials usually endanger the expert qualification of the official as well as the precise functioning of the bureaucratic mechanism. It also weakens the dependence of the officials upon the hierarchy. This holds at least for the large administrative bodies that are difficult to supervise. The superior qualification and integrity of federal judges, appointed by the President, as over against elected judges in the United States is well known, although both types of officials have been selected primarily in terms of party considerations. The great changes in American metropolitan administrations demanded by reformers have proceeded essentially from elected mayors working with an apparatus of officials who were appointed by them. These reforms have thus come about in a 'Caesarist' fashion. Viewed technically, as an organized form of authority, the efficiency of 'Caesarism,' which often grows out of democracy, rests in general upon the position of the 'Caesar' as a free trustee of the masses (of the army or of the citizenry), who is unfettered by tradition. The 'Caesar' is thus the unrestrained master of a body of highly qualified military officers and officials whom he selects freely and personally without regard to tradition or to any other considerations. This 'rule of the personal genius,' however, stands in contradiction to the formally 'democratic' principle of a universally elected officialdom.

(3.) Normally, the position of the official is held for life, at least in public bureaucracies; and this is increasingly the case for all similar structures. As a factual rule, *tenure for life* is presupposed, even where the giving of notice or periodic reappointment occurs. In contrast to the worker in a private enterprise, the official normally holds tenure. Legal or actual life-tenure, however, is not recognized as the official's right to the possession of office, as was the case with many structures of authority in the past. Where legal guarantees against arbitrary dismissal or transfer are developed, they merely serve to guarantee a strictly objective discharge of specific office duties free from all personal considerations. In Germany, this is the case for all juridical and, increasingly, for all administrative officials.

Within the bureaucracy, therefore, the measure of 'independence,' legally guaranteed by tenure, is not always a source of increased status for the official whose position is thus secured. Indeed, often the reverse holds, especially in old cultures and communities that are highly differentiated. In such communities, the stricter the subordination under the arbitrary rule of the master, the more it guarantees the maintenance of the conventional seigneurial style of living for the official. Because of the very absence of these legal guarantees of tenure, the conventional esteem for the official may rise in the same way as, during the Middle Ages, the esteem of the nobility of office rose at the expense of esteem for the freemen, and as the king's judge surpassed that of the people's judge. In Germany, the military officer or the administrative official can be removed from office at any time, or at least far more readily than the 'independent judge,' who never pays with loss of his office for even the grossest offense against the 'code of honor' or against social conventions of the salon. For this very reason, if other things are equal, in the eyes of the master stratum the judge is considered less qualified for social intercourse than are officers and administrative officials, whose greater dependence on the master is a greater guarantee of their conformity with status conventions. Of course, the average official strives for a civil-service law, which would materially secure his old age and provide increased guarantees against his arbitrary removal from office. This striving, however, has its limits. A very strong development of the 'right to the office' naturally makes it more difficult to staff them with regard to technical efficiency, for such a development decreases the career-opportunities of ambitious candidates for office. This makes for the fact that officials, on the whole, do not feel their dependency upon those at the top. This lack of a feeling of dependency, however, rests primarily upon the inclination to depend upon one's equals rather than upon the socially inferior and governed strata. The present conservative movement among the Badenia clergy, occasioned by the anxiety of a presumably threatening separation of church and state, has been expressly determined by the desire not to be turned 'from a master into a servant of the parish.'

(4.) The official receives the regular *pecuniary* compensation of a normally fixed *salary* and the old age security provided by a pension. The salary is not measured like a wage in terms of work done, but according to 'status,' that is, according to the kind of function (the 'rank') and, in addition, possibly, according to the length of service. The relatively great security of the official's income, as well as the rewards of social esteem, make the office a sought-after position, especially in countries which no longer provide opportunities for colonial profits. In such countries, this situation permits relatively low salaries for officials.

(5.) The official is set for a '*career*' within the hierachical order of the public service. He moves from the lower, less important, and lower paid to the higher positions. The average official naturally desires a mechanical fixing of the conditions of promotion: if not of the offices, at least of the salary levels. He wants these conditions fixed in terms of 'seniority,' or possibly according to grades achieved in a developed system of expert examinations. Here and there, such examinations actually form a character *indelebilis* of the official and have lifelong effects on his career. To this is joined the desire to qualify the right to office and the increasing tendency toward status group closure and economic security. All of this makes for a tendency to consider the offices as 'prebends' of those who are qualified by educational certificates. The necessity of taking general personal and intellectual qualifications into consideration, irrespective of the often subaltern character of the educational certificate, has led to a condition in which the highest political offices, especially the positions of 'ministers,' are principally filled without reference to such certificates.

# 34

# Bureaucracy and Social Reform

## SEYMOUR MARTIN LIPSET

Various writers and social scientists have long called attention to the fact that, in large-scale social organizations, administrative functions cannot be separated from policy-making power.[1] It is

Reprinted from *Research Studies*, Washington State University, 17 (1949), pp. 11–17, with permission of the publisher and the author. This paper is a summary of a chapter in *Agrarian Socialism* by Seymour Martin Lipset (Berkeley: University of California Press, 1950) Anchor Book edition 1967.
[1] See Harold Laski, *Democracy in Crisis* (London: George Allen and Unwin, Ltd.,

impossible to understand the operation of a government purely by analyzing the goals of the politicians in power, and the nongovernmental pressures on them. The members of the administrative bureaucracy, the Civil Service, constitute one of the major "Houses" of

1933), pp. 99–104; Max Weber, *Essays in Sociology* ed. by H. Gerth and C. W. Mills (New York: Oxford University Press, 1946), pp. 232–233; Herman Finer, *The Future of Government* (London: Methuen and Co., 1946), pp. 12–13.

government, and as such have the power to initiate, amend, and veto actions proposed by other branches. The goals and values of the Civil Service are at least as important a part of the total complex of forces responsible for state policy as those of the ruling political party.

The political problem of the power and influence of a permanent Civil Service is not important as long as the social and economic values of the bureaucracy and the governing politicians do not seriously conflict. The problem becomes crucial, however, when a new political movement takes office and proposes to enact reforms which go beyond the traditional frame of reference of previous government activity. It is especially important today, when the explicit formal goals of many democratic states are changing from the *laissez-faire* policeman regulation of society to those of the social-welfare-planning state.[2]

The tradition and concept of a merit nonpatronage Civil Service developed in many countries as a result of the needs of the dominant business groups which demanded cheap, efficient, and predictable service from the state. Kingsley has shown how in Great Britain, the policy of the impartial Civil Service grew with the increase in political power of the business class.[3] Business men desired an efficient state which would facilitate and protect the development of commerce. Permanent, nonpolitical officials insured continuity of government regulations and practices and made for stable relations with the state, regardless of party fortunes. The policy of the merit Civil Service was not challenged as long as party politics remained contests between groups which accepted the basic orientation and activities of the state and society.[4]

The establishment of reform and socialist governments, which propose radical changes in the functions of the state, necessarily raises the problem of whether the reforms that these governments are pledged to carry out can successfully be initiated and administered by a bureaucratic structure, which is organized to regulate a different set of norms, and whose members possess different values from those of the "radical" politicians.

Since the days of Karl Marx, some socialists have maintained that a successful socialist state "must destroy the old state apparatus," that is, erect a new administrative organization. In recent times, various individuals who have served in or studied socialist or "social welfare" governments have suggested that one crucial reason for their failure to proceed more vigorously toward the attainment of their goals has been the "bureaucratic conservative" influence of permanent Civil Servants. This point has been made about the Social-Democratic governments in Weimar (Germany), the various Labor governments in Great Britain, Australia, and New Zealand, the Popular Front governments in France, and the New Deal in the United States.[5]

[2] See J. Donald Kingsley, *Representative Bureaucracy* (Yellow Springs: The Antioch Press, 1944), pp. 287–305.
[3] *Ibid.*, pp. 42–72.

[4] See L. D. White and T. V. Smith, *Politics and Public Service* (New York: Harper and Brothers, 1939), pp. 132–33.
[5] See Arnold Brecht, "Bureaucratic Sabotage," *Annals of American Academy of Political and Social Science* (January, 1937), p. 5; Edgar Lansbury, *George Lansbury, My Father* (London: Sampson Low Masston and Co., Ltd., no date), p. 197; Charles Aiken, "The British Bureaucracy and the Origin of Parliamentary Policy, *American Political Science Review*, XXXIII (Feb., 1939), pp. 40–41; V. G. Childe, *How [Australian] Labour Governs* (London: Labour Publishing Co., Ltd., 1923), p. 16; J. Donald Kingsley, *op. cit.*, p. 274; and Leon Blum, *For All Mankind* (London: Victor Gollancz, 1946), p. 59.

The validity of the hypothesis about the "conservative" role of a permanent Civil Service was tested by the author in the course of a research study of a social-democratic movement which secured power towards the end of the last war.

The Cabinet Ministers in this government anticipated "sabotage" and resistance to their plans by the permanent Civil Service. In a pre-election speech, the head of the government stated his belief that the Civil Service must be sympathetic to the objectives of the government:

It is most necessary for any government that those in charge of various departments shall be competent and capable of absorbing new ideas and techniques. No matter how good legislation is, if those in charge of administering it are unsympathetic or incapable of a new approach, little good will come of it.

The government ministers entered office ready to change key Civil Servants as soon as they showed any signs of opposition to government proposals. The ministers, however, envisaged opposition as deliberate "sabotage" and explicit defiance of government proposals. The key Civil Servants, on the other hand, expected to be discharged or demoted soon after the socialists took office. A number of them, therefore had begun to look for other jobs or planned to retire. In the hope of maintaining their positions, however, many of these Civil Servants began to ingratiate themselves with their ministers.

Almost all of the leading Civil Servants were outwardly obsequious, flattered their ministers, and in general, did everything they could to convince the Cabinet that they were cooperative. In many departments, during the early period of the new government, the best "socialists" were in the top ranks of the government bureaucracy. The administratively insecure Cabinet ministers were overjoyed at the response which they secured from the Civil Servants. They were happy to find people in their departments who were friendly and helpful. To avoid making administrative blunders which would injure them in the eyes of the public and the party, the ministers gradually began to depend on the Civil Servants, who never criticized and knew the internal operations of the department.[6]

The failure to change key members of the Civil Service had important consequences for the future work of the government, as it was interpreted by many of the officials as revealing personal weakness on the part of their ministers and a lack of political strength on the part of the movement. The Civil Servants, soon realizing that there was no danger of being discharged, fell back into the bureaucratic pattern of maintaining the traditional practices and the equilibrium of their departments. Some Civil Servants succeeded in convincing their ministers that various proposed changes were administratively infeasible, or that they would incur too much opposition from im-

---

[6] "[Specialist] Ministers are likely to arrive in office, not with a complete body of specific plans, but with some general principles which the departments will be asked to test against the facts before they are given the share of a concrete measure. The inevitable tendency of the departments will be, for the Minister's own sake, to minimize the break with tradition. . . . They will be passionately and laudably anxious to save him from failure. Unless they share his own outlook—and this is unlikely enough—they will want time where he demands speed, the attack on the narrow front, where his instruction is for comprehensiveness.

". . . . this attitude in the civil service is wholly compatible with the tradition of neutrality. . . . My point is the quite different one that . . . the whole ethos of the service becomes one of criticism which looks towards delay instead of encouragement which looks toward action." Harold Laski, *op. cit.*, pp. 103–04.

portant groups in the community. Top-ranking Civil Servants exchanged information with each other on their techniques of "controlling" their ministers. It is difficult to demonstrate concretely and it would be revealing confidential information to do so, but it is a fact that in conversations with others, key officials have boasted of "running my department completely," and of "stopping hare-brained radical schemes."

The resistance of top-level Civil Servants to proposed new reforms was not necessarily a result of their conscious anti-socialist sympathies. Though there were probably instances in which direct partisan sabotage of the government took place, the most significant "bureaucratic conservative" influence on the government does not appear to be a result of attempts to injure the government. Many of the leading officials appeared to be honestly concerned with doing their jobs. These Civil Servants would probably have attempted to modify schemes of conservative governments which appeared unworkable to them. The bureaucracy, however, had become institutionalized under conservative governments. Its pattern of reacting to problems had been routinized. New methods of administration were often considered difficult or "impossible" to the incumbent bureaucrat, either because they had never been tried before, or because they would require the revamping of the work of a department. By opposing such changes, the Civil Servant was only taking the easy way out of preserving the *status quo* in his own area of working and living. Harold Laski has pointed this out as a characteristic of bureaucracy in general:

In all large scale enterprise men who are desirous of avoiding great responsibility (and the majority of men is so desirous) are necessarily tempted to avoid great experiments. In a political democracy this obviously becomes an official habit where there is a . . . bureaucratic system. . . .

The tendency accordingly has been a certain suspicion of experimentalism, a benevolence toward the 'safe' man. . . . Administrative codes . . . are applied simply from the conservatism of habit.[7]

Civil Service modification of government goals took three major forms: (1) the continuation by government departments of traditional and, from the socialist point of view, "reactionary" modes of procedure; (2) changes in the intent of new laws and regulations through administrative practices; and (3) direct and indirect methods of influencing Cabinet members to adopt policies advocated by top-level Civil Servants. Each of the above statements will be documented in a larger study of the work of this government.[8]

The sources of Civil Service action cannot be found in an unidimensional analysis. Civil Servants, like all individuals, do not operate in a social vacuum (though one suspects that some advocates of the "impartial" Civil Service believe that they do). Their opinions about relative "right" and "wrong" on a particular issue are determined by various pressures existing in their social milieu. A department official is not only interested in whether a minister's proposals can be effectively put into operation, but must also be concerned with the effect of such policies on the traditional practices of the department, and of the long-term relations of the department with other groups in the government and in the community. A reform which may be socially desirable, but which disrupts the continuity of practices, and inter-personal relations

---

[7] Harold Laski, "Bureaucracy," in *Encyclopedia of the Social Sciences*, Volume III, ed. by Edwin R. A. Seligman (New York: The Macmillan Company, 1935), p. 72.
[8] S. M. Lipset, *Agrarian Socialism, op. cit.*

within the department, will often be resisted by a top-ranking Civil Servant. He is obligated to protect those beneath him in the administrative hierarchy from the negative consequences of a change in policy.

Second, and as important in influencing the decisions of government officials, is the fact that their opinion of the feasibility of any proposal is necessarily colored by their social and political outlook and by the climate of opinion in the social group in which they move. Many of the top-ranking Civil Servants are members of the upper class socially in the capital city in which they live. Their social contacts are largely with people who believe that they will be adversely affected by many socialist policies. Civil Servants cannot avoid being influenced by the predicament of their own social group. Those government officials who belong to professional or economic groups, whose power or privileges are threatened by government policies, tend to accept the opinion of their group that reforms which adversely affect the group are wrong and will not work.[9] There are a number of examples of Civil Servants reducing the significance of reforms directed against their own groups.

The failure of this government to change the character of the top-level Civil Service precipitated a major conflict within the party between the Cabinet ministers and the majority of the non-office holding leaders of the movement. The majority of the members of the party's legislative group, the party executive, and annual convention delegates have demanded that the government replace old administrators by more sympathetic personnel. The members of these groups usually cite many examples of actions by the Civil Service which they consider to be "administrative sabotage." The attacks on

[9] See Max Weber, *op. cit.*, p. 234.

the Cabinet by the rest of the party has gradually forced the Cabinet to modify its public position on the question, and in the last two years it has accepted the principle of a partially politicized bureaucracy and has appointed a number of sympathetic experts to leading positions in the administrative apparatus.

Many of the new "radical" Civil Servants have suggested new policies or specific means of carrying out overall government policy which would probably never have been proposed if policy formation had been left to the Cabinet and the permanent Civil Service. The ministers did not have the technical knowledge to suggest needed changes in their own field, and the old Civil Servants were not imbued with the social-democratic values of finding means to reduce the wealth and power of private-interest groups and of using the agencies of the government to increase the standards of living of the people. In at least two departments the differences in orientation of the new and old Civil Service resulted in the two groups engaging in a covert struggle to determine department policy. The permanent Civil Servants in these departments repeatedly brought their ministers into contact with representatives of the more conservative groups in their field, whereas the new Civil Servants encouraged supporters of reform to visit the minister and impress him with the widespread public support for changes. Examination of the work of many government departments makes it apparent that there is a direct relationship between the extent and vigor of reform, and the degree to which the key administrative positions in a department are staffed by persons who adhered to the formal goals of the government.

In recent years many individuals have become concerned with the problem of "bureaucratic domination" in large-scale society. The justified concern with the dangers of oligarchic or "bureaucratic" domination of social organization has, however, led many persons to ignore the fact that it does make a difference to society which set of "bureaucrats" controls its destiny. To suggest, as many social scientists have, that trade unions, co-operatives, corporations, political parties, and states are large social organizations which must develop a bureaucratic structure in order to operate efficiently still leaves a large area of indeterminate social action for a bureaucratically organized society. No matter how structured a situation, every individual and group acts somewhat differently within it, as determined by his past background and present social pressures.

The emphasis on a single theory of bureaucracy has been encouraged by the lack of a sociological approach on the part of political scientists working in the field of governmental bureaucracies. For the most part, they have not raised questions about the social origins and values of government administrators and about the relationship of such factors to government policy.[10] The determinants of the role played by the Civil Servant in affecting government policy are analyzed largely on the bureaucratic level; that is, the actions of the bureaucracy are explained in terms of the self-preservation and efficiency goals of the Civil Service. These interests may be defined in terms of prestige and privilege, preservation of existent patterns of organization or relationships within a department, or maintenance of department traditions and policies. There is as yet little for-

mal recognition that the behavior of a governmental bureaucracy also varies with the nongovernmental social background and interests of those inhabiting the bureaucratic structure. Members of a Civil Service—like members of the judiciary, trade-unions, or business corporations—are also members of other nongovernmental social groups and classes. Social pressures from the multi-group affiliations and loyalties of individuals will determine their behavior. The behavior of an individual or group in a given situation cannot be considered as if the individual or group members had no other life outside of the given situation one is analyzing.

A permanent governmental bureaucracy which is part of or loyal to a minority social group can be an effective check against social reforms desired by the majority in a period of changing social values such as the present. There is no simple solution to the dilemma of keeping government administration efficient, as well as responsive to the will of the electorate. The increase in the power, functions, and sheer size of modern government necessitates the search for some means of controlling the bureaucracy. It is utopian to think that the electorate's changing the inexpert politician who formally heads the bureaucracy will by itself change the course of the activities of the government. As Max Weber stated:

The question is always who controls the existing bureaucratic machinery. And such control is possible only in a very limited degree to persons who are not technical specialists. Generally speaking, the trained permanent official is more likely to get his way in the long run than his nominal supervisor, the Cabinet Minister, who is not a specialist.[11]

[10] For two studies by sociologists which deal with this problem, see Reinhard Bendix, *Higher Civil Servants in American Society* (Boulder: University of Colorado Press, 1949), and Philip Selznick, *T.V.A. and the Grass Roots* (Berkeley: University of California Press, 1949).

[11] *The Theory of Social and Economic Organization*, translated by Talcott Parsons and A. R. Henderson (New York: Oxford University Press, 1947), p. 128.

# 35

# The Individual and Organization: Some Problems of Mutual Adjustment

## CHRIS ARGYRIS

It is a fact that most industrial organizations have some sort of formal structure within which individuals must work to achieve the organization's objectives. Each of these basic components of organization (the formal structure and the individuals) has been and continues to be the subject of much research, discussion, and writing. An extensive search of the literature leads us to conclude, however, that most of these inquiries are conducted by persons typically interested in one or the other of the basic components. Few focus on both the individual and the organization.

Since in real life the formal structure and the individuals are continuously interacting and transacting, it seems useful to consider a study of their simultaneous impact upon each other. It is the purpose of this paper to outline the beginnings of a systematic framework by which to analyze the nature of the relationship between formal organization and individuals and from which to derive specific hypotheses regarding their mutual impact. Although a much more detailed definition of formal organization will be given later, it is important to emphasize that this analysis is limited to those organizations whose original formal structure is defined by such traditional principles of organi-

zation as "chain of command," "task specialization," "span of control," and so forth. Another limitation is that since the nature of individuals varies from culture to culture, the conclusions of this paper are also limited to those cultures wherein the proposed model of personality applies (primarily American and some Western European cultures).

The method used is a simple one designed to take advantage of the existing research on each component. The first objective is to ascertain the basic properties of each component. Exactly what is known and agreed upon by the experts about each of the components? Once this information has been collected, the second objective follows logically. When the basic properties of each of these components are known, what predictions can be made regarding their impact upon one another once they are brought together?

## Some Properties of Human Personality

. . . The self, in this culture, tends to develop along specific trends which are operationally definable and empirically observable. The basic developmental trends may be described as follows. The human being, in our culture:

1. Tends to develop from a state of being passive as an infant to a state of increasing activity as an adult. (This is what E. H. Erikson has called self-initiative and Urie Bron-

Reprinted from *Administrative Science Quarterly* 1 (June 1957) pp. 1–24, with permission of the publisher and the author. This analysis is part of a larger study which is reported in Chris Argyris, *Personality and Organization* (New York: Harper & Row, 1957).

fenbrenner has called self-determination.[1])

2. Tends to develop from a state of dependence upon others as an infant to a state of relative independence as an adult. Relative independence is the ability to "stand on one's own two feet" and simultaneously to acknowledge healthy dependencies.[2] It is characterized by the individual's freeing himself from his childhood determiners of behavior (e.g., the family) and developing his own set of behavioral determiners. The individual does not tend to react to others (e.g., the boss) in terms of patterns learned during childhood.[3]

3. Tends to develop from being capable of behaving in only a few ways as an infant to being capable of behaving in many different ways as an adult.[4]

4. Tends to develop from having erratic, casual, shallow, quickly dropped interests as an infant to possessing a deepening of interests as an adult. The mature state is characterized by an endless series of challenges where the reward comes from doing something for its own sake. The tendency is to analyze and study phenomena in their full-blown wholeness, complexity, and depth.[5]

5. Tends to develop from having a short-time perspective (i.e., the present largely determines behavior) as an infant to having a much longer time perspective as an adult (i.e., the individual's behavior is more affected by the past and the future).[6]

6. Tends to develop from being in a subordinate position in the family and society as an infant to aspiring to occupy at least an equal and/or superordinate position relative to his peers.

7. Tends to develop from having a lack of awareness of the self as an infant to having an awareness of and control over the self as an adult. The adult who experiences adequate and successful control over his own behavior develops a sense of integrity (Erikson) and feelings of self-worth (Carl R. Rogers).[7]

These characteristics are postulated as being descriptive of a basic multi-dimensional developmental process along which the growth of individuals in our culture may be measured. Presumably every individual, at any given moment in time, could have his degree of development plotted along these dimensions. The exact location on each dimension will probably vary with each individual and even with the same individual at different times. Self-actual-

[1] E. H. Erikson, *Childhood and Society* (New York: W. W. Norton, 1950); Urie Bronfenbrenner, "Toward an Integrated Theory of Personality," in Robert R. Blake and Glenn V. Ramsey, *Perception* (New York: Ronald Press Co., 1951), pp. 206–257. See also R. Kotinsky, *Personality in the Making* (New York, 1952), pp. 8–25.
[2] This is similar to Erikson's sense of autonomy and Bronfenbrenner's state of creative interdependence.
[3] Robert W. White, *Lives in Progress* (New York: The Dryden Press, 1952), pp. 339 ff.
[4] Lewin and Kounin believe that as the individual develops need and abilities the boundaries between them become more rigid. This explains why an adult is better able than a child to be frustrated in one activity and behave constructively in another. See Kurt Lewin, *A Dynamic Theory of Personality* (New York: McGraw-Hill, 1935) and Jacob S. Kounin, "Intellectual Development and Rigidity," in R. Barker, J. Kounin, and H. R. Wright, eds., *Child Behavior and Development,* (New York: McGraw-Hill, 1943), pp. 179–198.
[5] Robert White, *op. cit.,* pp. 347 ff.
[6] Lewin reminds those who may believe that a long-time perspective is not characteristic of the majority of individuals of the billions of dollars that are invested in insurance policies. Kurt Lewin, *Resolving Social Conflicts* (New York: Harper, 1948), p. 105.
[7] Carl R. Rogers, *Client-Centered Therapy* (Boston: Houghton Mifflin, 1951).

ization may now be defined more precisely as the individual's plotted scores (or profile) along the above dimensions. . . .

One might say that an independent person is one whose behavior is not caused by the influence others have over him. Of course, no individual is completely independent. All of us have our healthy dependencies (i.e., those which help us to be creative and to develop). One operational criteria to ascertain whether an individual's desire to be, let us say, independent and active is truly a mature manifestation is to ascertain the extent to which he permits others to express the same needs. Thus an autocratic leader may say that he needs to be active and independent; he may also say that he wants subordinates who are the same. There is ample research to suggest, however, that his leadership pattern only makes him and his subordinates more dependence-ridden.

## Some Basic Properties of Formal Organization

The next step is to focus the analytic spotlight on the formal organization. What are its properties? What are its basic "givens"? What probable impact will they have upon the human personality? How will the human personality tend to react to this impact? What sorts of chain reactions are probable when these two basic components are brought together?

*Formal Organizations As Rational Organizations.* Probably the most basic property of formal organization is its logical foundation or, as it has been called by students of administration, its essential rationality. It is the planners' conception of how the intended consequences of the organization may best be achieved. The underlying assumptions made by the creators of formal organization is that within re-

spectable tolerances man will behave rationally, that is, as the formal plan requires him to behave. Organizations are formed with particular objectives in mind, and their structures mirror these objectives. Although man may not follow the prescribed paths, and consequently the objectives may never be achieved, Herbert A. Simon suggests that by and large man does follow these prescribed paths:

Organizations are formed with the intention and design of accomplishing goals; and the people who work in organizations believe, at least part of the time, that they are striving toward these same goals. We must not lose sight of the fact that however far organizations may depart from the traditional description . . . nevertheless most behavior in organizations is intendedly rational behavior. By "intended rationality" I mean the kind of adjustment of behavior to goals of which humans are capable—a very incomplete and imperfect adjustment, to be sure, but one which nevertheless does accomplish purposes and does carry out programs.[8]

The possibility that the formal organization can be altered by personalities, as found by Conrad M. Arensberg and Douglas McGregor [9] and Ralph M. Stogdill and Katheleen Koehler,[10] is not denied by formal organizational experts. Urwick,[11] for example, states . . . that the planner must take into account the human element. But it is interesting to note that he perceives

[8] Herbert A. Simon, *Research Frontiers in Politics and Government* (Washington, D.C.: 1955), ch. ii, p. 30.
[9] Conrad M. Arensberg and Douglas McGregor, Determination of Morale in an Industrial Company, *Applied Anthropology*, 1 (Jan.–March 1942), pp. 12–34.
[10] Ralph M. Stogdill and Katheleen Koehler, *Measures of Leadership Structure and Organization Change* (Columbus, O.: Ohio State University Press, 1952).
[11] L. Urwick, *The Elements of Administration*, (New York: Harper & Row, 1943).

these adjustments as "temporary deviations from the pattern in order to deal with idiosyncrasy of personality." If possible, these deviations should be minimized by careful preplanning.

The majority of experts on formal organization agree with Urwick. Most of them emphasize that no organizational structure will be ideal. None will exemplify the maximum expression of the principles of formal organization. A satisfactory aspiration is for optimum expression, which means modifying the ideal structure to take into account the individual (and any environmental) conditions. Moreover, they urge that the people must be loyal to the formal structure if it is to work effectively. Thus Taylor emphasizes that scientific management would never succeed without a "mental revolution." [12] Fayol has the same problem in mind when he emphasizes the importance of *esprit de corps*.

It is also true, however, that these experts have provided little insight into *why* they believe that people should undergo a "mental revolution," or why an *esprit de corps* is necessary if the principles are to succeed. The only hints found in the literature are that resistance to scientific management occurs because human beings "are what they are" or "because it's human nature." But *why* does "human nature" resist formal organizational principles? Perhaps there is something inherent in the principles which causes human resistance. Unfortunately too little research specifically assesses the impact of formal organizational principles upon human beings. . . .

*Task (Work) Specialization.* As James J. Gillespie suggests, the roots of these principles of organization may be traced back to certain principles of

industrial economics, the most important of which is the basic economic assumption held by builders of the industrial revolution that "the concentration of effort on a limited field of endeavor increases quality and quantity of output." [13] It follows from the above that the necessity for specialization should increase as the quantity of similar things to be done increases.

If concentrating effort on a limited field of endeavor increases the quality and quantity of output, it follows that organizational and administrative efficiency is increased by the specialization of tasks assigned to the participants of the organization.[14] Inherent in this assumption are three others. The first is that the human personality will behave more efficiently as the task that it is to perform becomes specialized. Second is the assumption that there can be found a one best way to define the job so that it is performed at greater speed.[15] Third is the assumption that any individual differences in the human personality may be ignored by transferring more skill and thought to machines.[16]

A number of difficulties arise concerning these assumptions when the properties of the human personality are recalled. First, the human personality we have seen is always attempting to actualize its unique organization of parts resulting from a continuous, emotionally laden, ego-involving process of growth. It is difficult, if not impossible, to assume that this process can be choked off and the resultant unique differences of individuals ignored. This

---

[12] For a provocative discussion of Taylor's philosophy, see Reinhard Bendix, *Work and Authority in Industry* (New York: Wiley, 1956), pp. 274–319.

[13] James J. Gillespie, *Free Expression in Industry* (London: 1948), pp. 34–37.
[14] Herbert A. Simon, *Administrative Behavior* (New York: The Macmillan Company, 1947), pp. 80–81.
[15] For an interesting discussion see Georges Friedman, *Industrial Society* (New York: The Free Press, 1955), pp. 54 ff.
[16] *Ibid.*, p. 20, Friedman reports that 79 per cent of Ford employees had jobs for which they could be trained in one week.

is tantamount to saying that self-actualization can be ignored. The second difficulty is that task specialization requires the individual to use only a few of his abilities. Moreover, as specialization increases, the less complex motor abilities are used more frequently. These, research suggests, tend to be of lesser psychological importance to the individual. Thus the principle violates two basic givens of the healthy adult human personality. It inhibits self-actualization and provides expression for few, shallow, superficial abilities that do not provide the "endless challenge" desired by the healthy personality.

Harold L. Wilensky and Charles N. Lebeaux correctly point out that task specialization causes what little skill is left in a job to become very important.[17] Now small differences in ability may make enormous differences in output. Thus two machine-shovel operators or two drill-press operators of different degrees of skill can produce dramatically different outputs. Ironically, the increasing importance of this type of skill for the healthy, mature worker means that he should feel he is performing self-satisfying work while using a small number of psychologically unchallenging abilities, when in actuality he may be predisposed to feel otherwise. Task specialization, therefore, requires a healthy adult to behave in a less mature manner, but it also requires that he feel good about it! . . .

*Chain of Command.* The principle of task specialization creates an aggregate of parts, each performing a highly specialized task. An aggregate of parts, each busily performing its particular objective, does not form an organization, however. A pattern of parts must be formed so that the interrelationships among the parts create the organiza-

tion. Following the logic of specialization, the planners create a new function (leadership) the primary responsibility of which is to control, direct, and coordinate the interrelationships of the parts and to make certain that each part performs its objective adequately. Thus the planner makes the assumption that administrative and organizational efficiency is increased by arranging the parts in a determinate hierarchy of authority in which the part on top can direct and control the part on the bottom.

If the parts being considered are individuals, then they must be motivated to accept direction, control, and coordination of their behavior. The leader, therefore, is assigned formal power to hire, discharge, reward, and penalize the individuals in order to mold their behavior in the pattern of the organization's objectives.

The impact of such a state of affairs is to make the individuals dependent upon, passive, and subordinate to the leader. As a result, the individuals have little control over their working environment. At the same time their time perspective is shortened because they do not control the information necessary to predict their futures. These requirements of formal organization act to inhibit four of the growth trends of the personality, because to be passive, subordinate, and to have little control and a short time perspective exemplify in adults the dimensions of immaturity, not adulthood. . . .

*Unity of Direction.* If the tasks of everyone in a unit are specialized, then it follows that the objective or purpose of the unit must be specialized. The principle of unity of direction states that organizational efficiency increases if each unit has a single activity (or homogeneous set of activities) that are planned and directed by the leader.[18]

[17] Harold L. Wilensky and Charles N. Lebeaux, *Industrialization and Social Welfare* (New York: Russell Sage Foundation, 1955), p. 43.

[18] The sacredness of these principles is questioned by a recent study. Gunnar Heckscher

This means that the goal toward which the employees are working, the path toward the goal, and the strength of the barriers they must overcome to achieve the goal are defined and controlled by the leader. Assuming that the work goals do not involve the egos of the employees, (i.e., they are related to peripheral, superficial needs), the ideal conditions for psychological failure have been created. The reader may recall that a basic given of a healthy personality is the aspiration for psychological success. Psychological success is achieved when each individual is able to define his own goals, in relation to his inner needs and the strength of the barriers to be overcome in order to reach these goals. Repetitive as it may sound, it is nevertheless true that the principle of unity of direction also violates a basic given of personality.

*Span of Control.* The principle of span of control [19] states that administrative efficiency is increased by limiting the span of control of a leader to no more than five or six subordinates whose work interlocks. . . .

Although the distance between in-dividuals in different units increases (because they have to find a common superior), the administrative distance between superior and subordinate within a given unit decreases. As Whyte correctly points out, the principle of span of control, by keeping the number of subordinates at a minimum, places great emphasis on close supervision.[20] Close supervision leads the subordinates to become dependent upon, passive to-ward, and subordinate to, the leader. Close supervision also tends to place the control in the superior. Thus we must conclude that span of control, if used correctly, will tend to increase the sub-ordinate's feelings of dependence, sub-missiveness, passivity, and so on. In short, it will tend to create a work situa-tion which requires immature, rather than mature, participants.

## An Incongruency Between the Needs of a Mature Personality and of Formal Organization

Bringing together the evidence re-garding the impact of mormal organiza-tional principles upon the individual, we must conclude that there are some basic incongruencies between the growth trends of a healthy personality in our culture and the requirements of formal organization. If the principles of formal organization are used as ideally defined, then the employees will tend to work in an environment where (1) they are provided minimal control over their work-a-day world, (2) they are expected to be passive, dependent, sub-ordinate, (3) they are expected to have a short-time perspective, (4) they are induced to perfect and value the fre-quent use of a few superficial abilities, and (5) they are expected to produce under conditions leading to psycholog-ical failure.

concludes that the principles of unity of command and unity of direction are formally violated in Sweden: "A fundamental prin-ciple of public administration in Sweden is the duty of all public agencies to cooperate directly without necessarily passing through a common superior. This principle is even embodied in the constitution itself, and in actual fact it is being employed daily. It is traditionally one of the most important char-acteristics of Swedish administration that especially central agencies, but also central and local agencies of different levels, cooper-ate freely and that this is being regarded as a perfectly normal procedure" (*Swedish Public Administration at Work* [Stockholm, 1955], p. 12).

[19] First defined by V. A. Graicunas in an article entitled "Relationship in Organiza-tion," in L. Gulick and L. Urwick, eds., *Papers on the Science of Administration,* 2d ed. (New York: Institute of Public Ad-ministration, Columbia University, 1947), pp. 183–187.

[20] William Whyte, "On the Evolution of Industrial Sociology" (mimeographed paper presented at the 1956 meeting of the Ameri-can Sociological Society).

All of these characteristics are incongruent to the ones healthy human beings are postulated to desire. They are much more congruent with the needs of infants in our culture. In effect, therefore, formal organizations are willing to pay high wages and provide adequate seniority if mature adults will, for eight hours a day, behave in a less mature manner. If this analysis is correct, this inevitable incongruency increases (1) as the employees are of increasing maturity, (2) as the formal structure (based upon the above principles) is made more clear-cut and logically tight for maximum formal organizational effectiveness, (3) as one goes down the line of command, and (4) as the jobs become more and more mechanized (i.e., take on assembly-line characteristics). . . .

It is not difficult to see why some students of organization suggest that immature and even mentally retarded individuals probably would make excellent employees in certain jobs. There is very little documented experience to support such a hypothesis. One reason for this lack of information is probably the delicacy of the subject. Examples of what might be obtained if a systematic study were made may be found in a recent work by Mal Brennan.[21] He cites the Utica Knitting Mill, which made arrangements during 1917 with the Rome Institution for Mentally Defective Girls to employ twenty-four girls whose mental age ranged from six to ten years of age. The girls were such excellent workers that they were employed after the war emergency ended. In fact, the company added forty more in another of their plants. It is interesting to note that the managers praised the subnormal girls highly. According to Brennan, in several important reports they said that

when business conditions required a reduction of the working staff, the hostel girls were never "laid off" in disproportion to the normal girls; that they were more punctual, more regular in their habits, and did not indulge in as much "gossip and levity." They received the same rate of pay, and they had been employed successfully at almost every process carried out in the workshops.

In another experiment reported by Brennan, the Works Manager of the Radio Corporation, Ltd., reported that of five young morons employed, "the three girls compared very favourably with the normal class of employee in that age group. The boy employed in the store performed his work with satisfaction. . . . Although there was some doubt about the fifth child, it was felt that getting the most out of him was just a matter of right placement." In each of the five cases, the morons were reported to be quiet, respectful, well behaved, and very obedient. The Works Manager was especially impressed by their truthfulness. A year later the same Works Manager was still able to advise that "in every case, the girls proved to be exceptionally well-behaved, particularly obedient, and strictly honest and trustworthy. They carried out work required of them to such a degree of efficiency that *we were surprised they were classed as subnormals for their age.*"

## Summary of Findings

If one were to put these basic findings in terms of propositions, one could state: *There Is a Lack of Congruency between the Needs of Healthy Individuals and the Demands of the Formal Organization.*

If one uses the traditional formal principles of organization (i.e., chain of command, task specialization, and so on) to create a social organization, and if one uses as an input agents who

[21] Mal Brennan, *The Making of a Moron* (New York: 1953), pp. 13–18.

tend toward mature psychological development (i.e., who are predisposed toward relative independence, activeness, use of important abilities, and so on), then one creates a disturbance, because the needs of healthy individuals listed above are not congruent with the requirements of formal organization, which tends to require the agents to work in situations where they are dependent, passive, use few and unimportant abilities, and so forth. The disturbance will vary in proportion to the degree of incongruency between the needs of the individuals and the requirements of the formal organization. An administrator, therefore, is always faced with a tendency toward continual disturbance inherent in the work situation of the individuals over whom he is in charge. . . .

Drawing on the existing knowledge of the human personality, a second proposition can be stated: *The Results of This Disturbance Are Frustration, Failure, Short-Time Perspective, and Conflict.*

If the agents are predisposed to a healthy, mature self-actualization, the following results will occur:

1. They will tend to experience frustration because their self-actualization will be blocked.
2. They will tend to experience failure because they will not be permitted to define their own goals in relation to their central needs, the paths to these goals, and so on.
3. They will tend to experience short-time perspective, because they have no control over the clarity and stability of their future.
4. They will tend to experience conflict, because, as healthy agents, they will dislike the frustration, failure, and short-time perspective which is characteristic of their present jobs. If they leave, however, they may not find new jobs easily, and even if new

jobs are found, they may not be much different.

Based upon the analysis of the nature of formal organization, one may state a third proposition: *The Nature of the Formal Principles of Organization Cause the Subordinate, at Any Given Level, to Experience Competition, Rivalry, Intersubordinate Hostility, and to Develop a Focus toward the Parts Rather than the Whole.*

1. Because of the degree of dependence, subordination, and so on of the subordinates upon the leader, and because the number of positions above any given level always tends to decrease, the subordinates aspiring to perform effectively and to advance will tend to find themselves in competition with, and receiving hostility from, each other.
2. Because, according to the formal principles, the subordinate is directed toward and rewarded for performing his own task well, the subordinate tends to develop an orientation toward his own particular part rather than toward the whole.
3. This part-orientation increases the need for the leader to coordinate the activity among the parts in order to maintain the whole. This need for the leader, in turn, increases the subordinates' degree of dependence, subordination, and so forth. This is a circular process whose impact is to maintain and/or increase the degree of dependence, subordination, and so on, as well as to stimulate rivalry and competition for the leader's favor. . . .

It is impossible in the short space available to present all of the results obtained from the analysis of the literature. For example, it can be shown that employees tend to adapt to the frustration, failure, short-time perspective, and conflict involved in their work situations by any one or a combination of the following acts:

1. Leaving the organization.
2. Climbing the organizational ladder.
3. Manifesting defense reactions such as daydreaming, aggression, ambivalence, regression, projection, and so forth.
4. Becoming apathetic and disinterested toward the organization, its make-up, and its goals. This leads to such phenomena as: (a) employees reducing the number and potency of the needs they expect to fulfill while at work; (b) employees goldbricking, setting rates, restricting quotas, making errors, cheating, slowing down, and so on.
5. Creating informal groups to sanction the defense reactions and the apathy, disinterest, and lack of self-involvement. . . .

Furthermore, it can also be shown that many managements tend to respond to the employees' behavior by:

1. Increasing the degree of their pressure-oriented leadership.
2. Increasing the degree of their use of management controls.
3. Increasing the number of "pseudo"-participation and communication programs.

These three reactions by management actually compound the dependence, subordination, and so on that the employees experience, which in turn cause the employees to increase their adaptive behavior, the very behavior management desired to curtail in the first place. . . . This dilemma between individual needs and organization demands is a basic, continual problem posing an eternal challenge to the leader. How is it possible to create an organization in which the individuals may obtain optimum expression and, simultaneously, in which the organization itself may obtain optimum satisfaction of its demands? Here lies a fertile field for future research in organizational behavior.

# 36

# Bureaucracy and Freedom

### ALFRED WEBER

It is almost commonplace to observe that we live in an era of increasing bureaucratization of our existence. To discuss bureaucracy and freedom meaningfully is to inquire into the common conditions of social life that are conducive to such bureaucratization; to ask what specific forms it assumes and to

Reprinted from the Modern Review, 3–4 (March–April, 1948), pp. 176–186, by permission of the publisher.

what extent it is avoidable and escapable; how we can evade the obvious implicit danger of its degenerating into totalitarianism or even terrorism; in brief, how to preserve liberty.

Historically, bureaucracy is not a novel phenomenon. Indeed, the history of advanced human civilization began with bureaucracies that upheld and gave shape to the entire social life of the time. The hieratically-organized priesthood that created and guarded the magically-sanctified way of life, under pharaohs and emperors in ancient Egypt and Babylon, was probably the most "totalitarian" bureaucracy history has ever known. In its all-pervading forms and formulae, it conditioned not only the outer but also the inner manifestations of life—which in their totality could not be tampered with if its magic forces were to be kept intact. But this apparatus required no special instrument of self-perpetuation—neither a strong police nor a standing army. Only some 1500 years later, about 2000 B.C., were such special institutions established in defense against the nomads pressing in from without. These first great totalitarian bureaucratic structures could afford not to stain themselves with instruments of compulsion; they never experienced freedom as their antagonist.

The primary civilizations of China and India were likewise permeated with a strong bureaucratic web, similarly established on a basis of magic acceptance. In India, it was at an early point replaced by the caste system developed by the carriers of this magic faith—the Brahmins—who utilized the primitive belief in the transmigration of the soul and infused a solid skeleton of hieratic, functional division of labor into the existential matrix. There was no longer any need for a distinct layer of professional officialdom. Little remained of individual freedom of action in either the practical or even the political sphere. But considerable intellectual freedom could thrive, particularly under the influence of the surviving noble caste of the Kshatriya. In China, the mandarins came to form a strata of learned scribes, supported by the magistic hierocracy. An extraordinarily powerful bureaucracy emerged; its enemy, however, is not to be found in the masses yearning for freedom but always in the imperial seraglio with its eunuchs. Yet considerable leeway remained for freedom in

practice. And, just as in India, a culture of great spontaneity, permeating all strata of society, could develop within this still relatively loose bureaucratic framework.

The ancient civilizations of the Middle East—above all, that of Persia—were also almost all built on a foundation of bureaucracy. But in the Persian Empire itself bureaucracy was not hieratically sanctified. Far-reaching tolerance and only loose cohesion among its components remained characteristic of the great empire. The Persian emperor did not become a semi-divinity or vicar of god equipped with a supporting and all-encompassing bureaucracy. The distinct ways of life among the conquered nationalities were left virtually untouched or even revived, as was best exemplified by the liberation of the Jewish aristocracy from Babylonic exile and the re-establishment of Jerusalem.

But neither this Jewish nor any other "unbureaucratized" state or social organism had any conscious notions of personal freedom. Among the Jews in particular, all inner and outer activity was far too ritualized and placed under the control, first of the Levites, later of the learned scribes. Spiritual effort was harnessed not for the achievement of personal freedom but for the collective fulfillment of the religious mission and its ethically-conceived unfolding and deepening. The struggle was not being waged for freedom as such.

The ancient Jewish community was one of the first highly-developed state edifices without a proper bureaucracy. But owing to the peculiar manner in which individualism and collectivism were here intertwined, it stood entirely outside the contest of freedom versus bureaucracy.

The first societies that were aware of this contest and whose consciousness of freedom grew and sharpened upon this awareness, were ancient Greece and Rome. Neither of them needed bureaucracy since both had found a suitable form of social organization in the *polis* and *urbs*, with their honorary offices, and required no rational division of functions or professional specialization in public life. With lesser success in Greece and with greater success in Rome, this social organization met the test. The priestly hierocracy remained almost unseen—mysticism, sacrifices, and oracles notwithstanding—since it found no means for its propagation into the workaday life in the form of a temporal bureaucracy. It remained impotent, deprived of the opportunity to limit the range of free decisions in any manner.

The concept of freedom, taken for granted ever since the days of the earlier horsemen, continued to be recognized in the continual social struggle which accompanied the transformations that both the Roman and the Greek state underwent on the thoroughly rational basis of liberty. It was this notion of freedom that became the articulate intellectual slogan voiced in the great fight against the bureaucratic east, a fight waged not only for the preservation of national independence but quite specifically directed against a world of "unfreedom." Herodotus was aware of this, and this Thucydides put into Pericles' mouth in his funeral oration: ". . . freely we order the commonwealth" and "not fetched by imitation of others, we are rather a model for them."

Leaving aside the worlds of Islam and Russia, which are too complex to be treated briefly, let us look at the Western world. While one does encounter strongly bureaucratic forms of organization in that part of the West which was once occupied by the Roman Empire, the West, both at its inception and for a considerable time thereafter, was as good as devoid of officialdom. For feudalism was the very opposite of bureaucracy, since it represented the non-professional and non-specialized

execution of functions. And this is why within and alongside the form of reciprocal feudal relationships—contractual, hence originally based on the premise of freedom—with the revival of classicism, the ancient consciousness of liberty could be revived and renewed. It could produce a symbiosis of the precultural sense of freedom, on the one hand, and a more deeply comprehensible and comprehended freedom produced by Christianity, on the other. In bending the old concept of natural rights to its ends, it could unfold the ideas of liberty and equality of a Locke.

Such was the great contest of bureaucracy and freedom in the past. The rise of the modern state was the occasion, and provided the framework for that strata of professional officialdom that was imported into the West from Byzantium over the Italian universities. This is also whence came its metaphysical sanction.

Less attention is usually paid to the fact that the bureaucratic stratification in the modern state has been produced as much by the emergence of standing armies as by the rise of civil officialdom. It is no accident that the modern standing army, with its rational gradations and schematic unification, has found its most striking expression in the military *casern*—admittedly, a factory with a bureaucratic head.

*Since the latter half of the nineteenth century, the bureaucratic stranglehold has rapidly spread, as if endowed with mystic power, from administrative offices and army barracks into almost all fields of human endeavor.* It has increasingly penetrated, affected, and transformed relations between man and man. Today industry is in large segments no less bureaucratic than are the public health services, in whose barrack-like hospitals the disease, and not the sick human being, assumes individuality—where, so to speak, the object replaces the subject. The same is true of modern social legislation, of the compulsory insurance schemes with their gigantic machines; of such labor organizations as trade unions, with their bureaucratic heads; of popular political organizations, with their caucuses. Not only the state and other official bureaucracies continue to swell in accordance with the "law of growing state functions" first formulated by Adolf Wegner; next to them we witness a growth —a rank growth—of innumerable private bureaucracies, which everywhere offer the same picture: the emergence of a closed bureaucratic leadership, largely autocratic in practice, and as specialized a division of labor as is rationally necessary or possible. In recent decades, the number of officials and civil servants has been growing far more rapidly than the number of workers. What we witness is a tremendous inflation of the bureaucratic head topping a more slowly growing body. And this, despite all democratic sugar-coating, means: the spread of authoritarian leadership through small cliques and staffs, tending not only rationally to divide the fulfillment of functions horizontally, if you will, but also to permeate it vertically in such a manner as to assure the uppermost bureaucratic nucleus, due to its organizational-technical position, preponderance against any endeavor to shape and express the will from below. This is the hidden master key to the over-all trends of present-day social organization.

If we ask for the way out, for an antitoxin, we must first take account of the following. Our modern world, interdependent as it has become, organized in large and increasingly inclusive units, necessarily bringing a specialization of functions in society, cannot be controlled except by large-scale formations, inherently gradated and bureaucratic in management. This is certainly true of the general organization of services and supplies. Just like the Egyptians and

Babylonians of old, with their canal system which had to be bureaucratically managed, so we "moderns" are caught in the gigantic web of railroads, postal services, electricity, and what not—a web which spans and upholds our very existence, a web within whose framework we live and die, and which by its very nature commands central bureaucratic direction and rational subdivision. On our level of civilization, this framework of social existence has become an artificially rational and bureaucratic stockade from which there is no escape.

Just as inescapably, the great dimensions of our world and the concomitant huge organizations that belong in it result in the transformation of a previously diversified society of individuals into a uniform mass. This is also inherent in the very nature of these vast dimensions, since they bracket and uniformly affect great masses of human beings in a standardized fashion. It is an optical illusion to see this trend toward mass uniformity only in its most obvious and almost accidental manifestation, namely, the uprooted, intermingled and compressed masses of our cities and industrial centers. Less visibly but just as effectively, this schematizing trend affects that part of the population which has remained geographically dispersed but is being supplied—day after day, hour after hour—with the same uniformly-prepared set of experiences and information—and this in such a manner that the victims are being flattened out, as if by a steamroller, without being capable of resisting this process. Today they cannot but react as a mass, which is being swayed daily and hourly in similar rhythm. Not to face this reality is to indulge in romantic self-deception.

But once we recognize how a limited number of central agencies can make and break public opinion and decisively shape the mental habitat of the masses, we understand how natural it is to try and utilize these psychic potentialities through appropriate organs and methods specifically patterned for this purpose. One more step, and an effort is made to recast this outwardly uniform mass into one that is a herd in inherent constitution and behavior—and thus gain complete control over it. The resulting political conception is the specific modern authoritarian party, with its various appendages such as the rational system of "party cells" and control by "block wardens." Intensive propaganda turns into terrorism. This is the base on which the modern terroristic dictatorships have flourished. In a sense, they are the sole alternative and antipode to democracy. Modern bureaucratization of all forms of life not only makes it possible to "lead" the masses but also is susceptible of becoming the tool of a demagogic clique and the authoritarian organization associated with it, for the definitive eviction of freedom.

*I would not think of proclaiming this transformation of modern bureaucracy and rationalization into dictatorship as inevitable.* After the terrible example which mankind recently experienced with the substitution of terroristic dictatorship for democracy in Germany, I will still maintain that those countries are, above all, most immune to it which have a historically-rooted tradition of liberty or, whenever challenged, have proved capable of soon re-establishing it anew. For countries like Switzerland or the Netherlands, for Sweden and Norway, for England and the United States, political freedom as a decisive counterweight to totalitarianism is virtually innate, as far as we can see today; their peoples seem to take freedom as much for granted as they do the limbs for the survival of the body. The problem facing *these* countries is limited to the first two aspects outlined above: the challenge of weakening, narrowing, and atrophying private initiative due to an unhealthy growth of bureaucracy and uniformity through modern techniques of standardization. But all three consequences must be understood as elements present in modern society, and must be grasped in their technical aspects as well.

Next to the *casern*, the factory provided the second locus around which the modern trend toward rationalization and mechanization could crystallize. Historically, it is matter of sheer accident that the factory system arose, of all things, under modern capitalism. Generally speaking, the factory is a purely cultural product: a Socialist system employing techniques and rational organization needs it as imperatively as does capitalism. But to the extent to which our large-scale existence demands effective organization in large units—for rational reasons of competition as well as because of the inherent nature of its dimensions—the principles of the factory system and the concomitant bureaucratization of institutions cannot be evaded. Perhaps spontaneous and free motivating forces of unbureaucratic hue could be injected into our social bloodstream. But even these must fit in with the overall skeleton—unless we wish artificially to preserve elements incommensurate with the great dimensions of our days; unless, so to speak, we choose to perpetuate forcibly isolated little hothouses around which the air of the wide spaces is allowed freely to circulate. Today most of the problems we here face can be correctly seen, felt, and dealt with only within this larger radius. Not only in the technical but especially in the mental and political realm there are definite limits beyond which there is no escape from the organization of society into large units, no escape from the bureaucratization connected with it.

Let us draw the consequences.

There exist today very substantial

tendencies which, while of sharply anti-fascist and anti-Nazi persuasion, *should* be anti-totalitarian as well, but which in effect represent but a different form of totalitarianism. Or else, in the sincere belief of working for human liberty and emancipation, they paradoxically further a process of all-bureaucratic enslavement, because they ignore the dangers outlined above. One such trend is Communism, in its current edition at least; official contemporary Democratic Socialism is the other.

Both are fanatically centralist and rationalist. Therein they are the genetic heirs of the nineteenth century. Present-day Communism sacrifices the rights of the individual and freedom in favor of the complete liquidation of the upper classes and the elimination of all productive private capital. This transformation, it holds, can be achieved only by totalitarian means, and for its achievement no sacrifice is too great. One cannot argue with such a radical attitude, as it is based on a peculiar scale of values. "Classical" Socialism, on the other hand, today passionately defends the democratic scale of values. But its actions lead it to a double paradox.

Constricted to the old, mid-nineteenth century formulae which stem from Marx' revelation of the nature of capitalism, this classical socialism looks for its panacea to the "*socialization* of the means of production," which is to bring in the wake of the elimination of private capital's power position the emancipation of the proletariat. This slogan, intentionally couched in very general and vague terms by Marx and Engels, is so fascinating in an atmosphere imbued with the tradition of class struggle that when the modern Socialist seeks to mold it into a plank or political program, can think of nothing better than the nationalization—or, coin a term, *etatization*—of the means of production. Enraptured as he is, he fails to perceive the danger of the unheard-of strengthening of concentrated and ubiquitous bureaucracy, which would transform the anticipated emancipation of the masses into its antithesis. The classical Socialist is oblivious of the danger of enslavement by the State and does not notice that he is in effect advocating state socialism—on the model once favored by those to whom civil liberties mattered little and the authoritarian state meant much. He who really should know something about historical dialectics, fails to perceive that he becomes its victim.

The other paradox consists in the sign of equality which the contemporary Social-Democrat, taking the State to be his only universe of discourse, places between public planning and Socialism. Planned economy as such—as imperative as it may be within limits under the present circumstances—has little to do with Socialism, *i.e.* with the emancipation of the masses. Planning in the economic sphere may mitigate crimes and blunt the impact of the resulting phenomenon of mass unemployment. But beyond this, it is merely a technique arising from such deficiency situations as result from war and economic disorder. That is why today planning is so widely accepted. But its impressive propagation, in turn, is apt to lead once again towards omnipotent bureaucracy, killing off in the process the end goal of Socialism—Freedom.

We who see these dangers—what can we do about them? Some will tell us that what we need is to organize society in smaller units, substitute federalism for centralism with its lethal tendencies. The limits within which this recipe can be carried out have already been outlined. They are—to repeat myself—partly material, and just as important, partly psychological and mental. Federalism creates, not less bureaucracy, but more. Under it, the unpenetrable abodes of officialdom multiply, in which decisions of greatest portent are made without the participation of the public. The same is true wherever a great-dimensional whole is split up under the slogan of federalism. The necessary decisions will still have to be made at the center in a bureaucratic manner. What you have then accomplished is the replacement of *one* bureaucracy by several superimposed bureaucracies—those of the subordinate limbs and that at the center—which co-exist under superfluous and paralyzing complications. The material limits for all forms of federalism are thus clearly indicated.

The over-expansion of the federative idea is just as dangerous in the political and mental sense. It fosters and facilitates rule and abuse by all sorts of small bureaucratic cliques. What we need today in the sphere of mind and politics is not the confinement to small empty rooms but, on the contrary, the approximation of the global and telluric, the espousal of dimensions which encompass all humanity. There, on the higher rung, federalism for the new and greater entities is again indicated. Federalism on such a higher level is probably the only salvation for Europe.

Of course every nation should organize on the richest possible communal and regional basis; and, depending on its traditions, it may follow the pattern of federation and *Bundesstaat*: of course, local government should remain as untouched as possible and be permitted to mold itself independently to a maximal extent. Of course small, historically warranted states have a right to exist today—especially today—along with the emerging supernational federations; above all, they have a moral function to fulfill. One must not forget, however, that those questions which are of moral and political importance are being settled not in small but in increasingly large entities and demand solution on such vast dimensions.

The most radical enemy of modern bureaucracy, one who has recognized its menace with considerable clairvoyance, is *neo-liberalism*. In strange ways this new and growing school of thought is at times wedded to the neo-federalist trend. The reason for this alliance is the tendency to misread the signs of the time—a tendency noticeable in both these movements. In neo-federalism it is the vision of an organically-germinating, easily scannable *small* unit of social organization that distorts the outlook, as it appears to require little bureaucracy and would seem to engender democratic spontaneity. In neo-liberalism it is romantic oblivion to the fact that since the 19th century we have had monopoly capitalism, which cannot be done away with by evading the word "capitalism" or by prohibiting its symptoms—cartels, syndicates, and trusts—and seeking to re-establish free competition with all its rules of the game. Such business combinations are but the forms in which the accumulative tendencies of capital find expression, which aim at the establishment of overt or covert monopolies and, in one form or another, do indeed, set up monopolies—unless they themselves are extinguished. Pretty verbiage about the restitution of competition and the prohibition of monopolies are of no use. Such legislation merely trims the beard, so to speak, without touching the foundations on which monopolies thrive. All sacrifices before the altar of competition are doomed to be futile whenever the market is dominated by some four or ten big business enterprises whose captains, over a glass of whiskey, can decide upon the conditions under which they will supply the market in what amounts to monopolistic or quasi-monopolistic manner. The efforts of the neo-liberals, well-meant as they are, can therefore be of only limited practical value, for they come as little to grips with the bases of bureaucratization as with the effective diversion of totalitarianism, whose menace they see but fail to trace to the end. Their approach is romantic—and this is an age which, whether it likes it or not, requires economic planning.

I can see but one effective barrier to these dangers: a new form of Socialism, distinct from its classical form. It must be a Socialism which, taking account of the social framework within which bureaucracy exists as a universal and inescapable trend, infuses organized counterforces into this framework in order to salvage liberty and accordingly seeks to exert a systematic influence on state and society. It must *socialize* all those segments of economy which have become monopolistic, bureaucratic, hence ripe for socialization —and thereby shatter the power of capitalist bureaucracy. It must do so not in order to replace private bureaucracy with state bureaucracy—*i.e.* merely change masters—in order to establish a society in which (along with a necessarily nationalized and bureaucratic transportation, communications, and supply system) all other monopolies are broken, dissolved into public, corporate-socialist, autonomous units which as free units on the market can survive in the form of such rationally-necessary technical organisms as public foundations, socially-useful concessions, or public corporations which would be constrained to adopt socialist behavior and organization. *This means above all: production without the capitalist profit motive; election of boards of directors by those concerned; a voice, and concern for the furtherance of the interests of the workers.* Such socialist organs, freely co-existing, would have to be under the control of economic senates, part of the judicial arm, which would be entirely independent of all influence of political parties. This would be a form of industrial organization which, once the above conditions

are fulfilled, could even make possible the reduction of bureaucratic planning along socialist lines, after the elimination of present economic shortages of production. Next to these organs there must be "democratic partnership" of employees in the economic sphere, on the model of most recent English practice in the non-socialized branches of economy; and the establishment of a network of production co-operatives in agriculture so as to reduce even there the bureaucracy of planning. It must be a Socialism whose *political* orientation would aim at undermining bureaucracy's intellectual and moral tendency to domineer. It must aim at reducing bureaucracy to its necessary technical functions.

These are but a few practical features, easy to multiply, of such a new, thoroughly realistic, Socialist orientation, which would aim at the emancipation, not only of the working class, but of the population as a whole. To this end—by transformation or, whenever impossible, by restrictions—it would infuse spontaneous forces in order to counteract the bureaucratization of societal life, to render totalitarianism impossible and, at the same time, to realize freedom for all mankind.

I have been compelled to ask myself bluntly whether human history is to end where it began more than 5,000 years ago; whether mankind is to lose the freedom it gained at such a high price in the course of its existence; whether it is to trade in its liberty for a man-made dungeon just as it once exchanged the barbaric absence of restrictions for a hierocracy that guided and shaped its existence? Such a monstrous and grotesque parody of all meaningful history is not inevitable. What I have sought to do is to stake out the road along which, perhaps, it is possible to escape it.

# D Race and Ethnic Relations

## INTRODUCTION

Virtually all modern nations include peoples of different racial, ethnic, and religious backgrounds. These differences are sometimes regarded as historical accidents, in contrast to the social class differences created and perpetuated by the major institutional structures of a society. Yet the populations of all civilized societies, even the very earliest ones, have been ethnically diverse. The earliest civilizations came into being by absorbing and welding together numerous primitive societies, each of which contributed elements of its own distinctive culture. Empires and, at a later date, nation states expanded by conquering alien peoples. In modern history mass migrations have added to the ethnic diversity of national populations. True, ethnic differences have often become attenuated over time. The development of a loyalty to a national culture that takes precedence over attachments to previously independent local cultures is a major consequence of modern nation building. Yet new ethnic divisions arise in a nation when it expands its territory or attracts immigrants from outside its borders after older divisions have become little more than historical memories. Thus ethnic diversity has always been a feature of civilized societies, as ubiquitous as class divisions. The enormous variety of historical processes creating ethnically diverse national populations is reviewed by Everett C. Hughes in the first selection reprinted here.

The term *ethnic group* has come to mean any group within a national society that possesses elements of a distinctive culture that are a source of solidarity among its members. The combination of a shared language, national origin, and religion is the most common and durable cultural bond fostering ethnic solidarity. Ethnic groups account for different proportions of the populations of various modern nation states. In some, a single ethnic group may form a majority of the population, as Englishmen do in Great Britain. Other nations, such as the United States, contain many groups, none of which constitutes a majority.

Nathan Glazer and Daniel Patrick Moynihan contend, in our second selection, that in the United States racial and religious differences are becoming more important and more permanent than differences in national origin arising out of past immigration. In the case of religion, the principle of religious tolerance embodied in the Constitution, combined with widespread approval of religion in general on the part of Americans, has encouraged the survival of religious differences. The diminishing importance of nationality groups has had the effect of strengthening religious loyalties as religious organizations have become one of the few remaining cohesive groups mediating between the individual and the impersonal institutions of mass society.

Race is a biological rather than a cultural phenomenon. A race is a population possessing some genes in common that create physical resemblances among its members. The social visibility of racial differences, engraved as they are on the very physiques of human beings, makes it possible for races to perpetuate their sense of difference from one another. When one race is the more power-ful and cherishes a belief in its innate superiority, it can create a whole structure of permanent institutions imposing severe disabilities on racial minorities. American Negroes, Orientals, Mexicans, and Indians have experienced such disabilities. Their situation is thus not comparable to that of European nation-ality groups who suffered a rejection by native-born Americans that was bound to diminish in force as second- and third-generation descendants of immigrants became fully Americanized.

All traces of the original African culture of American Negroes were destroyed when they were captured and brought to the New World and forced to endure the long ordeal of slavery. The experience of slavery and of the racial discrimina-tion that survived its abolition have given Negroes a distinctive version of American culture. Gradually Negroes have developed a strong sense of group solidarity in combatting the deprivations and indignities they have suffered, a process that Lester Singer calls *ethnogenesis* in one of the readings in this sec-tion. The rise of an organized black protest movement has been the major domestic political event in the United States in the past decade.

All four of the readings included in this section discuss at least some aspect of the circumstances of the American Negro. Everett Hughes compares the positions of American Negroes and French Canadians within their respective national societies and the protest movements each of these peoples has created to change and improve their positions. Professor Hughes has been kind enough to write an addition of two paragraphs to his original 1963 paper especially for the second edition of the present book, in which he summarizes his view of more recent developments. Glazer and Moynihan describe the economic situation and the political behavior of the Negro in New York City and compare them to those of the other groups making up the ethnic mosaic of this metrop-olis. Lester Singer interprets the history of Negroes in America as a continuing process of ethnogenesis. Finally, Stokely Carmichael and Charles Hamilton present the ideology of "Black Power," a phrase which became popular shortly after the appearance of their book from which the selection here is drawn and which has become the rallying cry of the entire black movement in the United States.

# 37

# Race Relations in World Perspective

### EVERETT C. HUGHES

What is there new to say about race relations? A colleague with great knowledge and deep experience of American race relations—he is a Negro—asked me that. I could have answered that new things are happening in race relations here and all over the world; things from which we can still learn.

A younger colleague who builds models and tries them out in the laboratory wanted to know to what general theoretical problem I would direct this discussion. I could have answered that race relations are so much a fea-

Reprinted from Everett C. Hughes, "Race Relations and the Sociological Imagination," *American Sociological Review* 28 (December 1963), pp. 879–887, with permission of the author and the publisher.

ture of most societies, and that they are in such flux that one could find in them a living laboratory for almost any problem of social interaction, social identity and social structure which one could imagine.

While these points are indeed part of my discussion, a deeper question concerning sociology and social life lurks in the background: Why did social scientists—and sociologists in particular—not foresee the explosion of collective action of Negro Americans toward immediate full integration into American society? It is but a special instance of the more general question concerning sociological foresight of and involvement in drastic and massive social changes and extreme forms of social action.

Robert E. Park defined race relations thus:

. . . the term . . . includes all the relations which exist between members of different ethnic and genetic groups which are capable of provoking race conflict and race consciousness, or of determining the relative status of the racial groups of which a community is composed.[1] . . .

Park's definition makes study of race relations a part of the study of society itself, not a peculiar problem requiring special concepts for its analysis.

In the same paper Park—it was in 1939—spoke of a great movement among "national minorities to control and direct their own destinies;" a movement "which began in Europe in the early part of the last century, and has now spread, as if it were contagious, to every part of the world; every part of the world at any rate, which has felt or still feels itself oppressed in its provincial, autonomous life, or for any other reason, inferior in its international status." [2]

We of this country ushered in that great movement for national independence a little earlier than the beginning of the 19th century. Never ethnically homogeneous, we became less so by swallowing the remnants of Spanish and French empires, by importing black labor from Africa, and by encouraging immigration from Europe and, for a time, from Asia. The movement continued in Central and South America; those new states were also, all of them, racially mixed. The Spanish- or Portuguese-speaking cities were surrounded by latifundia with indigenous,

African or mixed labor force, beyond which generally there lay a back country whose inhabitants were not part of any body politic. As in North America, immigration from Europe and even from Asia continued. To our North, Canada gradually took on national status, by a confederation of provinces, the oldest of which was French-speaking Quebec.[3]

In Europe the continental Empires began to break up; Belgium, Greece, Italy, Norway, Finland and the Balkan states became nation-states. At the end of the First World War, the process went on until a belt of independent states was formed between Russia and the west. Established in the name of the self-determination of peoples—of people of common language and culture governing themselves on their historic territory—not one of those nation-states corresponded to the ideal. Every one contained some minority of another people than the one in whose name independence had been claimed. Nor, indeed, was any one of the dominant states from which these peoples had got independence, made into a country of one language and people by this cleansing. Germany tried to reverse the trend under Hitler, but ended up smaller than ever, as two states each racially purer —in our broad sense—than any in Europe. In that sense, Hitler won.

The victors of the First World War were proponents of the self-determination of European peoples, but all had overseas empires to which they did not apply that principle—as Max Weber pointed out in a speech at the time.[4] Their turn came after World War II.

[1] Robert E. Park, "The Nature of Race Relations," pp. 3–45 in E. T. Thompson (ed.), Race Relations and the Race Problem. Durham, N.C.: Duke University Press, 1939. Reproduced in Park, Race and Culture, Glencoe, Ill.: The Free Press, 1950, pp. 81–116. See p. 82.
[2] Loc. cit.

[3] New Zealand, Australia and the Union of South Africa became, like Canada, self-governing states with minorities, either indigenous or European, or both.
[4] Max Weber, "Deutschland unter den europäischen Weltmächten (October, 1916)," pp. 73–93 in Gesammelte Politische Schriften. Munich: Drei Masken Verlag, 1921. See pp. 89–90.

Their Asiatic, Oceanic and African possessions then sought and got political independence. None of these former colonies is racially homogeneous. India, Indonesia, the Philippines all contain a variety of languages, historic religions, cultures and tribes. Mass migrations, some voluntary, some forced, have, if anything, made people more aware of those divisions. In the little artificial states of the old French Asiatic colonies, probably few people know what state they do live in. In the Near East and northern Africa, a series of states, supposedly Muslim in religion and Arab in culture, are in fact a mosaic of languages, sects, tribes, races, classes and "communities." Israel, enclaved among them, is itself an ethnic pressure-cooker; linguistic and patriotic conformity are insisted upon.

In the oldest state south of the Sahara, South Africa, the European population is divided into majority and minority, which are numerically but a fraction of the total population of the country. The black Africans, once tribal, are being welded into something like an entity by the effort of the Europeans to keep them from it. Among the Europeans themselves, the former minority of Afrikaners has become the dominant group in politics, although English South Africans still dominate the economy. The other countries and the few remaining colonies in sub-Saharan Africa are all diverse in language, culture, tribal loyalties and degree of integration into modern urban economy and life. So diverse are they that the language of the battle for independence is generally that of the oppressor from whom they seek emancipation; language, that is, in both senses, of letters and words and of political and social philosophy. A bit of African chant and rhythm make the rhetoric seem more indigenous than it is. Portugal has thus far saved her empire by not teaching the language of independence, in either sense, to her African subjects.

All of these African countries are observation posts for those interested in the process of nation-making on which Bagehot wrote a classic essay a century ago. The development of a feeling of national, rather than local or tribal, identity proceeds but painfully in some of them.[5] Lucy Mair thinks its growth depends not upon a state of mind induced by propaganda, but upon social structure. Cities, communications, education and experience of industrial employment will create people who identify themselves with a nation. "The structure of an industrial society," she says, "is such that no section of it can pursue its interests by trying to cut itself off from the rest." [6] Whether or not she is right on that point, certainly the new African states are not yet nations. It may be that the state makes the nation, and not the reverse.

This tremendous burgeoning of so-called nation-states took place in a time of colossal migrations, voluntary or forced, of people seeking land or wanted as labor for industrial agriculture, the extractive or more advanced industries. Migration makes diversified populations. Even Japan, of all nations perhaps the one with the strongest myth of national homogeneity, got a large population of strange people as she became industrial and an empire—Koreans, Okinawans, her traditional Eta and her tribal Ainu have given the Japanese something on which to exercise their racial exclusiveness. As a final twist, some of the centers of erstwhile empires are now getting a reverse migration from their former colonies. West Indian Negroes are entering the British labor force at the bottom, as are Al-

[5] Walter Bagehot, *Physics and Politics.* Chapters III and IV, "Nation-Making."
[6] Lucy Mair, "Divide and Rule in the New Countries?" *New Societies*, No. 37 (June 13, 1963), p. 18.

gerians in France and Puerto Ricans in New York.

The very era in which the concept of nation-state has been so powerful has been one of empire-building and empire-breaking; an era in which the idea has spread, as Park said, like a contagion; a queer contagion, since the European countries which spread it did their best to prevent others— those in their own empires, at any rate —from catching it. The nation-state, far from eliminating race relations, intensifies them; its ideology of the correspondence of cultural and racial with political boundaries makes internal problems of what were external or international problems in the days of empire or in the more primitive times of tribal rule. It has made great numbers of human individuals aware of race as a fateful personal characteristic, determining the terms of their struggle for a place. It has made whole groups of people conscious of themselves as having a status, not merely in their own region, but in the world. Race, in our broad sense, has been made a part of the political, economic and social processes of much of the world. The United Nations has become an organ of world opinion which makes every domestic racial problem again a diplomatic and international one as well.

The relations among races are now even more disturbed than when Park wrote. They offer a richer and more varied living laboratory than ever for any of us sociologists who would consider going abroad other than to attend conferences. But it is not precisely a laboratory which they offer, for we have but one chance to observe, to understand and to act.

Of course, we need not go abroad. Racial turmoil is here at home. In North America, two elderly nation-states—as those things go—contain two of the oldest established minorities of

the world, Negro Americans and French Canadians. When I call them old, I refer to the duration of their position in the nation-states of which they are a part. Negro Americans, aided by some others, are engaged in their most massive, determined, urgent and detailed struggle for equality. French Canadians are vigorously demanding an overhaul of the century-old bargain sealed by the Confederation of the provinces into a single dominion.

Although there have always been agitators in both minorities, there have been long periods of quiet in which there was an entente between the leading classes of each minority and the dominant groups and implicit acceptance of it by the masses of the people. During these periods the dominant group apparently thought that an equilibrium had been established for an indefinite period, with changes going on so slowly as not to upset it. One might have said of both American and Canadian society what Park says of all:

Every society represents an organization of elements more or less antagonistic to each other but united for the moment, at least, by an arrangement which defines the reciprocal relations and respective sphere of action of each. This accommodation, this *modus vivendi*, may be relatively permanent as in a society constituted by castes, or quite transistory as in societies made up of open classes. In either case, the accommodation, while it is maintained, secures for the individual or for the group of recognized status.

In the accommodation, then, antagonism of the hostile elements is, for the time being, regulated, and conflict disappears as overt action, although it remains latent as a potential force. With a change in the situation, the adjustments that had hitherto held in control the antagonistic forces fail. There is confusion and unrest which may result in open conflict. Conflict . . . invariably issues in a new accommodation or social order, which in general involves a changed status in the relations among the participants.[7]

Park's view of society is that status arrangements are always tentative and likely to be questioned. In our two minorities, many of the younger people are questioning the bargain—the status arrangement—made by their forebears and consented to by their elders (for failure to act is considered consent). But what is the time perspective of parties to a bargain? The group with the greatest interest in the status quo may be expected to think of the arrangement as permanent, and to justify it by various devices—such as the doctrine of racial superiority and inferiority. The group disadvantaged in status may use some principle of permanency, which has been violated by the status-bargain forced upon them. Thus a national minority, such as the French Canadian, will prove that it was there first; that it is an older nation than the oppressor. The function of folklore is to establish antiquity and the rights based upon it. Colonial tribal minorities can achieve a sort of apocalyptic eternity, as Nadine Gordimer says so well of Africans:

You can assure yourself of glory in the future, in a heaven, but if that seems too nebulous for you—and the Africans are sick of waiting for things—you can assure yourself of glory in the past. It will have exactly the same sort of effect on you, in the present. You'll feel yourself, in spite of everything, worthy of either your future or your past.[8]

In both our minorities, the Negro-American and the French-Canadian, the time perspectives of past bargains are being called into question; in both cases, the dominant group asks either

[7] R. E. Park and E. W. Burgess, *Introduction to the Science of Sociology*, Chicago: University of Chicago Press, 1921, p. 665.
[8] Nadine Gordimer, *Occasion for Loving*, New York: Viking, 1960, pp. 9–10.

that the bargain be permanent or that it be changed but slowly.

Why the great outbreak of unrest and demand for change in these two minorities at just this moment? Certainly there have been great changes in the situation of both. At the last census, French Canadians had become more urban than other Canadians; Negroes, more urban than other Americans. With the precipitous drop in the agricultural labor force of both countries, these minorities have undergone changes of occupational structure probably greater than those of the rest of the population. Both minorities, in the industrial and urban order in which their fate now lies, are concentrated at lower points of the socio-economic scale than are the dominant groups.

These similarities may appear strained. They cover great differences. French Canadians do not, and never have, suffered civil or personal disabilities; they have not had to give deference to others. No social rank inheres in being French Canadian; the only aristocracy Canada ever had was French. French institutions in Canada are more venerable than English. French Canadians have headed the national government and always control the governments of their province and of most cities within it.

The two minorities are alike in that they have gone from a rural condition to an urban and see themselves as thereby put into a position of increased disadvantage; and at precisely that time in history when such disadvantage is no longer a purely domestic matter. But they seek opposite remedies. The Negro Americans want to disappear as a defined group; they want to become invisible as a group, while each of them becomes fully visible as a human being. Only so will they, in the myriad relations of American life, be judged by the characteristics pertinent to each. They want to be seen, neither as

360

Sociology of Contemporary Society

Negroes nor as if they were not; but as if it did not matter. The French Canadians, on the other hand, struggle not for survival as individuals—in which their problems are those of other Canadians —but for survival as a group with full social, economic and political standing.

These two apparently opposite goals represent one of the dialectics of human beings and the groups with which they identify themselves and are identified. How like others, how different from them shall I, shall we, can I, can we, be? And in what respects? Jews in the western world are generally thought to find these questions difficult, and the solutions unstable. Such a group as Negro Americans is at one pole—where all is to be gained from reduction of the social perception of differences. Their end will have been gained when Negroid characteristics and African descent matter no more and no less than other physical traits and quirks of ancestry. At that point, there would be no racial bargain. Whether all persons known as Negroes—and their descendants of that future day—would be content to wipe out their collective past and all features of Negro-American culture is another matter.

Some Negro Americans have given up hope that white Americans will ever live up to the bargain of the American ideology of equal rights for all. They reject everything American—the country, the Christian religion, their Anglo-Saxon names; as so-called Black Muslims they claim complete and eternal difference from white Americans and seek to develop such solidarity among Negroes as will enable them to fight and bargain for a separate realm. To support their claim, they have imagined themselves a glorious past as the Muslims who were the scourge of Europe and Christianity throughout the centuries. They project themselves into an apocalyptic future when, in cargo-cult fashion, their ship will come in and the

evil white race will be destroyed.[9] This, mind you, is not in the South Seas, in Black Africa or among dispossessed American Indians, but among urban Americans. The question one must ask is this: at what point do people so far lose confidence in the "others" with whom they are destined to live as to reject all the collective symbols of their common society, and to erase from their talk all phrases which imply common humanity. Such symbolic Apartheid has not been the prevailing mind of Negro Americans, but it lurks ready to be called into the open with every alienating rebuff. The balance is still with the movement for complete integration.

Indeed it is so much so that some Negroes are claiming special treatment in order to make the integration more rapid, on the ground that past discrimination has loaded them with a competitive disadvantage which it will take a long time to overcome. Thus, for the moment, they appear to be asking that their Negro-ness be not forgotten, in order that, in the long run, it may be. It is the vigor and urgency of the Negro demand that is new, not its direction or the supporting ideas. It was that vigor and urgency that sociologists, and other people, did not foresee, even though they knew that Negroes would not be content forever with their situation, and should have sensed that the contradiction between "speed" and "deliberate" would become the object of both wit and anger.

In Canada, the tension between French and English has always existed,

[9] M. Eliade, " 'Cargo-Cults' and Cosmic Regeneration," pp. 139–143 in S. L. Thrupp (ed.), Millennial Dreams in Action. Comparative Studies in Society and History, Supplement II, The Hague, 1962. See other articles in this volume. The members of such cults are enjoined to prepare for the great day, not by political action, but by strict abstinence from all contact with the enemy and his works.

and has always turned upon the question of the survival and status of the French as a linguistic, cultural and political entity. French Canadians believe that a large proportion of English Canadians assume that French Canada will and ought to cease to exist, just as English Canadians believe that many Americans assume that Canada itself will and ought to cease to exist. From time to time, the tension becomes great and various French nationalist movements arise. In time of war, English Canadians accuse French Canadians of less than full devotion to the cause, while French Canadians resent the attempt of the others to tell them their duty. In the great depression there was tension over jobs and the burden of unemployment centering about the fact that management and ownership of industry were English, while labor was French.

The present movement is the first major one in time of peace and prosperity, when critics can say, and do, "They never had it so good. What do they want anyway?" To be sure it is a *drôle de paix* in which some other Canadians wish the French might join more heartily in the campaign against Castro—as they ought, it is said, being Catholics and therefore presumably leaders in the battle against Communism. Not only are the circumstances different from the times of earlier national upsurgings, but the very rhetoric is contrary, and some of the most ardent of earlier leaders are dubbed compromisers, or even traitors.

Most earlier French nationalist leaders called upon their fellow Canadians to respect the bargain of Confederation everywhere in Canada; bilingualism and public support of Catholic schools should prevail, or at least be tolerated, everywhere, not only in Quebec. The French were to have parity, their just proportion of all positions in government, and eventually in business and

industry. But to merit their survival French Canadians should retain their rural virtues, including a high birth rate which would win for them, in due time, a victory of the cradle. To retain those virtues, their unemployed and the extra sons of farmers should go north to clear and settle new lands. Only so would they save themselves from the vices of the city, which were alleged to be English, American—and Jewish. To document their charter-membership of Canada, they cultivated folklore and song; their novelists wrote of the clearing of the land, of the drive of logs down the rivers after the spring thaw, of the land passing from father to son. They emphasized their place as the true Canadians—*Canadiens* without qualifying adjective—while English Canadians were *Anglais*, or perhaps *Canadiens anglais*.

Thus equal rights with English in a common country was the theme of most of the earlier leaders, and was the sentiment of most French Canadians, whether active in any movement or not. But the new movement talks of separation of the State, not Province, of Quebec from Canada; if not separation, then a new constitution giving Quebec a special status. It calls the French people of Quebec by the name *Québecois*. English Canadians are called Canadians, with English spelling, and the French word Canadien, is avoided. The government in Ottawa is spoken of as an alien power maintaining unjust colonial rule; the *Québecois* are chid for allowing themselves to remain the only white colonized people in the world and, indeed, one of the few colonized peoples, white or colored. Instead of seeking bilingualism everywhere in Canada, the more extreme wing—and even some quite conservative groups—ask for a Quebec with one language, French, and complete fiscal independence from Canada. The movement takes the doctrine of the nation-state in its extreme form as defining the goal to be attained.

Instead of praising rural life, they speak of an urban and industrial Quebec, which will solve its problems by becoming master in its own house. They dismiss return to the land and the victory of the cradle as dreams that divert French Canadians from attaining realistic goals. Those goals of well-being for an urban and industrial people are to be gained by socialistic means, and by breaking the power of Yankee capitalism.

Some talk of Freud, Marx and alienation. In literary criticism, they talk of emancipation from obsession with the past, the frontiers, the land and France; not of denying the past and French identity, but of taking them for granted while they deal with their problems as North American city dwellers, as a people who need no justification except that they exist and have the same problems to write about as do others.

The new rhetoric may not be used in extreme form by many, but it has permeated a great deal of French-Canadian writing and political talk. It has spread much more rapidly than any one expected. There are indeed some extreme groups who have turned to the bombing of symbols of British hegemony—a statue of Queen Victoria, an army recruiting station, and mailboxes in what is considered a well-to-do English quarter. The members of this small terrorist sect are not the leaders of the separatist movement, but their existence and temper indicate the intensity of the general feeling of malaise. Those arrested and accused of the bombings are alienated young men of the city, not intellectuals, but part of the white-collar Lumpenproletariat, semi-employed. It has been said that the whole separatist movement is one of the little bureaucrats of business and government. In its more moderate form, the movement has certainly been joined by many people

of various classes, whose rhetoric also turns in the direction of a special status for the State of Quebec, of a renegotiation of the terms of Confederation.

To return to this country, the new things about the Negro movement are not its ultimate goals and its rhetoric, but its immediate goals, its mass and its structure. It got under way and took on mass as a struggle for the equal right to consume goods and services— food, transportation, education, housing and entertainment. This is a goal of people with at least some money to spend and with the aspiration to spend as others do. The Negro Americans who led those first sit-ins were indeed so American that they seem more humiliated by not being able to spend the dollar than they would be at not having a dollar to spend. "My money is as good as the other fellow's," is probably the ultimate expression of American democracy. Here we meet the great paradox in American social structure. While our race line is, next to South Africa's, the world's tightest, we have the times-over largest Negro middle class in the world, and the largest group of Negroes approaching middle-class western tastes and with the money to satisfy them in some measure. This may be due to the fact that we are that country in which industry first depended upon its own workers to be its best customers, and in which movement has gone farthest in that direction.[10] Handicapped though Negro Americans are in employment and income, they are well-enough off to re-

[10] F. P. Spooner shows that in South Africa the high standard of living of Whites rests upon the poverty of the Blacks; seven-eighths of the labor in mining, the industry that brings money to the country, is Black. The consumption industries import raw materials with the foreign exchange earned by mining, and produce at prices which only Whites can afford. *South African Predicament. The Economics of Apartheid*, New York: Praeger, 1960, pp. 181 *et seq.*

sent the barriers which prevent them from keeping up with the white Joneses. This reflects a great change in the Negro social structure itself; goal and social structure are doubtless functions of each other. In the struggle for consumption it appears generally to have been true that the Negro participants were of higher social class than the whites who have set upon them, or perhaps it is that racial struggles bring out the low-class side of white people.

Now that the movement for equality of the right to consume has moved into high gear—and especially in the South —the movement for equality in employment has taken on new momentum in the North. When, during the war, a number of us worked to get Negroes employed in industry in Chicago, our first objective was to get them moved into semi-skilled production jobs, and out of maintenance and unskilled work. The effort now is aimed higher—at the kinds of work controlled by craft unions, and especially those in construction. For in the precariously seasonal construction trades apprenticeships and jobs are notoriously held tightly in ethnic and family cliques. The battle for equality of right to consume may be essentially won long before access to all kinds of training and jobs is open. There are many inaccessible crevices in the American labor market. I have seen no good account of who the people are who are demonstrating at construction sites, but apparently many have been drawn in who never took part in demonstrations before. We may expect, I believe, that each new immediate objective, whether for the right to consume or to work, will draw in new kinds of participants.

One of the most striking cases of this is the apparent mobilization of the National [Negro] Medical Association. It was reported in the press that members of the National Medical Association were to picket the convention of the American Medical Association in Atlantic City and their headquarters in Chicago. The permanent executive secretary of the Negro association declared himself against the picketing as it would embarrass his good friends in the American Medical Association; but the young president was reported to have said he would himself lead the picketing. Negro physicians have been notoriously conservative in their attack on racial discrimination—even against themselves. Safely ensconced in general practice with patients whom white physicians did not want, they enjoyed a certain security provided they were content to practice in their own offices or in segregated hospitals, letting such Negro patients as could get into other hospitals go to white physicians. But that security is in danger. Negro physicians no longer have a near monopoly on Negro patients, for the patients may be part of insurance schemes which give them access to clinics or hospitals and which will pay their bills. The few segregated Negro hospitals are in generally sad and declining condition. Young Negro physicians do not want to tie their professional fate to them. Back of all this, however, lies a general change in the structure of medical organization. The capital goods of medicine are concentrated more and more in hospitals and clinics; patient and physician meet where the tools and machines and auxiliary personnel are found. If the Negro patient has more access to them than the Negro physician, the latter is in a poor position. Thus a general change in the social structure of medical institutions strikes hard at the position of one of the Negro-American elites. If the younger Negro physicians are to survive, they must get into the main institutions of modern medicine; that means specialization, access to clinics, hospitals and laboratories, membership of various colleague groups and ability to move freely. The American Medical Association is the bastion of the older organization of medicine, for the power to accept members lies completely in the hands of county medical associations, dominated by local physicians out of sympathy with the modern trends in medicine as well as likely to be opposed to recognizing Negroes as full colleagues.

Perhaps it took this combination of changes in the structure of medical institutions, plus the momentum of a great social movement to stir the relatively well-off and well-entrenched to such undignified action as picketing. The change in medical institutions gives the younger Negro physician a motive for rejecting the bargains of the older ones; the new movement gives them the will and the courage.

The older Negro middle class—in the clergy, teaching, law, medicine, insurance and undertaking—had its being in segregated institutions. They got support from white people and organizations with an implicit bargain that there was to be no Negro middle class except what could be supported by giving services to Negro clients and customers; as Park said, the accommodation gave certain Negroes a defined place and field of activity. Now that these institutions are undergoing changes much like those in medicine, the very basis of the older Negro elite would be shaky even without changes in the race line itself.[11]

But that line is changing. With every increase of access of Negroes to consumption and service institutions; the security of the older Negro middle class, which depended upon segregated delivery of services takes another blow; and another front is opened in the battle for equality in the production

and distribution of goods and services. Like so many battles in time of great change, it is in part a battle of the generations. In the larger, more itinerant and cosmopolitan system of distributing professional services in which younger men must make their careers, sponsorship of specialized colleagues and the good opinion of their peers about the country counts more than favor with a local clientele or local white leader. While the standards of judgment among professional peers are in some respects objective and universal, yet the specialized colleagueships of the academic, scientific and professional world are small and relations are quite personal. People are loath to hire a stranger. This is the front on which Negro scholars and professional men have to move forward.[12]

Another new feature of the present movement is that some white people have joined not merely in financial support but in direct action itself. A few white Protestant, Catholic and Jewish religious dignitaries have lent not merely their voices, but also their bodies to the demonstrations. Larger numbers of young white persons, mainly students, have joined, perhaps at somewhat greater risk, in marches,

---

[11] E. Franklin Frazier, *The Black Bourgeoisie*, New York: The Free Press, 1957. That was the middle class of which Frazier wrote so mordantly.

[12] I have not commented on the role in this movement of the older organizations established to improve the condition of Negroes, to win their rights, or to consolidate their position. The Urban Leagues originally had the form of social agencies, with boards of leading citizens and support by community chests as well as by gifts. The National Association for the Advancement of Colored People was originally both a fighting and an elite organization without the features of a philanthropic agency; it became the organ of legal action. The new direct action has been led by new people. A division of labor seems to be emerging among them, with the whole enlivened by the popular direct action. This is a common enough feature of social movements; as some organizations settle down to one style of negotiation or action, new styles of action spring up around new, unofficial, charismatic leaders.

demonstrations and sit-ins in both South and North. This is another matter on which Park commented, in 1923, just 40 years ago:

What has happened to other peoples in this modern world, has happened, is happening, to the Negro. Freedom has not given him the opportunity for participation in the common life of America and of the world that he hoped for. Negroes are restless and seeking. We are all restless, as a matter of fact.

In some respects, however, it seems to me the Negro, like all the other disinherited peoples, is more fortunate than the dominant races. He is restless, but he knows what he wants. The issues in his case, at least, are clearly defined. More than that, in this racial struggle, he is daily gaining not merely new faith in himself, but new faith in the world. Since he wants nothing except what he is willing to give to every other man on the same terms, he feels that the great forces that shape the destinies of peoples are on his side. It is always a source of great power to any people when they feel that their interests, so far from being antagonistic, are actually identified with the interests of the antagonists. We of the dominant, comfortable classes, on the other hand, are steadily driven to something like an obstinate and irrational resistance to the Negro's claims, or we are put in the position of sympathetic spectators, sharing vicariously in his struggles but never really able to make his cause whole-heartedly our own.[13]

The obstinate and irrational resistance of which Park spoke is certainly in evidence, and apparently more on the consumption front than on the job front. Perhaps the American ego is more centered on symbolic consumption of housing among the right neigh-

[13] Robert E. Park, "Negro Race Consciousness as Reflected in Race Literature," *American Review*, I (Sept.–Oct. 1923), 505–516, reproduced in R. E. Park, *Race and Culture*, New York: The Free Press, 1950, pp. 284–300.

bors than on having the right job and colleagues. But what about those white people who join in the lively action on behalf of Negro equality? Are they really nothing more than sympathetic spectators? This raises questions concerning the part of people without status disadvantage in the struggles of those who have a disadvantage. The clergy and many white people are, for the first time, going into overt action on behalf of an eternal principle which they presumably believed and preached all the time. In this case, conscience seems to have been aroused only after the movement, initiated and led by the injured party, got momentum and showed some signs of success. This somewhat cynical suggestion is no answer to this problem: What circumstances so re-define a social situation that some espoused eternal moral principle is considered not merely to apply to it, but to require immediate drastic action of kinds the keepers of the principle ordinarily would not consider proper? . . .

*   *   *

In 1963, when this paper was written, the balance of Negro American sentiment appeared to fall in the direction of integration; but it was on the verge of turning toward symbolic and organizational separation. The turn came quickly, sometimes with violence.

The organizational separation sought was not return of the old segregated schools, churches, and hospitals. It was rather a separation within existing institutions. The symbol of the new attitude is the name *Black*, which, more than the moderate word "Colored" and the exotic Portuguese word "Negro," makes the difference between the races polar—as distant as black from white. The immediate popular organizational goal is reorganization of many existing institutions so as to allow Blacks control of their own segment, with Black teaching Black about Blacks in the schools and universites, Blacks delivering professional services to Blacks, Blacks selling to Blacks. But one should be careful about predicting that this mood will continue or that all Blacks share it now or will share it in the future.

Some do, and more may, desire to play the game of equality and identity on the larger stage of all humanity. The aim of such a paper as mine was not to make predictions of events, but rather to develop sensitivity to the turns things may take, and to emphasize, as did Park, that "status arrangements are always tentative and likely to be questioned."

# 38

# Race and Religion in an American City

## NATHAN GLAZER AND
## DANIEL PATRICK MOYNIHAN

The idea of the melting pot is as old as the Republic. "I could point out to you a family," wrote the naturalized New Yorker, M-G. Jean de Crèvecoeur, in 1782, "whose grandfather was an Englishman, whose wife was Dutch, whose son married a French woman, and whose present four sons have now four wives of different nations. He is an American, who leaving behind him all his ancient prejudices and manners, receives new ones from the new mode of life he has embraced. . . . Here individuals of all nations are melted into a new race of men. . . ." [1] It was an idea close to the heart of the American self-image. But as a century passed, and the number of individuals and nations involved grew, the confidence that they could be fused together waned,

and so also the conviction that it would be a good thing if they were to be. In 1882 the Chinese were excluded, and the first general immigration law was enacted. In a steady succession thereafter, new and more selective barriers were raised until, by the National Origins Act of 1924, the nation formally adopted the policy of using immigration to reinforce, rather than further to dilute, the racial stock of the early America.

This latter process was well underway, had become in ways inexorable, when Israel Zangwill's play The Melting Pot was first performed in 1908. The play (quite a bad one) was an instant success. It ran for months on Broadway; its title was seized upon as a concise evocation of a profoundly significant American fact.

Behold David Quixano, the Russian Jewish immigrant—a "pogrom orphan"—escaped to New York City, exulting in the glory of his new country:

. . . America is God's Crucible, the great Melting Pot where all the races of Europe

Reprinted from Beyond the Melting Pot by Nathan Glazer and Daniel Patrick Moynihan, by permission of the M.I.T. Press, Cambridge, Massachusetts.
[1] J. Hector St. John Crèvecoeur (Michel-Guillaume Jean de Crèvecoeur), Letters from an American Farmer, New York: Fox, Duffeld & Co., 1904, pp. 54–55.

are melting and reforming! Here you stand, good folk, think I, when I see them at Ellis Island, here you stand in your fifty groups with your fifty languages and histories, and your fifty blood hatreds and rivalries, but you won't be long like that brothers, for these are the fires of God you've come to—these are the fires of God. A fig for your feuds and vendettas! German and Frenchman, Irishman and Englishman, Jews and Russians—into the Crucible with you all! God is making the American. . . .

The real American has not yet arrived. He is only in the Crucible, I tell you—he will be the fusion of all the races, the coming superman.[2]

Yet looking back, it is possible to speculate that the response to *The Melting Pot* was as much one of relief as of affirmation: more a matter of reassurance that what had already taken place would turn out all right, rather than encouragement to carry on in the same direction.

Zangwill's hero throws himself into the amalgam process with the utmost energy; by curtainfall he has written his American symphony and won his Muscovite aristocrat: almost all concerned have been reconciled to the homogeneous future. Yet the play seems but little involved with American reality. It is a drama about Jewish separatism and Russian anti-Semitism, with a German concertmaster and an Irish maid thrown in for comic relief. Both protagonists are New Model Europeans of the time. Free thinkers and revolutionaries, it was doubtless in the power of such to merge. But neither of these doctrines was dominant among the ethnic groups of New York City in the 1900's, and in significant ways this became less so as time passed. Individuals, in very considerable numbers to be sure, broke out of their mold, but the groups remained. The experience of Zangwill's hero and heroine was *not*

general. The point about the melting pot is that it did not happen.

Significantly, Zangwill was himself much involved in one of the more significant deterrents to the melting pot process. He was a Zionist. He gave more and more of his energy to this cause as time passed, and retreated from his earlier position on racial and religious mixture. Only eight years after the opening of *The Melting Pot* he was writing "It was vain for Paul to declare that there should be neither Jew nor Greek. Nature will return even if driven out with a pitchfork, still more if driven out with a dogma." [3]

We may argue whether it was "nature" that returned to frustrate continually the imminent creation of a single American nationality. The fact is that in every generation, throughout the history of the American republic, the merging of the varying streams of population differentiated from one another by origin, religion, outlook has seemed to lie just ahead—a generation, perhaps, in the future. This continual deferral of the final smelting of the different ingredients (or at least the different white ingredients) into a seamless national web as is to be found in the major national states of Europe suggests that we must search for some systematic and general causes for this American pattern of subnationalities; that it is not the temporary upsetting inflow of new and unassimilated immigrants that creates a pattern of ethnic groups within the nation, but rather some central tendency in the national ethos which structures people, whether those coming in afresh or the descendants of those who have been here for generations, into groups of different status and character.

It is striking that in 1963, almost forty years after mass immigration

[2] Israel Zangwill, *The Melting Pot*, New York: Macmillan, 1909, pp. 37–38.

[3] Joseph Leftwich, *Israel Zangwill*, New York: Thomas Yoseloff, 1957, p. 255.

from Europe to this country ended, the ethnic pattern is still so strong in New York City. It is true we can point to specific causes that have served to maintain the pattern. But we know that it was not created by the great new migrations of Southern Negroes and Puerto Ricans into the city; nor by the "new" immigration, which added the great communities of East European Jews and Italians to the city; it was not even created by the great migration of Irish and Germans in the 1840's. Even in the 1830's, while the migration from Europe was still mild, and still consisted for the most part of English-speaking groups, one still finds in the politics of New York State, and of the city, the strong impress of group differentiation. In a fascinating study of the politics of the Jacksonian period in New York State, Lee Benson concludes: "At least since the 1820's, when manhood suffrage became widespread, ethnic and religious differences have tended to be *relatively* the most widespread sources of political differences." [4]

There were ways of making distinctions among Welshmen and Englishment, Yorkers and New Englanders, long before people speaking strange tongues and practicing strange religions came upon the scene. The group-forming characteristics of American social life—more concretely, the general expectation among those of new and old groups that group membership is significant and formative for opinion and behavior—are as old as the city. The tendency is fixed deep in American life generally; the specific pattern of ethnic differentiation, however, in every generation is created by specific events.

We can distinguish four major events or processes that have structured this

pattern in New York during the past generation and whose effects will remain to maintain this pattern for some time to come—to be replaced by others we can scarcely now discern. These four formative events are the following:

First, the shaping of the Jewish community under the impact of the Nazi persecution of the Jews in Europe and the establishment of the state of Israel; second, the parallel, if less marked, shaping of a Catholic community by the reemergence of the Catholic school controversy; third, the migration of Southern Negroes to New York following World War I and continuing through the fifties; fourth, the influx of Puerto Ricans during the fifteen years following World War II.

## The Jews

Developments within the Jewish community have had the most immediate significance. A fourth of the city is Jewish; very much more than a fourth of its wealth, energy, talent, and style is derived from the Jews. Over the past thirty years this community has undergone profound emotional experiences, centered almost entirely on the fact of Jewishness, has been measurably strengthened by immigration, and has become involved in vast Zionist enterprises, the rationale of which is exclusively Jewish. There are two aspects of these developments as they affect melting pot tendencies, one negative, the other positive.

The negative aspect has prevented a change that might otherwise have occurred. Prior to the 1930's Jews contributed significantly to the ethnic pattern of New York politics by virtue of their radicalism. This kept them apart from the Catholic establishment in the Democratic party and the Protestant regime within the Republican party but did give them a distinct role of their own. At the time of *The Melting Pot*

[4] Lee Benson, *The Concept of Jacksonian Democracy*, Princeton, N.J.: Princeton University Press, 1961, p. 165.

there were, to be sure, a great many Democratic and Republican Jewish merchants and businessmen. Most East Side Jews probably voted the Tammany ticket. But indigenous Jewish politics, the politics of the *Jewish Daily Forward*, of the Workmen's Circle, and the needle-trades unions were predominantly socialist. The Russian Revolution, in which Russian Jews played a prominent role, had a strong attraction for a small but important number of their kinsmen in New York. It would appear, for example, that during the 1930's most Communist party members in New York City were Jewish.[5] It must be stressed that the vast majority of New York Jews had nothing whatever to do with Communism. Some of the strongest centers of anti-Communist activity were and are to be found within the New York Jewish community. Nonetheless there was an ethnic cast to this form of political radicalism in New York, as there had been to the earlier Socialist movement.

Both Socialism and Communism are now considerably diminished and both have lost almost entirely any ethnic base. But just as the moment when the last distinctly Jewish political activity might have disappeared, a transcendent Jewish political interest was created by the ghastly persecutions of the Nazis, the vast dislocations of World War II, and the establishment of the State of Israel. These were matters that no Jew or Christian could ignore. They were equally matters about which little could be done except through politics. From the beginnings of the Zionist movement a certain number of New York Jews have been involved on that account with the high politics of the nation. Since the mid-1930's, however, this involvement has reached deeper

and deeper into the New York Jewish community. They are the one group in the city (apart from the white Protestant financial establishment) of which it may fairly be said that among the leadership echelons there is a lively, active, and effective interest in who will be the next U.S. Secretary of State but one . . . or two, or three.

In a positive sense, events of the Nazi era and its aftermath have produced an intense group consciousness among New York Jews that binds together persons of widely disparate situations and beliefs. A pronounced religious revival has occurred. Among those without formal religious ties there is a heightened sense of the defensive importance of organized Jewish activity. Among intellectuals, the feeling of Jewishness is never far from the surface.

Now, as in the past, the Jewish community in New York is the one most actively committed to the principles of racial integration and group tolerance. But open housing is something different from the melting pot. There is no reason to think that any considerable portion of the Jewish community of New York ever subscribed to Israel Zangwill's vision of a nonreligious intermarried, homogeneous population, but it surely does not do so today. To the contrary, much of the visible activity of the community is aimed in directions that will intensify Jewish identity: Jewish elementary and secondary schools, Jewish colleges and universities, Jewish periodicals, Jewish investments in Israel, and the like. In the meantime Jewish politicians make more (or at least not less) of the "Jewish" vote.

This is not to say the Jewish community of New York has been *created* or *maintained* by these events of the thirties or forties: that would be too narrow a view of Jewish history, and would ignore the group-making char-

[5] See Nathan Glazer, *The Social Basis of American Communism*, New York: Harcourt, Brace & World, 1961, Chap. IV.

acteristics of American civilization. But
the Jewish community was *shaped* by
these events. Moving rapidly from
working-class to middle-class occupations and styles of life, many alternative courses of development were possible. Within the frame set by these
large social movements, the historical
drama shaped a community intensely
conscious of its Jewishness. Religion
plays in many ways the smallest part
of the story of American Jews. In New
York City in particular the religious
definition of the group explains least.
Here the formal religious groups are
weakest, the degree of affiliation to
synagogues and temples smallest. In a
city with 2,000,000 Jews, Jews need
make no excuses to explain Jewishness
and Jewish interests. On the one hand,
there is the social and economic structure of the community; on the other,
ideologies and emotions molded by the
specific history of recent decades. Together they have shaped a community
that itself shapes New York and will
for generations to come.[6]

## The Catholics

Outwardly, events since World War I
have brought Catholics, notably the
Irish Catholics, ever closer to the centers of power and doctrine in American
life. But following a pattern common
in human affairs, the process of closing
the gap has heightened resentment,
among some at all events, that a gap
should exist. Here, as in much else
concerning this general subject, it is
hardly possible to isolate New York
events from those of the nation generally, but because New York tends to be
the center of Catholic thinking and
publishing, the distinction is not cru-

[6] For the complex interplay of religious,
ideological, and socioeconomic factors within
the American Jewish community, see *American Judaism* by Nathan Glazer, Chicago:
University of Chicago Press, 1967.

cial. The great division between the
Catholic Church and the leftist and
liberal groups in the city during the
period from the Spanish Civil War to
the era of McCarthy has been narrowed,
with most elements of city politics con-
verging on center positions. However
issues of church-state relations have
become considerably more difficult, and
the issue of government aid to Catholic
schools has become acute.

Controversy over church-state relations is nothing new to the American
Catholic Church. What is new, however, and what is increasingly avowed,
is the extent to which the current controversy derives from Catholic-Jewish
disagreements rather than from traditional Catholic-Protestant differences.
Relations between the two latter groups
have steadily improved: to the point
that after three centuries of separation
Catholics in the 1960's began increasingly to talk of the prospects of re-
establishing Christian unity. In general
(there are, of course, many individual
exceptions) the dominant view within
Protestant and Catholic circles is that
the United States is and ought to be a
Christian commonwealth, to the point
at very least of proclaiming "In God
We Trust" on the currency and cele-
brating Christmas in the public schools.
However, as this *rapprochement* has
proceeded, within the Jewish community a contrary view has arisen which
asserts that the separation of church
and state ought to be even more complete than it has been, and that the
"Post-Protestant era" means Post-
Christian as well, insofar as government relations with religion are
concerned.

The most dramatic episode of this
development was the decision of the
United States Supreme Court on June
25, 1962, that the recitation of an official prayer in the New York school
system was unconstitutional. The case
was brought by five parents of children

in the public schools of the New York City suburb of New Hyde Park. Two of the parents were Jewish, one a member of the Ethical Culture Society, one a Unitarian, and one a non-believer. Before it concluded, however, the principal protagonists of the Catholic-Jewish controversy in New York City were involved. The attorney for the Archdiocese of New York, for example, argued in the Supreme Court for a group of parents who supported the prayer. The response to the decision could hardly have been more diametrical. Cardinal Spellman declared, "I am shocked and frightened. . . ." The New York Board of Rabbis, on the other hand, hailed the decision: "The recitation of prayers in the public schools, which is tantamount to the teaching of prayer, is not in conformity with the spirit of the American concept of the separation of church and state. All the religious groups in this country will best advance their respective faiths by adherence to this principle." The American Jewish Committee, the American Jewish Congress, and the Anti-Defamation League of B'nai B'rith strongly supported the Court. Only among the Orthodox was there mild disagreement with the Supreme Court decision.

Although the argument could certainly be made that the American Catholic Church ought to be the first to object to the spectacle of civil servants composing government prayers, and although many Catholic commentators noted that the decision strengthened the case for private Church-sponsored schools, the general Catholic reaction was most hostile. The Jesuit publication America, in an editorial "To our Jewish Friends," declared that Jewish efforts to assert an ever more strict separation of church and state were painting the Jewish community into a corner, where it would be isolated from the rest of Americans.

Significantly, Protestant reaction to the decision was mixed. The Brooklyn Tablet took the cue, stating that the crucial question raised by the decision was "What are the Protestants going to do about it? For, although this is a national problem, it is particularly a Protestant problem, given the large Protestant enrollment in the public schools. Catholics have been fighting long—and sometimes alone—against the Church-State extremists. May we count on Protestants to supply more leadership in this case? If so, we pledge our support to join efforts against the common enemy: secularism." [7]

The subject of aid to Catholic schools is only one aspect of the more general issue of church-state relations, and here again the ethnic composition of New York City tends to produce the same alignment of opposing groups. There are elements within the Jewish community, again the Orthodox, that favor public assistance for religious schools, but the dominant view is opposed. In 1961 the New York Republican party at the state level made a tentative move toward the Catholic position by proposing a Constitutional amendment that would have permitted state construction loans to private institutions of higher learning, sectarian as well as secular. Opposition from Jewish (as well as some Protestant) groups was pronounced, and the measure was beaten at the polls.

The situation developing in this area could soberly be termed dangerous. An element of interfaith competition has entered the controversy. As the costs of education mount, it becomes increasingly difficult to maintain the quality of the education provided by private schools deprived of public assistance. It is not uncommon to hear it stated in Catholic circles that the results of national scholarship competitions already point to the weakness of Catholic

[7] Quoted in the New York Herald Tribune, July 2, 1962.

education in fields such as the physical sciences. The specter is raised that a parochial education will involve sacrifice for the students as well as for their parents.

There is understandably much resentment within Catholic educational circles at the relative crudity of most such observations. At the same time this resentment is often accompanied by an unmistakable withdrawal. In a thoughtful address calling for more meticulous assessment of the qualities of Catholic education, Bishop McEntegart of the Diocese of Brooklyn went on to state that "Judgment on the effectiveness of an educational system should be something more profound and more subtle than counting heads of so-called intellectuals who happen to be named in Who's Who or the "Social Register." [8]

Whether the course of the controversy will lead Catholics further into separatist views of this kind is not clear. But it is abundantly evident that so long as Catholics maintain a separate education system and the rest of the community refuses to help support it by tax funds or tax relief, a basic divisive issue will exist. This will be an ethnic issue in measure that the Catho-

lic community continues to include the bulk of the Irish, Italian, and Polish population in the city, at least the bulk of those affiliated with organizations taking a position on the issue. If, as may very well happen, the Catholics abandon elementary and even secondary education to concentrate on their colleges and universities, the larger issue of church-state relations will no doubt subside.

But it is not the single issue of school aid, no matter how important and long-lived it is, that alone shapes the polarization between the Jewish and the emerging Catholic community. There have been other issues in the past—for example, the struggle over the legitimacy of city hospitals giving advice on birth control, which put Jews and liberal Protestants on one side and Catholics on the other. There are the recurrent disputes over government censorship of books and movies and magazines that have become freer and freer in their handling of sex and sexual perversion. This again ranges Jewish and Protestant supporters of the widest possible freedom of speech against Catholics who are more anxious about the impact of such material on young people and family life. One can see emerging such issues as the rigid state laws on divorce and abortion.[9]

Many of these issues involve Catholic *religious* doctrine. But there exists here a situation that is broader than a conflict over doctrines and the degree to which government should recognize them. What is involved is the emergence of two subcultures, two value systems, shaped and defined certainly in part by religious practice and experience and organization but by now supported by the existence of two communities. If the bishops and the rabbis

---

[8] *The Tablet*, February 17, 1962. In an address given in Washington on April 30, 1962, Very Reverend William F. Kelley, S.J., President of Marquette University, implicitly proposed a secondary role for Catholic education. As reported in *The Washington Post*, Father Kelley suggested that Catholic schools leave "research and the exploration for new knowledge" to "research institutes" like Hopkins, Harvard, and M.I.T., it being "perfectly respectable and professionally honorable" to concentrate on the transmission of the knowledge of the past:

It is an entirely sound plan to be trailing along at a respectable distance with a trained and educated citizenry competent to appreciate and consume the discovery of the successful investigator. Let us remember that if there are no followers, there can be no leader.

[9] See *A Tale of Ten Cities*, Albert Vorspan and Eugene Lipman, New York: *Union of American Hebrew Congregations*, 1962, pp. 175 ff.

were to disappear tomorrow, the sub-cultures and subcommunities would remain. One is secular in its attitudes, liberal in its outlook on sexual life and divorce, positive about science and social science. The other is religious in its outlook, resists the growing liberalization in sexual mores and its reflection in cultural and family life, feels strongly the tension between moral values and modern science and technology. The conflict may be seen in many ways—not least in the fact that the new disciplines such as psychoanalysis, particularly in New York, are so largely staffed by Jews.

Thus a Jewish ethos and a Catholic ethos emerge: they are more strongly affected by a specific religious doctrine in the Catholic case than in the Jewish, but neither is purely the expression of the spirit of a religion. Each is the result of the interplay of religion, ethnic group, American setting, and specific issues. The important fact is that the differences in values and attitudes between the two groups do not, in general, become smaller with time. On the contrary: there is probably a wider gap between Jews and Catholics in New York today than in the days of Al Smith.[10]

## Negroes and Puerto Ricans

A close examination of Catholic-Jewish relations will reveal some of the tendency of ethnic relations in New York to be a form of class relations as well.

[10] Gerhard Lenski, *The Religious Factor*, New York: Doubleday, 1961, gives a great deal of evidence to the effect that value differences between Catholics and white Protestants and Jews (the latter two often linked, but not always) in Detroit have increased as the groups move from working-class and immigrant generation to middle-class and later generations. Parochial schooling plays some part in these differences. For an interesting evocation of the milieu in which Jewish-Catholic political cooperation flourished, see *Al Smith*, by Oscar Handlin, Boston: Little, Brown, 1958.

However, the tendency is unmistakably clear with regard to the Negroes and Puerto Ricans. Some 22 percent of the population of the city is now Negro or Puerto Rican, and the proportion will increase. (Thirty-six percent of the births in 1961 were Negro or Puerto Rican.) To a degree that cannot fail to startle anyone who encounters the reality for the first time, the overwhelming portion of both groups constitutes a submerged, exploited, and very possibly permanent proletariat.

New York is properly regarded as the wealthiest city in the nation. Its more affluent suburbs enjoy some of the highest standards of living on earth. In the city itself while-collar wages are high, and skilled labor through aggressive trade union activity has obtained almost unprecedented standards. Bricklayers earn $5.35 an hour, plus 52¢ for pension, vacation, and insurance benefits. Electricians have a nominal twenty-five hour week and a base pay of $4.96 an hour plus fringe benefits.[11] But amidst such plenty, unbelievable squalor persists: the line of demarcation is a color line in the case of Negroes, a less definite but equally real ethnic line in the case of Puerto Ricans.

The relationship between the rise of the Negro-Puerto Rican labor supply and the decline of industrial wages is unmistakable. In 1950 there were 246,000 Puerto Ricans in the city. By 1960 this number has increased by two and one-half time to 613,000 or 8 percent. In 1950 the average hourly earnings of manufacturing production workers in New York City ranked tenth in the nation. By 1960 they ranked thirtieth. In the same period comparable wages in Birmingham, Alabama, rose from thirty-third to tenth. In 1959 median family income for Puerto Ricans was $3,811 as against $6,091 for all the city's families (and $8,052 for suburbs of Westches-

[11] U.S. Bureau of Labor Statistics for October, 1962.

374

Sociology of Contemporary Society

ter). In 1962 average weekly earnings of manufacturing production workers were 10 percent higher in Birmingham than in New York City, 15 percent higher in New Orleans, and almost 10 percent higher in the nation as a whole.

These economic conditions vastly reinforce the ethnic distinctions that serve to separate the Negro community and the Puerto Rican community from the rest of the city. The Negro separation is strengthened by the fact that the colored community is on the whole Protestant, and much of its leadership comes from Protestant clergy. Thus the Negroes provide the missing element of the Protestant-Catholic-Jew triad.

Housing segregation, otherwise an intolerable offense to the persons affected, serves nonetheless to ensure the Negroes a share of seats on the City Council and in the State Legislature and Congress. This power, as well as their voting power generally, has brought Negro political leaders to positions of considerable prominence. Following the 1961 mayoralty election, Mayor Wagner appointed the talented Harlem leader, J. Raymond Jones, as a political secretary through whom he would deal with all the Democratic party organizations of the city. Puerto Ricans have only begun to make their influence felt, but they are clearly on the way to doing so.

Their fate gives them an interest in the same issues: the housing of the poor in a city of perpetual housing shortage; the raising of the wages of the poorly paid semiskilled service occupations in which most of them work; the development of new approaches to raising motivation and capacity by means of education and training in the depressed areas of the city. They live adjacent to each other in vast neighborhoods. And they cooperate on many specific issues—for example, in fighting urban renewal programs that would displace them. But there are deeply

felt differences between them. The more Americanized group is also more deeply marked by color. The furtive hope of the new group that it may move ahead as other immigrants have without the barrier of color, and the powerful links of language and culture that mark off the Puerto Ricans, suggest that, despite the fact that the two groups increasingly comprise the proletariat of the city, their history will be distinct.

Thus the cast of major characters for the next decades is complete: the Jews; the Catholics, subdivided at least into Irish and Italian components; the Negroes; the Puerto Ricans; and, of course, the white Anglo-Saxon Protestants. These latter, ranging from the Rockefeller brothers to reform district leaders in the Democratic party are, man for man, among the most influential and powerful persons in the city, and will continue to play a conspicuous and creative role in almost every aspect of the life of the metropolis. . . .

## The Future

We have tried to show how deeply the pattern of ethnicity is impressed on the life of the city. Ethnicity is more than an influence on events; it is commonly the source of events. Social and political institutions do not merely respond to ethnic interests; a great number of institutions exist for the specific purpose of serving ethnic interests. This in turn tends to perpetuate them. In many ways, the atmosphere of New York City is hospitable to ethnic groupings: it recognizes them, and rewards them, and to that extent encourages them. . . .

[Ethnic] groups do not disappear, however, because of their *religious* aspect which serves as the basis of a subcommunity, and a subculture. Doctrines and practices are modified to some extent to conform to an American norm, but a distinctive set of values is nurtured in the social groupings defined by religious affiliation. This is quite contrary to early expectations. It apeared to de Crèvecoeur, for example, that religious as well as national identity was being melted into one by the process of mixed neighborhoods and marriage:

. . . This mixed neighborhood will exhibit a strange religious medley, that will be neither pure Catholicism nor pure Calvinism. A very perceptible indifference even in the first generation, will become apparent; and it may happen that the daughter of the Catholic will marry the son of the seceder, and settle by themselves at a distance from their parents. What religious education will they give their children? A very imperfect one. If there happens to be in the neighborhood any place of worship, we will suppose a Quaker's meeting; rather than not shew their fine clothes, they will go to it, and some of them may attach themselves to that society. Others will remain in a perfect state of indifference; the children of these zealous parents will not be able to tell what their religious principles are, and their grandchildren still less.

Thus all sects are mixed as well as all nations; thus religious indifference is imperceptibly disseminated from one end of the continent to the other; which is at present one of the strongest characteristics of the Americans.[12]

If this was the case in the late eighteenth century, it is no longer. Religious identities are strongly held by New Yorkers, and Americans generally, and they are for the most part transmitted by blood line from the original immigrant group. A great deal of intermarriage occurs among nationality groups of the three great religious groups, of the kind Ruby Jo Kennedy described in New Haven, Connecticut, under the general term of the Triple Melting Pot, [13]

[12] de Crèvecoeur, op. cit., pp. 65–66.
[13] Ruby Jo Reeves Kennedy, "Single or Triple Melting Pot: Intermarriage in New Haven," American Journal of Sociology, Vol. 58, No. 1, July, 1952, pp. 55–66.

but this does not weaken religious identity. When marriages occur between different religions, often one is dominant, and the result among the children is not indifference, but an increase in the numbers of one of the groups.

Religion and race seem to define the major groups into which American society is evolving as the specifically national aspect of ethnicity declines. In our large American cities, four major groups emerge: Catholics, Jews, white Protestants, and Negroes, each making up the city in different proportions. This evolution is by no means complete. And yet we can discern that the next stage of the evolution of the immigrant groups will involve a Catholic group in which the distinctions between Irish, Italian, Polish, and German Catholic are steadily reduced by intermarriage; a Jewish group, in which the line between East European, German, and Near Eastern Jews is already weak; the Negro group; and a white Protestant group, which adds to its Anglo-Saxon and Dutch old-stock elements German and Scandinavian Protestants, as well as, more typically, the white Protestant immigrants to the city from the interior.

The white Protestants are a distinct ethnic group in New York, one that has probably passed its low point and will now begin to grow in numbers and probably also in influence. It has its special occupations, with the customary freemasonry. This involves the banks, corporation front offices, educational and philanthropic institutions, and the law offices who serve them. It has its own social world (epitomized by, but by no means confined to, the Social Register), its own churches, schools, voluntary organizations and all the varied institutions of a New York minority. These are accompanied by the characteristic styles in food, clothing, and drink, special family patterns, special psychological problems, and ailments. For a long while political conservatism, as well as social aloofness, tended to keep the white Protestants out of the main stream of New York politics, much in the way that political radicalism tended to isolate the Jews in the early parts of the century. Theodore Roosevelt, when cautioned that none of his friends would touch New York politics, had a point in replying that it must follow that none of his friends were members of the governing classes.

There has been a resurgence of liberalism within the white Protestant group, in part based on its growth through vigorous young migrants from outside the city, who are conspicuous in the communications industry, law firms, and corporation offices of New York. These are the young people that supported Adlai Stevenson and helped lead and staff the Democratic reform movement. The influence of the white Protestant group on this city, it appears, must now grow as its numbers grow.

In this large array of the four major religio-racial groups, where do the Puerto Ricans stand? Ultimately perhaps they are to be absorbed into the Catholic group. But that is a long time away. The Puerto Ricans are separated from the Catholics as well as the Negroes by color and culture. One cannot even guess how this large element will ultimately relate itself to the other elements of the city; perhaps it will serve, in line with its own nature and genius, to soften the sharp lines that divide them.

Protestants will enjoy immunities in politics even in New York. When the Irish era came to an end in the Brooklyn Democratic party in 1961, Joseph T. Sharkey was succeeded by a troika (as it was called) of an Irish Catholic, a Jew, and a Negro Protestant. The last was a distinguished clergyman, who was at the same time head of the New York City Council of Protestant Churches. It would have been unlikely for a rabbi, unheard of for a priest, to hold such a position.

Religion and race define the next stage in the evolution of the American peoples. But the American nationality is still forming: its processes are mysterious, and the final form, if there is ever to be a final form, is as yet unknown.

# 39

# Ethnogenesis and Negro-Americans Today

## LESTER SINGER

The view of Negro-white relations in American society generally accepted by sociologists is that they are caste relations.[1] A competing view—which has

Reprinted from *Social Research*, 29 (Winter, 1962), pp. 422–432, with permission of the author and the publisher.
[1] For definitions see as examples W. L. Warner, "Formal Education and the Social Structure," *Journal of Educational Sociology*, vol. 19 (May 1936) pp. 524–31. W. L. Warner and A. Davis, "A Comparative Study of American Caste," in *Race Relations and the Race Problem*, ed. Thompson (Durham, N.C.: Duke University Press, 1939). A. Davis, B. B. and M. R. Gardner, *Deep South* (Chicago, Ill.: University of Chicago Press, 1941). G. Myrdal, *An American Dilemma* (New York: Harper & Bros., 1944).

not achieved wide acceptance, although the terminology persists—is that the phenomena are best understood as race relations.[2] The two approaches, regardless of the differences between them, deal primarily with the structure of Negro-white relations and with the factors serving to maintain that relational structure.[3]

My thesis is that these structural models fail to illuminate the character of the entities that occupy the various places in the relational structure. I had asked the question: In sociological terms, *what* are the Negroes in American society? And, at first, the answer appeared to be: They are a caste, or a race—and the whites must be one or the other also. Upon further consideration, however, it became clear that caste—as defined by Warner, Davis and Myrdal—and race—as defined by Cox—are not answers to the substantive question. The writers answer the question: *Where?* That is to say, they tell us the position of the Negroes in the structure of Negro-white relations. They do not indicate *what* the Negroes are, *what* they constitute as a social entity.

## Social Category, Social Entity, and Negro-Americans

Let me make clear the notions that underlie the use of the term "social entity" as contrasted with the term "social category." "Social category" has been defined by Bennett and Tumin as referring to "numbers of people who constitute an aggregate because they have a common characteristic(s) *about which* [italics mine] society expresses some views and which therefore in-

fluences their life chances."[4] The "members" of a social category are not necessarily involved in any relationship among themselves. Thus the terms "men," "women," "imigrants," and "divorcees" stand for social categories.[5] The term "social entity," on the other hand, refers to a number of people manifesting such qualities as patterned relationships, shared values, and self-recognition. Thus a team, a gang, a community, an ethnic group, and a society all constitute recognizable social entities.

For this writer, the nub of the contrast between the two terms is the presence or absence of internal structure and the accompanying cultural, or ideological, elements. This is somewhat like the difference between a bin full of spare parts and an engine which has been assembled from such spare parts. As with the bin full of spare parts, the social category contains elements that have no necessary relations to one another. The social entity, however, like the engine, can only be understood through an understanding of the elements in patterned relations.

In the work of both Myrdal and Cox are to be found the empirical generalizations that express the distinctive social attributes of Negro-Americans.

[4] J. W. Bennett and M. M. Tumin, *Social Life* (New York: Alfred A. Knopf, Inc., 1949), p. 140. Note that the authors go on to say, "For instance, in our society all people with dark skin may be considered as belonging to a social category."

[5] It may be added that social categories cannot interact in any sociological sense. For example, when we speak of the interaction of men and women, it may sound as if we are referring to the interaction of categories. But actually we are referring to the cumulative interaction of individuals or, more likely, to typical aspects of interaction situations that involve individuals. Certainly such interaction situations are influenced by the beliefs and values attached to the several category definitions but, just as certainly, it is incorrect to say that the social categories are interacting.

[2] See as an example O. C. Cox, *Caste, Class, and Race* (New York: Doubleday & Co., Inc., 1948).

[3] This structural emphasis and static quality is especially the case with the caste approach.

These attributes, when viewed as elements in a pattern rather than separately, make up a picture of Negroes as a social entity on the order of an ethnic group.[6] Among these qualities are, briefly, the following. 1) The existence of a separate Negro prestige continuum, that is "a social-class system." 2) The existence of a distinctive Negro culture pattern. [While it is true that the pattern is derived from that of the larger society—Myrdal calls it a "pathological" form and Cox a "truncated" form of the larger American culture pattern—such references to origin indicate, if we disregard their evaluative content, the distinctiveness of this pattern. This is not to say that it is completely different from the larger pattern but, rather, that it is not quite the same.] 3) The existence of various aspects of Negro solidarity vis-à-vis the "whites": its, heretofore, primarily defensive character; its tentativeness; the predominantly compromising nature of Negro leadership; the development of a self-image; the Negroes' conviction of their rights in the larger society; and the direction of collective Negro aspiration toward the realization of these rights within the larger society. 4) The existence of the uncountable relational networks and organizations (that is the internal structure) which, by virtue of discrimination and the defensive response of Negroes, are manned largely by Negroes.

If this pattern of qualities is sig-

nificant it means, as I indicated at the outset, that Negroes and, therefore, Negro-white relations, cannot be fully understood if only category concepts are used. The employment of such concepts results in interpretations that are not as inclusive as the data allow. Another important limiting effect of the use of these concepts is an emphasis on the static. Consequently, while a model based on category concepts may prepare the ground, it certainly does not facilitate an examination of process, development, and change.[7] And yet it is in precisely this latter direction that we must search if social entities, which come into existence and which disappear, are to be adequately understood. Thus, if Negroes in the United States are to be understood as an entity, that is as an ethnic group, it is necessary to attempt to answer such questions as: How did this entity commence to form? What are the factors tending to maintain or change the formative process? What are the circumstances under which such an entity will cease to exist? The remainder of this essay attempts to answer these questions.

## Ethnogenesis

During the seventeenth and eighteenth centuries the Africans who were brought to North America, as well as to other parts of the New World, were representatives of a variety of societies, cultural backgrounds, language groups, and so forth. Consequently, *as a totality* they can only be viewed as a social category; that is as "Africans" or "slaves." Removed from their various social contexts and thrown together as enslaved strangers they had, particularly in North America, no internal

[6] For a definition of ethnic group see note 11. Interestingly enough, both Myrdal and Cox approached the issue of Negroes as an entity, but neither one developed the implications of his own suggestive comments. See Myrdal's references to "a separate community" and "a nation within a nation" (note 1, above), pp. 680, 785, 1003–04 and Cox's reference to a "quasi-society" (note 2, above), p. 503. See also L. Singer, "A Comparative Analysis of Selected Approaches to Negro-White Relations in the United States" (Doctor's dissertation, Columbia University, 1958), pp. 140, 231–32, 270–72.

[7] This is a serious consideration when the investigator's concern is diachronic and developmental. But this is not to say that category concepts are useless, for they are precisely applicable to synchronic analysis.

organization. In fact, the evidence indicates that virtually all traces of African social organization disappeared under the impact of American slavery.[8] One method of accomplishing this was the intentional separation of members of the same society. This was done, among other reasons, to diminish the possibility of revolt. As R. E. Park says, "It was found easier to deal with the slaves, if they were separated from their kinsmen."[9]

It should be realized that during the period of slavery the newly arrived Africans came into contact with whites and acculturated slaves. In this way, cut off from their own background, they came to take on the culture of American society in whatever form it was available to them. With Emancipation the former Africans and their descendants became, as the federal government put it, "freedmen." This legal term, however, stands only for a social category; the freedman lacked determinate social group characteristics. But indications of what was to come had been evidenced earlier by the numerous slave revolts, [10] and the participation of runaway slaves and free Negroes in the Abolitionist movement and the Underground Railroad.

Following Emancipation, the group-forming process moved with much greater speed and intensity than before. I propose that this formative process be referred to as "ethnogenesis," meaning by this term the process whereby a people, that is an ethnic group, comes into

existence.[11] The process [12] appears to have the following form. 1) A portion of a population becomes distinguished, on some basis or bases, in the context of a power relationship. [The particulars are not important for the general outline of the process. The bases may be ideological differences, imputed intrinsic differences, particular functions in the division of labor, and so forth.] 2) The members of this distinguished population segment are "assigned" to a particular social role and fate; [13] that is, the division of labor becomes reorganized.[14] 3) As these people react to the

[11] The term ethnic group is derived from the Greek word *ethnos* meaning "a people." Ethnic group is used here to mean a set of persons that may be distinguished from other such sets by virtue of: 1) a shared pattern of values, beliefs, norms, tastes, and so forth 2) an awareness of their own distinctiveness, partially reflected in a "we-feeling"; (These two distinctions taken together make up their *ethos*.) 3) some structure of relationships among them; and 4) the tendency to maintain generational continuity by marriage within the group. This is very close to E. K. Francis' definition with its emphasis on the *Gemeinschaft* quality of an ethnic group. See, for example, his "The Nature of an Ethnic Group," *American Journal of Sociology*, vol. 52 (March 1947) pp. 393–400 and "The Russian Mennonites: from Religious to Ethnic Group," *American Journal of Sociology*, vol. 54 (September 1948) pp. 101–07. See also the definition given by R. M. MacIver and C. H. Page which specifies both primary and secondary relationships in *Society* (New York: Rinehart & Co., Inc.), p. 387. Compare with R. M. Williams, Jr., *The Reduction of Intergroup Tensions* (New York: Social Science Research Council, 1947), p. 42.

[12] This process seems to me to be one of several kinds of "group-forming" processes. Roscoe C. Hinkle, in a private communication, has suggested "socio-genesis" as the generic term.

[13] The distinguished population segment may become dominant, although this is not usually the case. See, for example, MacIver and Page, note 11, p. 388.

[14] In the case of the Africans in the English colonies this would mean, not slavery per se, but the qualities which slavery in America

[8] See E. F. Frazier, *The Negro in the United States* (New York: The Macmillan Co., 1949), pp. 6–21. This may be contrasted, for example, with Brazilian slavery. See D. Pierson, *Negroes in Brazil* (Chicago: University of Chicago Press, 1942), especially pp. 38–45, IX, and X.

[9] *Race and Culture* (New York: Free Press of Glencoe, Inc., 1950), p. 268.

[10] See H. Aptheker, *American Negro Slave Revolts* (New York: Columbia University Press, 1943).

situation in which they find themselves, they become involved with one another, if the situation permits. In other words, social structures develop among them; it is at this point that entity characteristics first become apparent. 4) Then these people become aware of their commonality of fate. The growth of such corporate self-awareness reinforces the structuring tendencies.[15] 5) The further development of the emerging ethnic group will then depend, in part, on the nature of the structures that develop, the content of the group's "self-image," and the shared conception of its destiny. This, of course, emphasizes internal development, which is our present concern. The other big area of causal factors—with which we are not here concerned except to indicate a context of power relations—is the specific character of the relationship with the other segment(s) of the population. Necessarily, internal group development and external (inter-group) relationships influence one another.

It has already been pointed out that the enslaved Africans were not a social group, although from the first they were a distinguishable portion, that is category, of the population. They were not merely physically distinguishable, as has been stressed in the literature, but also socially distinguishable by virtue of their depressed economic situation, with all of the occupational, educational, and associational consequences. With the passage of time it was the latter point that became the most important. Slavery, however, muted the overt, collective responses of the enslaved to the situation. Emancipation altered this picture.

Let us now briefly scan the phases of the processes of ethnogenesis as it has operated in the case of the Negroes.

*Reconstruction.* During the Reconstruction period the freedmen achieved physical mobility and, consequently, wide-ranging contacts with one another. Also, as a consequence of political participation and the struggle for land, some Negro political leaders emerged. A significant factor that influenced all of the subsequent developments was the failure of the freedman to obtain land and their consequent involvement in cotton farming on, for the most part, the lowest levels of tenancy of the plantation system. It is also significant that during the Reconstruction period the Negroes had to fight in a variety of ways, including organized militia, against the physical onslaughts of Southern whites.[16]

*The National Compromise and After.* The Reconstruction governments were overthrown by the end of the third quarter of the nineteenth century, and the last quarter of that century witnessed both the actual restoration and the political assertion of "white supremacy." During this period discriminatory practices increased and there developed a tendency to treat all Negroes alike regardless of social attributes. This marked a change from the previous period (Myrdal, note 1, pp. 578–82). *Pari passu*, behind the growing barriers there were developing distinctive structural and ideological attributes among the Negroes; for example, a "lower class" Negro family pattern, Negro businesses catering to Negroes, the expansion of the Negro Church (with

---

achieved by the end of the seventeenth century. It was only then that the European-Christian "slaves" and the African-heathen "slaves" became differentiated into servants—who would serve for a limited time—and chattel slaves—who would serve for the duration of their lives. See O. Handlin, *Race and Nationality in American Life* (New York: Doubleday Anchor Books, 1957), especially I.

[15] See, for example, A. Rose, *The Negro's Morale* (Minneapolis: University of Minnesota Press, 1949), especially II.

[16] From one point of view Reconstruction was "a prolonged race riot." G. B. Johnson, cited in Myrdal, note 1, p. 449.

Negro ministers representing the status quo as supernaturally sanctioned), and the emergence of Booker T. Washington as a national Negro leader.

*Early Twentieth Century.* The peak, or depth, of discriminatory tendencies was reached in the early twentieth century. By this time the Reconstruction state constitutions had been changed, legislation requiring "separate but equal" facilities had been declared constitutional, and in the preceding three decades approximately 2,500 Negroes had been lynched in the South. This last is an index of the community-wide methods of violence and intimidation used by the whites to maintain the situation.

In the first decade of this century, however, there appeared other entity, or ethnic group, characteristics among the Negroes; for example, organized protest in the form of the Niagara Movement and the National Association for the Advancement of Colored People and the attempts to create economic opportunities for Negroes in the form of the National Urban League. These, in turn, give evidence of the Negroes' conception of their destiny— full and unhampered participation in the larger society. This was first expressed organizationally in the statement of the Niagara Movement in 1905.

*World War I and After.* At the time of World War I there commenced the "Great Migration" to the Northern cities.[17] The advent of the Negroes was accompanied by a number of severe "race riots." (A "race riot" is a situation in which Negroes fight back against

extra-legal mob violence.) As a result of the disappointments and frustrations which followed the move North to "freedom" and the "war to save democracy," the 1920s saw the rise of the Garvey [Back-to-Africa] Movement. Although unsuccessful, it is significant because a fundamental part of the ideology of the movement was anti-white and separatist in orientation. (It is also significant that a movement with this orientation failed.) Further, no whites were involved in the leadership of the movement, as was not the case with the previously mentioned Negro lay organizations nor the Negro Church. This fact demonstrated, for the first time, that Negroes could organize Negroes as such. By this time, as Frazier points out (note 8, p. 531):

The impact of urban living . . . [and] . . . conflicts in the North tended not only to intensify the consciousness of being a Negro, but . . . also gave new meaning to being a Negro . . . [it] meant being a member of a group with a cause, if not a history. As in the case of the nationalistic struggles in Europe, the emergence of a . . . literature helped in the development of a consciousness. As we have seen, there appeared a Negro Renaissance following World War I. Much of the literature and art of the Negro Renaissance was not only militant but tended to give the Negro a conception of the mission and destiny of the Negro. The Negro newspapers, which began to influence the masses, tended to create a new . . . consciousness . . . [which] did not have separation from American life.[18]

The recent past and the present continue to yield evidence of both Negro ethnicity and the persistence of ethnogenesis. Such evidence is found in the assaults on the "white primary," segregated education at all levels, the

---

[17] See Myrdal, note 1, pp. 191–96. The bulk of the Negroes are still in the South, although the northward movement continues as well as the movement of Southern Negroes to Southern cities. It might be pointed out that Cox hypothesizes (note 2, p. xxxii) that, "In the future Negroes will probably become more highly urbanized than any other native-born population group in the country."

[18] For a similar view of the social-psychological consequences of the Negro press see Myrdal, note 1, pp. 908–24 and A. Rose, note 15, pp. 102–08.

increased efforts of Negroes to get Negroes out to vote, the increasing attempts of Southern Negroes to vote, the "sit-ins" in the South, and the "Freedom Riders." [19]

## Summary and Conclusion

To sum up, then, Negro-Americans are an instance of a people: 1) whose ancestors, as recently as four generations ago, showed little in the way of ethnic group characteristics and who in this *ante bellum* period could only be conceptualized as a social category; 2) who now form a distinct social and subcultural entity within the American society and are in the process of becoming a full-fledged ethnic group; 3) whose character as an emergent ethnic group is the consequence of factors outside themselves as well as their response to these factors.

The earlier ways of conceptualizing Negroes in Negro-white relations in the United States were called into question because they are based on static category concepts and, as such, appear not to do justice to the phenomenon. The available data seem to require an entity concept that will allow the developmental factors to be taken into account. If the ethnogenesis concept, which has been offered to replace these other conceptual tools, is to be properly evaluated, two questions must be answered: Does this new approach encompass the data and relate them adequately to one another? The answer to this is, ultimately, the task of future investigators. How fruitful is this new approach as a source of hypotheses?

This paper will close with some suggestions in answer to the second question.

1. In the light of the above, it may be suggested that the people whom we call the Negroes in this society are not comparable to the so-called Negroes of Brazil, Haiti, or the British West Indies. Negro-Americans are different from Brazilians, Cubans, Haitians, or Jamaicans who may happen to possess some negroid physical traits. In these latter instances, the use of the term Negro lays stress on biological similarities and blurs the sociological, cultural, and psychological differences.

2. Although there have been and are many instances of ethnogenesis,[20] this particular instance involving the Negroes has a contemporary uniqueness beyond the particularity which inheres in any single case. As stated above, the special aspect in this case resides in the forcible acculturation of the individual African progenitors in a completely strange setting and the loss of their African cultures in the process. An important consequence of this is that when ethnogenesis moved into high gear less than a century ago the freedmen were social persons"; that is, they were socialized individuals since they had been members of plantation households. Taken as a whole, however, they comprised a collection of unrelated individuals. Further, this collection of unrelated individuals was without the community of tradition, sentiment, and so forth, that has marked other populations and given rise to ethnic groups

[19] The "Freedom Riders" have a special significance in that whites are actively participating in the attempt to end discrimination in transportation. Both Myrdal and Cox hypothesize that Negro-Americans cannot achieve their aspirations without overt support from whites. The "sit-ins" are also especially significant because of the youth of the demonstrators.

[20] C. M. Arensberg in a private communication suggests such instances as "Italian-Americans in the U.S.A.; . . . Africans and East Indians in the Caribbean (cf. Trinidad); Hispanos (Puerto Ricans, and so forth) in New York (just started); Pennsylvania Dutch (1600–1800); 'white Southerners' paralleling Negroes in the U.S.A.; . . . In Israel, today, the Oriental Jews . . . are being welded into a self-conscious minority vis-à-vis the 'Askenazim' or 'Europeans' by all accounts. . . ."

such as the Italian immigrants.[21] Thus we have here a case of ethnogenesis starting *ab initio*, unlike all other current instances of ethnogenesis in which members of some ethnic groups become transformed into another ethnic group.[22]

3. To say that Negroes are involved in the process of ethnogenesis is not the same as saying that they are a full-fledged ethnic group. They are not. Full-fledged ethnicity would appear to be characterized by at least two qualities: long tradition and a marked, if not a general, tendency toward self-perpetuation. Concerning tradition, Negro-Americans have neither a legendary nor a long historic past. E. K. Francis writes of what would here be called a full-fledged ethnic group, "Since an ethnic group is based on an elementary feeling of solidarity, we must suppose that mutual adjustment has been achieved over a considerable length of time and that the memory of having possibly belonged to another system of social relationships must have been obliterated. Certainly, this is not the case with Negroes" (note 11, p. 396). As for self-perpetuation, this is usually achieved by endogamy. Now, despite the use of this term with reference to Negro-white relations in the United States,

it is quite clear that pressures outside the Negro group are primarily effective in preventing marriages between Negroes and the members of other ethnic groups rather than self-imposed restrictions.[23] The current tendency among Negroes to frown on intermarriage is a defensive *reaction*. It is suggested by various writers that this attitude is neither deep nor abiding (Myrdal, note 1, pp. 56–7 and 62–4 and Cox, note 2, pp. 447–50).

On the basis of the two points of tradition and self-perpetuation, while it is proper to regard the Negroes as an ethnic group, it is also proper to say that they are still in the *process of becoming* an ethnic group, that is, their ethnicity is still *developing*. Paradoxical as the formulation may appear, it is no stranger than applying the term "tree" to a young tree, to a mature tree, and to an old tree. Let us now turn to some predictive notions based on the view of the Negroes as a developing ethnic group.

4. As the Negroes become more of an ethnic group—more focused and organized—it may be expected that rather than *reacting* to the actions of white, they will increasingly *act* along paths of action chosen to achieve their goal of full, individual participation in the larger society. It can be added that any successes can be expected to pave the way for increased activity. It may be further hypothesized that, as the barriers to full participation yield and slowly crumble, frustration and impatience over the differences between actuality and aspirations may prompt segments of the Negro group to manifest radical and separatist (anti-white) sentiments, such as the "black Muslim" movement. It is doubtful that any of these organizations will be large. Size,

[21] Beyond the differences in prestige-ranking of field hands and house servants, the only common cultural element was the slave family. On the relative weakness of this structure see Frazier, note 8, II, especially 40–41.

[22] This is the sort of process which E. K. Francis refers to: "Yet even on the ground of our limited knowledge it becomes clear that, generally speaking, the stages of development traversed by ethnic groups are: expansion—fission—new combination." (note 11, p. 398). What we have here called ethnogenesis is related to Francis' sequence at two points. It is, on the one hand, temporally prior in that ethnic groups must have formed before they could expand. On the other hand, the last stage of the sequence is ethnogenesis. Consequently, the expanded sequence should be: ethnogenesis—expansion—fission—new combination (that is, ethnogenesis).

[23] See, for example, A. Davis and M. and B. Gardner, especially the section, "Endogamy-Keystone of Caste," pp. 24–44. Note also the various state laws, and not only in the deep South, prohibiting intermarriage.

however, should not be confused with importance. By defining one end of the spectrum of Negro responses, such groups will affect the thinking of all Negroes. Further, because of the impact upon the whites, they may contribute to the general struggle for Negro aspirations despite their separatist orientations.

5. A related hypothesis concerns the character of Negro leadership. Negro leaders in the latter part of the nineteenth century typically played the role of justifying the condition of Negroes.[24] Many Negro ministers fell into this category. It is important to add that such leaders were, either directly or as a result of the "veto power," chosen by dominant whites. (This type of leadership is called "accommodating leadership" by Myrdal while Cox refers to it as "the spirit of Uncle Tom.") By the turn of the century, a new kind of leadership had emerged typified by Booker T. Washington. (This type of leaderships is called "conciliatory leadership" by Frazier and "compromising leadership" by Myrdal.) It is Myrdal's thesis, as well as Cox's, that whites

were, and are, also influential in the selection of this type of leader. If my thesis is correct, then we may expect that in the coming period the character of Negro leadership will have more of the qualities exemplified earlier by W. E. B. DuBois and today by Martin Luther King, Thurgood Marshall, and James Farmer. We may also expect that the "Uncle Toms" and the conciliators will become fewer and fewer.

6. As a final point, it may be suggested that there are implications for psychological research in the social entity approach to the American Negro. The effects of identifying oneself with an emergent group that is no longer on the defensive but is coming more and more to act for itself as well as with a group that has strong leaders and hero figures should make a significant difference in the personalities of Negro-Americans. Indeed, I believe that as the self-image of the Negroes is internalized by individual Negroes, a redirection and transformation of Negro resentment and hostility and a redefinition of individual Negro selves will surely take place.

# 40

# The Ideology of Black Power

### STOKELY CARMICHAEL AND
### CHARLES V. HAMILTON

"To carve out a place for itself in the politico-social order," V. O. Key, Jr.

From Black Power (New York: Random House, Inc., 1967), pp. 34–56. Reprinted by permission of Random House and Jonathan Cape, Ltd.

[24] No slight is intended to Frederick Douglass by this comment. While it is true that he lived through the period and died in 1895, he is not typical of it.

wrote in Politics, Parties and Pressure Groups, "a new group may have to fight for reorientation of many of the values of the old order" (p. 57). This is especially true when that group is composed of black people in the American society—a society that has for centuries deliberately and systematically excluded them from political participation. Black people in the United States must raise hard questions, questions which challenge the very nature of the society itself: its long-standing values, beliefs and institutions.

To do this, we must first redefine ourselves. Our basic need is to reclaim our history and our identity from what must be called cultural terrorism, from the depredation of self-justifying white guilt. We shall have to struggle for the right to create our own terms through which to define ourselves and our relationship to the society, and to have these terms recognized. This is the first necessity of a free people, and the first right that any oppressor must suspend.

In *Politics Among Nations*, Hans Morgenthau defined political power as "the psychological control over the minds of men" (p. 29). This control includes the attempt by the oppressor to have *his* definitions, *his* historical descriptions, *accepted* by the oppressed. This was true in Africa no less than in the United States. To black Africans, the word "Uhuru" means "freedom," but they had to fight the white colonizers for the right to use the term. The recorded history of this country's dealings with red and black men offers other examples. In the wars between the white settlers and the "Indians," a battle won by the Cavalry was described as a "victory." The "Indians'" triumphs, however, were "massacres." (The American colonists were not unaware of the need to define their acts in their own terms. They labeled their fight against England a "revolution"; the English attempted to demean it by calling it "insubordination" or "riotous.")

The historical period following Reconstruction in the South after the Civil War has been called by many historians the period of Redemption, implying that the bigoted southern slave societies were "redeemed" from the hands of "reckless and irresponsible" black rulers. Professor John Hope Franklin's *Recon-* *struction* or Dr. W. E. B. Dubois' *Black Reconstruction* should be sufficient to dispel inaccurate historical notions, but the larger society persists in its own self-serving accounts. Thus black people came to be depicted as "lazy," "apathetic," "dumb," "shiftless," "good-timers." Just as red men had to be recorded as "savages" to justify the white man's theft of their land, so black men had to be vilified in order to justify their continued oppression. Those who have the right to define are the masters of the situation. Lewis Carroll understood this:

"When I use a word," Humpty Dumpty said in a rather scornful tone, "it means just what I choose it to mean—neither more nor less."

"The question is," said Alice, "whether you *can* make words mean so many different things."

"The question is," said Humpty Dumpty, "which is to be master—that's all." [1]

Today, the American educational system continues to reinforce the entrenched values of the society through the use of words. Few people in this country question that this is "the land of the free and the home of the brave." They have had these words drummed into them from childhood. Few people question that this is the "Great Society" or that this country is fighting "Communist aggression" around the world. We mouth these things over and over, and they become truisms not to be questioned. In a similar way, black people have been saddled with epithets.

"Integration" is another current example of a word which has been defined according to the way white Americans see it. To many of them, it means black men wanting to marry white daughters; it means "race mixing"—implying bed or dance partners. To black people, it has meant a way to improve their lives

[1] Lewis Carroll, *Through the Looking Glass.* New York: Doubleday Books, Inc., p. 196.

—economically and politically. But the predominant white definition has stuck in the minds of too many people.

Black people must redefine themselves, and only *they* can do that. Throughout this country, vast segments of the black communities are beginning to recognize the need to assert their own definitions, to reclaim their history, their culture; to create their own sense of community and togetherness. There is a growing resentment of the word "Negro," for example, because this term is the invention of our oppressor; it is *his* image of us that he describes. Many blacks are now calling themselves African-Americans, Afro-Americans or black people because that is *our* image of ourselves. When we begin to define our own image, the stereotypes—that is, lies—that our oppressor has developed will begin in the white community and end there. The black community will have a positive image of itself that *it* has created. This means we will no longer call ourselves lazy, apathetic, dumb, good-timers, shiftless, etc. Those are words used by white America to define us. If we accept these adjectives, as some of us have in the past, then we see ourselves only in a negative way, precisely the way white America wants us to see ourselves. Our incentive is broken and our will to fight is surrendered. From now on we shall view ourselves as African-Americans and as black people who are in fact energetic, determined, intelligent, beautiful and peace-loving.

There is a terminology and ethos peculiar to the black community of which black people are beginning to be no longer ashamed. Black communities are the only large segments of this society where people refer to each other as brother—soul-brother, soul-sister. Some people may look upon this as *ersatz*, as make-believe, but it is not that. It is real. It is a growing sense of community. It is a growing realization that black Americans have a com-

mon bond not only among themselves, but with their African brothers. In *Black Man's Burden*, John O. Killens described his trip to ten African countries as follows:

> Everywhere I went people called me brother. . . . "Welcome, American brother." It was a good feeling for me, to be in Africa. To walk in a land for the first time in your entire life knowing within yourself that your color would not be held against you. No black man ever knows this in America [p. 160].

More and more black Americans are developing this feeling. They are becoming aware that they have a history which pre-dates their forced introduction to this country. African-American history means a long history beginning on the continent of Africa, a history not taught in the standard textbooks of this country. It is absolutely essential that black people know this history, that they know their roots, that they develop an awareness of their cultural heritage. Too long have they been kept in submission by being told that they had no culture, no manifest heritage, before they landed on the slave auction blocks in this country. If black people are to know themselves as a vibrant, valiant people, they must know their roots. And they will soon learn that the Hollywood image of man-eating cannibals waiting for, and waiting on, the Great White Hunter is a lie.

With redefinition will come a clearer notion of the role black Americans can play in this world. This role will emerge clearly out of the unique, common experiences of Afro-Asians, Killens concludes:

> I believe furthermore that the American Negro can be the bridge between the West and Africa-Asia. We black Americans can serve as a bridge to mutual understanding. The one thing we black Americans have in common with the other colored peoples of the world is that we have all felt the cruel

and ruthless heel of white supremacy. We have all been "niggerized" on one level or another. And all of us are determined to "de-niggerize" the earth. To rid the world of "niggers" is the Black Man's Burden, human reconstruction is the grand objective [p. 176].

Only when black people fully develop this sense of community, of themselves, can they begin to deal effectively with the problems of racism in *this* country. That is what we mean by a new consciousness; this is the vital first step.

The next step is what we shall call the process of political modernization—a process which must take place if the society is to be rid of racism. "Political modernization" includes many things, but we mean by it three major concepts: (1) questioning old values and institutions of the society; (2) searching for new and different forms of political structure to solve political and economic problems; and (3) broadening the base of political participation to include more people in the decision-making process. These notions (we shall take up each in turn) are central to our thinking throughout this book and to contemporary American history as a whole. As David Apter wrote in *The Politics of Modernization*, ". . . . the struggle to modernize is what has given meaning to our generation. It tests our cherished institutions and our beliefs. . . . So compelling a force has it become that we are forced to ask new questions of our own institutions. Each country, whether modernized or modernizing, stands in both judgment and fear of the results. Our own society is no exception" (p. 2).

The values of this society support a racist system; we find it incongruous to ask black people to adopt and support most of those values. We also reject the assumption that the basic institutions of this society must be preserved. The goal of black people must *not* be to assimilate into middle-class America,

for that class—as a whole—is without a viable conscience as regards humanity. The values of the middle class permit the perpetuation of the ravages of the black community. The values of that class are based on material aggrandizement, not the expansion of humanity. The values of that class ultimately support cloistered little closed societies tucked away neatly in tree-lined suburbia. The values of that class do *not* lead to the creation of an open society. That class *mouths* its preference for a free, competitive society, while at the same time forcefully and even viciously denying to black people as a group the opportunity to compete.

We are not unmindful of other descriptions of the social utility of the middle class. Banfield and Wilson, in *City Politics*, concluded:

The departure of the middle class from the central city is important in other ways. . . . The middle class supplies a social and political leavening in the life of a city. Middle-class people demand good schools and integrity in government. They support churches, lodges, parent-teacher associations, scout troops, better-housing committees, art galleries, and operas. It is the middle class, in short, that asserts a conception of the public interest. Now its activity is increasingly concentrated in the suburbs [p. 14].

But this same middle class manifests a sense of superior group position in regard to race. This class wants "good government" *for themselves*; it wants good schools *for its children*. At the same time, many of its members sneak into the black community by day, exploit it, and take the money home at night to support their middle-class communities and their operas and art galleries and comfortable homes. When not actually robbing, they will fight off the handful of more affluent black people who seek to move in; when they approve or even seek token integration, it applies only to black people like themselves—as "white" as possible. *This class is the backbone of institutional racism in this country.*

Thus we reject the goal of assimilation into middle-class America because the values of that class are in themselves anti-humanist and because that class as a social force perpetuates racism. We must face the fact that, in the past, what we have called the movement has not really questioned the middle-class values and institutions of this country. If anything, it has accepted those values and institutions without fully realizing their racist nature. Reorientation means an emphasis on the dignity of man, not on the sanctity of property. It means the creation of a society where human misery and poverty are repugnant to that society, not an indication of laziness or lack of initiative. The creation of new values means the establishment of a society based, as Killens expresses it in *Black Man's Burden*, on "free people," not "free enterprise" (p. 167). To do this means to modernize—*indeed, to civilize*—this country.

Supporting the old values are old political and economic structures; these must also be "modernized." We should at this point distinguish between "structures" and "system." By system, we have in mind the entire American complex of basic institutions, values, beliefs, etc. By structures, we mean the specific institutions (political parties, interest groups, bureaucratic administrations) which exist to conduct the business of that system. Obviously, the first is broader than the second. Also, the second assumes the legitimacy of the first. Our view is that, given the illegitimacy of the system, we cannot then proceed to transform that system with existing structures.

The two major political parties in this country have become non-viable entities for the legitimate representation of the real needs of masses—especially blacks—in this country. Walter Lipp-

mann raised the same point in his syndicated column of December 8, 1966. He pointed out that the party system in the United States developed before our society became as technologically complex as it is now. He says that the ways in which men live and define themselves are changing radically. Old ideological issues, once the subject of passionate controversy, Lippmann argues, are of little interest today. He asks whether the great urban complexes—which are rapidly becoming the centers of black population in the U.S.—can be run with the same systems and ideas that derive from a time when America was a country of small villages and farms. While not addressing himself directly to the question of race, Lippmann raises a major question about our political institutions; and the crisis of race in America may be its major symptom.

Black people have seen the city planning commissions, the urban renewal commissions, the boards of education and the police departments fail to speak to their needs in a meaningful way. We must devise new structures, new institutions to replace those forms or to make them responsive. There is nothing sacred or inevitable about old institutions; the focus must be on people, not forms.

Existing structures and established ways of doing things have a way of perpetuating themselves and for this reason, the modernizing process will be difficult. Therefore, timidity in calling into question the boards of education or the police departments will not do. They must be challenged forcefully and clearly. If this means the creation of parallel community institutions, then that must be the solution. If this means that black parents must gain control over the operation of the schools in the black community, then that must be the solution. The search for new forms means the search for institutions that will, for once, make decisions in the interest of black people. It means, for example, a building inspection department that neither winks at violations of building codes by absentee slumlords nor imposes meaningless fines which permit them to continue their exploitation of the black community.

Essential to the modernization of structures is a broadened base of political participation. More and more people must become politically sensitive and active (we have already seen this happening in some areas of the South). People must no longer be tied, by small incentives or handouts, to a corrupting and corruptible white machine. Black people will choose their own leaders and hold those leaders responsible to *them*. A broadened base means an end to the condition described by James Wilson in *Negro Politics*, whereby "Negroes tended to be the objects rather than the subjects of civic action. Things are often done for, or about, or to, or because of Negroes, but they are less frequently done *by* Negroes" (p. 133). Broadening the base of political participation, then, has as much to do with the quality of black participation as with the quantity. We are fully aware that the black vote, especially in the North, has been pulled out of white pockets and "delivered" whenever it was in the interest of white politicians to do so. That vote must no longer be controllable by those who have neither the interests nor the demonstrated concern of black people in mind.

As the base broadens, as more and more black people become activated, they will perceive more clearly the special disadvantages heaped upon them as a group. They will perceive that the larger society is growing more affluent while the black society is retrogressing, as daily life and mounting statistics clearly show (see Chapters I and VIII). V. O. Key describes what often happens next, in *Politics, Parties and Pressure Groups:* "A factor of great significance in the setting off of political movements is an abrupt change for the worse in the status of one group relative to that of other groups in society. . . . A rapid change for the worse . . . in the relative status of any group . . . is likely to precipitate political action" (p. 24). Black people will become increasingly active as they notice that their retrogressive status exists in large measure because of values and institutions arraigned against them. They will begin to stress and strain and call the entire system into question. Political modernization will be in motion. We believe that it is now in motion. One form of that motion is Black Power.

The adoption of the concept of Black Power is one of the most legitimate and healthy developments in American politics and race relations in our time. The concept of Black Power speaks to all the needs mentioned in this chapter. It is a call for black people in this country to unite, to recognize their heritage, to build a sense of community. It is a call for black people to begin to define their own goals, to lead their own organizations and to support those organizations. It is a call to reject the racist institutions and values of this society.

The concept of Black Power rests on a fundamental premise: *Before a group can enter the open society, it must first close ranks.* By this we mean that group solidarity is necessary before a group can operate effectively from a bargaining position of strength in a pluralistic society. Traditionally, each new ethnic group in this society has found the route to social and political viability through the organization of its own institutions with which to represent its needs within the larger society. Studies in voting behavior specifically, and political behavior generally, have made it clear that politically the American pot has not melted. Italians vote for Rubino over O'Brien; Irish for Murphy over Goldberg, etc. This phenomenon may seem distasteful to some, but it has been and remains today a central fact of the American political system. There are other examples of ways in which groups in the society have remembered their roots and used this effectively in the political arena. Theodore Sorensen describes the politics of foreign aid during the Kennedy Administration in his book *Kennedy*:

No powerful constituencies or interest groups backed foreign aid. The Marshall Plan at least had appealed to Americans who traced their roots to the Western European nations aided. But there were few voters who identified with India, Colombia or Tanganyika [p. 351].

The extent to which black Americans can and do "trace their roots" to Africa, to that extent will they be able to be more effective on the political scene.

A white reporter set forth this point in other terms when he made the following observation about white Mississippi's manipulation of the anti-poverty program:

The war on poverty has been predicated on the notion that there is such a thing as a community which can be defined geographically and mobilized for a collective effort to help the poor. This theory has no relationship to reality in the deep South. In every Mississippi county there are two communities. Despite all the pious platitudes of the moderates on both sides, these two communities habitually see their interests in terms of conflict rather than cooperation. Only when the Negro community can muster enough political, economic and professional strength to compete on somewhat equal terms, will Negroes believe in the possibility of true cooperation and whites accept its necessity. En route to integration, the Negro community needs to develop a greater independence—a chance to run its own affairs and not cave in whenever "the man" barks—or so it seems to me, and to

most of the knowledgeable people with whom I talked in Mississippi. To OEO, this judgment may sound like black nationalism. . . .[2]

The point is obvious: black people must lead and run their own organizations. Only black people can convey the revolutionary idea—and it is a revolutionary idea—that black people are able to do things themselves. Only they can help create in the community an aroused and continuing black consciousness that will provide the basis for political strength. In the past, white allies have often furthered white supremacy without the whites involved realizing it, or even wanting to do so. Black people must come together and do things for themselves. They must achieve self-identity and self-determination in order to have their daily needs met.

Black Power means, for example, that in Lowndes County, Alabama, a black sheriff can end police brutality. A black tax assessor and tax collector and county board of revenue can lay, collect, and channel tax monies for the building of better roads and schools serving black people. In such areas as Lowndes, where black people have a majority, they will attempt to use power to exercise control. This is what they seek: control. When black people lack a majority, Black Power means proper representation and sharing of control. It means the creation of power bases, of strength, from which black people can press to change local or nation-wide patterns of oppression—instead of from weakness.

It does not mean *merely* putting black faces into office. Black visibility is not Black Power. Most of the black politicians around the country today are not examples of Black Power. The power must be that of a community, and emanate from there. The black politi-

[2] Christopher Jencks, "Accommodating Whites: A New Look at Mississippi," *The New Republic* (April 16, 1966).

cians must start from there. The black politicians must stop being representatives of "downtown" machines, whatever the cost might be in terms of lost patronage and holiday handouts.

Black Power recognizes—it must recognize—the ethnic basis of American politics as well as the power-oriented nature of American politics. Black Power therefore calls for black people to consolidate behind their own, so that they can bargain from a position of strength. But while we endorse the *procedure* of group solidarity and identity for the purpose of attaining certain goals in the body politic, this does not mean that black people should strive for the same kind of rewards (i.e., end results) obtained by the white society. The ultimate values and goals are not domination or exploitation of other groups, but rather an effective share in the total power of the society.

Nevertheless, some observers have labeled those who advocate Black Power as racists; they have said that the call for self-identification and self-determination is "racism in reverse" or "black supremacy." This is a deliberate and absurd lie. There is no analogy—by any stretch of definition or imagination—between the advocates of Black Power and white racists. Racism is not merely exclusion on the basis of race but exclusion for the purpose of subjugating or maintaining subjugation. The goal of the racists is to keep black people on the bottom, arbitrarily and dictatorially, as they have done in this country for over three hundred years. The goal of black self-determination and black self-identity—Black Power—is full participation in the decision-making processes affecting the lives of black people, and recognition of the virtues in themselves as black people. The black people of this country have not lynched whites, bombed their churches, murdered their children and manipulated laws and institutions to maintain op-

pression. White racists have. Congressional laws, one after the other, have not been necessary to stop black people from oppressing others and denying others the full enjoyment of their rights. White racists have made such laws necessary. The goal of Black Power is positive and functional to a free and viable society. No white racist can make this claim.

A great deal of public attention and press space was devoted to the hysterical accusation of "black racism" when the call for Black Power was first sounded. A national committee of influential black churchmen affiliated with the National Council of Churches, despite their obvious respectability and responsibility, had to resort to a paid advertisement to articulate their position, while anyone yapping "black racism" made front-page news. In their statement, published in the *New York Times* of July 31, 1966, the churchmen said:

We, an informal group of Negro churchmen in America, are deeply disturbed about the crisis brought upon our country by historic distortions of important human realities in the controversy about "black power." What we see shining through the variety of rhetoric is not anything new but the same old problem of power and race which has faced our beloved country since 1619.

. . . The conscience of black men is corrupted because having no power to implement the demands of conscience, the concern for justice in the absence of justice becomes a chaotic self-surrender. Powerlessness breeds a race of beggars. We are faced with a situation where powerless conscience meets conscienceless power, threatening the very foundations of our Nation.

We deplore the overt violence of riots, but we feel it is more important to focus on the real sources of these eruptions. These sources may be abetted inside the Ghetto, but their basic cause lies in the silent and covert violence which white middle class America inflicts upon the victims of the inner city.

. . . In short, the failure of American leaders to use American power to create equal opportunity *in life* as well as *law*, this is the real problem and not the anguished cry for black power.

. . . Without the capacity to participate with power, i.e., to have some organized political and economic strength to really influence people with whom one interacts, integration is not meaningful.

. . . America has asked its Negro citizens to fight for opportunity as *individuals*, whereas at certain points in our history what we have needed most has been opportunity for the *whole group*, not just for selected and approved Negroes.

. . . We must not apologize for the existence of this form of group power, for we have been oppressed as a group and not as individuals. We will not find our way out of that oppression until both we and America accept the need for Negro Americans, as well as for Jews, Italians, Poles, and white Anglo-Saxon Protestants, among others, to have and to wield group power.

It is a commentary on the fundamentally racist nature of this society that the concept of group strength for black people must be articulated—not to mention defended. No other group would submit to being led by others. Italians do not run the Anti-Defamation League of B'nai B'rith. Irish do not chair Christopher Columbus Societies. Yet when black people call for black-run and all-black organizations, they are immediately classed in a category with the Ku Klux Klan. This is interesting and ironic, but by no means surprising: the society does not expect black people to be able to take care of their business, and there are many who prefer it precisely that way.

In the end, we cannot and shall not offer any guarantees that Black Power, if achieved, would be non-racist. No one can predict human behavior. Social change always has unanticipated consequences. If black racism is what the larger society fears, we cannot help them. We can only state what we hope will be the result, given the fact that the present situation is unacceptable

and that we have no real alternative but to work for Black Power. The final truth is that the white society is not entitled to reassurances, even if it were possible to offer them.

We have outlined the meaning and goals of Black Power; we have also discussed one major thing which it is not. There are others of greater importance. The advocates of Black Power reject the old slogans and meaningless rhetoric of previous years in the civil rights struggle. The language of yesterday is indeed irrelevant: progress, non-violence, integration, fear of "white backlash," coalition. Let us look at the rhetoric and see why these terms must be set aside or redefined.

One of the tragedies of the struggle against racism is that up to this point there has been no national organization which could speak to the growing militancy of young black people in the urban ghettos and the black-belt South. There has been only a "civil rights" movement, whose tone of voice was adapted to an audience of middle-class whites. It served as a sort of buffer zone between that audience and angry young blacks. It claimed to speak for the needs of a community, but it did not speak in the tone of that community. None of its so-called leaders could go into a rioting community and be listened to. In a sense, the blame must be shared —along with the mass media—by those leaders for what happened in Watts, Harlem, Chicago, Cleveland and other places. Each time the black people in those cities saw Dr. Martin Luther King get slapped they became angry. When they saw little black girls bombed to death *in a church* and civil rights workers ambushed and murdered, they were angrier; and when nothing happened, they were steaming mad. We had nothing to offer that they could see, except to go out and be beaten again. We helped to build their frustration.

We had only the old language of love

and suffering. And in most places— that is, from the liberals and middle class—we got back the old language of patience and progress. The civil rights leaders were saying to the country: "Look, you guys are supposed to be nice guys, and we are only going to do what we are supposed to do. Why do you beat us up? Why don't you give us what we ask? Why don't you straighten yourselves out?" For the masses of black people, this language resulted in virtually nothing. In fact, their objective day-to-day condition worsened. The unemployment rate among black people increased while that among whites declined. Housing conditions in the black communities deteriorated. Schools in the black ghettos continued to plod along on outmoded techniques, inadequate curricula, and with all too many tired and indifferent teachers. Meanwhile, the President picked up the refrain of "We Shall Overcome" while the Congress passed civil rights law after civil rights law, only to have them effectively nullified by deliberately weak enforcement. "Progress is being made," we were told.

Such language, along with admonitions to remain non-violent and fear the white backlash, convinced some that that course was the *only* course to follow. It misled some into believing that a black minority could bow its head and get whipped into a meaningful position of power. The very notion is absurd. The white society devised the language, adopted the rules and had the black community narcotized into believing that that language and those rules were, in fact, relevant. The black community was told time and again how *other* immigrants finally won *acceptance*: that is, by following the Protestant Ethic of Work and Achievement. They worked hard; therefore, they achieved. We were not told that it was by building Irish Power, Italian Power, Polish Power or Jewish Power that these groups got themselves together and operated from

positions of strength. We were not told that "the American dream" wasn't designed for black people. That while today, to whites, the dream may *seem* to include black people, it cannot do so by the very nature of this nation's political and economic system, which imposes institutional racism on the black masses if not upon every individual black. A notable comment on that "dream" was made by Dr. Percy Julian, the black scientist and director of the Julian Research Institute in Chicago, a man for whom the dream seems to have come true. While not subscribing to "black power" as he understood it, Dr. Julian clearly understood the basis for it: "The false concept of basic Negro inferiority is one of the curses that still lingers. It is a problem created by the white man. Our children just no longer are going to accept the patience we were taught by our generation. We were taught a pretty little lie—excel and the whole world lies open before you. *I obeyed the injunction and found it to be wishful thinking.*" (Authors' italics) [3]

A key phrase in our buffer-zone days was non-violence. For years it has been thought that black people would not literally fight for their lives. Why this has been so is not entirely clear; neither the larger society nor black people are noted for passivity. The notion apparently stems from the years of marches and demonstrations and sit-ins where black people did not strike back and the violence always came from white mobs. There are many who still sincerely believe in that approach. From our viewpoint, rampaging white mobs and white night-riders must be made to understand that their days of free head-whipping are over. Black people should and must fight back. Nothing more quickly repels someone bent on destroying you than the unequivocal message: "O.K., fool,

[3] *The New York Times* (April 30, 1967), p. 30.

make your move, and run the same risk I run—of dying."

When the concept of Black Power is set forth, many people immediately conjure up notions of violence. The country's reaction to the Deacons for Defense and Justice, which originated in Louisiana, is instructive. Here is a group which realized that the "law" and law enforcement agencies would not protect people, so they had to do it themselves. If a nation fails to protect its citizens, then that nation cannot condemn those who take up the task themselves. The Deacons and all other blacks who resort to self-defense represent a simple answer to a simple question: what man would not defend his family and home from attack?

But this frightened some white people, because they knew that black people would now fight back. They knew that this was precisely what *they* would have long since done if *they* were subjected to the injustices and oppression heaped on blacks. Those of us who advocate Black Power are quite clear in our own minds that a "non-violent" approach to civil rights is an approach black people cannot afford and a luxury white people do not deserve. It is crystal clear to us—and it must become so with the white society—*that there can be no social order without social justice.* White people must be made to understand that they must stop messing with black people, or the blacks *will* fight back!

Next, we must deal with the term "integration." According to its advocates, social justice will be accomplished by "integrating the Negro into the mainstream institutions of the society from which he has been traditionally excluded." This concept is based on the assumption that there is nothing of value in the black community and that little of value could be created among black people. The thing to do is siphon off the "acceptable" black people into the surrounding middle-class white community.

The goals of integrationists are middle-class goals, articulated primarily by a small group of Negroes with middle-class aspirations or status. Their kind of integration has meant that a few blacks "make it," leaving the black community, sapping it of leadership potential and know-how. As we noted in Chapter I, those token Negroes—absorbed into a white mass—are of no value to the remaining black masses. They become meaningless show-pieces for a conscience-soothed white society. Such people will state that they would prefer to be treated "only as individuals, not as Negroes"; that they "are not and should not be preoccupied with race." This is a totally unrealistic position. In the first place, black people have not suffered as individuals but as members of a group; therefore, their liberation lies in group action. This is why SNCC —and the concept of Black Power— affirms that helping *individual* black people to solve their problems on an *individual* basis does little to alleviate the mass of black people. Secondly, while color blindness *may* be a sound goal ultimately, we must realize that race is an overwhelming fact of life in this historical period. There is no black man in this country who can live "simply as a man." His blackness is an ever-present fact of this racist society, whether he recognizes it or not. It is unlikely that this or the next generation will witness the time when race will no longer be relevant in the conduct of public affairs and in public policy decision-making. To realize this and to attempt to deal with it does not make one a racist or overly preoccupied with race; it puts one in the forefront of a significant *struggle*. If there is no intense struggle today, there will be no meaningful results tomorrow.

"Integration" as a goal today speaks to the problem of blackness not only in an unrealistic way but also in a despicable way. It is based on complete acceptance of the fact that in order to have a decent house or education, black people must move into a white neighborhood or send their children to a white school. This reinforces, among both black and white, the idea that "white" is automatically superior and "black" is by definition inferior. For this reason, "integration" is a subterfuge for the maintenance of white supremacy. It allows the nation to focus on a handful of Southern black children who get into white schools at a great price, and to ignore the ninety-four percent who are left in unimproved all-black schools. Such situations will not change until black people become equal in a way that means something, and integration ceases to be a one-way street. Then integration does not mean draining skills and energies from the black ghetto into white neighborhoods. To sprinkle black children among white pupils in outlying schools is at best a stop-gap measure. The goal is not to take black children out of the black community and expose them to white middle-class values; the goal is to build and strengthen the black community.

"Integration" also means that black people must give up their identity, deny their heritage. We recall the conclusion of Killian and Grigg: "At the present time, integration as a solution to the race problem demands that the Negro foreswear his identity as a Negro." The fact is that integration, as traditionally articulated, would abolish the black community. The fact is that what must be abolished is not the black community, but the dependent colonial status that has been inflicted upon it.

The racial and cultural personality of the black community must be preserved and that community must win its freedom while preserving its cultural integrity. Integrity includes a pride—in the sense of self-acceptance, not chauvinism—in being black, in the historical attainments and contributions of black people. No person can be healthy, complete and mature if he must deny a part of himself; this is what "integration" has required thus far. This is the essential difference between integration as it is currently practiced and the concept of Black Power.

The idea of cultural integrity is so obvious that it seems almost simple-minded to spell things out at this length. Yet millions of Americans resist such truths when they are applied to black people. Again, that resistance is a comment on the fundamental racism in the society. Irish Catholics took care of their own first without a lot of apology for doing so, without any dubious language from timid leadership about guard'ng against "backlash." Everyone understood it to be a perfectly legitimate procedure. Of course, there would be "backlash." Organization begets counter-organization, but this was no reason to defer.

The so-called white backlash against black people is something else: the embedded traditions of institutional racism being brought into the open and calling forth overt manifestations of individual racism. In the summer of 1966, when the protest marches into Cicero, Illinois, began, the black people knew they were not allowed to live in Cicero and the white people knew it. When blacks began to demand the right to live in homes in that town, the whites simply reminded them of the status quo. Some people called this "backlash." It was, in fact, racism defending itself. In the black community, this is called "White folks showing their color." It is ludicrous to blame black people for what is simply an overt manifestation of white racism. Dr. Martin Luther King stated clearly that the protest marches were not the cause of the racism but merely exposed a long-term cancerous condition in the society.

# E Social Stratification and Inequality

## INTRODUCTION

Although some primitive societies lack class differences, the populations of all known civilized societies have been divided into more or less distinct classes. Yet sociologists have not always agreed on the meaning of the term *class*, nor on the methods to be used in assigning individuals to particular classes. They have, however, agreed that classes (whatever their other characteristics may be) always consist of groups or categories of people that are *ranked* in relation to one another. Individuals differ in many respects—in age, sex, race, and ethnicity—but such differences do not in themselves constitute class differences. It is only when people are grouped into separate categories on the basis of selected differences and the categories are then ranked as "higher" or "lower," "superior" or "inferior," in relation to each other that we may speak of a class structure. The term *social stratification* is used by sociologists to describe this grouping of individuals into strata regarded as lying above or below one another like geological layers, or, to use a more homely analogy, like the layers of icing in a layer cake. Class systems are hierarchies of such layers that embrace nearly the entire population of a society. The important problem for the sociologist is to determine *which* of the many differences between individuals and groups are the most relevant criteria for classifying them into ranked, society-wide strata.

The problem is more easily solved in preindustrial societies than in contemporary industrial societies. In most of the great agrarian civilizations of the past, membership in a class constituted a recognized social role assigning definite rights, privileges, and duties to its incumbents. Class membership was usually assigned to individuals at birth on the basis of the class to which their parents belonged. Stratification systems in which *social mobility,* or the chance of changing one's original class in the course of a lifetime, was virtually impossible have been called *caste* systems. The best historical example of such rigid systems is the traditional Indian caste system. Class structures in which an individual can have a higher class position bestowed upon him by a ritual ceremony or legal proceeding have been called *estate* systems. Premodern Europe is perhaps the best-known historical example. The granting of a title of nobility to an individual, or the manumission of a slave, are examples of the types of social mobility possible under such a system.

Castes and estates, the basic units in such systems of stratification, were self-conscious, more or less cohesive social groups. Frequently they created councils and other representative bodies to serve as spokesmen for their collective interests in dealings with other classes and with the political authorities. Yet caste or estate members were not necessarily equal apart from their common social rank. Penurious noblemen and wealthy commoners existed in feudal Europe, although the former possessed a higher rank than the latter.

In postmodern industrial societies, clearly defined rank orders of groups like the Indian caste or European estate system no longer exist except as historical survivals in some of the older European countries which, unlike the United States, have a feudal past. Since the French Revolution, nation states have in principle, if not always in fact, been committed to the formal legal and political equality of all their citizens. And since the industrial revolution, continuing economic expansion has greatly increased opportunities for individuals to acquire through wealth and occupational success many of the possessions, manners, and attitudes associated with the traditional styles of life of the upper classes. Legal and political equality, the ideology of egalitarianism, a competitive market economy, merit and seniority systems of selecting people for bureaucratic roles, and the influence of mass production and mass communications have blurred older class distinctions.

On the other hand, the relative disappearance of clearly demarcated, cohesive ranked groups has in no sense meant that all men have become equal in wealth, social rank, and power. Nor has it meant, in spite of higher rates of social mobility, that opportunities for achievement are not still for the vast majority primarily determined by parental position, that is, by the stratification level on which people are born. Sociologists have defined three overlapping yet partially distinct pyramids of inequality in contemporary industrial societies: one of *wealth,* one of *prestige* or status, and one of *power.* The wealthy, the highly regarded and socially valued, and the powerful are often not the same persons, which justifies identifying these three separable dimensions of inequality in modern societies.

Our readings for this section open with an up-to-date statistical survey of income distribution in the United States and some other nations, by Herman P. Miller of the U.S. Bureau of the Census. Our next four selections describe four major groupings in American society that correspond roughly, though in different degrees, to social classes. E. Digby Baltzell describes the American upper class, particularly its Philadelphia branch, a group that in its cohesiveness, wealth, style of life, and stress on family origins resembles older European aristocracies. C. Wright Mills describes the new middle class of managers, salaried employees, and sales and office workers that has grown so rapidly in this century with the increase in the size and number of the bureaucratic organizations requiring their services. In contrast to Baltzell's Proper Philadelphians, Mills finds that this white-collar stratum is internally very heterogeneous in occupation, income, and prestige. Gerhard Lenski briefly describes the situation of the working class in contemporary industrial societies, while S. M. Miller and Frank Riessman discuss the values and life styles of American working-class culture.

Of the three groups described, only Baltzell's "business aristocracy" resembles a social class in traditional terms. Thus we have included as a final reading an analysis by Dennis H. Wrong of continuing changes in the postmodern world that make it necessary for the sociologist to distinguish clearly between persistent inequalities in income, status, and power, on the one hand, and the hierarchy of ranked social groups that sociologists have conventionally called "social stratification" or "the social class system," on the other.

# 41

# The Distribution of Personal Income in the United States

## HERMAN P. MILLER

The amount of income that is produced by a given country prescribes the levels of living that are possible for its inhabitants. A given amount of income may be widely distributed throughout the population and provide adequate levels of living for all, or it may be concentrated in the hands of a few persons and provide pyramids and palaces for princes and kings and nothing but hovels and hunger for everyone else. It is for this reason that statistics on income distribution are needed in addition to those on gross national product, particularly in a wealthy country like the United States.

India, with an annual income of only $80 or $90 per person, can do little to alleviate the poverty of its teeming masses by taxing the rich more and giving it to the poor. If the total income produced in India each year were more equally divided, it might prevent thousands of people from starving to death, but at best a redistribution of income in India would not provide more than a bare subsistence level of living.

In the United States, however, where the average income per person is over $4,000 per year, it is very important that we know how incomes are distributed,

for if there are large numbers of people with incomes too low to maintain a minimum level of living for this country it is possible to do something about it. Increases can be made in social security payments to the aged, in unemployment compensation for those unable to find work, and in public assistance to mothers with dependent children. There is even a proposal now to provide a guaranteed income for all the poor, regardless of where they live or with whom they live. It is also possible to help the poor by providing more and better services, such as low-cost public housing, training programs, and better schools and medical facilities.

Even in a very wealthy country like the United States, there are limits to the amount that the middle class and the well-to-do can be taxed without destroying their incentives to work, save, and invest which are the ultimate sources of our fabulous wealth. We do not know what these limits are. There is some evidence that they may be quite great and that it may be possible to tax ourselves more than we do without any serious reduction of incentives to work. One recent study of the economic behavior of rich people showed that seven-eighths of high-income respondents do not curtail their work at all because of the income tax and that

**Table 1**
Families by Income Level: 1968

| INCOME LEVEL | NUMBER OF FAMILIES | PERCENTAGE FAMILIES | PERCENTAGE INCOME |
|---|---|---|---|
| All families | 50.5 million | 100% | 100% |
| Under $3,000 | 5.2 million | 10 | 2 |
| Between $3,000 and $7,000 | 13.4 million | 27 | 14 |
| Between $7,000 and $10,000 | 11.8 million | 23 | 20 |
| Between $10,000 and $15,000 | 12.6 million | 25 | 31 |
| Between $15,000 and $25,000 | 6.1 million | 12 | 23 |
| Between $25,000 and $50,000 | 1.2 million | 2 | 7 |
| $50,0000 and over | 150,000 | 0.3 | 2 |
| Median income | $8,600 | | |
| Average (mean) income | $9,700 | | |

Note: Sums of tabulated figures in this chapter may not equal totals because of rounding. Derived from U.S. Bureau of the Census, *Current Population Reports*, Series P-60, No. 66.

income taxes do not appear to have any significant effect either on the timing of retirement or on the employment of wives. At least we can agree that although there are limits to taxation, there is a surplus among higher-income American families at present which could be used to alleviate the extremes of poverty, if such action were deemed necessary or desirable.

Statistics on income distribution are used for many different purposes. Their most important use, perhaps, was in revealing the existence of millions of poor people in the United States and thereby calling attention to the need for an attack on poverty early in the 1960's. These statistics were not only instrumental in starting that "war," they were also the single most important measure of year-to-year progress in that war—and they showed that we made progress.

. . . . . . . . . .

Below are figures showing the spread of income in the United States. They come from a study conducted by the U.S. Bureau of the Census in March 1969. You may be interested in finding out where you fit in the income picture. Since only seven different income groups are shown, these figures give an unrealistic view of the actual spread of income. It is really much greater than most people imagine. The noted economist Paul Samuelson has described income distribution in the following terms: "If we made an income pyramid out of a child's blocks, with each layer portraying $1,000 of income, the peak would be far higher than the Eiffel Tower, but almost all of us would be within a yard of the ground." This statement gives you some idea of the diversity that is compressed within these seven groupings.

About 5 million families received less than $3,000 in 1968. They represented about one-tenth of all families and received one-fiftieth (2 percent) of the income. Some lived on farms where their cash incomes were supplemented by food and lodging that they did not have to purchase. But even if this income were added to the total, the figures would not change much.

At the top income level were about 150,000 families with incomes of $50,000 and over. They represented 3/10 of 1 percent of all families and received 2 percent of all the income.

Another way to view these figures

**Table 2**

Share of Income Received by Each Fifth of Families
and by Top 5 Percent and Top 1 Percent: 1968

| FAMILIES RANKED FROM LOWEST TO HIGHEST | INCOME RANGE | PERCENTAGE OF INCOME RECEIVED |
|---|---|---|
| Lowest fifth | Under $4,600 | 6% |
| Second fifth | Between $4,600 and $7,400 | 12 |
| Middle fifth | Between $7,400 and $10,000 | 18 |
| Fourth fifth | Between $10,000 and $13,500 | 24 |
| Highest fifth | $13,500 and over | 41 |
| Top 5% | $23,000 and over | 14 |
| Top 1% | $42,500 and over | 5 |

Derived from U.S. Bureau of the Census, *Current Population Reports*, Series P-60, No. 66.

is to examine the share of income received by each fifth of the families, ranked from lowest to highest by income. Table 2 shows that in 1968, the poorest fifth of the families had incomes under $4,600; they received 6 percent of the total. In that same year, the highest fifth of the families had incomes over $13,500; they received 41 percent of the total.

Who sits at the top of the heap? The figures show that until you get to the very top the incomes are not so high. The top 5 percent of the families had incomes over $23,000. They received 14 percent of all the income. Families with incomes over $42,500 were in the top 1 percent and they received 5 percent of the total.

The figures in Table 2 show the distribution of income before taxes. Since families in the higher income groups pay a larger share of the taxes, their share of income should be smaller on an after-tax basis. It is, but not by as much as you might think. Table 3 shows the figures both ways for 1966, using data collected by the Survey Research Center of the University of Michigan. This table shows that the share of income received by the top fifth of the families and individuals is reduced by only two percentage points when taxes are taken into account. The reason taxes have such little impact is

that our tax structure is not very progressive. In fact, in 1965, families at each income level between $2,000 and $15,000 paid the same proportion of their income in taxes (see Table 4). There is some progressivity in the federal tax structure. Families in the $2,000 to $4,000 income class pay 16 percent of their income in federal taxes whereas those in the $15,000 and over class turn over 32 percent of their income to the federal treasury. State and local taxes, however, are regressive from beginning to end. Families with incomes under $2,000 pay one-fourth of their income in state and local taxes (mostly sales taxes at the bottom income class), whereas families in the top income class pay only 7 percent of their income in taxes to state and local governments.

The government not only takes money away from people, it also gives it back to some in the form of transfer payments like social security, unemployment compensation, public assistance, etc. When transfer payments are taken into account, a large measure of progressivity is added to the tax structure. Families at the very lowest income levels receive more in transfer payments than they pay in taxes to the federal, state, and local governments The share of income paid in taxes, less transfer payments, does rise with income level.

**Table 3**

Share of Income Received by Each Fifth of Families and Individuals, Before and After Taxes: 1966

| FAMILIES AND INDIVIDUALS, RANKED FROM | PERCENTAGE OF AGGREGATE INCOME RECEIVED | |
|---|---|---|
| LOWEST TO HIGHEST | BEFORE TAXES | AFTER TAXES |
| Lowest fifth | 5% | 5% |
| Second fifth | 11 | 11 |
| Middle fifth | 18 | 17 |
| Fourth fifth | 23 | 25 |
| Highest fifth | 43 | 41 |

Derived from University of Michigan, Survey Research Center, *Survey of Consumer Finances: 1967.*

One writer stated recently, in commenting on the impact of fiscal policy on the distribution of income, that from "reading conservative popular writers, one would assume that the federal government, in particular, did little else than redistribute income from those who work hard to those who do not. Reading the radical press would probably lead one to conclude that redis-

tribution is indeed taking place but that it is from the poor to the wealthy, further concentrating and distorting the original distribution by the economic system." Hard facts are difficult to come by in this area. Conservatives and radicals can undoubtedly interpret such information as is available as a confirmation of their views. The figures shown in Table 4 take into account taxes and transfer payments only; they make no allowance for benefits accruing to each income class as a result of government expenditures for public schools, roads, national defense, and similar activities. It takes some very heroic assumptions to get at the net impact of *all* public expenditures on the distribution of income. Such a study was made several years ago, initially as a doctoral dissertation submitted to Johns Hopkins University and later as an article in a book of essays on fiscal policy published by The Brookings Institution. In this article, the author, Irwin Gillespie, first distributed the tax burden by income class, using the following assumptions:

With regard to federal taxes, it is assumed

**Table 4**

Taxes and Transfers As a Percentage of Income: 1965

| INCOME CLASS | TAXES | | | TRANSFER PAYMENTS | TAXES LESS TRANSFERS |
|---|---|---|---|---|---|
| | FEDERAL | STATE AND LOCAL | TOTAL | | |
| Under $2,000 | 19% | 25% | 44% | 126% | −83%* |
| $2,000–$4,000 | 16 | 11 | 27 | 11 | 16 |
| $4,000–$6,000 | 17 | 10 | 27 | 5 | 21 |
| $6,000–$8,000 | 17 | 9 | 26 | 3 | 23 |
| $8,000–$10,000 | 18 | 9 | 27 | 2 | 25 |
| $10,000–15,000 | 19 | 9 | 27 | 2 | 25 |
| $15,000 and over | 32 | 7 | 38 | 1 | 37 |
| Total | 22 | 9 | 31 | 14 | 24 |

* The minus sign indicates that families and individuals in this class received more from federal, state, and local governments than they, as a group, paid to these governments in taxes.

Joseph A. Pechman, "The Rich, the Poor and the Taxes They Pay," *The Public Interest*, November 1969. The data are from the *Economic Report of the President*, 1969, p. 161.

that: the individual income tax is borne entirely by the individual; the estate and gift taxes fall entirely on those in the highest income bracket; two-thirds of the corporate profits tax is borne by the owners (and therefore is allocated by a distribution of dividends received), and one-third is shifted forward to consumers; excise and customs are shifted forward to consumers of the products taxed; social security contributions fall on wage earners (the employee's share and half the employer's share) and total consumption (half of the employer's share).

State and local taxes, including the individual income tax, estate and gift taxes, and the corporate profits tax are treated in the same way as their federal counterparts. In addition, it is assumed that: excise taxes are shifted to total consumption goods, while sales taxes are shifted to consumption goods less food product purchases; property taxes are borne equally by homeowners (and renters) and consumers; social security contributions are borne entirely by wage and salary earners.

Gillespie then attempts to estimate the benefits received from government expenditures by income class. The procedure is quite complex and is not summarized as neatly as the distribution of the tax burden. In the case of highways, for example, 75 percent of the expenditures was distributed as a benefit to highway users and 25 percent as a benefit to nonusers (i.e., as a benefit to property owners whose sites were increased in value); expenditures on education were distributed as a benefit to families with children in elementary and secondary schools and in colleges; expenditures on public health were assumed to be consumed equally by all families, etc. The one critical assumption which had to be made involved general expenditures, which includes national defense among other things, and accounted for $50 billion out of a total of $83 billion of government expenditures in 1960. Gillespie used four different assumptions to distribute the benefits of general expenditures. The one he regards as the standard case, and the one that is reported here, assumes that general expenditures are distributed proportionately to income and are therefore allocated according to the distribution of families by income levels.

**Table 5**

Percentage Change in Income, by Income Class, After Tax Payments and the Benefits of Government Expenditures: 1960

| INCOME CLASS | PERCENTAGE CHANGE IN INCOME |
|---|---|
| Under $2,000 | 55% |
| $2,000 to $2,999 | 44 |
| $3,000 to $3,999 | 19 |
| $4,000 to $4,999 | −1 |
| $5,000 to $7,499 | −3 |
| $7,500 to $9,999 | 2 |
| $10,000 and over | −13 |

Article by W. Irwin Gillespie, "Effect of Public Expenditures on the Distribution of Income" in Richard A. Musgrave, *Essays in Fiscal Federalism*, Washington, D.C.: The Brookings Institution, 1965, p. 162.

Table 5 shows how families at each income level are affected when the joint net impact of the burden of tax payments and the benefits of government expenditures are taken into account. The incomes of families at the lowest level (under $2,000) are increased by 55 percent and those at the $2,000–$3,000 level are increased by 44 percent. The incomes of families at the $10,000 and over level are reduced by 13 percent. Within the $4,000 to $10,000 there is very little change. It does appear, therefore, when all factors are taken into account, that the poor do benefit appreciably as a result of the government's efforts to redistribute income.

Are U.S. incomes too unequally distributed?

There is no objective answer to this question. It all depends on how equally you think incomes should be distributed.

Around the turn of the century, the

French poet and philosopher Charles Péguy wrote: "When all men are provided with the necessities, the real necessities, with bread and books, what do we care about the distribution of luxury?" This point of view went out of style with spats and high-button shoes. There is an intense interest in the distribution of luxury in the modern world.

Since we all cannot have as many material things as we should like, many people are of the opinion that those who are more productive should get more both as a reward for past performance and as an incentive to greater output in the future. This seems like a reasonable view, consistent with the realities of the world. Lincoln said: "That some should be rich shows that others may become rich and hence is just encouragement to industry and enterprise." The fact is that all modern industrial societies, whatever their political or social philosophies, have had to resort to some forms of incentives to get the most work out of their people.

Despite its reasonableness, this view has its critics. Some have argued that a man endowed with a good mind, drive, imagination, and creativity, and blessed with a wholesome environment in which these attributes could be nurtured, has already been amply rewarded. To give him material advantages over his less fortunate fellows would only aggravate the situation. The British historian R. H. Tawney wrote in his book *Equality*: ". . . some men are inferior to others in respect to their intellectual endowments. . . . It does not, however, follow from this fact that such individuals or classes should receive less consideration than others or should be treated as inferior in respect to such matters as legal status or health, or economic arrangements, which are within the control of the community."

. . . .. .. .. .. .. .. .. ..
Do the rich get a larger share of in-

come in the United States than they do in other countries? According to the available evidence this is not the case. The United States has about the same income distribution as Denmark, Sweden, and Great Britain and a much more equal distribution than most of the other countries for which data are shown.

The figures in Table 6 classify the top 5 percent as "rich." This is a rather low point on the income scale. In the United States it would include all families receiving more than $23,000 a year. A more interesting comparison would be the share of income received by the top 1 percent ($42,500 or more per year) or perhaps an even higher income group. Such information, however, is not available for most other countries.

A comprehensive study of international comparisons of income was made in 1960 by Professor Irving Kravis of the University of Pennsylvania. He summarized the income distribution among the countries for which data are available in the following way:

More nearly equal distribution than U.S.
    Denmark
    Netherlands
    Israel (Jewish population only)
About the same distribution as U.S.
    Great Britain
    Japan
    Canada
More unequal distribution than U.S.
    Italy
    Puerto Rico
    Ceylon
    El Salvador

## Growth in Average Family Income: 1929–1968

The year 1929 is a landmark in U.S. history. It was the year of the stock market crash. It is also the first year for which reliable statistics are available showing the distribution of families by income level. There are good figures showing changes in *average* income back

**Table 6**

Percentage of Income Received by Top 5 Percent of Families in Selected Countries

| COUNTRY | | INCOME PERCENTAGE |
|---|---|---|
| United States | (1950) | 20%* |
| Sweden | (1948) | 20 |
| Denmark | (1952) | 20 |
| Great Britain | (1951–52) | 21 |
| Barbados | (1951–52) | 22 |
| Puerto Rico | (1953) | 23 |
| India | (1955–56) | 24 |
| West Germany | (1950) | 24 |
| Italy | (1948) | 24 |
| Netherlands | (1950) | 25 |
| Ceylon | (1952–53) | 31 |
| Guatemala | (1947–48) | 35 |
| El Salvador | (1946) | 36 |
| Mexico | (1957) | 37 |
| Colombia | (1953) | 42 |
| Northern Rhodesia | (1946) | 45 |
| Kenya | (1949) | 51 |
| Southern Rhodesia | (1946) | 65 |

* The numbers represent total income before taxes received by families or spending units.

Simon Kuznets, "Quantitative Aspects of the Economic Growth of Nations," *Economic Development and Cultural Change*, Vol. XI, No. 2 (January 1963), Table 3.

to the turn of the century, but we have little more than rough approximations of the *distribution* of families by income level before 1929. We might therefore begin by asking what has happened to average family income since the onset of the great depression.

It is important to be very careful about dollars here because prices have risen and a dollar buys much less today than it did in 1929. Therefore, all figures will have to be expressed in dollars of constant purchasing power: 1968 dollars have been used for that purpose. Moreover, taxes have gone up as well as prices. In order to get a reasonable approximation of change in purchasing power, the income should be measured

after federal income taxes are deducted. The figures below satisfy both conditions. In view of the recent rise in social security taxes and the growing importance of state and local taxes, it would be desirable if these taxes were also deducted, in order to obtain an estimate of the disposable income available to consumers for personal spending or saving. The necessary data, however, are not readily available, and so we will have to be satisfied with family income less federal income taxes.

There are some very important lessons to be learned from this set of numbers. In the first place, you can see that there is nothing magical about economic growth. Nothing is built into the economic system to guarantee that purchasing power—levels of living—will automatically go up each year. Indeed these few figures show that a decline began in 1929, lasted for about a decade, and was not fully recovered until World War II broke out.

During the war years there was a tremendous growth in real income. This resulted in a huge growth in savings, since there were few consumer goods around to be purchased. Factories were working at full steam and prices were controlled. As a result, real incomes rose by $800 in five years, or about $160 per year.

The end of World War II did not bring the mass unemployment that so many economists had forecast, but the removal of price controls and the huge backlog of consumer demand backed by fat bank accounts forced prices up. The reduction in hours of work also reduced family income. Consequently there was a slight drop in purchasing power throughout most of the Truman Administration. Real family incomes were lower in 1952, when Truman left office, than they were in 1945, when he entered it.

The Eisenhower Administration concentrated heavily on the control of inflation. The figures show that this policy was quite successful in terms of producing increases in family purchasing power. During the eight years of the Eisenhower Administration real family income rose by nearly $1,000, or a little more than $100 a year.

Incomes continued to grow regularly during the Kennedy and Johnson years. Between 1961 and 1963 incomes rose by about $500, or by about $250 per year. During the five years of the Johnson Administration (1963–1968) incomes rose by $1,200, or by about $250 per year. Largely because of the sharp rise in prices in 1967 and 1968, the rate of growth in real income was distinctly lower in those years than it had been earlier in the decade.

The rising income levels between 1950 and 1970 suggest that a new type of individual is now appearing on the American scene, one who has never had firsthand experience with severe economic depression. People born in 1942 are reaching maturity. Most of them have completed their education. Many are already married and having families. These youngsters have been reared in a period in which there has been no major economic depression. There have been recessions, to be sure, but these are minor economic ripples compared with the national depressions each previous generation of Americans experienced. Some of these young people live in depressed areas where jobs are scarce, but these are the exceptions rather than the rule. Never in the postwar era has the whole country suffered the bleak despair of the economic famines that formerly came again and again—in 1837, 1857, 1893, 1907, 1921, and 1929.

The growth in income, as shown in Table 7, can be traced back much further than 1929. Since 1890, our national income, adjusted for price changes, has grown at the average rate of more than 3 percent per year compounded. It has doubled every twenty years. Even when allowance is made for population growth, income per person today is four times what it was in 1890. That growth was no accident. A better understanding of why it occurred in the past is the best guarantee that it will continue in the future. Our geographic location plays a very important role. While we have an abundance of good land, water, mineral resources, and timber, the importance of these factors should not be overemphasized. It has been pointed out that "at the time our Constitution was drawn up other countries had equally fertile soil, other countries had more abundant labor, larger amounts of capital, better educational institutions, better roads and other means of communication, and natural resources more adequate for the agrarian economies of those times." What we had in addition was a form of government and a general outlook which accepted and encouraged change. "Change and attempted improvement have been in the very genes of the millions of immigrants who have come to our land over the centuries. Many came seeking freedom in a very wide sense—freedom from government domination; freedom from church domination; freedom from class rigidity. An urge toward 'progress' has been part and parcel of our thinking, of our social environment, from the days of the earliest settlers. Our people, no matter whence they came, tended quickly to throw off the old and seek the new." Our wealth did not arise out of thin air. It is attributable to the fact that we were blessed with abundance of resources and that we have a set of values which encouraged the development of our physical and human resources.

.. .. .. .. .. .. .. .. ..

## Changes in the Distribution by Income Level: 1929–1968

Averages can be very misleading. All that an average tells you is the amount that each one would get if the total

**Table 7**
Average Income of Families and
Individuals, After Taxes (in 1968
Dollars)

| YEAR | AVERAGE INCOME |
|------|----------------|
| 1929 | $4,706 |
| 1935–36 | 4,055 |
| 1941 | 4,988 |
| 1944 | 6,344 |
| 1946 | 6,381 |
| 1947 | 5,794 |
| 1948 | 5,803 |
| 1949 | 5,635 |
| 1950 | 5,890 |
| 1951 | 5,917 |
| 1952 | 5,990 |
| 1953 | 6,255 |
| 1954 | 6,269 |
| 1955 | 6,610 |
| 1956 | 6,889 |
| 1957 | 6,885 |
| 1958 | 6,799 |
| 1959 | 7,061 |
| 1960 | 7,133 |
| 1961 | 7,174 |
| 1962 | 7,437 |
| 1963 | 7,648 |
| 1964 | 8,004 |
| 1965 | 8,324 |
| 1966 | 8,660 |
| 1967 | 8,781 |
| 1968 | 8,900 |

1948 to 1968, derived from unpublished
data of Office of Business Economics; 1929
and 1947, from "Size Distribution of Income in 1963," *Survey of Current Business,*
April 1964. Figures for 1935–36, 1941,
1944, and 1946 derived from Herman P.
Miller, *Income Distribution in the United
States,* Government Printing Office, 1966,
p. 9.

were equally divided. The total is not
equally divided and it makes a big
difference just how unequally divided
it is.

The increase in income since the depression of the thirties has been widespread throughout the population and
has resulted in a general movement of
families up the income scale. There
have, of course, been many exceptions.
The aged, uneducated, and unskilled

have not moved ahead as fast as the
others, but even for many of these
groups the sharp edge of poverty has
been blunted.

The typical picture, particularly since
the end of World War II, has been one
of gradually rising family incomes, due
not only to the full-time employment
of chief breadwinners but also to the rising tendency for wives to supplement
family income. These factors, in combination with the increasing productivity of American industry, have caused
a persistent drop in the number and
proportion of families at the lower income levels and a corresponding increase
in the middle- and upper-income brackets. The extent of the increase in family income can be seen most clearly in
the tables below. Here again, all the
numbers are expressed in terms of constant purchasing power, so that the
effects of inflation are eliminated. There
is a technical problem that must be
mentioned here. There are no figures
which are entirely comparable for the
complete period since 1929. The only
figures available are those prepared by
the Office of Business Economics covering family *personal* income for 1929–
1962 and those prepared by the Bureau
of the Census covering family *money*
income for 1947–1968. The difference
between the two series is that the OBE
data include nonmoney income and are
adjusted for underreporting of income,
which is characteristic of all income
data collected in household surveys. In
contrast, the census data cover money
income only and are not adjusted for
underreporting. During the years in
which the two series overlap (1947–
1962), they show remarkably similar
trends.

In 1959 Robert Heilbroner, in *The
Future as History,* wrote: "In the economic folklore of our country we still
look back to 1929 not only as a year of
great business prosperity but as a year
of widespread and fundamental well-

**Table 8**
Distribution of Families and Individuals by Personal Income (in 1968 Dollars)

| INCOME LEVEL | 1913 | 1929 | 1947 | 1967 |
|---|---|---|---|---|
| Under $3,000 | 61% | 50% | 24% | 17% |
| Between $3,000 and $6,000 | 27 | 32 | 36 | 34 |
| Between $6,000 and $8,000 | 6 | 8 | 18 | 9 |
| Between $8,000 and $10,000 | 2 | 4 | 8 | 13 |
| $10,000 and over | 4 | 6 | 14 | 27 |

Figures for 1929, 1947, and 1962 derived from "Size Distribution of Income in 1963," *Survey of Current Business*, April 1964, Table 4. Figures for 1913 are very rough approximations.

**Table 9**
Distribution of Families and Unrelated Individuals by Money Income (in 1968 Dollars)

| TOTAL MONEY INCOME | 1947 | 1957 | 1962 | 1968 |
|---|---|---|---|---|
| Number of families (thousands) | 45,402 | 54,131 | 58,011 | 64,313 |
| Median income | $4,183 | $5,397 | $6,044 | $7,434 |
| Under $3,000 | 34% | 28% | 26% | 19% |
| $3,000 to $5,999 | 37 | 28 | 24 | 21 |
| $6,000 to $7,999 | 13 | 19 | 17 | 15 |
| $8,000 to $9,999 | 7 | 12 | 12 | 13 |
| $10,000 and over | 9 | 13 | 21 | 33 |

Derived from *Current Population Reports*, Series P-60, No. 66, Table 5.

being. But when we examine the economy of 1929 critically, we find that the facade of business prosperity concealed an inner structure of widespread economic frailty."

This conclusion is clearly supported by the figures. If $3,000 is used as the poverty line, it can be noted that in 1913 about three-fifths of the families and individuals had incomes that would be regarded as substandard today. By the end of World War II this proportion was reduced to one-third and by 1968 it was further reduced to one-fifth.

The figures at the other end of the income scale show why ours is called an affluent society. In 1968 about one family out of every three had an income over $10,000. In many cases this high an income was achieved only because the wife and the husband were both working; but the income is there nonetheless and it is available for air conditioners, dishwashers, second cars, and prestige schools. In 1929, an income over $10,000 was achieved by only one family out of twenty.

# 42

# The American Metropolitan Upper Class

E. DIGBY BALTZELL

*The wealthier, or, as they would prefer to style themselves the "upper" classes, tend distinctly towards the bourgeois type, and an individual in the bourgeois stage of development, while honest, industrious, and virtuous, is also not unapt to be a miracle of timid and short-sighted selfishness. The commercial classes are only too likely to regard everything merely from the standpoint of "Does it pay?" and many a merchant does not take any part in politics because he is short-sighted enough to think that it will pay him better to attend purely to making money, and too selfish to be willing to undergo any trouble for the sake of abstract duty; while the younger men of this type are too much engrossed in their various social pleasures to be willing to give up their time to anything else.*

THEODORE ROOSEVELT

Conceived in a new world which was free of the traditional authority of an established church and a feudal nobility, and born in a revolt from the tyranny of a centralizing government symbolized in the British monarchy and mercantilism, American institutions have, virtually from the beginning, been shaped in a laissez-faire capitalist climate. The merchant, mining, manufacturing, railroad, and finance capitalists, each in their day, were the most powerful members of the elite in nineteenth- and early twentieth-century America. As "old family" is usually found to be synonymous with "old money," the leading capitalists in the pre-Civil War period were the "old-family" founders in America. In the 1870's, the families of these men and their descendants formed local business aristocracies in the older cities such as Boston, New York, and Philadelphia. Living near one another, on the gentle slope of Murray Hill in New York, on Beacon Street in Boston, or around Rittenhouse Square in Philadelphia, the members of these families knew "who" belonged within this formal and well-structured world of polite society.

In the last two decades of the nineteenth century, these provincial aristocracies of birth and breeding (old money) merged with a new and more conspicuously colorful world known as "Society." It was in the 1880's that New York Society with a capital "S," then moving uptown to the newly fashionable Fifth Avenue district, came under the tutelage of Mrs. Astor and her right-hand man, Ward McAlister. It was Mr. McAlister who coined the snobbish term "Four Hundred" and finally gave his official list to the New York *Times* on the occasion of Mrs. Astor's famous ball on February 1, 1892. During this same period, as millionaires multiplied and had to be accepted, as one lost track of "who" people were and had to recognize "what" they were worth, the *Social Register* became an index of a new upper class in America.

But this new upper class was soon to be organized on a national rather than a local scale. In an age which marked the centralization of economic power under the control of the finance capitalists, the gentlemen bankers and lawyers on Wall Street, Walnut Street, State Street, and La Salle Street began to send their sons to Groton, St. Mark's, or St. Paul's and afterwards to Harvard, Yale, or Princeton where they joined such exclusive clubs as Porcellian, Fence, or Ivy. These polished young men from many cities were educated together, and introduced to one another's sisters at debutante parties and fashionable weddings in Old Westbury, Mount Kisco, or Far Hills, on the Main Line or in Chestnut Hill, in Dedham, Brookline, or Milton, or in Lake Forest. After marriage at some fashionable Episcopal church, almost invariably within this select, endogamous circle, they lived in these same socially circumspect suburbs and commuted to the city where they lunched with their fathers and grandfathers at the Union, Philadelphia, Somerset, or Chicago clubs. Several generations repeat this cycle, and a centralized business aristocracy thus becomes a reality in America. The *Social Register*, first published in 1888, lists the families of this business aristocracy and their relatives and friends, in New York, Chicago, Boston, Philadelphia, Baltimore, San Francisco, St. Louis, Buffalo, Pittsburgh, Cleveland, Cincinnati-Dayton, and Washington, D.C. In 1940, approximately one-fourth of the residents of these twelve metropolitan areas who were listed in *Who's Who* in that year were also listed in the *Social Register*. Thus the members of this contemporary American upper class, descendants of leaders in American life from colonial times to the present, had considerable influence on the elite in 1940.

In 1940 the Proper Philadelphian tended "distinctly towards the bourgeois type" as Theodore Roosevelt would have put it. While 29 percent of the Philadelphians listed in *Who's Who* were also listed in the *Social Register*, the upper class contributed considerably more than its share of leaders within the business community: 75 percent of the bankers, 51 percent of the lawyers, 45 percent of the engineers, and 42 percent of the businessmen listed in *Who's Who* were also members of the upper class. In addition, of the 532 directorships in industrial and financial institutions reported by *all* the members of the elite, 60 percent were reported by members of the upper class. Finally, the leading bankers and lawyers in the city were members of the upper class. The presidents, and over 80 percent of the directors in the six largest banks were Proper Philadelphians, as were the senior partners in the largest law firms. And Dr. Thomas S. Gates, lawyer, former senior Morgan partner, and President of the University of Pennsylvania in 1940, was not only the most influential and respected member of the upper class but also the most powerful man in the city.

Within the upper class as a whole, moreover, business power tended to be correlated with the various attributes of high social class position. Thus, the members of the business elite, both those in the upper class and the rest, were more likely to live in the more fashionable neighborhoods, to attend the Episcopal churches, to have graduated from the right educational institutions, and to have grown up in the city (see Table 1).

In 1940 the ideal-typical Proper Philadelphian at the apex of the pyramid of social prestige and economic power in the city, may be said to have had the following attributes:

1. Of English or Welsh descent, his great-great-great-grandfather would have been a prominent Philadelphian in the great age of the new republic.

**Table 1**

Philadelphians in *Who's Who* in 1940—Attributes of High Social Class Position
As Related to Functional Elites

| | SOCIAL CLASS | | | |
| | Social Register | | Nonsocial Register | |
| ATTRIBUTES OF HIGH SOCIAL CLASS POSITION | BUSINESS ELITE MEMBERS | ALL OTHER ELITE MEMBERS | BUSINESS ELITE MEMBERS | ALL OTHER ELITE MEMBERS |
|---|---|---|---|---|
| Neighborhood: | | | | |
| Main Line & Chestnut Hill | 80% | 44% | 32% | 14% |
| Religion: | | | | |
| Episcopalian | 48 | 37 | 21 | 12 |
| Education: | | | | |
| Private School | 44 | 37 | 25 | 12 |
| Harvard-Yale-Princeton | 28 | 18 | 4 | 5* |
| Birthplace: | | | | |
| Philadelphia | 55 | 49 | 37 | 27 |
| (Number of cases) | (107) | (119) | (111) | (433) |

* Upper-class graduates of Harvard, Yale, or Princeton go into business, while the other graduates are more likely to go into church or education. This may explain this deviant case.

Somewhere along the line an ancestor would have made money, or married wisely. And along with money and social position, some good Quaker ancestor would have preferred the Episcopal Church, or have been banished from the Society of Friends for marrying "out of meeting."

2. His family would have been listed in the *Social Register* at the turn of the nineteenth century.

3. He would have been born on Walnut Street, facing Rittenhouse Square.

4. After an early education at the Episcopal Academy or some other private school in the city, he would have gone away to one of the fashionable Episcopalian boarding schools in New England.

5. Unless his parents felt an unusual loyalty and pride in local institutions, he would have gone to either Harvard, Yale, or Princeton where he would have belonged to one of the more exclusive clubs.

6. After attending the law school at the University of Pennsylvania, this young Proper Philadelphian would enter one of the fashionable and powerful law firms in the city and eventually become a partner; or enter the field of banking or finance. He would be on the board of directors of several cultural and economic institutions (Pennsylvania Railroad, a bank such as the Girard Trust Company, and perhaps the Fairmount Park Art Association).

7. Finally, the Proper Philadelphian would live either in Chestnut Hill or the Main Line in 1940, attend the Episcopal Church, be married with three or four children, and walk either up or down Walnut Street to lunch with his peers at the Rittenhouse, or preferably the Philadelphia Club.

As proper Philadelphia has been democratically assimilating new men of power and wealth into its ranks, most of the upper-class members of the elite in 1940, of course, do not measure up to this exalted ideal-typical status.

By way of a quantitative summary of the various attributes of social class position discussed throughout this book, the Philadelphia elite as a whole in 1940 has been broken down (in Table 2) into various levels which more or less approach this ideal-typical status. Columns 1 and 3 are made up of upper-class directors in certain prestige institutions discussed in the previous chapter; the men in column 1 were born in Philadelphia and were listed in the 1900 *Social Register*, while those in column 3 were not. Column 1, then, includes old-family men of power while column 3 includes men of newer power and position. The rest of the columns in Table 2 are self-explanatory. As we have said, the Philadelphia Club is both more socially circumspect and more influential than the younger Rittenhouse. In fact, the younger club is best understood as the first rung in the ladder of ascent into the upper class (except for columns 5 and 6, of course, the various subgroups in Table 2 have overlapping and not mutually exclusive memberships).

In a very real sense, Table 2 summarizes this book. Thus Proper Philadelphia was a business aristocracy in 1940 wherein social class position and commercial and financial power in the community were positively correlated variables in the total class situation. Throughout its history, and especially since the Civil War, the Philadelphia upper class closely approximated R. H. Tawney's description of the British aristocracy which most American patricians, of course, both emulate and respect: "It is a subtle combination of both—a blend of a crude plutocratic reality with the sentimental aroma of an aristocratic legend—which gives the English class system its peculiar toughness and cohesion. It is at once as businesslike as Manchester and as gentlemanly as Eton. . . ." [1]

[1] R. H. Tawney, *Equality*, New York: Harcourt, Brace & Co., 1931, p. 61.

After this brief summary of the characteristics of the Philadelphia upper class in 1940, several things pertaining to the American metropolitan upper class as a whole should be emphasized. . . .

It is important to stress once again the fact that, while there are many middle and lower classes in America, and in Philadelphia, there exists one metropolitan upper class with a common cultural tradition, consciousness of kind, and "we" feeling of solidarity which tends to be national in scope. The origin and development of this inter-city moneyed aristocracy in America quite naturally paralleled the rise of rapid communications and the national corporate enterprise. Moreover, just as economic control of the various local firms in the "Yankee Cities" and "Middletowns" of America have gradually gravitated to such metropolitan centers as Boston, New York, or Chicago, so upper-class prestige has, over the years, become increasingly centralized in the fashionable metropolitan suburbs.

The growth and structure of this national upper class has, in turn, been supported by various institutions. First and most important, of course, are the New England boarding schools and the fashionable Eastern universities. Whereas the older generation of Proper Philadelphians were educated at home or in local schools and colleges, at the turn of the century, and especially after the First World War, these national upper-class family-surrogates began to educate the children of the rich and well-born from all cities in ever-increasing numbers. At the same time, the Episcopal Church also developed into a national upper-class institution. By the end of the nineteenth century, the process of upper-class conversion, which had actually begun in the previous century, was virtually complete. In the twentieth century, the fashionable descendants of

**Table 2**

Philadelphians in *Who's Who* in 1940—Attributes of High Social Class Position
As Related to Specified Levels of Prestige and Power

| ATTRIBUTES OF HIGH SOCIAL CLASS POSITION | 1 "OLD FAMILY" PRESTIGE DIRECTORS | 2 PHILA- DELPHIA CLUB MEMBERS | 3 PRESTIGE DIRECTORS, NOT "OLD FAMILY" | 4 RITTEN- HOUSE CLUB MEMBERS | 5 SOCIAL REGISTER | 6 NON- SOCIAL REGISTER |
|---|---|---|---|---|---|---|
| Neighborhood: Main Line & Chestnut Hill | 88% | 77% | 77% | 67% | 61% | 18% |
| Religion: Episcopalian | 70% | 58% | 50% | 41% | 42% | 14% |
| Education: Private School | 70% | 52% | 28% | 35% | 41% | 15% |
| Harvard-Yale-Princeton | 33% | 37% | 33% | 21% | 22% | 5% |
| Birthplace: Philadelphia | 100% | 75% | 28% | 52% | 52% | 29% |
| Occupation: Banker | 42% | 25% | 22% | 18% | 11% | 1% |
| Lawyer | 21% | 12% | 17% | 17% | 9% | 4% |
| (Number of cases) | (24) | (57) | (18) | (66) | (226) | (544) |
| Family Size: Mean number of children per Male Parent | 3.50 | 3.30 | 3.20 | 2.89 | 2.80 | 2.61 |

staunch New England Calvinists or pious Philadelphia Quakers almost invariably worshipped in the Episcopal churches in the metropolitan suburbs of America. And the Episcopal Church is also an important part of the summer social life at such fashionable resorts as Mount Desert [Island, Maine] which do so much to foster inter-city family alliances.

Several things follow from the development of this national upper class and its supporting institutions. On the whole, of course, the family is weakened and increasingly replaced by an associational aristocracy. The family firm gives way to the large and anonymously owned corporation with the attending consequences of declining family pride and responsibility. The

entrepreneur who founded the family firm and fortune is replaced by the hired executive, and the corporation soon becomes an impersonal source of dividends which conveniently supports a suitable style of life. At the same time, the fashionable school, college, and club replace the family as the chief status-ascribing institutions: often isolated geographically as well as socially from the rest of the community, these fashionable associations tend to make for less social contact between classes than was the case in an earlier day when the members of polite society, although undoubtedly protected by a formal social distance recognized by all classes, may well have interacted more frequently in the local community with the members of the middle and lower classes. George Wharton Pepper, for instance, met and befriended a Negro boy while he was growing up in the neighborhood of stiff and fashionable Rittenhouse Square; his grandsons, reared in the social homogeneity of the Main Line and a New England boarding school, were more geographically isolated even though born in a more egalitarian age. Finally, the Episcopalianization of the whole American upper class also tends to foster uniformity and class isolation. This is, of course, part of a general trend throughout Protestantism. The Catholic Church has traditionally been an altar before which men of all walks of life bow down together, but the various Protestant denominations have, almost from the beginning, been organized along class lines. Certainly most Protestant churches today are social centers where families of similar backgrounds assemble together for worship. One often wonders if fashionable Episcopalians, in their aversion to the middle-class drabness of the "Protestant ethic," have not thereby substituted a convenient conventionality for their ancestors' more rigid convictions. At any rate, these developments in upper-class institutions tend to make for an increasing conformity and uniformity, a decline in local color and originality, and perhaps, at the same time, a new snobbishness which inevitably follows the increasing importance now attached to proper associational affiliation.

Arnold Toynbee has written that whereas Western civilization has been preoccupied for several generations with the building of roads, the challenge before us today is one of regulating the traffic thereon. American civilization, led by businessmen of daring enterprise and ingenuity ("know how"), has produced the highest standard of living the world has ever known. And these business leaders and producers of wealth have been the backbone of its upper class. "New occasions teach new duties," however, and today, in the atomic age of abundant consumption, the continuing, or perhaps, new greatness of America will presumably depend on the nation's ability to shoulder the burden of world leadership in creating and defending, to use Toynbee's analogy, some sort of world traffic rules. At the same time, domestic government, at the local, state, and national level, is playing a larger and larger role in the lives of American citizens, both as the defender of law and order and the redistributor of wealth in a host of welfare activities. In short, while entrepreneurial and financial genius may have built up America, statesmen and political leaders are rapidly becoming the most powerful and important members of the contemporary elite.

On the whole, the American upper class, with such outstanding exceptions as the Roosevelts, Adamses, Lodges, and Tafts, has produced few great statesmen in modern times. As we have seen, this has been especially true of Proper Philadelphia. As young Theodore Roosevelt once wrote: "There are not a few men of means who have always made the till their fatherland, and are always ready to balance a temporary interruption of money-making, or a temporary financial and commercial disaster, against the self-sacrifice necessary in upholding the honor of the nation and the glory of the flag." [2] The vigor and continuity of an upper class depends, not on its social prestige and style of life, but rather on its continuing contribution of men who are both willing and able to assume positions of power and leadership in the world of affairs. As the seat of power moves from State Street to the State House, from Wall Street to Washington, one

[2] Quoted in John P. Mallan, "Roosevelt, Brooks Adams, and Lea: The Warrior Critique of the Business Civilization," *American Quarterly*, 8 (Fall 1956), p. 219.

wonders if the American business aristocracy discussed in this volume will be capable of supplying its share of leaders in local, national, and international governmental affairs. There are several reasons for believing that it will.

First, Philadelphia has been going through a cultural, civic, and political renaissance since the close of the Second World War. The political renaissance has been led by two members of the upper class, Richardson Dilworth, a transplanted member of an old Pittsburgh family, and Joseph Sill Clark, descendant of Enoch W. Clark, founder of one of the city's leading banking families. Both men had distinguished war records; Dilworth with the Marine Corps at Guadalcanal and Clark with the United States Air Force in the Far East. Both were distinguished lawyers and former Republicans who became Democrats rather than attempt to reform the corrupt Republican party from within. Their fight for reform began when Dilworth ran for mayor in 1947 and was defeated by the entrenched Republican machine. Four years later, however, Clark and Dilworth waged a vigorous campaign and won; Clark became the city's first Democratic mayor in the twentieth century, and Dilworth was elected district attorney. Two years later the local Democratic revival was tested again when in Philadelphia Adlai Stevenson ran 162,000 votes ahead of Dwight D. Eisenhower in a conspicuous reversal of the national Republican landslide. Finally, in 1955, Dilworth was elected to succeed Clark as mayor.[3]

Ever since the reluctant gentlemen-revolutionists founded the Republic in the late eighteenth century, Philadel-

phians have preferred to have their radical reform movements guided by people of substance and position. While Clark and Dilworth were rejuvenating the Democratic party, other reform groups were forming in the city. Walter Phillips, a Proper Philadelphian and birthright Republican who as a student at Harvard during the Depression came all the way down from Cambridge (much against his father's will) in order to cast his vote for Franklin D. Roosevelt, organized and led the "Republicans for Clark and Dilworth."[4] At the same time, John Frederick Lewis, Jr. and his wife were instrumental in organizing the local chapter of the Americans for Democratic Action, a so-called radical group with a very responsible and politically concerned membership in Philadelphia.

John Frederick Lewis, Jr. was a wealthy Proper Philadelphia lawyer and philanthropist whose intellectual and nonconformist propensities . . . were more in the tradition of Proper Boston's greatest days when "everybody talked of reform." His grandfather, S. Weir Lewis, founded the family fortune in the China trade before the Civil War . . . and lived a few doors south of Holy Trinity Church on Rittenhouse Square. His father, John Frederick Lewis, Senior, a Philadelphia lawyer, augmented the family fortune by shrewd investments in urban real estate.

The Lewises have been leaders in the cultural life of Philadelphia for

---

[3] In this mayoralty contest it is interesting and perhaps a sign of the times, that Richardson Dilworth, one-time end on the Yale football team, and W. Thacher Longstretch, of Princeton gridiron fame, led their respective political parties.

[4] Phillips was also responsible for the founding of Philadelphia's first City Planning Commission (one of the nation's finest today). Appropriately enough, its first Chairman was Edward Hopkinson, Jr. He remained at the helm throughout Mayor Clark's Democratic administration but was replaced by Albert M. Greenfield after Richardson Dilworth became Mayor. Jared Ingersoll announced his resignation from the Commission after Greenfield's appointment as Chairman; such are the ways of social change.

two generations. John Frederick Lewis, Senior, was president of the Academy of the Fine Arts, Academy of Music, Mercantile Library, and the Historical Society of Pennsylvania. His son followed in his footsteps as president of the Academy of the Fine Arts and the Academy of Music. In accordance with his civic and cultural interests, John Frederick Lewis, Jr. limited his club memberships to the Franklin Inn and Art Alliance, in both of which he has held the office of president in recent years. The Philadelphia chapter of the Americans for Democratic Action was founded at an informal meeting in the Lewis mansion at 1916 Spruce Street, where the family has lived continuously since 1856.

On the national scene, men of means and background are following the example set by Franklin D. Roosevelt in the 1930's. In fact the Democratic party, in the tradition of Jefferson and that colorful frontier aristocrat, Andrew Jackson (who, of course, appealed to such patrician Philadelphians as Richard Rush and Charles Jared Ingersoll), has probably taken on more of an aristocratic pattern of leadership than at any other time in its long history. Such men as Adlai Stevenson of Choate School and Princeton, G. Mennen Williams of Salisbury School and Princeton, John F. Kennedy of Choate and Harvard, and both Dean Acheson and Averell Harriman of Groton and Yale are all representative of the trends.[5] Descendants of "robber barons" would hardly be sat-

isfied with the confining life of the corporation executive or a partnership in a large metropolitan law firm.

Even Proper Philadelphians are participating in this trend on the national scene. Apparently the voters of Pennsylvania, who re-elected President Eisenhower by an overwhelming majority, also had enough confidence in Proper Philadelphia's millionaire socialite, Joseph Sill Clark, to send him to Washington as their junior Senator. And he was the descendant of a long line of investment bankers who had never had the "itch for public office" in over one hundred years. Finally, of course, America's most important ambassadorial post was held recently by a Proper Philadelphian. The former American Ambassador to Moscow, ex-Philadelphian Charles E. Bohlen, a product of St. Paul's and Harvard (Porcellian), and his brother-in-law, Charles Wheeler Thayer, one of the few Proper Philadelphia graduates of West Point in modern times, are both thorough students of the Russian language and culture, having long since anticipated the present contest between this country and the Soviet Union. Perhaps gentlemen of means and secure leisure have often been leaders in new movements and ideas. After all, Thomas Jefferson, Oliver Cromwell, Franklin Roosevelt, and George Washington were country squires. Isaiah Berlin may well have a point when he writes:

There is something singularly attractive about men who retained, throughout life, the manners, the texture of being, the habits and style of a civilized and refined *milieu*. Such men exercise a peculiar kind of personal freedom which combines spontaneity with distinction. Their minds see large and generous horizons, and above all, reveal a unique intellectual gaiety of a kind that aristocratic education tends to produce. At the same time, they are intellectually on the side of everything that is new, progressive, re-

[5] A comparison of the biographies of Adlai Stevenson, Averell Harriman, and Dean Acheson as reported in Who's Who (British) and Who's Who in America reveals some interesting cultural contrasts. Hobbies are, of course, reported in the British version only. More interesting, however, is the fact that while all three report their boarding school in their British biographies, none does so in the American volume. One often observes this sort of reverse snobbism in this country where egalitarianism often is preferred to the truth.

bellious, young, untried, of that which is about to come into being, of the open sea whether or not there is land that lies beyond. To this type belong those intermediate figures, like Mirabeau, Charles James Fox, Franklin Roosevelt, who live near the frontier that divides old from new, between the *douceur de la vie* which is about to pass and the tantalising future, the dangerous new age that they themselves do much to bring into being.[6]

Perhaps America as a whole will benefit from the patrician's modern emancipation from the counting house.

One more question remains to be raised even if it cannot be answered: What is the future function of a predominantly Anglo-Saxon and Protestant upper class in an ethnically and religiously heterogeneous democracy? In many ways, this is the most important question of all. As Joseph Patrick Kennedy, Boston millionaire and American Ambassador to the Court of St. James under Roosevelt, once put it: "How long does our family have to be here before we are called Americans rather than Irish-Americans?" As has been shown throughout this volume, the American upper class has been from the beginning open to new men of talent and power and their families. By the middle of the twentieth century, however, upper-class status appears to be limited primarily to families of colonial and northern European stock and Protestant affiliations. Glancing back to the turn of the century, when a floodtide of immigrants came to these shores from southern and eastern Europe, to say nothing of the Irish Catholics who came earlier, one wonders if this American democracy has not produced somewhat of a caste situation at the upper-class level. Or are the talented and powerful descendants of these newer immigrants going to be assimilated into some future upperclass way of life and social organization?

It has been shown how parallel upper classes existed in Philadelphia in 1940. On a national scale, "café society" as well as the business executive society of rank, although perhaps not as permanent or community-rooted as the upper class, have been firmly institutionalized in recent decades as parallel social organizations. Whether this contemporary situation is a sign of a healthy social structure of leadership is a problem which needs a great deal of careful research. At any rate, the description of the wealthy and talented expense-account elite in A. C. Spectorsky's *The Exurbanites* or William H. Whyte, Jr.'s *The Organization Man* appears to suggest that large numbers of this new American elite are living in a nightmare of insecurity and conformity.[7] Nor does C. Wright Mills offer much hope; his *The Power Elite* adds up to a "higher immorality."[8]

In closing it should be said that, although a "classless society" is manifestly a contradiction in terms, this democracy surely cannot survive so long as upper-class status is still denied to those families with minority ethnic and religious affiliations. In this young nation, an ancient mansion of democracy, the stairway of social prestige has been "forever echoing with the wooden shoe going up, and the polished boot descending." When the echoes die, however, the ancient mansion will have been deserted.

---

[6] Isaiah Berlin, "A Marvelous Decade (IV)," *Encounter*, 6 (May 1956) p. 21.

[7] A. C. Spectorsky, *The Exurbanites*, Philadelphia: J. B. Lippincott, 1955. William H. Whyte, *The Organization Man*, New York: Simon and Schuster, 1956.

[8] C. Wright Mills, *The Power Elite*, New York: Oxford University Press, 1956.

# 43

# The New Middle Class

## C. WRIGHT MILLS

In the early nineteenth century, although there are no exact figures, probably four-fifths of the occupied population were self-employed enterprisers; by 1870, only about one-third, and in 1940, only about one-fifth, were still in this old middle class. Many of the remaining four-fifths of the people who now earn a living do so by working for the 2 or 3 percent of the population who now own 40 or 50 percent of the private property in the United States. Among these workers are the members of the new middle class, white-collar people on salary. For them, as for wage-workers, America has become a nation of employees for whom independent property is out of range. Labor markets, not control of property, determine their chances to receive income, exercise power, enjoy prestige, learn and use skills.

## Occupational Change

Of the three broad strata composing modern society, only the new middle class has steadily grown in proportion to the whole. Eighty years ago, there were three-quarters of a million middle-class employees; by 1940, there were over twelve and a half million. In that period the old middle class in-

### The Labor Force

|                   | 1870 | 1940 |
|-------------------|------|------|
| Old Middle Class  | 33%  | 20%  |
| New Middle Class  | 6    | 25   |
| Wage-Workers      | 61   | 55   |
| Total             | 100% | 100% |

### New Middle Class

|                       | 1870 | 1940 |
|-----------------------|------|------|
| Managers              | 14%  | 10%  |
| Salaried Professionals| 30   | 25   |
| Salespeople           | 44   | 25   |
| Office Workers        | 12   | 40   |
| Total                 | 100% | 100% |

creased 135 percent; wage-workers, 255 percent; new middle class, 1600 percent.

The employees composing the new middle class do not make up one single compact stratum. They have not emerged on a single horizontal level, but have been shuffled out simultaneously on the several levels of modern society; they now form, as it were, a new pyramid within the old pyramid of society at large, rather than a horizontal layer. The great bulk of the new middle class are of the lower middle-income brackets, but regardless of how social stature is measured, types of white-collar men and women range from almost the top to almost the bottom of modern society.

The managerial stratum, subject to minor variations during these decades, has dropped slightly, from 14 to 10 percent; the salaried professionals, displaying the same minor ups and downs, have dropped from 30 to 25 percent of the new middle class. The major shifts in over-all composition have been in the relative decline of the sales group, occurring most sharply around 1900, from 44 to 25 percent of the total new middle class; and the steady rise of the office workers, from 12 to 40 percent. Today the three largest occupational groups in the white-collar stratum are schoolteachers, salespeople in and out of stores, and

The Middle Classes

|                        | 1870  | 1940  |
|------------------------|-------|-------|
| Old Middle Class       | 85%   | 44%   |
| Farmers                | 62    | 23    |
| Businessmen            | 21    | 19    |
| Free Professionals     | 2     | 2     |
|                        |       |       |
| New Middle Class       | 15%   | 56%   |
| Managers               | 2     | 6     |
| Salaried Professionals | 4     | 14    |
| Salespeople            | 7     | 14    |
| Office Workers         | 2     | 22    |
| Total Middle Class     | 100%  | 100%  |

assorted office workers. These three form the white-collar mass.

White-collar occupations now engage well over half the members of the American middle class as a whole. Between 1870 and 1940, white-collar workers rose from 15 to 56 percent of the middle brackets, while the old middle class declined from 85 to 44 percent.

Negatively, the transformation of the middle class is a shift from property to no-property; positively, it is a shift from property to a new axis of stratification, occupation. The nature and well-being of the old middle class can best be sought in the condition of entrepreneurial property; of the new middle class, in the economics and sociology of occupations. The numerical decline of the older, independent sectors of the middle class is an incident in the centralization of property; the numerical rise of the newer salaried employees is due to the industrial mechanics by which the occupations composing the new middle class have arisen.

## Industrial Mechanics

In modern society, occupations are specific functions within a social division of labor, as well as skills sold for income on a labor market. Contemporary divisions of labor involve a hitherto unknown specialization of skill: from arranging abstract symbols, at $1000 an hour, to working a shovel, for $1000 a year. The major shifts in occupations since the Civil War have assumed this industrial trend: as a proportion of the labor force, fewer individuals manipulate *things*, more handle *people* and *symbols*.

This shift in needed skills is another way of describing the rise of the white-collar workers, for their characteristic skills involve the handling of paper and money and people. They are expert at dealing with people transiently and impersonally; they are masters of the commercial, professional, and technical relationship. The one thing they do not do is live by making things; rather, they live off the social machineries that organize and co-ordinate the people who do make things. White-collar people help turn what someone else has made into profit for still another; some of them are closer to the means of production, supervising the work of actual manufacture and recording what is done. They are the people who keep track; they man the paper routines involved in distributing what is produced. They provide technical and personal services, and they teach others the skills which they themselves practice, as well as all other skills transmitted by teaching.

As the proportion of workers needed for the extraction and production of things declines, the proportion needed for servicing, distributing, and co-ordinating rises. In 1870, over three-fourths, and in 1940, slightly less than one-half of the total employed were engaged in producing things.

|                | 1870  | 1940  |
|----------------|-------|-------|
| Producing      | 77%   | 46%   |
| Servicing      | 13    | 20    |
| Distributing   | 7     | 23    |
| Co-ordinating  | 3     | 11    |
| Total employed | 100%  | 100%  |

By 1940, the proportion of white-collar workers of those employed in industries primarily involved in the production of things was 11 percent; in service industries, 32 percent; in distribution, 44 percent; and in co-ordination, 60 percent. The white-collar industries themselves have grown, and within each industry the white-collar occupations have grown. Three trends lie back of the fact that the white-collar ranks have thus been the most rapidly growing of modern occupations: the increasing productivity of machinery used in manufacturing; the magnification of distribution; and the increasing scale of co-ordination.

The immense productivity of mass-production technique and the increased application of technologic rationality are the first open secrets of modern occupational change: fewer men turn out more things in less time. In the middle of the nineteenth century, as J. F. Dewhurst and his associates have calculated, some 17.6 billion horse-power hours were expended in American industry, only 6 percent by mechanical energy; by the middle of the twentieth century, 410.4 billion horse-power hours will be expended, 94 percent by mechanical energy. This industrial revolution seems to be permanent, seems to go on through war and boom and slump; thus 'a decline in production results in a more than proportional decline in employment; and an increase in production results in a less than proportional increase in employment.'

Technology has thus narrowed the stratum of workers needed for given volumes of output; it has also altered the types and proportions of skill needed in the production process. Know-how, once an attribute of the mass of workers, is now in the machine and the engineering elite who design it. Machines displace unskilled work-men, make craft skills unnecessary, push up front the automatic motions of the machine-operative. Workers composing the new lower class are predominantly semi-skilled: their proportion in the urban wage-worker stratum has risen from 31 percent in 1910 to 41 percent in 1940.

The manpower economies brought about by machinery and the large-scale rationalization of labor forces, so apparent in production and extraction, have not, as yet, been applied so extensively in distribution—transportation, communication, finance, and trade. Yet without an elaboration of these means of distribution, the wide-flung operations of multi-plant producers could not be integrated nor their products distributed. Therefore, the proportion of people engaged in distribution has enormously increased so that today about one-fourth of the labor force is so engaged. Distribution has expanded more than production because of the lag in technological application in this field, and because of the persistence of individual and small-scale entrepreneurial units at the same time that the market has been enlarged and the need to market has been deepened.

Behind this expansion of the distributive occupations lies the central problem of modern capitalism: to whom can the available goods be sold? As volume swells, the intensified search for markets draws more workers into the distributive occupations of trade, promotion, advertising. As far-flung and intricate markets come into being, and as the need to find and create even more markets becomes urgent, 'middle men' who move, store, finance, promote, and sell goods are knit into a vast network of enterprises and occupations.

The physical aspect of distribution involves wide and fast transportation networks; the co-ordination of marketing involves communication; the search for markets and the selling of goods involves trade, including wholesale and retail outlets as well as financial agencies for commodity and capital markets. Each of these activities engage more people, but the manual jobs among them do not increase so fast as the white-collar tasks.

Transportation, growing rapidly after the Civil War, began to decline in point of the numbers of people involved before 1930; but this decline took place among wage-workers; the proportion of white-collar workers employed in transportation continued to rise. By 1940, some 23 percent of the people in transportation were white-collar employees. As a new industrial segment of the U.S. economy, the communication industry has never been run by large numbers of free enterprisers; at the outset it needed large numbers of technical and other white-collar workers. By 1940, some 77 percent of its people were in new middle-class occupations.

Trade is now the third largest segment of the occupational structure, exceeded only by farming and manufacturing. A few years after the Civil War less than 5 out of every 100 workers were engaged in trade; by 1940 almost 12 out of every 100 workers were so employed. But, while 70 percent of those in wholesaling and retailing were free enterprisers in 1870, and less than 3 percent were white collar, by 1940, of the people engaged in retail trade 27 percent were free enterprisers; 41 percent white-collar employees.

Newer methods of merchandising such as credit financing, have resulted in an even greater percentage increase in the 'financial' than in the 'commercial' agents of distribution. Branch banking has lowered the status of many banking employees to the clerical level, and reduced the number of executive positions. By 1940, of all employees in finance and real estate 70 percent were white-collar workers of the new middle class.

The organizational reason for the expansion of the white-collar occupations is the rise of big business and big government, and the consequent trend of modern social structure, the steady growth of bureaucracy. In every branch of the economy, as firms merge and corporations become dominant, free entrepreneurs become employees, and the calculations of accountant, statistician, bookkeeper, and clerk in these corporations replace the free 'movement of prices' as the co-ordinating agent of the economic system. The rise of thousands of big and little bureaucracies and the elaborate specialization of the system as a whole create the need for many men and women to plan, co-ordinate, and administer new routines for others. In moving from smaller to larger and more elaborate units of economic activity, increased proportions of employees are drawn into co-ordinating and managing. Managerial and professional employees and office workers of varied sorts—floor-walkers, foremen, office managers—are needed; people to whom subordinates report, and who in turn report to superiors, are links in chains of power and obedience, co-ordinating and supervising other occupational experiences, functions, and skills. And all over the economy, the proportion of clerks of all sorts has increased: from 1 to 2 percent in 1870 to 10 or 11 percent of all gainful workers in 1940.

As the worlds of business undergo these changes, the increased tasks of government on all fronts draw still more people into occupations that regulate and service property and men. In response to the largeness and predatory complications of business, the crises of slump, the nationalization of the rural economy and small-town markets, the flood of immigrants, the urgencies of war and the march of technology disrupting social life, government increases its co-ordinating and regulating tasks. Public regulations, social services, and business taxes require more people to make mass records and to integrate people, firms, and goods, both within government and in the various segments of business and private life. All branches of government have grown, although the most startling increases are found in the executive branch of the Federal Government, where the needs for co-ordinating the economy have been most prevalent.

As marketable activities, occupations change (1) with shifts in the skills required, as technology and rationalization are unevenly applied across the economy; (2) with the enlargement and intensification of marketing operations in both the commodity and capital markets; and (3) with shifts in the organization of the division of work, as expanded organizations require co-ordination, management, and recording. The mechanics involved within and between these three trends have led to the numerical expansion of white-collar employees.

There are other less obvious ways in which the occupational structure is shaped: high agricultural tariffs, for example, delay the decline of farming as an occupation; were Argentine beef allowed to enter duty-free, the number of meat producers here might diminish. City ordinances and zoning laws abolish peddlers and affect the types of construction workers that prevail. Most states have bureaus of standards which limit entrance into professions and semi-professions; at the same time members of these occupations form associations in the attempt to control entrance into 'their' market. More successful than most trade unions, such professional associations as the American Medical Association have managed for several decades to level off the proportion of physicians and surgeons. Every phase of the slump-war-boom cycle influences the numerical importance of various oc-

cupations; for instance, the movement back and forth between 'construction worker' and small 'contractor' is geared to slumps and booms in building.

The pressures from these loosely organized parts of the occupational world draw conscious managerial agencies into the picture. The effects of attempts to manage occupational change, directly and indirectly, are not yet great, except of course during wars, when government freezes men in their jobs or offers incentives and compulsions to remain in old occupations or shift to new ones. Yet increasingly the class levels and occupational composition of the nation are managed; the occupational structure of the United States is being slowly reshaped as a gigantic corporate group. It is subject not only to the pulling of autonomous markets and the pushing of technology but to an 'allocation of personnel' from central points of control. Occupational change thus becomes more conscious, at least to those who are coming to be in charge of it.

## White-Collar Pyramids

Occupations, in terms of which we circumscribe the new middle class, involve several ways of ranking people. As specific activities, they entail various types and levels of *skill*, and their exercise fulfils certain *functions* within an industrial division of labor. These are the skills and functions we have been examining statistically. As sources of income, occupations are connected with *class* position; and since they normally carry an expected quota of prestige, on and off the job, they are relevant to *status* position. They also involve certain degrees of *power* over other people, directly in terms of the job, and indirectly in other social areas. Occupations are thus tied to class, status, and power as well as to skill and function; to understand the occupations composing the new middle class, we must consider them in terms of each of these dimensions.

'Class situation' in its simplest objective sense has to do with the amount and source of income. Today, occupation rather than property is the source of income for most of those who receive any direct income: the possibilities of selling their services in the labor market, rather than of profitably buying and selling their property and its yields, now determine the life-chances of most of the middle class. All things money can buy and many that men dream about are theirs by virtue of occupational income. In new middle-class occupations men work for someone else on someone else's property. This is the clue to many differences between the old and new middle classes, as well as to the contrast between the older world of the small propertied entrepreneur and the occupational structure of the new society. If the old middle class once fought big property structures in the name of small, free properties, the new middle class, like the wage-workers in latter-day capitalism, has been, from the beginning, dependent upon large properties for job security.

Wage-workers in the factory and on the farm are on the propertyless bottom of the occupational structure, depending upon the equipment owned by others, earning wages for the time they spend at work. In terms of property, the white-collar people are *not* 'in between Capital and Labor'; they are in exactly the same property-class position as the wage-workers. They have no direct financial tie to the means of production, no prime claim upon the proceeds from property. Like factory workers— and day laborers, for that matter—they work for those who do own such means of livelihood.

Yet if bookkeepers and coal miners, insurance agents and farm laborers, doctors in a clinic and crane operators in an open pit have this condition in common, certainly their class situations are not the same. To understand their class positions, we must go beyond the common fact of source of income and consider as well the amount of income.

In 1890, the average income of white-collar occupational groups was about double that of wage-workers. Before World War I, salaries were not so adversely affected by slumps as wages were but, on the contrary, they rather steadily advanced. Since World War I, however, salaries have been reacting to turns in the economic cycles more and more like wages, although still to a lesser extent. If wars help wages more because of the greater flexibility of wages, slumps help salaries because of their greater inflexibility. Yet after each war era, salaries have never regained their previous advantage over wages. Each phase of the cycle, as well as the progressive rise of all income groups, has resulted in a narrowing of the income gap between wage-workers and white-collar employees.

In the middle 'thirties the three urban strata, entrepreneurs, white-collar, and wage-workers, formed a distinct scale with respect to median family income: the white-collar employees had a median income of $1,896; the entrepreneurs, $1,464; the urban wage-workers, $1,175. Although the median income of white-collar workers was higher than that of the entrepreneurs, large proportions of the entrepreneurs received both high-level and low-level incomes. The distribution of their income was spread more than that of the white collar.

The wartime boom in incomes, in fact, spread the incomes of all occupational groups, but not evenly. The spread occurred mainly among urban entrepreneurs. As an income level, the old middle class in the city is becoming less an evenly graded income group, and more a collection of different strata, with a large proportion of lumpenbourgeoisie who receive very low incomes, and a small, prosperous bourgeoisie with very high incomes.

In the late 'forties (1948, median family income) the income of all white-collar workers was $4000, that of all urban wage-workers, $3300. These averages, however, should not obscure the overlap of specific groups within each stratum: the lower white-collar people—sales-employees and office workers—earned almost the same as skilled workers and foremen,[1] but more than semi-skilled urban wage-workers.

In terms of property, white-collar people are in the same position as wage-workers; in terms of occupational income, they are 'somewhere in the middle.' Once they were considerably above the wage-workers; they have become less so; in the middle of the century they still have an edge but the over-all rise in incomes is making the new middle class a more homogeneous income group.

As with income, so with prestige: white-collar groups are differentiated socially, perhaps more decisively than wage-workers and entrepreneurs. Wage earners certainly do form an income pyramid and a prestige gradation, as do entrepreneurs and rentiers; but the new middle class, in terms of income and prestige, is a superimposed pyramid, reaching from almost the bottom of the first to almost the top of the second.

People in white-collar occupations claim higher prestige than wage-workers, and, as a general rule, can cash in their claims with wage-workers as well as with the anonymous public. This fact has been seized upon, with much justification, as the defining characteristic of the white-collar strata, and although

[1] It is impossible to isolate the salaried foremen from the skilled urban wage-workers in these figures. If we could do so, the income of lower white-collar workers would be closer to that of semi-skilled workers.

there are definite indications in the United States of a decline in their prestige, still, on a nation-wide basis, the majority of even the lower white-collar employees—office workers and salespeople—enjoy a middling prestige.

The historic bases of the white-collar employees' prestige, apart from superior income, have included the similarity of their place and type of work to those of the old middle-classes' which has permitted them to borrow prestige. As their relations with entrepreneur and with esteemed customer have become more impersonal, they have borrowed prestige from the firm itself. The stylization of their appearance, in particular the fact that most white-collar jobs have permitted the wearing of street clothes on the job, has also figured in their prestige claims, as have the skills required in most white-collar jobs, and in many of them the variety of operations performed and the degree of autonomy exercised in deciding work procedures. Furthermore, the time taken to learn these skills and the way in which they have been acquired by formal education and by close contact with the higher-ups in charge has been important. White-collar employees have monopolized high school education—even in 1940 they had completed 12 grades to the 8 grades for wage-workers and entrepreneurs. They have also enjoyed status by descent: in terms of race, Negro white-collar employees exist only in isolated instances —and, more importantly, in terms of nativity, in 1930 only about 9 percent of white-collar workers, but 16 percent of free enterprisers and 21 percent of wage-workers, were foreign born. Finally, as an underlying fact, the limited size of the white-collar group, compared to wage-workers, has led to successful claims to greater prestige.

The power position of groups and of individuals typically depends upon factors of class, status, and occupation, often in intricate interrelation. Given occupations involve specific powers over other people in the actual course of work; but also outside the job area, by virtue of their relations to institutions of property as well as the typical income they afford, occupations lend power. Some white-collar occupations require the direct exercise of supervision over other white-collar and wage-workers, and many more are closely attached to this managerial cadre. White-collar employees are the assistants of authority; the power they exercise is a derived power, but they do exercise it.

Moreover, within the white-collar pyramids there is a characteristic pattern of authority involving age and sex. The white-collar ranks contain a good many women: some 41 percent of all white-collar employees, as compared with 10 percent of free enterprisers, and 21 percent of wage-workers, are women.[2] As with sex, so with age: free enterprisers average (median) about 45 years of age, white-collar and wage-workers, about 34; but among free enterprisers and wage-workers, men are about 2 or 3 years older than women; among white-collar workers, there is a 6- or 7-year difference. In the white-collar pyramids, authority is roughly graded by age and sex: younger women tend to be subordinated to older men.

The occupational groups forming the white-collar pyramids, different as they may be from one another, have certain common characteristics, which are central to the character of the new middle class as a general pyramid overlapping the entrepreneurs and wage-workers. White-collar people cannot be ade-

quately defined along any one possible dimension of stratification—skill, function, class, status, or power. They are generally in the middle ranges on each of these dimensions and on every descriptive attribute. Their position is more definable in terms of their relative differences from other strata than in any absolute terms.

On all points of definition, it must be remembered that white-collar people are not one compact horizontal stratum. They do not fulfil one central, positive *function* that can define them, although in general their functions are similar to those of the old middle class. They deal with symbols and with other people, co-ordinating, recording, and distributing; but they fulfil these functions as dependent employees, and the skills they thus employ are sometimes similar in form and required mentality to those of many wage-workers.

In terms of property, they are equal to wage-workers and different from the old middle class. Originating as propertyless dependents, they have no serious expectations of propertied independence. In terms of income, their class position is, on the average, somewhat higher than that of wage-workers. The overlap is large and the trend has been definitely toward less difference, but even today the differences are significant.

Perhaps of more psychological importance is the fact that white-collar groups have successfully claimed more prestige than wage-workers and still generally continue to do so. The bases of their prestige may not be solid today, and certainly they show no signs of being permanent; but, however vague and fragile, they continue to mark off white-collar people from wage-workers.

Members of white-collar occupations exercise a derived authority in the course of their work; moreover, compared to older hierarchies, the white-collar pyramids are youthful and feminine bureauc-

[2] According to our calculations, the proportions of women, 1940, in these groups are: farmers, 2.9%; businessmen, 20%; free professionals, 5.9%; managers, 7.1%; salaried professionals, 51.7%; salespeople, 27.5%; office workers, 51%; skilled workers, 3.2%; semi-skilled and unskilled, 29.8%; rural workers, 9.1%.

racies, within which youth, education, and American birth are emphasized at the wide base, where millions of office workers most clearly typify these differences between the new middle class and other occupational groups. White-collar masses, in turn, are managed by people who are more like the old middle class, having many of the social characteristics, if not the independence, of free enterprisers.

# 44

# The Industrial Working Class

### GERHARD LENSKI

In traditional agrarian societies the great majority of the population was concentrated in the peasant class. Though a remnant of the peasant or farm class still survives in more or less modified form in every industrial society, its place as the largest occupational class was taken long ago by the working class, a descendant of the old artisan class. Actually, the members of this new class are not, for the most part, descendants of the artisans of an earlier era. Rather, most of them are the displaced descendants of peasants and farmers forced off the land both by excess fertility and by the mechanization of agriculture.

Though the working class is the largest occupational class in the more advanced industrial societies, it has seldom had the numerical preponderance the peasant class once had. With the single exception of Britain, the working class has probably never constituted more than 60 per cent of the total male labor force, and usually it has totaled less than 50 per cent. So far, the relative size of the working class has been quite variable, standing, apparently, in a curvilinear relationship to the degree of industrialization in a society. In the earlier stages of industrialization, the proportion of workers in the labor force steadily rises as the proportion of farmers and farm laborers declines. Eventually, when the farm population has been reduced to a small minority and migration from the rural areas has been reduced to a trickle, a turning point is reached, and the working class, too, begins to decline, at least in relative terms.

Census data indicate that the proportion of manual workers in the *urban* part of the population is already declining in many industrial societies. In the United States, for example, the percentage of males in manual occupations in the urban labor force dropped from 70 per cent in 1870 to 60 per cent in 1960.[1] A recent nationwide study of mobility in Sweden revealed that only 61 per cent of the males in the urban labor force were in manual occupations, as compared with 73 per cent of the pre-

[1] Calculated from *Historical Statistics*, p. 74, and *1960 Census of Population*, vol. I, part 1.

vious generation.[2] The Hungarian census of 1949 indicated a similar decline between the last generation and the present; in the present generation only 72 per cent of males in the urban labor force were in manual occupations compared with 82 per cent in the previous generation.[3] Comparable trends can be observed in data from other countries, including France, Japan, Norway, and West Germany.[4]

The modern working class, like the peasantry before it, contains persons in varying circumstances. At one extreme are a handful of persons who earn wages higher than the median in the managerial or professional classes; at the other extreme are some who are unable to earn enough to support themselves and depend on welfare payments to supplement their earnings. Yet despite these differences, there is, as in the case of the peasantry, one attribute which makes it possible to treat them all as members of a single class in the occupational class system: *the resource on which each depends is a job involving a limited range of manual skills that could be performed by most other members of society after a relatively short period of training.*

As a consequence, members of the working class are always in a poor competitive position relative to the other classes we have examined. This has been especially true when they have sought to compete on an individual basis under anything approaching free

[2] These figures are calculated from Gosta Carlsson, *Social Mobility and Class Structure* (Lund: Gleerup, 1958), table 6.1. These figures might be distorted somewhat by differential fertility, but the effect of this would be to *reduce* (not increase) the difference between the two generations, since working class families were traditionally larger than middle class. The same applies to the Hungarian figures cited below.
[3] These figures are calculated from data reported in S. M. Miller, p. 72.
[4] Calculated from data assembled by Miller, *ibid.*

market conditions, because of the traditional oversupply of manual labor. Since the number of persons seeking these jobs normally exceeds the number of jobs available (or has in the past), the buyers of labor are usually in a position to hire at, or near, the subsistence level—*at least so long as truly free market conditions prevail.*

As a matter of historical fact, the situation of most members of the working class has not been nearly so grim as this, especially in the more advanced industrial societies. Other factors have intervened to improve the situation for the majority. To begin with, in the early stages of industrialization it often took highly skilled artisans a number of years to master their trade (though there is reason to think the apprenticeship period could usually have been shortened considerably if speed of training had been a major objective). This introduced a degree of inelasticity into the supply factor in the market situation. Those who wished to employ highly skilled laborers knew that they could not find many replacements on short notice. Thus, though the supply of craftsmen in a given field might potentially be almost unlimited, at any given time it was severely limited. This gave the members of such crafts a bargaining power which enabled them to demand and obtain wages above the subsistence level. The extent to which this was possible varied according to the ease and speed with which replacements could be trained.

Since the beginning of the Industrial Revolution, a host of new machines have been created, many of which can perform intricate tasks which men once spent months or years mastering. What is more, they perform them more rapidly and efficiently. While it is difficult to find a precise measure of the trend, rigidities in the labor market due to skill level alone are apparently declining and an ever-increasing percentage of manual trades require a shorter period of time for mastery by the average worker. Hence, while in the past the factor of skill provided some measure of protection for a considerable number of workingmen, its influence is declining and may eventually almost disappear.[5]

A second factor which has modified the situation is *union organization.* Though the union movement dates from the eighteenth century, its chief successes have been in the last two generations.[6] By acting collectively in negotiations with employers on wages, hours, and working conditions, workers have managed to gain a considerable measure of control over the supply of labor. When well organized, they have been able to create a situation in which no labor is available below a certain price. To accomplish this, they have usually had to prevent the use of strike-breakers recruited from the ranks of the unemployed. In earlier times this was accomplished by direct (often violent) action by the union itself; more recently this has been accomplished by political action.

There are, of course, limits beyond which unions cannot go in their efforts. Above all, they cannot drive the price of labor so high that their employer or their industry loses its competitive position. To do so would be to destroy the goose that lays the golden eggs. To some extent this is what the United Mine Workers seem to have done to the coal industry after World War II: by driving the cost of labor so high in the mining industry they at least hastened the substitution of oil for coal. In advanced industrial nations, the opportunities for substituting new materials for traditional ones are increasing all the time. The case of the coal industry illustrates another limit on collective bargaining and union activity. As wages in an industry rise, employers are provided with increased incentive to replace men with machines, thus reducing the number of workers who benefit from union activity.

Perhaps the chief effect of union activity has been to create a major cleavage within the working class, dividing workers who are organized into unions from those who are not. For the former, union membership is a valuable resource which raises their wages considerably above the subsistence level, improves their working conditions, and provides them with a measure of job security. For the rest, union membership is of little value except by indirect means.[7]

A third factor which, in the long run,

[5] See, for example, Gerhard Bry, *Wages in Germany, 1871–1945* (Princeton, N.J.: Princeton University Press, 1960), pp. 283–286, who reports declining wake differentials among manual workers in Germany, Britain, and the United States, and attributes this *in part* to "mass production techniques with an accompanying breakdown of skilled operations into simpler jobs." However, as he makes clear, other factors are also responsible. See also J. Frederic Dewhurst and Associates, *Europe's Needs and Resources* (New York: Twentieth Century Fund, 1961), appendix 3–5, which reports declining wage differentials between skilled and unskilled workers for eleven countries in Europe.
[6] On the early unions, see, for example, G. D. H. Cole, *The Common People, 1746–1946* (London: Methuen, 1956, first published 1938), chap. 14, or Carroll Daugherty, *Labor Problems in American Industry,* 5th ed. (Boston: Houghton Mifflin, 1941), pp. 318–324.

[7] There is evidence which indicates that in industries or communities in which a good part of the working class is organized, the employers of nonunion labor strive to keep their wages reasonably competitive to reduce the dangers of unionization of their employees. Also, to the extent that unions enter politics and secure minimum wage laws and the like, nonunion workers benefit. On the other hand, the practice of the union shop and closed shop prevents nonunion workers from competing for jobs for which they may even have superior qualifications.

has proven of greater importance than either skill level or union organization is *political organization*. So long as the machinery of government remained firmly in the hands of the propertied class and its allies, the very existence of labor unions remained in jeopardy. For example, the Combination Acts of 1799 and 1800 made union organization extremely dangerous; and, as recently as the 1930s, the property elite in Middletown (and many other American communities) used the machinery of local government to combat the unions.[8]

In most of the more advanced industrial nations, workers are now organized into Socialist, Labor, or Communist Parties, which either share in the governmental process or substantially influence it. In the United States there is no class-based party of this type, but the Democratic Party works with the labor unions and the working class. In Canada, even this is lacking: there the working-class vote is divided among the parties in much the same proportions as the vote of other classes.[9] In Communist countries, the Communist Party rules in the name of the working class, but as we have noted, it is no longer a workingmen's party in the same sense that the Socialist, Labor, and Communist Parties are in democratic nations.

Where the usual pattern prevails, workingmen's parties seek to restrict the free play of market forces, and to reduce their importance in the determination of wages. This is accomplished by various means. One of the first steps is often to curtail the supply of labor by legislative means, especially by limiting the employment of children. Later,

efforts are made to establish the legal right of workingmen to organize and bargain collectively, a principal which introduces monopsonistic or oligopsonistic elements into the market situation. Still later, the party usually tries to establish a legal minimum for wages above the subsistence level, thus reducing the range within which employers can compete for labor. Another major feature of the program of workers' parties is the establishment of rights to goods and services based on citizenship alone (see pages 428 to 430). Other policies have the same intent: to minimize the influence of the basic market factors of supply and demand in the determination of individual income. To put the matter in slightly different terms, one might say that *the efforts of workingmen's parties are aimed largely at making the distribution of goods and services subject to political, rather than economic, determination.*

Finally, the situation of the working class has been modified and improved by most of those factors which have contributed to the decline in political and economic inequality. In other words, the working class has benefited by the rise and spread of the new democratic-egalitarian ideology, the rising level of productivity, the reduction in the birthrate, and the increased involvement of the total population in warfare. All have helped raise the income for most workingmen well above the subsistence level.

It is difficult to say exactly what a bare subsistence wage would be in most industrial societies today, and therefore difficult to determine how far removed the average workingman is from it. However, there are studies of the trends in *real* wages, i.e., after adjustments for changes in the cost of living from year to year, in various nations, and they shed considerable light on the problem. For example, one recent study showed that in the period from 1871 to 1958, real

[8] On the Combination Acts, see G. D. H. Cole and R. W. Postgate, *The British Common People, 1746–1938* (New York: Knopf, 1939), chap. 14; on Middletown (Muncie, Indiana), see Lynd and Lynd, chap. 2.

[9] Robert Alford, *Party and Society: The Anglo-American Democracies* (Chicago: Rand McNally, 1963), chap. 9.

weekly wages in Germany more than doubled.[10] This same study indicated that real British wage rates nearly doubled between 1871 and 1944, while American wages rose more than fourfold. Since then still further increases have been recorded in both of the latter.[11] These gains were all made despite the substantial shortening of the work week, which in 1871 averaged about seventy-two hours in Germany and about sixty in the United States and Britain.[12] Data from Norway indicate a nearly twofold increase in real wages in the brief period from 1920 to 1955,[13] while figures from Italy show a 13.6 per cent increase in the single decade 1948–1959.[14] If we assume that the average wage was already above the subsistence level in the first period of each of these time series, then it follows that the average income of members of the working class is now considerably above the subsistence level in all of the more advanced industrial societies.

The wages of industrial workers have risen not only in absolute terms in the modern era, but also relative to the income of the more privileged classes as well. This is indicated, for example, by income data from the United States for the period from 1939 to 1959, which show the following rates of increase in money (not real) wages for male workers: [15]

*Nonmanual workers:*
| | |
|---|---|
| Professional and kindred workers | 366% |
| Proprietors, managers, and officials | 312% |
| Clerical and kindred workers | 337% |
| Salesmen | 391% |

*Manual workers:*
| | |
|---|---|
| Craftsmen, foremen, and kindred | 400% |
| Operatives | 427% |
| Laborers (nonfarm) | 438% |
| Service workers | 397% |

Data from France for the period from 1910 to 1954 show the same pattern, only more pronounced: whereas the money income of various managerial and professional occupations increased 100- to 170-fold in this period, for various occupations in the working class it increased 200- to 350-fold.[16] In Communist countries also, income differentials between the working and nonmanual classes have been reduced compared with the pre-Communist era. The gains of the working class have come not only from increased wages, however, but also, in large measure, from the changing nature and growing importance of the resource of citizenship.

These political and economic advances have combined with certain other developments to produce one other significant change in the social situation of the working classes. In the earlier stages of industrialization, a great cultural chasm separated manual workers from the middle classes. This

[10] Bry, calculated from tables A-50 and A-54.
[11] In the United States real wages rose 10 per cent from 1944 to 1959, which means a 4.4-fold increase from 1871 to 1959. For the period from 1944 to 1959 see Harold Vatter, *The U.S. Economy in the 1950's: An Economic History* (New York: Norton, 1963), table 8–2.
[12] *Ibid.*, pp. 274–275.
[13] Calculated from Walter Galenson, *Labor in Norway* (Cambridge, Mass.: Harvard University Press, 1949), table 3 for the period from 1920 to 1938, and Mark Leiserson, *Wages and Economic Control in Norway, 1945–1957* (Cambridge, Mass.: Harvard University Press, 1959), table 4 for the years 1938 to 1955.
[14] Daniel Horowitz, *The Italian Labor Movement* (Cambridge, Mass.: Harvard University Press, 1963), pp. 275–276.

[15] These percentages are based on 1939 figures from *Historical Statistics*, p. 168, and 1959 figures from the *U.S. Census of Population, 1960*, vol. I, part 1, table 208.
[16] Jean Fourastié, *The Causes of Wealth*, translated by Theodore Caplow (New York: Free Press, 1960, first published 1951), table 3.

is now disappearing, or at least being substantially reduced. In part, this change stems from improvements in the economic situation of workers and from the mass production of consumer goods which makes it possible for persons of limited incomes to purchase commodities which are not nearly so distinguishable from their more expensive counterparts as comparable goods of a half century or century ago. In addition, the political advances of the working class have greatly reduced antagonism toward existing political institutions, bringing the average worker's thinking more into line with that of the middle class. Most important, perhaps, the rise of free public schools and the mass media have stimulated a trend toward cultural convergence among the classes. The net effect of all these developments has been the adoption of many elements of middle class culture by the working class, and probably, as a result, some reduction in the traditional hostility of workers toward the existing social order.

# 45

# The Working Class Subculture: A New View

## S. M. MILLER AND FRANK RIESSMAN

### Introduction

A decade and a half ago the working class was depicted by Allison Davis and Robert J. Havighurst [1] as permissive and indulgent toward their children and free of the emotional strain of impulse-inhibition which characterized the middle class in the United States. Indeed, it was felt by many that the middle class had much to envy and imitate in the working class.[2] This romantic view of the working class has faded. It is now asserted that the working class (usually termed the "lower class") is incapable of deferring gratification [3] and consequently unable to make major strides in improving their conditions. Frequently accompanying this view is the belief that this lower class is "immoral," "uncivilized," "promiscuous," "lazy," "obscene," "dirty," and "loud." With the rising plane and standard of living of workers has come the argument that workers are middle class in their outlook and desires; the difficulties in attaining full middle-class status lead to juvenile delinquency on the part of those youth who fall back into the working and lower classes and to authoritarianism on the part of those who rise into the middle class. Recently, a further vigorous blow has felled any no-

Reprinted from *Social Problems* 9 (Summer, 1961), pp. 86–97, with permission of the publisher.
[1] Allison Davis and Robert J. Havighurst, "Social Class and Color Differences in Child Rearing," *American Sociological Review*, 11 (December, 1946), pp. 698–710.
[2] Cf. David Riesman in his introduction to Ely Chinoy's *American Workers and Their Dreams* (New York: Doubleday & Company, 1955).
[3] Louis Schneider and Sverre Lysgaard, "The Deferred Gratification Pattern: A Preliminary Study," *American Sociological Review*, 18 (April, 1953), pp. 142–9.

tions of desirable characteristics of workers: their economic liberalism is not paralleled by political liberalism for workers are said to be more authoritarian in outlook than are members of the middle class. The free, spontaneous worker is now seen as an aggressive, authoritarian, yet fettered person. . . .

In this paper, we can only present a few elements of what we believe is a more realistic picture of workers. This analysis is severely compressed and truncated in this presentation and it might be helpful therefore to indicate at the outset an important element of our general orientation. Our stress is much more on cognitive and structural factors than on the more commonly cited affectual and motivational ones. The nature of the conditions of working-class lives (jobs, opportunities, family structure) affects behavior more than has been frequently realized; similarly, modes of understanding the environment can be more important than deepseated personality factors in behavioral patterns. (For example, workers' low estimates of opportunities and high expectations of risk and loss may be more crucial in the unwillingness to undertake certain long-term actions than personality inadequacies involved in a presumed inability to defer gratification.) This is not to argue that motivational-psychological-affectual variables are unimportant but that they have been overstressed while cognitive and structural variables have been underemphasized. The recognition of the importance of the internal life of man has sometimes overshadowed the significance of the more manifest aspects of his existence.

Our definition of working class is simple: regular members of the non-agricultural labor force in manual occupations. Thus, we exclude the "lower class," irregular working people, although the analysis has some relevance to the lower class as will be mentioned

below. One of the greatest sources of difficulties in understanding non-upper and non-middle class behavior is that social scientists have frequently used the omnibus category of "lower class" to encompass the stable, and frequently mobile, fairly high income skilled workers, the semi-skilled factory worker, the worker in varied service trades, the unskilled worker and the irregular worker. This collection is probably more a congeries of fairly disparate groups than a category with similar life chances and circumstances. It is especially important to distinguish the segment which has irregular employment (and "voluntary" withdrawals from the labor force), unskilled jobs in service occupations (and is largely Negro and Puerto Rican now) from the other groupings, which are larger and have more of a commonness to them.

This latter group of regular workmen we call "working class" despite the reluctance of many social scientists today to use this historic term; the opprobrious term "lower class" might be applied to the irregular segment although it would probably be better all around if a less invidious term (perhaps "the unskilled") were employed.

The reluctance to make the distinction between "working class" and "lower class," despite useful discussions by Kahl[4] and others, not only is a topic worthy of independent study, but leads to error. For example, Hollingshead and Redlich in their important study have been interpreted as finding that the lower the class, the higher the rate of mental illness. Close examination of their data reveals, however, that the working class, Class IV, is closer to the upper and middle classes, Classes I, II and III, than to the lower class, Class V. Classes I through IV are similar, while Class V is quite dissimilar from all the

[4] Joseph A. Kahl, The American Class Structure (New York: Rinehart and Company, 1959), pp. 205 ff.

other classes, including the working class.[5]

Within the working class, we are primarily interested in the *stable* working-class subculture. We believe there is considerable variation within the working class, but the differences probably are variations upon the theme of the stable working-class pattern. While we think in terms of working-class subcultures, and, to some extent, lower-class subcultures, a key to understanding them, we believe, is likely to be the *stable* working-class subculture.

Our analysis is aimed at developing *themes* in working-class life. Thus, we are interpreting the *meaning* of findings rather than reporting new findings. We have utilized the published materials commonly employed plus our own interviews and observations of working-class people. . . .

## Basic Themes

Before discussing a few of the themes which we think are basic in working-class life, we present a brief overall picture of what we believe are the essential characteristics of the stable American worker today.

He is traditional, "old fashioned," somewhat religious, and patriarchal. The worker likes discipline, structure, order, organization and directive, definite (strong) leadership, although he does not see such strong leadership in opposition to human, warm, informal, personal qualities. Despite the inadequacy of his education, he is able to build abstractions, but he does so in a slow, physical fashion.[6] He reads ineffectively, is poorly

informed in many areas, and is often quite suggestible, although interestingly enough he is frequently suspicious of "talk" and "new fangled ideas."

He is family centered; most of his relationships take place around the large extended, fairly cooperative family. Cooperation and mutual aid are among his most important characteristics. While desiring a good standard of living, he is not attracted to the middle-class style of life with its accompanying concern for status and prestige. He is not class conscious although aware of class differences. While he is somewhat radical on certain economic issues, he is quite illiberal on numerous matters, particularly civil liberties and foreign policy. The outstanding weakness of the worker is lack of education. Strongly desiring education for his children, he shows considerable concern about their school work, although he feels estranged and alienated from the teacher and the school, as he similarly feels alienated from many institutions in our society.[7] This alienation is expressed in a ready willingness to believe in the corruptness of leaders and a general negative feeling toward "big shots."

He is stubborn in his ways, concerned with strength and ruggedness, interested in mechanics, materialistic, superstitious, holds an "eye for an eye" psychology, and is largely uninterested in politics.

*Stability and Security.* We suspect that one of the central determinants in working-class life is the striving for stability and security. External and internal factors promote instability and insecurity. Chief among the external factors is unemployment and layoff. Prosperity has of course barred the anguish of the prolonged depression of the 1930's, but the danger of occasional layoffs of some duration are not remote during the usually shaky

[5] For the original report, see A. B. Hollingshead and Frederick C. Redlich, *Social Class and Mental Illness* (New York: John Wiley and Sons, 1958). The point above is taken from S. M. Miller and Elliot G. Mishler, "Social Class, Mental Illness, and American Psychiatry," *Milbank Memorial Fund Quarterly,* XXXVII (April, 1959), pp. 174–99.
[6] For a review of the relevant literature, see Frank Riessman, *Education and the Culturally Deprived Child* (New York: Harper and Brothers, 1961).

[7] Riessman, *Education and the Culturally Deprived Child,* has a discussion of some of the relevant literature.

prosperity conditions which are inter-larded with episodes of recession, plant relocation, industry decline and strikes.[8]

Chief among the internal factors promoting instability are family discord, including divorce and desertion, inter-generational conflict, and the desire for excitement.

Coping with the instability threats becomes a dominant activity within the working-class family. Many practices, such as mutual aid and cooperation, extended family perspectives, are important as adjustive mechanisms. "Getting by" rather than "getting ahead" in the middle-class self-realization and advancement sense is likely to be dominant. For example, the limited desire to become foremen is partly a result of the economic insecurity resulting from the loss of job seniority in case of a layoff.[9]

Part of the ambivalence toward obtaining a college education reflects the same emphasis on security. Even a highly talented working-class youth is not sure what he can do with a college diploma, and he may fear the disruption of his familial, community and peer group security.[10]

The poll data indicating the unwillingness of workers to take economic risks and their greater concern for jobs with security, is part of the same pattern of a striving for stability.

*Traditionalism.* The American working class is primarily a migrant group; not only have people come from European farms and rural settlements to American factories but they also have migrated from America's rural life to the industrial scene.[11] Traditional practices, once thought to be infrequent in urbanized, industrialized, nuclear-oriented families, are very strong in working-class families. The pattern is patriarchal, extended (with many relevant cousins, grandparents, and aunts and uncles) and delineated by sharply separated sex roles. The family is not child-centered (or child-dominant or dominating), but parent-centered and controlled. Traditional values of automatic obedience by children are expected to be the norm even if not always observed in practice.

One probable consequence of this is that workers seem to be more authoritarian than they probably are. For while on the F-scale type of test, they tend to be "conventional," a characteristic of the authoritarian according to Adorno et al., it is doubtful, . . . that this conventionalism means the same in both the middle and working class.

The worker also has a traditional attitude toward discipline which again may be confused with authoritarianism. All the child-rearing data indicate that workers utilize physical punishment as a basic discipline technique. In the eyes of the worker punishment discourages people from wrong-doing whether the punishment is inflicted upon them or upon others who serve as "examples." There is also a "rightness" about punishment for a misdeed, for punishment is the other side of responsibility for one's actions. Thus, for example, acceptance of the death penalty may not be the result of a sado-masochistic character structure but the product of a belief in the efficacy of punishment in deterring others from

[8] Charles H. Hession, S. M. Miller and Curwen Stoddart, *The Dynamics of the American Economy* (New York: Alfred A. Knopf, 1956), Chapter 11.

[9] Ely Chinoy, *op. cit.*, and Charles R. Walker, *Steeltown* (New York: Harper and Brothers, 1950), have data showing the considerable reluctance of workers to become foremen.

[10] The initial attraction of many working-class youth to engineering is partly due to the apparently concrete and clear nature of the work and the presumed definiteness of the education for a particular type of job. Motivating working-class youth to go to college may require an expansion and sharpening of working-class children's interpretation of the job market.

[11] Lloyd Reynolds, *Labor Economics and Labor Relations* (Englewood Cliffs, N.J.: Prentice-Hall, Inc., 1949), pp. 7–23.

misdeeds and in the value of attaching responsibility to people's actions. Workers consequently do not easily accept the notion that an individual is not responsible for his crimes because of his emotional state at the time of their occurrence.

*Intensity.* We believe that one of the most neglected themes in working-class life and one of the most difficult to understand and interpret is that of intensity. This intensity is expressed in a number of different ways. It is found in the areas in which workers have belief and emotional involvement. While there are numerous areas about which workers are confused, and lacking in opinion (e.g., the high percentage of "no answer" and "don't know" on public opinion polls), there are important spheres in which they have definite convictions, and indeed, are highly stubborn. Their beliefs about religion, morality, superstition, diet, punishment, custom, traditional education, the role of women, intellectuals, are illustrative here. Many of these attitudes are related to their traditional orientation and they are held unquestioningly in the usual traditional manner. They are not readily open to reason and they are not flexible opinions.

Other possible sources of this intensity may be their physical (less symbolic) relation to life,[12] their person centeredness (to be discussed below), and their lack of education.

*Person-Centered.* Threaded through much of working-class life is a person-centered theme. On one level this theme has an informal, human quality, of easy, comfortable relationship to people where the affectionate bite of humor is appreciated. The factory "horse-play," the

ritualistic kidding, is part of this although by no means all of it. It is an expressive component of life.

At another level, it is the importance of personal qualities. One learns more from people than from books, it is said. At a political level, the candidate as a decent, human person is more important than the platform.

In the bureaucratic situation, the worker still tends to think of himself as relating to people, not to roles and invisible organizational structure. This orientation is an aspect of particularism, the reaction to persons and situations in terms of their personal qualities and relations to oneself rather than in terms of some universal characteristics of their social position. The neighbor or workmate who gets ahead is expected "not to put on airs"; he should like the "old gang" and accept them despite his new position. An individual is expected to transcend his office. A foreman is a s.o.b. not because he has stresses and demands on the job which force him to act forcibly and harshly, but because of his personal qualities. Contrariwise, one of the top executives is frequently regarded as one who would help the rank-and-file workers if he had the chance, because *he* is a "nice guy"; putting him in the stresses of a new position would not force him to act as others in that position have acted.[13] It is the man not the job that makes for behavior; this attitude is not a class-conscious one, far from it. Another example of particularism is the juvenile delinquent who reacts positively to the social worker or therapist who seems to be interested in him beyond the call of professional duty.

*Pragmatism and Anti-Intellectualism.* With workers, it is the end-result of action rather than the planning of ac-

---

[12] The discussion by Miller and Swanson on the "motoric" orientation of workers is one of the most suggestive in the literature. Daniel R. Miller and Guy E. Swanson, *Inner Conflict and Defense* (New York: Henry Holt and Company, 1960).

[13] S. M. Miller, *Union Structure and Industrial Relations: A Case Study of a Local Labor Union,* unpublished Ph.D. thesis, Princeton University, 1951.

tion or the preoccupation with means that counts. An action that goes astray is not liked for itself; it has to achieve the goal intended to be satisfactory.[14] It is results that pay off. While this orientation has an anti-intellectual dimension, it does somewhat reduce the reliance on personality (person-centered theme) by its emphasis on results. Workers like the specific action, the clear action, the understood result. What can be seen and felt is more likely to be real and true in the workers' perspectives, which are therefore likely to be limited. The pragmatic orientation of workers does not encourage them to see abstract ideas as useful. Education, for what it does for one in terms of opportunities, may be desirable but abstract intellectual speculation, ideas which are not rooted in the realities of the present, are not useful, indeed may be harmful.

On the other hand, workers often have an exaggerated respect for the ability of the learned. A person with intellectual competence in one field is frequently thought to be a "brain" with ability in all fields; partly this is due to the general abstract nature of ideas regardless of field. If a real obstacle comes up, they may expect "the brain" to have a ready solution for it, even if they may not be willing to adopt it.

At first glance, the anti-words orientation may appear to be incompatible with the possible appeal of the charismatic. But it is not. For the charismatic are charismatic because they can be emotional and expressive, qualities not usually associated with abstract ideas. Also, the charismatic leader may promise "pie in the sky" but it is a very concrete, specific set of ingredients with a clear distribution of the pie.

14 Melvin L. Kohn, "Social Class and the Exercise of Parental Authority," *American Sociological Review*, 24 (June, 1959), pp. 364–5.

*Excitement.* Another component in workers' lives is the appreciation of excitement, of moving out of the humdrum. News, gossip, new gadgets, sports, are consequently very attractive to workers. To some extent, the consumership of workers—the desire to have new goods, whether television sets or cars—is part of this excitement dimension. The excitement theme is often in contradiction with the traditional orientation.

It is worth nothing that different subgroups within the working class may favor one theme rather than another. Thus younger groups, and especially juvenile delinquents, are probably much more attracted to the excitement theme, are more alienated and less traditional. On the other hand, workers with a more middle-class orientation are probably less alienated, more traditional and pragmatic.

*Parsimony and Variation.* In the preceding remarks we have touched only very fleetingly on a few themes of working-class life and ignored other important themes, like cooperation and a physical orientation, almost completely. While we can sum up our analysis in a relatively few descriptive adjectives, such as person centered, traditional, pragmatic, etc., we have been unable to develop a parsimonious conceptualization, such as a non-deferred gratification pattern which attempts to explain by this single formulation or theme a vast array of behavior. Perhaps the simplest shorthand, if one wishes to use it, would be Parsons'; employing his criteria, we could say that workers are particularistic rather than universalistic, affective rather than neutral, ascriptive rather than achievement-minded, diffuse in definition of role rather than specific. But this summary may obscure more than it reveals.

Indeed, our analysis contains a number of themes which may, in part, be in opposition to each other. For example, traditionalism and alienation have certain conflicting features, as do pragmatism and person centeredness, and the resulting strains and adjustive mechanisms are important to analyze.

Let us make just two points to indicate the general value of the orientation that we have only sketchily presented here: (1) It may be possible to understand other working-class and lower-class styles by looking for sources of variation from the stable working-class pattern. (2) The development of the stable working-class style among lower-class and working-class youth might be the goal of educational and other socializing and remedial forces rather than instilling the middle-class value structure.

## Variations of Working-Class Culture

By stating that we are describing the *stable* worker we imply that there are other worker subcultures. We feel that the stable worker has been relatively ignored in the emphasis on the "underprivileged," "lower class," unskilled, irregular worker and the middle-class oriented worder. By understanding the stable worker, important leads are provided for understanding other subcultural variations.

The unskilled, irregular (read "lower class") worker lacks the disciplined, structured and traditional approach of the stable worker and stresses the excitement theme. He does less to cope with insecurity and instability. In the large industrial and commercial centers today the lower-class style of life (as distinct from the stable working-class style) is found particularly among peoples relatively new to industrial and urban life: Negroes, Puerto Ricans, transplanted Southern whites. They have not been able so far to make the kind of adjustment that stable workers have. Frequently, they have special problems not only of discrimination but of fairly menial (service) jobs at low pay, extremely poor housing and considerable overcrowding. Some children of stable workers do not develop the stable pattern and assume the lower-class style. A few children of middle-class parents become lower class: they have unskilled jobs and adopt the lower-class style of life. But the bulk of individuals with the lower-class style come from those who are children of unskilled workers and of farmers, thus including many of the ethnic people of whom we spoke earlier.[15]

Another deviant group from the main working-class pattern are those workers who are very much concerned with achievement of success for children and for the symbols of success in consumership. In many cases the families are secure and stable and have been able to make a workable accommodation to the stresses of their lives. But this is not enough for the middle-class orientation; in many cases there is a vague opportunity and motivational factor present.

Those of working-class origins who do move into the middle class and into the middle-class style of life are likely to have a middle-class cross-pressure in that they more frequently than other working-class children have relatives who were or are middle class. Their grandparents may have been middle class; their parents though in working-class occupations are more likely to have more education than is typical in the working class and to have other attributes of middle-class life. If we may give a literary example, in *Sons and Lovers*, the hero, brought up in a mining community, had a working-class father but his mother was a teacher and came from a middle-class community.

[15] The data to support this assertion can be computed from the two American studies detailed in the appendix to S. M. Miller, "Comparative Social Mobility," *Current Sociology*, 1961.

Undoubtedly, the hero, whose life follows that of D. H. Lawrence, received motivation from her to move into literary activities and probably also some early direct help in reading and school. The motivational factor is important but it is likely linked to the background and experiential factor of grandparental and paternal activities.

We have discussed these two styles in different ways. The lower-class style is considered to be the inability to develop an adequate measure of coping with the environment so that some degree of security and stability ensues. The origin of the middle-class style would seem to emerge from the stable pattern. A working-class family would likely first go through a stable period of accommodation before it or the children developed middle-class orientations. *It is not intrinsic in the stable pattern that a middle-class orientation emerge but the stable stage would seem to be a necessary step in most cases for the development of a middle-class orientation.*

Other variations in the subculture of workers exist. Religious, ethnic, educational, and regional factors are important in producing deviations from the pattern we have described.

## The Stable Style As Goal

Explicitly as well as implicitly, many agents of educational and other institutions that deal with working-class and lower-class youth attempt to "middle-classize" them. When any effort is extended toward the juvenile delinquent, it is usually with this orientation. Such endeavors are largely a failure because the middle-class outlook is alien to the experiences, prospects and values of these youth. Possibly there is a better chance of emphasizing working-class values; for example cooperation—as happens in group therapy—rather than vocational success in middle-class terms. We recognize that it is not easy to develop some of the working-class values but they are probably much easier to develop than the middle-class ones. In addition, emphasis on the former may develop a more favorable attitude on the part of the youth to both the institution and its agents than does the insistence on the middle-class values.

A basic value question is involved here: Do we attempt to make the middle-class style a model for all to follow? Or do we adopt a rigid cultural relativity position that the lower class has a right to its way of life regardless of the social effects? Or do we attempt to develop what appear to be the most positive elements, from the point of view of society and the individuals involved, of the styles of life closest to them? While we have some doubts about the answer, the possibility of the stable working-class style as the goal adds a new dimension to a deep problem that deserves more forthright scrutiny than it has received.

Our attempts at interpreting working-class life will undoubtedly prove inadequate. But we are certain that without an attempt at analyzing the contexts and the genotypes of working-class behavior and attitude, the *description* (and there is faulty description) and interpretation of working-class life will remain a reflex of social scientists' changing attitudes toward the middle class.

# 46

## Social Inequality Without Social Stratification

### DENNIS H. WRONG

Recently, several sociologists have, notwithstanding the increased preoccupation of their colleagues with the subject of class, argued that the concept of social class is becoming more and more irrelevant to understanding advanced industrial societies.[1] They have largely confined their remarks to the United States. Several European writers, however, have made similar suggestions with respect to the major countries of Western Europe, though rather more tentatively since much that has already become a reality in America remains a trend on the other side of the Atlantic.[2] On the whole, the new claim that social classes have disappeared or are disappearing has been rejected by the majority of American sociologists. For the most part their rejection has been based on little more than a preference for different definitions of class and has been offered good-humoredly as if the matter were merely a trivial issue of terminology. Yet, as so often in sociology, definitions defended on pragmatic or

A revised version of a paper presented at the annual meeting of the American Sociological Association in Los Angeles, August, 1963 and published in The Canadian Review of Sociology and Anthropology, 1:5–16. Reprinted with permission of the publisher.
[1] Arnold M. Rose, "The Concept of Class and American Sociology," Social Research, XXV, Spring, 1958, 53–69; Robert A. Nisbet, "The Decline and Fall of Social Class," Pacific Sociological Review, II, Spring, 1959, 11–17; Wilbert E. Moore, "But Some Are More Equal Than Others," American Sociological Review, XXVIII, February, 1963, 14–15.
[2] T. H. Marshall, "General Survey of Changes in Social Stratification in the Twentieth Century," Transactions of the Third World Congress of Sociology, International Sociological Association, 1956, III, 1–17; George Lichtheim, The New Europe: Today and Tomorrow (New York, Frederick A. Praeger, 1963), 198–215.

operational grounds turn out on closer examination to obscure full recognition of the contrast between past and present and of the new possibilities latent in contemporary social reality.

Sociologists who argue that social class is no longer a useful concept take what has been called a "realist" position regarding the existence of classes. They are committed to the view that, in the words of one of them, social classes "are groups possessed both of real and vital common economic interests and of a group-consciousness of their general position in the social scale."[3] Their contention that social classes are disappearing in industrial societies rests on the failure to locate such groups. The opposing "nominalist" point of view regards class as a useful classificatory concept, grouping together for purposes of analysis individuals who possess certain attributes in common, whether or not they feel any unity or are even aware of having something in common with their fellow class members. The sociologist, in effect, creates the "class structures" he describes, which are no more than a means of organizing his data on variations in human behavior within a society. He may find several different class systems or pyramids of stratification within a society, none of which are perceived or experienced as collective realities, as real social groups, by their members.

A denial of the existence of social classes as defined by the "realist" perspective in no way implies a trend toward general equality or social uniformity. Inequalities in the distribution of income, the invidious ranking of occupations with respect to prestige or

[3] Marshall, "General Survey of Changes in Social Stratification," 15.

status, and functional hierarchies of power and authority may remain solidly established in the absence of social classes. Individuals or social roles may be ranked with respect to varying income, status, or power, as is commonly done by sociological researchers, but the categories or percentiles into which individuals or roles are grouped are not social classes in the realist sense unless there is independent evidence that their members are internally cohesive and see themselves as a distinct collectivity with *common* rather than merely *like* goals, interests, and values.

The so-called "realist versus nominalist" dispute over the kind of objective reality that should be ascribed to social classes has long been a standard theoretical and methodological issue in discussions of social stratification. Yet it has not always been acknowledged that all of the major nineteenth- and twentieth-century theorists of class were unmistakably on the "realist" side, regardless of whether they thought classes were based on economic interests, shared values, or common access to social power.

To Marx, a class was not fully formed until it had ceased to be merely a potential membership-group (*Klasse an sich*) and had achieved a solidarity based on awareness of the common interests of its members in opposition to those of another class (*Klasse für sich*).

Joseph Schumpeter wrote: "Class is something more than an aggregation of class members. . . . A class is aware of its identity as a whole, sublimates itself as such, has its own peculiar life and characteristic 'spirit.' " [4]

Max Weber is frequently cited by American sociologists in support of the contention that stratification in modern societies involves at least three partially independent hierarchies, one of wealth,

one of prestige, and one of power. He is also often invoked to justify the treatment of status rankings of occupations as synonymous with "class structure." Weber is the source of the "wealth-status-power" triad so favored by contemporary sociologists, but he was clearly concerned with identifying relatively cohesive groups differentiated with respect to these three bases of stratification and did not consider each as forming a continuous scale on which individuals or positions could be located. Thus, defining "class," like Marx, in strictly economic terms, he saw classes as "possible, and frequent, bases for communal action," although he was less certain than Marx that aggregates of people sharing like interests would become aware of their common interests and resort to "communal action" to advance them. Commonly regarded as the first modern social theorist to stress the importance of status, Weber was chiefly concerned to describe "status groups" or *Stände*—a term that clearly designates self-conscious collectivities. With reference to power, he used the less fortunate term "party," which nevertheless is unambiguous in connoting a collective entity rather than an attribute with respect to which individuals or roles vary continuously.

Finally, W. Lloyd Warner has always insisted that the six social classes he discovered in Newburyport, Massachusetts, were ultimately derived from "the way in which people in American communities actually classify themselves," although his critics have repeatedly challenged the validity of this claim after re-analysing Warner's own data.

I doubt that any of these men would have devoted so much time and effort to the study of class had they thought it a matter of indifference whether classes "really" existed in the experience of their members or were no more than artifacts constructed by the sociologist as a means of ordering and sum-

[4] Joseph A. Schumpeter, *Imperialism and Social Classes* (New York, Meridian Books, 1955), 107.

marizing his observations. The categorizing together by the sociologist of individuals sharing a common position with respect to several distinct variables is a thoroughly legitimate and useful procedure in certain kinds of empirical research. But to call the resultant categories "social classes" is to risk confusion with the quite different meaning of class in the writings of the leading theorists of stratification. Those researchers who use such terms as "socioeconomic level" at least implicitly recognize the distinction. But there are others who persist in referring to combined measures of occupation, income, or education as "indexes" of social class, although the entity these measures allegedly indicate appears to have no independent reality and "class" becomes no more than a short-hand expression for the ensemble of the very variables that have been combined to form the index.[5]

Critics of the realist conception of social classes have attributed to it the necessary implication that members of a society must be fully aware of the class system and that its nature can therefore be determined by a simple opinion poll.[6] Surely, this is a specious argument. To assert that social controls and expectancies are present in the minds and sentiments of the people whose conduct they influence is not to maintain that these people can readily put them into words. Consider social norms in primary groups, which are clearly operative influences on behavior; those who conform to them are not always able to provide a coherent account of the codes that guide and restrain them in their day-to-day interactions with others.[7] The kind of awareness-in-behavior that frequently characterizes social class relations may involve still less self-consciousness since classes (except in small isolated local communities) are not even potential primary groups; hence the frequent use of the term "quasi-group" to describe them.

The existence of classes, however, is a matter of degree depending upon the extent to which their members are conscious of their unity and of the boundaries separating them from other classes.[8] But recognition of this does not invalidate the realist position. All the theorists previously mentioned, with the exception of the ahistorical Warner, dealt at length with what Schumpeter called *class formation* and saw it

---

[5] Marshall, "General Survey of Changes in Social Stratification," 5–6; Rose, "The Concept of Class," 65–9.

[6] See, for example, Bernard Barber, *Social Stratification* (New York, Harcourt, Brace, 1957), 76–7; Nelson N. Foote, Walter Goldschmidt, Richard Morris, Melvin Seeman and Joseph Shister, "Alternative Assumptions in Stratification Research," *Transactions of the Second World Congress of Sociology*, International Sociological Association, 1953, II, 386–7.

[7] William F. Whyte reports that his main informant, Doc, remarked to him: "Now when I do something, I have to think what Bill Whyte would want to know about it and how I can explain it. . . . Before I used to do these things by instinct." *Street Corner Society* (Chicago, University of Chicago Press, 1943), 10.

Many of the simplifications to which sociologists are prone in discussing the question of the degree to which people are aware of the determinants of their own behaviour result from a failure to take into account Ryle's distinction between "knowing how" and "knowing that." See Gilbert Ryle, *The Concept of Mind* (New York, Barnes & Noble, 1949), 25–61.

[8] As Andreas Miller has written: "A social class is a real group. Set aside from its social environment by natural boundaries . . . In a classless society one can speak of differences in social status. It would, however, be of no value to look for a class-system in a society without differences in social status . . . An adequate conception of the class-system can only be reached by answering the question whether the community investigated is divided into strata by clear boundaries, what is their number, location, and strength." "The Problem of Class Boundaries and Its Significance for Research into Class Structure," *Transactions of the Second World Congress of Sociology*, 1953, II, 343, 348–9.

as a process frequently falling short of the eventual emergence of fully developed classes. All of them attempted to specify the conditions under which aggregates of similarly situated individuals acquire cohesion and begin to behave as if they constitute at least a fictive membership-group. Nor does the existence of individuals or families whose position is marginal within the class structure pose special theoretical difficulties, for this is an inevitable result of inter-class mobility, which is also a temporal process of uncertain outcome.

Finally, if the existence of a class system implies *some* stratification, it is also possible for particular classes— most frequently new and rising classes —to exist which do not fit into an orderly hierarchical system.[9] Thus if we regard social stratification as a stratification of groups, classes may be formed in partial independence of stratification. But, more important, inequalities in the distribution of income, prestige, and power may exist in complete independence of it.

So far, my emphasis has been primarily definitional and I have done no more than insist on a number of distinctions that are widely recognized in principle, although often ignored in research practice. Applied to contemporary industrial societies, however, these distinctions are acquiring new relevance, for modern societies are unmistakably moving in the direction of maintaining considerable institutionalized inequality in the absence of a class system, a condition that the Polish sociologist, Stanislaw Ossowski, has characterized as "non-egalitarian classlessness." [10] This

condition has not yet been fully achieved even in the United States, much less in Western Europe. But the steady approach toward it increasingly transforms social classes into "ghost" communities preserving a fitful and wavering identity rooted in historical memories, similar to that ascribed by Nathan Glazer to the "ghost nations" of third-generation American immigrants which continue to play a minor role in American politics.[11]

Since so many American sociologists have failed to see any significance in the disappearance of social classes in view of the survival of pronounced status inequalities, I shall briefly suggest several differences between societies where classes to some degree are present and societies where social inequality is relatively detached from stratification.

1. Income, educational, and status mobility are experienced differently in the two societies. The person who moves upward (or downward) in a classless society does not encounter a class boundary in addition to the career obstacles he has to overcome in order to rise. Surely, it is the relative absence of classes in American society, whatever the historical causes for this absence, that accounts for the general belief that mobility is greater in the United States than in Europe, a belief that Lipset and Bendix have shown to be unfounded.[12] Quite minor improvements in status or income are more readily perceived as mobility where no class boundary has to be crossed or confronted. There have been no real counterparts in the United

[9] Stanislaw Ossowski, "Old Notions and New Problems: Interpretations of Social Structure in Modern Society," *Transactions of the Third World Congress of Sociology,* 1956, III, 18–25.
[10] Stanislaw Ossowski, *Class Structure in the Social Consciousness* (New York, The Free Press, 1963), 100–18.

[11] Nathan Glazer, "Ethnic Groups in America: From National Culture to Ideology," in Morroe Berger, Charles H. Page and Theodore Abel, editors, *Freedom and Control in Modern Society* (New York, Van Nostrand, 1954), 172–3.
[12] Seymour Martin Lipset and Reinhard Bendix, *Social Mobility in Industrial Society* (Berkeley, University of California Press, 1959), 11–75.

States to the British "angry young men"; persons of provincial and working-class origin who rise through educational or occupational attainment but become embittered on experiencing real or imagined exclusion when they try to cross a class line. The closest American equivalent is the experience of upwardly mobile Negroes and members of ethnic or religious minorities. The fact that occupational status rankings are similar in America and Britain, and indeed in all advanced industrial societies,[13] merely underlines the difference between these rankings and a social class system.

2. More important, a distinction between stratification and social inequality aids us in understanding the political sociology of modern industrial societies. The distinction holds, it should be noted, regardless of whether economic interest or style-of-life is considered the essential basis of class. The latter—the "Marx vs. Warner" issue—is a separate definitional problem. However, last-ditch defenders of the relevance of the class concept, such as Rudolph Heberle in a recent paper,[14] fall back on the Marxist view of classes as interest-groups divided by ownership or non-ownership of the means of production. They plausibly argue that, although classes separated by sharp status and associational boundaries have been largely supplanted by a continuous hierarchy of status, conflicts of interest have by no means disappeared and the major opposing groups continue to think and act in concert politically, at the very least in their voting behavior. The prediction of American Marxists in the 1930's that national cleavages of economic interest would increasingly supersede regional

and ethnic divisions as the main basis of political alignment has on the whole been borne out.

But a second part of the prediction was that more tightly drawn class lines would result in an intensification of the political class struggle between Left and Right. The opposite has occurred: "class" has become a more important determinant of voting at the same time that the bitterness of class struggle has unmistakably abated.[15] While it may, therefore, be formally correct to insist that the term "class" in the Marxist sense is still applicable where society-wide conflicts of interest find political expression, it is surely more relevant to the understanding of modern politics to recognize that today economic interest-groups and the political associations based on them do not, in T. H. Marshall's words, "permeate the whole lives of their members, as social classes do, nor are they always in action, and at times the constituent sub-groups may be more important than the largest aggregates."[16]

Ralf Dahrendorf attributes the obsolescence of the Marxist two-class system to what he aptly calls the "institutional isolation of industry" in modern society. But he tries to preserve the emphasis on conflict and change in Marxist class theory by re-defining classes as the result of tension between power-holders and their subordinates, arguing that the division between owners and non-owners of property, and even conflicts of economic interest in general, are merely special cases of this more fundamental phenomenon.[17] Dahrendorf does not hesitate to conclude that there are as many class systems in a modern society

[13] Alex Inkeles and Peter H. Rossi, "National Comparisons of Occupational Prestige," *American Journal of Sociology*, LXI, January, 1956, 329–39.
[14] Rudolph Heberle, "Recovery of Class Theory," *Pacific Sociological Review*, II, Spring, 1959, 18–28.
[15] Seymour Martin Lipset, *Political Man* (New York, Doubleday & Co., 1960), especially chapters IX and XIII.
[16] Marshall, "General Survey of Changes in Social Stratification," 13.
[17] Ralf Dahrendorf, *Class and Class Conflict in Industrial Society* (Stanford, Calif., Stanford University Press, 1959), especially Part Two.

as there are functional hierarchies of power and that a single individual may therefore simultaneously be a member of several different classes if he belongs to several associations each with its own structure of authority. In effect, Dahrendorf makes three main contentions: that social conflict is generated by differences in power; that classes are conflict-groups; and that all conflict-groups are classes. He may be right on the first two points (I am inclined to think that he is), but the third assertion surely represents the most quixotic effort to uphold the continuing usefulness of the concept of class in recent sociological writing.[18] Moreover, it would seem to be of no use at all in understanding the major political divisions in modern societies, although this has been precisely the most valuable feature of class theories which take their point of departure from Marx. Yet notwithstanding the inadequacies of his own class theory, Dahrendorf shows a far more acute grasp of the many differences between stratified and non-egalitarian classless societies than most American sociologists.

3. The absence of classes also helps account for the invisibility of poverty in the United States, to which several writers have recently called attention. The poor are composed of a number of categories of persons with particular demographic characteristics whose economic plight is no longer clearly linked to what Marx or Weber would consider a "class situation." [19] Both in status and

in economic terms, only the American Negroes come close to constituting a definable and cohesive deprived group, with the possible exception of tenant farmers and laborers in certain sectors of the agricultural economy. There is indeed some justification for calling Negroes *the* American lower class.[20]

The emerging social structure of post-bourgeois industrial society can best be understood if, except for secondary purposes and for historical analysis, we abandon the concept of social class and re-define much of the work done under this label as a contribution to the sociology of equality and inequality. But American sociologists have been unwilling to make this necessary redefinition, in part for ideological reasons.

Celebrations of the United States have traditionally affirmed its "classlessness" and extolled at the same time the equality of opportunity to attain unequal rewards it allegedly provides. In challenging the reality of the latter, sociologists have been unwilling to concede any truth to the claim of classlessness lest they should appear to be denying the facts of inequality and barriers to opportunity. A spirit of liberal muckraking still pervades much American sociological writing on stratification whether the writer's intent is to deplore or, like W. Lloyd Warner, to counsel adjustment to the "brute facts" of inequality that are concealed or minimized by the official egalitarian ideology.

---

[18] Both Kurt B. Mayer and Lewis A. Coser have similarly criticized Dahrendorf's thesis in reviews of his book. See Mayer's review of the German edition, *American Sociological Review*, XXIII, October, 1958, 592–3, and of the English edition, *ibid.*, XXV, April, 1960, 288; and Coser, *American Journal of Sociology*, LXV, March, 1960, 520–1.

[19] An exhaustive forthcoming study of poverty in the United States by Oscar Ornati indicates that the following were "poverty-linked characteristics" in 1960: Non-white, Female head of household. Age 65 and over, Age 14–24 head of household, Rural Farm,

Residence in South, Non-wage earner, Part-time wage earner, More than Six Children under 18, Education less than 8 years. None of the groups defined by these characteristics, with the possible exception of Rural Farm, represents a socioeconomic class. Ornati, *Poverty in an Affluent Society*, Preliminary Draft, New York: The New School for Social Research and The Twentieth Century Fund (Mimeographed), chapter 5. For a discussion of the non-class nature of contemporary American poverty see Henry M. Pachter, "The Income Revolution," *Dissent*, IV, Summer, 1957, 315–18.

[20] Rose, "The Concept of Class," 64.

444 Sociology of Contemporary Society

The result has been that sociologists have perpetuated the very confusion of classlessness with equality that the official ideology makes.

American sociologists have failed to see that the absence of classes may both in ideology and social fact *more* effectively conceal existing inequalities than a social structure clearly divided into recognizable classes. The invisibility of poverty in the United States, already referred to, suggests such a conclusion, as does the fact that income distribution has become more unequal in the past decade,[21] the very decade of the "affluent society," which has witnessed so much individual and collective mobility, the mass diffusion of formerly restricted status symbols, and the breakdown of long-standing ethnic, religious, and even racial barriers to opportunity.

In distinguishing conceptually between stratification and inequality and noting some of the consequences of their increasing factual separation in contemporary society, I have avoided direct discussion of mobility and equality of opportunity. Many writers who have insisted as I have that stratification involves a hierarchy of groups rather than of positions or of individuals possessing unequal amounts of income, prestige, and power, have gone on to argue that stratified groups, or social classes, must necessarily be hereditary.[22] By transmitting the unequal privileges of one generation to the next through the family, classes thus inevitably prevent the full institutionalization of equality of opportunity.

The class systems of the past have

undeniably been hereditary, though permitting sufficient mobility to justify distinguishing them from *caste* systems. But need this be so in the future? Historically, biological continuity has been the major means of preserving the internal solidarity and the distinctive ethos of classes from generation to generation, but is it necessarily the only possible means? George Orwell wrote: "The essence of oligarchical rule is not father-to-son inheritance, but the persistence of a certain world-view and a certain way of life imposed by the dead upon the living. A ruling group is a ruling group so long as it can nominate its successors. Who wields power is not important, provided that the hierarchical structure remains always the same." [23] Orwell was writing of political elites, but his point that permanence of structure need not depend on biological continuity may well have a broader relevance. Hereditary social classes may not be succeeded by non-egalitarian classlessness but by new classes whose members are not recruited by the intergenerational transmission of privileges through the family and whose cohesion does not depend on familial socialization.

Equality of opportunity could literally be achieved in full only by a method of allocating individuals to social positions that was strictly random, such as drawing lots. In contrasting equal opportunity with the inheritance of social position, however, sociologists obviously mean by the former the allocation of individuals to positions according to the single criterion of demonstrated ability to carry out the position's requirements. They have usually assumed that equality of opportunity thus defined is not only morally superior to any hereditary principle but would also prove to be more humanly tolerable, eliminating the social gulf that has ex-

[21] I am indebted to Oscar Ornati for having shown me the data from a later section of his study, *Poverty in an Affluent Society*, indicating this to be unmistakably the case.
[22] See especially Walter Buckley, "Social Stratification and the Functional Theory of Social Differentiation," *American Sociological Review*, XXIII, August, 1958, 369–75; and Kurt B. Mayer, "The Changing Shape of the American Class Structure," *Social Research*, XXX, Winter, 1963, 458–68.

[23] *Nineteen Eighty-Four* (New York, Harcourt, Brace, 1949), 370–1.

isted between hereditary social classes and removing the envy and sense of injustice of low-status individuals who feel deprived of social rewards only by the accident of birth.

There is some evidence that the absence of clear-cut class lines in the United States and the prevailing "democracy of manners" make it easier for low-status individuals to tolerate hereditary inequalities provided they continue to believe that at least *some* opportunity to rise is available to them and their children.[24] but the most devastating attack on the belief that an inegalitarian order combined with full equal opportunity would reduce social conflict has been made by the English sociologist, Michael Young, in his brilliant sociological satire *The Rise of the Meritocracy: 1870–2073*.[25] This book has been completely ignored by American sociologists, failing even to receive reviews in the journals, although it contributes vastly more to our theoretical understanding of class and inequality than the innumerable continuing studies of community class structures or of correlations between "class affiliation" and various kinds of behavior.[26]

Young's book is cast in the form of an historical interpretation written by a sociologist in the year 2033. His meritocratic social order is located in England, rather than "nowhere," and its evolution under the pressure of social forces powerfully at work in today's world is fully described. Although like other anti-Utopian writers Young's purpose is to warn rather than to prophesy, the form he has chosen gives his book a sociological relevance greater than that of many similar efforts which do not succeed in becoming more than a kind of sociological science-fiction or satiric caricatures of contemporary society.

The meritocracy is the result of three forces: the attack by socialists on all hereditary privileges, the pace of international economic competition requiring Britain to maintain high rates of economic growth,[27] and improvements in intelligence testing which have made it possible to reorganize the school system so that students can be segregated by intelligence at progressively earlier ages and trained for their eventual positions in the social order. The testing centers and in the school system thus have become the vehicles for selecting the ruling elite of meritocrats. Possessing a monopoly of ability, the meritocracy easily prevails in conflicts of interest with the lower strata, who are completely bereft of leadership since all their potential leaders have been elevated into the meritocracy, and who must live with the knowledge that they have been scientifically proven to be inferior in ability to their rulers. The family, however, has survived in its present form and, echoing the functional theory of inequality, Young sees this as the Achilles heel of the regime. The meritocratic parents of inferior children and women, whose occupational skills suffer as a result of their withdrawal to bear and raise children, become infected with a discontent that eventually leads to revolution.

In Young's account the meritocracy

[24] Robert E. Lane, *Political Ideology: Why the American Common Man Believes What He Does* (New York: The Free Press, 1962), 57–81.

[25] London, Thames and Hudson, 1958, passim.

[26] See Dennis H. Wrong, "The Functional Theory of Stratification: Some Neglected Considerations," *American Sociological Review*, XXIV, December, 1959, 778–82; and "All Men Are Equal But Some . . . ," *Dissent*, VII, Spring, 1960, 207–10.

[27] Several writers have recently argued that the maintenance of high rates of economic growth sets severe limits to the achievement of greater equality of condition as distinct from equality of opportunity. See Lichtheim, *The New Europe* (New York: Frederick A. Praeger, 1963), 188–9; also C. A. R. Crosland, *The Conservative Enemy* (New York, Schocken Books, 1962), 29–34.

clearly constitutes a unified ruling group, sharing common interests and a similar style of life, even though it is not recruited by heredity. And the same is true to a lesser degree of the "technicians" —the regime's euphemism for the industrial working class. Rather than defining class and stratification by the hereditary principle and calling the meritocracy a "classless" or unstratified society, it is surely more reasonable to see it as a new form of class society.

Yet one must raise some doubts about the general relevance of Young's meritocracy to contemporary trends in advanced industrial societies. One might question, to begin with, his assumption that the family will remain cohesive and unchanged when so much else has been transformed. More important, the very plausibility of Young's account depends heavily on the roots of the meritocracy in English history with its characteristic "inevitability of gradualness." Thus Young sees the sharpness of class lines and the steepness of the status hierarchy that have existed in English society from feudalism to the present day as surviving even when birth has been entirely supplanted by merit as the basis of status. While the independence of stratification in general from the particular form of stratification by hereditary social classes is thus brilliantly suggested, one is forced to wonder whether a meritocracy would have the same consequences in an industrial society that lacked the pervasive continuities of English history—in, say, the United States.

I know of only one even sketchy account of a possible American meritocracy. It is provided, not by a sociologist, but by a lawyer and unsuccessful politician, Stimson Bullitt, in his perceptive little book *To Be a Politician*.[28] Bullitt envisages an American meritocratic order as being far more stable and less riven by class conflict than Young's Britain. He writes:

The free flow up and down and the narrow range of variations in revealed ability among members of the great majority will make class differences less sharp. Also, the classes will be equally well fed and in most ways equally free; people on different levels of talent will be closer in many ways than were the social classes of the past. All people will have greater understanding, and therefore sympathy, for persons on other levels of talent than used to be the case between classes whose members lived like different species. (177–8)

While Bullitt attributes the absence of class tensions in a meritocratic United States in part to general prosperity and a high degree of material equality—conditions which are absent in Young's less economically self-sufficient England—the traditional classlessness of American society clearly leads him to anticipate an American meritocracy that would resemble a continuous hierarchy of unequal positions rather than Young's more stratified order.

Will the decline of hereditary social classes and the trend toward meritocracy eventuate in non-egalitarian classlessness or in a new class society allocating individuals by specialized abilities rather than by birth? What will be the peculiar discontents of each order? What form will the ancient dream of an egalitarian society, equally frustrated by both, take under these conditions? These are likely to be the questions, only dimly adumbrated in our present imperfectly affluent society, with which future sociologists of inequality will concern themselves. We are not likely to make much progress in answering them if we cling to a conceptual apparatus that does not distinguish between stratification in general and the particular form it has taken in the hereditary class societies of the past.

[28] (New York, Doubleday Anchor Books, 1961), 162–93.

# F  The Political Economy

## INTRODUCTION

The social changes of the twentieth century have so increased the interdependence of politics and economics in advanced industrial societies that the old term *political economy* has acquired a new relevance. No longer is it useful to think of the state and the economy as separate, autonomous institutional orders. Indeed the habit of so conceiving them always led to some distortion of reality and helped provide ideological support for nineteenth-century *laissez-faire* capitalism. It did, however, encourage the growth of economics and political science as specialized disciplines. Yet today no economist trying to understand the relations between the supply of goods, consumer demand, savings, and investment in a national economy can ignore the influence of political decisions on these quantities. And no political scientist can fail to see that conflict over the distribution of the national economic product has become the main domestic issue in the politics of democracies—the "democratic class struggle," as it has been aptly called.

The idea of capitalism held by both its defenders and its socialist critics in the nineteenth century has become so obsolete that some writers have claimed that the modern economic order in Western Europe and North America can no longer meaningfully be characterized as "capitalist"—a view at least implied by John Kenneth Galbraith in his discussion of the great American corporations and their industrial planning, though rejected by Robert Heilbroner who nevertheless recognizes most of the changes noted by Galbraith, in two of the selections we have reprinted in this section. The principal changes include the intervention of governments striving to control and even direct the capitalist market economy, the organization of much of the economy into large, powerful corporations—the "corporatization" of the economy—the partial militarization of both government and economy in World War II and the cold war, and the enormously increased complexity of modern technology.

Political democracy has resulted in the organization of parties to advance the interests of those groups suffering most severely from the unregulated workings of the market. Even in countries where these working-class and socialist parties have rarely been elected to office, the necessity of appealing for votes from their adherents has led conservative parties to adopt and enact parts of their program. Thus government protection of the rights of trade unions, minimum wage laws, social services financed out of taxation, the redistribution of income through

447

taxation, the use of fiscal controls to avert depressions and prevent unemployment, and the nationalization of some public utilities and basic industries have become permanent features of modern government. Collectively, they are often labeled the "welfare state."

Welfare-state measures have been more fully accepted in Europe than in the United States, although the latter was the first nation to enact some of them as part of Roosevelt's New Deal in the 1930's. All major European political parties favor preserving and even strengthening the welfare state, whereas significant segments of American conservative opinion remain in opposition even to existing measures. European socialists and even some nonsocialists, as in Gaullist France, are committed to increasing the public sector of the economy and instituting far-reaching national economic planning, measures that would further reduce the autonomy of private capitalists. Powerful support for such a program is lacking in the United States. Although the working class and ethnic minority groups have long supported the Democratic party and the Republican party has always had the support of the business community, socialist ideas and programs have never won a large following in America.

Yet, as Galbraith argues, the huge size of business organizations dictated by the cost and intricacy of the new technology enables them in effect to plan their production and sales schedules in virtual independence of autonomous market forces. Heilbroner alludes to America's lack of a precapitalist and feudal past in accounting for the greater prestige of businessmen in this country. The dominant form of business enterprise, the giant corporation, has been fostered by the size and continental expanse of the American market and the labor shortages that stimulated the invention of mass-production technology. So great is the control of large corporations over the American economy that they possess autonomous decision-making powers in many other areas of social life. Although in no way accountable to political authority, they function as political institutions, deciding issues unrelated to the search for profits as such. Andrew Hacker discusses their role in American society, stressing that they concentrate power in bureaucratic organizations rather than in individuals or families.

One area that rests almost entirely within the control of the corporations is the rate of technological change. Automation and its potential effects on the labor force are reviewed by Daniel Bell in another reading. Bell's analysis underlines the very important fact that the political economy is the pacemaker of social change in modern industrial societies, profoundly shaping other institutions and the entire fabric of social life. Bell indicates the far-reaching consequences of technical innovation, suggesting, for example, that work shifts required by automated production are likely to affect the marital relations and sex lives of the workers and that the very concept of self, long tied to work as a central life activity, may be altered if man ceases to be *Homo faber* as a result of automation.

The legislator is the prototype of the professional politician in American society. That he does not always feel his lot to be a happy one is suggested by Edward Shils' perceptive analysis of his role. American political parties are such loose coalitions of groups, lacking clear-cut national programs, that the legislator feels himself continuously exposed to the demands of his constituents, who are far from Washington and insensitive to the pressures of all the powerful centralized institutions in American life that are brought to bear upon him in Congress. A symbol of democracy and yet often a man from the provinces lacking secure tenure in his job, he feels at an enormous disadvantage in confronting the more urbane and secure representatives of the executive bureaucracy, the Pentagon, and the corporate elite. Small wonder, Shils argues, that he often develops a fear and hatred of those forces identified with the trend toward bigness and centralized power in American life.

New movements among students and the intelligentsia in the Western world have arisen in recent years to protest the bureaucratization and militarization of capitalism, the American war in Vietnam, and the relations between the relatively affluent Western societies and the poorer countries of the "third world," many of them past victims of Western imperialism. Richard Flacks presents one view of these movements in the essay we have reprinted.

# 47

# The New Industrial State

## JOHN KENNETH GALBRAITH

### I

A curiosity of modern economic life is the role of change. It is imagined to be very great; to list its forms or emphasize its extent is to show a reassuring grasp of the commonplace. Yet not much is supposed to change. The economic system of the United States is praised on all occasions of public ceremony as a largely perfect structure. This is so elsewhere also. It is not easy to perfect what has been perfected. There is massive change but, except as the output of goods increases, all remains as before.

As to the change there is no doubt. The innovations and alterations in economic life in the last seventy years, and more especially since the beginning of World War II, have, by any calculation, been great. The most visible has been the application of increasingly intricate and sophisticated technology to the pro-

duction of things. Machines have replaced crude manpower. And increasingly, as they are used to instruct other machines, they replace the cruder forms of human intelligence.

Seventy years ago the corporation was still confined to those industries—railroading, steamboating, steel-making, petroleum recovery and refining, some mining—where, it seemed, production had to be on a large scale. Now it also sells groceries, mills grain, publishes newspapers and provides public entertainment, all activities that were once the province of the individual proprietor or the insignificant firm. The largest firms deploy billions of dollars' worth of equipment and hundreds of thousands of men in scores of locations to produce hundreds of products. The five hundred largest corporations produce close to half of all the goods and services that are available annually in the United States.

Seventy years ago the corporation was the instrument of its owners and a projection of their personalities. The names of these principals—Carnegie,

Rockefeller, Harriman, Mellon, Guggenheim, Ford—were known across the land. They are still known, but for the art galleries and philanthropic foundations they established and their descendants who are in politics. The men who now head the great corporations are unknown. Not for a generation have people outside Detroit and the automobile industry known the name of the current head of General Motors. In the manner of all men, he must produce identification when paying by check. So with Ford, Standard Oil and General Dynamics. The men who now run the large corporations own no appreciable share of the enterprise. They are selected not by the stockholders but, in the common case, by a Board of Directors which narcissistically they selected themselves.

Equally it is a commonplace that the relation of the state to the economy has changed. The services of Federal, state and local governments now account for between a fifth and a quarter of all economic activity. In 1929 it was about eight per cent. This far exceeds the government share in such an avowedly socialist state as India, considerably exceeds that in the anciently social democratic kingdoms of Sweden and Norway, and is not wholly incommensurate with the share in Poland, a Communist country which, however, is heavily agricultural and which has left its agriculture in private ownership. A very large part (between one-third and one-half) of public activity is concerned with national defense and the exploration of space. This is not regarded even by conservatives as socialism. Elsewhere the nomenclature is less certain.

Additionally, in the wake of what is now called the Keynesian Revolution, the state undertakes to regulate the total income available for the purchase of goods and services in the economy. It seeks to insure sufficient purchasing power to buy whatever the current labor force can produce. And, more tentatively and with considerably less sanction in public attitudes, it seeks, given the resulting high employment, to keep wages from shoving up prices and prices from forcing up wages in a persistent upward spiral. Perhaps as a result of these arrangements, and perhaps only to test man's capacity for feckless optimism, the production of goods in modern times has been notably high and remarkably reliable.

Previously, from the earliest appearance of capitalism until the beginning of Hitler's war, expansion and recession had followed each other, at irregular intervals, but in steady procession. The business cycle had become a separate subject of economic study; the forecasting of its course and the explanation of its irregularities had become a modest profession in which reason, divination, incantation and elements of witchcraft had been combined in a manner not elsewhere seen save in the primitive religions. In the two decades following World War II, there was no serious depression; from 1947 until this writing (1966) there has been only one year in which real income in the United States has failed to rise.

Three further changes are less intimately a part of the established litany of accomplishment. First, there has been a further massive growth in the apparatus of persuasion and exhortation that is associated with the sale of goods. Measurement of the exposure, and susceptibility, of human beings to this persuasion is itself a flourishing science.

Second, there has been the beginning of the decline of the trade union. Union membership in the United States reached a peak in 1956. Since then employment has continued to grow; union membership in the main has gone down. Friends of the labor movement, and those who depend on it for a livelihood, picture this downturn as temporary or cyclical. Quite a few others have not noticed it. There is a strong presumption that it is deeply rooted in related and deeper change.

Finally, there has been a large expansion in enrollment for higher education together with a somewhat more modest increase in the means for providing it. This has been attributed to a new and penetrating concern for popular enlightenment. As with the fall in union membership, it has deeper roots. Had the economic system need only for millions of unlettered proletarians, these, very plausibly, are what would be provided.

## 2

These changes or most of them have been much discussed. But to view them in isolation from each other, the usual practice, is greatly to minimize their effect. They are related to each other as cause to consequence. All are part of a yet larger matrix of change. In its effect on economic society this matrix has been more than the sum of its parts.

Thus mention has been made of machines and sophisticated technology. These require, in turn, heavy investment of capital. They are designed and guided by technically sophisticated men. They involve, also, a greatly increased elapse of time between any decision to produce and the emergence of a salable product.

From these changes come the need and the opportunity for the large business organization. It alone can deploy the requisite capital; it alone can mobilize the requisite skills. It can also do more. The large commitment of capital and organization well in advance of result requires that there be foresight and also that all feasible steps be taken to insure that what is foreseen will transpire. It can hardly be doubted that General Motors will be better able to influence the world around it—the prices and wages at which it buys and

the prices at which it sells—than a man in suits and cloaks.

Nor is this all. The high production and income which are the fruits of advanced technology and expansive organization remove a very large part of the population from the compulsions and pressures of physical want. In consequence their economic behavior becomes in some measure malleable. No hungry man who is also sober can be persuaded to use his last dollar for anything but food. But a well-fed, well-clad, well-sheltered and otherwise well-tended person can be persuaded as between an electric razor and an electric toothbrush. Along with prices and costs, consumer demand becomes subject to management. This adds an important further element of control over environment.

When investment in technological development is very high, a wrong technical judgment or a failure in persuading consumers to buy the product can be extremely expensive. The cost and associated risk can be greatly reduced if the state pays for more exalted technical development or guarantees a market for the technically advanced product. Suitable justification—national defense, the needs of national prestige, support to indispensable industries such as supersonic travel—can readily be found. Modern technology thus defines a growing function of the modern state.

And technology and associated requirements in capital and time lead even more directly to the regulation of demand by the state. A corporation, contemplating an automobile of revised aspect, must be able to persuade people to buy it. It is equally important that people be able to do so. This is vital where heavy advance commitments of time and money must be made and where the product could as easily come to market in a time of depression as of prosperity. So there must be stabilization of overall demand.

Affluence adds to the need for such

stabilization of aggregate demand. A man who lives close to the margin of subsistence must spend to exist and what he spends is spent. A man with ample income can save, and there is no assurance that what he saves will be offset by the spending or investment of others. Moreover, a rich society owes its productivity and income, at least in part, to large-scale organization—to the corporation. Corporations also have the option of retaining or saving from earnings—and can exercise it with the unique sense of righteousness of men who are imposing thrift on others. There is no guarantee that this corporate saving will be offset by spending. In consequence, in a community of high well-being, spending and hence demand are less reliable than in a poor one. They lose their reliability precisely when high costs and the long period of gestation imposed by modern technology require greater certainty of markets. The Keynesian Revolution occurred at the moment in history when other change had made it indispensable. Like the other changes with which this chapter began, it is intimately a cause and consequence of yet other change.

## 3

In economics, unlike fiction and the theater, there is no harm in a premature disclosure of the plot: it is to see the changes just mentioned and others as an interlocked whole. I venture to think that modern economic life is seen much more clearly when, as here, there is effort to see it whole.

I am also concerned to show how, in this larger context of change, the forces inducing human effort have changed. This assaults the most majestic of all economic assumptions, namely that man in his economic activities is subject to the authority of the market. Instead, we have an economic system which, whatever its formal ideological

billing, is in substantial part a planned economy. The initiative in deciding what is to be produced comes not from the sovereign consumer who, through the market, issues the instructions that bend the productive mechanism to his ultimate will. Rather it comes from the great producing organization which reaches forward to control the markets that it is presumed to serve and, beyond, to bend the customer to its needs. And, in so doing, it deeply influences his values and beliefs—including not a few that will be mobilized in resistance to the present arguument. One of the conclusions that follows from this analysis is that there is a broad convergence between industrial systems. The imperatives of technology and organization, not the images of ideology, are what determine the shape of economic society. This, on the whole, is fortunate although it will not necessarily be welcomed by those whose intellectual capital and moral fervor are invested in the present images of the market economy as the antithesis of social planning. Nor will it be welcomed by their disciples who, with lesser intellectual investment, carry the banners of free markets and free enterprise and therewith, by definition, of the free nations into political, military or diplomatic battle. Nor will it be welcomed by those who identify planning exclusively with socialism. These are not, alas, the ideas of the consensus.

Nor is the good fortune unqualified. The subordination of belief to industrial necessity and convenience is not in accordance with the greatest vision of man. Nor is it entirely safe. On the nature of this subjugation, and its consequences, I also dwell at some length.

·   ·   ·   ·   ·   ·   ·   ·   ·   ·

## 4

Until the end of World War II, or shortly thereafter, planning was a moderately evocative word in the United States. It implied a sensible concern for what might happen in the future and a disposition, by forehanded action, to forestall avoidable misfortune. As persons won credit for competent planning of their lives, so communities won credit for effective planning of their environment. It was thought good to live in a well-planned city. The United States government had a National Resources Planning Board. During the war, postwar planning acquired the status of a modest industry in both the United States and the United Kingdom; it was felt that it would reassure those who were fighting as to the eventual utility as civilians.

With the cold war, however, the word planning acquired ideological overtones. The Communist countries not only socialized property, which seemed not a strong likelihood in the United States, but they planned, which somehow seemed more of a danger. Since liberty was there circumscribed, it followed that planning was something that the libertarian society should avoid. Modern liberalism carefully emphasizes tact rather than clarity of speech. Accordingly it avoided the term and conservatives made it one of opprobrium. For a public official to be called an economic planner was less serious than to be charged with Communism or imaginative perversion, but it reflected adversely nonetheless. One accepted and cherished whatever eventuated from the untrammeled operation of the market. Not only concern for liberty but a reputation for economic hardihood counseled such a course.

For understanding the economy and polity of the United States and other advanced industrial countries, this reaction against the word planning could hardly have been worse timed. It occurred when the increased use of technology and the accompanying commitment of time and capital were forcing extensive planning on all industrial

communities. This has now been sensed. And, in many quarters, the word planning is again acquiring a measure of respectability.

Still what is not supposed to exist is often imagined not to exist. In consequence, the role of planning in the modern industrial society remains only slightly appreciated. Additionally, it is the sound instinct of conservatives that economic planning involves, inevitably, the control of individual behavior. The denial that we do any planning has helped to conceal the fact of such control even from those who are controlled.

## 5

In the market economy the price that is offered is counted upon to produce the result that is sought. Nothing more need be done. The consumer, by his offer to pay, obtains the necessary responding action by the firm that supplies his needs. By offering to pay yet more he gets more. And the firm, in its turn, by similar offers gets the labor, materials and equipment that it requires for production.

Planning exists because this process has ceased to be reliable. Technology, with its companion commitment of time and capital, means that the needs of the consumer must be anticipated—by months or years. When the distant day arrives the consumer's willingness to buy may well be lacking. By the same token, while common labor and carbon steel will be forthcoming in response to a promise to pay, the specialized skills and arcane materials required by advanced technology cannot similarly be counted upon. The needed action in both instances is evident: in addition to deciding what the consumer will want and will pay, the firm must take every feasible step to see that what it decides to produce is wanted by the consumer at a remunerative price. And it must see that the labor, materials and equipment that it needs will be available at a cost consistent with the price it will receive. It must exercise control over what is sold. It must exercise control over what is supplied. It must replace the market with planning.

That, as more time elapses and more capital is committed, it will be increasingly risky to rely on the untutored responses of the consumer needs no elaboration. And this will be increasingly so the more technically sophisticated the product. There is a certain likelihood that even two or three years hence there will be a fairly reliable consumer demand for strawberries, milk and fresh eggs. There is no similar assurance that people will want, so spontaneously, an automobile of particular color or contour, or a transistor of particular size or design.

The effect of technology, and related change, in reducing the reliability of the market for labor or equipment and in making imperative the planning of their procurement, is equally clear and can be seen in the simplest case.[1] If men use picks and shovels to build a road, they can be called out on the same morning that the decision is taken to do the job. The picks and shovels serve a variety of purposes; accordingly, the market stocks them in readily available quantities. It will help in getting manpower if, as Marx thought necessary, there is an industrial reserve army of the unemployed. But an equally prompt beginning is possible by raiding the work force of another employer of unskilled labor with the simple market promise of more pay.

When specifications are raised to modern superhighway standards and heavy machinery is introduced, the market no longer works as well. Engineers, draftsmen, drainage experts and those who arrange the elimination of trees, grass, parkland, streams and the other environmental amenities may not be readily available even in response to a substantial advance in pay. Bulldozers and heavy earth-moving equipment cannot be bought with the same facility as picks and shovels. In all of these cases anticipatory steps must be taken to insure that the necessary supply is available at an appropriate wage or price. Market behavior must be modified by some measure of planning.[2]

For inertial systems engineers, digital circuit design specialists, superconductivity research specialists, aeroelasticity investigators and radio test and evaluation engineers as also for titanium alloys in comparison with steel, and space vehicles as compared with motorcycles, the market is greatly less dependable. Need must be elaborately anticipated and arranged. The language of both industry and government reflects the modern fact. Civil War quartermasters went into the market for their needs. So, in turn, did the contractors who filled these orders. The equivalent procurement would now be programmed.

As viewed by the industrial firm, planning consists in foreseeing the actions required between the initiation of production and its completion and preparing for the accomplishment of these actions. And it consists also of foreseeing, and having a design for meeting, any unscheduled developments, favor-

---

[1] In technical terms the supply price of highly specialized materials, components and labor is inelastic. So is the demand for highly technical products. In the first instance large (and punishing) increases in prices will bring no added supply. In the second case large (and equally punishing) decreases will bring no added customers.

[2] That planning is necessary does not mean that it is well done. At any given time on any particular construction site, as everyone has observed, nothing much is happening. Planning, to anticipate and arrange material, machinery, manpower and subcontractor requirements, is necessary. But, in context, it is done with great imprecision or incompetence. Accordingly, something is normally being awaited.

able or otherwise, that may occur along the way.[3] As planning is viewed by the economist, political scientist or pundit, it consists of replacing prices and the market as the mechanism for determining what will be produced, with an authoritative determination of what will be produced and consumed and at what price. It will be thought that the word planning is being used in two different senses.

In practice, however, the two kinds of planning, if such they may be called, are inextricably associated. A firm cannot usefully foresee and schedule future action or prepare for contingencies if it does not know what its prices will be, what its sales will be, what its costs including labor and capital costs will be and what will be available at these costs. If the market is unreliable, it will not know these things. Hence it cannot plan. If, with advancing technology and associated specialization, the market becomes increasingly unreliable, industrial planning will become increasingly impossible unless the market also gives way to planning. Much of what the firm regards as planning consists in minimizing or getting rid of market influences.

## 6

A variety of strategies are available for dealing with the increasing unreliability of markets. Not all, in fact, require their replacement. If the item is unimportant, market uncertainty can be ignored. For General Electric it is a matter of considerable interest to know the price at which it will be able to buy high alloy steel or sell large generators, and the quantities that will be forthcoming or which can be sold. No similar urgency attaches to knowledge of the price at which flatware will be available for the plant cafeterias. And size is a solvent for uncertainty that cannot otherwise be eliminated. In the late nineteen-fifties and early nineteen-sixties, the Convair Division of General Dynamics Corporation lost $425 million on the manufacture of jet transports. Part of this was the result of uncertainties associated with research and development; its 880 and 990 passenger jets cost more to bring into being than expected. But a major factor was the failure of the market—or more precisely default on or failure to obtain the contracts that were meant to reduce market uncertainty. The company did not fail (although it was a near thing) because it had annual revenues of around $2 billion from—in addition to aircraft—such diverse artifacts as missiles, building materials, submarines and telephones.[4] None of these was affected by the misfortunes of Convair. For a smaller company, with one product, a $425 million loss would have been uncomfortable. We have here an important explanation of one of the more notable corporate developments of recent times, the growth of the so-called polyglot corporation. It combines great size with highly diverse lines of manufacture. Thus it can absorb the adverse consequences of uncertainty that cannot otherwise be eliminated. Uncontrolled aversion of customers to one product, such as aircraft, is unlikely to affect telephones or building materials. The effects of market uncertainty are thus contained in what will often be a relatively small part of the total planning unit.

[3] "In practice [business management] . . . aims to minimise uncertainty, minimise the consequences of uncertainty, or both." Robin Marris, The Economic Theory of "Managerial" Capitalism (New York: The Free Press of Glencoe, 1964), p. 232.

[4] Richard Austin Smith, Corporations in Crisis (New York: Doubleday, 1963), pp. 91 et seq. The company's misfortunes in the sale of aircraft were intimately bound up with the contemporary difficulties of Howard Hughes at TWA.

But the more common strategies require that the market be replaced by an authoritative determination of price and the amounts to be sold or bought at these prices. There are three ways of doing this:

(1) The market can be superseded.
(2) It can be controlled by sellers or buyers.
(3) It can be suspended for definite or indefinite periods by contract between the parties to sale and purchase.

All of these strategies are familiar features of the industrial system.

7

The market is superseded by what is commonly called vertical integration. The planning unit takes over the source of supply or the outlet; a transaction that is subject to bargaining over prices and amounts is thus replaced with a transfer within the planning unit. Where a firm is especially dependent on an important material or product— as an oil company on crude petroleum, a steel firm on ore,[5] an aluminum company on bauxite or Sears, Roebuck on appliances—there is always danger that the requisite supplies will be available only at inconvenient prices. To have control of supply—to rely not on the market but on its own sources of supply—is an elementary safeguard. This does not eliminate market uncertainty; rather, the large and unmanageable uncertainty as to the price of ore or crude is replaced by the smaller, more diffuse and more manageable uncertainties as to the costs of labor, drilling, ore transport and yet more remote raw materials. But this is a highly beneficial exchange. For Socony-Vacuum or Sohio, a change in the cost of crude is a serious matter, a change in the cost of drilling equipment a detail.

As viewed by the firm, elimination of a market converts an external negotiation and hence a partially or wholly uncontrollable decision to a matter for purely internal decision. Nothing, we shall see, better explains modern industrial policy in regard to capital and labor than the desire to make these highly strategic cost factors subject to purely internal decision.

Markets can also be controlled. This consists in reducing or eliminating the independence of action of those to whom the planning unit sells or from whom it buys. Their behavior being subject to control, uncertainty as to that behavior is reduced. At the same time the outward form of the market, including the process of buying and selling, remains formally intact.

This control of markets is the counterpart of large size and large size in relation to the particular market. A Wisconsin dairy farm cannot influeunce the price that it pays for fertilizer or machinery. Being small, its decision to purchase or not to purchase is of no appreciable significance to the supplier. The same is true of its sales. Having no control over its suppliers or its customers it pays and receives the going prices.

Not so with General Motors. Its decision to buy or not to buy will usually be very important to its suppliers; it may be a matter of survival. This induces a highly cooperative posture. So

[5] This problem has been of importance in the difficulties experienced in recent years by Wheeling Steel, a non-integrated producer. "Thus under its contracts Wheeling in the late 1950's and early 1960's, found itself powerless to trim ore supplies as sales fluctuated. . . . Moreover by the early 1960's the operating efficiencies of using beneficiated ores . . . were fully apparent, but Wheeling, tied to outmoded sources of supply, lagged behind many in the industry in using such ores." Fortune, June, 1965.

with any large firm.[6] Should it be necessary to press matters, General Motors,
unlike the dairyman, has always the
possibility of supplying a material or
component to itself. The option of eliminating a market is an important source
of power for controlling it.[7]

Similarly, size allows General Motors
as a seller to set prices for automobiles,
diesels, trucks, refrigerators and the rest

[6] Economists, in the past, have been at pains
to disassociate large absolute size from large
size in relation to the particular market.
"Concentration [i.e. small numbers and
hence large size in relation to the market]
has nothing to do with size of firms, no matter by what resounding name it is called—
big business, colossal corporation, financial
giantism, etc. . . . most of my fellow economists would agree that 'absolute size is
absolutely irrelevant.'" M. A. Adelman,
Hearings before the Subcommittee on Anti-
trust and Monopoly of the Committee on
the Judiciary, United States Senate, Eighty-
Eighth Congress, Second Session, Pursuant
to S. Res. 262, Part I. Economic Concentration. Overall and Conglomerate Aspects
(1964), p. 228. This contention, although
wrong, is deeply grounded in contemporary
economic attitudes.

Market power is associated by economists
not with planning but with monopoly. Market concentration or monopoly in the conventional view is inimical to efficient employment of resources by the market and
has strong overtones of illegality. If big business and monopoly power tend to be identical, then all big business is inefficient and
presumptively illegal. This, however, given
the evident role of large firms in the modern
economy is absurd. So disassociation of absolute from relative size is important if
traditional antipathy to monopoly is to
seem sensible and big business is to be legitimate. In fact, large absolute size and large
size relative to the market do go together.
Great firms—General Motors, Standard Oil,
Ford, United States Steel—are invariably
large in relation to their principal markets.
On this see the sensible remarks of Carl
Kaysen, "The Corporation: How Much
Power? What Scope?" in The Corporation
in Modern Society, Edward S. Mason, ed.
(Cambridge: Harvard University Press,
1959), p. 89.
[7] There are similar, although more complex,
possibilities for control of the labor market
to which I will return.

of its offering and be secure in the
knowledge that no individual buyer, by
withdrawing its custom, can force a
change. The fact that GM is one of a
few sellers adds to its control. Each
seller shares the common interest in
secure and certain prices; it is to the advantage of none to disrupt this mutual
security system. Competitors of General
Motors are especially unlikely to initiate
price reductions that might provoke
further and retributive price-cutting. No
formal communication is necessary to
prevent such actions; this is considered
naïve and arouses the professional wrath
of company counsel. Everyone knows
that the survivor of such a contest would
not be the aggressor but General
Motors. Thus do size and small numbers of competitors lead to market
regulation.

Control of prices is only a part of
market control; if uncertainty is to be
eliminated there must also be control
of the amount sold. But size also makes
this possible. It allows advertising, a
well-nutured sales organization and careful management of product design
which can help to insure the needed
customer response. And since General
Motors produces some half of all the
automobiles, its designs do not reflect
the current mode, but are the current
mode. The proper shape of an automobile, for most people, will be what the
automobile majors decree the current
shape to be. The control of demand, as
we shall see later, is not perfect. But
what is imperfect is not unimportant
for reducing market uncertainty.

Finally, in an economy where units
are large, firms can eliminate market
uncertainty for each other. This they
do by entering into contracts specifying
prices and amounts to be provided or
bought for substantial periods of time.
A long-term contract by a Wisconsin
dairy farmer to buy fertilizer or sell
milk accords no great certainty to the
fertilizer dealer or the dairy receiving

the milk. It is subject to the capacity of the farmer to fulfill it; death, accident, drought, high feed costs and contagious abortion can all supervene. But a contract with the United States Steel Corporation to supply sheet steel or to take electric power is extremely reliable. In a world of large firms, it follows, there can be a matrix of contracts by which each firm eliminates market uncertainty for other firms and, in turn, gives to them some of its own.

Outside of the industrial system, most notably in agriculture, the government also intervenes extensively to set prices and insure demand and thus to suspend the operation of the market and eliminate market uncertainty. This it does because the participating units—the individual farms—are not large enough to control prices. Technology and the associated commitment of capital and time require nonetheless that there be stable prices and assured demand. But within the industrial system, similar action is also required where exacting technology, with extensive research and development, mean a very long production period and a very large commitment of capital. Such is the case in the development and supply of modern weapons, in the exploration of space and in the development of a growing range of modern civilian products or services including transport planes, high-speed ground transport and various applied uses of nuclear energy. Here the state guarantees a price sufficient with suitable margin, to cover costs. And it undertakes to buy what is produced or to compensate fully in the case of contract cancellation. Thus, effectively, it suspends the market with all associated uncertainty. One consequence, as we shall see, is that in areas of most exacting and advanced technology the market is most completely replaced and planning is therefore most secure. As a further consequence this has become for the participants a very attractive part of the industrial system.

The fully planned economy, so far from being unpopular, is warmly regarded by those who know it best.

8

Two things of some interest are evident from this analysis. It is clear, first of all, that industrial planning is in unabashed alliance with size. The large organization can tolerate market uncertainty as a smaller firm cannot. It can contract out of it as the smaller firm cannot. Vertical integration, the control of prices and consumer demand and reciprocal absorption of market uncertainty by contracts between firms all favor the large enterprise. And while smaller firms can appeal to the state to fix prices and insure demand, this security is also provided by the state to the big industrial firm when it is most needed. Those circumstances—the exacting technology, large commitments of time and capital—make it fairly certain that most of this government work will be done by large organizations.[8]

[8] In 1960, 384 firms with 5,000 employees or more accounted for an estimated 85 per cent of all industrial research-and-development expenditure. Firms employing fewer than 1,000 people, though numbering 260,-000, accounted for only 7 per cent of such expenditure. An estimated 65 per cent of these funds were supplied by the Federal Government. (M. A. Adelman, Hearings before the Subcommittee on Antitrust and Monopoly of the Committee on the Judiciary, United States Senate, Eighty-Ninth Congress, First Session, Pursuant to S. Res. 70, Part III. *Economic Concentration. Concentration, Invention and Innovation* [1965], pp. 1137, 1140.) In recent years the high degree of market security in the use of Federal funds—a secure coverage of all costs and a secure market for the product—has allowed a considerable number of small firms to enter the manufacture of highly technical products. These firms line highways adjacent to major educational centers, most notably in Massachusetts and California, and have encouraged the belief that the small firm has a major foothold in the manufacture of highly technical products and components particularly for defense and space exploration. Their share of the total is, in fact, negligible.

By all but the pathologically romantic, it is now recognized that this is not the age of the small man. But there is still a lingering presumption among economists that his retreat is not before the efficiency of the great corporation, or even its technological proficiency, but before its monopoly power. It has superior capacity to extract profits. Therein lies its advantage. "Big business will undertake only such innovations as promise to enhance its profits and power, or protect its market position . . . free competitive men have always been the true innovators. Under the stern discipline of competition they must innovate to prosper and to survive." [9]

This, by the uncouth, would be called drivel. Size is the general servant of technology, not the special servant of profits. The small firm cannot be restored by breaking the power of the larger ones. It would require, rather, the rejection of the technology which since earliest consciousness we are taught to applaud. It would require that we have simple products made with simple equipment from readily available materials by unspecialized labor. Then the period of production would be short; the market would reliably provide the labor, equipment and materials required for production; there would be neither possibility nor need for managing the market for the finished product. If the market thus reigned there would

be, and could be, no planning. No elaborate organization would be required. The small firm would then, at last, do very well. All that is necessary is to undo nearly everything that, at whatever violence to meaning, has been called progress in the last half century. There must be no thought of supersonic travel, or exploring the moon, and there will not be many automobiles.

We come thus to the second conclusion which is that the enemy of the market is not ideology but the engineer. In the Soviet Union and the Soviet-type economies, prices are extensively managed by the state. Production is not in response to market demand but given by the overall plan. In the western economies, markets are dominated by great firms. These establish prices and seek to insure a demand for what they have to sell. The enemies of the market are thus to be seen, although rarely in social matters has there been such a case of mistaken identity. It is not socialists. It is advanced technology and the specialization of men and process that this requires and the resulting commitment of time and capital. These make the market work badly when the need is for greatly enhanced reliability—when planning is essential. The modern large corporation and the modern apparatus of socialist planning are variant accommodations to the same need. It is open to every freeborn man to dislike this accommodation. But he must direct his attack to the cause. He must not ask that jet aircraft, nuclear power plants or even the modern automobile in its modern volume be produced by firms that are subject to unfixed prices and unmanaged demand. He must ask instead that they not be produced.

[9] Horace M. Gray, Hearings before the Subcommittee on Antitrust and Monopoly of the Committee on the Judiciary, United States Senate, Eighty-Ninth Congress, First Session, Pursuant to S. Res. 70, Part III. *Economic Concentration. Concentration, Invention and Innovation* (1965), p. 1164.

# 48

# The Social and Economic Power of Corporations

### ANDREW HACKER

Problems like poverty, civil rights and juvenile delinquency may have been "discovered" only in the past few years, but such can hardly be said about the issue of bigness in American business. On and off, for the last three-quarters of a century, the question has been raised whether the nation's large corporations have reached the point where they can cut a swath through society without having to account for the consequences of their actions.

Allusions to "the trusts," "robber barons" and even "Wall Street" may have an archaic ring. Nevertheless, the frequency and magnitude of recent corporate mergers, the high level of profits despite the persistence of poverty and the latest furor over safety in the country's leading industry are bringing renewed life to a debate that has as much importance for 1966 as did for 1896, 1912 and 1932.

Our large corporations are very large indeed. General Motors, for example, employs more than 600,000 people, a figure exceeding the combined payrolls of the state Governments of New York, California, Illinois, Pennsylvania, Texas and Ohio. The annual sales of Standard Oil of New Jersey are over $10 billion, more than the total tax collections of Wisconsin, Connecticut and Massachusetts, in addition to the six states just mentioned. In fact, our 50 largest companies have almost three times as many people working for them as our 50 states, and their combined sales are

over five times greater than the taxes the states collect.

Yet here, as elsewhere, statistics can be made to tell several stories. For example, is big business getting bigger? Between 1957 and 1965, non-agricultural employment in the United States rose by about 10 percent. But during that same period the number of persons employed by the nation's largest industrial companies went up by 15 percent. Measured in this way, the big corporations seem to be taking three steps for every two taken by the economy as a whole.

At the same time it must be acknowledged that corporate America is by no means the fastest-growing sector in the country. Government employment, especially at the local level, is increasing at a higher rate; from 1957 to 1965 the public payroll, excluding the military, rose by 25 percent. Even higher was the percentage increase in service industries. Enterprises like boatyards, car washes and carry-out restaurants—many of them small and locally based—have come to constitute the most vital area of economic growth.

Moreover, the advent of automated processes in large-scale production has actually cut down corporate employment in several dominant industries. At the outset of 1965, for instance, such companies as General Electric and Gulf Oil and United States Steel actually had *fewer* people working for them than they had eight years earlier. While these firms are not yet typical, they may be harbingers of things to come—the apparent ability of corporations to increase their sales, production and profits with a decreasing work force.

If corporate size has a variety of

yardsticks, corporate power is beyond precise measurement. It is not an overstatement to say that we know too much about the economics of big business and not nearly enough about the social impact of these institutions. Professional economists tend to focus on the freedom of large firms to set or manage prices, with the result that attention is deflected from the broader but less tangible role played by corporations in the society as a whole.

By the same token it is all too easy to to expose egregious defects in consumer products or advertising or packaging. Congressional hearings make good forums for periodic charges of "irresponsibility," whether the target of the year happens to be automobiles or pharmaceuticals or cigarettes. It is true that the buyer is often stung—and sometimes laid to rest—by the products of even the most prestigeful of corporations. But the quality of merchandise, like the ability to fix prices, is only a secondary aspect of corporate power.

What calls for a good deal more thought and discussion is the general and pervasive influence of the large corporate entity in and on the society. For the decisions made in the names of these huge companies guide and govern, directly and indirectly, all of our lives.

The large corporations shape the material contours of the nation's life. While original ideas for new products may come from a variety of sources, it is the big companies that have the resources to bring these goods to the public. The argument that the consumer has "free will," deciding what he will and will not buy, can be taken just so far. (Too much can be made of the poor old Edsel.) For in actual fact we *do* buy much or even most of what the large corporations put on the shelves or in the showrooms for us.

To be sure, companies are not unsophisticated and have a fair idea of what the consumer will be willing to purchase. But the general rule, with fewer exceptions than we would like to think, is that if they make it we will buy it. Thus we air-condition our bedrooms, watch color television in our living rooms, brush our teeth electrically in the bathroom and cook at eyelevel in the kitchen. It is time for frankness on this score: the American consumer is not notable for his imagination and does not know what he "wants." Thus he waits for corporate America to develop new products and, on hearing of them, discovers a longfelt "need" he never knew he had.

And more than any other single force in society, the large corporations govern the character and quality of the nation's labor market. The most visible example of this process has been the decision of companies to introduce computers into the world of work, bringing in train an unmistakable message to those who must earn a living. Millions of Americans are told, in so many words, what skills they will have to possess if they are to fill the jobs that will be available. A company has the freedom to decide *how* it will produce its goods and services, whether its product happens to be power mowers or life insurance or air transportation. And having made this decision, it establishes its recruiting patterns accordingly. Individuals, in short, must tailor themselves to the job if they want to work at all. Most of us and all of our children, will find ourselves adjusting to new styles of work whether we want to or not.

The impact of corporate organization and technology on the American educational system deserves far closer attention than it has been given. Whether we are talking of a vocational high school in Los Angeles or an engineering college in Milwaukee or a law school in New Haven, the shape of the curriculum is most largely determined by the job needs of our corporate enterprises. The message goes out that certain kinds of people having certain kinds of knowledge are needed. All American education, in a significant sense, is vocational. Liberal-arts students may enjoy a period of insulation but they are well aware that they will eventually have to find niches for themselves in offices or laboratories.

While many college graduates go into non-corporate or non-business employment, the fact remains that much of their educational tune is still being determined by corporate overtures. Even the liberal-arts college in which I teach has recently voted to establish within its precincts a department of "computer science." It is abundantly clear that while I.B.M. and Sperry Rand did not command Cornell to set up such a department, the university cannot afford to be insensitive to the changing character of the job market.

Our large firms both have and exercise the power to decide where they will build their new factories and offices. And these decisions, in their turn, determine which regions of the country will prosper and which will stagnate. The new face of the South is, in largest measure, the result of corporate choices to open new facilities in what was hitherto a blighted area. Not only has this brought new money to the region, but new kinds of jobs and new styles of work have served to transform the Southern mentality. The transition to the 20th century has been most rapid in the communities where national corporations have settled. You cannot remain an unrepentant Confederate and expect to get on in Du Pont.

By the same token the regions which have not prospered in postwar years have been those where corporations have opted not to situate. Too much can be made of the New England "ghost towns." Actually corporations have "pulled out" of very few places; more critical has been their failure to establish or expand facilities in selected parts of the country. Thus patterns of migration—from the countryside to the city and from the city to the suburb—are reflections of corporation decisions on plant and office location. If men adjust to machines, they also move their bodies to where the jobs are.

Related to this have been the corporate decisions to rear their headquarters in the center of our largest cities, especially the East Side of New York. Leaving aside the architectural transformation and the esthetic investment with which we will have to live for many years, the very existence of these prestige-palaces has had the effect of drawing hundreds of thousands of people into metropolitan areas not equipped to handle them. Thus not only the traffic snarls and the commuter crush, but also the burgeoning of suburbs for the young-marrieds of management and the thin-walled apartments for others in their twenties, fifties and sixties.

Much—perhaps too much—has been made of ours being an age of "organization men." Yet there is more than a germ of truth in this depiction of the new white-collar class which is rapidly becoming the largest segment of the American population. The great corporations created this type of individual, and the habits and style of life of corporate employment continue to play a key role in setting values and aspirations for the population as a whole. Working for a large organization has a subtle but no less inevitable effect on a person's character. It calls for the virtues of adaptability, sociability, and that certain caution necessary when one knows one is forever being judged.

The types of success represented by the man who has become a senior engineer at Western Electric or a branch manager for Metropolitan Life are now models for millions. Not only does the prestige of the corporation rub off on the employe, but he seems to be affixed to an escalator that can only move in an upward direction. Too much has been made of the alleged "repudiation" of business and the corporate life by the current generation of college students. This may be the case at Swarthmore, Oberlin and in certain Ivied circles. But in actual fact, the great majority of undergraduates, who are after all at places like Penn State and Purdue, would like nothing better than a good berth in Ford or Texaco. Indeed, they are even now priming themselves to become the sort of person that those companies will want them to be.

The pervasive influence of the large corporations, in these and other areas, derives less from how many people they employ and far more from their possession of great wealth. Our largest firms are very well-off indeed, and they have a good deal of spare cash to spend as and where they like. These companies make profits almost automatically every year, and they find it necessary to give only a fraction of those earnings back to their stockholders in the form of dividends.

(If the largest companies are "competitive" it is only really in the sense that we all are: all of us have to keep working at our jobs if we are to survive as viable members of the society. Quite clearly the biggest corporations stand no risk of going out of business. Of the firms ranking among the top 40 a dozen years ago all but two are still in preeminent positions. And the pair that slipped—Douglas Aircraft and Wilson meat-packing—continue to remain in the top 100.)

Thus the big firms have had the money to create millions of new white-collar jobs. Department heads in the large companies ask for and are assigned additional assistants, coordinators, planners and programmers who fill up new acres of office space every year. What is ironic, considering that this is the business world, is that attempts are hardly ever made to discover whether these desk-occupiers actually enhance the profitability or the productivity of the company. But everyone keeps busy enough: attending meetings and conferences, flying around the country, and writing and reading and amending memoranda.

White-collar featherbedding is endemic in the large corporation, and the spacious amenities accompanying such employment make work an altogether pleasant experience. The travel and the transfers and the credit-card way of life turn work into half-play and bring with them membership in a cosmopolitan world. That a large proportion of these employes are not necessary was illustrated about 10 years ago when the Chrysler Corporation had its back to the wall and was forced to take the unprecedented step of firing one-third of its white-collar force. Yet the wholesale departure of these clerks and executives, as it turned out, had no effect on the company's production and sales. Nevertheless, Chrysler was not one to show that an empire could function half-clothed, and it hired back the office workers it did not need just as soon as the cash was again available.

If all this sounds a bit Alice-in-Wonderland, it would be well to ponder on what the consequences would be were all of our major corporations to cut their white-collar staffs to only those who were actually needed. Could the nation bear the resulting unemployment, especially involving so many people who have been conditioned to believe that they possess special talents and qualities of character?

Corporate wealth, then, is spent as a corporation wishes. If General Motors wants to tear down the Savoy-Plaza and erect a corporate headquarters for itself at Fifth Avenue and 59th Street, it will go ahead and do so. Quite obviously an office building could, at a quarter of the cost, have been located on Eleventh Avenue and 17th Street. But why should cost be the prime consideration? After all, the stockholders have been paid their dividends, new production facilities have been put into operation, and there is still plenty of money left over. Nor is such a superfluity of spare cash limited to the very largest concerns. Ford, which is generally thought of as General Motors' poor sister, was sufficiently well-heeled to drop a quarter of a billion dollars on its Edsel and still not miss a dividend.

If our large corporations are using their power to reshape American society, indeed to reconstruct the American personality, the general public's thinking about such concentrated influence still remains ambiguous.

There persists, for example, the ideology of anti-trust and the fond place in American hearts still occupied by small business. Thus politicians can count on striking a resonant chord when they call for more vigorous prosecutions under the Sherman Law and for greater appropriations for the Small Business Administration. Most Americans, from time to time, do agree that our largest companies are too big and should somehow or other be broken up into smaller units. But just how strong or enduring this sentiment is is hard to say. No one really expects that Mobil Oil or Bethlehem Steel can or will be "busted" into 10 or a dozen entirely new and independent companies. Thus, if the ideology that bigness equals badness lingers on, there is no serious impetus to translate that outlook into action.

Part of the problem is that if Americans are suspicious of bigness, they are not really clear about just what it is about large corporations that troubles them. Despite the periodic exposures of defective brake cylinders or profiteering on polio vaccine, the big story is not really one of callous exploitation or crass

irresponsibility. Given the American system of values, it is difficult to mount a thoroughgoing critique of capitalism or to be "anti-business" in an unequivocal way. The result is that our commentaries in this area are piecemeal and sporadic in character. We have the vocabularies for criticizing both "big government" and "big labor" but the image of the large corporation is a hazy one, and despite its everyday presence in our midst our reaction to its very existence is uncertain.

Take the question of who owns our big enterprises. In terms of legal title the owners are the stockholders, and management is accountable to that amorphous group. But it is well known that in most cases a company's shares are so widely dispersed that the managers of a corporation can run the firm pretty well as they please. Yet even assuming that the executives are acting with the tacit consent of their company's theoretical owners, it is worth inquiring just who these stockholders are.

Interestingly, a rising proportion of the stockholders are not people at all but rather investing institutions. Among these non-people are pension funds, insurance companies, brokerage houses, foundations and universities. Thus some of the most significant "voters" at the annual meetings of the big companies are the Rockefeller Foundation, Prudential Life and Princeton University. And these institutions, out of habit and prudence, automatically ratify management decisions.

It is instructive that the corporations' own public-relations departments have just about given up trying to persuade us that these stockholder gatherings are just another version of the local town meeting. The last report I saw that did this was filled with photographs showing average-citizen stockholders rising to question the board of directors on all manner of company policies. "A sizable number of share-holders participated in the lively discussion periods," the reader is told. "Many more spoke individually with directors and other executives about the affairs of the company." However, in small type in the back of the report is an accounting of the five votes that were actually taken at the meeting. In no case did the management receive less than 96 percent of the ballots (i.e., shares) that were cast.

From these observations at least one answer is possible: yes, there is a "power élite" presiding over corporate America. Yet the problem with this term is that the "élite" in question consists not so much of identifiable personalities—how many of the presidents of our 20 largest corporations can any of us name?—but rather of the chairs in the top offices.

The typical corporation head stays at his desk for only about seven years. The power he exercises is less discretionary than we would like to believe, and the range of decisions that can be called uniquely his own is severely limited. (It is only in the small companies on the way up, such as the Romney days at American Motors, that the top men impress their personalities on the enterprise.) John Kenneth Galbraith once noted that when a corporation president retires and his successor is named, the price of the company's stock, presumably a barometer of informed opinion, does not experience a perceptible change.

Unfortunately it is far easier to think in terms of actual individuals than of impersonal institutions. Therefore it must be underlined that the so-called "élite" consists not of Frederic Donner and Frederick Kappel and Fred Borch but rather of *whatever* person happens to be sitting in the top seat at General Motors and A.T.&T. and General Electric. We are reaching the point where corporate power is a force in its own right, for all intents and purposes independent of the men who in its name make the decisions.

The modern corporation is not and cannot be expected to be a "responsible" institution in our society. For all the self-congratulatory handouts depicting the large firm as a "good citizen," the fact remains that a business enterprise exists purely and simply to make more profits—a large proportion of which it proceeds to pour back into itself. (True, the big companies do not seek to "maximize" their profits: their toleration of make-work and high living is enough evidence for this.)

But corporations, like all businesses whether large or small, are in the primary business of making money; indeed, they do not even exist to produce certain goods or services that may prove useful or necessary to society. If Eli Lilly or Searle and the other drug companies discovered that they could chalk up larger profits by getting out of vaccines and manufacturing frozen orange juice instead, they would have no qualms or hesitation about taking such a step.

A corporation, then, cannot be expected to shoulder the aristocratic mantle. No one should be surprised that in the areas of civil rights and civil liberties our large companies have failed to take any significant initiative. The men who preside over them are not philosopher-kings, and no expectation should be held out that they may become so. At best they can be counted on to give some well-publicized dollars to local community chests and university scholarships. But after those checks are written (and the handing-over of them has been photographed) it is time to get back to business.

And this is as it should be. Corporate power is great—in fact, far more impressive than corporation executives are willing to admit—and were large corporations to become "socialminded," their impact would be a very mixed blessing. For then the rest of us would have to let corporate management define just what constitutes "good citizenship," and we would have to accept such benefactions without an excuse for comment or criticism.

Therefore, when corporations, in the course of doing their business, create social dislocations there is no point in chiding or exhorting them to more enlightened ways. It would be wrong, of course, to lay the blame for all of our social ills at the doorsteps of the large firms. If the drug companies manufacture cheap and effective birth control pills it is a trifle presumptuous to take them to task for whatever promiscuity occurs as a consequence.

Nevertheless, the American corporation, in the course of creating and marketing new merchandise, presents us with temptations—ranging from fast cars to color television—to which we sooner or later succumb. There is nothing intrinsically wrong with color television. It is, rather, that the money we spend for a new set is money that can no longer be put aside for the college education of our children. (Thus, no one should be surprised when, 15 years from now, there is a demand for full Federal scholarships for college students. Not the least reason for such a demand will be that we were buying color TV back in 1966.)

Specific questions can be framed easily enough. It is the answers that are far from clear. We have unemployment: how far is it because corporations have not been willing or able to create enough jobs for the sorts of people who need them? We have a civil rights problem: how far is it because corporations have been reluctant to hire and train Negroes as they have whites? We have a shortage of nurses: how far is it because corporations outbid and undercut the hospitals by offering girls secretarial jobs at higher pay for less work? We have whole waves of un-

wanted and unneeded immigrants pouring into our large cities: how far is it because corporations have decided to locate in Ventura County in California rather than Woodruff County in Arkansas?

Questions like these may suggest differing answers but they do add up to the fact that a good measure of laissez-faire continues to exist in our corporate economy. For all their ritual protestations over Government intervention and regulation, our large companies are still remarkably free: free to make and sell what they want, free to hire the people they want for the jobs they have created, free to locate where they choose, free to dispose of their earnings as they like—and free to compel the society to provide the raw materials, human and otherwise, necessary for their ongoing needs.

The task of picking up the pieces left by the wayside belongs to Government. This is the ancient and implicit contract of a society committed to freedom of enterprise. But whether the agencies of Government have the resources or the public support to smooth out the dislocations that have been caused to our economy and society is not at all clear. Negro unemployment, the pollution of the Great Lakes, the architectural massacre of Park Avenue and the wasteland of television seem to be beyond the power and imagination of a Government that has traditionally understood its secondary and complementary role.

Corporate America, with its double-edged benefactions and its unplanned disruptions, is in fact creating new problems at a rate faster than our Governmental bureaus can possibly cope with them. Given that the articulate segments of the American public seem at times to show more confidence in United States Steel than in the United States Senate, the prognosis must be that the effective majority today prefers a mild but apparently bearable chaos to the prospect of serious Government allocation and planning.

The American commitment to private property means, at least for the foreseeable future, that we will be living with the large corporation. On the whole, Americans seem vaguely contented with this development, unanticipated as it may have been. In light of this stolidity the order of the day—to reverse Karl Marx's dictum—is to understand our world rather than change it; to identify, with as much clarity and precision as is possible, the extent to which a hundred or so giant firms are shaping the contours of our contemporary and future society. Only if we engage in such an enterprise will we be able to make any kind of considered judgment concerning the kind of nation in which we wish to live and the sort of people we want to be.

# 49

## The Role of the Legislator

### EDWARD A. SHILS

In the United States, as in any other large democratic government, the burden on the legislator is great. The volume of legislation is vast and its complexity beyond the judgment of laymen. Even an expert could not hope to understand and master fully all the bills which are produced. In Great Britain, where the party leadership strictly controls the introduction of legislation and private members' bills are the exceptions, the detailed mastery of all proposed legislation is beyond the power of all Members of Parliament. In the United States, where so many nearly similar bills are produced on the same subject, where the number of subjects on which legislation is proposed is vast, and where individual legislators often have their own legislative ambitions in addition to the program of their party leaders and of the Executive, the burden is especially great. The legislator is

Reprinted by permission of the publisher from *The Torment of Secrecy* by Edward A. Shils. Copyright 1956 by The Free Press, A Corporation.

overwhelmed by his legislative work alone. He frequently votes on measures on which he has not formed his own judgment and on which he has not had his judgment authoritatively and reassuringly formed for him by his party organization. The fact that he leaves so much uncovered has a disquieting effect on him; it causes him to feel that matters are slipping beyond his control. The American legislator does not inherit a tradition of a political class who have a sense of having been born to rule. American legislators come from a great diversity of backgrounds, but for a long time they have come from moderate provincial circumstances in which there was no sense of a natural affinity to authority. The self-esteem of a traditional political class has been lacking in the tradition of American politics, and the effects of the absence have been aggravated by the prestige of the "people."

The discipline of the British parliamentary party and the power of the national headquarters lightens the burden of judgment and worry for the British M.P. If he behaves himself reasonably well, he can count on the support of his party for re-election. The decentralized structure of the American party system and absence of disciplinary power of the party leadership in Congress accentuate, on the contrary, the strains on the American legislator. He is very much on his own. The national party does not arrange his candidacy; it has little control over the machine on which the Congressman depends for his re-election; and its financial aid for the conduct of his campaign is much less than adequate. He must keep his machine going. Like an ambassador who is uneasy that his enemies at home are undoing his work and undermining his position while he is away, the legislator must always keep his eye on the machine at home—fearing that it might break out of his control during his absence in Washington.

American constituents, at least a sector of them, are often very outspoken in their demands. The American legislator is moreover hypersensitive to the faintest whisper of a constituent's voice. Unable to depend on the national party for re-election, he must cultivate and nurture the more active elements in his constituency more than legislators in Great Britain where constituents are less clamorous and parties are stronger at the center.

To satisfy the demands of some of his constituents the American legislator expends much of his time and energy running errands for them in Washington and receiving them when they visit the capital for business or for sightseeing purposes. He himself is often quite pleased to have this opportunity for personal contact with his constituents, even though it distracts him from his job in Washington.

In addition to trying to please those whom he sees, he is constantly harried in his mind's eye by those whom he does not see. His remoteness from them does not make him less sensitive to their sentiments or less fearful of their displeasure. The distance from the voters and their anonymity make the sensitivity even greater and more delicate. The nature of the recruitment process favors the man with a delicate ear for the voters' sentiments and an eagerness to gain their approbation. The populistic ethos of the American electorate and the traditions of American politics favor the person who can present himself as a man of the people, who is proud of the fact that he deviates from them in no significant way and who fears that any known deviations would be interpreted as snobbery or standoffishness.

This eagerness to gratify an unseen constituency and to rank high in their favor helps us to understand why it is that legislators who have no strong convictions on a given topic might sometimes be among its most fervent investigators. They do so simply because they believe it will appeal to their constituents and because they cannot allow any rival for the affection and votes of their constituents to preempt this theme.

Far from his home base and insecure about his tenure and support, he is hard put to find a procedure for keeping in touch with his constituents and fixing himself in their minds. The press conference, the cultivation of newspapermen, the radio and the television program, and the congressional investigation are often the best-suited instruments for the legislator's need to remind his constituents of his existence. That is the reason why investigations often involve such unseemly uses of the organs of publicity. By giving material to the press, he pleases the journalists and reaches the eyes of his constituents. Publicity is the next best thing to the personal contact which the legislator must forego. It is his substitute offering by which he tries to counteract the personal contact which his rivals at home have with his constituents.

The frequent recourse to personal intervention on behalf of individual constituents has greater consequences than the maintenance of a sensitive attachment of the legislator to his audible constituency and the wasteful expenditure of his time. It encourages in him expectation of personal service by the bureaucracy, an expectation long entrenched in the traditions of patronage politics and populism.

The American legislator, whose professional traditions date back to a social order in which government intervention played no great part and in which patronage was the main method of the recruitment of civil servants, tends to look on the administrator's role and tasks as properly the legislator's own responsibility—which are only transiently delegated to the administrator. He draws no fine line between legislation and administration and he likes to cooperate in and assist in administration as well as to specify, scrutinize, and control the administrator's tasks and powers. The modern separation of powers is indeed often felt as an implicit rebuff.

To these particular strains in the vocational life of an American legislator should be added the more general strains. For one thing, the career of the professional politician is full of hazards. In all demoncracies the legislator is recurrently in danger of not being re-elected. In the event of being unsuccessful he must go back to a career which he has neglected. In the United States very few of our professional politicians are recruited from the classes which live from inherited wealth. If he is in the professions or business, he will, if defeated for re-election, have to make up the distance which his contemporaries have gained on him. Although he might have improved certain "connections," some of his skill other than political skill might well have deteriorated. He will probably have allowed some of his professional connections to lapse. Whatever the effect on his skill he often faces the humiliation of return as a political failure, and the need to begin at a lower level than those who were his equals a few years before. Moreover, since our politicians do not come from classes which have as part of their tradition a normal expectation of entering a political career, they tend to a greater extent to be selected from among persons who enjoy the game of politics, to whom it has a special psychological appeal. For such persons, the threat of exclusion from politics through failure is especially unsatisfactory. Thus the situation of the political career in the United States makes legislators faced with the possibility of failure take eager refuge in devices which will recommend them to their constituents and reassure their continuation in office. Activity as a member of an investigative committee bathed in publicity is one of these devices.

Even when successful, however, the professional politician in the United States cannot always have the unalloyed pleasure and comfort of feeling that he is participating in a highly honored profession. The fact that he is so often made into an errand boy or a handmaiden to his constituents is indicative of their attitude towards him and of his attitude towards himself. Government in the United States, where established institutions are not usually objects of deep reverence, is far from the most esteemed of institutions. Living from the public treasury, from the taxpayer's money, whether as legislator or administrator, has until recently been rather looked down upon by the hardworking taxpayer and his journalistic spokesmen. This view is still alive in American public opinion. The image of the politician in the organs of mass communication is not a laudatory one. Pomposity, vanity, an unbalanced sense of importance and occasionally sheer dishonesty are part of the traditional American concept of the professional politician—although the reality has been far different. Even though this popular image has been changing in the past decades, the term "politician" still has a derogatory overtone.

It is significant that there is no word in current usage to describe the legislator which is free from either cant or delegation. The word "politician" in the United States brings a wrinkle—and scarcely a smiling one—to the nose. There is no other word save "statesman" for the job, and it always evokes uneasiness and visions of diplomatic chancelleries and of elegant gentlemen who have a rather hard time at the hands of the politicians. The fact that the United States is simultaneously the freest of great states and at the same time the scene of some of the most unworthy departures from the principles of liberty and the rule of law is closely connected with the devaluation of the politician in American life.

The occasional outbursts of an excessive desire to please on the one hand, and of vindictive aggressiveness on the other, are both products of this perception by the professional politician of his ambiguous status. The legislator's suspicion of the administrator as one who lives wastefully on the taxpayer's money is also an expression of the discomfiture which arises from the uneasy feeling that he himself is doing exactly that. Congressional investigations often provide favorable occasions for the manifestations of this deep-lying distrust.

It is not only the social status of politics that influences the legislator's mood. The geographical location of the center of national political life also has its effect. The almost exclusive position of politics as the chief preoccupation of Washington has an influence on the life of the legislator. It means that he is forced to live almost entirely in an atmosphere of politics. It is true, of course, that many enjoy this type of life with its incessant stress on influence, rivalry, ambition and frustration—it sharpens political wits and has a brilliance of its own. It does, however, strengthen and even overdevelop the political orientation of men who have already entered voluntarily upon such a career. It aggravates the exclusive preoccupation with political events to the point where every human activity becomes evaluated not in terms of its intrinsic value in its own appropriate sphere, but in terms of its political significance.

In London, a legislator can carry on his own profession if he is fortunate, which is more frequently the case than in Washington. He can also associate more easily with persons in other professions, with businessmen, scientists, writers, clergymen, in fact with all the groups which the diversified life of a great city which is not merely the political and administrative capital of a great country makes possible. A diversity of interests and a reduction of the primacy of politics is more practicable in this kind of situation.

In Washington, however, legislators must associate in their leisure hours almost entirely with other legislators or with journalists, administrators, and businessmen whose presence in Washington is almost always evidence of their own predominantly political interests. In such a society, where the talk is invariably centered about who is getting what from whom, both the sensitivity and the insecurity of the legislator are increased. It strengthens his tendency to interpret everything in political terms and to look on the world as engaged at every moment in arranging political combinations, intended to advance some individual or group and to ruin another. This type of social life offers no respite from the tensions and anxieties of the individual legislator's own political career. It provides a stimulant rather than a soothing calm. The gossip and rumors agitate him and cause him to worry more about his own political fortunes. Hearing so much of what others are doing or are having done for them to secure their political fortunes, he feels he must exert himself more to establish and advance his own prestige. Whoever blocks him is his enemy. Whoever has a deficiency, real or imputable, which can be attacked in the name of a major political value, becomes a fair target in the competition to keep oneself politically afloat. He is more susceptible to excitation by rumors and by the passing currents of opinion.

As a result of these factors—not all of which operate equally for all legislators—the life of the American politician holding a seat in the Senate or in the House of Representatives is far from an easy one. He is always confronted with more demands on him than he can satisfy. He is always in danger of displeasing some people and he is never sure of just what it will take to please them or how he can do it when he knows what it is. He is always dependent on someone else's judgment for his equanimity and for his security, and he tends to be a person with a desire to please. The result is a state of stress and disquiet, often flaring up into rage and sometimes into vindictiveness.

If we bear in mind the populistic atmosphere in which the political career is conducted, and the populistic dispositions which many of our political leaders carry with them as a product of their own spontaneous outlook and as a product of the need to read and please their constituents' minds, we begin to understand why political life in the United States is often so stormy, and why so many politicians seek their salvation in publicity. We also begin to see why politicians have conspiracies on their minds and why they are preoccupied with secrecy. . . .

# 50

# The Future of Work in the Modern Economy

DANIEL BELL

## Arcadia and Utopia

In the history of human hopes and longing, the polar images of arcadia and utopia meet at some point in the curving universe. Men have always looked back to some golden age or forward to some golden idyl. Two thou-

Reprinted by permission of the publisher from *The End of Ideology* by Daniel Bell. Copyright 1960 by The Free Press, A Corporation.

sand years ago a Greek poet of Cicero's day acclaimed the invention of the water wheel for grinding corn as giving freedom to female slaves: "Sleep late even if the crowing cocks announce the dawn . . . the Nymphs perform the work of your hands . . . turn the heavy concave Nisyrian millstones." Aristotle predicted that slavery would disappear when looms would weave by themselves, for then the chief workmen would not need helpers, nor masters slaves. The romantics would have none of these visions. In Samuel Butler's *Erewhon*, inventions were prohibited; Bellamy's *Looking Backward*, with its conscript industrial army, was called by William Morris a "horrible cockney dream." In the Gothic revival, it was the primitive that was ennobled: to shoot, to trap, to chop trees, to hold a plow, to prospect a seam—these were the virtues of work.

Today we stand at a point where those hopes and longings seem to converge. While the assembly line brought the work to the workers, tending to grip them bodily to the rhythm of the line, the vast development of automatic controls and the continuous flow creates the possibility of eliminating the workers from production completely. On its present scale and complexity, the continuous-flow innovation dates back only to 1939, when Standard Oil of New Jersey and M. W. Kellogg Company erected the first of the oil industry's great fluid-catalytic crackers. In these new plants, the raw material, fluid or gas, flows continuously in at one end, passes through intricate processing stages, and debouches in a 24-hour stream of products at the other. The whole plant is run from central control rooms by a few men at the control panels, while mobile maintenance crews take care of any breakdowns. The new Ford engine plant in Cleveland, opened in 1952, provides almost a continuous operation from the original pouring of sand and the casting of molds to the flow of molten iron and the shaking-out of fully cast engine blocks, with few human hands involved in the operation other than to speed the flow of work by checking empty gauges and to operate the high overhead cranes which lift the mass of metals. Thus foundry work, the grimiest of human denigration, has given way to the machine.

The new industrial revolution is symbolized in the word "automation." The term itself was coined in 1948 by the engineering division of the Ford Motor Company to describe the operations of some new "transfer machines" which mechanically unload the stampings from the body presses and position them before machine tools that automatically drill and bore the holes for other parts to be inserted. The purists among the engineers dismiss the Ford process as "advanced mechanization," or grudgingly call it "Detroit automation." For the term "automation" is reserved for processes in which high-speed, self-correcting (i.e., feedback) instruments control the operations of other machines.[1] Automatic devices, they point out, are quite ancient. The Romans had a hydraulic float valve to regulate the water level in their storage tanks. The Dutch used such devices to keep windmills facing into the wind. James Watt devised a "flyball governor" to keep his steam engine clacking at constant speed. Quite ingeniously, the old Yankee flour mills of a hundred and fifty years ago operated with true "automation" principles: the grain from wagons was unloaded into a hopper where, after being mechanically weighed, it was carried by a screw-type conveyor and bucket elevator to the top floor; there, by force of gravity, the grain flowed into hoppers which regulated the amounts fed into the millstones; the ground grain, now flour, was sifted mechanically through screens into barrels and conveyed away by barge or wagon.

Whatever the claims of the ancients, what is new today is the simultaneous introduction of many different processes whereby direct human labor has been eliminated and mechanical or electronic

[1] A toaster is automatic, but it follows a "pre-set" cycle of operations, and cannot adjust for variations, whereas an "automated" machine, by feedback, corrects itself for variations.

devices regulate the flow of work. These processes are of four orders:

1. Continuous flow or automatic handling operations such as in the oil refineries or in the new engine casting plants. Here the worker is a dial adjuster, maintenance man, skilled repairman.

2. Data-processing systems, or the use of giant electronic "brains" which can store millions of bits of information and select the required item in a fraction of a second. The United States Steel Corporation has installed a data-processing system whereby incoming orders are simultaneously translated, through tapes, into production, scheduling, traffic, and shipping orders for the relevant plant; into volume and income information for the company's operating and financial records; and into billing, invoicing, and price notices to the customers. The Bank of America has a 25-ton "bank clerk," an electronic machine made up of 17,000 radio tubes and a million feet of electric wire, coyly named "Erma," which is capable of handling the bookkeeping details on 50,000 checking accounts a day. It accepts "stop" payments and "hold" orders, catches overdrawn accounts, and prints monthly statements at a speed of 600 lines a minute.

3. Self-correcting control devices which "instruct" machines through punched tapes, very much like the ones in old player-pianos. An automatic lathe developed by the Arma Corporation, through punched-tape instructions, machined a workpiece in four minutes to tolerances of 0.0003 of an inch, which normally was machined in thirty minutes by a skilled machinist working with drawings. A concrete-mixing plant, in use by the Cleveland Builders Supply Company, loads onto ready-mix trucks any one of 1,500 different mixing formulas. A punched card, coded for the formula, is inserted into an electronic control panel, and the desired mixture is delivered by conveyors onto the waiting truck; the control mechanisms even measure and compensate for any deficiency or excess of water in the sand, coarse rock, and slag that go into the mixture.

4. Automatic assembly. Admiral Corporation and several other major electrical manufacturing companies have machines that can "spit out" completely assembled radios. A machine called Autofab, produced by General Mills, will put together in one minute the number of electronic units that previously took a worker a full day to assemble.

While some of these plants resemble the image of the "robot factory" which science-fiction writers have conjured up for decades, they are still one step away from "true" automation. Today, fully automatic assembly is possible only when a large output of a single product is called for, but such inflexible, single-purpose machinery is too costly for medium or short production runs, and consequently the adoption of such machines tends to "freeze" the design and the technological stage of the product. True automation, as envisaged by Eric Leaver and John J. Brown, would design products in terms of a multi-purpose machine, rather than a machine for each product. If such machines ever were produced, they would create a revolution not only in technology but in aesthetics as well. The concept of what a radio or a stove should look like, for example, might have to change drastically. In the first industrial revolution, fixed aesthetic habit dominated the design of a machine. When, in the famous Crystal Palace Exhibit of 1851, iron was introduced for the first time into construction other than machinery, the first structures and artifacts, true to the predominant imagination, were ornamental and baroque rather than utilitarian. Only gradually did the "modern" emphasis that the form should express, rather than hide, the function gain the upper hand. Yet, although the designer is no longer conservative, the engineer still is. It is easier for him to create single-purpose automatic machinery that can produce quick, spectacular results. But the adoption of these expensive machines will only delay the coming of the flexible automatic machines, capable of turning out a wide variety of products, and producing a true machine revolution.

Americans, with their tendency to exaggerate innovations, have conjured up wild fears about changes that automation may bring. Norbert Wiener, whose book on "cybernetics" was responsible in part for the vogue of "communication theory," has pictured a dismal world of unattended factories turning out mountains of goods which a jobless population will be unable to buy. Such projections are silly. Even if automatic controls were suddenly introduced, regardless of cost considerations, into all the factories that could use them, only about eight percent of the labor force would be directly affected.

It is evident that automation will produce disruptions; and many workers, particularly older ones, may find it difficult to ever find suitable jobs again. It is also likely that small geographical pockets of the United States may find themselves becoming "depressed areas" as old industries fade or are moved away. But it is unlikely that the economic effects of automation will be any greater, say, than the social disruptions which follow shifts in taste, or substitution of products, or changes in mores. The rise of a functional style in architecture, for example, has meant a decrease in the ranks of brick masons,

plasterers, painters, and molders. The substitution of oil for coal has cut in half the required number of miners. The fact that young people now marry at an earlier age has produced a sharp slump in the textile and clothing industries, for marrying earlier means that one dresses up less, dresses more casually, and spends more of the family budget for house and furniture.

Whether the nation can absorb all such disruptions depends on the general level of economic activity, and this itself is a function of the productive growth of the economy. Over the last decade and a half Americans have learned, through a flexible tax and fiscal policy, how to regulate the economy and to stimulate its growth. The government, as gyroscope, can offset overproduction and underconsumption. The question is largely one of politics rather than economics, of the willingness of the government to act when necessary.

Automation, however, will have enormous social effects. Just as factory work impressed its rhythms on society, so the rhythms of automation will give a new character to work, living, and leisure.

Automation will change the basic composition of the labor force, creating a new *salariat* instead of a *proletariat*, as automatic processes reduce the number of industrial workers required in production. In the chemical industry, for example, output rose, from 1947 to 1954, over 50 percent, while the number of "blue-collar" workers increased only 1.3 percent. At the same time, the number of non-production workers, that is, professional, supervisory, clerical, and sales personnel, increased by 50 percent. In 1947, the ratio of production workers to non-production workers was 3:1. In 1954, in a seven-year period, the ratio had dropped to 2:1.

In its most important consequence, the advent of automation means that a corporation no longer has to worry about a large labor supply. This means that new plants can be located away from major cities and closer to markets or to sources of raw materials and fuels. Sylvania, for example, which has forty-three plants, has built its most recent ones in such out-of-the-way places as Nelsonville, Ohio; Burlington, Iowa; and Shawnee, Oklahoma. The company has also insisted that its plants be smaller, and it placed a limit of 700 persons to be employed in a plant. In this way, the corporation can exercise new social controls. The works manager can know all the men personally, and the social divisions of the small town will recapitulate the social gradations in the plant. Under these conditions a new manorial society may be in the making.

The decentralization of industry may equally revolutionize the social topography of the United States as a whole. As new plants are built on the outskirts of towns and as more and more workers live along the radial fringes of the spreading city, the distinction of the urban and the suburban becomes increasingly obliterated. In its place may appear one scenery, standard for town, suburb, countryside, and wild. An environment, as William James has noted, is an extension of ego. In the new topography, we may arrive at what the editors of the British *Architectural Review* have called "subtopia."

But more than topographical changes are involved. The very matutinal patterns will change as well. The major economic fact is that, under automation, depreciation rather than labor becomes the major cost. And when labor is relatively cheap, it becomes uneconomical to keep an enormously expensive machine idle. To write off the high capital investment, more and more of the automated plants may expand shift operations in order to keep the plant running twenty-four hours a day. And so more and more workers may find themselves working "out of hours." In

such work communities, the rhythms of sleeping, eating, social, and sexual life become skewed. A man on the regular eight-to-four shift follows a cycle of *work, recreation, and sleep,* while during the same day the fellow on the four-to-twelve shift is on a cycle of *recreation, work, and sleep,* while the night man goes through his twenty-four hours in *sleep, recreation, and work.* Where this occurs, friendship patterns may change abruptly. When the wife and children follow a "normal" routine while the man sleeps through the day, home and sex life become disjointed.

This breakup of the workday—and why should men work while the sun is shining? the practice is a relic of rustic days—is accentuated by a different aspect of the changing economic pattern of the country. As incomes rise and hours are reduced, more and more families begin to spend increasing amounts of money on recreation and travel. This rising demand for entertainment and services, for hotels, motels, vacation resorts, garages, theaters, restaurants, television, requires more individuals to work "out-of-hours"—evenings and weekends —in catering to these desires. In the next decade, perhaps a fourth or more of the labor force will be working special hours. The multiplication of such special work groups, with their own internal life and modes of recreation, is one of the features of a consumer-oriented culture.

For the individual worker, automation may bring a new concept of self. For in automation men finally lose the "feel" of work. Whatever the derogating effects, the men who use power-driven tools sense these instruments, almost as in driving an automobile, as an extension and enlargement of their own bodies, their machines responding, almost organically, to their commands and adding new dexterity and power to their own muscle skills. As a machine tender, a man now stands outside work, and whatever control once existed by "setting a bogey" (i.e., restricting output) is finally shattered. As one steelworker said, "You can't slow down the continuous annealer in order to get some respite." With the new dial-sets, too, muscular fatigue is replaced by mental tension, by the interminable watching, the endless concentration. (In the Puritan morality, the devil could always find work for "idle hands," and the factory kept a man's hands busy. But that morality ignored the existence of the fantasy life and its effects. Now, with machine-watching, there will be idle hands but no "idle minds." An advance in morality?)

Yet there is a gain for the worker in these new processes. Automation requires workers who can think of the plant as a whole. If there is less craft, less specialization, there is the need to know more than one job, to link boiler and turbine, to know the press and the borer and to relate their jobs to each other.

Most important, perhaps, there may be an end, too, to the measurement of work. Modern industry began not with the factory but with the measurement of work. When the worth of the product was defined in production units, the worth of the worker was similarly gauged. Under the unit concept, the time-study engineers calculated that a worker would produce more units for more money. This was the assumption of the wage-incentive schemes (which actually are output-incentive schemes) and of the engineering morality of a "fair day's pay for a fair day's work."

But under automation, with continuous flow, a worker's worth can no longer be evaluated in production units. Hence output-incentive plans, with their involved measurement techniques, may vanish. In their place, as Adam Abruzzi foretells, may arise a new work morality. Worth will be defined not in terms of a "one best way," not by the slide rule and stop watch, not in terms of fractioned time or units of production, but on the basis of planning and organizing and the continuous'y smooth functioning of the operation. Here the team, not the individual worker, will assume a new importance; and the social engineer will come into his own. And work itself?

## Ananke and Thanatos

In Western civilization, work, whether seen as curse or as blessing, has always stood at the center of moral consciousness. "In the sweat of thy brow," says Genesis, "shalt thou eat bread." The early Church fathers were intrigued about what Adam did before the Fall; in the variety of speculations, none assumed he was idle. He devotel himself to gardening, "the agreeable occupation of agriculture," said St. Augustine.

In the Protestant conception, all work was endowed with virtue. "A housemaid who does her work is no farther away from God than the priest in the pulpit," said Luther. Every man is "called" [to an occupation], not just a few, and every place, not just a church, is invested with godliness. With Zwingli, even with dour Calvin, work was connected with the joy of creating and with exploring even the wonders of creation.

In the nineteenth century, beginning with Carlyle, man was conceived as *homo faber*, and human intelligence was defined as the capacity for inventing and using tools. If man in the Marxist sense was "alienated" from himself, the self was understood as a man's potential for "making" things, rather than alienation as man being broken into a thing itself. (Man will be free when "nature is his work and his reality" and he "recognizes himself in a world he has himself made," said Marx in his early philosophical-economic manuscripts, adopting an image that A. E. Housman later turned into a lament.) In the same vein, John Dewey argued that a man "learned by doing," but the phrase, now a progressive-school charade, meant simply that men would grow not by accepting prefigured experiences but by seeking problems that called for new solutions. ("Unlike the handling of a tool," said Dewey, "the regulation of a machine does not challenge man or teach him anything; therefore he cannot grow through it.")

All these are normative conceptions. In Western history, however, work has had a deeper "moral unconsciousness." It was a way, along with religion, of confronting the absurdity of existence and the beyond. Religion, the most pervasive of human institutions, played a singular symbolic role in society because it faced for the individual the problem of death. Where death was but a prelude to eternal life, hell and heaven could be themes of serious discourse, and domination on earth had a reduced importance. But with the decline in religious belief went a decline in the power of belief in eternal life. In its place arose the stark prospect that death meant the total annihilation of the self. (Hamlet, as Max Horkheimer points out, "is the embodiment of the idea of individuality for the very reason that he fears the finality of death, the terror of the abyss.")

Many of these fears were staved off by work. Although religion declined, the significance of work was that it could still mobilize emotional energies into creative challenges. (For Tolstoy, as later for the Zionists in the Israeli *kibbutzim*, work was a religion; A. D. Gordon, the theoretician of the cooperative communities, preached redemption through physical labor.) One could eliminate death from consciousness by minimizing it through work. As *homo faber*, man could seek to master nature and to discipline himself. Work, said Freud, was the chief means of binding an individual to reality. What will happen, then, when not only the worker but work itself is displaced by the machine?

# 51

## Young Intelligentsia in Revolt

RICHARD FLACKS

Karl Marx expected that capitalist exploitation of industrial workers would lead them to oppose the culture of capitalism—that is, that workers would organize not only on behalf of their own interests but ultimately on behalf of human liberation. What now seems

clear is that opposition to capitalist culture arose less in the working class than among tiny groups of artists and intellectuals. Obviously, such people were too few in number and too isolated from the productive process to have any historical significance in Marx's eyes. To the extent that he had any hope for a revolutionary contribution from them, it was that they would follow his example and join the working-class struggle, which of course few did.

What Marx could not anticipate, however, was that the antibourgeois intellectuals of his day were the first representatives of what has become in our time a mass intelligentsia, a group possessing many of the cultural and political characteristics of a class in Marx's sense. By intelligentsia I mean those engaged vocationally in the production, distribution, interpretation, criticism and inculcation of cultural values. Most of the occupations in which the intelligentsia work are located outside the capitalist sector of the economy, either as free professions or in nonprofit educational institutions or other public bureaucracies. If, as in the case of the mass media, they are coordinated by private corporations, the intelligentsia are often officially depicted as serving such values as pleasure, art and truth, rather than commercial values.

It is important to note that these occupations are among the most rapidly growing, numerically, of any in the society. This is due in part to increasing governmental investment in educational, scientific and social service activities, and in part to the increase in leisure time and the consequent demand for entertainment and recreation. But more fundamentally, it is a function of the need in advanced industrial society for people to do the work of planning, prediction, innovation and systematic training, and socialization that the system now requires for its survival and growth. In the past century, then, the intelligentsia has been transformed from a tiny group of marginal status to a fast-growing, increasingly organized mass playing a key role in the functioning of the system.

Several years ago, when some of us at the University of Chicago looked into the social backgrounds of New Left students, we found that our group of activists was distinct from other college students in the degree to which they aspired to be part of the intelligentsia. But we also found, after interviewing their parents, that there was a substantial continuity between basic values and aspirations of the two generations. Both the activists and their parents were hostile to the self-denying, competitive, status-oriented individualism of bourgeois culture, and both sought a way of life that emphasized self-expression, humanism, openness to experience and community. In addition, both the students and their parents were substantially disaffected from the political system—though the students, of course, were more thoroughly alienated than their parents. It seemed clear to us that the students, through their activism, were for the most part attempting to fulfill and extend to ideological and cultural tradition already present in their families, rather than rebelling against the values on which they had been raised.

The fact that there have been, in the United States and Europe, a number of previous examples of political and cultural movements, based in the intelligentsia, with parallel ideological overtones, suggests, as does the generational continuity within activists' families, that the current youth radicalism is an expression of a definite historical process. This process may be described as the effort by many in the ranks of the intelligentsia to articulate and implement values which would serve as alternatives to those prevailing in capitalist culture.

## Intellectuals As a Class

Historically, the revolt against bourgeois culture has taken many, quite divergent, ideological forms, ranging from socialism on the left to romanticism on the right, and it was acted out in a variety of ways, from direct participation in revolutionary movements to withdrawal into bohemian communities. In the first years of this century, however, a characteristically American intellectual radicalism began to emerge, which differed in important respects from the perspectives that prevailed in Europe. Like the Europeans, the new radical American intellectuals expressed their disaffection in a variety of ways: muckraking journalism, literary and social criticism in little magazines, realistic novels, avant-garde poetry and painting, salon conversation, scholarly radicalism, progressive politics, labor-organizing, the socialist movement. But unlike their European counterparts, American intellectuals tended to have a relatively optimistic and rationalist perspective. They believed that social, political and personal reforms were possible, especially if science and reason were brought to bear on pressing problems.

Significantly, the revolt of American writers and intellectuals coincided with the rise of the feminist movement. One consequence of the impact of feminism on the perspective of American intellectuals was a tendency for the boundaries between private and public issues to become blurred or obliterated. Political reform in the larger society was linked to reform of family life and individual character, with the result that many intellectuals emphasized conscious, deliberate and scientific reform of the socializing institutions, the family and the school in order to create new values and character types and thereby to facilitate social change.

## Optimism of the Intelligentsia

The specific hopes of the early twentieth century radical intellectuals were largely abortive. But their assault on Victorianism, the Protestant Ethic and business values had a wide impact. Progressive education, social work, child psychology, psychotherapy—a host of

new professions emerged which had their original impulse in the desire to cure the effects of the dominant culture and which embodied implicit or explicit criticism of it. An important result of these new ideas, when combined with the rising status of women, was to create a new kind of middle-class family—less authoritarian, less hierarchical, more childcentered, more democratic, more self-conscious in its treatment of children. In these ways, the criticism of capitalist culture by tiny groups of European and American intellectuals became rooted in American life and incorporated into the value system of large numbers of middle-class Americans who attended the universities or were influenced by university-centered thought.

Now it is not the case, of course, that the rising intelligentsia was predominantly radical politically or unconventional culturally. Rather, what has been characteristic of this class politically is its very substantial optimism about the direction of the society and a wholehearted acceptance of the legitimacy of the national political system, coupled with a strong hostility to those aspects of politics and culture identifiable as reactionary and regressive. What supported their optimism was their faith in three interrelated instruments of change.

First, they believed that the federal government could be molded into a force for social amelioration, economic progress and equality. This hope was, of course, crystallized during the New Deal and solidified during World War II and the immediate postwar period. Second, they believed that the new vocations, the service, helping and educational professions they had entered, would be significant in curing and preventing social and psychological pathology, extending the possibilities for democracy and upward mobility and raising the intellectual and cultural level of the people. Third, they tended to believe that the values they held were best implemented through self-conscious efforts to create families and a personal life style embodying demo-cratic, humanistic, egalitarian principles, in contradiction to the authoritarian, repressed, Victorian, anti-intellectual and acquisitive style of life they per-ceived as characteristic of other middle-class people.

These beliefs emerged most strongly in the twenties and thirties, and it was possible to maintain them all during the New Deal period and the forties when it appeared that there was a real chance for the welfare state actually to be realized. Moreover, the horrors of fascism and Stalinism permitted many of the educated to feel that the United States, whatever its flaws, was the major defender of democratic values. Post-World War II prosperity greatly raised living standards and cultural possibili-ties for this group and also seemed to be creating the conditions for social equality. Thus, the parents of the pres-ent generation of student activists, despite their antipathy to traditional capitalist culture, maintained a generally complacent view of American society when they themselves were young and in the years when their children were growing up.

By the late fifties, however, some of this complacency undoubtedly began to break down. The Eisenhower years were a period of political stagnation and anti-Communist hysteria in which it became evident that the drive toward a welfare state and social equality might not be inherent in American political institu-tions. It also became clear that Amer-ica's international role was incongruent with humanist, democratic values and beliefs. At a more fundamental level, many of the educated, as they reached middle age, began to have some doubts about the moral worth of their own occupations and about the degree to which they too had participated in the pursuit of status and material comfort. The late 1950s was a period of increas-ing social criticism much of which revolved around the collapse of mean-ing in vocation and about the moral callousness of the American middle class.

By 1960, then, the development of the American intelligentsia as a class had come to this. Demographically, it had grown over several decades from small pockets of isolated, independent intellectuals to a substantial stratum of the population, including many in new white-collar vocations. Culturally, it had begun to develop a family structure and value system at odds with the tradi-tional capitalist, Protestant Ethic, middle-class culture. Politically, it had passed through a period of optimistic reformism and seemed to be moving into a period of increasing disillusion-ment. The newest and largest genera-tion of this stratum was thronging the nation's colleges, at just that point historically when the sustaining ideol-ogies of industrial society—liberalism, socialism, communism—had reached exhaustion. At the same time, the cold war and anticommunism had ceased to be a workable framework for American international policy, and the colored population in the United States and around the world was breaking into active revolt.

## Coming Together

In the decade since 1960, the off-spring of the intelligentsia have become politicized and increasingly radicalized, despite the fact that, having been born to relatively high privilege and social advantage, they saw society opening ever wider vistas for personal success and enrichment. Why have they, in large numbers, refused to follow their fathers and mothers—adopting a stance of slightly uneasy acceptance of the prevailing social order while trying to establish a personal life on a somewhat different cultural basis?

In part, the disaffection of these youth is a direct consequence of the values and impulses their parents transmitted to them. The new generation had been raised in an atmosphere that encouraged personal autonomy and individuality. Implicitly and explicitly it had been taught to be skeptical about the intrinsic value of money-making and status and to be skeptical about the claims of established authority. It incorporated new definitions of sex roles. Having seen their parents share authority and functions more or less equally in the family, and having been taught to value aesthetic and intellectual activity, these were boys who did not understand masculinity to mean physical toughness and dominance, and girls who did not understand femininity to mean passivity and domesticity. Moreover, they were young people—young people for whom the established means of social control were bound to be relatively ineffective (and here they were particularly different from the older generation). Growing up with economic security in families of fairly secure status, the normal incentives of the system—status and income—were of relatively minor importance, and indeed many of their parents encouraged them to feel that such incentives ought to be disdained.

In retrospect, it seems inevitable that young people of this kind should come into some conflict with the established order. Because of their central values, they, like the earlier generations of intellectuals, would necessarily be social critics. Because of their material security, they, like earlier generations of high status youth, were likely to be experimental, risk-taking, open to immediate experience, relatively unrepressed. Because of their character structure, they would very likely come into con-

flict with arbitrary authority in school and other situations of imposed restriction. Because of their values and sex role identifications, they would find themselves out of harmony with the conventional youth culture with its frivolity, anti-intellectualism and stereotypic distinctions between the sexes.

Furthermore, their impulses to autonomy and individuality, their relative freedom from economic anxiety and their own parents' ambivalence toward the occupational structure would make it difficult for them to decide easily on a fixed vocational goal or life style, would make them aspire to construct their lives outside conventional career lines, would make them deeply critical of the compromise, corruption and unfreedom inherent in the occupations of their fathers—the very occupations for which they were being trained.

Much of this had happened before, but the situation of the young intelligentsia of the sixties differed radically from that of their precursors. First, their numbers were enormously greater than ever before. Second, they faced, not a scarcity of jobs, but an abundance of careers—yet the careers for which they were being trained no longer held the promise of social melioration and personal fulfillment that their parents had anticipated. Third, these youth sensed not only the narrowness and irrationality of the prevailing culture but the deeper fact that the dominant values of bourgeois society, appropriate in an age of scarcity and entrepreneurial activity, had become irrelevant to a society which was moving beyond scarcity and competitive capitalism. Thus, by the late fifties, more youth were feeling more intensely than ever before a sense of estrangement from capitalist culture—an estrangement which could not be assuaged by the promise of material security the system offered.

The cultural crisis these youth experienced provided the ground for their coming together. But the transformation of cultural alienation into political protest, and eventually into revolutionary action, was due to more immediate and concrete pressures. It was the emergence of the southern civil rights movement which, more than any other single event, led the young intelligentsia in the early sixties to see the relevance of political opposition and social change to their own problems. The nonviolent movement showed, for one thing, how small groups of committed youth could undertake action that could have major historical impact. It demonstrated how such action could flow directly from humanistic values. But above all, it confronted these white students with the fact that all of their opportunities for personal fulfillment were based on white upper-middle-class privilege and that continued passivity in the face of racism meant that one was in fact part of the oppressive apparatus of society, no matter what one's private attitudes might be.

## Hopes of SDS

Participation in the civil rights struggle seemed, however, to offer a way out of this dilemma, and civil rights protest helped to open the consciousness of many students to other political issues. It made them aware that there was more to their problems than the fact that the culture offered litle support for their personal aspirations; it also threatened their existence. But at the same time numbers of students became rapidly sensitive to the fact that the nuclear arms race, the cold war and the militarization of society were not simply facts of life but deliberate, therefore reversible, policies. It was not long before the protest tactics acquired in the civil rights movement began to be applied to the demand for peace.

When one reads today the Port Huron Statement (June 1962) and other documents of the early Students for a Democratic Society (SDS) and the New Left, one is struck by the degree to which the early New Left conceived of itself largely as a political reform movement rather than in clearly revolutionary terms. While it's true, as Todd Gitlin has suggested, that the early new radicals of the sixties were filled with "radical disappointment" with the American way of life, it is also the case that they retained a good deal of optimism about the possibilities for change in the context of American politics. In particular, it was hoped that the labor movement, the religious community, the liberal organizations, the intellectual community, the civil rights movement all could eventually unite around a broad-based program of radical reform.

The role of the student movement was seen by the early SDS leaders as providing the intellectual skills needed for such a new movement and, somewhat later, as important for producing people who would help to catalyze grass root activities in a variety of places. Direct action such as the sit-ins, freedom rides and other forms of protest and civil disobedience was seen, on the one hand, as a vital tactic for the winning of reform and, on the other hand, as a method by which the more established institutions such as the labor movement could be induced to move in the direction of more vigorous action. In this early phase of the student movement, SDS and other New Left leaders were little aware of the possibility that a mass movement of students on the campus could be created and engaged in collective struggles against university authority. Rather the New Left's role on the campus was seen primarily as one of breaking through the atmosphere of apathy, educating students about political issues, so that they could begin to take a role off the campus in whatever struggles were going on.

But the early reformism of the New

Left was soon abandoned. The failure of the established agencies of reform to create a political opposition and to mobilize mass support for political alternatives was most decisive in preventing the new movement of the young intelligentsia from becoming absorbed by conventional politics, thereby following in the footsteps of previous movements of American intellectuals. This collapse of the so-called liberal establishment thus marked a new stage in the consciousness of the American intelligentsia —beyond cultural alienation, beyond social reform, beyond protest—toward active resistance and revolution.

The emergence of the student movement in the sixties, then, signifies a more fundamental social change and is not simply a species of "generational conflict." The convergence of certain social structural and cultural trends has produced a new class, the intelligentsia, and, despite the apparent material security of many in this class, its trajectory is toward revolutionary opposition to capitalism. This is because, first, capitalism cannot readily absorb the cultural aspirations of this group—aspirations that fundamentally have to do with the abolition of alienated labor and the achievement of democratic community. Second, the incorporation of this group is made more difficult by the concrete fact of racism and imperialism—facts which turn the vocations of the intelligentsia into cogs in the machinery of repression rather than means for self-fulfillment and general enlightenment. Third, the numerical size of this group and the concentration of much of it in universities make concerted oppositional political action extremely feasible. Finally, the liberal default has hastened the self-consciousness of students and other members of this class, exacerbated their alienation from the political system and made autonomous oppositional politics a more immediate imperative for them.

Thus, a stratum, which under certain conditions might have accepted a modernizing role within the system, has instead responded to the events of this past decade by adopting an increasingly revolutionary posture.

In part, this development grows out of the antiauthoritarian impulses in the fundamental character structure of the individual members which provide much of the motivation and emotional fuel for the movement. But, as the history of the movement shows, there was an early readiness to consider whether established political alternatives were in fact viable. That such readiness has virtually disappeared is almost entirely due to the failure of the political system itself—a failure most manifest in the crises of race, poverty and urban life on the one hand and the international posture of the United States on the other.

Over the last decade the American government has consistently failed to enforce new or existing legislation guaranteeing civil rights. It has consistently failed to implement promised reforms leading to social and economic equality. It has demonstrated a stubborn unwillingness and/or incompetence in dealing with the deepening crises of urban life, and it has supported essentially repressive, rather than ameliorative, policies with respect to the black revolt.

Even more crucial in undermining the legitimacy of the system for young people was, of course, the war in Vietnam—the fact that the United States was unable to win the war; the fact that it dragged on endlessly to become the longest war in American history; the fact that the United States in Vietnam was involved in an effort to suppress a popular uprising; the fact that the United States in Vietnam committed an interminable series of atrocities and war crimes, especially involving the destruction of civilian life; the fact that the war was accompanied by a military draft and that alongside the draft a system involving the social tracking of all young males in America had grown up; the fact that the war in Vietnam was not simply an accident of policy but an essential ingredient of what became increasingly identified as a worldwide imperialist policy involving the suppression of popular revolution and the maintenance and extension of American political and corporate power throughout the Third World.

Moreover, alongside the growth of conventional and nuclear military power and the penetration of American institutions, including especially the universities, by military priorities, there grew up a paramilitary establishment which had attempted to control and manipulate organizations and events throughout the world and also at home. This development was perhaps best symbolized for students by the fact that the Central Intelligence Agency had subsidized the National Student Association and had extensive ties with American academics. Finally, the war continued and escalated despite vast expressions of popular discontent.

This, more than anything else, reinforced the New Left's disbelief in the efficacy of conventional political means of affecting policy. By the time of the Democratic Convention in 1968, a very large number of young people were convinced that only extreme action of a disruptive sort could have any substantial effect on major policy and that "working through the system" was a trap, rather than a means to effect change.

Obviously, many young people, fearing the consequences of a full-scale delegitimation of authority, continue to search for a more responsive political alternative within the system. But the stagnation of liberalism in these years along with the astonishing series of assassinations of spokesmen for its revi-

talization have made such hopes appear increasingly unrealistic. Thus the growth of revolutionary sentiment among the students proceeds apace. As the legitimacy of national authority declines, a process of delegitimation occurs for all in authoritative positions—for instance, university officials—and proposals for melioration and compromise are viewed with deepening suspicion. Political polarization intensifies, and those in the opposition feel, on the one hand, the imperative of confrontation as a means of further clarifying the situation and, on the other hand, that the entire structure of social control is being organized for the purpose of outright repression. And for American students confrontation is made more urgent by the moral pressure of the black liberation movement, which continuously tests the seriousness of their proclaimed revolutionary commitment.

## New Front Line

The early New Left frequently criticized university life as well as the larger society, but it was also quite ambivalent toward the university as an institution. University authority was seen as paternalistic and as subservient to dominant interests in the society. University education was regarded as a contributor to student indifference towards social questions. At the same time, the Port Huron Statement and other early New Left writing viewed the university as a potential resource for movements for change, university intellectuals as potentially useful to such movements and the university as a relatively free place where political controversy could flourish provided it was catalyzed.

Prior to the fall of 1964, sds leaders ignored the campus as a base of operation, persuading a considerable number of students to either leave school or to work off the campus in the efforts to organize the urban poor. In large measure, university reform campaigns were felt by the most committed activists to be both irrelevant and, in a certain sense, immoral, when people in the South were putting their bodies on the line. The Berkeley free speech movement of 1964 helped to change this perception of the campus. The police action at Berkeley, the first of numerous large-scale busts of student protestors, suggested that a campus struggle could be the front line. And the political impact of Berkeley in California, and indeed internationally, suggested that there was nothing parochial or irrelevant about an on-campus struggle. Moreover, these events, coincided with the turning away of portions of the civil rights movement, especially the Student Nonviolent Coordinating Committee, from efforts to work with white students. Further, Berkeley coincided with the escalation of the war in Vietnam and with the discovery, only dimly realized before, that the universities were major resources in the development of the military potential of the United States.

Beginning in the fall of 1966 attacks on military research installations, on ROTC, on connections between the university and military agencies, on military recruitment and recruitment by defense corporations became the prime activity of SDS and other student groups for a number of months. Every major confrontation mobilized hundreds of students for highly committed direct action and many thousands more for supportive action. Typically the issues raised by the student movement on a campus were supported by as many as two-thirds of the student body, even though large numbers of students were unwilling to participate in disruptive actions as such. And as previously uncommitted students joined these actions, many were radicalized by the experience of participation in a community of struggle, by the intransigence

and obtuseness of university administrators and by the violence of police repression of the protests. Institutional resistance was fostering student "class consciousness."

By the late sixties, the movement was no longer the exclusive property of those I've been calling the young intelligentsia. It was having a widening impact on students at nonelite campuses, in junior colleges and high schools, and on nonstudent youth in the streets and in the Armed Forces. To a great extent, the availability of larger numbers of young people for insurgent ideas and actions is rooted in the cultural crisis we alluded to at the outset of this paper. For all youth experience the breakdown of traditional culture, the irrelevance of ideologies based on scarcity. Vast numbers of youth in America today are in search of a less repressed, more human, more spontaneous life style.

The radicalization of youth is enhanced by the peculiar social position of high school and college students, who have achieved some degree of independence from family authority but are not yet subject to the discipline of work institutions. The high school and college situation is, on the one hand, extremely authoritarian but, on the other hand, functions to segregate young people, maintaining them in a peculiar limbo combining dependency with irresponsibility. The impact of the cultural crisis on the school situation is to make really vast numbers of young people ready for new and more liberating ideas, while they have the freedom and energy to spend time in examination and criticism of prevailing values and ideologies.

In addition, the situation of youth is exacerbated by the demands of the imperialist system for manpower and by the increasing bureaucratization of both education and vocation. More concretely, the draft is the reality that undermines the endless promises made to American youth. What the draft means is that one is not really free to pursue self-fulfillment, even though one has been taught that self-fulfillment is the highest goal and purpose of the system. Not only is that promise undermined by the necessity to serve in the army and die in the mud of some distant jungle, a fate reserved for relatively few young men, but the draft serves to facilitate control over the careers of all young men by serving explicitly as a means for tracking youth into occupations believed to be in the interest of the state. The result for school youth is postponement or avoidance of the military but subjugation to an educational system that reproduces many of the worst features of the larger society in terms of authoritarianism, competitiveness, individualism and dehumanization. The growth of a mass youth movement depended on the emergence of a group of young intelligentsia whose own socialization was particularly at odds with the dominant culture, but once such a circle of youth emerged, their expressions, both cultural and political, spread like wildfire.

Thus, the story of the student movement in the United States over the past decade has been one of continued self-transformation. Once student activism was characteristic of tiny groups of campus rebels, the offspring, as we have suggested, of the educated middle class, who faced severe value and vocational crisis, could find no moral way to assimilate into American society and so searched for a new basis for living in cultural avant-gardism and moralistic dedication to social reform. In the past decade, obviously, the movement has spread well beyond this original group. It has transformed itself from a non-ideological movement for vague principles of social justice into a new radical movement in quest of a new social vision and a new framework for social criticism, and finally into a movement spearheaded by revolutionaries tending, more and more, to look to classical revolutionary doctrine as a guiding principle and to embody, more and more, classical models of revolutionary action as their own.

It is a movement that rejects and is at the same time entangled by its roots in what I have called the intelligentsia. Yet it has expressed most clearly the fundamental aspirations of the rising generation of that class for a new social order in which men can achieve autonomy and full participation in determining the conditions of their lives, in which hierarchy and domination are replaced by community and love, in which war, militarism and imperialism are obsolete and in which class and racial distinctions are abolished. It is a movement of surprising strength. It has touched the minds of millions and changed the lives of thousands of young people, both here and abroad. It has severely shaken the stability of the American empire and challenged the basic assumptions of its culture. But its most sensitive adherents have become increasingly despairing, as the movement has reached the limit of its possibilities. This despair is rooted first in the unresponsiveness of the political system to pressure for reform; second, in the narrow class base of the movement; third, in the seemingly overwhelming capacity of the authorities to manage social control. Out of this despair arises the sense that revolution is an urgent, if impossible, necessity, that the movement must transcend its social base, that it must make common cause with other enemies of the empire around the world.

## Co-optation

Given this new consciousness, what can be said about the future of the movement? It seems to me that one can envision several possibilities. First, any student and youth movement has the potential of becoming a relatively insulated expression of generational revolt. This is not the explicit intention of very many spokesmen for the New Left, but it certainly appears to be the implicit expectation of many agencies of social control. A generational movement may be understood as a movement of cultural and social innovation whose impact has been contained within the framework of existing society. For agencies of social control, the ideal circumstance would be the opportunity to eliminate those elements in the movement that are most disruptive and destructive, while putting into effect some of the cultural, social and political innovations and reforms the movement advocates.

Accordingly, you put Yippies in jail but work out some means to legalize the use of marijuana. You put draft-resisters in jail or into exile while abolishing conscription. You expel SDS from the campus while admitting student representatives to the board of trustees. You deride and derogate the women's liberation movement while liberalizing abortion laws. You break up and harass hippie urban communities while providing fame and fortune to some rock music groups. This is all done with the aid of ideological perspectives that emphasize that what is going on is a generational revolt, that there is a generation gap, that the big problem is one of communication between the old and the young. The hope is that if reforms can be made that will liberalize the cultural and social atmosphere, particularly in relation to sex, drug use, art, music, censorship and so forth, the mass of youth will not become tempted by the message of the radical vanguard.

If the new political and cultural radicalism were to become channeled more fully in the direction of genera-

tional revolt, it would then be serving stabilizing and modernizing functions for the going system, and it would not be the first time that a radical movement in the United States ended up functioning this way. But from the point of view of New Left activists, such an outcome for the movement would represent profound failure, particularly if it meant, as it does now seem to mean, that the most active and militant of the participants of the movement would suffer, rather than benefit, from any social change that might be forthcoming.

There is a substantial likelihood, however, that the student movement and the New Left of the sixties will move in the direction we have just outlined. The most important fact supporting this outcome is that the movement has, in the ten years of its existence, failed very largely to break out of its isolation as a movement of the young, and particularly of the relatively advantaged young. There are reasons to think that this isolation could be broken in the near future, and we shall suggest some of these shortly, but it is important to recognize that most of the public understanding of what is happening has revolved around the generational problem, rather than the substantive political and social questions that the movement has raised. Most of the expressed sympathy for the movement on the part of the elders has been couched in terms of solving the problems of youth and liberalizing the cultural atmosphere, rather than in joining in the making of a social revolution.

At the same time, however, despite the very large-scale public discussion of the need for reform and innovation, the prevailing tendencies of the state and other dominant institutions do not seem to be primarily in this direction. Even such apparently unthreatening changes as liberalization of laws governing drug use, the 18-year-old vote, the involvement of students in direct participation in university government or the abolition of the draft meet very strong resistance and do not now seem to be on the agenda. Instead, what is in prospect is further tightening of drug laws, further restrictions and harassment of the communal outcroppings of the youth culture, further efforts at censorship, a continuation of the draft and a generally more hostile climate with respect to even the modest aspirations for change of most young people today. All of this, of course, could change in a relatively short period of time as those who are now young move into full citizenship and have the opportunity directly to influence public and institutional policies. But what happens in the intervening years is likely to be crucial.

Another reason for believing that the New Left has considerable capacity for resisting this kind of incorporation into the culture is that the movement is profoundly suspicious of and sensitive to the dangers of co-optation. Most movement participants are aware at one level or another that the classic American pattern for controlling revolutionary and quasi-revolutionary movements is to destroy or isolate the most militant sections while implementing, at least on paper, the programmatic thrust of the movement. This is what happened in the labor movement. It is what is happening in the black liberation movement, and it is certainly what is being advocated for the student movement. In this way the American political system has served to contain the revolutionary thrust of movements that develop within it, while keeping these movements fragmented, preventing their outreach into sectors of the population beyond those that form the original constituency of the movement.

As I say, new leftists wish to avoid at all costs the buying off of the movement through piecemeal reform. This is one reason why the movement is so hesitant to propose concrete reforms and to proclaim its interest in short-range goals. A greater danger, however, is that the movement has been unable to offset pressures, both internal and external, that maintain it as a movement of youth.

The future of the New Left depends now on its ability to break out of its isolation and to persuade the majority of Americans that their interests depend on the dismantling of imperialism and the replacement of capitalism with a fully democratized social order. The movement cannot afford to be encapsulated as a generational revolt. It cannot wait until the present young "take over." It cannot survive in a climate of repression and polarization unless large numbers of people are moving in a similar political direction. It cannot survive and ought not survive if it conceives itself to be an elite band of professional revolutionaries, aiming to "seize power" in the midst of social chaos and breakdown.

What are the structural conditions that might open up the possibility of the New Left transcending its present age and class base? Here are at least some:

☐ The class base of the movement is rapidly changing as the "youth culture" spreads to the high schools and junior colleges, to army bases and young workers. Along with this cultural diffusion, the mood of resistance spreads—protest is now endemic in high schools, it is evident in the armed forces, it is growing in the junior colleges.

☐ Inflation and high taxes have led to a decline in real wages. Current fiscal policies generate rising unemployment. A new period of labor militance may have already begun. This situation converges with the influx of postwar youth into the labor force, with the militant organization of black caucuses in unions, with intensifying organization and militance among public employees and with the first efforts by former student radicals to "reach" workers. It may be that in spite of the Wallace phenomenon, racism and the alleged conservatism of the American working class a new radicalism is about to become visible among factory, government and other workers.

□ The impoverishment and disintegration of public services, the systematic destruction of the natural environment, urban squalor, the tax burden—all are deeply felt troubles which are directly traceable to the profit system and the military priority. The sense of crisis and frustration that these problems generate throughout society offers the ground for the formulation and promulgation of radical program, action and organization.

□ Political repression, although obviously dangerous for the survival of radicalism, can have the effect of intensifying rather than weakening insurgency. This would be particularly true if repression is seen as an assault on whole categories of persons, rather than on handfuls of "outside agitators." So, for instance, many participants in the youth culture now connect their own harassment by the police with the Chicago Conspiracy trial and other government attacks on radicals. Repression at this writing seems more likely to stiffen the mood of resistance among young people than it is to end attacks on "law and order."

□ By 1975 there will be well over 50 million adults born since 1940. Most of these will have achieved political consciousness in the past decade. This fact alone suggests a major transformation of the political landscape by the second half of the seventies.

□ In the next five years the proportion of the labor force definable as "intelligentsia" will have substantially increased. Current Bureau of Labor Statistics manpower projections for "professional, technical and kindred workers" are for a 40 percent increase in this category between 1966 and 1975, reaching a total of about 13 million in 1975. If my analysis in this essay is correct, this group should be a major source of radicalism in the coming period. The situation of these workers is now dramatically changing from one of high opportunity to relative job scarcity due to current federal and state budgetary policies. Thus one can expect that the radicalization of the intelligentsia will continue to intensify in the years ahead.

One might suggest that these conditions provide the opportunity for a large-scale and successful "new politics" of liberal reform to assert itself. But the current exhaustion of political liberalism may well mean that a new "center-Left" coalition cannot be formed—that we have finally arrived in this country at the point where reformism is no longer viable.

An alternative possibility would be the emergence of a popular socialist party oriented to both "parliamentary" and "extraparliamentary" activity. Although this would certainly facilitate the transcendence of the New Left, there are as yet no signs that such a development is even incipient. In any case, the most important insight of the New Left is that political organization is not enough—the heart of revolution is the reconstruction of civil society and culture.

## "The Long March"

It may well be that the singular mission of the new mass intelligentsia is to catalyze just such a transformation—to undertake what Rudi Dutschke called "the long march through the institutions of society." This march began in the universities. In coming years it may well continue through all significant cultural, educational, public service and professional institutions. It would have a double aim: to force these institutions to serve the people rather than the corporate system and the state and to engage cultural workers and professionals in struggles to control their work and govern the institutions that coordinate it and determine its use.

It is possible that such struggle by the intelligentsia could stimulate similar struggles in the primary economic institutions—to build a basis for workers' control and for the abolition of technologically unnecessary labor.

In addition to such institutional struggle, the reconstruction of civil society and culture requires the further development of self-organization of communities and especially of exploited and oppressed minorities. Such self-organization—of racial and ethnic minorities and of women—is necessary for any general cultural transformation. Struggle by communities for control of their own development and services prepares the basis for a decentralized and democratized civil society. It is obvious that all such developments have profound need for the services of professional, intellectual, cultural and scientific workers.

It is natural to assume that the development of political, civil and cultural struggle requires central, disciplined organization. My own feeling is that it requires something prior to, and perhaps instead of, the classical revolutionary party. What is really crucial is the organization of local "collectives," "affinity groups," "communes," "cells" of people who share a revolutionary perspective, a common locale of activity, a sense of fraternity, a willingness to bind their fates together. Each such group can be free to work out its priorities, projects and work style. What is necessary is that these groups generally conceive of themselves as catalysts of mass action rather than as utopian communities or

elite terrorists. Most of the dramatic movements of the sixties occurred because small groups of friends undertook action that was catalytic or exemplary to larger masses. Most of the exciting cultural development in this period occurred in a similar way. Many of the problems the party is supposed to exist to solve can be coped with without centralization. Problems of communication can be handled by the underground media—which up to now have been the expression of a host of small collectives. National action projects can be coordinated by ad hoc coalitions and umbrella organizations. The generation of resources can be managed through movement banks and quasi foundations. There is no reason why collectives in different or similar milieus cannot meet together to exchange experience. If the purpose of a revolutionary movement is not to seize power but to educate the people to take it for themselves, then a maximally decentralized mode of work is appropriate. And in a period of tightening repression, a cellular rather than centralized mode of organization is obviously advantageous.

The revolution in advanced capitalist society is not a single insurrection. It is not a civil war of pitched battles fought by opposing armies. It is a long, continuing struggle—with political, social and cultural aspects inextricably intertwined. It is already underway. It is not simply a socialist revolution—if by that one means the establishment of a new form of state power that will introduce social planning and redistribute income. It is more than that. For it must be a revolution in which the power to make key decisions is placed in the hands of those whose lives are determined by those decisions. It is not, in short, a revolution aimed at seizing power but a revolution aimed at its dispersal.

It is possible that the New Left's current return to Old Left styles and models signifies that the kind of revolution of which I speak is premature, that the classes and groups that would be most active in producing it have not achieved full consciousness. We are not yet in an age of "postscarcity," and consequently the revolutionary visions appropriate to that age will have a difficult time establishing their reality. Perhaps, then, the New Left of the sixties is not destined to be the catalyst of the new revolution. I am personally convinced, however, that whatever the immediate destiny of the movement might be, the social and cultural changes that pro-

duced it and were accelerated by it are irreversible and cannot be contained within a capitalist framework. Once the material basis for human liberation exists, men will struggle against the institutions that stand in its way. The rise of the student movement in the United States and other industrial societies is a crucial demonstration of the truth of this proposition. For it is a sign that a revolutionary class consciousness appropriate to the era of monopoly capital, advanced technology and dying imperialism is in existence.

# 52

## The Future of Capitalism

### ROBERT L. HEILBRONER

For roughly the last century and a half the dominant system of economic organization in most of the West has been that of capitalism. In all likelihood, barring the advent of a catastrophic war, capitalism will continue as the dominant system of the Western world during the remainder of this century and well into the next. Although it will inevitably change, will likely suffer considerable duress over the next decades, and in the longer run will gradually give way to a very different kind of social order, for our lives and for those of our children, capitalism bids fair to confront us as the prevailing form of social organization in those nations where it is now solidly entrenched.

It seems to me that all serious social analysis and prediction must start from some such premise. At any rate, it is

Reprinted from *Commentary* 41 (April, 1966), pp. 23–35, with permission of the author and the publisher.

my premise, and I propose to explore —with all the uncertainties and risks inherent in such an enterprise—the social changes available to us within the limits of capitalism in the future.

But how can we establish these "limits"? Perhaps we can shed an initial light on the question if we imagine asking some perceptive observer in, say, 13th-century France what were the limits of feudalism. Our observer might be hard put to find an answer, particularly if he looked about him at the striking variety of forms that feudalism assumed in the various domains of Europe. Yet undoubtedly we could have suggested an answer to him that would have sounded reasonable. It is that certain kinds of economic and social change were unimaginable—indeed impossible—in 13th-century France because they would have implied the establishment of some totally different form of social organization. To take a central instance, it would have been impossible to have replaced the traditional ties, established customs, and fixed obligations by which the manorial economy hung together with some radically different system, such as the cash markets that were already disrupting the settled tenor of feudal economic life, because a change of this dimension would have critically undermined the power of the lord, elevated out of all proportion that of the parvenu class of merchants, and thereby destroyed the fixed hierarchy of status that was the very backbone of the feudal social structure. Thus, one meaning we can give to the idea of "limits" in a society is very simple: It is those boundaries of change that would so alter the functional base of a society, or the structure of privilege built on that base, as to displace a given social order by a new one.

In terms of the immediate subject of our essay, this draws the broad limits of American capitalism in the last third of the 20th century with reasonable fixity. To take a few examples: it is certainly beyond the present limits of capitalism to replace the guiding principle of production for profit by that of production for use; it is impossible to nationalize the great corporations or to end the private ownership of the means of mass communication; and it is impossible to end the concentration of wealth in private hands. One can debate whether all or any of these changes are desirable, but there is little point in debating whether they are realizable. Barring only some disaster that would throw open the gates to a radical reconstruction of society, they are not.

What we have established thus far, however, is only the first and most obvious answer to the question of what we mean by the "limits" of social change. For if we now return to the 13th century, we could imagine suggesting to our medieval observer another approach to the idea of feudal limits.

Rather than pointing out to him the contemporary incompatibility of the market system, we might be able to show him the immense long-term historical momentum of the emergent forces of the monetized economy. Indeed, we might even be able to bring him to see that by the end of another four or five centuries, feudalism would have virtually disappeared, and that an economic organization of society once incompatible with feudalism would have triumphed over it.

From such a perspective, the task of delineating the limits of feudalism becomes a different one. It is no longer to discover what cannot be done in the short run, but to explore what *can* be done, and how, in doing it, the social structure may slowly and subtly alter, making possible still further change in the future.

It need hardly be said that one cannot project such a long evolutionary—or possibly revolutionary—advance in close detail. The precise route to be taken, the pace of progress, the roadblocks where the invading forces of a new society may be temporarily halted or even thrown back—all this surpasses any power of analysis we now have. But the grand line of march is not beyond our ability to foresee. Looking back at 13th-century France, we can see how defenseless were its castle walls against the insinuating influence of the market system. In similar fashion, it should be possible to explore the limits of capitalism in America, not alone in terms of changes that cannot now be accommodated by the business system, but in terms of those forces that are altering capitalism, like feudalism in an earlier day, in ways that will eventually cause its social and economic structure to be displaced by another.

# I

We cannot, however, explore change until we answer a prior question: Why do societies resist change? A full explanation of social inertia must reach deep into the psychological and technical underpinnings of the human community. But in the process of gradual social adjustment it is clear enough where to look for the main sources of the resistance to change. They are to be found in the structure of privilege inherent in all social systems.

Privilege is not an attribute we are accustomed to stress when we consider the construction of our social order. When pressed, we are, of course, aware of its core institutions in capitalism—the right to reap private benefits from the use of the means of production and the right to utilize the dynamic forces of the marketplace for private enrichment. The element of privilege in these institutions, however—that is, their operative result in favoring certain individuals and classes—is usually passed over in silence in favor of their purely functional aspects. Thus, private property is ordinarily explained as being no more than a convenient instrumentality for the efficient operation of an economic system, or the market elements of Land, Labor, and Capital as purely neutral "factors of production."

Now these institutions and relationships do indeed fulfill the purposes for which they are advertised. But this is not the only use they have. Land, Labor, and Capital are not just functional parts of a mechanism but are categories of social existence that bring vast differences in life chances with them. It is no just Labor on the one hand, and Land or Capital on the other; it is the Bronx on the one hand and Park Avenue on the other. Similarly, private property is not merely a pragmatic arrangement devised for the facilitation of production, but a social institution that brings to some members of the community a style of life qualitatively different from that afforded to the rest. In a word, the operation of capitalism as a *functional* system results in a structure of wealth and income characteristic of capitalism as a *system of privilege*—a structure in which the top two per cent of American families own between two-thirds and three-quarters of all corporate stock, and enjoy incomes roughly ten times larger than the average received within the nation as a whole.

The mere presence of these concentrations of wealth or large disparities of income does not in itself differentiate the system of privilege under capitalism from those of most other societies in history. Rather, what marks off our system is that wealth and income within capitalism are not mainly derived from non-economic activity, such as war, plunder, extortionate taxation, etc., but arise from the activity of marketers or the use of property by its owners.

This mixture of the functional and the privileged aspects of capitalism has a curious but important political consequence. It is that privilege under capitalism is much less "visible," especially to the favored groups, than privilege under other systems. The upper classes in feudalism were keenly alive to the gulf that separated them from the lower classes, and perfectly open about the need for preserving it. The upper groups under capitalism, on the other hand, are typically unaware that the advantages accruing to them from following the paths of the market economy constitute in any sense or fashion a "privilege."

This lack of self-awareness is rendered even more acute by virtue of another differentiating characteristic of privilege under capitalism. It is that privilege is limited to the advantages inherent in the economic structure of society. That is, the same civil and criminal law, the same duties in war and peace, apply to both economically privileged and unprivileged. It would be a mistake to concentrate on obvious differences in the application of the law as being of the essence. Rather, one must contrast the single system of law and obligation under capitalism—however one-sidedly administered—with the *differing* systems that apply to privileged and unprivileged in other societies.

The divorce of economic from political or social privilege brings up the obvious fact that, at least in democratic societies like America, the privileged distribution of economic rewards is exposed to the corrective efforts of the democratic electorate. The question is, however, why the structure of privilege has remained relatively intact, despite so long an exposure to the potentially leveling influences of the majority.

In part, we can trace the answer to they very "invisibility" of privilege we have just described. Furthermore, in all stable societies the structure of privilege appears to the general public not as a special dispensation, but as the natural order of things, with which their own interests and sentiments are identified. This is especially true under capitalism, where the privileges of wealth are open, at least in theory, and to some extent in practice, to all comers. Finally, the overall results of capitalism, particularly in America during the entire 20th century and recently in Europe as well, have been sufficiently rewarding to hold anti-capitalist sentiment to a relatively small segment of the population.

That the defense of privilege is the active source of resistance to social and economic change may appear so obvious as scarcely to be worth emphasizing. Obvious or not, it is a fact too often passed over in silence. It seems to me impossible to analyze the nature of the opposition to change without stressing the vulgar but central fact that every person who is rich under capitalism is a beneficiary of its inherent privileges. Taking the American system as it now exists, it seems fair to assert that the chance to own and acquire wealth constitutes a primary—perhaps even a dominating—social motivation for most men, and that those who enjoy or aspire to these privileges will not readily acquiesce in changes that will substantially lessen their chances of maintaining or gaining them.

## II

The touchstone of privilege provides an indispensable key when we now return to our main theme. If it does not give us an exact calculus by which to compute what changes wil land will not be acceptable, it does give us an angle of entry, a point of view, without which attempts to cope with the problem of social change are apt to have no relevance at all.

Take, for example, the problem of the poverty that now afflicts some 30 or 40 million Americans. One alleged cause of this poverty has always directly stressed the privileges of capitalism. This is the view that poverty under capitalism is largely ascribable to wage exploitation. There is clearly an element of truth here, in that the affluence of the favored groups in capitalism does indeed stem from institutions that divert income from the community at large into the channels of dividends, interest, rent, monopoly returns, etc. It is by no means clear, however, that the amount of this diversion, if redistributed among the masses, would spell the difference between their poverty and their well-being. On the contrary, it is now generally acknowledged that the level of wages reflects workers' productivity more than any other single factor, and that this productivity in turn is primarily determined by the quantity and the quality of the capital equipment of the economic system.

Certainly, the productivity of the great mass of workers under capitalism has steadily increased, and so have their real wages. Today, for example, industrial workers in America cannot be classified as "poor" by prevailing absolute standards, if we take $4,000 a year as defining a level of minimum adequacy for a small family. Although wage poverty is clearly present in capitalism, it is primarily restricted to the agricultural areas and to the lowest categories of skills in the service trades. No small part of it is accounted for by discrimination against Negroes, and by the really shocking levels of income of Negro farm and service labor. On the other hand, the proportion of the labor force that is afflicted with this poverty is steadily diminishing. Farmers, farm managers, and farm laborers together will probably constitute only 5 per cent of the labor force within a decade. The low-paid non-farm common laborer, who constituted over 12 per cent of the working force in 1900, makes up only 5 per cent of it today and will be a smaller percentage tomorrow.

There remains, nevertheless, the question of how much the existing level of wages could be increased if the categories of capitalist privilege did not exist. Since it is difficult to estimate accurately the total amount of "privileged" income under capitalism, let us take as its convenient representation the sum total of all corporate profits before tax. In the mid 1960's, these profits exceeded $70 billion a year. If this sum were distributed equally among the 70 million members of the work force, the average share would be $1,000. For the lowest-paid workers, such as migrant farm laborers, this would represent an increase in annual incomes of 100 percent or more—an immense gain. For the average industrial worker, however, the gain would be in the neighborhood of 20–25 percent, certainly a large increase but not one that would fundamentally alter his living standards.

Thus, insofar as the institutions of capitalism constitute a drain upon non-privileged groups, it can be fairly said

that they are only marginally responsible for any inadequacy in the prevailing general level of income. Individual companies may indeed be capable of vastly improving the lot of their workers—General Motors makes nearly as much gross profit on a car as it pays out in wages, and "could," therefore, virtually double its wages. But for the economy as a whole, no such large margin of redistribution is possible. So long, then, as the defense of these privileges does not result in substantially *increasing* the share of national income accruing to the privileged elements of the nation, it seems fair to conclude that the level of material well-being under capitalism is limited mainly by the levels of productivity it can reach. If the trend of growth of the past century is continued, the average level of real wages for industrial labor should double in another two to three decades. This would bring average earnings to a level of about $10,000 and would effectively spell the abolition of wage poverty, under any definition.

This conclusion does not close our investigation into the relationship between poverty and privilege, but rather directs it toward what is now revealed as the principal cause of poverty. This is the fact that large groups within the population—the aged, the handicapped, the sick, the unemployed, the castaways in rural backwaters—have no active tie into the market economy and must therefore subsist at the very meager levels to which non-participants in the work process are consigned. There is only one way that their condition can be quickly alleviated, but that one way would be very effective indeed. This is to redistribute to them enough income earned or received by more favored members of the community to bring them to levels of economic decency. A program with this objective would require some $10 to $12 billion above the public assistance that the poor now receive in this country. Such a sum would amount to approximately a seventh of corporate profits before tax. Alternatively, shared among the 11 or 12 million consumer units who constitute the top 20 percent of the nation's income receivers, it would require an average additional tax of roughly $1,000 on incomes that average $16,000.

In both cases, in other words, a program to eliminate sheer need among the poor would constitute a sizable incursion into the incomes enjoyed by favored groups, although hardly such an invasion as to constitute the elimination of these privileges. Thus, the failure to carry out such a program cannot be laid to the "objective" or functional difference that such a redistribution would entail, but simply to the general unwillingness of those who enjoy higher incomes to share their good fortune with those who do not. As Adam Walinsky has very aptly put it, "The middle class knows that the economists are right when they say that poverty could be eliminated if we only will it; they simply do not will it."

To what extent does that conclusion, then, lead to the prospect of alleviating poverty within the next generation or so? In the short run the outlook is not very hopeful. Given the temptations of luxury consumption and the general lack of deep concern in a nation lulled by middle-class images of itself, it is doubtful that very effective programs of social rescue can be launched within the next decade or two. Yet, of all the problems confronting capitalism, poverty seems the least likely to be blocked permanently by the resistance of privilege. Tax receipts are now growing at the rate of some $6 billion a year simply as a consequence of the growth of the level of output, and this flow of funds to the government will increase over the future. It may be that these receipts will be used for larger arms expenditures for some years, but assuming that full-scale

war will be averted, sooner or later the arms budget must level off. Thereafter the funds will become available for use either in the form of tax reductions—an operation which normally favors the well-to-do—or as the wherewithal for a major assault on the slums, etc. In this choice between the claims of privilege and those of social reform, the balance is apt to be tipped by the emerging new national elites, especially from government. In addition, a gradual liberalization of the prevailing business ideology is likely to ease opposition to measures that clearly promise to improve the quality of society without substantially affecting its basic institutions of privilege.

It is idle to predict when Harlem will be reconstructed and Appalachia reborn, since so much depends on the turn of events in the international arena. Yet it seems to me that the general dimensions of the problem make it possible to envisage the substantial alleviation—perhaps even the virtual elimination—of massive poverty within the limits of capitalism three or four decades hence, or possibly even sooner.

The elimination of poverty is, however, only part of a larger problem within capitalism—the problem of income distribution. Hence, we might now look to the chances that capitalism will alter the moral anomalies of wealth as well as those of poverty.

Here it is not so easy to foresee a change in the operational results of the system of privilege. Since the 1930's, the political intent of the public has clearly been to bring about some lessening of the concentration of income that goes to the very rich, and some diminution of the enclaves of family wealth that have passed intact from one generation to the next. Thus, we have seen the introduction of estate taxes that levy imposts of about one-third on net estates of only $1 million, and of fully half on net estates of $5 million; and these rates have been supplemented by measures to prevent the tax-free passage of wealth before death by gift.

Since the enactment of these taxes, a full generation has passed, and we would therefore expect to see some impact of the legislation in a significant lowering of the concentration of wealth among the top families. Instead, we find that the share held by the top families has decreased only slightly—from 33 percent of all personal wealth in 1922, to 29 percent in 1953 (the last year for which such calculations exist). Concentrations of stock—the single most important medium for the investment of large wealth—has shown no tendency to decline since 1922. Equally recalcitrant before egalitarian measures is the flow of income to topmost groups. Legal tax rates on top incomes have risen from 54 percent under President Hoover to over 90 percent in the 1940's and early 1950's, and to 72 percent in the mid 1960's. The presumed higher incidence of taxes at the peak of the income pyramid has, however, been subverted by innumerable stratagems of trusts, family sharing of income, capital gains, deferred compensation, or other means of tax avoidance or outright tax evasion.

There is no indication that this resistive capacity of the system of privilege is likely to weaken, at least within the time span of a generation. Nor is there any sign that the "natural workings" of the system will lessen the flow of income to the top. The statistics of income distribution clearly show a slow but regular drift *toward* the upper end of the spectrum. Three percent of all income was received by income receivers in the $15,000-and-up brackets in 1947; in 1963, in terms of constant dollars, this fraction had grown to eight. This determined self-perpetuation of large concentrations of private wealth is likely to continue—afflicting the social order with that peculiar irresponsibility that is the unhappy hallmark of the sys-

tem. The power of wealth is by no means the only source of power in America and may, in fact, be expected to decline. But the voice of money still speaks very loudly, and the capacity of wealth to surmount the half-acquiescent opposition of a democratic political system promises that it will continue to resound in America for a long while to come.

## III

The maldistribution of income and the social problems that spring from it can no longer be said to threaten the viability—although it may seriously jeopardize the social peace—of capitalism. This cannot be said, however, of a second problem—the economic malfunction that has periodically racked capitalism over the last hundred years and that nearly caused its demise in the 1930's.

The persistent breakdowns of the capitalist economy can all be traced to a single underlying cause: the anarchic or planless character of capitalist production. So long as the output of individual firms is guided solely by the profitable opportunities open to each, without regard to the state of the market as a whole, economic short-circuits must result whenever the output of all firms fails to dovetail with the structure of demand, or when the production plans of the business community as a whole are not adequate to cope with the independently formulated savings plans of the community at large. In a milieu of huge enterprises and enormous fixed investments, such miscalculations or imbalances carry the potential of a major disruptive impact.

Hence, it is not surprising that reformers have long advocated planning as the remedy for capitalist depressions or stagnation. The trouble has been, however, that much of the planning which its partisans have urged upon it has been incompatible with the institutions of capitalism. For example, proposals to nationalize the core of heavy industry or to convert the biggest corporations into quasi-public utilities, may have much to recommend them along strictly economic lines, but they all infringe the preserves of private property or of the market to a degree intolerable to the American business community.

This does not mean, however, that planning is therefore ruled out. On the contrary, a great deal of planning is virtually inevitable over the coming decades, but it is likely to be used in support of the main institutions of capitalism rather than as a means of replacing them.

One such planning instrument is certain to be the reliance on the government's fiscal powers to maintain aggregate demand. Although we are still only in the early stages of experience with public demand-creation, there is little doubt that a bold use of fiscal mechanisms can virtually guarantee a steady or rising level of total expenditure. Moreover, since demand-creation involves little or no interference with individual markets or business, it impinges little, if at all, on the preserves of privilege. Tax cuts, for example, are certain to be welcomed by business and upper-income groups. Additional spending, so long as it is within the established areas of public concern— arms, roads, schools, rivers and harbors, conservation, and perhaps now social welfare—is also welcomed as a source of new business.

There remains, to be sure, a body of ideological resistance to the use of fiscal measures of a compensatory sort, compounded of an ignorance of public finance and a shrewd foreboding that the assumption of public economic responsibility, no matter how useful at the moment, is freighted with serious long-term implications. Yet it seems likely that this is a view of dwindling

importance. A very considerable segment of business backed the controversial Kennedy tax cut, and the undoubted success of that policy should pave the way for further measures of the same kind. In addition, the nonbusiness elites, especially from the academic and government establishments, are strongly in favor of fiscal controls to buoy up the system, and their influence in securing the bold use of these measures may be very important or even decisive. Thus, there seems a reasonable expectation that measures to safeguard the economy against the collapse of effective demand lie well within the ambit of capitalism today.

What is more difficult to judge is the extent to which capitalism will be able to go beyond general fiscal planning on a more detailed basis for the achievement of broad welfare objectives. Here the experience of Europe since the war is relevant. In nearly every nation of Europe we have seen the formulation of planning techniques that go considerably beyond the mere application of fiscal leverage, to the conscious "design" of the economic future. The very fact that European capitalism has taken this turn puts it beyond argument that a considerable amount of indirect planning is compatible with the main institutions of capitalism.

On the other hand, the growth of European planning owes much to the particular traditions of European capitalism, including the more or less formalized structures of employers' federations and the prounced "*étatist*" tradition in many states. The absence of comparable institutions and history makes doubtful the possibility of a wholesale transplantation of European forms of planning to America. Furthermore, unlike its sister capitalisms across the Atlantic, the United States has not become accustomed to the public ownership of transportation or utilities, or to a large public-housing sector, or to the development of a strong system of public welfare.

As a result, the United States has always entertained an exaggerated suspicion of all invasions by the public authority into private terrain. Hence the extent and speed with which American capitalism may evolve in the direction of detailed economic planning would seem to depend primarily on whether circumstances arise that require such techniques. If, for example, the continued incursion of technology, coupled with a very large inflow of young people into the labor market, should create an employment crisis during the next decade, some form of industrial planning would quite possibly emerge as an instrument of social policy. In that case, policies designed deliberately to create employment through a substantial enlargement of public activities at state or local levels, or—looking farther ahead—the designation of a civil sector, such as the rebuilding of the cities, as the peacetime equivalent of the military sector, might well show up as part of the practicable social agenda.

Capitalism, then, can achieve considerable change within the boundaries imposed by its market mechanisms and privileges of private property. But there are also important limits beyond which it cannot go—at least within the foreseeable future. Primary among these is the continuing requirement that the economic participants in a capitalistic world—even in a planned capitalist world—behave in the manner that is required of them if the market mechanism is to work. That is, they must act as "economic men," buying cheap and selling dear, allowing relative remunerations to weigh heavily in their choices of occupations or employment, setting acquisitive aims high in the hierarchy of life goals. These marketing traits are not merely pervasive private idiosyncrasies that can be dispensed with if they are no longer esteemed. They are integral to, and necessary for, the successful operation of a market system. In a setting of bare subsistence and newly-risen entrepreneurs there is little difficulty in adducing the acquisitive behavior required to run a capitalist economy. But in a more advanced and affluent society, where the primary drives of self-preservation begin to fail, the necessary marketing behavior must be sustained by supplementary motives of emulation and competitive striving. Thus, the endless and relentless exacerbation of economic appetites in advanced capitalism is not merely a surface aberration, but a deeply-rooted functional necessity to provide the motivations on which the market system depends.

This thralldom to an overweening economic imperative of sales and profits and its accompanying worship of a calculus of income are features of capitalism that cannot be eliminated by planning. A planned capitalism of the future, however rid of its growth malfunctions, will nonetheless be one in which men are subservient to the economic demands of a market environment.

Nowhere is this apt to pose a more serious problem than along the extended frontier where technology interacts with society. This interaction takes two forms. One, which we may call the *direct effect*, is revealed as the immediate change in the environment brought about by the application of a new technique such as the computerized control of production, or the use of a new product such as a jet transport. This effect, as we know from experience, may bring radical changes into economic or social life, but these changes have, at least, been consciously introduced into society (although often with inadequate appreciation of their immediate impact).

But there is as well an *indirect effect*

of technology that diffuses throughout society as the secondary consequence of new machinery or new processes. Thus, the indirect effect of the new technology of automation is unemployment; the indirect effect of the new technology of medicine and health is an aging population; the indirect effect of the technology of war is the creation of a military-industrial economic sector. Not least we find, as a general indirect effect of all modern technology, an increasing complexity, size, and hierarchical organization of production, which gives rise in turn to a growing need for public intervention into the economic process itself.

Against this tremendous invasion of technology, a market economy offers but one instrument of control—the profit or loss stemming from the direct effect of a particular technology. As to its side-effects, the market mechanism proper has no controls whatsoever. As a result, the invasion of technology becomes an essentially disruptive force, continuously upsetting the patterns of life in a haphazard manner. Under a system that abdicates as much decision-making as possible to the rule of profit, the possibilities for a rational restraint over this force that rearranges our lives thus shrinks to a minimum. Capitalism is essentially defenseless before the revolutionizing impact of its technical drive. Of all the limits to which capitalism is subject, this is the most unyielding—although, as we shall see, it is this very helplessness of the system before the technological onslaught that holds out the most important promise for the long-term remaking of capitalism itself.

Our next concern lies with the reach and inhibitions of what we might call the *capitalist imagination.*

The quality of this imagination is most clearly revealed if we think for a moment of the "visionary" glimpses of the future often spelled out for us by business spokesmen—a future of enormous affluence, technical marvels, widespread leisure, etc. There is, in these vistas, much that is genuinely new and rich with possibilities for material betterment. But there is also something inherent in all these visions that remains unmentioned. It is that these imagined societies of the future still depend on "workers," however well off, who work for "businessmen," however enlightened, in a system motivated and directed by the commercial impulse, however tempered or refined. A society in which there were no workers or businessmen as we understand the terms; or in which the categories of privilege had been fundamentally altered; or where the pressures of the marketplace had been replaced by some other means of assuring economic continuity—all these possibilities are absent from the capitalist imagination. More than that, they are dismissed as "utopian."

Albeit unwittingly, this is set forth all too clearly in the peroration of a recent book by Frederick R. Kappel, President of A.T.&T.:

We are involved in one of the great ideological struggles of all times. Essentially it is a contest between two quite basic concepts. One is that men are capable of faith in ideas that lift their minds and hearts, ideas that raise their sights and give them hope, energy, and enthusiasm. Opposing this is the belief that the pursuit of material ends is all that life on this earth is about.

The words are eloquent enough, but alas, what do they reveal? Which side, ours or theirs, is the side of "ideas that lift minds and hearts," which the side that believes "the pursuit of material ends is all that life on this earth is about"? In the breathtaking ambiguity of this intended affirmation of business faith, the unseeing confusion of identities meant to be so clearly polarized, lies an all too clear exposition of the weakness that inhabits the very center of the capitalist imagination.

We cannot be sure what effect such a constricted view of the future may have on the aspirations and attitudes of most American citizens. It is likely that for the majority who are understandably concerned with their material lot, it would make no difference whatsoever. But for a not unimportant minority— I think of college youth and of the intellectual community—the absence of any transcendent secular goal is apt to present an oppressive limitation to thought and spirit. Indeed, in my opinion the present anarchic mood of youth may well be due to just such a lack of a visionary future to which to bend its hopes and efforts.

## IV

Whatever the ultimate effect of this stifling at home, there is another area where the limitations of the capitalist imagination are likely to be of very great importance. This is in the contest with Communism for the guidance of future world society.

It is hardly necessary to speak of the power of Communism as a force bearing on American capitalism. Yet in appraising that force, we often fail to articulate that which is most threatening about it to ourselves as members or protagonists of the capitalist way of life. This is the presence of Communism as a viable social system that has dispensed with our institutions of privilege, and that therefore faces capitalism with the living refutation of their necessity. In this fundamental sense, Communism puts capitalism on trial before the bar of history. In this trial it matters not that Communism has its own system of privilege, in some ways more primitive than our own. Nor does it count for much that capitalist performance on many fronts is manifestly superior to that of Communism. What

matters is that Communism has demonstrated the mutability and historic transiency of our particular social order, and that that social order can never again feel entirely secure in its claims to permanence and legitimacy.

I believe it is this sense of historic unease that lies behind the deep, uncritical, and often unreasoning hostility of America toward Communism. The reasons we cite for our fear and hatred —the undeniable acts of cruelty and repression, of aggression and intolerance, of intrigue and untrustworthiness—can be duplicated in many non-Communist countries: in Portugal, in Spain, in the Union of South Africa, in various Latin American dictatorships, past and present. There, however, they have never roused in us the fervor or revulsion they do when discovered in the Communist world. In part, this is no doubt because these other nations are small and weak and do not constitute centers of national power comparable to Russia or China (although hardly Cuba); in part, because they do not seek to export their particular world-views. But more deeply, especially among the conservative interests of this country, I think it is because the existence of Communism frightens American capitalism, as the existence of Protestantism once frightened the Catholic Church; or the French Revolution the English aristocracy.

The fundamental threat of Communism is not likely to decline over the next generation. Rather, it is apt to grow. In Russia, the prospect is clearly for substantial economic expansion; for the gradual improvement of the still dreary life of its people; for a continuation of its massive scientific advances; for further intellectual, and perhaps political, liberalization. For China, no such sanguine assurances can be given, but its continuing emergence as the unquestioned leader of Asia seems hardly likely to be reversed. In Latin America and

Africa, the outlook can only be for political turmoil as the aspirations of excited masses outdistance any conceivable pace of progress. In the ensuing unrest, radical leaders are bound to emerge, and it would be a miracle if they were not inclined, to some degree, toward Communism or some kind of national collectivism.

This tendency is apt to be reinforced by the very ideological limitations of capitalism we have been concerned with. If we look to the developing nations, we find in nearly all of them a yearning, not alone for material progress, but for a great social and political, even spiritual, transformation. However millennial these hopes, however certain to be dashed, they are not to be lightly disregarded. The leaders and elites of the young nations, like those of our own youth, are looking for a model of a society that will fire them to great efforts, and it is unlikely that they will find this model in the market-based and wealth-protecting philosophy of capitalism.

All these considerations point to the very great likelihood that Communism or radical national collectivism will make substantial inroads during the coming generation or two, perhaps by conquest or subversion, but more probably by the decay of existing orders unable to handle the terrible demands of political awakening and economic reformation.

Given this grave outlook, what would be its impact on America?

We have already witnessed the initial impact in the substantial militarization of American capitalism. The so-called military-industrial complex (to which should be added "political" as an equal partner) today contributes between eight and ten percent to the Gross National Product. In the 1960's, military expenditure has regularly exceeded the sum total of all personal income taxes, has accounted for one-fourth of all federal public works, has directly employed some 3.2 million

workers in defense industries and another 1.1 million as civilian employees of the Defense Department and the services, has subsidized about one-third of all research in the United States; and not least, has come to be accepted as a normal and permanent fixture of American life by all groups, including the academic. The fact is that American capitalism is now a semi-militarized economy and will very probably become even more so during the next decade.

In this dangerous situation, it is important for us to clarify the specific influence over the direction of events that can be ascribed to the business interest in society. According to Marxism—or more properly Leninism—the business structure itself inherently presses the state toward armed conflict. The fierce economic conflicts of capitalist nations prior to World War II, the long history of capitalist suppression of colonials continuing down to the present in some parts of Africa, the huge and jealously guarded interests of the United States and other capitalist nations in the oil regions of the Near East or Latin America—all make it impossible to dismiss such a picture of a belligerent capitalist imperialism. At the same time, even a cursory review of the nations initating aggressive actions since 1945 should raise doubts as to the exclusive capitalist predisposition to war. More important, an analysis of the roots of belligerency in the more warlike capitalism, specifically pre-war Germany or Japan, must emphasize the leading role played by purely military or lingering feudal elements, and the largely passive, although not always reluctant, part taken by capitalist groups.

On somewhat more Marxian lines, Victor Perlo has made a determination of the direct economic interest of the top American corporations in war or peace. He concludes that the economic self-interest of the biggest corporations is more or less evenly divided, with half profiting from a defense economy, and half—including such giants as General Motors and U.S. Steel—being penalized by it. Assuming that big businessmen would be motivated to oppose or support disarmament on such grounds, it is important to note that nothing like a monolithic "pro-war" economic interest can be said to exist within American capitalism.

Further, the imperialist thrust that increased both the chances and the causes of war in the late 19th century seems to be giving way to less dangerous forms of international relationship. Property interests that once had to be defended by force of arms are now protected by government insurance. International relationships that formerly allowed large capitalist enterprises to intervene directly into the economic and political life of colonial nations have been succeeded by relationships in which the independence of action of foreign companies is severely restricted. In a word, the politics of nationalism has asserted its preeminence over the economics of imperialism, with the salutary consequence of a diminution in the role of business as the active initiator of foreign economic policy.

Thus, the role of business proper in the struggle for world power does not seem intrinsically warlike. Unfortunately, that does not mean the chances for conflict are therefore small. Business is not the only power center within capitalist societies, and in America the military and the civil branches of government contain more than their share of belligerent-minded leaders who are in a position to influence foreign policy. Then, too, we must reckon with the generalized hatred of Communism among the lower and middle classes, a hatred that may originally have been implanted but that now flourishes as a self-maintaining source of aggression.

In this situation, given the reciprocal posture of the other side, it is difficult to see how a major conflict could be avoided, were not the consequences of all-out war so terrifying. On both sides, only the instinct of self-preservation—fortunately the single most powerful instinct—holds back the military-minded, the fundamentalist, the ambitious, or simply the self-righteous. As a result, the most probable outlook becomes a continuation of the military-political struggle on the scale of Korea or Vietnam. The danger is that a succession of such involvements may encourage the rise of a strict garrison state, one that is marked by an atmosphere of internal repression and external belligerence.

This grave possibility may well be the single most dangerous eventuality during the next decade or two, when the chances for Communist "takeovers" will be greatest. But the longer-term future is far from foreclosed along such lines. On both sides of the great divide, forces are at work that can lessen the intensity of hostilities. One of these is the enhanced prospect for international stabilization, once the worst is over and those nations that are going to go Communist or national-collectivist have done so. A second hopeful possibility is the growth of a greater degree of isolationism in American politics—or perhaps one should say a lesser degree of interventionism—compounded in part of disillusion, in part of fear, and in part of a more realistic appreciation of our inability to affect the unruly tides of world history. Yet another force for peaceful accommodation is the possibility that the specter of Communist "world domination" will be dispelled by the sight of Communist nations in intense rivalry, just as the Communist world may be relieved by the continuing evidence of inter-capitalist frictions.

And finally, we can hope that within a generation or so, new concerns posed by enormous world populations, interlocked global technical devices for communications, transport, power, and other uses, vanishing fossil fuel supplies, a worldwide polluted atmosphere, etc., will cause the present ideological fervor to subside under more pressing problems, just as did the great religious animosities of the past.

Not all the preconditions for such a turn of events lie in our own hands. Much depends on the continuation of the present trend toward the fragmentation and gradual liberalization of the Communist world. But given this opportunity, there seems at least a reasonable chance that American and European capitalism can find a *modus vivendi* with the other side. There again, I believe, the critical determination of direction is apt to reside with the new elites rising within capitalism. Indeed, if there are limits to the adaptability of capitalism before the untoward development of world events, these limits appear to reside, more than is the case with the other challenges before the system, in the quality of the "new men" who are rising to positions of power within it.

## V

It is time to revert to the question we set ourselves at the outset. What limits, we asked, were inherent in the capitalist system as such? The answer at which we have arrived is necessarily of a speculative nature. Yet, it does not appear entirely fanciful. What seems possible is to bring about social change that stops short of a direct assault on the economic machinery of privilege that all elites—indeed, that even the general public—in a capitalist society are normally eager to protect. This enables us to draw the general boundaries of short-term evolution for capitalism. The distribution of wealth can be corrected at the bottom, albeit slowly, but not at the top. The control over output can be improved very greatly but the essential commercial character of a market system, with its surrender to the acquisitive impulse, is incorrigible. A considerable accommodation can be made with the noncapitalist world, but the imagination of that world cannot be captured by a basically conservative outlook. There are, in a word, deep-seated attributes to the quality of life that constitute an impregnable inner keep of the system of American capitalism as we know it.

And yet, if we now recall our earlier concern with feudalism, we will recall that despite the seeming impregnability of its institutions in the 13th century, by the 18th century, somehow, the system had nonetheless changed out of all recognition. How did feudalism expire? It gave way to capitalism as part of a subversive process of historic change in which a newly-emerging attribute of daily life proved to be as irresistibly attractive to the privileged orders of feudalism as it was to be ultimately destructive of them. This subversive influence was the gradual infiltration of commercial relationships and cash exchanges into the everyday round of feudal life, each act of marketing binding men more fully into the cash nexus and weakening by that degree the traditional duties and relationships on which feudalism was based. Against this progressive monetization the old order struggled in vain, for the temptations and pleasures of the cash economy were greater than the erosion of privileges that went with it.

Could there be in our day an equivalent of that powerfully disintegrative and yet constitutive force—a force sufficiently overwhelming to render impotent the citadel of capitalism, and yet as irresistibly attractive to it as the earlier current of exchange was to feudalism? I think there is such a force, and that it already bulks very large within our world. This revolutionary power is the veritable explosion of organized knowledge, and its applied counterpart, scientific technology.

The extraordinary rate of expansion of this explosion is sufficiently familiar to require only a word of exposition. There is, for instance, the often-quoted but still astonishing statement that of all the scientists who have ever lived in all of history, half are alive today. There is the equally startling calculation that the volume of scientific publication during the last ten to fifteen years is as large as, or larger than, that of all previous ages. Such examples serve accurately enough to convey the notion of the exponential growth of scientific inquiry in our day. As to the equally phenomenal growth of the powers of the technology, if that needs any demonstration, there is the contrast cited by Kenneth Boulding between the centuries needed to recuperate from the physical destruction that accompanied the collapse of the Roman Empire, and the scant twenty years in which the shattered and burned cities of modern Europe and Japan were rebuilt after the Second World War.

This explosion of science and technology is often thought of as a product *of* capitalism, insofar as it arose in an age dominated by capitalism. Yet the association was far more one of coexistence than of casual interrelation. At best we can say that the secular air of bourgeois culture was compatible with, perhaps even conducive to, scientific investigation, but we can hardly credit the acceleration of scientific activities around the middle of the 19th century to the direct stimulus or patronage of capitalism itself.

Even scientific technology exhibits but little debt to the existence of capitalism. The technology on which capitalism began its long course of growth was strictly of a pragmatic, intuitive, pre-scientific kind. Watt, for example, invented the steam engine over fifty years before the basic formulation of the law of thermodynamics. The English textile, iron and steel, or chemical industries were founded and prospered with no "scientific" underpinnings at all. The same is true for the young railroad industry, for canal building, or road-laying. The deliberate employment of scientific investigation to create or refine the technology of production was considerably delayed in arriving. In this country the first private industrial laboratory was not built until 1900 by the General Electric company, and organized research and development on a large scale did not really get under way until 1913.

Thus, we find the flowering of science and the application of science to technology—the very hallmarks of the modern era—to be currents that arose *within* capitalism, but that do not owe their existence directly to capitalism. Rather, science and its technology emerge as a great underground river whose tortuous course has finally reached the surface during the age of capitalism, but which springs from far distant sources. Having now surfaced, that river must cut its own channels through the existing social landscape. Indeed, if we ask what force in our day might in time be strong enough to undercut the bastions of privilege of capitalism and to create its own institutions and social structures in their place, the answer must surely be the one force that dominates our age—the power of science and of scientific technology.

There is, I suspect, little to argue about as to the commanding pressure of science in modern times. What is likely to be a good deal less readily accepted, however, is the contention that this force will cause drastic modifications in, or even the eventual supersession of, capitalism. For at first glance this new current of history seems to have imparted an immense momentum to capitalism by providing it with a virtually inexhaustible source of invention and innovation to insure its economic growth. Merely to review in our minds the broad areas of investment and economic output that owe their existence *entirely* to the laboratory work of the last three decades—the nuclear and space establishments, electronics, the computerization of industry, the creation of new materials such as plastics —is to reveal the breadth of this new gulf stream of economic nourishment.

Yet, like the attractions of the cash market for the feudal lord, the near-term advantages of science and technology conceal long-term conflicts and incompatibilities between this new force of history and its host society. Indeed, the insinuation of science and technology into the interstices of business enterprise promises to alter the fundamental working arrangements of capitalism.

At least one of these alterations is already familiar to us. This is the tendency of technology to create social problems that require public controls to correct or forestall. In part, these agencies of control are contained and concealed *within* the centers of production themselves, where they show up as rising echelons of corporate administration and supervision. In part, the controls show up in the familiar bureaus of government that cope, with greater or lesser success, with the social repercussions of transportation, nuclear energy, drugs, air pollution, etc. In still a different aspect, the controls invade areas of social life rather than production, as in the astonishing network of government required solely to manage the automobile (an effort that requires the labor of one out of every ten persons employed by all state and local governments). Meanwhile, in the background of the social system the controls are manifest as the growing apparatus of regulation over wages and prices, and over the total flow of economic activity —all ultimately traceable to the need to intervene more closely into an econ-omy of increasing technological disruption.

Not that the disruptive effect of technology is itself a new phenomenon. The dislocations of the technology of the pre-scientific age—say the spinning jenny—were quite as great as those of the modern age. The difference is that in an earlier age the repair of technological disturbances was largely consigned to the adaptive powers of the individual and his family, of the ameliorative efforts of small-scale local government, and to the annealing powers of the market itself. Today, however, these traditional agencies of social repair can no longer cope effectively with the entrance of technology. The individual, now typically a member of a small urban family rather than of a large extended rural family, is much less capable of withstanding economic displacement without external assistance. The local community, faced with large-scale problems of unemployment or ecological maladjustment brought about by technical change, has no recourse but to turn to the financial help and expertise available only from larger government units. The market, which no longer "clears" when the marketers are enormous firms rather than atomistic business units, also discovers that the only antidote to grave economic disjunction is the countervailing influence or *force majeur* of the central governing authority. In a word, technology seems to be exerting a steady push from many levels and areas of the economy in the direction of a society of *organization*.

To this well-known effect of technical progress we must now add another— the capacity of technology to render redundant the physical energies of man. That is, machines do man's work for him, thereby freeing him from the bonds of toil and, not less important in the context of our inquiry, from the hegemony of the market process.

We see this disemployment effect

most dramatically in the case of agriculture. But equally startling is the labor-displacing effect of modern technology in that congeries of activities associated with the extraction of basic materials from nature and their fabrication, assembly, conversion, or transport to point of sale. Since 1900, science and technology have given us a stupendous array of new products, each requiring large quantities of human effort—the automobile, the whole range of consumer durables, the communications industry, office machinery, new metals, fabrics, and materials of all kinds, to name but a few. Yet at the end of that period, the total requirements on the labor force for all these goods-centered industries had risen by only *two percentage points*. During the era of the greatest increase in factory production ever known, virtually no increase in the distribution of labor in favor of the goods sector was needed—indeed, since the hours of work fell, there was actually a *relatively decreased* need for human effort in the output of these goods.

Today we stand at the threshold of a new stage in the application of scientific technology to human activities: automation. What is most threatening about this technology is that it has begun to invade a sanctuary of hitherto relatively unmechanized work—the vast numbers of jobs in the office, administrative, and service occupations. By 1960, more than half the labor force was in these jobs. And now, into this varied group of occupations, technology is starting to penetrate in the form of machines as complex as those that can read and sort checks, or as relatively simple as those that dispense coffee and sandwiches.

This is not to maintain that no new areas of employment exist. Certainly there remain very large and still untapped possibilities for work in the reconstruction of the cities; the pro-

vision of education; the improvement of health and recreation facilities; the counseling of the young and the care of the aged; the beautification of the environment. Provided only that demand can be marshaled for these activities, there is surely no dearth of job prospects for the coming generation.

But that is precisely the point. The incursion of technology has pushed the frontiers of work into a spectrum of jobs whose common denominator is that they require *public action and public funds* for their initiation and support. The employment-upsetting characteristics of technology thus act to speed capitalism along the general path of planning and control down which it is simultaneously impelled by the direct environment-upsetting impact of technological change.

If we look further ahead, the necessity for planning is apt to become still more pressing. The day of a "fully automated" society is by no means a fantasy, although its realization may well require another century, or more. That is to say, we can, without too much difficulty, imagine a time when as small a proportion of the labor force as now suffices to overprovide us with food, will serve to turn out the manufactured staples, the houses, the transportation, the retail services, even the governmental supervision that will be required.

What the leisured fraction of the population will then do with itself is an interesting and important question. It may possibly find avenues of remuneration that are resistive to mechanical duplication, so that instead of taking in one another's wash, we buy one another's paintings. But even in this best outcome, the underlying process of production, now enormously mechanized and intricately interconnected, would require some form of coordination other than the play of market forces. If we think of the network of controls over output and disposal that now characterize the agricultural sector, we catch some idea of the controls required to operate an economy where manpower requirements generally would have been reduced to a level comparable to that of farming today. And, if the leisured population does not find adequate remuneration in unmechanizable private employments, it will have to be given the direct right to share in society's output—another vital infringement on the market's function.

But the erosion of the market goes deeper yet. For the introduction of technology has one last effect whose ultimate implications for the metamorphosis of capitalism are perhaps greatest of all. This is the effect of technology in steadily raising the average level of well-being, thereby gradually bringing to an end the condition of material need as an effective stimulus for human behavior.

Everyone recognizes that the end to want would represent the passage over an historic watershed for mankind. But it must be equally clear that such a passage will also represent a basic revision of the existential situation that has hitherto provided the main impetus for work. As needs diminish, the traditional stimuli of capitalism begin to lose their force, occupations become valued for their intrinsic pleasures rather than for their extrinsic rewards. The very decision to work or not becomes a matter of personal preference rather than of economic necessity. More telling, the drive for profit—the nuclear core of capitalist energy—becomes blunted, as the purchasable distinctions of wealth decline. In a society of the imaginable wealth implicit in another hundred years of technical progress, who will wish to be the rich man's servant at any price?

All this is no doubt a gain in human dignity. But that is not an end to it. As a result of this inestimable gain in personal freedom, a fundamental assurance for social viability also vanishes, for the market stimuli that bring about social provisioning are no longer met with obedient responses. One has but to imagine employees in an industry of central importance going on strike, not with the slim backing of unemployment insurance and a small union supplement, as today, but with liquid assets sufficient to maintain them, if need be, for a year or more, to envisage the potential for social disorder inherent in the attainment of a genuinely widespread and substantial affluence.

Yet it is precisely such an affluence that is within clear sight, provided that the impetus of science and technology continue to propel the economy for another century. In this impasse there is but one possible solution. *Some authority other than the market must be entrusted with the allocation of men to the essential posts of society, should they lack for applicants.*

We have concerned ourselves so far only with the curious two-edged effect of science and technology on the functional aspects of capitalism. Now we must pay heed to a second and perhaps even more critical effect, the conquest of the capitalist imagination by science and scientific technology.

I think it is fair to say that capitalism as an *idea* has never garnered much enthusiasm. All efforts to raise money-making to the level of a positive virtue have failed. The self-interest of the butcher and the baker to which Adam Smith appealed in lieu of their benevolence may serve as powerful sources of social energy, but not as powerful avatars of the social imagination.

By way of contrast, I think it is also fair to say that science *is* the burning idea of the 20th century, comparable in its impact on men's minds to the flush of democratic enthusiasm of the late 18th century or to the political commitment won by Communism in the early 20th. The altruism of science, its "purity," the awesome vistas it opens and the venerable path it has followed, have won from all groups exactly that passionate interest and conviction that is so egregiously lacking to capitalism as a way of life.

It is not alone that science carries a near-religious ethos of conviction and even sacrifice. Within Communism as within capitalism, the new elites arising within the framework of the old society owe their ascendancy and their allegiance in large part to science. The scientific cadres proper, the social scientists, the government administrative personnel—even the military—look to science not merely as the vehicle of their expertise, but as the magnetic North of their compass of values. These new elites have not as yet divorced their social goals from those of the society to which they are still glad to pay allegiance, and no more than the 13th-century merchants huddled under the walls of a castle, do they see themselves as the potential architects and lords of a society built around their own functions. But as with the merchants, we can expect that such notions will in time emerge and assert their primacy over the aims of the existing order.

What sorts of notions are these apt to be?

One general direction of thought will surely be the primacy of scientific discovery as a central purpose of society, a *raison d'être* for its existence, perhaps even a vehicle for its religious impulses. No doubt the distribution of social resources and of privileges will reflect this basic orientation toward scientific exploration and application. Not less characteristic will be an emphasis on rational solutions to social problems. The key word of the new society is apt to be *control*. Not alone economic affairs (which should become of secondary importance), but the num-

bers and location of the population and its genetic quality, the manner of social domestication of children, the choice of life-work—even the very duration of life itself—are all apt to become subjects for scientific investigation and direction.

It is tempting, but idle, to venture beyond these few suggestions. What manner of life, what institutions, what ideologies may serve the purposes of a society dedicated to the accumulation of scientific knowledge and power, we cannot foretell; variations may well be as great as those observable in societies dedicated to the accumulation of material wealth. Nor does there seem to be much point in attempting to foresee by what precise stratagems the elites and ideas of the future may finally assert their claims. Historic projection is rarely, if ever, a matter of simple extrapolation from the present and recent past. Should there arise radical parties in America, broadly-based and aimed at a rational reorganization of economic affairs, the pace of transition would be quicker. Should there not, change will still occur, but more slowly. Veblen was too impatient for his engineers to take over; Schumpeter, more realistic when he advised the intelligentsia to be prepared to wait in the wings for possibly a century, a "short run" in affairs of this kind, he said.

So, too, the examples of the past discourage us from attempting to prophesy the manner of demise of the system to be superseded. The new protagonists of social and economic control will lack for some time an articulate conception of a purposively constituted and consciously directed social system. The old ideas of the proper primacy of economic aims will linger side-by-side with newer ideas of the priority of scientific interests. And no doubt the privileges of the older order will endure side-by-side with those of the new, just as titles of nobility exist to this very day. It is conceivable that violence may attend the transfer of power and responsibility from one elite to another, but more probably the transfer will be imperceptible; managed by the sons of the old elite entering the profession of the new.

All these are the merest speculations, difficult to avoid entirely, not to be taken too literally. Only one thing is certain. It is the profound incompatibility between the new idea of the active use of science within society and the idea of capitalism.

The conflict lies in the ideas that ultimately inform both worlds. The world of science as it is applied to society is committed to the idea of man as a being who shapes his collective destiny; the world of capitalism to an idea of man as one who permits his common social destination to take care of itself. The essential idea of a society built on scientific engineering is to impose human will on the social universe; that of capitalism to allow the social universe to unfold as if it were beyond human interference.

Before the activist philosophy of science as a social instrument, this inherent social passivity of capitalism becomes archaic, and eventually intolerable. The "self-regulating" economy that is its highest social achievement stands condemned by its absence of meaning and intelligence, and each small step taken to correct its deficiencies only advertises the inhibitions placed on the potential exercise of purposeful thought and action by its remaining barriers of ideology and privilege. In the end, capitalism is weighed in the scale of science and found wanting, not alone as a system but as a philosophy.

That an ascendant science, impatient to substitute reason for blind obedience, inquiry for ideology, represents a great step forward for mankind, I do not doubt. Yet it seems necessary to end on a cautionary note. Just as the prescient medievalist might have foreseen in capitalism the possibilities for the deformation of human life as well as for its immense improvement, so the approaching world of scientific predominance has its darker side. There lurks a dangerous collectivist tinge in the prospect of controls designed for the enlargement of man but inherently capable of his confinement as well. But beyond that, there is, in the vista of a scientific quest grimly pursued for its own sake, a chilling reminder of a world where economic gains are relentlessly pursued for their own sake. Science is a majestic driving force from which to draw social energy and inspiration, but its very impersonality, its "value-free" criteria, may make its tutelary elites as remote and unconcerned as the principles in whose name they govern.

Against these cold and depersonalizing tendencies of a scientifically organized world, humanity will have to struggle in the future, as it has had to contend against not dissimilar excesses of economic involvement in this painful—but also liberating—stage of human development. Thus, if the dawn of an age of science opens larger possibilities for mankind than it has enjoyed heretofore, it does not yet promise a society in which the overriding aim of mankind will be the cultivation and enrichment of all human beings, in all their diversity, complexity, and profundity. That is the struggle for the very distant future, which must be begun, nonetheless, today.

# G Man in Mass-Total Society

## INTRODUCTION

Many sociologists, both classical and contemporary, have described and analyzed the tendency of urban-industrial societies to become organized into larger and larger social units. Auguste Comte and Ferdinand Tonnies, for example, pointed to the importance of studying the large cities and nation states into which the European populations were being organized in the nineteenth century, whereas Karl Marx and Max Weber called attention to the significance of increasing size in industry, business, and government. The processes of metropolitanization and bureaucratization and trends in the political economy discussed in previous sections illustrate this trend toward largeness and complexity in the organization of modern social life. The importance of the individual is undoubtedly reduced in the larger and more complex social organizations. People are gradually forced to adjust to these changes in their life situation and to evolve beliefs, values, and personalities compatible with the new forms of social organization.

Alexis de Tocqueville, in his classic nineteenth-century study *Democracy in America*, pointed to the increasing size of government and the enlargement of its areas of activity as a "kind of despotism" which he felt "democratic nations have to fear." Americans today have witnessed the growth of government activity in many areas of life, including business, health, education, communication, and even recreation. Such activity does lead to centralization of political power. Many Americans also fear it reduces individual initiative and creates complacency in the population by seeming to provide for most men's needs without calling for assertive action on their part. On the other hand, the struggles of the working class for effective unions in the 1930's and the Negro struggle for equality today indicate that disadvantaged groups in the population can and do still fight to assert their interests.

The tendency toward bigness and complexity is to be found in the organization of most areas of modern social life, including, for example, education, health and medical care, and even recreation. Modern man's social life is, therefore, enacted within the context of large-scale organizations. Harry Gracey, in his brief essay, points to one kind of adjustment people make to gaining a living in large-scale bureaucracies. He calls this the development of an "exploitative orientation," and points out that people on all levels of the social structure—upper class, middle class, and working class—and in many different occupations, come to regard the organizations they work for as great impersonal units which they may freely exploit for their own benefit whenever the opportunity arises. Gracey rejects the view that this is to be regarded as an outbreak of individual immorality, and instead suggests it is a rational adaptation of individuals to their new social environment.

David Riesman's conception of the "other-directed man" makes sense in the context of the developing total organization of modern society. The other-directed man is socialized to develop great sensitivity to the demands of others and an anxious desire to please them by conforming to their wishes. This man has few firm standards of conduct or inflexible values of his own, but is, instead, willing to adjust his actions and beliefs to those prevalent in his social groups. Riesman claims that other-direction is an adaptive personality structure for people living in a highly mobile, rapidly changing society such as ours. It is also adaptive, it can be added, for people who will spend their lives interacting with others in great impersonal social organizations which require continued association with large numbers of little-known people to whose demands the individual must be ready to accommodate himself.

Philip Slater writes of three "human deficiencies" of modern society, stressing the separateness and ensuing loneliness of the people in the "lonely crowds" of mass-total society. He points out that American culture, or perhaps more accurately, the organization of modern society, makes it impossible for most of the population to establish the supportive and cooperative bonds of community. The decline of community as a form of social group in modern society has been commented upon by many contemporary sociologists and was a theme in the writings of the classic sociologists. Maurice Stein in his book *Eclipse of Community* traces this theme in American community studies and develops some of the personal difficulties which the absence of community creates for modern man. Slater contends that American society also frustrates the human desire for direct engagement with others in working for solutions to the important problems facing the society. Slater also feels that Americans at any rate are denied the opportunity for a certain amount of necessary human dependence, specifically in sharing responsibility for self-control and self-direction with others in a trusting relationship. Modern man, Slater concludes, is "deeply and uniquely frustrated" in his needs for community, engagement, and dependence on his fellow men.

# 53

# What Sort of Despotism Democratic Nations Have to Fear

### ALEXIS DE TOCQUEVILLE

I had remarked during my stay in the United States that a democratic state

From *Democracy in America* by Alexis de Tocqueville, Volume II, Book IV, Chapter VI. First published in English in 1840.

of society, similar to that of the Americans, might offer singular facilities for the establishment of despotism; and I perceived, upon my return to Europe, how much use had already been made, by most of our rulers, of the notions, the sentiments, and the wants created by this same social condition, for the purpose of extending the circle of their power. This led me to think that the nations of Christendom would perhaps eventually undergo some oppression like that which hung over several of the nations of the ancient world.

A more accurate examination of the subject, and five years of further meditation, have not diminished my fears, but have changed their object.

No sovereign ever lived in former ages so absolute or so powerful as to undertake to administer by his own agency, and without the assistance of intermediate powers, all the parts of a great empire; none ever attempted to subject all his subjects indiscriminately to strict uniformity of regulation and personally to tutor and direct every member of the community. The notion of such an undertaking never occurred to the human mind; and if any man had conceived it, the want of information, the imperfection of the administrative system, and, above all, the natural obstacles caused by the inequality of conditions would speedily have checked the execution of so vast a design.

When the Roman emperors were at the height of their power, the different nations of the empire still preserved usages and customs of great diversity; although they were subject to the same monarch, most of the provinces were separately administered; they abounded in powerful and active municipalities; and although the whole government of the empire was centered in the hands of the Emperor alone and he always remained, in case of need, the supreme arbiter in all matters, yet the details of social life and private occupations lay for the most part beyond his control. The emperors possessed, it is true, an immense and unchecked power, which allowed them to gratify all their whim-

sical tastes and to employ for that purpose the whole strength of the state. They frequently abused that power arbitrarily to deprive their subjects of property or of life; their tyranny was extremely onerous to the few, but it did not reach the many; it was confined to some few main objects and neglected the rest; it was violent, but its range was limited.

It would seem that if despotism were to be established among the democratic nations of our days, it might assume a different character; it would be more extensive and more mild; it would degrade men without tormenting them. I do not question that, in an age of instruction and equality like our own, sovereigns might more easily succeed in collecting all political power into their own hands and might interfere more habitually and decidedly with the circle of private interests than any sovereign of antiquity could ever do. But this same principle of equality which facilitates despotism tempers its rigor. We have seen how the customs of society become more humane and gentle in proportion as men become more equal and alike. When no member of the community has much power or much wealth, tyranny is, as it were, without opportunities and a field of action. As all fortunes are scanty, the passions of men are naturally circumscribed, their imagination limited, their pleasures simple. This universal moderation moderates the sovereign himself and checks within certain limits the inordinate stretch of his desires.

Independently of these reasons, drawn from the nature of the state of society itself, I might add many others arising from causes beyond my subject; but I shall keep within the limits I have laid down.

Democratic governments may become violent and even cruel at certain periods of extreme effervescence or of great danger, but these crises will be rare and brief. When I consider the petty passions of our contemporaries, the mildness of their manners, the extent of their education, the purity of their religion, the gentleness of their morality, their regular and industrious habits, and the restraint which they almost all observe in their vices no less than in their virtues, I have no fear that they will meet with tyrants in their rulers, but rather with guardians.

I think, then, that the species of oppression by which democratic nations are menaced is unlike anything that ever before existed in the world; our contemporaries will find no prototype of it in their memories. I seek in vain for an expression that will accurately convey the whole of the idea I have formed of it; the old words *despotism* and *tyranny* are inappropriate: the thing itself is new, and since I cannot name, I must attempt to define it.

I seek to trace the novel features under which despotism may appear in the world. The first thing that strikes the observation is an innumerable multitude of men, all equal and alike, incessantly endeavoring to procure the petty and paltry pleasures with which they glut their lives. Each of them, living apart, is as a stranger to the fate of all the rest; his children and his private friends constitute to him the whole of mankind. As for the rest of his fellow citizens, he is close to them, but he does not see them; he touches them, but he does not feel them; he exists only in himself and for himself alone; and if his kindred still remain to him, he may be said at any rate to have lost his country.

Above this race of men stands an immense and tutelary power, which takes upon itself alone to secure their gratifications and to watch over their fate. That power is absolute, minute, regular, provident, and mild. It would be like the authority of a parent if, like that authority, its object was

to prepare men for adulthood; but it seeks, on the contrary, to keep them in perpetual childhood: it is well content that the people should rejoice, provided they think of nothing but rejoicing. For their happiness such a government willingly labors, but it chooses to be the sole agent and the only arbiter of that happiness; it provides for their security, foresees and supplies their necessities, facilitates their pleasures, manages their principal concerns, directs their industry, regulates the descent of property, and subdivides their inheritances: what remains, but to spare them all the care of thinking and all the trouble of living?

Thus it every day renders the exercise of the free agency of man less useful and less frequent; it circumscribes the will within a narrower range and gradually robs a man of all the uses of himself. The principle of equality has prepared men for these things; it has predisposed men to endure them and often to look on them as benefits.

After having thus successively taken each member of the community in its powerful grasp and fashioned him at will, the supreme power then extends its arm over the whole community. It covers the surface of society with a network of small complicated rules, minute and uniform, through which the most original minds and the most energetic characters cannot penetrate, to rise above the crowd. The will of man is not shattered, but softened, bent, and guided; men are seldom forced by it to act, but they are constantly restrained from acting. Such a power does not destroy, but it prevents existence; it does not tyrannize, but it compresses, enervates, extinguishes, and stupefies a people, till each nation is reduced to nothing better than a flock of timid and industrious animals, of which the government is the shepherd.

I have always thought that servitude of the regular, quiet, and gentle kind which I have just described might be combined more easily than is commonly believed with some of the outward forms of freedom, and that it might even establish itself under the wing of the sovereignty of the people.

Our contemporaries are constantly excited by two conflicting passions: they want to be led, and they wish to remain free. As they cannot destroy either the one or the other of these contrary propensities, they strive to satisfy them both at once. They devise a sole, tutelary, and all-powerful form of government, but elected by the people. They combine the principle of centralization and that of popular sovereignty; this gives them a respite: they console themselves for being in tutelage by the reflection that they have chosen their own guardians. Every man allows himself to be put in leading-strings, because he sees that it is not a person or a class of persons, but the people at large who hold the end of his chain.

By this system the people shake off their state of dependence just long enough to select their master and then relapse into it again. A great many persons at the present day are quite contented with this sort of compromise between administrative despotism and the sovereignty of the people; and they think they have done enough for the protection of individual freedom when they have surrendered it to the power of the nation at large. This does not satisfy me: the nature of him I am to obey signifies less to me than the fact of extorted obedience.

I do not deny, however, that a constitution of this kind appears to me to be infinitely preferable to one which, after having concentrated all the powers of government, should vest them in the hands of an irresponsible person or body of persons. Of all the forms that democratic despotism could assume, the latter would assuredly be the worst.

When the sovereign is elective, or

narrowly watched by a legislature which is really elective and independent, the oppression that he exercises over individuals is sometimes greater, but it is always less degrading; because every man, when he is oppressed and disarmed, may still imagine that, while he yields obedience, it is to himself he yields it, and that it is to one of his own inclinations that all the rest give way. In like manner, I can understand that when the sovereign represents the nation and is dependent upon the people, the rights and the power of which every citizen is deprived serve not only the head of the state, but the state itself; and that private persons derive some return from the sacrifice of their independence which they have made to the public. To create a representation of the people in every centralized country is, therefore, to diminish the evil that extreme centralization may produce, but not to get rid of it.

I admit that, by this means, room is left for the intervention of individuals in the more important affairs; but it is not the less suppressed in the smaller and more private ones. It must not be forgotten that it is especially dangerous to enslave men in the minor details of life. For my own part, I should be inclined to think freedom less necessary in great things than in little ones, if it were possible to be secure of the one without possessing the other.

Subjection in minor affairs breaks out every day and is felt by the whole community indiscriminately. It does not drive men to resistance, but it crosses them at every turn, till they are led to surrender the exercise of their own will. Thus their spirit is gradually broken and their character enervated; whereas that obedience which is exacted on a few important but rare occasions only exhibits servitude at certain intervals and throws the burden of it upon a small number of men. It is in vain to summon a people who have been rendered so dependent on the central power to choose from time to time the representatives of that power; this rare and brief exercise of their free choice, however important it may be, will not prevent them from gradually losing the faculties of thinking, feeling, and acting for themselves, and thus gradually falling below the level of humanity.

I add that they will soon become incapable of exercising the great and only privilege which remains to them. The democratic nations that have introduced freedom into their political constitution at the very time when they were augmenting the despotism of their administrative constitution have been led into strange paradoxes. To manage those minor affairs in which good sense is all that is wanted, the people are held to be unequal to the task; but when the government of the country is at stake, the people are invested with immense powers; they are alternately made the playthings of their ruler, and his masters, more than kings and less

than men. After having exhausted all the different modes of election without finding one to suit their purpose, they are still amazed and still bent on seeking further; as if the evil they notice did not originate in the constitution of the country far more than in that of the electoral body.

It is indeed difficult to conceive how men who have entirely given up the habit of self-government should succeed in making a proper choice of those by whom they are to be governed; and no one will ever believe that a liberal, wise, and energetic government can spring from the suffrages of a subservient people.

A constitution republican in its head and ultra-monarchical in all its other parts has always appeared to me to be a shortlived monster. The vices of rulers and the ineptitude of the people would speedily bring about its ruin; and the nation, weary of its representatives and of itself, would create freer institutions or soon return to stretch itself at the feet of a single master.

# 54

# Morality in the Organized Society

## HARRY L. GRACEY

During the past decade the investigating units of various governmental bodies have brought to light illegal and unethical practices in almost all areas of organized social life. These "scandals," which have been exposed in industry, labor, government, entertainment, and other institutions of society, with such regularity that they periodically chase one another across the pages of the daily press, share the common

feature of individuals acting solely or primarily to secure for themselves as much money, power, and prestige as they can. Their behavior is regarded as "scandalous" when they employ illegal and unethical means to exploit the social institutions for their own ends.

This behavior has been popularly interpreted as an outbreak of "immorality" among individual Americans. Public discussion of the problem consists primarily of moral condemnation and pleas for individual moral rehabilitation. *The New York Times*, for example, editorializes on the "moral decline" of the United States and, as a solution, urges Americans to throw off "the moral slothfulness that makes success more important than the methods for achieving it." A major religious body took the same line when it proclaimed recently, "the nation's life is marked by a disintegration of moral and ethical behavior" and urged "every American to adopt personal integrity and morality as part of his code of life."

By posing the problem as one of individual misbehavior, the popular discussion avoids the crucial question of what it is about life in our society which produces such a widespread exploitative orientation. To paraphrase C. Wright Mills, if a few people showed this exploitative orientation toward social institutions we would look to their character for the explanation, but when many people from all social levels show this orientation we must examine the structure and functioning of social institutions to find the causes of their behavior.

This exploitative orientation is one important part of the malaise which seems to infect the social organism today, and is therefore worth a serious effort at understanding.

Recent investigations by the Kefauver Committee and the Justice Department have shown that corporations manufacturing such diverse products as electrical equipment, autos, steel, drugs, and bread engage in illegal price fixing to the end of securing a constantly increasing profit. These policies are, of course, set by responsible top executives and board members of the corporations (regardless of who takes the rap when they are discovered) whose wealth, status, and corporate privileges are enhanced by ever-increasing company profits. When caught at their illegal activities, company executives justify their actions as having been in the best interests of their companies, and seem to regret only the damage they have done to their companies' reputations—and thus the danger to their own privileged positions in society. The stockholders also seem to feel that the companies should pursue any policies which assure them of ever-increasing monetary returns. At the year's annual meetings, the majority of General Electric stockholders present, whose dividends have been increasing with the annual increases in GE's profits, jeered anyone who tried to question top management policy and voted down all motions condemning illegal practices.

The exploitative orientation of middle-level bureaucrats is regularly documented in the case of government employees charged with inspecting the work of private contractors. Often it is the rule, rather than the exception, that people in such positions accept and even demand money from the contractors for passing on work which either does or does not meet the legal specifications. The petty bureaucrats in government are probably not getting rich on this graft, but it does contribute to their ability to live up to the middle-class consumption standards upon which their families' status depends. Bribery and graft, therefore, seem to provide middle-level bureaucrats with the means for living the middle-class version of the good life.

It has long been known that the people at the bottom of the American status heap, the blue-collar workers, regard their routine, monotonous, and dehumanizing jobs solely as sources of income. It has recently been shown that members of the teamsters' union have the same orientation toward their union. The attitude of the teamsters is essentially the same as that of the GE stockholders—they support their organization as long as it provides them with an ever-increasing income. The fact that their president, James Hoffa, has been accused of illegal and unethical practices seems to be unimportant to the majority of union members, so long as he brings home the annual wage increases.

The exploitative orientation toward social institutions is not confined to business, government, and labor. It can be found in almost any institution of contemporary society. In higher education, for example, we have witnessed the much-publicized basketball scandals. Equally unethical, but unpublicized, is the politics of academic grant-getting by which university faculty members use research funds from the government and private foundations for purposes other than those for which they were allocated. In many cases, the administrators of the grants know that the money will be misused. Everyone is involved in the status function of academic grant-getting, which is to build the prestige of the faculty member and the university as a basis for getting more grants, and thus providing a means for increasing the wealth of both.

The majority of Americans today live in urban communities in which most aspects of their lives are organized by large bureaucratic structures. The exploitative orientation, I shall contend, is a product of the mass bureaucratic nature of contemporary society.

The small community in the preindustrial, or early industrial, society was a social organization on a more personal scale. It was a static place with a rigid social structure, but it provided many opportunities for intimate, emotionally fulfilling social relations. Few aspects of one's life were free from the scrutiny of neighbors, but most people had a secure place in a network of informal social relations in which they were assigned status on the basis of their family background, size and source of

income, community activities, and conformity to community morality.

Today the metropolis is replacing the small community as the home of the majority of people. In metropolitan life social relations tend to become limited, formal, and rationally calculating in nature. Opportunities for lasting, comprehensive, and intimate associations tend to decrease, though they continue to exist in some stable neighborhoods of large cities and in suburban communities in which the population has become stabilized over a period of time. As the opportunity for intimate associations decreases, people have less knowledge of one another upon which to base their judgments of each other. Under these conditions, material possessions, signifying varying expenditures of money, become an important basis upon which people judge and rank one another. Accurate knowledge of how the money has been obtained is difficult to get, and therefore cannot be easily subject to judgment. The urban mass society thus provides opportunities for personal privacy impossible in small rural communities at the same time that it isolates people from intimate contact with each other.

Upon this base of an individuated urban mass have arisen the great bureaucratic structures which organize almost all areas of social life outside of the family and small friendship groups. Bureaucracy is the product of two major trends in industrial society: the trend toward greater functional specialization and the trend toward larger organizations. It is the only form of social organization yet invented for coordinating the work of many specialists in the accomplishment of many interrelated tasks in large business, government, education, and other areas of modern life. All important decision-making power is vested in the top offices of bureaucracies and in the private bureaucracies of business and industry, the manipulation of the organization by those at the top to maximize their own gain is the accepted and expected behavior under the profit system. Laws, ethics, and "social responsibility" must be viewed in a pragmatic and utilitarian light by those who would succeed in such positions. The lower bureaucratic employees, both blue collar and white ·collar, in both public and private bureaucracies have little control over organization policy and thus over their own futures. This powerlessness of bureaucratic employees to influence organizational policy makes it rational for them to exploit their present positions to gain whatever wealth, power, or prestige they can.

Morals are products of social life and can be expected to change as the life experiences of people in their society change. Man in the mass society —isolated from much intimate contact with others, relying heavily on con-

spicuous consumption for his social standing and self-respect, and for the most part powerless in the organizations which determine his own future —has little reason to regard the organizations in which he participates as anything other than sources of private gain. The mass-bureaucratic nature of social life today, in other words, probably produces so many individuals with the exploitative orientation toward modern social organizations. Without significant primary groups to enforce traditional moral standards in these organizations, there is no reason to expect the mass man to reject any means which are convenient for attaining his own end. Finally, individuals living in such a society cannot be expected to feel much responsibility for anyone's welfare but their own and certainly cannot be expected to "rise in indignation" when others are shown to be exploiting the social institutions too.

# 55

# The Other-Directed Man

DAVID RIESMAN

## Types of Social Character

. . . The typology of character set forth in *The Lonely Crowd* is at the same time a typology of societies. In terms of models, we speak of a society depending on *tradition-direction* if in it conformity to tradition is the characteristic achievement both of institutions and of individuals; this conformity is

From *Faces in the Crowd* by David Riesman. Copyright © 1952 by the Yale University Press. Reprinted by permission òf the Yale University Press.

assured by a type of character we term tradition-directed. We posit such a society and such a character type as typical for preliterate and peasant cultures in most of the world, while recognizing that there may be instances (such as the Manus of the Admiralty Islands, as described by Margaret Mead) where "primitives" are anything but traditional in outlook. In the Western world as a whole we see emerging over the course of the post-medieval period an expanding and dynamic form of society which we speak of as depending on *inner-direction*—one in which individuals are trained to conform not to external tradition but to internalized norms; this conformity is assured by a type of character we term inner-directed. This type must still be considered the dominant mode of conformity of the dominant classes of the West; hence we cannot speak as yet of a whole society depending on *other-direction*, a third form of conformity; we can only say that adumbrations of such a society appear in contemporary America, especially in the larger metropolitan areas, and in the middle and, notably, the upper-middle strata. In such areas and groups individuals are trained to conform neither to tradition nor to internalized goals but to the ever-changing expectations of ever-changing contemporaries; this conformity is assured by a type of character we term other-directed.

It will be seen that it is through the concept of the mode of conformity that character and society are linked in our analysis, for each type of society is seen as instilling a particular mode of conformity in its members, who then perpetuate the society as they go about its business, including the rearing of the young. I shall postpone discussion of some of the more or less obvious difficulties presented by such a formulation and turn first to a brief picture of each of the three character types.

*The Tradition-Directed Type.* In the type of society depending on tradition-direction, social change is at a minimum, though upsets in personal life may be violent and catastrophic. Conformity is assured by inculcating in the young a near-automatic obedience to tradition, as this is defined for the particular social role toward which the individual is headed by his sex and station at birth. That obedience, with all its gratifying rewards, is taught by the large circumambient clan and, after childhood, usually by members of one's own sex group. In this way one learns to master increasingly admired and difficult techniques and to avoid the shame that befalls the violator of the given norms. Since this type in its pristine form is almost nonexistent in today's America, it is not necessary to say more about it at this point.

*The Inner-Directed Type.* In historical sequence, the tradition-directed type gave way to a new pattern of conformity resting less on continuously encouraged obedience to customs and more on obedience to internalized controls instilled in childhood by the individual's parents and other adult authorities. This change in the source of direction was both cause and consequence of the creation, in western Europe and its conquered territories, of historically new social roles for which children could not possibly be prepared by rigorous or amiable attention to traditional mores. Hence the parent—and, for the first time, there *is* a parent in control, rather than an extended family ménage—equipped his child with an inflexible determination to achieve any of the possible goals which an expanding society seemed to suggest.

The inner-directed type can be described by a related congeries of attitudes toward work, toward the self, toward leisure, toward children, toward history, and so on. Among these no one readily isolable criterion is definitive. What is central, however, to the concept of inner-direction is that one's whole life is guided, for good or ill, by very generalized goals—such as wealth, fame, goodness, achievement—which were implanted early by identification with the modeling upon one's parents and other influential adults. One may be torn among these goals, fail to achieve them, or fight their tug; but one never doubts that life is goal-directed and that the inner voice is the principal source of that direction. Metaphorically, one may think of such people as *gyroscopically* driven—the gyroscope being implanted by adults and serving to stabilize the young even in voyages occupationally, socially, or geographically far from the ancestral home.

*The Other-Directed Type.* The inner-directed type, as just indicated, is prepared to cope with fairly rapid social change, and to exploit it in pursuance of individualistic ends. But the very possession of these ends makes the type less resilient, in the face of exceedingly quick change, than the other directed type whose conformity rests not so much on the incorporation of adult authority as on sensitive attention to the expectations of contemporaries. In the place of lifelong goals toward which one is steered as by a gyroscope, the other-directed person obeys a fluctuating series of short-run goals picked up (to continue with metaphor) by a *radar*. This radar, to be sure, is also installed in childhood, but the parents and other adults encourage the child to tune in to the people around him at any given time and share his preoccupation with their reactions to him and his to them.

The development of this character type, with its mode of sensitivity to others, is both cause and consequence of sweeping and accelerated changes in the social structure of contemporary industrial society: the rise of the "new" middle class; the preoccupation with consumption rather than production, and, within the sphere of production, with the "human factor"; the weakening of parental assurance and control over children; and so on down a long list. Again, a new congeries of attitudes toward all major spheres of life—toward work, consumption, sex, politics, and the self—reflect and confirm the shifts in character structure and in social structure. The world of interpresonal relations almost obscures from view the world of physical nature and the supernatural as the setting for the human drama.

Other-direction makes its appearance in a society in which the problems not only of mere subsistence but also of large-scale industrial organization and production have been for the most part surmounted, freeing for other concerns both the small leisure class and the large leisure masses. In such a society the customer can only be wrong if he remains an ascetic Puritan, haunted by ideas of thrift and fears of scarcity. Outside of America such a state of affairs has only been spottily attained —in parts of Sweden, in Australia and New Zealand, and perhaps in a few other centers. But even within America other-direction has not yet become equivalent to "the American way" and inner-directed types are still important.

*Some Essential Qualifications.* We are a long way from being able to say that other-direction can be equated with contemporary metropolitan America, or that the people of this or that preliterate society actually have been found to be tradition-directed. And doubtless, by the time such empirical tests are made we shall have better models to work with. Meanwhile it should be clear that the very nature of the typology, which is overlapping rather than discrete in its categories, implies the necessity of going through a number of further steps before such concrete test, against individuals or against societies, could even be fruitfully undertaken. In human affairs one seldom deals with all-or-none situations, and our typology is designed to grapple with the interrelationships rather than with the discontinuities in social life; this commitment, at least at the present stage of the work, rules out any neat litmus-paper test for character.

In fact, the discerning reader may

already have realized that in the nature of the case there can be no such thing as a society or a person wholly dependent on tradition-direction, inner-direction, or other-direction: each of these modes of conformity is universal, and the question is always one of the degree to which an individual or a social group places principal reliance on one or the other of the three available mechanisms. Thus, all human beings are inner-directed in the sense that, brought up as they are by people older than they, they have acquired and internalized some permanent orientations from them. And, conversely, all human beings are other-directed in the sense that they are oriented to the expectations of their peers and to the "field sitlation" (Kurt Lewin) or "definition of the situation" (W. I. Thomas) that these peers at any moment help create. . . .

## An Example of Other-Direction

Inner-direction and other-direction, as leading contenders for American allegiance, set up crosscurrents which are nicely illustrated by the fact that one of the radio programs to which the inner-directed Mr. Burns listens is written (along with others) by a Hollywood script-writer whom I have chosen as an example of other-direction; I shall call him Shelton. This writer, in his thirties, was too busy to allow the interview to be completed, but enough transpired to show how constant is his need to be liked and reassured about himself. Though claiming to be bored by his $1000-a-week job, he could not help overplaying his role as clever comic; nor does he appear to relax his stance even in the midst of his own family; and, though often anxious when he is with others, he cannot bear to be alone.

Indeed, for him the separation of work and play is almost nonexistent.[1] Asked what movies he prefers, he states:

[Repeated question out loud to himself.] I enjoy a comedy because I'm in that branch of the writing business. [Much more of this, then:] I like pictures with a pertinent theme. Pictures like *Possessed*, with Joan Crawford, a psychiatric study, is the best of its kind in the last couple of years. It gave me a feeling of realism. I always considered movies a form of escapism, but when you get realism in them you become more aware of the cares of the world.

Asked about his reading tastes, he declares:

If someone has given me a book or I hear of something entertaining, I'll read it. [He mentioned a book about Colonel Evans Carlson—"great admiration for the man"— and *Wind in the Olive Trees*—"pertinent to Spain."] In other words, if they are significant books. On the other hand, I have had *Inside U.S.A.* for some months and haven't finished it.

But he does "scan the newspaper at home every day"—mainly for columnists, including show-business ones; he adds: "Now and again I glance at a column like Pegler's to see who he is attacking and the reasons; to see how the other half lives. I used to read sports a lot." Who are his heroes?

Well, how far back can I go? Colonel Evans Carlson—I'll start early. Wendell Willkie. Franklin Roosevelt. Henry Wallace. Eugene Debs. Lincoln. A man like Edison. Da Vinci. There's quite a list. Collectively they have foresight, ingenuity, humanity, perseverance—the main things collectively.

In these responses the manner quite as much as the matter gives indications

[1] True, he tells us: "I go to wrestling matches very occasionally, but only for a source of amusement," commenting also that "I dislike boxing matches—fights—unless they're really top fighters." . . . But here as elsewhere it is clear that he is concerned with the status of his leisure pursuits, and in that sense he works at them.

of the self-consciousness, the concern with the other's reaction, the tendency to rate one's experiences, and the lack of long-term aims that are among the criteria for other-direction. The political section of the interview exhibits Shelton as a not exceptional Hollywood "lib-lab" without real conviction, with that combination of cynicism about "what really goes on" and idealism about the heroes just named which can so readily be manipulated by Stalinist commissars in the writers' guilds. His cultural judgments are held with like deference to opinion leaders: timid toward the supposedly highbrow milieu of the interviewer, he is yet drawn to his own vulgarities by an equal fear of losing the common touch.

In one of those "real-life" encounters that are worth more than any number of questions, Shelton invites the interviewer to have dinner with him and his family at a night club. Here he is described as the genial host—so genial as never to relax for a moment; his generosity, which he mentions in the interview—and which may be a show-business convention as much as an individual character trait [2]—is borne out in his treatment of waiters and guests. In the interview, asked what he would do if he had six months to live and could do just as he pleased [3]—a question

[2] To put matters this way, of course, polarizes the individual from his milieu in a way which is usually unjustified. For it is "no accident" that Shelton is in show business: occupations have differential appeals to different character types, and their traditions are carried not only in surface behavior but also in the character structure of many, though not all, of those who are drawn to and remain in the given roles.

[3] This question in our interview, like a number of others, was taken from preliminary reports of the Berkeley study which eventuated in The Authoritarian Personality. We adapted other questions (particularly concerning work attitudes) from long interviews by C. Wright Mills which were preparatory to his White Collar (New York, Oxford University Press, 1951).

which was frequently productive— Shelton has said: "I'd probably travel for a good part of it. Then I would like to write something that would be profound enough to live a while." Even in this hypothetical crisis Shelton sees himself as aimless, hoping both to travel—a frequent, and usually aimless, answer to this question—and still find time to write something of moment. However, at the night club he gives additional reasons for his desire to write a novel or serious play: he wants to lift himself out of the group of more or less anonymous and hence insecure script-writers—an effort, that is, at "marginal differentiation"; [4] beyond such pressing competitive needs, the unwritten opus seems to stand as a kind of culturally accepted symbol for the deficiencies Shelton senses in his way of life. Yet it develops that in his job he always works in tandem with other writers, jealousy of whom he represses in bursts of generosity which he then resents.

Leaving the night club, he jokes about an abstract painting to hide his self-consciousness about "art"—but, as with so much else he does, the very act of hiding is revealing, and the interviewer suspects that he *wants* to reveal, to share, to be warm and intimate. Asked in the interview about guilt feelings, he had said that he more than lives up to his community obligations but that "I've been told I've neglected obligations to myself." He seems unwilling to make this claim, or confession, on his own behalf, and the interview is devoid of strong complaints; he declares drably: "My past few years have been happy ones. I survived a war. I came back—after a short period of struggle I regained

[4] For a description of this phenomenon, see the portrait of Higgins, p. 577, n. 5; also my article, "Some Observations Concerning Marginality," Phylon, 12 (1951), 113, 116 ff.

my position. I'm content with my wife."

In Shelton's case, character, Hollywood culture (on one of its levels), and occupational role all seem to reinforce one another. (We can also see that, as an influential writer, he will tend, as a media model, to spread the ethos characteristic of other-directed types even when—as in his preference for "message" films—he may appear to react against "entertainment" or the consumer outlook.) More than metaphorically, he lives by his radar, and the interview shows that the scanning never stops. And yet even this man, who seems successful and "adjusted," has strivings of another sort—some generosity, perhaps, which transcends (or is rationalized by) what others expect of him; some deeply repressed desires for fulfillment of obligations to himself, which bespeak his "humanistic conscience" (in Erich Fromm's sense), his wish for autonomy.

And we can also see that were such a man to be put in another milieu— say, a Hartford insurance office or a southern university—his very sensitivity might enable him to wear, on short notice, a seemly cloak of inner-directed attitudes.[5] By the same token, of course, the *content* of his answers, especially when taken one by one, does not demonstrate that Shelton is, in fact, other-directed; as always, it is the Gestalt, the total mechanism, which counts. Furthermore, the fact that Shelton may strike many readers as, in comparison with Burns, an unattractive "character" (as Shelton himself would be the first to anticipate) should not lead them to

[5] Cf. Theodore Newcomb, *Personality and Social Change* (New York, Dryden Press, 1943), a study of the ways in which the attitudes and values of Bennington College girls shifted during the four-year course in a "liberal" direction, in consonance with the atmosphere created by the faculty and older students.

a hasty verdict on other-direction per se; for here again a wide gamut of individuals could be brought together under that designation. And Shelton's all-too-evident insecurities can be laid at the door of his occupation, the excess of his income (which includes his childless wife's high earnings as an interior decorator) over his inherited capital and cultural background, and perhaps his very strivings toward less ephemeral accomplishment, quite as much as to the defects inherent in other-direction as a conformity-mechanism. Many observers would be inclined to say that Shelton handles his "high income guilt" in a distinctly more graceful way than many, and that his other-directed effortfulness succeeds in achieving genuine hospitalities quite beyond Burns' ken.

Turning again to our collection of interviews we find a very different type of other-direction in the case of a thirty-eight-year-old navy commander, home on a visit from his Honolulu headquarters station. Son of a Vermont small-town contractor, he took an advanced agronomist degree at the University of Vermont, got a commission in 1939, and has remained in the navy since. Yet there is nothing stereotypically "rural" or "braid" in his very urbane interview. His friendly, calm responses aim to show him as cosmopolitan and tolerant. In his unusually well-informed political remarks he emphasizes the insincerity of the Russians as the basis of international discord. In his navy command his interests seem to be entirely in the sphere of human relations, divorced from any technical matters; speaking of his pep talks to junior officers, he observes:

Sometimes it was good to fly into a rage or sometimes to say well, we're all good friends, and we want to do the best we can, and we're all in this together. If I used the same method it would have lost its effectiveness.

In fact it was good to change the method by throwing them off balance—especially if they thought I would rant and rage and then I was friendly—that threw them off balance until they were working in the right direction.

As his best trait he names "ability to see the other person's side," and as his worst a certain intolerance when "he doesn't see yours." The whole interview shows him as amiably people-oriented and consumption-oriented rather than job-oriented.

Yet here again it is necessary to distinguish between the content and the mechanisms of direction. An interest in personnel, as an occupational matter, is not necessarily a sign of other-direction in character. I recall the dismay of one of my students who discovered that a group of personnel men in a large company were, in the main, inner-directed rather than other-directed. She had assumed that, since such work involved concern for morale and group mood, it would draw only other directed types; she overlooked (among many other possibilities which in any given case can quite reverse "normal" expectations of this sort) the fact that personnel work has for many years been a crusade as well as a career for many inner-directed people—whose organizational zeal later on made places in industry available for men of a different mold.

To return to our naval officer, we cannot be sure, then, about his character. It is striking that he has made with such apparent ease the transition from small-town Vermont and soil science to the "smooth" and worldly executive. Just such transitions of role and locale, however, are characteristic of these still very fluid United States, and the high-school and university system is the navigational lock ordinarily used to by-pass the rapids of becoming a self-made man. Thus, the fact of transition says nothing about whether a person is inner-directed or other-directed; many types can make it, and their character influences the form and style of ascent rather than the ascent itself. It is again the whole quality of the interview which leads to an interpretation that the commander is, on the whole, governed by the mechanism of other-direction.

Save in rare cases, however, such an interpretation must remain tentative. In the study of lengthy interviews the experience I often have is to come upon an answer for which I am totally unprepared, one which fits neither my own nor any other frame of interpretation known to me. We can therefore never be sure that, had the army officer said more, or been asked questions of a different genre, he might not have compelled the interpreter to realign all the rest of the answers. Thus, studying an interview with a highly cultivated, skeptical, and intelligent clubwoman, we say to ourselves: yes, here is a person on the whole other-directed, typical of her suburban set in the League of Women Voters (in which she is active)—until we come to her answer to the question whether she would like to have been born in some other age, and we see her matter-of-fact declaration that she probably has been—she believes in reincarnation! There is, so far as I can see, nothing in the previous answers to prepare for this; on the contrary, everything else makes it most unlikely. And then, in interpreting such an interview, in trying to find clues to character and social orientation, we may be led to see this as not only more salient but more significant, for this particular person, than the general schematic question of the degrees of inner-direction or other-direction. . . .

# 56

# Human Deficiencies of American Culture

PHILIP SLATER

I would like to suggest three human desires that are deeply and uniquely frustrated by American culture:

(1) The desire for *community*—the wish to live in trust and fraternal cooperation with one's fellows in a total and visible collective entity.

(2) The desire for *engagement*—the wish to come directly to grips with social and interpersonal problems and to confront on equal terms an environment which is not composed of ego-extensions.

(3) The desire for *dependence*—the wish to share responsibility for the control of one's impulses and the direction of one's life.

When I say that these three desires are frustrated by American culture, this need not conjure up romantic images of the individual struggling against society. In every case it is fair to say that we participate eagerly in producing the frustration we endure—it is not something merely done to us. For these desires are in each case subordinate to their opposites in that vague entity called the American Character. The thesis of this chapter is that Americans have voluntarily created and voluntarily maintain a society which increasingly frustrates and aggravates these secondary yearnings, to the point where they threaten to become primary. Groups that in any way personify this threat are therefore feared in an exaggerated way, and will be until Americans as a group are able to recognize and accept those needs within themselves.

## Community and Competition

We are so accustomed to living in a society that stresses individualism that

From *The Pursuit of Loneliness* (Boston: Beacon Press, 1970). Reprinted by permission.

we need to be reminded that "collectivism" in a broad sense has always been the more usual lot of mankind, as well as of most other species. Most people in most societies have been born into and died in stable communities in which the subordination of the individual to the welfare of the group was taken for granted, while the aggrandizement of the individual at the expense of his fellows was simply a crime.

This is not to say that competition is an American invention—all societies involve some sort of admixture of cooperative and competitive institutions. But our society lies near or on the competitive extreme, and although it contains cooperative institutions I think it is fair to say that Americans suffer from their relative weakness and peripherality. Studies of business executives have revealed, for example, a deep hunger for an atmosphere of trust and fraternity with their colleagues (with whom they must, in the short run, engage in what Reisman calls "antagonistic cooperation"). The competitive life is a lonely one, and its satisfactions are very short-lived indeed, for each race leads only to a new one.

In the past, as so many have pointed out, there were in our society many oases in which one could take refuge from the frenzied invidiousness of our economic system—institutions such as the extended family and the stable local neighborhood in which one could take pleasure from something other than winning a symbolic victory over one of his fellows. But these have disappeared one by one, leaving the individual more and more in a situation in which he must try to satisfy his affiliative and invidious needs in the same place. This has made the balance a more brittle one

—the appeal of cooperative living more seductive, and the need to suppress our longing for it more acute.

In recent decades the principal vehicle for the tolerated expression of this longing has been the mass media. Popular songs and film comedies have continually engaged in a sentimental rejection of the dominant mores, maintaining that the best things in life are free, that love is more important than success, that keeping up with the Joneses is absurd, that personal integrity should take precedence over winning, and so on. But these protestations must be understood for what they are: a safety valve for the dissatisfactions that the modal American experiences when he behaves as he thinks he should. The same man who chuckles and sentimentalizes over a happy-go-lucky hero in a film would view his real-life counterpart as frivolous and irresponsible, and suburbanites who philosophize over their back fence with complete sincerity about their "dog-eat-dog-world," and what-is-it-all-for, and you-can't-take-it-with-you, and success-doesn't-make-you-happy-it-just-gives-you-ulcers-and-a-heart-condition—would be enraged should their children pay serious attention to such a viewpoint. Indeed, the degree of rage is, up to a point, a function of the degree of sincerity: if the individual did not feel these things he would not have to fight them so vigorously. The peculiarly exaggerated hostility that hippies tend to arouse suggests that the life they strive for is highly seductive to middle-aged Americans.

The intensity of this reaction can in part be attributed to a kind of circularity that characterizes American individualism. When a value is as strongly held as is individualism in America the illnesses it produces tend to be treated by increasing the dosage, in the same way an alcoholic treats a hangover or a drug addict his withdrawal symptoms.

Technological change, mobility, and the individualistic ethos combine to rupture the bonds that tie each individual to a family, a community, a kinship network, a geographical location—bonds that give him a comfortable sense of himself. As this sense of himself erodes, he seeks ways of affirming it. But his efforts at self-enhancement automatically accelerate the very erosion he seeks to halt.

It is easy to produce examples of the many ways in which Americans attempt to minimize, circumvent, or deny the interdependence upon which all human societies are based. We seek a private house, a private means of transportation, a private garden, a private laundry, self-service stores, and do-it-yourself skills of every kind. An enormous technology seems to have set itself the task of making it unnecessary for one human being ever to ask anything of another in the course of going about his daily business. Even within the family Americans are unique in their feeling that each member should have a separate room, and even a separate telephone, television, and car, when economically possible. We seek more and more privacy, and feel more and more alienated and lonely when we get it. What accidental contacts we do have, furthermore, seem more intrusive, not only because they are unsought but because they are unconnected with any familiar pattern of interdependence.

Most important, our encounters with others tend increasingly to be competitive as a result of the search for privacy. We less and less often meet our fellow man to share and exchange, and more and more often encounter him as an impediment or a nuisance: making the highway crowded when we are rushing somewhere, cluttering and littering the beach or park or wood, pushing in front of us at the supermarket, taking the last parking place, polluting our air and water, building a highway through our house, blocking our view, and so on. Because we have cut off so much communication with each other we keep bumping into each other, and thus a higher and higher percentage of our interpresonal contacts are abrasive.

We seem unable to foresee that the gratification of a wish might turn out to be something of a monkey's paw if the wish were shared by many others. We cheer the new road that initially shaves ten minutes off the drive to our country retreat but ultimately transforms it into a crowded resort and increases both the traffic and the time. We are continually surprised to find, when we want something, that thousands or millions of others want it, too —that other human beings get hot in summer and cold in winter. The worst traffic jams occur when a mass of vacationing tourists departs for home early to "beat the traffic." We are too enamored of the individualistic fantasy that everyone is, or should be, different —that each person could somehow build his entire life around some single, unique eccentricity without boring himself and everyone else to death. Each of us of course has his quirks, which provide a surface variety that is briefly entertaining, but aside from this human beings have little basis for their persistent claim that they are not all members of the same species.

Since our contacts with others are increasingly competitive, unanticipated, and abrasive, we seek still more apartness and accelerate the trend. The desire to be somehow special inaugurates an even more competitive quest for progressively more rare and expensive symbols—a quest that is ultimately futile since it is individualism itself that produces uniformity.

This is poorly understood by Americans, who tend to confuse uniformity with "conformity," in the sense of compliance with or submission to group demands. Many societies exert far more pressure on the individual to mold himself to fit a particularized segment of a total group pattern, but there is variation among these circumscribed roles. Our society gives far more leeway to the individual to pursue his own ends, but, since *it* defines what is worthy and desirable, everyone tends, independently but monotonously, to pursue the same things in the same way. The first pattern combines cooperation, conformity, and variety; the second, competition, individualism, and uniformity.

These relationships are exemplified by two familiar processes in contemporary America: the flight to the suburb and the do-it-yourself movement. Both attempt to deny human interdependence and pursue unrealistic fantasies of self-sufficiency. The first tries to overlook our dependence upon the city for the maintenance of the level of culture we demand. "Civilized" means, literally, "citified," and the state of the city is an accurate index of the condition of the culture as a whole. We behave toward our cities like an irascible farmer who never feeds his cow and then kicks her when she fails to give enough milk. But the flight to the suburb is in any case self-defeating, its goals subverted by the mass quality of the exodus. The suburban dweller seeks peace, privacy, nature, community, and a child-rearing environment which is healthy and culturally optimal. Instead he finds neither the beauty and serenity of the countryside, the stimulation of the city, nor the stability and sense of community of the small town, and his children are exposed to a cultural deprivation equaling that of any slum child with a television set. Living in a narrow age-graded and class-segregated society, it is little wonder that suburban families have contributed so little to the national talent pool in proportion to their numbers, wealth, and other social advantages.[1] And this transplantation, which has caused the transplants to atrophy, has blighted the countryside and impoverished the city. A final irony of the suburban dream is that, for many Americans, reaching the pinnacle of one's social ambitions (owning a house in the suburbs) requires one to perform all kinds of menial tasks (carrying garbage cans, mowing lawns, shoveling snow, and so on) that were performed for him when he occupied a less exalted status.

Some of this manual labor, however, is voluntary—an attempt to deny the elaborate division of labor required in a complex society. Many Americans seem quite willing to pay this price for their reluctance to engage in interpersonal encounters with servants and artisans—a price which is rather high unless the householder particularly relishes the work (some find in it a tangible relief from the intangibles they manipulate in their own jobs) or is especially good at it, or cannot command a higher rate of pay in the job market than the servant or artisan.

The do-it-yourself movement has accompanied, paradoxically, increasing specialization in the occupational sphere. As one's job narrows, perhaps, one seeks the challenge of new skill-acquisition in the home. But specialization also means that one's interpersonal encounters with artisans in the home proliferate and become more imper-

sonal. It is not a matter of a familiar encounter with the local smith or grocer—a few well-known individuals performing a relatively large number of functions, and with whom one's casual interpersonal contacts may be a source of satisfaction, and are in any case a testimony to the stability and meaningful interrelatedness of human affairs. One finds instead a multiplicity of narrow specialists—each perhaps a stranger (the same type of repair may be performed by a different person each time). Every relationship, such as it is, must start from scratch, and it is small wonder that the householder turns away from such an unrewarding prospect in apathy and despair.

Americans thus find themselves in a vicious circle, in which their extra-familial relationships are increasingly arduous, competitive, trivial, and irksome, in part as a result of efforts to avoid or minimize potentially irksome or competitive relationships. As the few vestiges of stable and familiar community life erode, the desire for a simple, cooperative life style grows in intensity. The most seductive appeal of radical ideologies for Americans consists in the fact that all in one way or another attack the competitive foundations of our society. Each touches a responsive doubt, and the stimuli arousing this doubt must be carefully unearthed and rooted out, just as the Puritan must unearth and root out the sexual stimuli that excite him.[2]

[1] Using cities, small towns, and rural areas for comparison. The small Midwestern town achieves its legendary dullness by a process akin to evaporation—all the warm and energetic particles depart for coastal cities, leaving their place of origin colder and flatter than they found it. But the restless spirit in a small town knows he lives in the sticks and has a limited range of experience, while his suburban counterpart can sustain an illusion of cosmopolitanism in an environment which is far more constricted (a small town is a microcosm, a suburb merely a layer).

[2] Both efforts are ambivalent, since the "seek and destroy" process is in part a quest for the stimulus itself. The Puritanical censor both wants the sexual stimulus and wants to destroy it, and his job enables him to gratify both of these "contradictory" desires. There is a similar prurience in the efforts of groups such as the House UnAmerican Activities Committee to "uncover subversion." Just as the censor gets to experience far more pornography than the average man, so the Congressional red-baiter gets to hear as much Communist ideology as he wants, which is apparently quite a lot.

Now it may be objected that American society is far less competitive than it once was, and the appeal of radical ideologies should hence be diminished. A generation of critics has argued that the entrepreneurial individualist of the past has been replaced by a bureaucratic, security-minded, Organization Man. Much of this historical drama was written through the simple device of comparing yesterday's owner-president with today's assistant sales manager; certainly these nostalgia-merchants never visited a nineteenth-century company town. Another distortion is introduced by the fact that it was only the most ruthlessly competitive robber barons who survived to tell us how it was. Little is written about the neighborhood store that extended credit to the poor, or the small town industry that refused to lay off local workers in hard times—they all went under together. And as for the organization men—they left us no sagas.

Despite these biases real changes have undoubtedly occurred, but even if we grant that the business world as such was more competitive, the total environment contained more cooperative, stable, and personal elements. The individual worked in a smaller firm with lower turnover in which his relationships were more enduring and less impersonal, and in which the ideology of Adam Smith was tempered by the fact that the participants were neighbors and might have been childhood playmates. Even if the business world was as "dog-eat-dog" as we imagine it (which seems highly unlikely), one encountered it as a deviant episode in what was otherwise a more comfortable and familiar environment than the organization man can find today in or out of his office. The organization man complex is simply an attempt to restore the personal, particularistic, paternalistic environment of the family business and the company town; and the other-directed "group-think" of the suburban community is a desperate attempt to bring some old-fashioned small-town collectivism into the transient and impersonal life-style of the suburb. The social critics of the 1950's were so preoccupied with assailing these rather synthetic substitutes for traditional forms of human interdependence that they lost sight of the underlying pathogenic forces that produced them. Medical symptoms usually result from attempts made by the body to counteract disease, and attacking such symptoms often aggravates and prolongs the illness. This appears to be the case with the feeble and self-defeating efforts of twentieth-century Americans to find themselves a viable social context.

## Engagement and Uninvolvement

Many of the phenomena we have discussed can also be linked to a compulsive American tendency to avoid confrontation of chronic social problems. This avoiding tendency often comes as a surprise to foreigners, who tend to think of Americans as pragmatic and down-to-earth. But while trying to solve long-range social problems with short-run "hardware" solutions produces a lot of hardware—a down-to-earth result, surely—it can hardly be considered practical when it aggravates the problems, as it almost always does. American pragmatism is deeply irrational in this respect, and in our hearts we have always known it. One of the favorite themes of American cartoonists is the man who paints himself into a corner, saws off the limb he is sitting on, or runs out of space on the sign he is printing. The scientist of science-fiction and horror films, whose experimentation leads to disastrously unforeseen consequences, is a more anxious representation of this same awareness that the most future-oriented nation in the world shows a deep incapacity to plan ahead. We are, as a people, perturbed by our inability to anticipate the consequences of our acts, but we still wait optimistically for some magic telegram, informing us that the tangled skein of misery and self-deception into which we have woven ourselves has vanished in the night. Each month popular magazines regale their readers with such telegrams: announcing that our transportation crisis will be solved by a bigger plane or a wider road, mental illness with a pill, poverty with a law, slums with a bulldozer, urban conflict with a gas, racism with a goodwill gesture. Perhaps the most grotesque of all these telegrams was an article in *Life* showing a group of suburbanites participating in a "Clean-Up Day" in an urban slum. Foreigners are surprised when Americans exhibit this kind of naïvité and/or cynicism about social problems, but their surprise is inappropriate. Whatever realism we may display in technical areas, our approach to social issues inevitably falls back on cinematic tradition, in which social problems are resolved by gesture. Deeply embedded in the somnolent social consciousness of the broom-wielding suburbanites is a series of climactic movie scenes in which a long column of once surly natives, marching in solemn silence and as one man, framed by the setting sun, turn in their weapons to the white chief who has done them a good turn, or menace the white adventurer's enemy (who turns pale at the sight), or rebuild the missionary's church, destroyed by fire.

When a social problem persists (as they tend to do) longer than a few days, those who call attention to its continued presence are viewed as "going too far" and "causing the pendulum to swing the other way." We can make war on poverty but shrink from the extensive readjustments required to stop breeding it. Once a law is passed, a commission set up, a study made, a report written, the problem is expected to have been "wiped out" or "mopped up." Bombs abroad are matched by "crash programs" at home—the terminological similarity reveals a psychological one. Our approach to transportation problems has had the effect, as many people have observed, of making it easier and easier to travel to more and more places that have become less and less worth driving to. Asking us to consider the manifold consequences of chopping down a forest, draining a swamp, spraying a field with poison, making it easier to drive into an already crowded city, or selling deadly weapons to everyone who wants them arouses in us the same impatience as a chess problem would in a hyperactive six-year-old.

The avoiding tendency lies at the very root of American character. This nation was settled and continuously repopulated by people who were not personally successful in confronting the social conditions obtaining in their mother country, but fled these conditions in the hope of a better life. This series of choices (reproduced in the westward movement) provided a complex selection process—populating America disproportionately with a certain kind of person.

In the past we have always, explicitly or implicitly, stressed the positive side of this selection, implying that America thereby found itself blessed with an unusual number of energetic, mobile, ambitious, daring, and optimistic persons. Now there is no reason to deny that a number of traits must have helped to differentiate those who chose to come from those who chose to stay, nor that these differences must have generated social institutions and habits of mind that tended to preserve and reproduce these characteristics. But very little attention has been paid to the more negative aspects of the selection. If we gained the energetic and daring we also gained the lion's share of the rootless, the unscrupulous, those who value money over relationships, and those who put self-aggrandizement ahead of love and loyalty. And most of all, we gained a critically undue proportion of persons who, when faced with a difficult situation, tended to chuck the whole thing and flee to a new environment. Escaping, evading, and avoiding are responses which lie at the base of much that is peculiarly American—the suburb, the automobile, the self-service store, and so on.

These responses also contribute to the appalling discrepancy between our material resources and our treatment of those who cannot adequately care for themselves. This is not an argument against institutionalization: American society is not geared to handle these problems in any other way, and this is in fact the point I wish to make. One cannot successfully alter one facet of a social system if everything else is left the same, for the patterns are interdependent and reinforce one another. In a cooperative, stable society the aged, infirm, or psychotic person can be absorbed by the local community, which knows and understands him. He presents a difficulty which is familiar and which can be confronted daily and directly. This condition cannot be reproduced in our society today—the burden must be carried by a small, isolated, mobile family unit that is not really equipped for it.

But understanding the forces that require us to incarcerate those who cannot function independently in our society does not give us license to ignore the significance of doing so. The institutions we provide for those who cannot care for themselves are human garbage heaps—they result from and reinforce our tendency to avoid confronting social and interpersonal problems. They make life "easier" for the rest of society, just as does the automobile. And just as we find ourselves having to devise ridiculous exercises to counteract the harmful effects of our dependence upon the

automobile, so the "ease" of our non-confronting social technology makes us bored, flabby, and interpersonally insensitive, and our lives empty and mechanical.

Our ideas about institutionalizing the aged, psychotic, retarded, and infirm are based on a pattern of thought that we might call the Toilet Asumption—the notion that unwanted matter, unwanted difficulties, unwanted complexities and obstacles will disappear if they are removed from our immediate field of vision. We do not connect the trash we throw from the car window with the trash in our streets, and we assume that replacing old buildings with new expensive ones will alleviate poverty in the slums. We throw the aged and psychotic into institutional holes where they cannot be seen. Our approach to social problems is to decrease their visibility: out of sight, out of mind. This is the real foundation of racial segregation, especially its most extreme case, the Indian "reservation." The result of our social efforts has been to remove the underlying problems of our society farther and farther from daily experience and daily consciousness, and hence to decrease, in the mass of the population, the knowledge, skill, resources, and motivation necessary to deal with them.

When these discarded problems rise to the surface again—a riot, a protest, an exposé in the mass media—we react as if a sewer had backed up. We are shocked, disgusted, and angered, and immediately call for the emergency plumber (the special commission, the crash program) to ensure that the problem is once again removed from consciousness.

The Toilet Assumption is not merely a facetious metaphor. Prior to the widespread use of the flush toilet all of humanity was daily confronted with the immediate reality of human waste and its disposal. They knew where it was and how it got there. Nothing miraculously vanished. Excrement was conspicuously present in the outhouse or chamber pot, and the slops that went out the window went visibly and noticeably into the street. The most aristocratic Victorian ladies strolling in fashionable city parks thought nothing of retiring to the bushes to relieve themselves. Similarly, garbage did not disappear down a disposal unit—it remained nearby.

As with physical waste, so with social problems. The biblical adage, "the poor are always with us," had a more literal meaning before World War I. The poor were visible and all around. Psychosis was not a strange phenomenon in a textbook but a familiar neighbor or village character. The aged were in every house. Everyone had seen animals slaughtered and knew what they were eating when they ate them; illness and death were a part of everyone's immediate experience.

In contemporary life the book of experience is filled with blank and mysterious pages. Occupational specialization and plumbing have exerted a kind of censorship over our understanding of the world we live in and how it operates. And when we come into immediate contact with anything that does not seem to fit into the ordinary pattern of our somewhat bowdlerized existence our spontaneous reaction is to try somehow to flush it away, bomb it away, throw it down the jail.

But in some small degree we also feel bored and uneasy with the orderly chrome and porcelain vacuum of our lives, from which so much of life has been removed. Evasion creates self-distaste as well as comfort, and radical confrontations are exciting as well as disruptive. The answering chord that they produce within us terrifies us, and although we cannot entirely contain our fascination, it is relatively easy to project our self-disgust onto the perpetrators of the confrontations.

This ambivalence is reflected in the mass media. The hunger for confrontation and experience attracts a lot of attention to social problems, but these are usually dealt with in such a way as to reinforce the avoidance process. The TV documentary presents a tidy package with opposing views and an implication of progress. Reports in popular magazines attempt to provide a substitute for actual experience. Important book and film reviews, for example, give just the blend of titillation and condescension to make the reader imagine that he is already "in" and need not undergo the experience itself—that he has not only participated in the novel adventure but already outgrown it. Thus the ultimate effect of the media is to reinforce the avoiding response by providing an effigy of confrontation and experience. There is always the danger with such insulating mechanisms, however, that they at times get overloaded, like tonsils, and become carriers of precisely the agents against which they are directed. This is an increasingly frequent event in our society today.

A corollary of this latent desire for social confrontation is the desire for an incorruptible man—a man who cannot be bribed, who does not have his price. Once again this desire is a recessive trait, relegated largely to the realm of folk drama and movie script, but it exists nonetheless, as a silent rebellion against the oppressive democratic harmony of a universal monetary criterion.

In the hard reality of everyday life, however, the incorruptible man is at best an inconvenience, an obstacle to the smooth functioning of a vast institutional machinery. Management leaders, for example, tend to prefer corrupt union leaders—"people you can do business with"—to those who might introduce questions and attitudes lying outside the rules of a monetary game. The man who cannot be bought tends to be mistrusted as a fanatic, and the fact that incorruptible men are so often called Communists may be understood in the same light. As in the case of the mass media, however, this mechanism has become overloaded, so that having been jailed and/or called a Communist or traitor is now regarded by young adults as a medal attesting to one's social concern.

Also closely related to the latent desire for confrontation is an inarticulate wish to move in an environment consisting of something other than our own creations. Human beings evolved as organisms geared to mastery of the natural environment. Within the past few thousand years we have learned to perform this function so well that the natural environment poses very little threat to civilized peoples. Our dangers are self-made ones—subtle, insidious, and meaningless. We die from our own machines, our own poisons, our own weapons, our own despair. Furthermore, we are separated from primitive conditions by too few millennia to have evolved any comfortable adaptation to a completely man-made environment. We still long for and enjoy struggling against the elements, even though such activity can only occasionally be considered meaningful or functional.[3] We cross the ocean in artificially primitive boats, climb mountains we could fly over, kill animals we do not eat. Natural disasters, such as floods, hurricanes, blizzards, and so on, generate a cheerfulness

which would seem inappropriate if we did not all share it. It is as if some balance between man and nature had been restored, and with it man's "true function." Like the cat that prefers to play with a ball around the obstacle of a chair leg, so man seems to derive some perverse joy from having a snowstorm force him to use the most primitive mode of transportation. It is particularly amusing to observe people following the course of an approaching hurricane and affecting a proper and prudent desire that it veer off somewhere, in the face of an ill-concealed craving that it do nothing of the kind. There is a satisfaction that comes from relating to nature on equal terms, with respect and even deference to forms of life different from ourselves—as the Indian respects the deer he kills for food and the tree that shields him from the sun.

We interact largely with extensions of our own egos. We stumble over the consequences of our past acts. We are drowning in our own excreta (another consequence of the Toilet Assumption). We rarely come into contact with a force which is clearly and cleanly Not-Us. Every struggle is a struggle with ourselves, because there is a little piece of ourselves in everything we encounter—houses, clothes, cars, cities, machines, even our foods. There is an uneasy, anesthetized feeling about this kind of life—like being trapped forever inside an air-conditioned car with power steering and power brakes and only a telephone to talk to. Our world is only a mirror, and our efforts mere shadowboxing—yet shadowboxing in which we frequently manage to hurt ourselves.

Even that part of the world which is not man-made impinges upon us through a symbolic network we have created. We encounter primarily our own fantasies: we have a concept and image of a mountain, a lake, or a forest almost before we ever see one. Travel posters tell us what it means to be in a

---

[3] The cholesterol problem provides an illustration: one theory proposes that the release of cholesterol into the bloodstream was functional for hunting large animals with primitive weapons. Since the animal was rarely killed but only wounded, he had to be followed until he dropped, and this was a matter of walking or running for several days without food or rest. A similar response would be activated today in fields such as advertising, in which a sustained extra effort over a period of time (to obtain a large contract, for example) is periodically required. But these peak efforts do not involve any physical release—the cholesterol is not utilized.

strange land, the events of life become news items before they actually happen —all experience receives preliminary structure and interpretation. Public relations, television drama, and life become indistinguishable.

The story of Pygmalion is thus the story of modern man, in love with his own product. But like all discreet fairy tales, that of Pygmalion stops with the consummation of his love. It does not tell us of his ineffable boredom at having nothing to love but an excrescence of himself. But we know that men who live surrounded by that which and those whom they have molded to their desires —from the Caliph of Baghdad to Federico Fellini—suffer from a fearsome ennui. The minute they assume material form our fantasies cease to be interesting and become mere excreta.

## Dependence and Independence

Independence training in American society begins almost at birth—babies are held and carried less than in most societies and spend more time in complete isolation—and continues, despite occasional parental ambivalence, throughout childhood and adolescence. When a child is admonished to be a "big boy" or "big girl" this usually means doing something alone or without help (the rest of the time it involves strangling feelings, but this norm seems to be on the wane). Signs of independence are usually rewarded, and a child who in too obvious a manner calls attention to the fact that human intelligence is based almost entirely on the process of imitation is ridiculed by calling him a copycat or a monkey (after the paradoxical habit humans have of projecting their most uniquely human attributes onto animals). There have been many complaints in recent years that independence training is less rigorous than it once was, but again, as in the case of competitiveness,

this is hard to assess. To be on one's own in a simple, stable, and familiar environment requires a good deal less internal "independence" than to be on one's own in a complex, shifting, and strange one. Certainly a child could run about more freely a century ago without coming to harm, and his errors and misdeeds had far more trivial consequences than today; but this decline in the child's freedom of movement says nothing about the degree to which the child is asked to forego the pleasures of depending upon his parents for nurturance and support. If the objective need is greater, it may offset a small increase in parental tolerance for dependent behavior, and cause the child to experience the independence training as more severe rather than less.

In any case, American independence training is severe relative to most of the rest of the world, and we might assume this to have emotional consequences. This is not to say that such training is not consonant with the demands of adult society: the two are quite in accord. Sociologists and anthropologists are often content to stop at this point and say that as long as this accord exists there is no problem worth discussing. But the frustration of any need has its effects (one of them being to increase the society's vulnerability to social change) and these should be understood.

An example might help clarify this issue. Ezra and Suzanne Vogel observe that Japanese parents encourage dependency as actively as American parents push independence, and that healthy children and adults in Japan rely heavily on others for emotional support and decisions about their lives. A degree of dependence on the mother which in America would be considered "abnormal" prepares the Japanese for a society in which far more dependency is expected and accepted than in ours. The Japanese firm is highly paternalistic and takes a great deal of responsibility for making the individual employee secure and comfortable. The Vogels observe, however, that just as the American mother tends to complain at the success of her efforts and feel that her children are *too* independent, so the Japanese mother tends to feel that her children are too *dependent*, despite the fact that she has trained them this way.

What I am trying to point out is that regardless of the congruence between socialization practices and adult norms, any extreme pattern of training will produce stresses for the individuals involved. And just as the mothers experience discomfort with the effects of these patterns, so do the children, although barred by cultural values from recognizing and naming the nature of their distress, which in our society takes the form of a desire to relinquish responsibility for control and decision-making in one's daily life. Deeply felt democratic values usually stand in the way of realizing this goal through authoritarian submission, although our attitudes toward democracy are not without ambivalence, as has been suggested elsewhere; but the temptation to abdicate self-direction in more subtle ways is powerful indeed. Perhaps the major problem for Americans is that of choice: Americans are forced into making more choices per day, with fewer "givens," more ambiguous criteria, less environmental stability, and less social structural support, than any people in history.

Many of the mechanisms through which dependency is counteracted in our society have already been discussed in the preceding sections, but a word should be said about the complex problem of internalized controls. In stable societies, as many authors have pointed out, the control of human impulses is usually a collective responsibility. The individual is viewed as not having within

himself the controls required to guarantee that his impulses will not break out in ways disapproved by the community. But this matters very little, since the group is always near at hand to stop him or shame him or punish him should he forget himself.

In more fluid, changing societies we are more apt to find controls that are internalized—that do not depend to so great an extent on control and enforcement by external agents. This has long been characteristic of American society —de Tocqueville observed in 1830 that American women were much more independent than European women, freer from chaperonage, and able to appear in what a European would consider "compromising" situations without any sign of sexual involvement.

Chaperonage is in fact the simplest way to illustrate the difference between external and internalized controls. In chaperon cultures—such as traditional Middle-Eastern and Latin societies—it simply did not occur to anyone that a man and woman could be alone together and not have sexual intercourse. In America, which represents the opposite extreme, there is almost no situation in which a man and a woman could find themselves in which sexual intercourse could not at least be considered problematic (Hollywood comedies have exploited this phenomenon—well past the point of exhaustion and nausea— over the past 35 years). Americans are virtuosi of internalized control of sexual expression (the current relaxation of sexual norms in no way changes this), and this has caused difficulties whenever the two systems have come into contact. An unchaperoned girl in a bikini or mini-skirt means one thing in America, another in Baghdad. It is a mistake to consider a chaperon society more prudish—the compliment is likely to be returned when the difference is understood. Even Americans consider some situations inherently sexual: if a girl from some mythical culture came to an American's house, stripped, and climbed into bed with him, he would assume she was making a sexual overture and would be rather indignant if he found that she was merely expressing casual friendship according to her native customs. He would also be puzzled if *he* were called prudish, and we need not speculate as to what he would call *her*.

But how are internalized controls created? We know that they are closely tied to what are usually called "love-oriented" techniques of discipline in childhood. These techniques avoid physical punishment and deprivation of privileges and stress reasoning and the withdrawal of parental affection. The basic difference between "love-oriented" and "fear-oriented" techniques (such as physical punishment) is that in the latter case the child simply learns to avoid punishment while in the former he tends to incorporate parental values as his own in order to avoid losing parental love and approval. When fear-oriented techniques prevail, the child is in the position of inhabitants of an occupied country, who obey to avoid getting hurt but disobey whenever they think they can get away with it. Like them, the child does not have any emotional commitment to his rulers—he does not fear losing their love.

Love-oriented techniques require by definition that love and discipline emanate from the same source. When this happens it is not merely a question of avoiding the punisher: the child wishes to anticipate the displeasure of the loved and loving parent, wants to be like the parent, and takes into himself as a part of himself the values and attitudes of the parent. He wants to please, not placate, and because he has taken the parent's attitudes as his own, pleasing the parent comes to mean making him feel good about himself. Thus while individuals raised with fear-oriented techniques tend to direct anger outward under stress, those raised with love-oriented techniques tend to direct it inward in the form of guilt—a distinction that has important physiological correlates.

Under stable conditions external controls work perfectly well. Everyone knows his own place and his neighbor's, and deviations from expected behavior will be quickly met from all sides. When social conditions fluctuate, social norms change, and people move frequently from one social setting to another and are often among strangers, this will no longer do. An individual cannot take his whole community with him wherever he goes, and in any case the rules differ from place to place. The mobile individual must travel light, and internalized controls are portable and transistorized, as it were.

Anger directed inward is also made for mobile conditions. In a stable community two youths who start to get into a fight will be held back by their friends —they depend upon this restraint and can abandon themselves to their passion, knowing that it will not produce harmful consequences. But where one moves among strangers it becomes increasingly important to have other mechanisms for handling aggression. In situations of high mobility and flux the individual must have a built-in readiness to feel himself responsible when things go wrong.

Most modern societies are a confused mixture of both systems, a fact that enables conservative spokesmen to attribute rising crime rates to permissive child-rearing techniques. The overwhelmingly majority of ordinary crimes, however, are committed by individuals who have *not* been reared with love-oriented techniques, but, insofar as the parent or parents have been able to rear them at all, by the haphazard use of fear-oriented discipline. Love-oriented child-rearing techniques are a luxury that slum parents, for example, can seldom afford.

Furthermore, it is rather misleading to refer to the heavily guilt-inducing socialization techniques of middle-class parents as "permissive." Misbehavior in a lower class child is more often greeted with a cuff, possibly accompanied by some non-informative response such as "stop that!" But it may not be at all clear to the child which of the many motions he is now performing "that" is; and, indeed, "that" may be punished only when the parent is feeling irritable. A child would have to have achieved an enormously high intelligence level (which, of course, it has not, for this very reason) to be able to form a moral concept out of a hundred irritable stop-thats. What he usually forms is merely a crude sense of when the "old man" or the "old lady" is to be avoided. The selfconscious, highly verbal, middle-class parent is at the opposite extreme. He or she feels that discipline should relate to the child's act, not the parent's own emotional state, and is very careful to emphasize verbally the principle involved in the misbehavior ("it's bad to hit people" or "we have to share with guests"). Concept-formation is made very easy for the middle-class child, and he tends to think of moral questions in terms of principles.

As he grows older this tendency is reinforced by his encounter with different groups with different norms. In a mobile society, one cannot simply accept the absolute validity of any rule because one experiences competing moral codes. As a result the middle-class child tends to evolve a system of meta-rules, that is, rules for assessing the relative validity of these codes. The meta-rules tend to be based upon the earliest and most general principles expressed by the parents; such as prohibitions on violence against others, egalitarianism, mutuality, and so on. This ability to treat rules in a highly secular fashion while maintaining a strong moral position is baffling to those whose control mechanisms are more primitive, but it presupposes a powerful and articulate conscience. Such an individual can expose himself to physical harm and to violence-arousing situations without losing control and while maintaining a moral position. This may seem inconceivable to an uneducated working-class policeman whose own impulses are barely held in line by a jerry-built structure of poorly articulated and mutually contradictory moral absolutes. Hence he tends to misinterpret radical middle-class behavior as a hypocritical mask for mere delinquency.

The point of this long digression, however, is that internalization is a mixed blessing. It may enable one to get his head smashed in a good cause, but the capacity to give oneself up completely to an emotion is almost altogether lost in the process. Where internalization is high there is often a feeling that the controls themselves are out of control—that emotion cannot be expressed when the individual would like to express it. Life is muted, experience filtered, emotion anesthetized, affective discharge incomplete. Efforts to shake free from this hypertrophied control system include not only drugs, and sensation-retrieval techniques such as those developed at the Esalen Institute in California, but also confused attempts to reestablish external systems of direction and control—the vogue currently enjoyed by astrology is an expression of this. The simplest technique, of course, would be the establishment of a more authoritarian social structure, which would relieve the individual of the great burden of examining and moderating his own responses. He could become as a child, lighthearted, spontaneous, and passionate, secure in the knowledge that others would prevent his impulses from causing harm.

Realization of this goal is prevented by democratic values and the social conditions that foster them (complexity, fluidity, change). But the desire plays a significant part in conventional reactions to radical minorities, who are all felt to be seeking the abandonment of self-restraints of one kind or another and at the same time demanding *more* responsible behavior from the establishment. This is both infuriating and contagious to white middle-class adults, who would like very much to do the same, and their call for "law and order" (that is, more *external* control) is an expression of that desire as well as an attempt to smother it. This conflict over dependency and internalization also helps explain why official American anticommunism always lays so much stress on the authoritarian (rather than the socialistic) aspects of Communist states.

## Individualism Reassessed

The three variables we have been discussing—community, engagement, dependency—can all trace their suppression in American society to our commitment to individualism. The belief that everyone should pursue autonomously his own destiny has forced us to maintain an emotional detachment (for which no amount of superficial gregariousness can compensate) from our social and physical environment, and aroused a vague guilt about our competitiveness and indifference to others; for, after all, our earliest training in childhood does not stress competitiveness, but cooperation, sharing, and thoughtfulness—it is only later that we learn to reverse these priorities. Radical challenges to our society, then, always tap a confused responsive chord within us that is far more disturbing than anything going on outside. They threaten to reconnect us with each other, with nature, and with ourselves, a possibility that is thrilling but terrifying—as if we had grown a shell-like epidermis and someone was threatening to rip it off.

Individualism finds its roots in the attempt to deny the reality and importance of human interdependence. One of the major goals of technology in America is to "free" us from the necessity of relating to, submitting to, depending upon, or controlling other people.[4] Unfortunately, the more we have succeeded in doing this the more we have felt disconnected, bored, lonely, unprotected, unnecessary, and unsafe.

Individualism has many expressions: free enterprise, self-service, academic freedom, suburbia, permissive gun-laws, civil liberties, do-it-yourself, oil-depletion allowances. Everyone values some of these expressions and condemns others, but the principle is widely shared. Criticisms of our society since World War II have almost all embraced this value and expressed fears for its demise—the organization man, the other-directed man, conformity, "groupthink," and so on. In general these critics have failed to see the role of the value they embrace so fervently in generating the phenomena they so detest.

The most sophisticated apologist for individualism is David Riesman, who recognizes at least that uniformity and community are not the same thing, and does not shrink from the inso'uble dilemmas that these issues create. Perhaps the definitive and revealing statement of what individualism is all about

---

[4] The peculiar germ-phobia that pervades American life (and supports several industries) owes much to this insulation machinery. So far we have carried the fantasy of individual autonomy that we imagine each person to have his own unique species of germs, which must therefore not be mixed and confused with someone else's. We are even disturbed at the presence of the germs themselves: despite the fact that many millions of them inhabit every healthy human body from the cradle to the grave we regard them as trespassers. We feel that nature has no business claiming a connection with us, and perhaps one day we will prove ourselves correct.

is his: "I am insisting that no ideology, however noble, can justify the sacrifice of an individual to the needs of the group."

Whenever I hear such sentiments I recall Jay Haley's discussion of the kind of communication that characterizes the families of schizophrenics. He points out that people who communicate with one another necessarily govern each other's behavior—set rules for each other. But an individual may attempt to avoid this human fate—to become independent, uninvolved: ". . . he may choose the schizophrenic way and indicate that nothing he does is done in relationship to other people." The family of the schizophrenic establishes a system of rules like all families, but also has "a prohibition on any acknowledgement that a family member is setting rules. Each refuses to concede that he is circumscribing the behavior of others, and each refuses to concede that any other family member is governing him." The attempt, of course, fails. "The more a person tries to avoid being governed or governing others, the more helpless he becomes and so governs others by forcing them to take care of him." In our society as a whole this caretaking role is assigned to technology, like so much else.

Riesman overlooks the fact that the individual is sacrificed either way. If he is never sacrificed to the group the group will collapse and the individual with it. Part of the individual is, after all, committed to the group. Part of him wants what "the group" wants, part does not. No matter what is done some aspect of the individual—id, ego, or whatever—will be sacrificed.

An individual, like a group, is a motley collection of ambivalent feelings, contradictory needs and values, and antithetical ideas. He is not, and cannot be, a monolithic totality, and the mod-

ern effort to bring this myth to life is not only delusional and ridiculous, but also acutely destructive, both to the individual and to his society.

Recognition of this internal complexity would go a long way toward resolving the dilemma Riesman implicitly poses. For the reason a group needs the kind of creative deviant Riesman values is the same reason it needs to sacrifice him: the failure of the group members to recognize the complexity and diversity and ambivalence within themselves. Since they have oversimplified and rejected parts of themselves, they not only lack certain resources but also are unable to tolerate their naked exposure by others. The deviant is a compensatory mechanism to mitigate this condition. He comes along and tries to provide what is "lacking" in the group (that is, what is present but denied, suppressed). His role is like that of the mutant—most are sacrificed but a few survive to save the group from itself in times of change. Individualism is a kind of desperate plea to save all mutants, on the grounds that we do not know what we are or what we need. As such it is horribly expensive—a little like setting a million chimps to banging on a typewriter on the grounds that eventually one will produce a masterpiece.

But if we abandon the monolithic pretense and recognize that any group sentiment, and its opposite, represents a part of everyone but only a part, then the prophet is unnecessary since he exists in all of us. And should be appear it will be unnecessary to sacrifice him since we have already admitted that what he is saying is true. And in the meantime we would be able to exercise our humanity, governing each other and being governed, instead of encasing ourselves in the leaden armor of our technological schizophrenia.

# H Sociology in Modern Society

## INTRODUCTION

In recent years the relation of sociology itself to the political and social conflicts of contemporary history has become the subject of intense debate among sociologists. We have therefore included this final section of three readings that both report on and adopt rather different positions in this ongoing debate. The rise of New Left protest movements, drawing the bulk of their adherents from the ranks of students and younger college and university teachers, has perhaps affected sociology more deeply than any other academic discipline. A large contingent of student radicals, campus protesters, and political activists on the Left have, as Alvin Gouldner notes in our first reading in this section, been undergraduate and graduate students of sociology and junior faculty members of sociology departments. There are indications that this is true of the student Left in European countries as well as in the United States, although sociology is a newer and less established discipline with far fewer practitioners both absolutely and relatively in Europe. Both factual knowledge of the social conditions against which political protest is mounted and many of the leading ideological themes of the protesters have, as Gouldner argues, been derived from, or at least heavily influenced by, exposure to the research and teachings of academic sociology. Gouldner makes this point in order to temper the total rejection of sociology by many student radicals, while at the same time expressing his political solidarity with them and endorsing their major criticism of sociology and sociologists for excessive willingness to serve established governmental and private bureaucratic organizations.

One of the main targets of the radicals has been the canon that the sociologist should separate his political and moral values from his scholarly work and strive for "objectivity" or "value-neutrality." Gouldner recognizes that this conviction often conveniently enables the sociologist to define himself as a mere technician for hire by the powerful, free of any obligation to be concerned with the uses to which his research may be put by his employers, but he nevertheless rejects the total equation of sociology with political ideology by some of the radical sociologists while applauding their unmasking of the conservative assumptions he sees as underlying much contemporary sociology. Robert Nisbet, in our second reading, regards the rejection of the ideal of objectivity in a far graver light. Nisbet clearly does not share Gouldner's sympathy with the political objec-

tives of the New Left: his main concern is with the threat posed by the politicization of the social sciences to the survival of social science itself as a major
achievement of Western scholarship. That he is not simply deploring the loss of
public reputation and access to government consultantships and research funds
which may result from the spread of the "epistemological nihilism" he condemns, is evident in his closing remarks where he agrees with Gouldner that
many social scientists have earned the censure of the radicals by their "naive and
rapacious eagerness" to collaborate on and even initiate questionable projects
financed by the government and especially the military establishment, such as
the ill-fated Project Camelot. Nisbet also condemns the "emergence of the
Higher Capitalism on the American campus during the 50's" with the effervescence of research institutes whose well-paid staff, withdrawn from teaching, succeeded in bureaucratizing much of the social science enterprise.

Our last selection by William Gamson considers several possible explanations
as to why the new demands for a more politically engaged sociology and the
rejection of scientific or scholarly detachment are raised by younger sociologists
and often resisted by older men. He finds most plausible the conclusion that
younger sociologists have been recruited from more economically comfortable
and higher status backgrounds and that they do not, like the older generation,
perceive their sociological careers as a means of upward mobility. He also notes
that the very successes of sociology in establishing itself as an influential and
burgeoning field makes the younger men less defensive in their affiliation with
it and less motivated therefore to strive to borrow from the prestige of physical
science in order to legitimize the discipline.

# 57

# Toward the Radical Reconstruction of Sociology

## ALVIN W. GOULDNER

The repeated denunciations of sociology, precisely because they are so
often merely repeated but not deepened,
threaten to smother legitimate criticism under a dead weight of clanking
cliches. Their very repetition denies our
ability to analyze the state of sociology
and to develop a rational praxis that
might do something about it. Denun-
ciation is a rhetoric appropriate to the
stage of political mobilization, to the
gathering of forces. While this stage

From *Social Policy*, May–June 1970. Reprinted by permission.

is by no means complete so far as the
reconstruction of sociology is concerned,
still it is now well advanced, as demonstrated by the August meetings of the
Sociology Liberation Movement in San
Francisco, and the time has come to
open a more interior dialogue among
those of us who believe that something
is deeply wrong with sociology.

At issue is not merely what sociologists think, what they profess, nor even
how they work. It is all of these and
more. It is a question of how they live
and what they live for, and of how this

affects their working and thinking. Now, as the opposition to "sociology as usual" has passed from preliminary mobilization to emerging organizational forms, from scattered complaints to coalescing rebellion, the issue increasingly becomes what can and should be done about the state of academic sociology. And this requires an estimate, on the one side, of the character of conventional sociology today and, on the other, of the developing strength of the forces that have gathered in rebellion against it. These are difficult questions. What follows is not meant to be a definitive answer, but only some provisional ideas that may launch a more collective discussion out of which we might reach a deeper appraisal.

. . . . . . . . .

Many radical sociologists think of themselves as "activists," often as free-floating community organizers fighting local battles as they happen to emerge. In effect, they have defined the radical sociologist only as a political radical, and almost entirely in terms of his political rather than his intellectual tasks. This is due largely to the fact that most conventional sociologists have long ignored the political implications of their position, the better to do business with the status quo, and have manifested a bland moral indifference to the dominant political issues of our time, thus preserving their availability as the technicians of the powerful. The political activism of the radical sociologist is thus a natural reaction to the political irresponsibility of the conventional sociologist, but it is no less lopsided.

For vital though I believe political activism to be in defining the radical sociologist, I also believe that it is a serious mistake to consider this the only important aspect of the radical sociologist's mission. Such a conception of the radical sociologist deprecates the role of social theory and social science for politics as such, and surrenders them to the conventional Establishment figures in sociology and the ASA.

In brief, the task of the radical sociologist is not only to participate in radical political action but also, and in part through this, to radicalize his own work, *as a sociologist*. His task is to radicalize (by which I do not mean politicize) sociology itself, and to do this in his intellectual work as well as by direct political activities. He has, in short, the obligation of contributing to a radical sociology—i.e., to a critical understanding and transformation of society and of sociology. The radical sociologist who does not get into the political fray is not much of a radical; and the one who is not involved in transforming sociology is not much of a sociologist. Many radical sociologists, however, divorce their radicalism and their sociology and write a conventional sociology which is often scarcely distinguishable from that of their apolitical or conservative brethren.

This may be related to the fact that the intellectual heroes of radical sociologists—e.g., Sorokin, Mannheim, Mills—almost invariably are dead, while their living heroes usually lack intellectual accomplishments or intellectual distinction, as sociologists. The operating system by which the radical caucus allocates esteem to the living is based largely on the manifestation of political courage and activism; only rarely is it given for contributions as sociologists.

One basic reason for this imbalance is that the youthful members of the radical caucus have not had time to make important intellectual contributions. Yet insofar as intellectual creativity (which I do not equate with one's bibliography) does not become one standard for esteem within the movement, to that extent the movement undermines its own capacity to shape intellectual developments in sociology, largely abdicating that role to the very Establishment sociologists whom they detest. The danger is that such a system is apt to transform radical sociologists into another Left political grouping, indistinguishable from any other radical action group, and devoid of any distinctive societal mission.

The divorce between their sociology and their politics is convenient to junior faculty members who lack such protection as tenure may provide, for an emphasis on community activism, away from the university and apart from sociology, reduces the danger of career-crippling reprisals. While conservative and liberal elements within the university scarcely relish it when the junior faculty's community activities make the newspapers, nonetheless traditions of academic freedom and role-separation ("He was not speaking as a member of the university.") impose a claim on their forbearance. But when activists operate militantly within the university itself to change its structures and traditions, they are then threatening the *Pax Academica* so important to the liberals themselves. In a similar vein, there is a tendency for young radicals to denounce Establishment sociologists in other universities but not in their own.

In emphasizing the danger of abandoning efforts to transform sociology and the university . . . I still remain convinced that it is tremendously important for radical sociologists to participate actively in efforts to change the larger community. My aim has not been to deprecate the importance of such efforts but to stress the significance of a two-way flow between sociology as an intellectual discipline and political radicalism. Each, I believe, can deepen and enhance the other. In addition to its value to the community, radical political activity can transform the persons involved in it. It can activate a new structure of sentiments and generate a new experience with the world that can transform the pre-theoretical impulses from which new, articulate sociologies

can emerge. The "radicalization" of the sociologist thus generates infrastructures conducive to new and better sociologies and to the transformation of sociology itself.

In the last analysis, a radical's appraisal of the divorce between politics and sociology must rest on his appraisal of academic sociology itself, of its intellectual worth and ideological meanings. Stated tersely, my appraisal follows.

Sociology, even academic sociology with its profoundly conservative structure, still retains politically liberative potentialities that can be useful in transforming the community. Even with its neglect of the importance of power, property, conflict, force and fraud, academic sociology has (not despite, but because of, this) focused attention on some of the new sources and sites of social change in the modern social world.

For example, and to be provocatively invidious about it, it was not the Marxists but Talcott Parsons and other functionalists who early spotted the importance of the emerging "youth culture," and at least lifted it out as an object for attention. It was the academic sociologists, not the Marxists, in the United States who helped many to get their first concrete picture of how Blacks and other subjugated groups live, and who contributed to such practical political developments as the Supreme Court's desegregation decision. It is the ethnography of conventional academic sociologists that has also given us the best picture of the emerging psychedelic and drug cultures, which are hardening the separation and conflict of generations.

Again, it was Max Weber and other academic sociologists who forced us to confront the problem of bureaucracy in the modern world in all of its profundity and pervasiveness. Unlike many Marxists, the academic sociologists refused to confine their view of bureaucracy to the state level alone. They did not view it as a social epiphenomenon that automatically would be overcome with the achievement of socialism, as Karl Kautsky did; and, unlike certain Soviet scholars, they did not view bureaucracy as some kind of social "vestige" possessed of an unexplained viability in the contemporary world.

It is precisely because so much of academic sociology is polemically and compulsively anti-Marxist and antisocialist that it was led to explore parts of the social world ignored by the Marxists and to focus on, and often to exaggerate, every new social development that meant bad news for Marxism. That academic sociology has commonly been animated by these politically inspired motives does not necessarily vitiate the fact that it has often explored hitherto unknown social worlds, and that what it has found is often usable in transforming the modern world.

The task then is not simply to denounce academic sociology, but to understand that it contains viable elements and liberative potentialities. The problem is to crack these out of the conservative ideological structure in which they are embedded, to rework them thoroughly, and to assimilate them in a social theory which is not limited and confined to the assumptions of our present society. The problem is not only to denounce academic sociology as it is, but also to transcend it.

From the standpoint of its political character and social role, academic sociology since Comte has always been ready to lend support to any established social system; it is this, and not that it is specifically the "tool" of corporate capitalism, that most deeply engraves it with a conservative character. Academic sociology has been geared to maintaining whatever social order exists, as its recent emergence in the Soviet Union makes plain once again. Its strong linkages to the state began during World War II, and while American sociology's military involvements remain important, its predominant character is now shaped by its support from the welfare sector of the state, the National Institute of Mental Health and the Office of Economic Opportunity. To this extent then, sociology increasingly serves as the Market Researcher for the Welfare State and its political character, within the spectrum of American politics, is predominantly liberal in ideology, Democratic in affiliation, and thus essentially conservative in its societal function.

But unless one thinks that liberals and social democrats are all social fascists at bottom and that it is useless to distinguish between liberal Democrats on the one side, and the followers of Senator Goldwater and Governor Wallace on the other, sociology cannot be viewed simply as a reactionary ideology which holds no promise of development and which radicals must extirpate root and branch. The root-and-branch view of sociology held by some radicals is lodged in a desperate politics that has no base other than among the most militant Blacks and students. But one does not have to be a Weatherman to see the storm gathering on the Right, and the Left's need for allies to cope with it. Even in its most conservative posture, academic sociology has been and promises to remain an ally against the rising Right.

That, one might say, is the situation in academic sociology at its worst. And even this is a very static picture of academic sociology. The obvious significance of the rise of the radical caucus in sociology is that it indicates a movement to the Left in sociology itself. It plainly implies that sociologists have a potential for further movement leftward. The radical caucus did not emerge as a desperate effort to stem a new "rightist" development in sociology, but rather from (1) a rejection of the galloping alliance between sociology and the Welfare State, as well as from (2) the radicalization of many young sociologists by their participation in efforts to transform the character of the university.

This very participation by young sociologists, however, is in itself significant in helping us gauge the character and potentiality of academic sociology; it suggests that, far from being unequivocally reactionary, sociology has somehow attracted more than its share of militants and within the university has played a relatively liberative role. The fact that sociologists are prominent among those who have been or are in the process of being fired at Simon Fraser University, at San Francisco State and the University of Connecticut plainly implies that sociologists are not an undifferentiated mass of fat cats and fuddy-duddies.

A transformed sociology, a radicalized and radical sociology, could very well develop an important social base in the university system and among youth who are emerging as a new and increasingly important social stratum. An assessment of the potential of such a transformed sociology should not, however, be confined to its role among university students but should also be seen in its potential for the larger community. Classical Marxism was an effective guide in resisting a venal economy when the social struggle was fluidly organized around class lines. It may be that a transformed sociology can provide useful guidelines for changing a social world which has been carved up into bureaucratic establishments that are superimposed upon the class system, and for conducting a structure-by-structure struggle in each of them.

Any estimate of the potentialities for change possessed by modern academic sociology will differ, according to whether one sees it as a stable and integrated whole or whether one is aware

of the tension-laden contradictions in the work of sociologists. It is therefore useful to review briefly certain of the contradictions inherent in contemporary sociology as such.

One of the central contradictions of modern sociology, especially in the United States, actually derives from its role as the Market Researcher for the Welfare State. This role exposes sociologists to two contradictory, even if not equally powerful, experiences: on one side, it limits the sociologist to the reformist solutions of the Welfare State; on the other, it exposes him to the failures of this State and of the society with whose problems it seeks to cope. Such sociologists have a vested interest in the very failures of this society—in a real sense their careers depend upon it; but at the same time their work may make them intimately familiar with the human suffering engendered by these failures. If it is the special business of such sociologists to help clean up the vomit of modern society, they are also sometimes revolted by what they see. Thus the sociologist's funding-tie to the Welfare State does not produce an unambivalent loyalty to the social system that it seeks to maintain. To be bought and to be paid for are two different things—and that is a contradiction of the Welfare State not peculiar to its relations with sociologists.

A similar contradiction is involved in the call for "objectivity" so central to the methodological canons of academic sociology. While a belief in objectivity fosters the sociologist's accommodation to the way things are, it also fosters and expresses a certain amount of distance from the society's dominant values. The sociologist's claim to objectivity is not simply a disguise for his devotion or capitulation to the status quo, nor is it an expression of a true neutrality toward it. For some sociologists, the claim to objectivity serves as a facade for their own alienation and resentment toward a society which, even today, basically treats them as the Romans treated their Greek slaves: as skilled servants, as useful but lower beings.

The call for "objectivity" serves as "sacred" justification for withholding the reflexive loyalty that the society demands, and provides protective covering for the critical impulses of the timid. Under this protection the sociologist sometimes engages in a bitchy and carping, a tacit and partial, unmasking of society's failures. Challenged, he can dodge behind the parapet of his "objectivity," claiming that he has not pronounced a judgment on society, but that the impersonal facts have spoken. In its present, historically developed form, as a claim of the contemporary professional social sciences, "objectivity" is largely the ambivalent ideology of those whose resentment is shackled by their timidity and privilege. Behind objectivity, there is a measure of alienation.

Another basic contradiction lies in the very assumptions fundamental to the sociological perspective. This is the contradiction between sociology's *focal* assumption that society makes man, and its *tacit* assumption that man makes society. The first assumption is focal partly because it is in the vested interest of academic sociology to emphasize the manner in which society, groups, social relations, social positions, and culture shape and infuse men. While this assumption served to liberate men from biological or supernatural conceptions of their destiny, it becomes an increasingly repressive element in a more fully secularized and bureaucratized society such as our own, particularly when it views social forces as independent reality, apart and autonomous from men's actions. If this assumption began by liberating men from their position as puppets of God and biology, it came to envision them as the passive raw materials of society and culture, inviting them to bow the knee in gratitude to "society," upon which, they are told, nothing less than their humanness depends.

There is an important truth in the vision of society as an autonomous force. It reflects the despair of secularized men who, believing they made the world, nonetheless found it out of their control and not really theirs. But the sociologist's conception of society and social forces as autonomous tacitly takes this alienated condition as *normal* and inevitable rather than as a pathology to be fought and surmounted, an effort supported by the view that it is. men who do indeed make society.

These central assumptions of sociology and their structure—i.e., the present dominance of the assumption that social forces shape men, and the subordination of the assumption that men make society—not only reflect the larger alienation of industrial societies since the French Revolution, but they are also rooted in and confirmed by the special experience of academicians, particularly in the daily reality of their servitude in the university and in their docility toward its authorities.

For tenured faculty, the university is the realm of congenial and leisured servitude. It is a realm in which the academician is both esteemed for his learning and castrated as a political being. Indeed, it is this tradeoff, in which the academician may be a tiger in the classroom but must be a pussycat in the Dean's office, that contributes so much to the irrational posturings and theatrics of the classroom. Like other academics, the sociologist learns from the routine experience of his dependency within the university that he can strike terror only in the hearts of the very young—and now they want to strip him of even that privilege!—but that he himself is the gelded servant of the system in which he is, ostensibly, the vaunted star. He thus believes with an intuitive conviction that "society shapes men" because the assumption conforms to what he lives; it is his autobiography objectified.

It is precisely here that the praxis of the radical sociologist has its greatest intellectual potentiality for, through it, he learns and teaches a different set of assumptions: that men can resist successfully; that they are not simply the raw materials of social systems; that they can be the shakers and makers of worlds that are and worlds that might be. It is such praxis that can help transcend the contradictions of sociology and release its liberative side. No "sociologist" has ever written a single sentence; no sociologist has ever done a single research or had a single idea. It is the entire man who makes sociology and those who are whole men, or struggle against their incompleteness, will make a very different sociology than those who passively accept the crippling that their worlds inflict upon them.

In its political and ideological character then, academic sociology is an ambivalent structure which has both liberative and repressive sides. Although its conservative-repressive dimension dominates, academic sociology is not unequivocally such. To miss this is to miss the opportunity and the task. To miss this is also to increase the danger of fostering a primitivistic regression to an orthodox (if not vulgar) Marxism, and to encourage a mindless knownothingism content with the delusion that academic sociology has accomplished absolutely nothing at all in the last thirty years, thereby inhibiting its use as one important stimulus for a continuing development of Marxism itself.

Unless one sees the ambivalent character of academic sociology, it seems impossible to understand why, throughout Europe and North America—from Nanterre to Columbia to Berkeley—

students of sociology have contributed a disproportionately large share of the leaders of the New Left. C. Wright Mills was not a mysterious aberration in sociology and did indeed raise up others in his image. If academic sociology were unambivalently conservative, how could it have attracted so many who were or became student militants? Recognizing this, some have held that their attraction was simply a case of mistaken identity; that is, they argue that those who were already militants came to sociology thinking it was something more liberative than closer involvement with it later revealed.

While there is truth in this judgment, I believe it is on the whole misleading. The young militants who came to sociology were correct in perceiving its liberative component. It was and is there to be seen. Where the young militants probably went wrong initially was in failing to see that this liberative component is only one part of an ambivalent system whose overall, or dominant, character is conservative and which, upon closer acquaintance, led them to feel betrayed. Yet it is precisely because sociology does contain both this promise and its betrayal, this openness to what is happening in the modern world and a surrender to it, that sociology, more than any of the other social sciences, has come under the heaviest attack from the New Left. The special bitterness is due to the betrayal of expectations that sociology itself arouses.

There are undeniably powerful contradictions within sociology which provide leverage for its transformation. These suggest that one cannot deal with sociology as Rome dealt with Carthage. Just as Marx extricated the liberative potentialities of a Hegelianism previously dominated by its conservative aspect, and delivered from it a left or neo-Hegelianism, so, too, it is possible to transcend contemporary academic sociology and to deliver from it a left or neo-sociology.

The strategy and tactics of the radical sociologist require a larger vision of the fundamental lineaments of the historical development of modern social theory and social science, some understanding that academic sociology and Marxism are together the basic structures into which world sociology became differentiated in the nineteenth century These systems were and still are in the nature of mirror images, each conditioning the other, now as earlier; and it may be that this structural cleavage in world social theory has moved to a new historical level in which, through struggle and praxis, a new theoretical synthesis is being readied.

The two most important sources of leverage to effect this synthesis are: (1) the praxis of the radical sociologist through which he transforms himself as a total person and thereby creates the human basis for a new sociology, and (2) a heightening of the direct, mutual exposure, tension and theoretical struggle between academic sociology and Marxism. The theoretical transformations that such mutual interaction produces, however, will not and cannot be one-sided; it will not simply be academic sociology that is transformed in the process, but also Marxism itself. The transformation of sociology will then not be brought about in isolation from Marxism; and it will not be brought about by a struggle in which Marxism swallows academic sociology whole, leaving itself intact and unchanged. The two need each other for their mutual regeneration.

# 58

# A Most Extraordinary Thing: The Debate over Objectivity in Sociology

ROBERT NISBET

In a memorable address to his faculty colleagues at Harvard last spring (reprinted in part in the Winter issue of The Public Interest) the economic historian Alexander Gerschenkron likened the events there to those unfolded in the Hans Christian Andersen tale "The Most Unbelievable Thing."

A king once offered the hand of his daughter, the princess, to the man who could do the most unbelievable thing in the arts. There was great competi-

From "Subjectivity Si! Objectivity No!" New York Times Book Review, March 15, 1970. Reprinted by permission.

tion. At last it was decided that the most unbelievable thing among entries was a combined clock and a calendar of ingenious design and surpassing beauty, the product of many years of work. Not only was the time given, the clock showed the ages back and forth into the past and future. And circling the clock were sculptured figures representing the greatest spiritual and cultural minds in the history of human society.

All assembled were agreed that this clock was without question the most unbelievable thing and that the hand of the princess must be given to the clock's handsome creator. But as judgment was about to be pronounced, a lowbrow competitor appeared, sledgehammer in hand. With a single blow he destroyed forever the marvelous clock. And everybody said, why, to destroy so beautiful a thing, this is surely the most unbelievable thing of all. And that was how the judges had to judge.

And, Mr. Gerschenkron concluded, in our own time of troubles the most unbelievable thing, surely, is not the fragile entity that is the university, product of centuries of love of learning for its own sake, but, rather, the acts of those, whether armed with student battering ram and torch or with faculty vote, who would seek to destroy the university in a matter of days.

Most of us would agree with Mr. Gerschenkron that this is indeed the most unbelievable thing at the present time. What, then, is the *next* most unbelievable thing? The answer is possibly not so clear. There must be many entries possible. But I will suggest one: the very recently begun, fast-accumulating nihilistic repudiation in the social sciences of the ancient Western ideal of dispassionate reason, of objective inquiry, in the study of man and society.

I will come in a moment to a few of the symptoms of the ongoing repudiation of objectivity. First, though, it might be noted that as recently as 1960 had any social scientist been asked, "What is the most unbelievable thing?" he would undoubtedly have replied: "Why the fact that after many decades of effort by social scientists to achieve honored place in the community of science, we appear to be finally there." Such a social scientist could have observed that the works of such 20th-century titans as William I. Thomas, Edward Tolman, Joseph Schumpeter, A. L. Kroeber and V. O. Key—I limit myself to a few of the greater ones in this country—had at last taken effect.

The august National Academy of Sciences was beginning to open its doors to social scientists as members; the physical and biological scientists on the campus had begun to make the possessive "our" include economists, sociologists, and political scientists. In a few places the hoary science requirement was being fulfilled by undergraduates with courses drawn from the social sciences. Surely, all of this would have seemed to any social scientist in 1960 as the most unbelievable thing.

But not in 1970. One is obliged by the evidence, I think, to conclude that the most unbelievable thing is the astonishing reversal of belief in the scientific, that is, the objective, the detached, the dispassionate character of the social sciences. What makes it unbelievable is that this reversal is to be found, not among physical scientists, government officials, or citizens. Not yet anyhow. Its locus is the social sciences themselves; more precisely, in the minds of a constantly increasing number of younger social scientists and among these most crucially, of students, graduate as well as undergraduate, in the social sciences.

What are the prime manifestations of this revolt against objectivity, this scuttling of the ideal of dispassionate reason in the study of man and society? I will limit myself to two or three of the more striking ones.

First, the declaration by self-styled *radical* social scientists that objectivity of inquiry is not even a proper end of the social sciences. From radical sociologist to radical political scientist to radical anthropologist, all across the spectrum of the social sciences, the refrain is the same: "Social scientists have heretofore sought to understand society. The point, however, is to destroy and then remake society." It is not, obviously, the mature Marx, who was capable of devoting himself for many years in the British Museum to the study of capitalism and society, but the youthful romantic Marx that these voices choose to echo. If anyone thinks I exaggerate the impact at the present time of the self-styled radical social scientist, I invite him to any annual meeting of one of the learned societies.

Let us look briefly at symptom number two. It is for me somewhat more chilling inasmuch as it makes inevitable a recollection of the Nazi Rosenberg and his efforts in the 1930's to demonstrate differences between German or Aryan science on the one hand and Jewish or plutocratic science on the other. I refer here to widening belief at the present time to what can only be called *the necessary ethnic roots of science*.

It is being said, by white and black alike, chiefly with respect though to studies of blacks, chicanos, and other ethnic minorities, that it is not possible by any stretch of one's dedication to objectively for the white to understand the black or the black to understand the white. There is black science and there is white science, and the twain shall never meet. More recently (and I can scarcely believe my eyes as I write the words) there have been intimations of a women's social science. As though one were dealing with public rest rooms.

How the gods must be laughing. We had no sooner started to erase (admittedly, *just* started) some of the more preposterous kinds of ethnic segregation in American society when there began —and began, let it be emphasized, among those forming the vanguard of reform—to be manifest a far more deadly type of segregation: deadly because it deals with the epistemological roots of the scientific study of man.

Let ‚us concede immediately: One must be a Negro to understand what it is like being a Negro. The same is exactly true of being a Wasp, a Puerto Rican, a mountain climber, a college professor. It is impossible for men to understand women, and women men. All of this has been said a long time, and in the sense that is usually meant I am willing to stipulate that it will always be true; just as I am willing to trumpet the imperishable truth that no one—not my wife, children, lawyer, physician, least of all, friends—will ever understand me. No one to my knowledge has ever challenged the existence in each of us, in each ethnic or cultural strain, of some doubtless forever unreachable essence. And, as the immortal Charlie Brown has concluded, it is probably good, all things considered, that this essence is unreachable.

But we are talking about science, not the metaphysics of identity or being. The movement I refer to among younger social scientists today is directed to the nature of science, *social science*. What used to be said by engineers, chemists, and the lay public is now being said by an ever widening group of social scientists themselves: particularly the younger ones. An objective understanding of social behavior is impossible; such understanding will always be limited by the political, or ethnic, or social and economic position one occupies in the social order. Its embedded values must become the values of the investigator and, hence, the bias of his conclusions. There is nothing that can be done about this.

Therefore it behooves us to abandon the vain pursuit of knowledge, objective knowledge and to throw ourselves into action oriented toward values we can cherish. The remarkable study of conditions of classroom achievement in the schools completed a year or two ago by James Coleman, sociologist at Johns Hopkins University, cannot be believed because, fist, Coleman is white and second, his massive study was financed by the Federal Government. So runs the argument of what I can only think of as the most unbelievable thing today in the social sciences.

That it is hard to achieve objectivity, especially in the social sciences, admits of no doubt. The philosophical literature of the West is filled with notations of the idols of the mind—as they were called by Francis Bacon—that incessantly seek to engage our attention. I assume that not the most dedicated practitioner of science, even physical science, would cavil at this. In all scientific work, however good, there is no doubt some lingering element of personal predilection, some thrust that is rooted in bias.

But this said, is there, then, no significant difference between the gathering of ethnic data by an Otto Klineberg or a James Coleman, and the interpretation of these data, and the gathering and the interpretation of such data by a George Wallace? I assume all but the most hopelessly fanatical would say, yes, there is a difference. But, given the crisis of the times, the roles into which we are being forced by history and by the impending revolution, the difference is not worth emphasizing. Better, it is said, for the Klinebergs and the Colemans to abandon the idle conceit of a value-free science and to join directly the fight against George Wallace. It is quicker that way.

That it is also suicidal, on the evidence of history, seems not to enter the minds of the radical social scientists. Or if it does, it seems not to matter greatly. Without wanting to put too fine a point on the matter it is hard to resist the conclusion sometimes that this generation of the left has a rendezvous with suicide. Retreat to drugs, to sensitivity sessions, to illusory communitarianism, and to the calculatedly clownish behavior of the Chicago Seven would suggest it.

All that is beside the point. I am writing here about the revolt against objectivity I find everywhere in the country today, even among young social scientists who are not conspicuously left or conspicuously anything. There is nothing remarkable in preoccupation with objectivity. That is old. What is new is the profound difference one finds today in attitude toward the *ideal* of objectivity, toward the goal of protection from the ideals of the mind in one's work. *This* is the most unbelievable thing.

How unbelievable it is may perhaps be sensed from a reading of several very recently published books now on my desk. Here, for instance, is "Knowledge Into Action: Improving the Nation's Use of the Social Sciences" (Government Printing Office). It is the report of the Special Commission on the Social Sciences of the National Board, published by the National Science Foundation. It is excellent. The nihilistic movement I refer to is, however, making it seem as obsolete as one of those tracts written in the 1930's on planned economy. I cannot conquer the feeling, reading it, that the pious are converting the pious.

Here is Gunnar Myrdal, "Objectivity in Social Research" (Pantheon). With insight, wit, and elegance one of the towering social scientists of the age deals once again with what I called above the Baconian idols. But the waters of nihilism lap unfelt at his feet. His book would produce, not dissent, but yawning indifference in any audience of young social scientists today. Hearing his message, they would ignore it. Who needs it? He doesn't feel, he is white, he is nonpolitical, he doesn't *understand* man!

Or "Politics and the Social Sciences," edited by Seymour Martin Lipset (Oxford), one of the most creative sociologists of our time, contributed to by minds of the luster of Scott Greer, Giovanni Sartori and Fred Greenstein. Mr. Lipset has brought together some splendid pieces on the relationships of the study of politics and the other social sciences. But I can find little if any evidence in the volume of recognition of that special form of nihilism that today spreads out from politically radical and ethnic sources.

And finally, here is "The Political Sciences: General Principles of Selection in Social Science and History" (Basic Books) by the Australian, Hugh Stretton. It is a fascinating and in many ways original book even if the author does not seem to realize the overkill conferred so recently by time and events upon his academic argument. Mr. Stretton is as merciless and witty in his judgments as he is learned. I should wish to be spared the circle of Dante's hell to which Mr. Stretton has consigned functionalists, systems-makers, along with dustbowl empiricists: and with their authors the tedious taxonomies and limping methodologies that have been passing themselves off for 20 years now as science. The howls and wails would be dreadful to have to listen to.

I rather suspect that Hugh Stretton is likely to become something of a hero in certain of the more literate quarters of the epistemological nihilism I write of in this essay. His learning is considerable, and he is a master of the one-two punch, setting his victim up with the faint jab of apparent praise, then coming through with a murderous right. But beyond this are the thrilling last lines of the book. The scientist's duty, Mr. Stretton writes, in today's conflict "goes beyond discovering and understanding. It becomes his business to win." That last sentence has the nice touch of the barricades seen from scholar's nest that can always be counted on to win applause in our day, no matter how badly the act has been going before. And, in Mr. Stretton's case, the act, I repeat, has been going well throughout.

As I say, I predict weeks, if not months, of magisterial status for this book in those quarters of the American academic left that ordinarily allow only days. Furthermore there is the proper element of Britannic establishment in the manner of Mr. Stretton's book that the American left invariably finds seductive even when the message is considerably to the political right of Mr. Stretton's.

But even Mr. Stretton—perhaps because he is at the University of Adelaide instead of Berkeley, Wisconsin, Brandeis, or Harvard—seems to me slightly archaic. His book and its message would have had more powerful impact a few years ago. The revolution of epistemological nihilism has left him, as well as others of its leaders, a mile or two behind.

No more than Gunnar Myrdal does he seem really aware of the recent, tempestlike ferocity of the movement that has been built around the slogan: *The scientist's business is to win*—that is, at the barricades, not in the laboratory or study. Mr. Stretton is anything but Auden's immured scholar of the 1930's "lecturing on navigation while the ship is going down." He is more nearly an elegant Bernard McFadden preaching the gospel of fresh air as the hurricane gathers. I cannot conquer the feeling that though he will certainly enjoy brief heroic status in this country, he will yet become like certain refugees from Berkeley who, having sown the wind, avoided the whirlwind by retreating behind institute door or else snuggling under eastern ivy. Whirlwinds, alas, are no respecters of degrees—using that word in both its senses.

What the disciples of social-science-as-action can never seem to understand is that if action is the magic word, there are always others, less burdened by the trained incapacities of scholarship, who can act more swiftly. And ruthlessly. What the man of action looks to the scholar and scientist for is knowledge, not barricade gymnastics. There is something about the cap-touching of graduate students and the genuflections of administrators' wives that unfits American university professors for the simple egalitarian civilities of the revolution.

All this would seem obvious enough; at least over Sunday morning coffee, if not Saturday night martinis. What we must ask, however, is, how is the revolution of nihilism in the social sciences at the present time to be explained? By the political objectives of the New Left, it has become fashionable to declare in academic circles—tenure circles —and by the stubborn unwillingness of members of the left to learn to become social scientists the way we did. Both explanations are variations on Original Sin. Let us look further into the matter, borrowing from the poet George Meredith: no villain need be; passions spin the plot; the wrong is mixed. Could we, the social scientists, have somehow betrayed ourselves during the past couple of decades by what is false within? Has there been anything resembling what Julien Benda called a *trahison des clercs?* I call to witness:

First, the special kind of hubris that attacked the social sciences in this country during the 1950's. With only the slenderest resources, they not only accepted invitations from all the men of power in Washington and elsewhere but actually started knocking on doors demanding invitations. Project Camelot, which can best be thought of as the social sciences' Black Sox scandal, was no doubt a fitting dénouement. (A more or less clandestine "research" project based in Washington through which more or less clandestine investigation would be made in selected foreign countries of types of insurgency and counter-insurgency. Sponsored, and heavily financed by the U.S. Army, it was mercifully killed by Executive Order before it was more than barely launched.) But even after its odor spread internationally, few American social scientists got the point. The air filled quickly with imprecations of Congress, of the Executive Office, of the State Department, and other agencies in Washington for having saved the social sciences from even worse consequences of their appalling combination of naïveté and rapacity.

Second, the vastly greater affinity that built up throughout the 1950's and 1960's between the sciences generally (but not excluding the social sciences) and the military establishment. It is, especially for the social sciences, a strange affinity. Not strange economically. That's where the money is. But Willie Sutton's celebrated words fit the robbing of banks better than they do the image of the social sciences that continued to persist in the minds of the young. Even at this very moment it is necessary to go to Congress to find substantial opposition to the affinity between the Pentagon and the sciences, social included. The latter seem to find instant absolution by repeating a hundred times a day the words "pure," "basic," and "theoretical." Few if any social scientists (except, that is, for those of the political far left) do anything beyond that save to join committees to appoint committees to find proper terminology for converting rape into legitimate union. (Still, it's never clear just who is raping whom.)

Third, the whole emergence of the Higher Capitalism on the American campus during the 1950's. I'm not referring to the by-definition capitalist trustees. I have in mind the New Entrepreneurs of the sciences, social as well as physical, through which research started to become merchandised by the piece and the hour. In institute, bureau, and center instead of factory. Hours 8 to 5, by appointment only. By the early 1960's there were as many institute and center directors on the American campus as there were officers in the old Mexican Army. They were doing good, of course, but also doing well. That is, until the revolt came and annual meetings became Bastilles stormed by disillusioned *sans-culottes*.

The physical sciences have been spared very much in the way of revolt, and heaven knows, they began the Higher Capitalism. But physical scientists have had more sense throughout than to spice their lectures to students with quotations from Rousseau, Marx and Lenin. The social scientists thought they were being pious in so doing when in fact they were lighting matches before open kerosene. The combination of capitalist luxury in what the Science magazine reporter, D. S. Greenberg irreverently calls the Institute for the Absorption of Federal Funds and the ritual radicalism of its owners was to prove by 1965 to be too explosive for further containment.

There are other reasons that might be offered here. These, however, will suffice to make clear that the revolution of nihilism presently attacking that most precious of intellectual ideals, objectivity, has roots beyond the commonly cited invincible ignorance of the revolutionaries. The wrong is indeed mixed. Though I persist in believing that there are villains.

# 59

# Sociology's Children of Affluence

## WILLIAM A. GAMSON

The American Sociological Association staged a happening in San Francisco near the end of the summer of 1967. This happening was called the 62nd Annual Meeting and for those of you who missed it, I would like to invoke something of the mood. I suppose I realized that this convention was to be a bit different when, upon arrival, a friend informed me that he had been handed a leaflet in the Haight-Ashbury advising all hippies to get their tape recorders out and go down to the Hilton Hotel where they could "observe sociologists in their natural habitat."

This intelligence was followed by a string of events in a similar vein. A local rock group called, I believe, the Second Coming, took over the main

From the *American Sociologist*, November 1968. Reprinted by permission.

ballroom at the Hilton to stage, for the benefit of the assembled sociologists, a light show and accompanying sound barrage. This affair began with a large group of observers but first a few and then a larger number began to dance until the remaining observers were relegated to the sidelines and replaced by participant nonobservers in the middle of the floor.

The next few days found a similar irreverence in the air. The corridors had a few sandled, loose-shirted young men with convention name tags. There seemed to me more displays of emotion and expressive behavior than usual, more laughter and more intensity in the discussions in the sessions I attended. One author of a paper submitted a poem for his abstract. In a session on sociology and public policy, one of the speakers addressed the familiar issues of a "value-free" sociology. He argued, as one might predict from the topic, for an engaged sociology but his paper was more scholarly than polemic. What interested me most was an incident that occurred in the audience discussion which followed the presentation of the papers. A young sociologist rose to defend the importance of detachment in examining major policy issues. The author of the paper responded graciously, suggesting that this was certainly a legitimate and widely shared point of view although his paper argued against it as a categorical policy. However, four or five other members of the audience rose to put down the questioner with considerable ferocity. By this time the author had had enough and he seized the first opportunity to assert that he had put his point badly and that he also favored involvement of sociologists on policy questions under the proper circumstances. The deviant thus censured, the meeting moved on to its conclusion, and I was left with my private musings about the rapidity with which yesterday's orthodoxy becomes heresy and the pitfalls for the eager young who learn their lessons too well.

Another session I attended on student activism had a Berkeley Free Speech Movement leader as a discussant. Her exhortations were rather predictable and, I felt, banal in content but they were written and delivered with style and were warmly applauded. In another session, some rather pompous and pedestrian remarks, to the effect that the hippie phenomenon could easily be understood with traditional sociological concepts, were met with laughter. It was not a happy time in San Francisco for decorum and respect for the importance and seriousness of the sociological enterprise.

While the hippie influences were making their way through the windows,

the political activists were storming the front door. The target, of course, was the government's Vietnam policy. However, government being seen as but one member of the species called establishment, some of the hostility inevitably bounced off onto the sociological member of that species. Things came to a head in the normally dull general business sessions of the convention, and these had enough angry and absurd moments to leave many of the older heads shaking with wonder and disapproval. It was as if the sociological house were suddenly full of Eartha Kitts, fed up to the teeth with sanctimony and irrelevance, and unwilling or unable to give decorum its accustomed due.

What was going on? A large part, of course, is that sociology is very much feeling and reflecting the strains that the society at large is experiencing at the moment. The universities are particularly sensitive to the forces for change which are generated by these strains and the structure of the university amplifies this impact for many people. In such periods, sociology is especially attractive to students with an activist orientation. In short, "The Movement" is having its influence on the sociological profession and I interpret events in San Francisco as evidence for this impact.[1]

How deep or enduring this impact will be is a matter of conjecture. It depends on the course of events in the society at large. My intuition is that we are dealing with in part a cyclical phenomenon but this is no more than intuition, and I don't wish to defend this point here. Aside from these outside forces which impinge on the profession and dispose its fate, there are longer term, more internal factors which

[1] The Boston meetings of the ASA occurred some time after this paper was written but provided additional evidence of such influence.

would lead me to predict that some part of the change will be permanent. Before offering this argument, I would like to spell out the hypothesized changes—changes for which the San Francisco events are the surface manifestation.

## Changing Role Conceptions

A significant number of younger sociologists and sociology graduate students embrace a conception of their professional role that differs in at least two important respects from earlier and still dominant conceptions in the profession. My intent in describing this newer conception is not to persuade those who do not share it but to identify the underlying premises which make it differ from the more traditional view. My device for doing this is to take two rather innocent looking statements which might be made by an older sociologist and to point out why, in my view, these apparently plausible statements are unconvincing to many younger colleagues.

1. *Statement Number One:* "The Sociological Association as such has no right to take an official position on political issues. There are other organizations appropriate to this function and it subverts the association to use it for this purpose."

Implicit in this view is the premise that the Vietnam issue, for example, is part of a category called "political issues." It is a special case of a more general principle and, therefore, one must be wary of setting a precedent that will compromise an important general policy. Even if the category is "important political issues," the argument continues to hold because the judgment of importance is highly individual and subject to disagreement. The fear is that the association will be diverted from its "proper" functions to deal continually with one or another partisan de-

mand by a small group of its members.

In contrast, many younger sociologists view the Vietnam issue and the attendant urban crisis in an Armageddon spirit. In many cases, they believe themselves confronted with a moral test on a par with that faced by German intellectuals during the 1930's. Implicit in such a view is a categorization which removes such "unprecedented" issues from the more general category of political issues. They may even fully concede the statement quoted above but find it irrelevant, given the unique character of the present crisis.

One speaker at the San Francisco convention compared the actions of the American government in Vietnam to the killer of eight nurses in Chicago and to the sniper who killed more than a dozen innocent people from atop the tower at the University of Texas. "Psychologists must ask themselves," he argued, "What kind of person is capable of such acts? As sociologists, we must ask ourselves the same question about our Vietnam actions. What kind of society is capable of watching its duly elected government carry out such actions in its name?" One may disagree with such a view and believe that our society is merely passing through a temporary turbulent period. But it is important to recognize this Armageddon spirit if one is to address those in its ambience about the proper functions of the American Sociological Association.

2. Related but somewhat different points may be made about *Statement Number Two:* "When I take a stand on political issues and do not draw on any special body of sociological knowledge, I do so as citizen, not as sociologist. If we do not make this distinction, we are no more than con men, exploiting our cachet and ultimately destroying it, since the laity will eventually find us out, if indeed they have not done so already."

This argument would, I believe, be

taken by many younger sociologists as an indication of either naïveté or hypocrisy. Hoult (1968) puts the hypocrisy argument forcefully in a recent issue of *The American Sociologist:* " . . . it is notable that people who say 'I only take a stand as a man, not as a social scientist,' are almost always the very same people who take no stands at all. . . . Although greed and sloth may account for a significant number of those who choose to remain on what they *think* is dead center so far as controversial social issues are concerned, I am personally convinced that *cowardice* is the most important single explanation."

The emphasis on the differentiation of sociologist and citizen roles, in this view, is a convenient ideology which serves as a protective cover for complacency.[2] The argument is viewed as rationalization; hence, it is not fruitful to take it at face value and meet it on its own terms. Any sociologist will be happy to recognize different degrees of consensus in interpreting data and events and in translating these interpretations into policy judgments. But the demands for documentation and consensus in interpretation may be made so stringent that the only possible response is to defer judgment, pending "further investigation." For example, Ralph Turner (1968:54) in a letter to *The American Sociologist,* criticizes the unscholarly nature of the San Francisco Member's Resolution condemning American policy in Vietnam. He asks, "Where is the scholarly investigation

to justify the assurance that Americans would have been willing to commit more money to urban ghettoes if there were no Vietnam war?" He might have asked, "Where is the sociological analysis?" but, then, those who supported the resolution would have been happy to supply one, although it might not have convinced everyone and been shared by all sociologists.

The point, then, is that Statement Number Two is unconvincing not because some sociologists believe no distinctions can be made between assertions based on shared interpretations and those based on interpretations that may be challenged by their colleagues. Nor do they believe that careful collection of data and closely argued analysis make no contribution to achieving that degree of consensus we call "knowledge." The statement is unconvincing because it is regarded as an argument which is disingenuously trotted out on those special occasions when interpretations of data and events threaten the power or status of the sociological guild.

## Why the Change?

Accept, for the sake of argument, the existence of the following facts which I cannot document: that the percentage of sociologists who feel that it is appropriate for the American Sociological Association as such to take a position on an issue like the war in Vietnam is higher now [3] than it would have been a few years ago; and that younger sociologists and graduate students are substantially over-represented among those who take this position. How might one explain these alleged facts?

1. *Failure of Professional Socializa-*

[2] It is not the only protective cover. Gouldner (1968) turns this point around and argues that an emphasis on value-commitment can also, if one is not careful, play a similar self-serving purpose. Of the assertion that a value-free sociology is impossible, he suggests that "we should try to notice, when men complain about the bonds that ~ them, whether their tone is one of ~nted resentment or of comfortable ~odation."

[3] It is still a minority, as the recent vote of the membership on the association's endorsement of the Vietnam resolution demonstrates.

*tion.* The young, it might be argued, have not had a chance to imbibe fully the ways and wisdom of their elders. The higher frequency of the attitude described above can be accounted for by the greater incidence of youthful and incompletely socialized sociologists during the rapid growth period of the last decade.

This argument implies that, if we distinguish among young sociologists on their degree of integration into the profession, we ought to find that those who are least integrated and, hence, least socialized to professional norms, are more likely to manifest this attitude than those who are most integrated. However, if studies of student activists are any guideline (Z. Gamson, 1967; Sampson, 1967; Westby and Braungart, 1966), those who are most rewarded and involved in the university will be *most* likely to manifest this attitude. These studies show that, by and large, student activists compared to non-activists come from higher status backgrounds with more liberal than average parents, are more deeply embedded in student sub-cultures which support their attitudes, are performing better academically, and are reflecting the intellectual and value thrust of their college experience. They are not those who are least integrated—academic and social failures who are compensating for their isolation by finding outlets in student politics. Instead, we are forced to ponder what it means when "a social system's successes lead the protests against it" (Z. Gamson et al., 1967).

We might expect similar results in contrasting those with an "activist" attitude about the proper role of the ASA with those who do not share this attitude within similar age and status groups. In other words, those graduate students who are most successful and are awarded the most recognition from their elders, those among the young with the best jobs and with degrees from the best schools, will be most likely to reject the older, non-activist conception of the role of the sociologist. If this prediction is correct, it suggests that the explanation does not lie in a failure of professional socialization unless this term is defined in some tautological manner.

2. *The Arrogance of Youth.* Not too long ago, *Newsweek* devoted a feature to middle-age, basing much of their discussion on the work of sociologists. One symptom, they suggested, is the feeling that one has seen it all before and been through it all before. There is, indeed, something arrogant about the youthful belief that one lives in a unique time. But it is worth reminding those sociologists who lived through the turbulence of the 1930's and World War II that there is a whole generation of sociologists who have grown up without these formative events. I suppose it is a faith-enhancing experience to see a society recover from the depths of a depression as creatively as American society did. Those who experienced these events feel, no doubt, that they have some perspective on the current crisis and perhaps they do. Those who came of age after these events do not share this faith and sometimes view it as incomprehensible complacency. One hypothesis, then, is that the current times *are* more unique for younger sociologists than for older ones and that their conceptions of appropriate action reflect this.

3. *Changing Base of Recruitment.* The explanation which I find most promising, however, is that the type of concerns and social background of people being attracted into sociology has changed. The field has always attracted a very substantial group with a strong concern about social issues and many older sociologists have taken quiet pleasure in the increasing recruitment of more technically oriented students without such concerns. However, our enter-

prise thrives on the ills of society, and bad times mean many sociology recruits. These are bad times and so we have more people turning to our trade, and the people attracted resemble those who were attracted in other, earlier bad times.

This much may be an ephemeral product of the times without long-term implications for the profession. The important difference between the young people now being attracted and those of an earlier era may not be in their social concern but in their status security. Sociology, I am hypothesizing, is less an avenue of upward mobility for those who are attracted to it today than for those of a previous generation. Having fewer status concerns, the new recruits are less concerned about being regarded as "unscientific," more likely to take the status of the field for granted and to assume that others give their field its due and then some. They are less defensive about it with outsiders and less in need of reassurance about it among themselves. Their professional specter is more likely to be the technician than the preacher.

Examine, in contrast, the themes of those who are concerned and dismayed about what went on in San Francisco. Wilbert Moore (1967), for example, criticizes some sociologists for being unable to distinguish organizations according to function and wonders if, in light of such failures, "there is any reason our students or a possibly ignorant . . . laity should take us seriously on anything." Similarly, Ralph Turner (1968) fears that the unsubstantiated nature of the claims in the members' Vietnam resolution may result in a reduction in "the effectiveness of our representations in those circumstances when we should be able to speak with authority." Between the lines, I read the message: "We have worked a long be taken seriously and are still ccepted, and you people jeop-

ardize it all by confirming everyone's suspicion that we are all a bunch of charlatans."

The lack of sensitivity to such issues by young sociologists is, I suspect, a case of the Third Generation Phenomenon. Mama and Papa did not take their Americanism lightly but for the kids, the whole issue is the hang-up of another generation. Kurtz and Maio'o (1968) reflect this younger view in their call for a "chapterectomy" for introductory sociology texts. "Sociology stands out," they suggest, "in its lengthy attempt to defend its place in the world of science." They interpret the preoccupation of opening chapters with philosophy of science issues as a manifestation of feelings of inadequacy. "Is it necessary for sociology to argue for its existence at all?" they ask. Instead of wasting the time of our students while we manage our status insecurity with proofs of our legitimacy as a science, we should, they argue, get down immediately to our real *raison d'être*, our subject matter.

In sum, I am suggesting two hypotheses which, if confirmed, would buttress the explanation offered here. First, that a larger proportion of sociologists are now being drawn from backgrounds with relatively high socio-economic status. This makes them less likely to be threatened by events which may lower the status of the profession. Second, within this group, those who are most confident and secure of their position *within* the profession will lead the attack on a role conception which offers protection from a threat they do not feel.

This change, this greater security about our prestige and worth, is likely to be a permanent one although it will be gradual and some time in coming. If, as critics of a sharp citizen-scientist separation have charged, this earlier role-conception served defensive purposes for many sociologists, then this defense will be unnecessary for more and more members of the trade in the future. In this case, the changing conception of the sociologist's role may be more permanent and less a product of the historical moment. The grounds of attack have *already* shifted from sociology as "meaningless" to sociology as "handmaiden." The change is well captured by the altering of the traditional battle cry of "Knowledge for What" to the present one of "Knowledge for Whom." Surely the life span of the minotaur must be in doubt when the central theme of an annual meeting of the ASA is "On the Gap between Sociology and Social Policy" and Whitney Young takes sociologists to task at a plenary meeting.

## References

1. GAMSON, ZELDA F., JEFFRY GOODMAN, and GERALD GURIN (1967) "Activists, moderates, and bystanders during a university protest," paper read at San Francisco Meetings of American Sociological Association, August, 1967.
2. GOULDNER, ALVIN W. (1968) "The sociologist as partisan: sociology and the welfare state." American Sociologist 3 (May):103–16.
3. HOULT, THOMAS FORD (1968) ". . . Who shall prepare himself to the battle?" American Sociologist 3 (February):3–7.
4. KURTZ, RICHARD A., and JOHN R. MAIOLO (1968) "Surgery for sociology: the need for introductory text opening chapterectomy." American Sociologists 3 (February):39–41.
5. MOORE, WILBERT E. (1967) Letter to the editor. American Sociologist 2 (November):221.
6. SAMPSON, EDWARD E. (ed.) (1967) "Stirrings out of apathy: student activism and the decade of protest." Journal of Social Issues 23 (July):1–137.
7. TURNER, RALPH H. (1968) Letter to the editor. American Sociologist 3 (February):54–55.
8. WESTBY, DAVID L., and RICHARD G. BRAUNGART (1966) "Class and politics in the family backgrounds of student political activists." American Sociological Review 31 (October):690–692.